NIETZSCHE

NIETZSCHE

Thus Spake Zarathustra ✷ Ecce Homo
Beyond Good and Evil

ARCTURUS

Disclaimer

Throughout the text readers may find that some of the language used and sentiments expressed are offensive and unacceptable by today's standards. These reflect the attitudes and usage common at the time the book was written. In no way do they reflect the attitude of the publishers.

This edition published in 2020 by Arcturus Publishing Limited
26/27 Bickels Yard, 151–153 Bermondsey Street,
London SE1 3HA

ISBN: 978-1-78950-989-2
AD007836UK

Printed in China

CONTENTS

INTRODUCTION

FRIEDRICH Nietzsche was born on 15 October 1844 in the small Prussian town of Röcken bei Lützen in Saxony. His father, Karl Ludwig, was appointed Röcken's Lutheran minister by King Friedrich Wilhelm IV. In 1849, Karl died and the family moved to Naumburg, where Nietzsche lived with his mother, sister, grandmother and two aunts. In 1858, he was accepted into the Schulpforta, one of Germany's most prestigious boarding schools.

Upon graduating in 1864, Nietzsche enrolled as a theology and classical philology student at the University of Bonn. Two terms later, he transferred to the University of Leipzig to follow Professor Friedrich Wilhelm Ritschl. Under Ritschl's tutelage, Nietzsche thrived in Leipzig, learning the philosophy of Arthur Schopenhauer and Immanuel Kant.

In 1869, Ritschl recommended the 24-year-old Nietzsche for a professorship in philology at the University of Basel. Basel was hesitant; Nietzsche had left the university for a year of military service and hadn't completed his doctoral thesis. But Ritschl heaped praise on Nietzsche, stating that he hadn't found another student like him in 40 years of teaching. So the University of Basel appointed him as an extraordinary professor of classical philology, and promoted him to full professor the following year.

Nietzsche took leave in August 1870 to work as a medical orderly during the Franco-German War. While helping transport the wounded, he contracted dysentery and diphtheria, which resulted in poor health, migraines, insomnia, and near blindness for the rest of his life. In October, he returned to university, but found himself struggling between his deteriorating health, constant pain and the demands of teaching. In 1879, he resigned from his position at the age of 34.

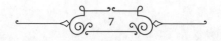

Written in biblical-narrative form while he battled with illness between 1883 and 1885, *Thus Spake Zarathustra* was the culmination of his philosophical career. Following the fictional travels of the prophet Zarathustra, Nietzsche laid out the core tenets of his philosophy. Two concepts lay at the heart of his writing: 'the death of God' and the *übermensch* (the superman). Seeking to free humanity from the strictures of religion and traditional authority, Nietzsche encouraged the mastery of one's self while at the same time accepting one's own fate. Fiercely critical of Christianity, he sought to establish a new system of values suitable for the modern age. Later appropriated by Nazi intellectuals and distorted for their own anti-Semitic purposes, *Thus Spake Zarathustra* became one of the most influential works of modern philosophy.

The work received a poor reception initially, leading Nietzsche to rework his ideas into *Beyond Good and Evil* in 1886. This new book was a scathing critique of his fellow philosophers and articulated a new morality. In 1888, Nietzsche wrote his last book. Initially titled *Why I Am So Wise*, it was finally published ten years later as *Ecce Homo*. It was an unusual and controversial autobiography, where Nietzsche examines his literary outputs over the years and questions whether the arguments he presented still hold true.

Less than a year after he finished writing the book, aged 44, he suffered a severe a nervous breakdown. Nietzsche then spent a number of years in psychiatric asylums, before returning to live with his mother until her death in 1897. He then moved into the household of his sister Elisabeth and her husband Bernhard Förster, a politically active anti-Semite. After Förster's suicide in 1889, Elisabeth worked diligently to keep her husband's dreams of 'racial purity' alive. She took control of Nietzsche's estate and used his writings to promote him as a supporter of Förster's work.

Throughout Nietzsche's philosophy, he offered an insightful and open-minded view of man's spirituality. Unlike the hateful message of his sister, he aimed to broaden the minds of his readers and urged them to take control of their own lives.

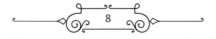

Thus Spake Zarathustra

Translated by
Thomas Common

CONTENTS

Zarathustra's Prologue

1

WHEN Zarathustra was thirty years old, he left his home and the lake of his home, and went into the mountains. There he enjoyed his spirit and his solitude, and for ten years did not weary of it. But at last his heart changed, and rising one morning with the rosy dawn, he went before the sun, and spake thus unto it:

'Thou great star! What would be thy happiness if thou hadst not those for whom thou shinest!

For ten years hast thou climbed hither unto my cave: thou wouldst have wearied of thy light and of the journey, had it not been for me, mine eagle, and my serpent.

But we awaited thee every morning, took from thee thine over-flow, and blessed thee for it.

Lo! I am weary of my wisdom, like the bee that hath gathered too much honey; I need hands outstretched to take it.

I would fain bestow and distribute, until the wise have once more become joyous in their folly, and the poor happy in their riches.

Therefore must I descend into the deep: as thou doest in the evening, when thou goest behind the sea, and givest light also to the netherworld, thou exuberant star!

Like thee must I *go down*, as men say, to whom I shall descend.

Bless me, then, thou tranquil eye, that canst behold even the greatest happiness without envy!

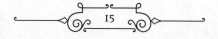

Bless the cup that is about to overflow, that the water may flow golden out of it, and carry everywhere the reflection of thy bliss!

Lo! This cup is again going to empty itself, and Zarathustra is again going to be a man.'

Thus began Zarathustra's down-going.

2

ZARATHUSTRA went down the mountain alone, no one meeting him. When he entered the forest, however, there suddenly stood before him an old man, who had left his holy cot to seek roots. And thus spake the old man to Zarathustra:

'No stranger to me is this wanderer: many years ago passed he by. Zarathustra he was called; but he hath altered.

Then thou carriedst thine ashes into the mountains: wilt thou now carry thy fire into the valleys? Fearest thou not the incendiary's doom?

Yea, I recognize Zarathustra. Pure is his eye, and no loathing lurketh about his mouth. Goeth he not along like a dancer?

Altered is Zarathustra; a child hath Zarathustra become; an awakened one is Zarathustra: what wilt thou do in the land of the sleepers?

As in the sea hast thou lived in solitude, and it hath borne thee up. Alas, wilt thou now go ashore? Alas, wilt thou again drag thy body thyself?'

Zarathustra answered: 'I love mankind.'

'Why,' said the saint, 'did I go into the forest and the desert? Was it not because I loved men far too well?

Now I love God: men, I do not love. Man is a thing too imperfect for me. Love to man would be fatal to me.'

Zarathustra answered: 'What spake I of love! I am bringing gifts unto men.'

'Give them nothing,' said the saint. 'Take rather part of their

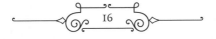

load, and carry it along with them – that will be most agreeable unto them: if only it be agreeable unto thee!

If, however, thou wilt give unto them, give them no more than an alms, and let them also beg for it!'

'No,' replied Zarathustra, 'I give no alms. I am not poor enough for that.'

The saint laughed at Zarathustra, and spake thus: 'Then see to it that they accept thy treasures! They are distrustful of anchorites, and do not believe that we come with gifts.

The fall of our footsteps ringeth too hollow through their streets. And just as at night, when they are in bed and hear a man abroad long before sunrise, so they ask themselves concerning us: Where goeth the thief?

Go not to men, but stay in the forest! Go rather to the animals! Why not be like me – a bear amongst bears, a bird amongst birds?'

'And what doeth the saint in the forest?' asked Zarathustra.

The saint answered: 'I make hymns and sing them; and in making hymns I laugh and weep and mumble: thus do I praise God.

With singing, weeping, laughing, and mumbling do I praise the God who is my God. But what dost thou bring us as a gift?'

When Zarathustra had heard these words, he bowed to the saint and said: 'What should I have to give thee! Let me rather hurry hence lest I take aught away from thee!' – And thus they parted from one another, the old man and Zarathustra, laughing like schoolboys.

When Zarathustra was alone, however, he said to his heart: 'Could it be possible! This old saint in the forest hath not yet heard of it, that *God is dead!*'

3

WHEN Zarathustra arrived at the nearest town which adjoineth the forest, he found many people assembled in the marketplace; for it had

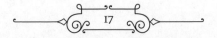

been announced that a rope-dancer would give a performance. And Zarathustra spake thus unto the people:

'*I teach you the Superman*. Man is something that is to be surpassed. What have ye done to surpass man?

All beings hitherto have created something beyond themselves: and ye want to be the ebb of that great tide, and would rather go back to the beast than surpass man?

What is the ape to man? A laughing-stock, a thing of shame. And just the same shall man be to the Superman: a laughing-stock, a thing of shame.

Ye have made your way from the worm to man, and much within you is still worm. Once were ye apes, and even yet man is more of an ape than any of the apes.

Even the wisest among you is only a disharmony and hybrid of plant and phantom. But do I bid you become phantoms or plants?

Lo, I teach you the Superman!

The Superman is the meaning of the earth. Let your will say: The Superman *shall be* the meaning of the earth!

I conjure you, my brethren, *remain true to the earth*, and believe not those who speak unto you of superearthly hopes! Poisoners are they, whether they know it or not.

Despisers of life are they, decaying ones and poisoned ones themselves, of whom the earth is weary: so away with them!

Once blasphemy against God was the greatest blasphemy; but God died, and therewith also those blasphemers. To blaspheme the earth is now the dreadfulest sin, and to rate the heart of the unknowable higher than the meaning of the earth!

Once the soul looked contemptuously on the body, and then that contempt was the supreme thing: the soul wished the body meagre, ghastly, and famished. Thus it thought to escape from the body and the earth.

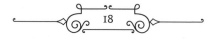

Oh, that soul was itself meagre, ghastly, and famished; and cruelty was the delight of that soul!

But ye, also, my brethren, tell me: What doth your body say about your soul? Is your soul not poverty and pollution and wretched self-complacency?

Verily, a polluted stream is man. One must be a sea, to receive a polluted stream without becoming impure.

Lo, I teach you the Superman: he is that sea; in him can your great contempt be submerged.

What is the greatest thing ye can experience? It is the hour of great contempt. The hour in which even your happiness becometh loathsome unto you, and so also your reason and virtue.

The hour when ye say: "What good is my happiness! It is poverty and pollution and wretched self-complacency. But my happiness should justify existence itself!"

The hour when ye say: "What good is my reason! Doth it long for knowledge as the lion for his food? It is poverty and pollution and wretched self-complacency!"

The hour when ye say: "What good is my virtue! As yet it hath not made me passionate. How weary I am of my good and my bad! It is all poverty and pollution and wretched self-complacency!"

The hour when ye say: "What good is my justice! I do not see that I am fervour and fuel. The just, however, are fervour and fuel!"

The hour when we say: "What good is my pity! Is not pity the cross on which he is nailed who loveth man? But my pity is not a crucifixion."

Have ye ever spoken thus? Have ye ever cried thus? Ah! would that I had heard you crying thus!

It is not your sin – it is your self-satisfaction that crieth unto heaven; your very sparingness in sin crieth unto heaven!

Where is the lightning to lick you with its tongue? Where is the frenzy with which ye should be inoculated?

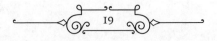

Lo, I teach you the Superman: he is that lightning, he is that frenzy!'

When Zarathustra had thus spoken, one of the people called out: 'We have now heard enough of the rope-dancer; it is time now for us to see him!' And all the people laughed at Zarathustra. But the rope-dancer, who thought the words applied to him, began his performance.

4

ZARATHUSTRA, however, looked at the people and wondered. Then he spake thus:

'Man is a rope stretched between the animal and the Superman – a rope over an abyss.

A dangerous crossing, a dangerous wayfaring, a dangerous look-ing-back, a dangerous trembling and halting.

What is great in man is that he is a bridge and not a goal: what is lovable in man is that he is an *over-going* and a *down-going*.

I love those that know not how to live except as down-goers, for they are the over-goers.

I love the great despisers, because they are the great adorers, and arrows of longing for the other shore.

I love those who do not first seek a reason beyond the stars for going down and being sacrifices, but sacrifice themselves to the earth, that the earth of the Superman may hereafter arrive.

I love him who liveth in order to know, and seeketh to know in order that the Superman may hereafter live. Thus seeketh he his own down-going.

I love him who laboureth and inventeth, that he may build the house for the Superman, and prepare for him earth, animal, and plant: for thus seeketh he his own down-going.

I love him who loveth his virtue: for virtue is the will to down-going, and an arrow of longing.

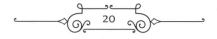

I love him who reserveth no share of spirit for himself, but wanteth to be wholly the spirit of his virtue: thus walketh he as spirit over the bridge.

I love him who maketh his virtue his inclination and destiny: thus, for the sake of his virtue, he is willing to live on, or live no more.

I love him who desireth not too many virtues. One virtue is more of a virtue than two, because it is more of a knot for one's destiny to cling to.

I love him whose soul is lavish, who wanteth no thanks and doth not give back: for he always bestoweth, and desireth not to keep for himself.

I love him who is ashamed when the dice fall in his favour, and who then asketh: "Am I a dishonest player?" – for he is willing to succumb.

I love him who scattereth golden words in advance of his deeds, and always doeth more than he promiseth: for he seeketh his own down-going.

I love him who justifieth the future ones, and redeemeth the past ones: for he is willing to succumb through the present ones.

I love him who chasteneth his God, because he loveth his God: for he must succumb through the wrath of his God.

I love him whose soul is deep even in the wounding, and may succumb through a small matter: thus goeth he willingly over the bridge.

I love him whose soul is so overfull that he forgetteth himself, and all things are in him: thus all things become his down- going.

I love him who is of a free spirit and a free heart: thus is his head only the bowels of his heart; his heart, however, causeth his down-going.

I love all who are like heavy drops falling one by one out of the dark cloud that lowereth over man: they herald the coming of the lightning, and succumb as heralds.

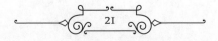

Lo, I am a herald of the lightning, and a heavy drop out of the cloud: the lightning, however, is the *Superman*.'

5

WHEN Zarathustra had spoken these words, he again looked at the people, and was silent. 'There they stand,' said he to his heart; 'there they laugh: they understand me not; I am not the mouth for these ears.

Must one first batter their ears, that they may learn to hear with their eyes? Must one clatter like kettledrums and penitential preachers? Or do they only believe the stammerer?

They have something whereof they are proud. What do they call it, that which maketh them proud? Culture, they call it; it distinguisheth them from the goatherds.

They dislike, therefore, to hear of "contempt" of themselves. So I will appeal to their pride.

I will speak unto them of the most contemptible thing: that, however, is *the last man!*'

And thus spake Zarathustra unto the people:

'It is time for man to fix his goal. It is time for man to plant the germ of his highest hope.

Still is his soil rich enough for it. But that soil will one day be poor and exhausted, and no lofty tree will any longer be able to grow thereon.

Alas! There cometh the time when man will no longer launch the arrow of his longing beyond man – and the string of his bow will have unlearned to whizz!

I tell you: one must still have chaos in one, to give birth to a dancing star. I tell you: ye have still chaos in you.

Alas! There cometh the time when man will no longer give birth to any star. Alas! There cometh the time of the most despicable man, who can no longer despise himself.

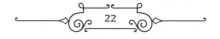

Lo! I show you *the last man*.

"What is love? What is creation? What is longing? What is a star?" – so asketh the last man and blinketh.

The earth hath then become small, and on it there hoppeth the last man who maketh everything small. His species is ineradicable like that of the ground-flea; the last man liveth longest.

"We have discovered happiness" – say the last men, and blink thereby.

They have left the regions where it is hard to live; for they need warmth. One still loveth one's neighbour and rubbeth against him; for one needeth warmth.

Turning ill and being distrustful they consider sinful: they walk warily. He is a fool who still stumbleth over stones or men!

A little poison now and then: that maketh pleasant dreams. And much poison at last for a pleasant death.

One still worketh, for work is a pastime. But one is careful lest the pastime should hurt one.

One no longer becometh poor or rich; both are too burdensome. Who still wanteth to rule? Who still wanteth to obey? Both are too burdensome.

No shepherd, and one herd! Every one wanteth the same; every one is equal: he who hath other sentiments goeth voluntarily into the madhouse.

"Formerly all the world was insane," say the subtlest of them, and blink thereby.

They are clever and know all that hath happened: so there is no end to their raillery. People still fall out, but are soon reconciled – otherwise it spoileth their stomachs.

They have their little pleasures for the day, and their little pleasures for the night, but they have a regard for health.

"We have discovered happiness," say the last men, and blink thereby.'

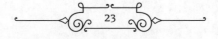

And here ended the first discourse of Zarathustra, which is also called 'The Prologue': for at this point the shouting and mirth of the multitude interrupted him. 'Give us this last man, O Zarathustra,' they called out. 'Make us into these last men! Then will we make thee a present of the Superman!' And all the people exulted and smacked their lips. Zarathustra, however, turned sad, and said to his heart:

'They understand me not: I am not the mouth for these ears.

Too long, perhaps, have I lived in the mountains; too much have I hearkened unto the brooks and trees: now do I speak unto them as unto the goatherds.

Calm is my soul, and clear, like the mountains in the morning. But they think me cold, and a mocker with terrible jests.

And now do they look at me and laugh: and while they laugh they hate me too. There is ice in their laughter.'

6

THEN, however, something happened which made every mouth mute and every eye fixed. In the meantime, of course, the rope-dancer had commenced his performance: he had come out at a little door, and was going along the rope which was stretched between two towers, so that it hung above the marketplace and the people. When he was just midway across, the little door opened once more, and a gaudily-dressed fellow like a buffoon sprang out, and went rapidly after the first one. 'Go on, halt-foot,' cried his frightful voice, 'go on, lazy bones, interloper, sallow-face! – lest I tickle thee with my heel! What dost thou here between the towers? In the tower is the place for thee, thou shouldst be locked up; to one better than thyself thou blockest the way!' – And with every word he came nearer and nearer the first one. When, however, he was but a step behind, there happened the frightful thing which made every mouth mute and every eye fixed – he uttered a yell like a devil, and jumped over the other who was in his

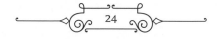

way. The latter, however, when he thus saw his rival triumph, lost at the same time his head and his footing on the rope; he threw his pole away, and shot downwards faster than it, like an eddy of arms and legs, into the depth. The marketplace and the people were like the sea when the storm cometh on: they all flew apart and in disorder, especially where the body was about to fall.

Zarathustra, however, remained standing, and just beside him fell the body, badly injured and disfigured, but not yet dead. After a while consciousness returned to the shattered man, and he saw Zarathustra kneeling beside him. 'What art thou doing there?' said he at last, 'I knew long ago that the devil would trip me up. Now he draggeth me to hell: wilt thou prevent him?'

'On mine honour, my friend,' answered Zarathustra, 'there is nothing of all that whereof thou speakest: there is no devil and no hell. Thy soul will be dead even sooner than thy body: fear, therefore, nothing any more!'

The man looked up distrustfully. 'If thou speakest the truth,' said he, 'I lose nothing when I lose my life. I am not much more than an animal which hath been taught to dance by blows and scanty fare.'

'Not at all,' said Zarathustra, 'thou hast made danger thy calling; therein there is nothing contemptible. Now thou perishest by thy calling: therefore will I bury thee with mine own hands.'

When Zarathustra had said this the dying one did not reply further; but he moved his hand as if he sought the hand of Zarathustra in gratitude.

7

MEANWHILE the evening came on, and the marketplace veiled itself in gloom. Then the people dispersed, for even curiosity and terror become fatigued. Zarathustra, however, still sat beside the dead man on the ground, absorbed in thought: so he forgot the time. But at last

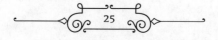

it became night, and a cold wind blew upon the lonely one. Then arose Zarathustra and said to his heart:

'Verily, a fine catch of fish hath Zarathustra made today! It is not a man he hath caught, but a corpse.

Sombre is human life, and as yet without meaning: a buffoon may be fateful to it.

I want to teach men the sense of their existence, which is the Superman, the lightning out of the dark cloud – man.

But still am I far from them, and my sense speaketh not unto their sense. To men I am still something between a fool and a corpse.

Gloomy is the night, gloomy are the ways of Zarathustra. Come, thou cold and stiff companion! I carry thee to the place where I shall bury thee with mine own hands.'

8

WHEN Zarathustra had said this to his heart, he put the corpse upon his shoulders and set out on his way. Yet had he not gone a hundred steps, when there stole a man up to him and whispered in his ear – and lo! he that spake was the buffoon from the tower. 'Leave this town, O Zarathustra,' said he, 'there are too many here who hate thee. The good and just hate thee, and call thee their enemy and despiser; the believers in the orthodox belief hate thee, and call thee a danger to the multitude. It was thy good fortune to be laughed at: and verily thou spakest like a buffoon. It was thy good fortune to associate with the dead dog; by so humiliating thyself thou hast saved thy life today. Depart, however, from this town, or tomorrow I shall jump over thee, a living man over a dead one.' And when he had said this, the buffoon vanished; Zarathustra, however, went on through the dark streets.

At the gate of the town the gravediggers met him: they shone their torch on his face, and, recognizing Zarathustra, they sorely derided him. 'Zarathustra is carrying away the dead dog: a fine thing

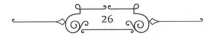

that Zarathustra hath turned a gravedigger! For our hands are too cleanly for that roast. Will Zarathustra steal the bite from the devil? Well then, good luck to the repast! If only the devil is not a better thief than Zarathustra! – he will steal them both, he will eat them both!' And they laughed among themselves, and put their heads together.

Zarathustra made no answer thereto, but went on his way. When he had gone on for two hours, past forests and swamps, he had heard too much of the hungry howling of the wolves, and he himself became hungry. So he halted at a lonely house in which a light was burning.

'Hunger attacketh me,' said Zarathustra, 'like a robber. Among forests and swamps my hunger attacketh me, and late in the night.

Strange humours hath my hunger. Often it cometh to me only after a repast, and all day it hath failed to come: where hath it been?'

And thereupon Zarathustra knocked at the door of the house. An old man appeared, who carried a light, and asked: 'Who cometh unto me and my bad sleep?'

'A living man and a dead one,' said Zarathustra. 'Give me something to eat and drink, I forgot it during the day. He that feedeth the hungry refresheth his own soul, saith wisdom.'

The old man withdrew, but came back immediately and offered Zarathustra bread and wine. 'A bad country for the hungry,' said he; 'that is why I live here. Animal and man come unto me, the anchorite. But bid thy companion eat and drink also, he is wearier than thou.' Zarathustra answered: 'My companion is dead; I shall hardly be able to persuade him to eat.' 'That doth not concern me,' said the old man sullenly; 'he that knocketh at my door must take what I offer him. Eat, and fare ye well!'

Thereafter Zarathustra again went on for two hours, trusting to the path and the light of the stars: for he was an experienced night-walker, and liked to look into the face of all that slept. When the

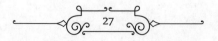

morning dawned, however, Zarathustra found himself in a thick forest, and no path was any longer visible. He then put the dead man in a hollow tree at his head – for he wanted to protect him from the wolves – and laid himself down on the ground and moss. And immediately he fell asleep, tired in body, but with a tranquil soul.

9

LONG slept Zarathustra; and not only the rosy dawn passed over his head, but also the morning. At last, however, his eyes opened, and amazedly he gazed into the forest and the stillness, amazedly he gazed into himself. Then he arose quickly, like a seafarer who all at once seeth the land; and he shouted for joy: for he saw a new truth. And he spake thus to his heart:

'A light hath dawned upon me: I need companions – living ones; not dead companions and corpses, which I carry with me where I will.

But I need living companions, who will follow me because they want to follow themselves – and to the place where I will. A light hath dawned upon me. Not to the people is Zarathustra to speak, but to companions! Zarathustra shall not be the herd's herdsman and hound!

To allure many from the herd – for that purpose have I come. The people and the herd must be angry with me: a robber shall Zarathustra be called by the herdsmen.

Herdsmen, I say, but they call themselves the good and just. Herdsmen, I say, but they call themselves the believers in the orthodox belief.

Behold the good and just! Whom do they hate most? Him who breaketh up their tables of values, the breaker, the lawbreaker: he, however, is the creator.

Behold the believers of all beliefs! Whom do they hate most? Him who breaketh up their tables of values, the breaker, the lawbreaker – he, however, is the creator.

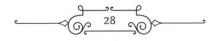

Companions, the creator seeketh, not corpses – and not herds or believers either. Fellow-creators the creator seeketh – those who grave new values on new tables.

Companions, the creator seeketh, and fellow-reapers: for everything is ripe for the harvest with him. But he lacketh the hundred sickles: so he plucketh the ears of corn and is vexed.

Companions, the creator seeketh, and such as know how to whet their sickles. Destroyers, will they be called, and despisers of good and evil. But they are the reapers and rejoicers.

Fellow-creators, Zarathustra seeketh; fellow-reapers and fellow-rejoicers, Zarathustra seeketh: what hath he to do with herds and herdsmen and corpses!

And thou, my first companion, rest in peace! Well have I buried thee in thy hollow tree; well have I hid thee from the wolves.

But I part from thee; the time hath arrived. 'Twixt rosy dawn and rosy dawn there came unto me a new truth.

I am not to be a herdsman, I am not to be a gravedigger. Not any more will I discourse unto the people; for the last time have I spoken unto the dead.

With the creators, the reapers, and the rejoicers will I associate: the rainbow will I show them, and all the stairs to the Superman.

To the lone-dwellers will I sing my song, and to the twain – dwellers; and unto him who hath still ears for the unheard, will I make the heart heavy with my happiness.

I make for my goal, I follow my course; over the loitering and tardy will I leap. Thus let my on-going be their down-going!'

10

THIS had Zarathustra said to his heart when the sun stood at noontide. Then he looked inquiringly aloft, for he heard above him the sharp call of a bird. And behold! An eagle swept through the air in

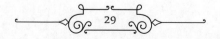

wide circles, and on it hung a serpent, not like a prey, but like a friend: for it kept itself coiled round the eagle's neck.

'They are mine animals,' said Zarathustra, and rejoiced in his heart.

'The proudest animal under the sun, and the wisest animal under the sun, they have come out to reconnoitre.

They want to know whether Zarathustra still liveth. Verily, do I still live?

More dangerous have I found it among men than among animals; in dangerous paths goeth Zarathustra. Let mine animals lead me!'

When Zarathustra had said this, he remembered the words of the saint in the forest. Then he sighed and spake thus to his heart:

'Would that I were wiser! Would that I were wise from the very heart, like my serpent!

But I am asking the impossible. Therefore do I ask my pride to go always with my wisdom!

And if my wisdom should some day forsake me: alas! It loveth to fly away! May my pride then fly with my folly!'

Thus began Zarathustra's down-going.

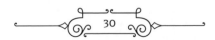

Part One

1. The Three Metamorphoses

'THREE metamorphoses of the spirit do I designate to you: now the spirit becometh a camel, the camel a lion, and the lion at last a child.

Many heavy things are there for the spirit, the strong load-bearing spirit in which the reverence dwelleth: for the heavy and the heaviest longeth its strength.

What is heavy? so asketh the load-bearing spirit; then kneeleth it down like the camel, and wanteth to be well laden.

What is the heaviest things, ye heroes? asketh the load-bearing spirit, that I may take it upon me and rejoice in my strength.

Is it not this: To humiliate oneself in order to mortify one's pride? To exhibit one's folly in order to mock at one's wisdom?

Or is it this: To desert our cause when it celebrateth its triumph? To ascend high mountains to tempt the temper?

Or is it this: To feed on the acorns and grass of knowledge, and for the sake of truth to suffer hunger of soul?

Or is it this: To be sick and dismiss comforters, and make friends of the deaf, who never hear thy requests?

Or is it this: To go into foul water when it is the water of truth, and not disclaim cold frogs and hot toads?

Or is it this: To love those who despise us, and to give one's hand to the phantom when it is going to frighten us?

All these heaviest things the load-bearing spirit taketh upon itself:

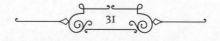

and like the camel, which, when laden, hasteneth into the wilderness, so hasteneth the spirit into its wilderness.

But in the loneliest wilderness happeneth the second metamorphosis: here the spirit becometh a lion; freedom will it capture, and lordship in its own wilderness.

Its last Lord it here seeketh: hostile will it be to him, and to its last God; for victory will it struggle with the great dragon.

What is the great dragon which the spirit is no longer inclined to call Lord and God? 'Thou-shalt,' is the great dragon called. But the spirit of the lion saith, 'I will.'

'Thou-shalt,' lieth in its path, sparkling with gold – a scale-covered beast; and on every scale glittereth golden, 'Thou shalt!'

The values of a thousand years glitter on those scales, and thus speaketh the mightiest of all dragons: 'All the values of things – glitter on me.

All values have already been created, and all created values – do I represent. Verily, there shall be no 'I will' any more.' Thus speaketh the dragon.

My brethren, wherefore is there need of the lion in the spirit? Why sufficeth not the beast of burden, which renounceth and is reverent?

To create new values – that, even the lion cannot yet accomplish: but to create itself freedom for new creating – that can the might of the lion do.

To create itself freedom, and give a holy Nay even unto duty: for that, my brethren, there is no need of the lion.

To assume the ride into new values – that is the most formidable assumption for a load-bearing and reverent spirit. Verily, unto such a spirit it is preying, and the work of a beast of prey.

As its holiest, it once loved 'Thou-shalt': now it is forced to find illusion and arbitrariness even in the holiest things, that it may capture freedom from its love: the lion is needed for this capture.

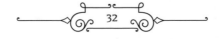

But tell me, my brethren, what the child can do, which even the lion could not do? Why hath the preying lion still to become a child?

Innocence is the child, and forgetfulness, and a new beginning, a game, a self-rolling wheel, a first movement, a holy Yea.

Aye, for the game of creating, my brethren, there is needed a holy Yea unto life: *its own* will, willeth now the spirit; *his own* world winneth the world's outcast.

Three metamorphoses of the spirit have I designated to you: how the spirit became a camel, the camel a lion, and the lion at last a child.'

Thus spake Zarathustra. And at that time he abode in the town which is called The Pied Cow.

2. *The Academic Chairs of Virtue*

PEOPLE commended unto Zarathustra a wise man, as one who could discourse well about sleep and virtue: greatly was he honoured and rewarded for it, and all the youths sat before his chair. To him went Zarathustra, and sat among the youths before his chair. And thus spake the wise man:

'Respect and modesty in presence of sleep! That is the first thing! And to go out of the way of all who sleep badly and keep awake at night!

Modest is even the thief in the presence of sleep: He always stealeth softly through the night. Immodest, however, is the night-watchman; immodestly he carrieth his horn.

No small art is it to sleep: it is necessary for that purpose to keep awake all day.

Ten times a day must thou overcome thyself: that causeth wholesome weariness, and is poppy to the soul.

Ten times must thou reconcile again with thyself; for overcoming is bitterness, and badly sleep the unreconciled.

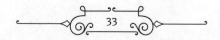

Ten truths must thou find during the day; otherwise wilt thou seek truth during the night, and thy soul will have been hungry.

Ten times must thou laugh during the day, and be cheerful; otherwise thy stomach, the father of affliction, will disturb thee in the night.

Few people know it, but one must have all the virtues in order to sleep well. Shall I bear false witness? Shall I commit adultery?

Shall I covet my neighbour's maidservant? All that would ill accord with good sleep.

And even if one have all the virtues, there is still one thing needful: to send the virtues themselves to sleep at the right time.

That they may not quarrel with one another, the good females! And about thee, thou unhappy one!

Peace with God and thy neighbour: so desireth good sleep. And peace also with thy neighbour's devil! Otherwise it will haunt thee in the night.

Honour to the government, and obedience, and also to the crooked government! So desireth good sleep. How can I help it, if power liketh to walk on crooked legs?

He who leadeth his sheep to the greenest pasture, shall always be for me the best shepherd: so doth it accord with good sleep.

Many honours I want not, nor great treasures: they excite the spleen. But it is bad sleeping without a good name and a little treasure.

A small company is more welcome to me than a bad one: but they must come and go at the right time. So doth it accord with good sleep.

Well, also, do the poor in spirit please me: they promote sleep. Blessed are they, especially if one always give in to them.

Thus passeth the day unto the virtuous. When night cometh, then take I good care not to summon sleep. It disliketh to be summoned – sleep, the lord of the virtues!

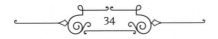

But I think of what I have done and thought during the day. Thus ruminating, patient as a cow, I ask myself: What were thy ten overcomings?

And what were the ten reconciliations, and the ten truths, and the ten laughters with which my heart enjoyed itself?

Thus pondering, and cradled by forty thoughts, it overtaketh me all at once – sleep, the unsummoned, the lord of the virtues.

Sleep tappeth on mine eye, and it turneth heavy. Sleep toucheth my mouth, and it remaineth open.

Verily, on soft soles doth it come to me, the dearest of thieves, and stealeth from me my thoughts: stupid do I then stand, like this academic chair.

But not much longer do I then stand: I already lie.'

When Zarathustra heard the wise man thus speak, he laughed in his heart: for thereby had a light dawned upon him and thus spake he to his heart:

'A fool seemeth this wise man with his forty thoughts: but I believe he knoweth well how to sleep.

Happy even is he who liveth near this wise man! Such sleep is contagious – even through a thick wall it is contagious.

A magic resideth even in his academic chair. And not in vain did the youths sit before the preacher of virtue.

His wisdom is to keep awake in order to sleep well. And verily, if life had no sense, and I had to choose nonsense, this would be the desirablest nonsense for me also.

Now know I well what people sought formerly above all else when they sought teachers of virtue. Good sleep they sought for themselves, and poppyhead virtues to promote it!

To all those belauded sages of the academic chairs, wisdom was sleep without dreams: they knew no higher significance of life.

Even at present, to be sure, there are some like this preacher of

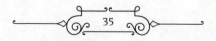

virtue, and not always so honourable: but their time is past. And not much longer do they stand: there they already lie.

Blessed are those drowsy ones: for they shall soon nod to sleep.'

Thus spake Zarathustra.

3. Backworldsmen

'ONCE on a time, Zarathustra also cast his fancy beyond man, like all backworldsmen. The work of a suffering and tortured God, did the world then seem to me.

The dream – and diction – of a God, did the world then seem to me; coloured vapours before the eyes of a divinely dissatisfied one.

Good and evil, and joy and woe, and I and thou-coloured vapours did they seem to me before creative eyes. The creator wished to look away from himself, thereupon he created the world.

Intoxicating joy is it for the sufferer to look away from his suffering and forget himself. Intoxicating joy and self-forgetting, did the world once seem to me.

This world, the eternally imperfect, and internal contradiction's image and imperfect image – an intoxicating joy to its imperfect creator: thus did the world once seem to me.

Thus, once on a time, did I also cast my fancy beyond man, like all backworldsmen. Beyond man, forsooth?

Ah, ye brethren, that God whom I created was human work and human madness, like all gods!

A man was he, and only a poor fragment of a man and ego. Out of mine own ashes and glow it came unto me, that phantom. And verily, it came not unto me from beyond!

What happened, my brethren? I surpassed myself, the suffering one; I carried mine own ashes to the mountain; a brighter flame I contrived for myself. And lo! Thereupon the phantom *withdrew* from me!

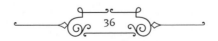

To me the convalescent would it now be suffering and torment to believe in such phantoms: suffering would it now be to me, and humiliation. Thus I speak to backworldsmen.

Suffering was it, and impotence – that created all backworlds; and the short madness of happiness, which only the greatest sufferer experienceth.

Weariness, which seeketh to get the ultimate one leap, with a death-leap; a poor ignorant weariness, unwilling even to will any longer: that created all gods and backworlds.

Believe me, my brethren! It was the body which despaired of the body – it groped with the fingers or the infatuated spirit at the ultimate walls.

Believe me, my brethren! It was the body which despaired of the earth – it heard the bowels of existence speaking unto it.

And then it sought to get through the ultimate walls with its head – and not with its head only – into "the other world".

But that "other world" is well concealed from man, that dehumanised, inhuman world, which is a celestial naught; and the bowels of existence do not speak unto man, except as a man.

Verily, it is difficult to prove all being, and hard to make it speak. Tell me, ye brethren, is not the strangest of all things best proved?

Yea, this ego, with its contradiction and perplexity, speaketh most uprightly of its being – this creating, willing, evaluing ego, which is the measure and value of things.

And this most upright existence, the ego – it speaketh of the body, and still implieth the body, even when it museth and raveth and fluttereth with broken wings.

Always more uprightly learneth it to speak, the ego; and the more it learneth, the more doth it find titles, and honours for the body and the earth.

A new pride taught me mine ego, and that teach I unto men:

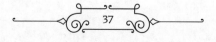

no longer to thrust one's head into the sand of celestial things, but to carry it freely, a terrestrial head, which giveth meaning to the earth!

A new will teach I unto men: to choose that path which man hath followed blindly, and to approve of it – and no longer slink aside from it, like the sick and perishing!

The sick and perishing – it was they who despised the body and the earth, and invented the heavenly world, and the redeeming blood drops; but even those sweet and sad poisons they borrowed from the body and the earth!

From their misery they sought to escape, and the stars were too remote for them. Then they sight: "O that there were heavenly paths by which to steal into another existence and into happiness!" Then they contrived for themselves their bypaths and bloody draughts!

Beyond the sphere of their body and this earth they now fancied themselves transported, these ungrateful ones. But to what did they owe the convulsion and rapture of their transport? To their body and this earth.

Gentle is Zarathustra to the sickly. Verily, he is not indignant of their modes of consolation and ingratitude. May they become convalescents and overcomers, and create higher bodies for themselves!

Neither is Zarathustra indignant at a convalescent who looketh tenderly on his delusions, and at midnight stealeth round the grave of his God; but sickness and a sick frame remain even in his tears.

Many sickly ones have there always been among those who muse, and languish for God; violently they hate the discerning ones, and the latest of virtues, which is uprightness.

Backward they always gaze toward dark ages: then, indeed, were delusion and faith something different. Raving of the reason was likeness to God, and doubt was sin.

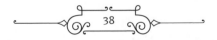

Too well do I know those godlike ones: they insist on being believed in, and that doubt is sin. Too well, also, do I know what they themselves most believe in.

Verily, not in backworlds and redeeming blood drops: but in the body do they also believe most; and their own body is for them the thing-in-itself.

But it is a sickly thing to them, and gladly would they get out of their skin. Therefore hearken they to the preachers of death, and themselves preach backworlds.

Hearken rather, my brethren, to the voice of the healthy body; it is a more upright and pure voice.

More uprightly and purely speaketh the healthy body, perfect and square-built; and it speaketh of the meaning of the earth.'

Thus spake Zarathustra.

4. The Despisers of the Body

'TO THE despisers of the body will I speak my word. I wish them neither to learn afresh, nor teach anew, but only to bid farewell to their own bodies, and thus be dumb.

"Body am I, and soul" – so saith the child. And why should one not speak like children?

But the awakened one, the knowing own, saith: "Body am I entirely and nothing more; and soul is only the name of something in the body."

The body is a big sagacity, a plurality with one sense, a war and a peace, a flock and a shepherd.

An instrument of thy body is also thy little sagacity, my brother, which thou callest a "spirit" – a little instrument and plaything of thy big sagacity.

"Ego," sayest thou, and art proud of that word. But the greater

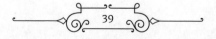

thing – in which thou are unwilling to believe – is thy body with its big sagacity; it saith not "ego", but doeth it.

What the sense feeleth, what the spirit discerneth, hath never its end in itself. But sense and spirit would fain persuade thee that they are the end of all things: so vain are they.

Instruments and plaything are sense and spirit: behind them there is still the Self. The Self seeketh with the eyes of the senses, it hearkeneth also with the ears of the spirit.

Ever hearkeneth the Self, and seeketh; it compareth, mastereth, conquereth, and destroyeth. It ruleth, and is also the ego's ruler.

Behind thy thoughts and feelings, my brother, there is a mighty lord, and unknown sage – it is called Self; it dwelleth in thy body, it is thy body.

There is more sagacity in thy body than in thy best wisdom. And who then knoweth why thy body requireth just thy best wisdom?

Thy Self laugheth at thine ego, and its proud prancings. "What are these prancings and flights of thought unto me?" it saith to itself. "A byway to my purpose. I am the leading-string of the ego, and the prompter of its notions."

The Self saith unto the ego: "Feel pain!" And thereupon it suffereth, and thinketh how it may put and end thereto – and for that very purpose it *is meant* to think.

To the despisers of the body will I speak a word. That they despise is caused by their esteem. What is it that created esteeming and despising and worth and will?

The creating Self created for itself esteeming and despising, it created for itself joy and woe. The creating body created for itself spirit, as a hand to its will.

Even in your folly and despising ye each serve your Self, ye despisers of the body. I tell you, your very self wanteth to die, and turneth away from life.

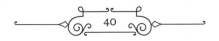

No longer can your Self do that which it desireth most: create beyond itself. That is what it desireth most; that is all its fervour.

But it is now too late to do so: so your Self wisheth to succumb, ye despisers of the body.

To succumb – so wisheth your Self; and therefore have ye become despisers of the body. For ye can no longer create beyond yourselves.

And therefore are ye now angry with life and with the earth. And unconscious envy is in the sidelong look of your contempt.

I go not your way, ye despisers of the body! Ye are no bridges for me to the Superman!'

Thus spake Zarathustra.

5. *Joys and Passions*

'MY BROTHER, when thou hast a virtue, and it is thine own virtue, thou hast it in common with no one.

To be sure, thou wouldst call it by name and caress it; thou wouldst pull its ears and amuse thyself with it.

And lo! Then hast thou its name in common with the people, and hast become one of the people and herd with thy virtue!

Better for thee to say: "Ineffable is it, and nameless, that which is pain and sweetness to my soul, and also the hunger of my bowels."

Let thy virtue be too high for the familiarity of names, and if thou must speak of it, be not ashamed to stammer about it.

Thus speak and stammer: "That is *my* good, that do I love, thus doth it please me entirely, thus only do *I* desire the good.

Not as the law of a God do I desire it, not as a human law or a human need do I desire it; it is not to be a guide-post for me to superearths and paradises.

An earthly virtue is it which I love: little prudence is therein, and the least everyday wisdom.

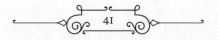

But that bird built its nest beside me: therefore, I love and cherish it – now sitteth it beside me on its golden eggs."

Thus shouldst thou stammer, and praise thy virtue.

Once hadst thou passions and calledst them evil. But now hast thou only thy virtues: they grew out of thy passions.

Thou implantedst thy highest aim into the heart of those passions: then became they thy virtues and joys.

And though thou wert of the race of the hot-tempered, or of the voluptuous, or of the fanatical, or the vindictive;

All thy passions in the end became virtues, and all thy devils angels.

Once hadst thou wild dogs in thy cellar: but they changed at last into birds and charming songstresses.

Out of thy poisons brewedst thou balsam for thyself; thy cow, affliction, milkedst thou – now drinketh thou the sweet milk of her udder.

And nothing evil groweth in thee any longer, unless it be the evil that groweth out of the conflict of thy virtues.

My brother, if thou be fortunate, then wilt thou have one virtue and no more: thus goest thou easier over the bridge.

Illustrious is it to have many virtues, but a hard lot; and many a one hath gone into the wilderness and killed himself, because he is weary of being the battle and battlefield of virtues.

My brother, are war and battle evil? Necessary, however is the evil; necessary are the envy and the distrust and the back-biting among the virtues.

Lo! How each of thy virtues is covetous of the highest place; it wanteth thy whole spirit to be *its* herald, it wanteth thy whole power, in wrath, hatred, and love.

Jealous is every virtue of the others, and a dreadful thing is jealousy. Even virtues may succumb by jealousy.

He whom the flame of jealousy encompasseth, turneth at last, like the scorpion, the poisoned sting against himself.

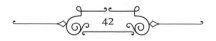

Ah! My brother, hast thou never seen a virtue backbite and stab itself?

Man is something that hath to be surpassed: and therefore shalt thou love thy virtues, for thou wilt succumb by them.'

Thus spake Zarathustra.

6. The Pale Criminal

'YE DO not mean to slay, ye judges and sacrificers, until the animal hath bowed its head? Lo! The pale criminal hath bowed his head: out of his eye speaketh the great contempt.

"Mine ego is something which is to be surpassed: mine ego is to me the great contempt of man": so speaketh it out of that eye.

When he judged himself – that was his supreme moment; let not the exalted one relapse again into his low estate!

There is no salvation for him who thus suffereth from himself, unless it be speedy death.

Your slaying, ye judges, shall be pity, and not revenge; and in that ye slay, see to it that ye yourselves justify life!

It is not enough that ye should reconcile with him whom ye slay. Let your sorrow be love to the Superman: thus will ye justify your own survival!

"Enemy" shall ye say but not "villain," "invalid" shall ye say but not "wretch", "fool" shall ye say but not "sinner."

And thou, red judge, if thou would say audibly all thou hast done in thought, then would every one cry: "Away with the nastiness and the virtulent reptile!"

But one thing is the thought, another thing is the deed, and another thing is the idea of the deed. The wheel of causality doth not roll between them.

An idea made this pale man pale. Adequate was he for his deed

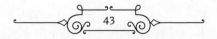

when he did it, but the idea of it, he could not endure when it was done.

Evermore did he now see himself as the doer of one deed. Madness, I call this: the exception reversed itself to the rule in him.

The streak of chalk bewitcheth the hen; the stroke he struck bewitched his weak reason. Madness *after* the deed, I call this.

Hearken, ye judges! There is another madness besides, and it is *before* the deed. Ah! Ye have not gone deep enough into this soul!

Thus speaketh the red judge: "Why did this criminal commit murder? He meant to rob." I tell you, however, that his soul wanted blood, not booty: he thirsted for the happiness of the knife!

But his weak reason understood not this madness, and it persuaded him. "What matter about blood!" it said; "wishest thou not, at least, to make booty thereby? Or take revenge?"

And he hearkened unto his weak reason: like lead lay its words upon him – thereupon he robbed when he murdered. He did not mean to be ashamed of his madness.

And now once more lieth the lead of his guilt upon him, and once more is his weak reason so benumbled, so paralysed, and so dull.

Could he only shake his head, then would his burden roll off; but who shaketh that head?

What is this man? A mass of diseases that reach out into the world through the spirit; there they want to get their prey.

What is this man? A coil of wild serpents that are seldom at peace among themselves – so they go forth apart and seek prey in the world.

Look at that poor body! What it suffered and craved, the poor soul interpreted to itself – it interpreted it as murderous desire, and eagerness for the happiness of the knife.

Him who now turneth sick, the evil over taketh which is now the evil: he seeketh to cause pain with that which causeth him pain. But there have been other ages, and another evil and good.

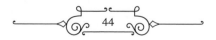

Once was doubt evil, and the will to Self. Then the invalid became a heretic or sorcerer; as heretic or sorcerer he suffered, and sought to cause suffering.

But this will not enter your ears; it hurteth your good people, ye tell me. But what doth it matter to me about your good people!

Many things in your good people cause me disgust, and verily, not their evil. I would that they had a madness by which they succumbed, like this pale criminal!

Verily, I would that their madness were called truth, or fidelity, or justice: but they have their virtue in order to live long, and in wretched self-complacency.

I am railing alongside the torrent; whoever is able to grasp me may grasp me! Your crutch, however, I am not.'

Thus spake Zarathustra.

7. *Reading and Writing*

'OF ALL that is written, I love only what a person hath written with his blood. Write with blood, and thou wilt find that blood is spirit.

It is no easy task to understand unfamiliar blood; I hate the reading idlers.

He who knoweth the reader, doeth nothing more for the reader. Another century of readers – and the spirit itself will stink.

Every one being allowed to learn to read, ruineth in the long run not only writing but also thinking.

Once spirit was God, then it became man, and now it even becometh populace.

He that writeth in blood and proverbs doth not want to be read, but learned by heart.

In the mountains the shortest way is from peak to peak, but for

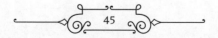

that route thou must have long legs. Proverbs should be peaks, and those spoken to should be big and tall.

The atmosphere rare and pure, danger near and the spirit full of a joyful wickedness: thus are things well matched.

I want to have goblins about me, for I am courageous. The courage which scareth away ghosts, createth for itself goblins – it wanteth to laugh.

I no longer feel in common with you; the very cloud which I see beneath me, the blackness and heaviness at which I laugh – that is your thunder-cloud.

Ye look aloft when ye long for exaltation; and I look downward because I am exalted.

Who among you can at the same time laugh and be exalted?

He who climbeth on the highest mountains, laugheth at all tragic plays and tragic realities.

Courageous, unconcerned, scornful, coercive – so wisdom wisheth us; she is a woman, and ever loveth only a warrior.

Ye tell me, "Life is hard to bear." But for what purpose should ye have your pride in the morning and your resignation in the evening?

Life is hard to bear: but do not affect to be so delicate! We are all of us fine sumpter asses and she-asses.

What have we in common with the rose-bud, which trembleth because a drop of dew hath formed upon it?

It is true we love life; not because we are wont to live, but because we are wont to love.

There is always some madness in love. But there is always, also, some method in madness.

And to me also, who appreciate life, the butterflies, soap-bubbles, and whatever is like them amongst us, seem most to enjoy happiness.

To see these light, foolish, pretty, lively little sprites flit about – that moveth Zarathustra to tears and songs.

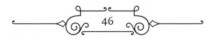

I should only believe in a God that would know how to dance.

And when I saw my devil, I found him serious, thorough, profound, solemn: he was the spirit of gravity – through him all things fall.

Not by wrath, but by laughter, do we slay. Come, let us slay the spirit of gravity!

I learned to walk; since then have I let myself run. I learned to fly; since then I do not need pushing in order to move from a spot.

Now am I light, now do I fly; now do I see myself under myself. Now there danceth a God in me.'

Thus spake Zarathustra.

8. *The Tree on the Hill*

ZARATHUSTRA'S eye had perceived that a certain youth avoided him. And as he walked alone one evening over the hills surrounding the town called 'The Pied Cow,' behold, there found he the youth sitting leaning against a tree, and gazing with wearied look into the valley. Zarathustra thereupon laid hold of the tree beside which the youth sat, and spake thus:

'If I wished to shake this tree with my hands, I should not be able to do so.

But the wind, which we see not, troubleth and bendeth it and it listeth. We are sorest bent and troubled by invisible hands.'

Thereupon the youth arose disconcerted, and said: 'I hear Zarathustra, and just now was thinking of him!' Zarathustra answered:

'Why art thou frightened on that account? But it is the same with man as with the tree.

The more he seeketh to rise into the height and light, the more vigorously do his roots struggle earthward, downward, into the dark and deep – into the evil.'

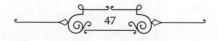

'Yea, into the evil!' cried the youth. 'How is it possible that thou hast discovered my soul?'

Zarathustra smiled, and said: 'Many a soul one will never discover, unless one first invent it.'

'Yea, into the evil!' cried the youth once more.

'Thou saidst the truth, Zarathustra. I trust myself no longer since I sought to rise into the height, and nobody trusteth me any longer; how doth that happen?

I change too quickly: my today refuteth my yesterday. I often overleap the steps when I clamber; for so doing, none of the steps pardons me.

When aloft, I find myself always alone. No one speaketh unto me; the frost of solitude maketh me tremble. What do I seek on the height?

My contempt and my longing increase together; the higher I clamber, the more do I despise him who clambereth. What doth he seek on the height?

How ashamed I am of my clambering and stumbling! How I mock at my violent panting! How I hate him who flieth! How tired I am on the height!'

Here the youth was silent. And Zarathustra contemplated the tree beside which they stood, and spake thus:

'This tree standeth here on the hills; it hath grown up high above man and beast.

And if it wanted to speak, it would have none who could understand it: so high hath it grown.

Now it waiteth and waiteth, – for what doth it wait? It dwelleth too close to the seat of the clouds; it waiteth perhaps for the first lightning?'

When Zarathustra had said this, the youth called out with violent gestures: 'Yea, Zarathustra, thou speakest the truth. My destruction I longed for, when I desired to be on the height, and thou art the

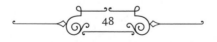

lightning for which I waited! Lo! What have I been since thou hast appeared amongst us? It is mine envy of thee that hath destroyed me!' Thus spake the youth, and wept bitterly. Zarathustra, however, put his arm around him, and led the youth away with him.

And when they had walked a while together, Zarathustra began to speak thus:

'It rendeth my heart. Better than thy words express it, thine eyes tell me all thy danger.

As thou art not free; thou still *seekest* freedom. Too unslept hath thy seeking made thee, and too wakeful.

On the open height wouldst thou be; for the stars thirsteth thy soul. But thy bad impulses also thirst for freedom.

Thy wild dogs want liberty; they bark for joy in their cellar when thy spirit endeavoureth to open all prison doors.

Still art thou a prisoner – it seemeth to me – who deviseth liberty for himself: ah! Sharp becometh the soul of such prisoners, but also deceitful and wicked.

To purify himself, is still necessary for the freedman of the spirit. Much of the prison and the mould still remaineth in him: pure hath his eye still to become.

Yea, I know thy danger. But by my love and hope I conjure thee: cast not thy love and hope away!

Noble thou feelst thyself still, and noble others also feel thee still, though they bear thee a grudge and cast evil looks. Know this, that to everybody a noble one standeth in the way.

Also to the good, a noble one standeth in the way: and even when they call him a good man, they want thereby to put him aside.

The new, would the noble man create, and a new virtue. The old, wanteth the good man, and that the old should be conserved.

But it is not the danger of the noble man to turn a good man, but lest he should become a blusterer, a scoffer, or a destroyer.

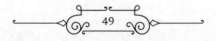

Ah! I have known noble ones who lost their highest hope. And then they disparaged all high hopes.

Then lived they shamelessly in temporary pleasures, and beyond the day had hardly an aim.

'Spirit is also voluptuousness,' said they. Then broke the wings of their spirit; and now it creepeth about, and defileth where it gnaweth.

Once they thought of becoming heroes; but sensualists are they now. A trouble and a terror is the hero to them.

But by my love and hope I conjure thee: cast not away the hero in thy soul! Maintain holy thy highest hope!'

Thus spake Zarathustra.

9. The Preachers of Death

'THERE are preachers of death: and the earth is full of those to whom desistance from life must be preached.

Full is the earth of the superfluous; marred is life by the many-too-many. May they be decoyed out of this life by the "life eternal"!

"The yellow ones": so are called the preachers of death, or "the black ones". But I will show them unto you in other colours besides.

There are the terrible ones who carry about in themselves the beast of prey, and have no choice except lusts or self-laceration. And even their lusts are self-laceration.

They have not yet become men, those terrible ones: may they preach desistance from life, and pass away themselves!

There are the spiritually consumptive ones: hardly are they born when they begin to die, and long for doctrines of lassitude and renunciation.

They would fain be dead, and we should approve of their wish! Let us beware of awakening those dead ones, and of damaging those living coffins!

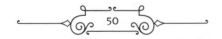

They meet an invalid, or an old man, or a corpse – and immediately they say: "Life is refuted!"

But they are only refuted, and their eye, which seeth only one aspect of existence.

Shrouded in thick melancholy, and eager for the little casualties that bring death: thus do they wait, and clench their teeth.

Or else, they grasp at sweetmeats, and mock at their childishness thereby: they cling to their straw of life, and mock at their still clinging to it.

Their wisdom speaketh thus: "A fool, he who remaineth alive; but so far are we fools! And that is the foolishest thing in life!"

"Life is only suffering": so say others, and lie not. Then see to it that *ye* cease! See to it that the life ceaseth which is only suffering!

And let this be the teaching of your virtue: "Thou shalt slay thyself! Thou shalt steal away from thyself!" – "Lust is sin," – so say some who preach death – "let us go apart and beget no children!"

"Giving birth is troublesome," – say others – "why still give birth? One beareth only the unfortunate!" And they also are preachers of death.

"Pity is necessary," – so saith a third party. "Take what I have! Take what I am! So much less doth life bind me!"

Were they consistently pitiful, then would they make their neighbours sick of life. To be wicked – that would be their true goodness.

But they want to be rid of life; what care they if they bind others still faster with their chains and gifts!

And ye also, to whom life is rough and labour is disquiet, are ye not very tired of life? Are ye not very ripe for the sermon of death?

All ye whom rough labour is dear, and the rapid, new, and strange – ye put up with yourselves badly; your diligence is flight, and the will to self-forgetfulness.

If ye believed more in life, then would ye devote yourselves less

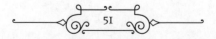

to the momentary. But for waiting, ye have not enough capacity in you – nor even for idling!

Everywhere resoundeth the voices of those who preach death; and the earth is full of those whom death hath to be preached.

Or "life eternal"; it is all the same to me – if only they pass away quickly!'

Thus spake Zarathustra.

10. War and Warriors

'BY OUR best enemies we do not want to be spared, nor by those either whom we love from the very heart. So let me tell you the truth!

My brethren in war! I love you from the very heart. I am, and was ever, your counterpart. And I am also your best enemy. So let me tell you the truth!

I know the hatred and envy of your hearts. Ye are not so great enough to not know of hatred and envy. Then be great enough not to be ashamed of them!

And if ye cannot be saints of knowledge, then, I pray to you, be at least its warriors. They are the companions and forerunners of such saintship.

I see many soldiers; could I but see many warriors! "Uniform" one calleth what they wear; may it not be uniform what they therewith hide!

Ye shall be those whose eyes ever seek for an enemy – for *your* enemy. And with some of you there is hatred at first sight.

Your enemy shall ye seek; your war shall ye wage, and for the sake of your thoughts! And if your thoughts succumb your uprightness shall still shout triumph thereby!

Ye shall love peace as a means to new wars – and the short peace more than the long.

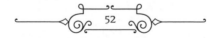

You I advise not to work, but to fight. You I advise not to peace, but to victory. Let your work be a fight, let your peace be a victory!

One can only be silent and sit peacefully when one hath arrow and bow; otherwise one prateth and quarrelleth. Let your peace be a victory! Ye say it is the good cause which halloweth even war? I say unto you: it is the good war which halloweth every cause.

War and courage have done more great things than charity. Not your sympathy, but your bravery hath hitherto saved the victims.

"What is good?" ye ask. To be brave is good. Let the little girls say: "To be good is what is pretty, and at the same time touching."

They call you heartless: but your heart is true, and I love the bashfulness of your goodwill. Ye are ashamed of your flow, and others are ashamed of their ebb.

Ye are ugly? Well then, my brethren, take the sublime about you, the mantle of the ugly!

And when your soul becometh great, then doth it become haughty, and in your sublimity there is wickedness. I know you.

In wickedness the haughty man and the weakling meet. But they misunderstand one another. I know you.

Ye shall only have enemies to be hated, but not enemies to be despised. Ye must be proud of your enemies; then, the successes of your enemies are also your successes.

Resistance – that is the distinction of the slave. Let your distinction be obedience. Let your commanding itself be obeying!

To the good warrior soundeth "thou shalt" pleasanter than "I will." And all that is dear unto you, ye shall first have it commanded unto you.

Let your love to life be love to your highest hope; and let your highest hope be the highest thought of life!

Your highest thought, however, ye shall have it commanded unto you by me – and it is this: man is something that is to be surpassed.

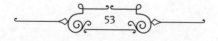

So live your life of obedience and of war! What matter about long life! What warrior wisheth to be spared!

I spare you not, I love you from my very heart, my brethren in war!'

Thus spake Zarathustra.

11. The New Idol

'SOMEWHERE there are still peoples and herds, but not with us, my brethren: here there are states.

A state? What is that? Well! Open now your ears unto me, for now I will say unto you my word concerning the death of peoples.

A state, is called the coldest of all cold monsters. Coldly lieth it also; and this lie creepeth from its mouth: "I, the state, am the people."

It is a lie! Creators were they who created peoples, and hung a faith and a love over them: thus they served life.

Destroyers, are they who lay snares for many, and call it the state: they hang a sword and a hundred cravings over them.

Where there is still a people, there the state is not understood, but hated as the evil eye, and as sin against laws and customs.

This sign I give unto you: every people speaketh its language of good and evil: this its neighbour understandeth not. Its language hath it devised for itself in laws and customs.

But the state lieth in all languages of good and evil; and whatever it saith it lieth; and whatever it hath it hath stolen. False is everything in it; with stolen teeth it biteth, the biting one. False are even its bowels.

Confusion of language of good and evil; this sign I give unto you as the sign of the state. Verily, the will to death, indicateth this sign! Verily, it beckoneth unto the preachers of death!

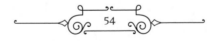

Many too many are born: for the superfluous ones was the state devised!

See just how it enticeth them to it, the many-too-many! How it swalloweth and cheweth and recheweth them!

"On earth there is nothing greater than I: it is I who am the regulating finger of God" – thus roareth the monster. And not only the long-eared and short-sighted fall upon their knees!

Ah! Even in your ears, ye great souls, it whispereth its gloomy lies! Ah! It findeth out the rich hearts which willingly lavish themselves!

Yea, it findeth you out too, ye conquerors of the old God! Weary ye became of the conflict, and now your weariness serveth the new idol!

Heroes and honourable ones, it would fain set up around it, the new idol! Gladly it basketh in the sunshine of good consciences, the cold monster!

Everything will it give *you*, if *ye* worship it, the new idol: thus it purchaseth the lustre of your virtue, and the glance of your proud eyes.

It seeketh to allure by means of you, the many-too-many. Yea, a hellish artifice hath here been devised, a death-horse jingling with the trappings of divine honours!

Yea, a dying for many hath here been devised, which glorifieth itself as life: verily, a hearty service unto all preachers of death!

The state, I call it, where all are poison-drinkers, the good and the bad: the state, where all lose themselves, the good and the bad: the state, where the slow suicide of all is called "life."

Just see these superfluous ones! They steal the works of the inventors and the treasures of the wise. Culture, they call their theft – and everything becometh sickness and trouble unto them!

Just see these superfluous ones! Sick are they always; they vomit

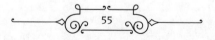

their bile and call it a newspaper. They devour one another, and cannot even digest themselves.

Just see these superfluous ones! Wealth they acquire and become poorer thereby. Power they seek for, and above all, the lever of power, much money – these impotent ones!

See them clamber, these nimble apes! They clamber over one another, and thus scuffle into the mud of the abyss.

Towards the throne they all strive: it is their madness – as if happiness sat on the throne! Oft-times sitteth filth on the throne – and oft-times also the throne on filth.

Madmen they all seem to me, and clambering apes, and too eager. Badly smelleth their idol to me, the cold monster: badly they all smell to me, these idolaters.

My brethren, will ye suffocate in the fumes of their maws and appetites! Better break the windows and jump into the open air!

Do go out of the way of the bad odour! Withdraw from the idolatry of the superfluous!

Do go out of the way of the bad odour! Withdraw from the steam of these human sacrifices!

Open still remaineth the earth for great souls. Empty are still many sites for lone ones and twain ones, around which floateth the odour of the tranquil seas.

Open still remaineth a free life for great souls. Verily, he who possesseth little is so much the less possessed: blessed be the moderate poverty!

There, where the state ceaseth – there only commenceth the man who is not superfluous: there commenceth the song of the necessary ones, the single and irreplaceable melody.

There, where the state *ceaseth* – pray look thither, my brethren! Do you not see it, the rainbow and the bridges of the Superman?'

Thus spake Zarathustra.

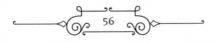

12. *The Flies in the Marketplace—Place*

'Flee, my friend, into thy solitude! I see thee deafened with the noise of the great men, and stung all over with the stings of the little ones.

Admirably do forest and rock know how to be silent with thee. Resemble again the tree which thou lovest, the broad-branched one- silently and attentively it o'erhangeth the sea.

Where solitude endeth, there beginneth the marketplace; and where the marketplace beginneth, there beginneth also the noise of the great actors, and the buzzing of the poison-flies.

In the world even the best things are worthless without those who represent them: those representers, the people call great men.

Little do the people understand what is great – that is to say, the creating agency. But they have a taste for all representers and actors of great things. Around the devisers of new values revolveth the world: invisibly it revolveth. But around the actors revolve the people and the glory: such is the course of things.

Spirit, hath the actor, but little conscience of the spirit. He believeth always in that wherewith he maketh believe most strongly – in *himself!*

Tomorrow he hath a new belief, and the day after, one still newer. Sharp perceptions hath he, like the people, and changeable humours.

To upset – that meaneth with him to prove. To drive mad – that meaneth with him to convince. And blood is counted by him as the best of all arguments.

A truth which only glideth into fine ears, he calleth falsehood and trumpery. Verily, he believeth only in gods that make a great noise in the world!

Full of clattering buffoons is the marketplace, and the people glory in their great men! These are for them the masters of the hour.

But the hour presseth them; so they press thee. And also from

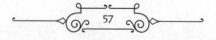

thee they want Yea or Nay. Alas! Thou wouldst set thy chair betwixt For and Against?

On account of those absolute and impatient ones, be not jealous, thou lover of truth! Never yet did truth cling to the arm of an absolute one.

On account of those abrupt ones, return into thy security: only in the marketplace is one assailed by Yea? or Nay?

Slow is the experience of all deep fountains: long have they to wait until they know *what* hath fallen into their depths.

Away from the marketplace and from fame taketh place all that is great: away from the marketplace and from fame have ever dwelt the devisers of new values. Flee, my friend, into thy solitude: I see thee stung all over by the poisonous flies. Flee thither, where a rough, strong breeze bloweth!

Flee into thy solitude! Thou hast lived too closely to the small and the pitiable. Flee from their invisible vengeance! Towards thee they have nothing but vengeance.

Raise no longer an arm against them! Innumerable are they, and it is not thy lot to be a fly-flap.

Innumerable are the small and pitiable ones; and of many a proud structure, raindrops and weeds have been the ruin.

You are not stone; but already hast thou become hollow by the numerous drops. Thou wilt yet break and burst by the numerous drops.

Exhausted I see thee, by poisonous flies; bleeding I see thee, and torn at a hundred spots; and thy pride will not even upbraid.

Blood would they have from thee in all innocence; blood their bloodless souls crave for – and they sting, therefore, in all innocence.

But thou, profound one, thou sufferest too profoundly even from small wounds; and ere thou hadst recovered, the same poison-worm crawled over thy hand.

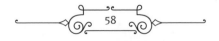

Too proud art thou to kill these sweet-tooths. But take care lest it be thy fate to suffer all their poisonous injustice!

They buzz around thee also with their praise: obtrusiveness is their praise. They want to be close to thy skin and thy blood.

They flatter thee, as one flattereth a God or devil; they whimper before thee, as before a God or devil; what doth it come to! Flatterers are they and whimperers, and nothing more.

Often, also, do they show themselves to thee as amiable ones.

But that hath always been the prudence of cowards. Yea! Cowards are wise!

They think much about thee with their circumscribed souls – thou art always suspect to them! Whatever is much thought about is at last thought suspicious.

They punish thee for all thy virtues. They pardon thee in their inmost hearts only for thy errors.

Because thou art gentle and of upright character, thou sayest: "Blameless are they for their small existence." But their petty souls think: "Blamable is all great existence."

Even when thou art gentle towards them, they still feel themselves despised by thee; and they repay thy beneficence with secret maleficence.

Thy silent pride is always counter to their taste; they rejoice if once thou are humble enough to be frivolous.

What we recognize in a man, we also irritate in him. Therefore be on your guard against the small ones!

In thy presence they feel themselves small, and their baseness gleameth and gloweth against thee in invisible vengeance.

Sawest thou not how often they became dumb when thou approachedst them, and how their energy left them like the smoke of an extinguishing fire?

Yea, my friend, the bad conscience art thou of thy neighbours;

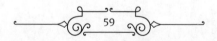

for they are unworthy of thee. Therefore they hate thee, and would fain suck thy blood.

Thy neighbours will always be poisonous flies; what is great in thee – that itself must make them more poisonous, and always more fly-like.

Flee, my friend, into thy solitude – and thither, where a rough strong breeze bloweth. It is not thy lot to be a fly-flap.'

Thus spoke Zarathustra.

13. Chastity

'I LOVE the forest. It is bad to live in cities: there, there are too many of the lustful.

Is it not better to fall into the hands of a murderer than into the dreams of a lustful woman?

And just look at these men: their eye saith it – they know nothing better on earth than to lie with a woman.

Filth is at the bottom of their souls; and alas! if their filth hath still spirit in it!

If that ye were perfect – at least as animals! But to animals belongeth innocence.

Do I counsel you to slay your instincts? I counsel you to innocence in your instincts.

Do I counsel you to chastity? Chastity is a virtue with some, but with many almost a vice.

These are continent, to be sure: but doggish lust looketh enviously out of all that they do.

Even into the heights of their virtue and into their cold spirit doth this creature follow them, with its discord.

And how nicely can doggish lust beg for a piece of spirit, when a piece of flesh is denied it!

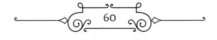

Ye love tragedies and all that breaketh the heart? But I am distrustful of your doggish lust.

Ye have too cruel eyes, and ye look wantonly towards the sufferers. Hath not your lust just disguised itself and taken the name of fellow-suffering?

And also this parable give I to you: Not a few who meant to cast out their devil, went thereby into the swine themselves.

To whom chastity is difficult, it is to be dissuaded: lest it become the road to hell – to filth and lust of soul.

Do I speak of filthy things? That is not the worst thing for me to do.

Not when the truth is filthy, but when it is shallow, does the discerning one go unwillingly into its waters.

Verily, there are chaste ones from their very nature; they are gentler of heart, and laugh better and oftener than you.

They laugh also at chastity, and ask: "What is chastity?"

Is chastity not folly? But this folly came unto us, and not we unto it.

We offered that guest harbour and heart: now it dwelleth with us – let it stay as long as it will!'

Thus spake Zarathustra.

14. The Friend

'"ONE is always too many about me" – thinks the anchorite. "Always once one – that maketh two in the long run!"

I and me are always too deeply in conversation: how could it be endured, if there were not a friend?

The friend of the anchorite is always the third one: the third one is the cork which prevents the conversation of the two sinking into the depth.

Ah! There are too many depths for all anchorites. Therefore, do they long so much for a friend and for his elevation.

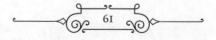

Our faith in others betrayeth that we would fain have faith in ourselves. Our longing for a friend is our betrayer.

And often with our love we want merely to overleap envy. And often we attack and make ourselves enemies, to conceal that we are vulnerable.

"Be at least my enemy!" – thus speaketh the true reverence, which dares not venture to solicit friendship.

If one would have a friend, then must one also be willing to wage war for him: and in order to wage war, one must be *capable* of being an enemy.

One ought still to honour the enemy in one's friend. Canst thou go nigh unto your friend, and not go over to him?

In one's friend one shall have one's best enemy. Thou shalt be closest unto him with thy heart when thou withstandest him.

Thou wouldst wear no raiment before thy friend? It is in honour of thy friend that thou showest thyself to him as thou art? But he wisheth thee to the devil on that account!

He who maketh no secret of himself shocketh: so much reason have ye to fear nakedness! Aye, if ye were gods, ye could then be ashamed of clothing!

Thou canst not adorn thyself fine enough for thy friend; for thou shalt be unto him an arrow and a longing for the Superman.

Sawest thou ever thy friend asleep – and know how he looketh? What is usually the countenance of thy friend? It is thine own countenance, in a coarse and imperfect mirror.

Sawest thou ever thy friend asleep? Wert thou not dismayed at thy friend looking so? O my friend, man is something that hast to be surpassed.

In divining and keeping silence shall the friend be a master: not everything must thou wish to see. Thy dreams shall disclose unto thee what thy friend doeth when awake.

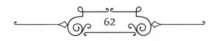

Let thy pity be a divining: to know first if thy friend wanteth pity. Perhaps he loveth in thee the unmoved eye, and the look of eternity.

Let thy pity for thy friend be hid under a hard shell; thou shalt bite out a tooth upon it. Thus will it have delicacy and sweetness.

Art thou pure air and solitude and bread and medicine to thy friend? Many a one cannot loosen his own fetters, but is nevertheless his friend's emancipator.

Art thou a slave? Then thou canst not be a friend. Art thou a tyrant? Then thou canst not have friends.

Far too long have slave and tyrant been concealed in woman. On that account woman is not yet capable of friendship: she knows only love.

In woman's love there is injustice and blindness to all she does not love. And even in woman's conscious love, there is still always attack and lightning and night, along with the light.

As yet woman is not capable of friendship: women are still cats and birds. Or at best, cows.

As yet woman is not capable of friendship. But tell me, you men, who of you is capable of friendship?

Oh! Your poverty, you men, and your sparingness of soul! As much as you give to your friend, I will give even to my enemy, and will not become poorer for it.

There is comradeship: may there be friendship!'

Thus spoke Zarathustra.

15. The Thousand and One Goals

'MANY lands saw Zarathustra, and many peoples: thus he discovered the good and bad of many peoples. No greater power did Zarathustra find on earth than good and bad.

No people could live without first valuing; if a people will maintain itself, however, it must not value as its neighbour valueth.

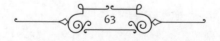

Much that passed for good with one people was regarded with scorn and contempt by another: thus I found it. Much I found here called bad, which was there decked with purple honours.

Never did the one neighbour understand the other: ever did his soul marvel at his neighbour's delusion and wickedness.

A tablet of excellences hangeth over every people. Lo! It is the tablet of their triumphs; behold, it is the voice of their Will to Power.

It is laudable, what they think hard; what is indispensable and hard they call good; and what relieveth in the direst distress, the unique and hardest of all, they extol as holy.

Whatever makes them rule and conquer and shine, to the dismay and envy of their neighbours, they regard as the high and foremost thing, the test and the meaning of all else.

Verily, my brother, if thou only knewest but a people's need, its land, its sky, and its neighbour, then you wouldst divine the law of its surmountings, and why it climbth up that ladder to its hope.

"Always shall thou be the foremost and prominent above all others: no one shall thy jealous soul love, except the friend" – that made the soul of a Greek thrill: thereby went he his way to greatness.

"To speak truth, and be skilful with bow and arrow" – so seemed it alike pleasing and hard to the people from whom cometh my name – the name which is alike pleasing and hard to me.

"To honour father and mother, and from the root of the soul to do their will" – this table of surmounting hung another people over them, and became powerful and permanent thereby.

"To have fidelity, and for the sake of fidelity to risk honour and blood, even in evil and dangerous courses" – teaching itself so, another people mastered itself, and thus mastering itself, became pregnant and heavy with great hopes.

Verily, men have given unto themselves all their good and bad.

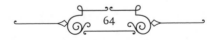

Verily, they took it not, they found it not, it came not unto them as a voice from heaven.

Values did man only assign to things in order to maintain himself – he created only the significance of things, a human significance! Therefore, calls he himself "man", that is, the valuator.

Valuing is creating: hear it, ye creating ones! Valuation itself is the treasure and jewel of all valued things.

Through valuation only is there value; and without valuation the nut of existence would be hollow. Hear it, ye creating ones!

Change of values – that means, change of the creating ones. Always doth he destroy, who hath to be a creator.

Creating ones were first of all peoples, and only in late times individuals; verily, the individual himself is still the latest creation.

Peoples once hung over them tables of the good. Love which would rule and love which would obey, created for themselves such tables.

Older is the pleasure in the herd than pleasure in the ego: and as long as the good conscience is for the herd, the bad conscience only saith: "ego".

The crafty ego, the loveless one, that seeks its advantage in the advantage of many – it is not the origin of the herd, but its downfall.

It was always loving ones and creators that created good and bad. Fire of love gloweth in the names of all the virtues, and fire of wrath.

Many lands saw Zarathustra, and many peoples: no greater power did Zarathustra find on earth than the creations of the loving ones – "good" and "bad" are their names.

Verily, a prodigy is this power of praising and blaming. Tell me, ye brethren, who will master it for me? Who will put a fetter upon the thousand necks of this animal?

A thousand goals have there been hitherto, for a thousand peoples have there been. Only the fetter for the thousand necks is still lacking; there is lacking the one goal. As yet humanity has not a goal.

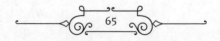

But pray tell me, my brethren, if the goal of humanity be still lacking, is there not still lacking humanity itself?'

Thus spoke Zarathustra.

16. Neighbour Love

'YE CROWD around your neighbour, and have fine words for it. But I say to you: your neighbour-love is your bad love of yourselves.

You flee unto your neighbour from yourselves, and would rather make a virtue of it: but I fathom your 'unselfishness'.

The *Thou* is older than the *I*; the *Thou* has been consecrated, but not yet the *I*: so man presses near to his neighbour.

Do I advise you to neighbour-love? Rather do I advise you to neighbour-flight and to furthest love!

Higher than love of your neighbour is love to the furthest and future ones; higher still than love to men, is love to things and phantoms.

The phantom that runs on before thee, my brother, is fairer than thou; why dost thou not give unto it thy flesh and thy bones? But thou fearest, and runnest unto thy neighbour.

Ye cannot endure it with yourselves, and do not love yourselves sufficiently: so ye seek to mislead your neighbour into love, and would fain gild yourselves with his error.

Would that ye could not endure it with any kind of near ones, or their neighbours; then would ye have to create your friend and his overflowing heart out of yourselves.

Ye call in a witness when ye want to speak well of yourselves; and when ye have misled him to think well of you, ye also think well of yourselves.

Not only does he lie, who speaketh contrary to his knowledge, but more so, he who speaketh contrary to his ignorance. And thus

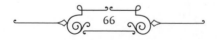

speak ye of yourselves in your intercourse, and belie to your neighbour with yourselves.

Thus says the fool: "Association with men spoils the character, especially when one hath none."

The one goeth to his neighbour because he seeketh himself, and the other because he would fain lose himself. Your bad love of your-selves makes solitude a prison to you.

The farthest ones are they who pay for your love to the near ones; and when there are five of you together, a sixth must always die.

I love not your festivals either: too many actors found I there, and even the spectators often behaved like actors.

Not the neighbour do I teach you, but the friend. Let the friend be the festival of the earth to you, and a foretaste of the Superman.

I teach you the friend and his overflowing heart. But one must know how to be a sponge, if one would be loved by over-flowing hearts.

I teach you the friend in whom the world stands complete, a capsule of the good, the creating friend, who hath always a complete world to bestow.

And as the world unrolled itself for him, so rolleth it together again for him in rings, as the growth of good through evil, as the growth of purpose out of chance.

Let the future and the furthest be the motive of thy today; in thy friend you shall love the Superman as thy motive.

My brethren, I advise you not to neighbour-love – I advise you to furthest love!'

Thus spoke Zarathustra.

17. The Way of the Creating One

'WOULDST thou go into isolation, my brother? Wouldst thou seek the way unto thyself? Tarry yet a little and hearken unto me.

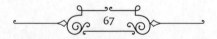

"He who seeketh may easily get lost himself. All isolation is wrong": so say the herd. And long didst thou belong to the herd.

The voice of the herd will still echo in you. And when thou sayest, "I have no longer a conscience in common with you," then will it be a plaint and a pain.

Lo, that pain itself did the same conscience produce; and the last gleam of that conscience still gloweth on thine affliction.

But thou wouldst go the way of your affliction, which is the way unto thyself? Then show me thine authority and thy strength to do so!

Are you a new strength and a new authority? A first motion? A self-rolling wheel? Canst thou also compel the stars to revolve around thee?

Alas! There is so much lusting for loftiness! There are so many convulsions of the ambitions! Show me that thou are not a lusting and ambitious one!

Alas! There are so many great thoughts that do nothing more than the bellows: they inflate, and make emptier than ever.

Free, do you call thyself? Thy ruling thought would I hear of, and not that thou hast escaped from a yoke.

Art thou one *entitled* to escape from a yoke? Many a one hath cast away his final worth when he hath cast away his servitude.

Free from what? What doeth that matter to Zarathustra! Clearly, however, shall thine eye show unto me: free *for what?*

Canst thou give unto thyself thy bad and thy good, and set up thy will as a law over thee? Canst thou be judge for thyself, and avenger of thy law?

Terrible is aloneness with the judge and avenger of one's own law. Thus is a star projected into desert space, and into the icy breath of aloneness.

Today sufferest thou still from the multitude, thou individual; today hast thou still thy courage unabated, and thy hopes.

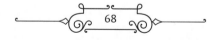

But one day will the solitude weary thee; one day will thy pride yield, and thy courage quail. Thou wilt one day cry: "I am alone!"

One day wilt thou see no longer thy loftiness, and see too closely thy lowliness; thy sublimity itself will frighten thee as a phantom. Thou wilt one day cry: "All is false!"

There are feelings which seek to slay the lonesome one; if they do not succeed, then must they themselves die! But art thou capable of this – to be a murderer?

Hast thou ever known, my brother, the word "disdain"? And the anguish of thy justice in being just to those that disdain thee?

Thou forcest many to think differently about thee; that, charge they heavily to thine account. Thou camest nigh unto them, and yet wenteth past: for that they never forgive thee.

Thou goest beyond them: but the higher thou risest, the smaller doth the eye of envy see thee. Most of all, however, is the flying one hated.

"How could ye be just unto me!" – must thou say – "I choose your injustice as my allotted portion."

Injustice and filth cast they at the lonesome one: but, my brother, if thou wouldst be a star, thou must shine for them none the less on that account!

And be on thy guard against the good and just! They would fain crucify those who devise their own virtue – they hate the lonesome ones.

Be on thy guard, also, against holy simplicity! All is unholy to it that is not simple; fain, likewise, would it play with the fire – of the faggot and the stake.

And be on thy guard, also, against the assaults of thy love! Too readily doth the recluse reach his hand to any one who meeteth him.

To many a one mayest thou not give thy hand, but only thy paw; and I want thy paw to have claws.

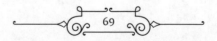

But the worst enemy thou canst meet, wilt thou thyself always be; thou waylayeth thyself in caverns and forests.

Thou lonesome one, thou goest the way to thyself! And past thyself and thy seven devils leadeth thy way!

A heretic wilt thou be to thyself, and a wizard and a soothsayer, and a fool, and a doubter, and a reprobate, and a villain.

Ready must thou be to burn thyself in thine own flame; how couldst thou become new if thou have not first become ashes!

Thou lonesome one, thou goest the way of the creating one: a God wilt thou create for thyself out of thy seven devils!

Thou lonesome one, thou goest the way of the loving one: thou lovest thyself, and on that account you despisest thyself, as only the loving ones despise.

To create, desireth the loving one, because he despiseth! What knoweth he of love who hath not been obliged to despise just what he loved!

With thy love, go into thine isolation, my brother, and with thy creating; and late only will justice limp after thee.

With my tears, go into thine isolation, my brother. I love him who seeketh to create beyond himself, and thus succumbeth.'

Thus spoke Zarathustra.

18. Old and Young Women

'WHY stealeth thou along so furtively in the twilight, Zarathustra? And what hideth thou so carefully under thy mantle?

Is it a treasure that hath been given thee? Or a child that hath been born thee? Or goeth thou thyself on a thief's errand, thou friend of the evil?'

'Verily, my brother', said Zarathustra, 'it is a treasure that hath been given me: it is a little truth which I carry.

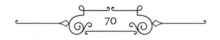

'But it is naughty, like a young child; and if I hold not its mouth, it screameth too loudly.

As I went on my way alone today, at the hour when the sun declineth, there met me an old woman, and she spake thus unto my soul:

"Much has Zarathustra spoken also to us women, but never spake he to us concerning woman."

And I answered her: "Concerning woman, one should only talk unto men."

"Talk also unto me of woman," said she; "I am old enough to forget it presently."

And I obliged the old woman and spake thus unto her:

"Everything in woman is a riddle, and everything in woman hath one answer – it is called pregnancy.

Man is for woman a means: the purpose is always the child. But what is woman for man?

Two different things wanteth the true man: danger and diversion. Therefore he wanteth woman, as the most dangerous plaything.

Man shall be trained for war, and woman for the recreation of the warrior: all else is folly.

Too sweet fruits – these the warrior liketh not. Therefore liketh he woman; bitter is even the sweetest woman.

Better than man doeth woman understand children, but man is more childish than woman.

In the true man there is a child hidden: it wanteth to play. Up then, ye women, and discover the child in man!

A plaything let woman be, pure and fine like the precious stone, illumined with the virtues of a world not yet come.

Let the beam of a star shine in your love! Let your hope say: 'May I bear to the Superman!'

In your love let there be valour! With your love shall ye assail him who inspireth you with fear!

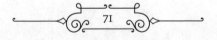

In your love be your honour! Little doth woman understand otherwise about honour. But let this be your honour: always to love more than you are loved, and never to be second.

Let man fear woman when she loveth: then she maketh every sacrifice, and everything else she regardeth as worthless.

Let man fear woman when she hateth: for man in his innermost soul is merely evil; woman, however, is mean.

Whom hateth woman most? – Thus spoke the iron to the magnet: 'I hate thee most, because thou attractest, but art too weak to draw unto thee.'

The happiness of man is, 'I will.' The happiness of woman is, 'He will.'

'Lo! Lo! Now hath the world become perfect!' Thus thinks every woman when she obeyeth with all her love.

Obey must the woman, and find a depth for her surface. Surface is woman's soul, a mobile, stormy film on shallow water.

Man's soul, however, is deep, its current gusheth in subterranean caverns: woman surmiseth its force, but comprehendeth it not."

Then answered me the old woman: "Many fine things hath Zarathustra said, especially for those who are young enough for them.

Strange! Zarathustra knoweth little about woman, and yet he is right about them! Does this happen, because with woman nothing is impossible?

And now accept a little truth by way of thanks! I am old enough for it!

Swaddle it up and hold its mouth: otherwise it will scream too loudly, the little truth."

"Give me woman, your little truth!" I said. And thus spake the old woman:

"Thou goest to women? Do not forget thy whip!'"

Thus spoke Zarathustra.

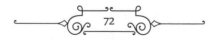

19. *The Bite of the Adder*

ONE day had Zarathustra fallen asleep under a fig tree, owing to the heat, with his arm over his face. And there came an adder and bit him in the neck, so that Zarathustra screamed with pain. When he had taken his arm from his face he looked at the serpent; and then did it recognize the eyes of Zarathustra, wriggled awkwardly, and tried to get away. 'Not at all,' said Zarathustra, 'as yet hast thou not received my thanks! Thou hast awakened me in time; my journey is yet long.' 'Your journey is short,' said the adder sadly; 'my poison is fatal.' Zarathustra smiled. 'When did ever a dragon die of a serpent's poison?' – said he. 'But take thy poison back! Thou art not rich enough to present it to me.' Then the adder fell again on his neck, and licked his wound.

When Zarathustra once told this to his disciples they asked him: 'And what, O Zarathustra, is the moral of thy story?' And Zarathustra answered them thus:

'The destroyer of morality, the good and just call me: my story is immoral.

When, however, ye have an enemy, then return him not good for evil: for that would abash him. But prove that he hath done something good to you.

And rather be angry than abash anyone! And when you are cursed, it pleaseth me not that ye should desire to bless. Rather curse a little also!

And should a great injustice befall you, then do quickly five small ones besides. Hideous to behold is he whom injustice presseth alone.

Did you know this? A shared injustice is half justice. And he who can bear it, should take the injustice upon himself!

A small revenge is more humane than no revenge at all. And if the punishment be not also a right and an honour to the transgressor, I do not like your punishment.

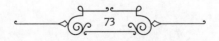

Nobler is it to own oneself in the wrong than to establish one's right, especially if one be in the right. Only, one must be rich enough to do so.

I do not like your cold justice; out of the eye of your judges there always glanceth the executioner and his cold steel.

Tell me: where find we justice, which is love with seeing eyes?

Devise me, then, the love which not only beareth all punishment, but also all guilt!

Devise me, then, the justice which acquiteth every one, except the judges!

And would ye hear this likewise? To him who seeketh to be just from the heart, even the lie becometh philanthropy.

But how could I be just from the heart! How can I give every one his own! Let this be enough for me: I give unto every own mine own.

Finally, my brethen, guard against doing wrong to any anchorite. How could a anchorite forget! How could he requite!

Like a deep well is a anchorite. Easy it is to throw in a stone: if it sinks to the bottom, however, tell me, who will bring it out again?

Guard against injuring the anchorite! If you have done so however, well then kill him also!'

Thus spoke Zarathustra.

20. Child and Marriage

'I HAVE a question for thee alone, my brother: like a sounding-lead, cast I this question into thy soul, that I may know its depth.

Thou art young, and desirest child and marriage. But I ask thee: Art thou a man *entitled* to desire a child?

Art thou the victorious one, the self-conqueror, the ruler of thy passions, the master of thy virtues? Thus do I ask thee.

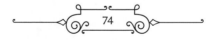

Or does the animal speak in thy wish, and necessity? Or isolation? Or discord in thee?

I would have thy victory and freedom long for a child. Living monuments shalt thou build to thy victory and emancipation.

Beyond thyself shalt thou build. But first of all must thou be built thyself, rectangular in body and soul.

Not only onward shalt thou propagate thyself, but upward! For that purpose may the garden of marriage help thee!

A higher body shalt thou create, a first movement, a spontaneously rolling wheel – a creating one shalt thou create.

Marriage: so call I the will of the twain to create the one that is more than those who created it. The reverence for one another, as those exercising such a will, call I marriage.

Let this be the significance and the truth of thy marriage. But that which the many-too-many call marriage, those superfluous ones – ah, what shall I call it?

Ah, the poverty of soul in the twain! Ah, the filth of soul in the twain! Ah, the pitiable self-complacency in the twain!

Marriage they call it all; and they say their marriages are made in heaven.

Well I do not like it, that heaven of the superfluous! No, I do not like them, those animals tangled in the heavenly toils!

Far from me also be the God who limpeth thither to bless what he hath not matched!

Laugh not at such marriages! What child has not had reason to weep over its parents?

Worthy did this man seem, and ripe for the meaning of the earth: but when I saw his wife, the earth seemed to me a home for madcaps.

Yea, I would that the earth shook with convulsions when a saint and a goose mate with one another.

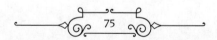

This one went forth in quest of truth as a hero, and at last got for himself a small dressed-up lie: his marriage he calleth it.

That one was reserved in intercourse and chose choicely. But one time he spoilt his company for all time: his marriage he calleth it.

Another sought a handmaid with the virtues of an angel. But all at once he became the handmaid of a woman, and now would he need also to become an angel.

Careful, have I found all buyers, and all of them have astute eyes. But even the most astute of them buyeth his wife in a sack.

Many short follies – that is called love by you. And your marriage putteth an end to your many short follies, with one long stupidity.

Your love of woman, and woman's love of man – ah, would that it were sympathy for suffering and veiled deities! But generally two animals alight on one another.

But even your best love is only an enraptured simile and a painful ardour. It is a torch to light loftier paths for you.

Beyond yourselves shall ye love some day! Then *learn* first of all to love. And on that account ye had to drink the bitter cup of your love.

Bitterness is in the cup even of the best love; thus doth it cause longing for the Superman; thus doth it cause thirst in thee, the creating one!

Thirst in the creating one, arrow and longing for the Superman: tell me, my brother, is this thy will to marriage?

Holy call I such a will, and such a marriage.'

Thus spoke Zarathustra.

21. *Voluntary Death*

'MANY die too late, and some die too early. Yet strange soundeth the precept: "Die at the right time!"

Die at the right time: so teacheth Zarathustra.

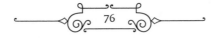

To be sure, he who never liveth at the right time, how could he ever die at the right time? Would that he had never been born! Thus do I advise the superfluous ones.

But even the superfluous ones make much ado about their death, and even the hollowest nut wanteth to be cracked.

Every one regardeth dying as a great matter: but as yet death is not a festival. Not yet have people learned to inaugurate the finest festivals.

The consummating death I show unto you, which becometh a stimulus and promise to the living.

His death, dieth the consummating one triumphantly, surrounded by hoping and promising ones.

Thus should one learn to die; and there should be no festival at which such a dying one doeth not consecrate the oaths of the living!

Thus to die is best; the next best, however, is to die in battle, and squander a great soul.

But to the fighter equally hateful as to the victor, is your grinning death which stealeth nigh like a thief, – and yet cometh as master.

My death, praise I unto you, the voluntary death, which cometh unto me because *I* want it.

And when shall I want it? He that has a goal and an heir, wants death at the right time for the goal and the heir.

And out of reverence for the goal and the heir, he will hang up no more withered wreaths in the sanctuary of life.

Verily, not the rope-makers will I resemble: they lengthen out their cord and thereby go ever backward.

Many a one, also, waxeth too old for his truths and triumphs; a toothless mouth hath no longer the right to every truth.

And whoever wanteth to have fame, must take leave of honour betimes, and practice the difficult art of going at the right time.

One must discontinue being feasted upon when one tasteth best: that is known by those who want to be long loved.

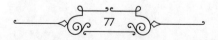

Sour apples are there, no doubt, whose lot is to wait until the last day of autumn: and at once they become ripe, yellow, and shrivelled.

In some the heart ages first, and in others the spirit. And some are hoary in youth, but the late young keep long young.

To many men life is a failure; a poison-worm gnaweth at their heart. Then let them see to it that their dying is all the more a success.

Many never become sweet; they rot even in the summer. It is cowardice that holdeth them fast to their branches.

Far too many live, and far too long do they hang on their branches. Would that a storm would come and shook all this rottenness and worm-eatenness from the tree!

Would that here came preachers of *speedy* death! Those would be the appropriate storms and agitators of the trees of life! But I hear only the slow death preached, and patience with all that is "earthly".

Ah! You preach patience with what is earthly? This earthly is it that hath too much patience with you, ye blasphemers!

Verily, too early died that Hebrew whom the preachers of slow death honour: and to many has it proved a calamity that he died too early.

As yet had he known only tears, and the melancholy of the Hebrews, together with the hatred of the good and just – the Hebrew Jesus: then was he seized with the longing for death.

Had he but remained in the wilderness, far from the good and just! Then perhaps would he have learned to live and love the earth – and laughter also!

Believe me, my brethren! He died too early; he himself would have disavowed his doctrine had he reached my age! Noble enough was he to disavow!

But he was still immature. Immaturely loveth the youth, immaturely also hateth the man and earth. Confined and awkward are still his soul and the wings of his spirit.

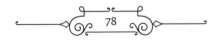

But in man there is more of the child than in the youth, and less of melancholy: better understandeth he about life and death.

Free for death, and free in death; a holy Naysayer, when there is no longer time for Yea: thus understandeth he about death and life.

That your dying may not be a reproach to man and the earth, my friends: that do I solicit from the honey of your soul.

In your dying, shall your spirit and your virtue still shine like an evening afterglow around the earth: otherwise your dying hath been unsatisfactory.

Thus I will die myself, that ye, my friends, may love the earth more for my sake; and earth will I again become, to have rest in her that bore me.

Verily, a goal had Zarathustra; he threw his ball. Now be ye, my friends, the heirs of my goal; to you I throw the golden ball.

Best of all, do I see you, my friends, throw the golden ball! And so tarry I a little while on the earth – pardon me for it!'

Thus spoke Zarathustra.

22. The Bestowing Virtue

1

WHEN Zarathustra had taken leave of the town to which his heart was attached, the name of which is The Pied Cow, there followed him many people who called themselves his disciples, and kept him company. Thus they came to a crossroads. Then Zarathustra told them that he now wanted to go alone; for he was fond of going alone. His disciples, however, presented him at his departure with a staff, on the golden handle of which a serpent twined round the sun. Zarathustra rejoiced on account of the staff, and supported himself thereon; then spake he thus to his disciples:

'Tell me, pray: how come gold to the highest value? Because it

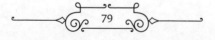

is uncommon, and unprofiting, and beaming, and soft in lustre; it always bestoweth itself.

Only as image of the highest virtue came gold to the highest value. Goldlike, beameth the glance of the bestower. Gold-lustre maketh peace between moon and sun.

Uncommon is the highest virtue, and unprofiting, beaming is it, and soft of lustre: a bestowing virtue is the highest virtue.

Verily, I divine you well, my disciples: ye strive like me for the bestowing virtue. What would ye have in common with cats and wolves?

It is your thirst to become sacrifices and gifts yourselves: and therefore have ye thirst to accumulate all riches in your soul.

Insatiably striveth your soul for treasures and jewels, because your virtue is insatiable in desiring to bestow.

Ye constrain all things to flow towards you and into you, so that they shall flow back again out of your fountain as the gifts of your love.

Verily, an appropriator of all values must such bestowing love become; but healthy and holy, call I this selfishness.

Another selfishness is there, an all-too-poor and hungry kind, which would always steal the selfishness of the sick, the sickly selfishness.

With the eye of the thief it looketh upon all that is lustrous; with the craving of hunger it measureth him who hath abundance; and ever does it prowl round the tables of bestowers.

Sickness speaketh in such craving, and invisible degeneration; of a sickly body, speaketh the larcenous craving of this selfishness.

Tell me, my brother, what do we think bad, and worst of all? Is it not degeneration? And we always suspect degeneration when the bestowing soul is lacking.

Upward goes our course from genera on to super-genera. But a horror to us is the degenerating sense, which saith: "All for myself."

Upward soareth our sense: thus is it a simile of our body, a simile of an elevation. Such similes of elevations are the names of the virtues.

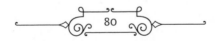

Thus goeth the body through history, a becomer and fighter. And the spirit – what is that to the body? Its fights and victories herald, its companion and echo.

Similes, are all names of good and evil; they do not speak out, they only hint. A fool who seeketh knowledge from them!

Give heed, my brethren, to every hour when your spirit would speak in similes: there is the origin of your virtue.

Elevated is then your body, and raised up; with its delight, enraptureth it the spirit, so that it becometh creator, and valuer, and lover, and everything's benefactor.

When your heart overfloweth broad and full like the river, a blessing and a danger to the lowlanders: there is the origin of your virtue.

When ye are exalted above praise and blame, and your will would command all things, as a loving one's will: there is the origin of your virtue.

When ye despise pleasant things, and the effeminate couch, and cannot couch far enough from the effeminate: there is the origin of your virtue.

When ye are willers of one will, and when that change of every need is needful to you: there is the origin of your virtue.

Verily, a new good and evil is it! Verily, a new deep murmuring, and the voice of a new fountain!

Power is it, this new virtue; a ruling thought is it, and around it a subtle soul: a golden sun, with the serpent of knowledge around it.'

2

Here paused Zarathustra awhile, and looked lovingly on his disciples. Then he continued to speak thus – and his voice had changed: 'Remain faithful to the earth, my brothers, with the power of your virtue! Let your giving love and your knowledge be devoted to the the meaning of the earth! Thus do I pray and conjure you.

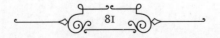

Let it not fly away from the earthly and beat against eternal walls with its wings! Ah, there hath always been so much flown-away virtue!

Lead, like me, the flown-away virtue back to the earth – yeah, back to body and life: that it may give to the earth its meaning, a human meaning!

A hundred times hitherto hath spirit as well as virtue flown away and blundered. Alas! In our body dwelleth still all this delusion and blundering: body and will hath it there become.

A hundred times hitherto hath spirit as well as virtue attempted and erred. Yea, an attempt hath man been. Alas, much ignorance and error hath embodied in us!

Not only the rationality of millennia – also their madness, breaketh out in us. Dangerous is it to be an heir.

Still fight we step by step with the giant Chance, and over all mankind hath hitherto ruled nonsense, the lack-of-sense.

Let your spirit and your virtue be devoted to the sense of the earth, my bretheren: let the value of everything be determined anew by you! Therefore shall ye be fighters! Therefore shall ye be creators!

Intelligently doth the body purify itself; attempting with intelligence it exalteth itself; to the discerners all impulses sanctify themselves; to the exalted the soul becometh joyful.

Physcian, heal thyself: then wilt thou also heal thy patient. Let it be his best cure to see with his eyes him who maketh himself whole.

A thousand paths are there which have never yet been trodden; a thousand salubrities and hidden islands of life. Unexhausted and undiscovered is still man and man's world.

Awake and listen, you that are lonely! From the future come winds with stealthy wings, and to subtle ears good tidings are proclaimed.

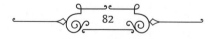

You that are lonely today, you that withdraw, you shall one day be a people: out of you, who have chosen yourselves, shall arise a chosen people: and out of them, the Superman.

The earth shall become a place of healing! And there already is a new fragrance surrounding it, a salvation-bringing fragrance – and a new hope!'

3

When Zarathustra had spoken these words, he paused, like one who had not yet said his last word; and long did he balance the staff doubtfully in his hand. At last he spoke thus – and his voice had changed:

'I now go alone, my disciples! You too go now, alone! Thus I want it.

I advise you: depart from me, and guard yourselves against Zarathustra! And better still: be ashamed of him! Perhaps he has deceived you.

The man of knowledge must be able not only to love his enemies, but also to hate his friends.

One requites a teacher badly if one remains merely a student. And why will you not pluck at my wreath?

You venerate me; but what if your veneration should some day collapse? Beware lest a statue crush you!

You say you believe in Zarathustra? But what matters Zarathustra! You are my believers: but what matters all believers! You had not yet sought yourselves: then you found me. So do all believers; thus all belief matters so little.

Now I bid you lose me and find yourselves; and only when you have all denied me will I return to you.

With other eyes, my brothers, shall I then seek my lost ones; with another love shall I then love you.

And once again you shall become friends to me, and children of

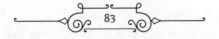

one hope: then I will be with you for the third time, to celebrate the great noontide with you.

And it is the great noontide, when man is in the middle of his course between animal and Superman, and celebrates his advance to the evening as his highest hope: for it is the advance to a new morning.

Then will the down-goer bless himself, for being an over-goer; and the sun of his knowledge will be at noontide.

"Dead are all Gods: now we want the Superman to live." Let this be our final will at the great noontide!'

Thus spoke Zarathustra.

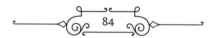

Part Two

23. *The Child with the Mirror*

AFTER this Zarathustra returned again into the mountains to the solitude of his cave, and withdrew himself from men, waiting like a sower who has scattered his seed. His soul, however, became impatient and full of longing for those whom he loved: because he had still much to give them. For this is hardest of all: to close the open hand out of love, and keep modest as a giver.

Thus passed with the lonesome one months and years; his wisdom meanwhile increased, and caused him pain by its abundance.

One morning, however, he awoke before the rosy dawn, and having meditated long on his couch, at last spake thus to his heart:

'Why did I startle in my dream, so that I awoke? Did not a child come to me, carrying a mirror?

"O Zarathustra" – said the child unto me – "look at thyself in the mirror!"

But when I looked into the mirror, I shrieked, and my heart throbbed: for not myself did I see therein, but a devil's grimace and derision.

Verily, all too well do I understand the dream's portent and monition: my *doctrine* is in danger; tares want to be called wheat!

My enemies have grown powerful and have disfigured the likeness of my doctrine, so that my dearest ones have to blush for the gifts that I gave them.

Lost are my friends; the hour has come for me to seek my lost ones!'

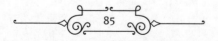

With these words Zarathustra started up, not however like a person in anguish seeking relief, but rather like a seer and a singer whom the spirit inspires. With amazement did his eagle and serpent gaze upon him: for a coming bliss overspread his countenance like the rosy dawn.

'What has happened to me, my animals?' said Zarathustra. 'Am I not transformed? Has not bliss come to me like a whirlwind?

Foolish is my happiness, and foolish things will it speak: it is still too young – so have patience with it!

Wounded am I by my happiness: all sufferers shall be physicians to me!

To my friends can I again go down, and also to my enemies! Zarathustra can again speak and give, and show his best love to his loved ones!

My impatient love overflows in streams, down towards sunrise and sunset. Out of silent mountains and storms of affliction, rushes my soul into the valleys.

Too long have I longed and looked into the distance. Too long has solitude possessed me: thus have I unlearned to keep silence.

Utterance have I become altogether, and the brawling of a brook from high rocks: downward into the valleys will I hurl my speech.

And let the stream of my love sweep into unfrequented channels! How should a stream not finally find its way to the sea! Forsooth, there is a lake in me, sequestered and self- sufficing; but the stream of my love beareth this along with it, down – to the sea!

New paths do I tread, a new speech comes to me; tired have I become – like all creators – of the old tongues. No longer will my spirit walk on worn-out soles.

Too slowly runs all speaking for me: into thy chariot, O storm, do I leap! And even you will I whip with my spite!

Like a cry and an huzza will I traverse wide seas, till I find the Happy Isles where my friends sojourn.

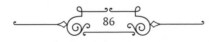

And mine enemies amongst them! How I now love every one to whom I may but speak! Even my enemies pertain to my bliss.

And when I want to mount my wildest horse, then does my spear always help me up best: it is my foot's ever ready servant:

The spear which I hurl at my enemies! How grateful am I to my enemies that I may at last hurl it!

Too great has been the tension of my cloud: 'twixt laughters of lightnings will I cast hail-showers into the depths.

Violently will my breast then heave; violently will it blow its storm over the mountains: thus comes its assuagement.

Like a storm comes my happiness, and my freedom! But my enemies shall think that the evil one roars over their heads.

Yes, you also, my friends, will be alarmed by my wild wisdom; and perhaps you will flee therefrom, along with my enemies.

Ah, that I knew how to lure you back with shepherds' flutes! Ah, that my lioness wisdom would learn to roar softly! And much have we already learned with one another!

My wild wisdom became pregnant on the lonesome mountains; on the rough stones did she bear the youngest of her young.

Now runneth she foolishly in the arid wilderness, and seeketh and seeketh the soft sward-mine old, wild wisdom!

On the soft sward of your hearts, my friends! On your love, would she fain couch her dearest one!'

Thus spake Zarathustra.

24. In the Happy Isles

'THE figs fall from the trees, they are good and sweet; and in falling the red skins of them break. A north wind am I to ripe figs.

Thus, like figs, do these doctrines fall for you, my friends: imbibe

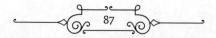

now their juice and their sweet substance! It is autumn all around, and clear sky, and afternoon.

Lo, what fullness is around us! And out of the midst of super-abundance, it is delightful to look out upon distant seas.

Once did people say God, when they looked out upon distant seas; now, however, have I taught you to say, Superman.

God is a conjecture: but I do not wish your conjecturing to reach beyond your creating will.

Could ye *create* a God? Then, I pray you, be silent about all gods! But ye could well create the Superman.

Not perhaps ye yourselves, my brethren! But into fathers and forefathers of the Superman could ye transform yourselves: and let that be your best creating! God is a conjecture: but I should like your conjecturing restricted to the conceivable.

Could you conceive a God? But let this mean Will to Truth to you, that everything be transformed into the humanly conceivable, the humanly visible, the humanly sensible! Your own discernment shall you follow out to the end!

And what you have called the world shall but be created by you: your reason, your likeness, your will, your love, shall it itself become! And verily, for your bliss, you discerning ones!

And how would you endure life without that hope, you discerning ones? Neither in the inconceivable could you have been born, nor in the irrational.

But that I may reveal my heart entirely to you, my friends: if there were gods, how could I endure it to be no God! Therefore there are no gods.

Yes, I have drawn the conclusion; now, however, does it draw me.

God is a conjecture: but who could drink all the bitterness of this conjecture without dying? Shall his faith be taken from the creator, and from the eagle his flights into eagle-heights?

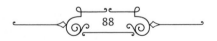

God is a thought – it makes all the straight crooked, and all that stands reel. What? Time would be gone, and all the perishable would be but a lie?

To think this is giddiness and vertigo to human limbs, and even vomiting to the stomach: verily, the reeling sickness do I call it, to conjecture such a thing.

Evil do I call it and misanthropic: all that teaching about the one, and the plenum, and the unmoved, and the sufficient, and the imperishable!

All the imperishable – that's but a parable, and the poets lie too much. But of time and of becoming shall the best parables speak: a praise shall they be, and a justification of all perishing!

Creating – that is the great salvation from suffering, and life's alleviation. But for the creator to appear, suffering itself is needed, and much transformation.

Yes, much bitter dying must there be in your life, you creators! Thus are you advocates and justifiers of all perishing.

For the creator himself to be the new-born child, he must also be willing to be the child-bearer, and endure the pangs of the child-bearer.

Through a hundred souls went I my way, and through a hundred cradles and birth-throes. Many a farewell have I taken; I know the heart-breaking last hours.

But so wills it my creating Will, my fate. Or, to tell you it more candidly: just such a fate wills my Will.

All feeling suffers in me, and is in prison: but my willing ever comes to me as my emancipator and comforter.

Willing emancipates: that is the true doctrine of will and emancipation – so teaches you Zarathustra.

No longer willing, and no longer valuing, and no longer creating! Ah, that that great debility may ever be far from me!

And also in discerning do I feel only my will's procreating and

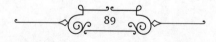

evolving delight; and if there be innocence in my knowledge, it is because there is will to procreation in it.

Away from God and gods did this will allure me; what would there be to create if there were gods!

But to man does it ever impel me anew, my fervent creative will; thus impels it the hammer to the stone.

Ah, you men, within the stone slumbers an image for me, the image of my visions! Ah, that it should slumber in the hardest, ugliest stone! Now rages my hammer ruthlessly against its prison. From the stone fly the fragments: what's that to me?

I will complete it: for a shadow came to me – the still and lightest of all things once came to me!

The beauty of the Superman came to me as a shadow. Ah, my brothers! Of what account now are the gods to me!'

Thus spoke Zarathustra.

25. The Pitiful

'MY FRIENDS, there has arisen a satire on your friend: "Behold Zarathustra! Walks he not amongst us as if amongst animals?"

But it is better said in this wise: "The discerning one walks amongst men as amongst animals."

Man himself is to the discerning one: the animal with red cheeks.

How has that happened to him? Is it not because he has had to be ashamed too oft?

O my friends! Thus speaks the discerning one: shame, shame, shame – that is the history of man!

And on that account does the noble one enjoin on himself not to abash: bashfulness does he enjoin himself in presence of all sufferers.

I like them not, the merciful ones, whose bliss is in their pity: too destitute are they of bashfulness.

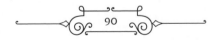

If I must be pitiful, I dislike to be called so; and if I be so, it is preferably at a distance. Preferably also do I shroud my head, and flee, before being recognized: and thus do I bid you do, my friends!

May my destiny ever lead unafflicted ones like you across my path, and those with whom I may have hope and repast and honey in common!

I have done this and that for the afflicted: but something better did I always seem to do when I had learned to enjoy myself better.

Since humanity came into being, man has enjoyed himself too little: that alone, my brothers, is our original sin!

And when we learn better to enjoy ourselves, then do we unlearn best to give pain to others, and to contrive pain.

Therefore do I wash the hand that has helped the sufferer; therefore do I wipe also my soul.

For in seeing the sufferer suffering – thereof was I ashamed on account of his shame; and in helping him, sorely did I wound his pride.

Great obligations do not make men grateful, but revengeful; and when a small kindness is not forgotten, it becomes a gnawing worm.

"Be shy in accepting! Distinguish by accepting!" – thus do I advise those who have naught to give.

I, however, am a giver: willingly do I give as friend to friends. Strangers, however, and the poor, may pluck for themselves the fruit from my tree: thus does it cause less shame.

Beggars, however, one should entirely do away with! It annoys one to give to them, and it annoys one not to give to them.

And likewise sinners and bad consciences! Believe me, my friends: the sting of conscience teaches one to sting. The worst things, however, are the petty thoughts. Better to have done evilly than to have thought pettily!

To be sure, you say: "The delight in petty evils spares one many a great evil deed." But here one should not wish to be sparing.

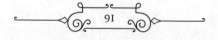

Like a boil is the evil deed: it itches and irritates and breaks forth – it speaks honourably.

"Behold, I am disease," says the evil deed: that is its honourableness.

But like infection is the petty thought: it creeps and hides, and wants to be nowhere – until the whole body is decayed and withered by the petty infection.

To him however, who is possessed of a devil, I would whisper this word in the ear: "Better for you to rear up your devil! Even for you there is still a path to greatness!"

Ah, my brothers! One knows a little too much about every one! And many a one becomes transparent to us, but still we can by no means penetrate him.

It is difficult to live among men because silence is so difficult.

And not to him who is offensive to us are we most unfair, but to him who does not concern us at all.

If, however, you have a suffering friend, then be a resting-place for his suffering; like a hard bed, however, a camp-bed: thus will you serve him best.

And if a friend does you wrong, then say: "I forgive you what you have done to me; that you have done it to yourself, however – how could I forgive that!"

Thus speaks all great love: it overcomes even forgiveness and pity.

One should hold fast one's heart; for when one lets it go, how quickly does one's head run away!

Ah, where in the world have there been greater follies than with the pitiful? And what in the world has caused more suffering than the follies of the pitiful?

Woe to all loving ones who have not an elevation which is above their pity!

Thus spoke the devil to me, once on a time: "Even God has his hell: it is his love for man."

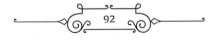

And lately, did I hear him say these words: "God is dead: of his pity for man has God died."

So be you warned against pity: from thence there yet comes to men a heavy cloud! I understand weather-signs!

But attend also to this word: All great love is above all its pity: for it seeks – to create what is loved!

"Myself do I offer to my love, and my neighbour as myself" – such is the language of all creators.

All creators, however, are hard.'

Thus spoke Zarathustra.

26. The Priests

AND one day Zarathustra made a sign to his disciples and spoke these words to them:

'Here are priests: but although they are my enemies, pass them quietly and with sleeping swords!

Even among them there are heroes; many of them have suffered too much: so they want to make others suffer.

Bad enemies are they: nothing is more revengeful than their meekness. And readily does he soil himself who touches them. But my blood is related to theirs; and I want withal to see my blood honoured in theirs.'

And when they had passed, a pain attacked Zarathustra; but not long had he struggled with the pain, when he began to speak thus:

'It moves my heart for those priests. They also go against my taste; but that is the small matter to me, since I am among men.

But I suffer and have suffered with them: prisoners are they to me, and stigmatized ones. He whom they call Saviour put them in fetters:

In fetters of false values and fatuous words! Oh, that some one would save them from their Saviour!

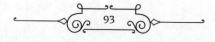

On an isle they once thought they had landed, when the sea tossed them about; but behold, it was a slumbering monster!

False values and fatuous words: these are the worst monsters for mortals – long slumbers and waits the fate that is in them.

But at last it comes and awakes and devours and engulfs whatever has built tabernacles upon it.

Oh, just look at those tabernacles which those priests have built themselves! Churches, they call their sweet-smelling caves!

Oh, that falsified light, that mustified air! Where the soul may not fly aloft to its height!

But so enjoins their belief: "On your knees, up the stair, you sinners!"

Rather would I see a shameless one than the distorted eyes of their shame and devotion!

Who created for themselves such caves and penitence-stairs? Was it not those who sought to conceal themselves, and were ashamed under the clear sky? And only when the clear sky looks again through ruined roofs, and down upon grass and red poppies on ruined walls – will I again turn my heart to the seats of this God.

They called God that which opposed and afflicted them: and verily, there was much hero-spirit in their worship!

And they knew not how to love their God otherwise than by nailing men to the cross!

As corpses they thought to live; in black drapes they their corpses; even in their talk do I still feel the evil flavour of charnel-houses.

And he who lives near to them lives near to black pools, wherein the toad sings his song with sweet gravity.

Better songs would they have to sing, for me to believe in their Saviour: more! Like saved ones would his disciples have to appear to me!

Naked, would I like to see them: for beauty alone should preach penitence. But whom would that disguised affliction convince!

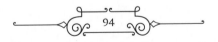

Their saviours themselves came not from freedom and freedom's seventh heaven! They themselves never trod the carpets of knowledge!

Of defects did the spirit of those saviours consist; but into every defect had they put their illusion, their stop-gap, which they called God.

In their pity was their spirit drowned; and when they swelled and o'erswelled with pity, there always floated to the surface a great folly.

Eagerly and with shouts drove they their flock over their foot-bridge; as if there were but one footbridge to the future! Those shepherds also were still of the flock!

Small spirits and spacious souls had those shepherds: but my brothers, what small domains have even the most spacious souls hitherto been!

Characters of blood did they write on the way they went, and their folly taught that truth is proved by blood.

But blood is the very worst witness to truth; blood taints the purest teaching, and turns it into delusion and hatred of heart.

And when a person goes through fire for his teaching – what does that prove! It is more, verily, when out of one's own burning comes one's own teaching!

Sultry heart and cold head; where these meet, there arises the blusterer, the "Saviour".

Greater ones, verily, have there been, and higher-born ones, than those whom the people call saviours, those rapturous blusterers!

And by still greater ones than any of the saviours must you be saved, my brothers, if you would find the way to freedom!

Never yet has there been a Superman. Naked have I seen both of them, the greatest man and the small man.

All-too-similar are they still to each other. Even the greatest found I all-too-human!'

Thus spoke Zarathustra.

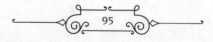

27. *The Virtuous*

'WITH thunder and heavenly fireworks must one speak to indolent and somnolent senses.

But beauty's voice speaks gently: it appeals only to the most awakened souls. Gently vibrated and laughed to me today my buckler; it was beauty's holy laughing and thrilling.

At you, you virtuous ones, laughed my beauty today. And thus came its voice to me: "They want – to be paid besides!"

You want to be paid besides, you virtuous ones! You want reward for virtue, and heaven for earth, and eternity for your today?

And now you upbraid me for teaching that there is no reward-giver, nor paymaster? And verily, I do not even teach that virtue is its own reward.

Ah! This is my sorrow: into the basis of things have reward and punishment been insinuated – and now even into the basis of your souls, you virtuous ones!

But like the snout of the boar shall my word grub up the basis of your souls; a ploughshare will I be called by you.

All the secrets of your heart shall be brought to light; and when you lie in the sun, grubbed up and broken, then will also your falsehood be separated from your truth.

For this is your truth: you are too pure for the filth of the words: vengeance, punishment, recompense, retribution.

You love your virtue as a mother loves her child; but when did one hear of a mother wanting to be paid for her love?

It is your dearest Self, your virtue. The ring's thirst is in you: to reach itself again struggles every ring, and turns itself.

And like the star that goes out, so is every work of your virtue: ever is its light on its way and travelling – and when will it cease to be on its way?

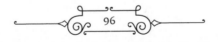

Thus is the light of your virtue still on its way, even when its work is done. Be it forgotten and dead, still its ray of light lives and travels.

That your virtue is your Self, and not an outward thing, a skin, or a cloak: that is the truth from the basis of your souls, ye virtuous ones!

But sure enough there are those to whom virtue meaneth writhing under the lash: and ye have hearkened too much unto their crying!

And others are there who call virtue the slothfulness of their vices; and when once their hatred and jealousy relax the limbs, their "justice" becometh lively and rubbeth its sleepy eyes.

And others are there who are drawn downwards: their devils draw them. But the more they sink, the more ardently gloweth their eye, and the longing for their God.

Ah! Their crying also hath reached your ears, ye virtuous ones: "What I am not, that, that is God to me, and virtue!" And others are there who go along heavily and creakingly, like carts taking stones downhill: they talk much of dignity and virtue – their drag they call virtue!

And others are there who are like eight-day clocks when wound up; they tick, and want people to call ticking virtue.

Verily, in those have I mine amusement: wherever I find such clocks I shall wind them up with my mockery, and they shall even whirr thereby!

And others are proud of their modicum of righteousness, and for the sake of it do violence to all things: so that the world is drowned in their unrighteousness.

Ah! How ineptly cometh the word "virtue" out of their mouth! And when they say: "I am just," it always soundeth like: "I am just – revenged!"

With their virtues they want to scratch out the eyes of their enemies; and they elevate themselves only that they may lower others.

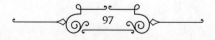

And again there are those who sit in their swamp, and speak thus from among the bulrushes: "Virtue – that is to sit quietly in the swamp.

We bite no one, and go out of the way of him who would bite; and in all matters we have the opinion that is given us."

And again, there are those who love attitudes, and think that virtue is a sort of attitude.

Their knees continually adore, and their hands are eulogies of virtue, but their heart knoweth naught thereof.

And again there are those who regard it as virtue to say: "Virtue is necessary"; but after all they believe only that policemen are necessary.

And many a one who cannot see men's loftiness, calleth it virtue to see their basness far too well: thus calleth he his evil eye virtue.

And some want to be edified and raised up, and call it virtue: and others want to be cast down, and likewise call it virtue.

And thus do almost all think that they participate in virtue; and at least every on claimeth to be an authority on "good" and "evil."

But Zarathustra came not to say unto all those liars and fools: "What do *ye* know of virtue! What *could* ye know of virtue!" –

But that ye, my friends, might become weary of the old words which ye have learned from the fools and liars:

That ye might become weary of the words "reward," "retribution," "punishment," "righteous vengeance."

That ye might become weary of saying: 'That an action is good because it is unselfish.'

Ah! my friends! That *your* very Self be in your action, as the mother is in the child: let that be *your* formula for virtue! Verily, I have taken from you a hundred formulae and your virtue's favourite playthings; and now you upbraid me, as children upbraid.

They played by the sea – then came there a wave and swept their playthings into the deep: and now do they cry.

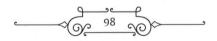

But the same wave shall bring them new playthings, and spread before them new speckled shells!

Thus will they be comforted; and like them shall you also, my friends, have your comforting – and new speckled shells!'

Thus spoke Zarathustra.

28. *The Rabble*

'LIFE is a well of delight; but where the rabble also drink, there all fountains are poisoned.

To everything cleanly am I well disposed; but I hate to see the grinning mouths and the thirst of the unclean.

They cast their eye down into the fountain: and now glances up to me their odious smile out of the fountain.

The holy water have they poisoned with their lustfulness; and when they called their filthy dreams delight, then poisoned they also the words.

Indignant becomes the flame when they put their damp hearts to the fire; the spirit itself bubbles and smokes when the rabble approach the fire.

Mawkish and over-mellow becomes the fruit in their hands: unsteady, and withered at the top, does their look make the fruit-tree. Mawkish and over-mellow becomes the fruit in their hands: unsteady, and withered at the top, does their look make the fruit-tree.

And many a one who has turned away from life, has only turned away from the rabble: he hated to share with them fountain, flame, and fruit.

And many a one who has gone into the wilderness and suffered thirst with beasts of prey, disliked only to sit at the cistern with filthy camel-drivers.

And many a one who has come along as a destroyer, and as a

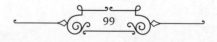

hailstorm to all cornfields, wanted merely to put his foot into the jaws of the rabble, and thus stop their throat.

And it is not the mouthful which has most choked me, to know that life itself requires enmity and death and torture-crosses.

But I asked once, and suffocated almost with my question: What? Is the rabble also necessary for life?

Are poisoned fountains necessary, and stinking fires, and filthy dreams, and maggots in the bread of life?

Not my hatred, but my loathing, gnawed hungrily at my life! Ah, oft-times became I weary of spirit, when I found even the rabble spiritual!

And on the rulers turned I my back, when I saw what they now call ruling: to traffic and bargain for power – with the rabble!

Amongst peoples of a strange language did I dwell, with stopped ears: so that the language of their trafficking might remain strange to me, and their bargaining for power.

And holding my nose, I went morosely through all yesterdays and todays: verily, badly smell all yesterdays and todays of the scribbling rabble!

Like a cripple become deaf, and blind, and dumb – thus have I lived long; that I might not live with the power-rabble, the scribe-rabble, and the pleasure-rabble.

Toilsomely did my spirit mount stairs, and cautiously; alms of delight were its refreshment; on the staff did life creep along with the blind one.

What has happened to me? How have I freed myself from loathing? Who has rejuvenated my eye? How have I flown to the height where no rabble any longer sit at the wells?

Did my loathing itself create for me wings and fountain-divining powers? To the loftiest height had I to fly, to find again the well of delight!

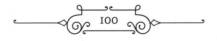

Oh, I have found it, my brothers! Here on the loftiest height bubbles up for me the well of delight! And there is a life at whose waters none of the rabble drink with me!

Almost too violently do you flow for me, you fountain of delight! And often emptiest you the goblet again, in wanting to fill it!

And yet must I learn to approach you more modestly: far too violently does my heart still flow towards you:

My heart on which my summer burns, my short, hot, melancholy, over-happy summer: how my summer heart longs for your coolness!

Past, the lingering distress of my spring! Past, the wickedness of my snowflakes in June! Summer have I become entirely, and summer-noontide!

A summer on the loftiest height, with cold fountains and blissful stillness: oh, come, my friends, that the stillness may become more blissful!

For this is our height and our home: too high and steep do we here dwell for all uncleanly ones and their thirst.

Cast but your pure eyes into the well of my delight, my friends! How could it become turbid thereby! It shall laugh back to you with its purity. On the tree of the future build we our nest; eagles shall bring us lone ones food in their beaks!

Verily, no food of which the impure could be fellow-partakers! Fire, would they think they devoured, and burn their mouths!

Verily, no abodes do we here keep ready for the impure! An ice-cave to their bodies would our happiness be, and to their spirits!

And as strong winds will we live above them, neighbours to the eagles, neighbours to the snow, neighbours to the sun: thus live the strong winds.

And like a wind will I one day blow amongst them, and with my spirit, take the breath from their spirit: thus willeth my future.

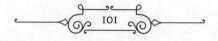

Verily, a strong wind is Zarathustra to all low places; and this counsel counselleth he to his enemies, and to whatever spitteth and speweth: "Take care not to spit against the wind!".'

Thus spake Zarathustra.

29. The Tarantulas

'LO, THIS is the tarantula's den! Wouldst thou see the tarantula itself? Here hangeth its web: touch this, so that it may tremble.

There cometh the tarantula willingly: Welcome, tarantula! Black on thy back is thy triangle and symbol; and I know also what is in thy soul. Revenge is in your soul: wherever you bite, there arises black scab; with revenge, your poison makes the soul giddy!

Thus do I speak to you in parable, you who make the soul giddy, you preachers of equality! Tarantulas are you to me, and secretly revengeful ones!

But I will soon bring your hiding-places to the light: therefore do I laugh in your face my laughter of the height.

Therefore do I tear at your web, that your rage may lure you out of your den of lies, and that your revenge may leap forth from behind your word "justice".

Because, *for man to be redeemed from revenge* – that is for me the bridge to the highest hope, and a rainbow after long storms.

Otherwise, however, would the tarantulas have it. "Let it be very justice for the world to become full of the storms of our vengeance" – thus do they talk to one another.

"Vengeance will we use, and insult, against all who are not like us" – thus do the tarantula-hearts pledge themselves.

"And 'Will to Equality' – that itself shall henceforth be the name of virtue; and against all that has power will we raise an outcry!"

Ye preachers of equality, the tyrant-frenzy of impotence cries thus

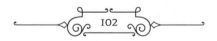

in you for "equality": your most secret tyrant-longings disguise themselves thus in virtue-words!

Fretted conceit and suppressed envy – perhaps your fathers' conceit and envy: in you break they forth as flame and frenzy of vengeance.

What the father has hid comes out in the son; and oft have I found in the son the father's revealed secret.

Inspired ones they resemble: but it is not the heart that inspires them – but vengeance. And when they become subtle and cold, it is not spirit, but envy, that makes them so.

Their jealousy leadeth them also into thinkers' paths; and this is the sign of their jealousy – they always go too far: so that their fatigue hath at last to go to sleep on the snow.

In all their lamentations soundeth vengeance, in all their eulogies is maleficence; and being judge seemeth to them bliss.

But thus do I counsel you, my friends: distrust all in whom the impulse to punish is powerful!

They are people of bad race and lineage; out of their countenances peer the hangman and the sleuth-hound.

Distrust all those who talk much of their justice! Verily, in their souls not only honey is lacking.

And when they call themselves "the good and just", forget not, that for them to be Pharisees, nothing is lacking but – power!

My friends, I will not be mixed up and confounded with others.

There are those who preach my doctrine of life, and are at the same time preachers of equality, and tarantulas.

That they speak in favour of life, though they sit in their den, these poison-spiders, and withdrawn from life – is because they would thereby do injury.

To those would they thereby do injury who have power at present: for with those the preaching of death is still most at home.

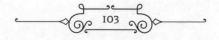

Were it otherwise, then would the tarantulas teach otherwise: and they themselves were formerly the best world-maligners and heretic-burners.

With these preachers of equality will I not be mixed up and confounded. For thus speaketh justice *unto me*: "Men are not equal".

And neither shall they become so! What would be my love to the Superman, if I spake otherwise?

On a thousand bridges and piers shall they throng to the future, and always shall there be more war and inequality among them: thus do my great love make me speak!

Inventors of figures and phantoms shall they be in their hostilities; and with those figures and phantoms shall they yet fight with each other the supreme fight!

Good and evil, and rich and poor, and high and low, and all names of values: weapons shall they be, and sounding signs, that life must again and again overcome itself!

Aloft will it build itself with columns and stairs – life itself into remote distances would it gaze, and out towards blissful beauties – therefore does it require elevation!

And because it requires elevation, therefore does it require steps, and variance of steps and climbers! To rise strives life, and in rising to overcome itself.

And just behold, my friends! Here where the tarantula's den is, rises aloft an ancient temple's ruins – just behold it with enlightened eyes!

He who here towered aloft his thoughts in stone, knew as well as the wisest ones about the secret of life!

That there is struggle and inequality even in beauty, and war for power and supremacy: that does he here teach us in the plainest parable.

How divinely do vault and arch here contrast in the struggle:

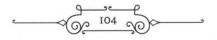

how with light and shade they strive against each other, the divinely striving ones.

Thus, steadfast and beautiful, let us also be enemies, my friends! Divinely will we strive against one another!

Alas! There has the tarantula bit me myself, my old enemy! Divinely steadfast and beautiful, it has bit me on the finger!

"Punishment must there be, and justice" – so thinks it: "not gratuitously shall he here sing songs in honour of enmity!"

Yes, it has revenged itself! And alas! Now will it make my soul also dizzy with revenge!

That I may not turn dizzy, however, bind me fast, my friends, to this pillar! Rather will I be a pillar-saint than a whirl of vengeance!

No cyclone or whirlwind is Zarathustra: and if he be a dancer, he is not at all a tarantula-dancer!'

Thus spoke Zarathustra.

30. The Famous Wise Men

'THE people have you served and the people's superstition – not the truth! All you famous wise ones! And just on that account did they pay you reverence.

And on that account also did they tolerate your unbelief, because it was a pleasantry and a by-path for the people. Thus does the master give free scope to his slaves, and even enjoys their presumptuousness.

But he who is hated by the people, as the wolf by the dogs – is the free spirit, the enemy of fetters, the non-adorer, the dweller in the woods.

To hunt him out of his lair – that was always called "sense of right" by the people: on him do they still hound their sharpest-toothed dogs.

"For there the truth is, where the people are! Woe, woe to the seeking ones!" – thus has it echoed through all time.

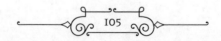

Your people would you justify in their reverence: that called you "Will to Truth", you famous wise ones!

And your heart has always said to itself: "From the people have I come: from thence came to me also the voice of God".

Stiff-necked and artful, like the ass, have you always been, as the advocates of the people.

And many a powerful one who wanted to run well with the people, has harnessed in front of his horses – a donkey, a famous wise man.

And now, you famous wise ones, I would have you finally throw off entirely the skin of the lion!

The skin of the beast of prey, the speckled skin, and the dishevelled locks of the investigator, the searcher, and the conqueror!

Ah! For me to learn to believe in your "conscientiousness", you would first have to break your venerating will.

Conscientious – so call I him who goes into God-forsaken wildernesses, and has broken his venerating heart.

In the yellow sands and burnt by the sun, he doubtless peers thirstily at the isles rich in fountains, where life reposes under shady trees.

But his thirst does not persuade him to become like those comfortable ones: for where there are oases, there are also idols.

Hungry, fierce, lonesome, God-forsaken: so does the lion-will wish itself.

Free from the happiness of slaves, redeemed from deities and adorations, fearless and fear-inspiring, grand and lonesome: so is the will of the conscientious.

In the wilderness have ever dwelt the conscientious, the free spirits, as lords of the wilderness; but in the cities dwell the well-foddered, famous wise ones – the draught-beasts.

For, always do they draw, as asses – the people's carts!

Not that I on that account upbraid them: but serving ones do

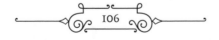

they remain, and harnessed ones, even though they glitter in golden harness.

And often have they been good servants and worthy of their hire. For thus says virtue: "If you must be a servant, seek him to whom your service is most useful!

The spirit and virtue of your master shall advance by you being his servant: thus will you yourself advance with his spirit and virtue!"

And verily, you famous wise ones, you servants of the people! You yourselves have advanced with the people's spirit and virtue – and the people by you! To your honour do I say it!

But the people you remain for me, even with your virtues, the people with purblind eyes – the people who know not what spirit is!

Spirit is life which itself cuts into life: by its own torture does it increase its own knowledge, did you know that before?

And the spirit's happiness is this: to be anointed and consecrated with tears as a sacrificial victim, did you know that before?

And the blindness of the blind one, and his seeking and groping, shall yet testify to the power of the sun into which he has gazed, did you know that before?

And with mountains shall the discerning one learn to build! It is a small thing for the spirit to remove mountains, did you know that before?

You know only the sparks of the spirit: but you do not see the anvil which it is, and the cruelty of its hammer!

You know not the spirit's pride! But still less could you endure the spirit's humility, should it ever want to speak!

And never yet could you cast your spirit into a pit of snow: you are not hot enough for that! Thus are you unaware, also, of the delight of its coldness.

In all respects, however, you make too familiar with the spirit; and out of wisdom have you often made an alms-house and a hospital for bad poets.

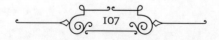

You are not eagles: thus have you never experienced the happiness of the alarm of the spirit. And he who is not a bird should not camp above abysses.

You seem to me lukewarm ones: but coldly flows all deep knowledge. Ice-cold are the innermost wells of the spirit: a refreshment to hot hands and handlers.

Respectable do you there stand, and stiff, and with straight backs, you famous wise ones! No strong wind or will impels you.

Have you ne'er seen a sail crossing the sea, rounded and inflated, and trembling with the violence of the wind?

Like the sail trembling with the violence of the spirit, does my wisdom cross the sea – my wild wisdom!

But you servants of the people, you famous wise ones – how could you go with me!'

Thus spoke Zarathustra.

31. The Night Song

'TIS night: now do all gushing fountains speak louder. And my soul also is a gushing fountain.

'Tis night: now only do all songs of the loving ones awake. And my soul also is the song of a loving one.

Something unappeased, unappeasable, is within me; it longs to find expression. A craving for love is within me, which speaks itself the language of love.

Light am I: ah, that I were night! But it is my lonesomeness to be begirt with light!

Ah, that I were dark and nightly! How would I suck at the breasts of light!

And you yourselves would I bless, you twinkling starlets and glow-worms aloft! and would rejoice in the gifts of your light.

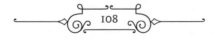

But I live in my own light, I drink again into myself the flames that break forth from me.

I know not the happiness of the receiver; and oft have I dreamt that stealing must be more blessed than receiving.

It is my poverty that my hand never ceases giving; it is my envy that I see waiting eyes and the brightened nights of longing.

Oh, the misery of all givers! Oh, the darkening of my sun! Oh, the craving to crave! Oh, the violent hunger in satiety!

They take from me: but do I yet touch their soul? There is a gap 'twixt giving and receiving; and the small gap has finally to be bridged over.

A hunger arises out of my beauty: I should like to injure those I illumine; I should like to rob those I have gifted: thus do I hunger for wickedness.

Withdrawing my hand when another hand already stretches out to it; hesitating like the cascade, which hesitates even in its leap: thus do I hunger for wickedness!

Such revenge does my abundance think of such mischief wells out of my lonesomeness.

My happiness in giving died in giving; my virtue became weary of itself by its abundance!

He who ever gives is in danger of losing his shame; to him who ever dispenses, the hand and heart become callous by very dispensing.

My eye no longer overflows for the shame of suppliants; my hand has become too hard for the trembling of filled hands.

Whence have gone the tears of my eye, and the down of my heart? Oh, the lonesomeness of all givers! Oh, the silence of all shining ones!

Many suns circle in desert space: to all that is dark do they speak with their light – but to me they are silent.

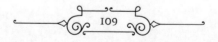

Oh, this is the hostility of light to the shining one: unpityingly does it pursue its course.

Unfair to the shining one in its innermost heart, cold to the suns: thus travels every sun.

Like a storm do the suns pursue their courses: that is their travelling. Their inexorable will do they follow: that is their coldness.

Oh, you only is it, you dark, nightly ones, that extract warmth from the shining ones! Oh, you only drink milk and refreshment from the light's udders!

Ah, there is ice around me; my hand burns with the iciness! Ah, there is thirst in me; it pants after your thirst!

'Tis night: alas, that I have to be light! And thirst for the nightly! And lonesomeness!

'Tis night: now do my longings break forth in me as a fountain, for speech do I long.

'Tis night: now do all gushing fountains speak louder. And my soul also is a gushing fountain.

'Tis night: now do all songs of loving ones awake. And my soul also is the song of a loving one.'

Thus sang Zarathustra.

32. The Dance Song

ONE evening went Zarathustra and his disciples through the forest; and when he sought for a well, lo, he lighted upon a green meadow peacefully surrounded by trees and bushes, where maidens were dancing together. As soon as the maidens recognised Zarathustra, they ceased dancing; Zarathustra, however, approached them with friendly mien and spoke these words:

'Cease not your dancing, you lovely maidens! No game-spoiler has come to you with evil eye, no enemy of maidens.

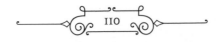

God's advocate am I with the devil: yet he is the spirit of gravity. How could I, you light-footed ones, be hostile to divine dances? Or to maidens' feet with fine ankles?

To be sure, I am a forest, and a night of dark trees: but he who is not afraid of my darkness, will find banks full of roses under my cypresses.

And even the little God may he find, who is dearest to maidens: beside the well lies he quietly, with closed eyes.

In broad daylight did he fall asleep, the sluggard! Had he perhaps chased butterflies too much?

Upbraid me not, you beautiful dancers, when I chasten the little God somewhat! He will cry, certainly, and weep – but he is laughable even when weeping!

And with tears in his eyes shall he ask you for a dance; and I myself will sing a song to his dance:

A dance-song and satire on the spirit of gravity my supremest, powerfulest devil, who is said to be "lord of the world".

And this is the song that Zarathustra sang when Cupid and the maidens danced together:

Of late did I gaze into your eye, O Life! And into the unfathomable did I there seem to sink.

But you pulled me out with a golden angle; derisively did you laugh when I called you unfathomable.

"Such is the language of all fish," said you; "what they do not fathom is unfathomable.

But changeable am I only, and wild, and altogether a woman, and no virtuous one:

Though I be called by you men the 'profound one,' or the 'faithful one,' 'the eternal one,' 'the mysterious one.'

But you men endow us always with your own virtues – alas, you virtuous ones!"

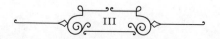

Thus did she laugh, the unbelievable one; but never do I believe her and her laughter, when she speaks evil of herself.

And when I talked face to face with my wild Wisdom, she said to me angrily: "You will, you crave, you love; on that account alone do you praise Life!"

Then had I almost answered indignantly and told the truth to the angry one; and one cannot answer more indignantly than when one "tells the truth" to one's Wisdom.

For thus do things stand with us three. In my heart do I love only Life – and verily, most when I hate her!

But that I am fond of Wisdom, and often too fond, is because she reminds me very strongly of Life!

She has her eye, her laugh, and even her golden angle-rod: am I responsible for it that both are so alike?

And when once Life asked me: "Who is she then, this Wisdom?" – then said I eagerly: "Ah, yes! Wisdom!

One thirsts for her and is not satisfied, one looks through veils, one grasps through nets.

Is she beautiful? What do I know! But the oldest carps are still lured by her.

Changeable is she, and wayward; often have I seen her bite her lip, and pass the comb against the grain of her hair.

Perhaps she is wicked and false, and altogether a woman; but when she speaks ill of herself, just then does she seduce most."

When I had said this to Life, then laughed she maliciously, and shut her eyes. "Of whom do you speak?" said she. "Perhaps of me?

And if you were right – is it proper to say that in such wise to my face! But now, pray, speak also of your Wisdom!"

Ah, and now have you again opened your eyes, O beloved Life! And into the unfathomable have I again seemed to sink.

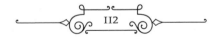

Thus sang Zarathustra. But when the dance was over and the maidens had departed, he became sad.

"The sun has been long set," said he at last, "the meadow is damp, and from the forest comes coolness.

An unknown presence is about me, and gazes thoughtfully. What! you live still, Zarathustra?

Why? Wherefore? Whereby? Where? Where? How? Is it not folly still to live?

Ah, my friends; the evening is it which thus interrogates in me. Forgive me my sadness!

Evening has come on: forgive me that evening has come on!'"

Thus sang Zarathustra.

33. The Grave Song

"'YONDER is the grave – island, the silent isle; yonder also are the graves of my youth. There will I carry an evergreen wreath of life."

Resolving thus in my heart, did I sail o'er the sea.

Oh, you sights and scenes of my youth! Oh, all you gleams of love, you divine fleeting gleams! How could you perish so soon for me! I think of you today as my dead ones.

From you, my dearest dead ones, comes to me a sweet savour, heart-opening and melting. It convulses and opens the heart of the lone seafarer.

Still am I the richest and most to be envied – I, the most lonesome one! For I have possessed you, and you possess me still. Tell me: to whom has there ever fallen such rosy apples from the tree as have fallen to me?

Still am I your love's heir and heritage, blooming to your memory with many-hued, wild-growing virtues, O you dearest ones!

Ah, we were made to remain near to each other, you kindly

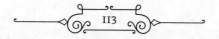

strange marvels; and not like timid birds did you come to me and my longing – no, but as trusting ones to a trusting one!

Yes, made for faithfulness, like me, and for fond eternities, must I now name you by your faithlessness, you divine glances and fleeting gleams: no other name have I yet learnt.

Too early did you die for me, you fugitives. Yet did you not flee from me, nor did I flee from you: innocent are we to each other in our faithlessness.

To kill me, did they strangle you, you singing birds of my hopes! Yes, at you, you dearest ones, did malice ever shoot its arrows – to hit my heart!

And they hit it! Because you were always my dearest, my possession and my possessedness: on that account had you to die young, and far too early!

At my most vulnerable point did they shoot the arrow – namely, at you, whose skin is like down – or more like the smile that dies at a glance!

But this word will I say to my enemies: What is all manslaughter in comparison with what you have done to me!

Worse evil did you do to me than all manslaughter; the irretrievable did you take from me: thus do I speak to you, my enemies!

Slew you not my youth's visions and dearest marvels! My playmates took you from me, the blessed spirits! To their memory do I deposit this wreath and this curse.

This curse upon you, my enemies! Have you not made my eternal short, as a tone dies away in a cold night! Scarcely, as the twinkle of divine eyes, did it come to me – as a fleeting gleam!

Thus spoke once in a happy hour my purity: "Divine shall everything be to me".

Then did you haunt me with foul phantoms; ah, where has that happy hour now fled!

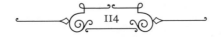

"All days shall be sacred to me" – so spoke once the wisdom of my youth: verily, the language of a joyous wisdom!

But then did you enemies steal my nights, and sold them to sleepless torture: ah, where has that joyous wisdom now fled?

Once did I long for happy auspices: then did you lead an owl – monster across my path, an adverse sign. Ah, where did my tender longing then flee?

All loathing did I once vow to renounce: then did you change my nigh ones and nearest ones into ulcerations. Ah, where did my noblest vow then flee?

As a blind one did I once walk in blessed ways: then did you cast filth on the blind one's course: and now is he disgusted with the old footpath.

And when I performed my hardest task, and celebrated the triumph of my victories, then did you make those who loved me call out that I then grieved them most.

It was always your doing: you embittered to me my best honey, and the diligence of my best bees.

To my charity have you ever sent the most impudent beggars; around my sympathy have you ever crowded the incurably shameless. Thus have you wounded the faith of my virtue.

And when I offered my holiest as a sacrifice, immediately did your "piety" put its fatter gifts beside it: so that my holiest suffocated in the fumes of your fat.

And once did I want to dance as I had never yet danced: beyond all heavens did I want to dance. Then did you seduce my favourite minstrel.

And now has he struck up an awful, melancholy air; alas, he tooted as a mournful horn to my ear!

Murderous minstrel, instrument of evil, most innocent instrument! Already did I stand prepared for the best dance: then did you kill my rapture with your tones!

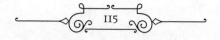

Only in the dance do I know how to speak the parable of the highest things: and now has my grandest parable remained unspoken in my limbs!

Unspoken and unrealized has my highest hope remained! And there have perished for me all the visions and consolations of my youth!

How did I ever bear it? How did I survive and overcome such wounds? How did my soul rise again out of those sepulchres?

Yes, something invulnerable, unburiable is with me, something that would rend rocks asunder: it is called my Will. Silently does it proceed, and unchanged throughout the years.

Its course will it go upon my feet, my old Will; hard of heart is its nature and invulnerable.

Invulnerable am I only in my heel. Ever live you there, and are like yourself, you most patient one! Ever have you burst all shackles of the tomb!

In you still lives also the unrealizedness of my youth; and as life and youth sit you here hopeful on the yellow ruins of graves.

Yes, you are still for me the demolisher of all graves: Hail to you, my Will! And only where there are graves are there resurrections.'

Thus sang Zarathustra.

34. Self-overcoming

'"WILL to Truth" do you call it, you wisest ones, that which impels you and makes you ardent?

Will for the thinkableness of all being: thus do I call your will!

All being would you make thinkable: for you doubt with good reason whether it be already thinkable.

But it shall accommodate and bend itself to you! So wills your will. Smooth shall it become and subject to the spirit, as its mirror and reflection.

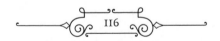

That is your entire will, you wisest ones, as a Will to Power; and even when you speak of good and evil, and of estimates of value.

You would still create a world before which you can bow the knee: such is your ultimate hope and ecstasy.

The ignorant, to be sure, the people – they are like a river on which a boat floats along: and in the boat sit the estimates of value, solemn and disguised.

Your will and your valuations have you put on the river of becoming; it betrays to me an old Will to Power, what is believed by the people as good and evil.

It was you, you wisest ones, who put such guests in this boat, and gave them pomp and proud names – you and your ruling Will!

Onward the river now carries your boat: it must carry it. A small matter if the rough wave foams and angrily resists its keel!

It is not the river that is your danger and the end of your good and evil, you wisest ones: but that Will itself, the Will to Power – the unexhausted, procreating life-will.

But that you may understand my gospel of good and evil, for that purpose will I tell you my gospel of life, and of the nature of all living things.

The living thing did I follow; I walked in the broadest and narrowest paths to learn its nature.

With a hundred-faced mirror did I catch its glance when its mouth was shut, so that its eye might speak to me. And its eye spoke to me.

But wherever I found living things, there heard I also the language of obedience. All living things are obeying things.

And this heard I secondly: Whatever cannot obey itself, is commanded. Such is the nature of living things.

This, however, is the third thing which I heard – namely, that commanding is more difficult than obeying. And not only because the

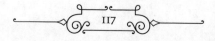

commander bears the burden of all obeyers, and because this burden readily crushes him:

An attempt and a risk seemed all commanding to me; and whenever it commands, the living thing risks itself thereby.

Yes, even when it commands itself, then also must it atone for its commanding. Of its own law must it become the judge and avenger and victim.

How does this happen! So did I ask myself. What persuades the living thing to obey, and command, and even be obedient in commanding?

Hearken now to my word, you wisest ones! Test it seriously, whether I have crept into the heart of life itself, and into the roots of its heart!

Wherever I found a living thing, there found I Will to Power; and even in the will of the servant found I the will to be master.

That to the stronger the weaker shall serve – thereto persuades he his will who would be master over a still weaker one. That delight alone he is unwilling to forego.

And as the lesser surrenders himself to the greater that he may have delight and power over the least of all, so do even the greatest surrender himself, and stakes – life, for the sake of power.

It is the surrender of the greatest to run risk and danger, and play dice for death.

And where there is sacrifice and service and love-glances, there also is the will to be master. By byways do the weaker then slink into the fortress, and into the heart of the mightier one – and there steals power.

And this secret spoke Life herself to me. "Behold," said she, "I am that which must ever overcome itself.

To be sure, you call it will to procreation, or impulse towards a goal, towards the higher, remoter, more manifold: but all that is one and the same secret.

Rather would I perish than disown this one thing; and verily,

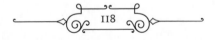

where there is perishing and leaf-falling, lo, there does Life sacrifice itself – for power!

That I have to be struggle, and becoming, and purpose, and cross-purpose – ah, he who divines my will, divines well also on what crooked paths it has to tread!

Whatever I create, and however much I love it, soon must I be adverse to it, and to my love: so wills my will.

And even you, discerning one, are only a path and footstep of my will: verily, my Will to Power walks even on the feet of your Will to Truth!

He certainly did not hit the truth who shot at it the formula: 'Will to existence': that will – does not exist!

For what is not, cannot will; that, however, which is in existence – how could it still strive for existence!

Only where there is life, is there also will: not, however, Will to Life, but – so teach I you – Will to Power!

Much is reckoned higher than life itself by the living one; but out of the very reckoning speaks – the Will to Power!"—

Thus did Life once teach me: and thereby, you wisest ones, do I solve you the riddle of your hearts.

I say to you: good and evil which would be everlasting – it does not exist! Of its own accord must it ever overcome itself anew.

With your values and formulae of good and evil, you exercise power, you valuing ones: and that is your secret love, and the sparkling, trembling, and overflowing of your souls.

But a stronger power grows out of your values, and a new over-coming: by it breaks egg and egg-shell.

And he who has to be a creator in good and evil – verily, he has first to be a destroyer, and break values in pieces.

Thus does the greatest evil pertain to the greatest good: that, however, is the creating good.

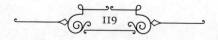

Let us speak thereof, you wisest ones, even though it be bad. To be silent is worse; all suppressed truths become poisonous.

And let everything break up which – can break up by our truths! Many a house is still to be built!'

Thus spoke Zarathustra.

35. The Sublime Ones

'CALM is the bottom of my sea: who would guess that it hides droll monsters!

Unmoved is my depth: but it sparkles with swimming enigmas and laughters.

A sublime one saw I today, a solemn one, a penitent of the spirit: Oh, how my soul laughed at his ugliness!

With upraised breast, and like those who draw in their breath: thus did he stand, the sublime one, and in silence:

O'erhung with ugly truths, the spoil of his hunting, and rich in torn raiment; many thorns also hung on him – but I saw no rose. Not yet had he learned laughing and beauty. Gloomy did this hunter return from the forest of knowledge.

From the fight with wild beasts returned he home: but even yet a wild beast gazes out of his seriousness – an unconquered wild beast!

As a tiger does he ever stand, on the point of springing; but I do not like those strained souls; ungracious is my taste towards all those self-engrossed ones.

And you tell me, friends, that there is to be no dispute about taste and tasting? But all life is a dispute about taste and tasting!

Taste: that is weight at the same time, and scales and weigher; and alas for every living thing that would live without dispute about weight and scales and weigher!

Should he become weary of his sublimeness, this sublime one,

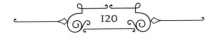

then only will his beauty begin – and then only will I taste him and find him savoury.

And only when he turns away from himself will he o'erleap his own shadow – and verily! into his sun.

Far too long did he sit in the shade; the cheeks of the penitent of the spirit became pale; he almost starved on his expectations.

Contempt is still in his eye, and loathing hides in his mouth. To be sure, he now rests, but he has not yet taken rest in the sunshine.

As the ox ought he to do; and his happiness should smell of the earth, and not of contempt for the earth.

As a white ox would I like to see him, which, snorting and lowing, walks before the plough-share: and his lowing should also laud all that is earthly!

Dark is still his countenance; the shadow of his hand dances upon it. O'ershadowed is still the sense of his eye.

His deed itself is still the shadow upon him: his doing obscures the doer. Not yet has he overcome his deed.

To be sure, I love in him the shoulders of the ox: but now do I want to see also the eye of the angel.

Also his hero-will has he still to unlearn: an exalted one shall he be, and not only a sublime one: the ether itself should raise him, the will-less one!

He has subdued monsters, he has solved enigmas. But he should also redeem his monsters and enigmas; into heavenly children should he transform them.

As yet has his knowledge not learned to smile, and to be without jealousy; as yet has his gushing passion not become calm in beauty.

Not in satiety shall his longing cease and disappear, but in beauty! Gracefulness belongs to the munificence of the magnanimous.

His arm across his head: thus should the hero repose; thus should he also overcome his repose.

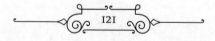

But precisely to the hero is beauty the hardest thing of all. Unattainable is beauty by all ardent wills.

A little more, a little less: precisely this is much here, it is the most here.

To stand with relaxed muscles and with unharnessed will: that is the hardest for all of you, you sublime ones!

When power becomes gracious and descends into the visible – I call such condescension, beauty.

And from no one do I want beauty so much as from you, you powerful one: let your goodness be your last self-conquest.

All evil do I accredit to you: therefore do I desire of you the good.

I have often laughed at the weaklings, who think themselves good because they have crippled paws!

The virtue of the pillar shall you strive after: more beautiful does it ever become, and more graceful – but internally harder and more sustaining – the higher it rises.

Yes, you sublime one, one day shall you also be beautiful, and hold up the mirror to your own beauty.

Then will your soul thrill with divine desires; and there will be adoration even in your vanity!

For this is the secret of the soul: when the hero has abandoned it, then only approach it in dreams – the super-hero.'

Thus spoke Zarathustra.

36. The Land of Culture

'TOO far did I fly into the future: a horror seized upon me.

And when I looked around me, behold, there time was my sole contemporary.

Then did I fly backwards, homewards – and always faster. Thus did I come to you: you present-day men, and into the land of culture.

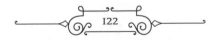

For the first time brought I an eye to see you, and good desire: verily, with longing in my heart did I come.

But how did it turn out with me? Although so alarmed – I had yet to laugh! Never did my eye see anything so motley-coloured!

I laughed and laughed, while my foot still trembled, and my heart as well. "Here, is the home of all the paint-pots", – said I.

With fifty patches painted on faces and limbs – so sat ye there to my astonishment, ye present-day men!

And with fifty mirrors around you, which flattered your play of colours, and repeated it!

Verily, ye could wear no better masks, ye present-day men, than your own faces! Who could – *recognize* you!

Written all over with the characters of the past, and these characters also pencilled over with new characters – thus have ye concealed yourselves well from all decipherers!

And though one be a trier of the reins, who still believeth that ye have reins! Out of colours ye seem to be baked, and out of glued scraps.

All times and peoples gaze divers-coloured out of your veils; all customs and beliefs speak divers-coloured out of your gestures.

He who would strip you of veils and wrappers, and paints and gestures, would just have enough left to scare the crows.

Verily, I myself am the scared crow that once saw you naked, and without paint; and I flew away when the skeleton ogled at me.

Rather would I be a day-labourer in the nether-world, and among the shades of the by – gone! – Fatter and fuller than ye, are the nether-worldlings!

This, yea this, is bitterness to my bowels, that I can neither endure you naked nor clothed, ye present-day men!

All that is unhomelike in the future, and whatever maketh strayed birds shiver, is verily more homelike and familiar than your 'reality.'

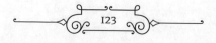

For thus speak you: "Real are we wholly, and without faith and superstition": thus do you plume yourselves – alas! even without plumes!

Indeed, how would ye be *able* to believe, you divers-coloured ones! You who are pictures of all that has ever been believed!

Perambulating refutations are you, of belief itself, and a dislocation of all thought. Untrustworthy ones: thus do I call you, you real ones!

All periods prate against one another in your spirits; and the dreams and pratings of all periods were even realer than your awakeness!

Unfruitful are you: therefore do you lack belief. But he who had to create, had always his presaging dreams and astral premonitions – and believed in believing!

Half-open doors are you, at which gravediggers wait. And this is your reality: "Everything deserves to perish."

Alas, how you stand there before me, you unfruitful ones; how lean your ribs! And many of you surely have had knowledge thereof.

Many a one has said: "There has surely a God filched something from me secretly whilst I slept? Enough to make a girl for himself therefrom!"

"Amazing is the poverty of my ribs!" thus has spoken many a present-day man.

Yes, you are laughable to me, you present-day men! And especially when you marvel at yourselves!

And woe to me if I could not laugh at your marvelling, and had to swallow all that is repugnant in your platters!

As it is, however, I will make lighter of you, since I have to carry what is heavy; and what matter if beetles and May bugs also alight on my load!

It shall not on that account become heavier to me! And not from you, you present-day men, shall my great weariness arise.

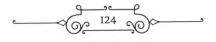

Ah, where shall I now ascend with my longing! From all mountains do I look out for fatherlands and motherlands.

But a home have I found nowhere: unsettled am I in all cities, and decamping at all gates.

Alien to me, and a mockery, are the present-day men, to whom of late my heart impelled me; and exiled am I from fatherlands and motherlands.

Thus do I love only my children's land, the undiscovered in the remotest sea: for it do I bid my sails search and search.

To my children will I make amends for being the child of my fathers: and to all the future – for this present-day!'

Thus spoke Zarathustra.

37. *Immaculate Perception*

'WHEN yester-eve the moon arose, then did I fancy it about to bear a sun: so broad and teeming did it lie on the horizon.

But it was a liar with its pregnancy; and sooner will I believe in the man in the moon than in the woman.

To be sure, little of a man is he also, that timid night-reveller. With a bad conscience does he stalk over the roofs.

For he is covetous and jealous, the monk in the moon; covetous of the earth, and all the joys of lovers.

No, I like him not, that tom-cat on the roofs! Hateful to me are all that slink around half-closed windows!

Piously and silently does he stalk along on the star-carpets: but I like no light-treading human feet, on which not even a spur jingles.

Every honest one's step speaks; the cat however, steals along over the ground. Behold, cat-like does the moon come along, and dishonestly.

This parable speak I to you sentimental dissemblers, to you, the "pure discerners!" You do I call – covetous ones!

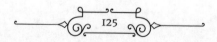

Also you love the earth, and the earthly: I have divined you well! But shame is in your love, and a bad conscience – you are like the moon!

To despise the earthly has your spirit been persuaded, but not your bowels: these, however, are the strongest in you!

And now is your spirit ashamed to be at the service of your bowels, and goes in byways and lying ways to escape its own shame.

"That would be the highest thing for me" – so says your lying spirit to itself – "to gaze upon life without desire, and not like the dog, with hanging-out tongue:

To be happy in gazing: with dead will, free from the grip and greed of selfishness – cold and ashy grey all over, but with intoxicated moon-eyes!

That would be the dearest thing to me" – thus does the seduced one seduce himself, "to love the earth as the moon loves it, and with the eye only to feel its beauty.

And this do I call immaculate perception of all things: to want nothing else from them, but to be allowed to lie before them as a mirror with a hundred facets."

Oh, you sentimental dissemblers, you covetous ones! You lack innocence in your desire: and now do you defame desiring on that account!

Not as creators, as procreators, or as jubilators do you love the earth!

Where is innocence? Where there is will to procreation. And he who seeks to create beyond himself, has for me the purest will.

Where is beauty? Where I must will with my whole Will; where I will love and perish, that an image may not remain merely an image.

Loving and perishing: these have rhymed from eternity. Will to love: that is to be ready also for death. Thus do I speak to you cowards!

But now does your emasculated ogling profess to be "contemplation!"

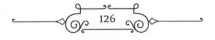

And that which can be examined with cowardly eyes is to be christened "beautiful!" Oh, you violators of noble names!

But it shall be your curse, you immaculate ones, you pure discerners, that you shall never bring forth, even though you lie broad and teeming on the horizon!

You fill your mouth with noble words: and we are to believe that your heart overflows, you cozeners?

But my words are poor, contemptible, stammering words: gladly do I pick up what falls from the table at your repasts.

Yet still can I say therewith the truth – to dissemblers! Yes, my fish-bones, shells, and prickly leaves shall – tickle the noses of dissemblers!

Bad air is always about you and your repasts: your lascivious thoughts, your lies, and secrets are indeed in the air!

Dare only to believe in yourselves – in yourselves and in your inward parts! He who does not believe in himself always lies.

A God's mask have you hung in front of you, you "pure ones": into a God's mask has your execrable coiling snake crawled.

Verily you deceive, you "contemplative ones!" Even Zarathustra was once the dupe of your godlike exterior; he did not divine the serpent's coil with which it was stuffed.

A God's soul, I once thought I saw playing in your games, you pure discerners! No better arts did I once dream of than your arts!

Serpents' filth and evil odour, the distance concealed from me: and that a lizard's craft prowled thereabouts lasciviously.

But I came near to you: then came to me the day, and now comes it to you, at an end is the moon's love affair!

See there! Surprised and pale does it stand – before the rosy dawn!

For already she comes, the glowing one, her love to the earth comes! Innocence, and creative desire, is all solar love!

See there, how she comes impatiently over the sea! Do you not feel the thirst and the hot breath of her love?

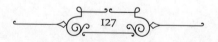

At the sea would she suck, and drink its depths to her height: now rises the desire of the sea with its thousand breasts.

Kissed and sucked would it be by the thirst of the sun; vapour would it become, and height, and path of light, and light itself!

Like the sun do I love life, and all deep seas.

And this means to me knowledge: all that is deep shall ascend – to my height!'

Thus spoke Zarathustra.

38. Scholars

'WHEN I lay asleep, then did a sheep eat at the ivy-wreath on my head, it ate, and said thereby: "Zarathustra is no longer a scholar."

It said this, and went away clumsily and proudly. A child told it to me.

I like to lie here where the children play, beside the ruined wall, among thistles and red poppies.

A scholar am I still to the children, and also to the thistles and red poppies. Innocent are they, even in their wickedness.

But to the sheep I am no longer a scholar: so wills my lot-blessings upon it!

For this is the truth: I have departed from the house of the scholars, and the door have I also slammed behind me.

Too long did my soul sit hungry at their table: not like them have I got the knack of investigating, as the knack of nut-cracking.

Freedom do I love, and the air over fresh soil; rather would I sleep on ox-skins than on their honours and dignities.

I am too hot and scorched with my own thought: often is it ready to take away my breath. Then have I to go into the open air, and away from all dusty rooms.

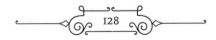

But they sit cool in the cool shade: they want in everything to be merely spectators, and they avoid sitting where the sun burns on the steps.

Like those who stand in the street and gape at the passers-by: thus do they also wait, and gape at the thoughts which others have thought.

Should one lay hold of them, then do they raise a dust like flour-sacks, and involuntarily: but who would divine that their dust came from corn, and from the yellow delight of the summer fields?

When they give themselves out as wise, then do their petty sayings and truths chill me: in their wisdom there is often an odour as if it came from the swamp; and verily, I have even heard the frog croak in it!

Clever are they – they have dexterous fingers: what does my simplicity pretend to beside their multiplicity! All threading and knitting and weaving do their fingers understand: thus do they make the hose of the spirit!

Good clockworks are they: only be careful to wind them up properly! Then do they indicate the hour without mistake, and make a modest noise thereby.

Like millstones do they work, and like pestles: throw only seed-corn to them! They know well how to grind corn small, and make white dust out of it.

They keep a sharp eye on one another, and do not trust each other the best. Ingenious in little artifices, they wait for those whose knowledge walks on lame feet, like spiders do they wait.

I saw them always prepare their poison with precaution; and always did they put glass gloves on their fingers in doing so.

They also know how to play with false dice; and so eagerly did I find them playing, that they perspired thereby.

We are alien to each other, and their virtues are even more repugnant to my taste than their falsehoods and false dice.

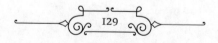

And when I lived with them, then did I live above them. Therefore did they take a dislike to me.

They want to hear nothing of any one walking above their heads; and so they put wood and earth and rubbish between me and their heads.

Thus did they deafen the sound of my tread: and least have I hitherto been heard by the most learned.

All mankind's faults and weaknesses did they put between themselves and me: they call it "false ceiling" in their houses.

But nevertheless I walk with my thoughts above their heads; and even should I walk on my own errors, still would I be above them and their heads.

For men are not equal: so speaks justice. And what I will, they may not will!'

Thus spoke Zarathustra.

39. Poets

'SINCE I have known the body better' – said Zarathustra to one of his disciples – 'the spirit has only been to me symbolically spirit; and all the 'imperishable' – that is also but a parable.'

'So have I heard you say once before,' answered the disciple, 'and then you added: "But the poets lie too much." Why did you say that the poets lie too much?'

'Why?' said Zarathustra. 'You ask why? I do not belong to those who may be asked after their Why.

Is my experience but of yesterday? It is long ago that I experienced the reasons for my opinions.

Should I not have to be a cask of memory, if I also wanted to have my reasons with me?

It is already too much for me even to retain my opinions; and many a bird flies away.

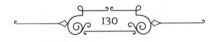

And sometimes, also, do I find a fugitive creature in my dovecote, which is alien to me, and trembles when I lay my hand upon it.

But what did Zarathustra once say to you? That the poets lie too much? – But Zarathustra also is a poet.

Believe you that he there spoke the truth? Why do you believe it?'

The disciple answered: 'I believe in Zarathustra.' But Zarathustra shook his head and smiled.

'Belief does not sanctify me', said he, 'least of all the belief in myself.

But granting that some one did say in all seriousness that the poets lie too much: he was right – we do lie too much.

We also know too little, and are bad learners: so we are obliged to lie.

And which of us poets has not adulterated his wine? Many a poisonous hotchpotch has evolved in our cellars: many an indescribable thing has there been done.

And because we know little, therefore are we pleased from the heart with the poor in spirit, especially when they are young women!

And even of those things are we desirous, which old women tell one another in the evening. This do we call the eternally feminine in us.

And as if there were a special secret access to knowledge, which chokes up for those who learn anything, so do we believe in the people and in their "wisdom."

This, however, do all poets believe: that whoever pricks up his ears when lying in the grass or on lonely slopes, learns something of the things that are between heaven and earth.

And if there come to them tender emotions, then do the poets always think that nature herself is in love with them:

And that she steals to their ear to whisper secrets into it, and

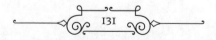

amorous flatteries: of this do they plume and pride themselves, before all mortals!

Ah, there are so many things between heaven and earth of which only the poets have dreamed!

And especially above the heavens: for all gods are poet-symbolizations, poet-sophistications!

Ever are we drawn aloft – that is, to the realm of the clouds: on these do we set our gaudy puppets, and then call them gods and supermen:

Are not they light enough for those chairs! All these gods and supermen?

Ah, how I am weary of all the inadequate that is insisted on as actual! Ah, how I am weary of the poets!'

When Zarathustra so spoke, his disciple resented it, but was silent. And Zarathustra also was silent; and his eye directed itself inwardly, as if it gazed into the far distance. At last he sighed and drew breath.

'I am of today and heretofore', said he then; 'but something is in me that is of the morrow, and the day following, and the hereafter.

I became weary of the poets, of the old and of the new: superficial are they all to me, and shallow seas.

They did not think sufficiently into the depth; therefore their feeling did not reach to the bottom.

Some sensation of voluptuousness and some sensation of tedium: these have as yet been their best contemplation.

Ghost-breathing and ghost-whisking, seems to me all the jingle-jangling of their harps; what have they known hitherto of the fervour of tones!

They are also not pure enough for me: they all muddle their water that it may seem deep.

And rather would they thereby prove themselves reconcilers: but mediaries and mixers are they to me, and half-and-half, and impure!

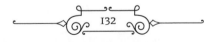

Ah, I cast indeed my net into their sea, and meant to catch good fish; but always did I draw up the head of some ancient God.

Thus did the sea give a stone to the hungry one. And they themselves may well originate from the sea.

Certainly, one finds pearls in them: thereby they are the more like hard molluscs. And instead of a soul, I have often found in them salt slime.

They have learned from the sea also its vanity: is not the sea the peacock of peacocks?

Even before the ugliest of all buffaloes does it spread out its tail; never does it tire of its lace-fan of silver and silk.

Disdainfully does the buffalo glance thereat, nigh to the sand with its soul, closer still to the thicket, nighest, however, to the swamp.

What is beauty and sea and peacock-splendour to it! This parable I speak to the poets.

Their spirit itself is the peacock of peacocks, and a sea of vanity!

Spectators seeks the spirit of the poet – should they even be buffaloes!

But of this spirit became I weary; and I see the time coming when it will become weary of itself.

Yes, changed have I seen the poets, and their glance turned towards themselves.

Penitents of the spirit have I seen appearing; they grew out of the poets.'

Thus spoke Zarathustra.

40. Great Events

THERE is an isle in the sea – not far from the Blessed isles of Zarathustra – on which a volcano ever smokes; of which isle the people, and especially the old women amongst them, say that it is placed as

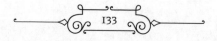

a rock before the gate of the underworld; but that through the volcano itself the narrow way leads downwards which conducts to this gate.

Now about the time that Zarathustra sojourned on the Blessed isles, it happened that a ship anchored at the isle on which stands the smoking mountain, and the crew went ashore to shoot rabbits. About the noontide hour, however, when the captain and his men were together again, they saw suddenly a man coming towards them through the air, and a voice said distinctly: 'It is time! It is the highest time!' But when the figure was nearest to them (it flew past quickly, however, like a shadow, in the direction of the volcano), then did they recognize with the greatest surprise that it was Zarathustra; for they had all seen him before except the captain himself, and they loved him as the people love: in such wise that love and awe were combined in equal degree.

'Behold!' said the old helmsman, 'there goes Zarathustra to hell!'

About the same time that these sailors landed on the fire-isle, there was a rumour that Zarathustra had disappeared; and when his friends were asked about it, they said that he had gone on board a ship by night, without saying where he was going.

Thus there arose some uneasiness. After three days, however, there came the story of the ship's crew in addition to this uneasiness – and then did all the people say that the devil had taken Zarathustra. His disciples laughed, sure enough, at this talk; and one of them said even: 'Sooner would I believe that Zarathustra has taken the devil.' But at the bottom of their hearts they were all full of anxiety and longing: so their joy was great when on the fifth day Zarathustra appeared amongst them.

And this is the account of Zarathustra's interview with the fire-dog:

'The earth', said he, 'has a skin; and this skin has diseases. One of these diseases, for example, is called "man."

And another of these diseases is called "the fire-dog": concerning

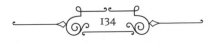

him men have greatly deceived themselves, and let themselves be deceived.

To fathom this mystery did I go o'er the sea; and I have seen the truth naked, verily! barefooted up to the neck.

Now do I know how it is concerning the fire-dog; and likewise concerning all the spouting and subversive devils, of which not only old women are afraid.

"Up with you, fire-dog, out of your depth!" cried I, "and confess how deep that depth is! Whence comes that which you snort up?

You drink copiously at the sea: that does your embittered eloquence betray! In sooth, for a dog of the depth, you take your nourishment too much from the surface!

At the most, I regard you as the ventriloquist of the earth: and ever, when I have heard subversive and spouting devils speak, I have found them like you: embittered, mendacious, and shallow.

You understand how to roar and obscure with ashes! You are the best braggarts, and have sufficiently learned the art of making dregs boil.

Where you are, there must always be dregs at hand, and much that is spongy, hollow, and compressed: it wants to have freedom.

'Freedom' you all roar most eagerly: but I have unlearned the belief in 'great events,' when there is much roaring and smoke about them.

And believe me, friend Hullabaloo! The greatest events – are not our noisiest, but our still hours.

Not around the inventors of new noise, but around the inventors of new values, does the world revolve; inaudibly it revolves.

And just own to it! Little had ever taken place when your noise and smoke passed away. What, if a city did become a mummy, and a statue lay in the mud!

And this do I say also to the o'erthrowers of statues: It is certainly the greatest folly to throw salt into the sea, and statues into the mud.

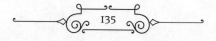

In the mud of your contempt lay the statue: but it is just its law, that out of contempt, its life and living beauty grow again!

With diviner features does it now arise, seducing by its suffering; and verily! it will yet thank you for o'erthrowing it, you subverters!

This counsel, however, do I counsel to kings and churches, and to all that is weak with age or virtue – let yourselves be o'erthrown! That you may again come to life, and that virtue – may come to you!"

Thus spoke I before the fire-dog: then did he interrupt me sullenly, and asked: "Church? What is that?"

"Church?" answered I, 'that is a kind of state, and indeed the most mendacious. But remain quiet, you dissembling dog! you surely know your own species best!

Like yourself the state is a dissembling dog; like you does it like to speak with smoke and roaring – to make believe, like you, that it speaks out of the heart of things.

For it seeks by all means to be the most important creature on earth, the state; and people think it so."

When I had said this, the fire-dog acted as if mad with envy. "What!" cried he, "the most important creature on earth? And people think it so?" And so much vapour and terrible voices came out of his throat, that I thought he would choke with vexation and envy.

At last he became calmer and his panting subsided; as soon, however, as he was quiet, I said laughingly:

"You are angry, fire-dog: so I am in the right about you!

And that I may also maintain the right, hear the story of another fire-dog; he speaks actually out of the heart of the earth.

Gold does his breath exhale, and golden rain: so does his heart desire. What are ashes and smoke and hot dregs to him!

Laughter flits from him like a variegated cloud; adverse is he to your gargling and spewing and grips in the bowels!

The gold, however, and the laughter – these does he take out of

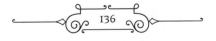

the heart of the earth: for, that you mayst know it, the heart of the earth is of gold."

When the fire-dog heard this, he could no longer endure to listen to me. Abashed did he draw in his tail, said "bow-wow!" in a cowed voice, and crept down into his cave.'

Thus told Zarathustra. His disciples, however, hardly listened to him: so great was their eagerness to tell him about the sailors, the rabbits, and the flying man.

'What am I to think of it!' said Zarathustra. 'Am I indeed a ghost?

But it may have been my shadow. You have surely heard something of the Wanderer and his Shadow?

One thing, however, is certain: I must keep a tighter hold of it; otherwise it will spoil my reputation.'

And once more Zarathustra shook his head and wondered. 'What am I to think of it!' said he once more.

'Why did the ghost cry: "It is time! It is the highest time!"

For what is it then – the highest time?'

Thus spake Zarathustra.

41. The Soothsayer

'AND I saw a great sadness come over mankind. The best turned weary of their works.

A doctrine appeared, a faith ran beside it: "All is empty, all is alike, all hath been!"

And from all hills there re-echoed: "All is empty, all is alike, all hath been!"

To be sure we have harvested: but why have all our fruits become rotten and brown? What was it fell last night from the evil moon?

In vain was all our labour, poison has our wine become, the evil eye hath singed yellow our fields and hearts.

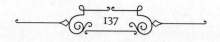

Arid have we all become; and fire falling upon us, then do we turn dust like ashes: yea, the fire itself have we made aweary.

All our fountains have dried up, even the sea has receded. All the ground tries to gape, but the depth will not swallow!

"Alas! where is there still a sea in which one could be drowned?" so soundeth our plaint – across shallow swamps. Even for dying have we become too weary; now do we keep awake and live on – in sepulchres.'

Thus did Zarathustra hear a soothsayer speak; and the foreboding touched his heart and transformed him. Sorrowfully did he go about and wearily; and he became like to those of whom the soothsayer had spoken.

Said he to his disciples, 'a little while, and there comes the long twilight. Alas, how shall I preserve my light through it!

That it may not smother in this sorrowfulness! To remoter worlds shall it be a light, and also to remotest nights!'

Thus did Zarathustra go about grieved in his heart, and for three days he did not take any meat or drink: he had no rest, and lost his speech. At last it came to pass that he fell into a deep sleep. His disciples, however, sat around him in long night-watches, and waited anxiously to see if he would awake, and speak again, and recover from his affliction.

And this is what Zarathustra said when he awoke; his voice, however, came to his disciples as from afar:

'Hear, I pray you, the dream that I dreamed, my friends, and help me to divine its meaning!

A riddle is it still to me, this dream; the meaning is hidden in it and encaged, and do not yet fly above it on free pinions.

All life had I renounced, so I dreamed. Night-watchman and grave-guardian had I become, aloft, in the lone mountain-fortress of Death.

There did I guard his coffins: full stood the musty vaults of those

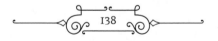

trophies of victory. Out of glass coffins did vanquished life gaze upon me.

The odour of dust-covered eternities did I breathe: sultry and dust-covered lay my soul. And who could have aired his soul there!

Brightness of midnight was ever around me; lonesomeness cowered beside her; and as a third, death-rattle stillness, the worst of my female friends.

Keys did I carry, the rustiest of all keys; and I knew how to open with them the most creaking of all gates.

Like a bitterly angry croaking ran the sound through the long corridors when the leaves of the gate opened: ungraciously did this bird cry, unwillingly was it awakened.

But more frightful even, and more heart-strangling was it, when it again became silent and still all around, and I alone sat in that malignant silence.

Thus did time pass with me, and slip by, if time there still was: what do I know thereof! But at last there happened that which awoke me.

Thrice did there peal peals at the gate like thunders, thrice did the vaults resound and howl again: then did I go to the sate.

Alpa! cried I, who carries his ashes to the mountain? Alpa! Alpa! who carries his ashes to the mountain?

And I pressed the key, and pulled at the gate, and exerted myself. But not a finger's-breadth was it yet open:

Then did a roaring wind tear the folds apart: whistling, whizzing, and piercing, it threw to me a black coffin.

And in the roaring and whistling and whizzing, the coffin burst open, and spouted out a thousand peals of laughter.

And a thousand caricatures of children, angels, owls, fools, and child-sized butterflies laughed and mocked, and roared at me.

Fearfully was I terrified thereby: it prostrated me. And I cried with horror as I ne'er cried before.

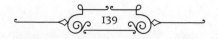

But my own crying awoke me: and I came to myself.'

Thus did Zarathustra relate his dream, and then was silent: for as yet he knew not the interpretation thereof. But the disciple whom he loved most arose quickly, seized Zarathustra's hand, and said:

'Your life itself interprets to us this dream, O Zarathustra!

Are you not yourself the wind with shrill whistling, which bursts open the gates of the fortress of Death?

Are you not yourself the coffin full of many-hued malices and angel – caricatures of life?

Like a thousand peals of children's laughter comes Zarathustra into all sepulchres, laughing at those night-watchmen and grave-guardians, and whoever else rattles with sinister keys.

With your laughter will you frighten and prostrate them: fainting and recovering will you demonstrate your power over them.

And when the long twilight comes and the mortal weariness, even then will you not disappear from our firmament, you advocate of life!

New stars have you made us see, and new nocturnal glories: verily, laughter itself have you spread out over us like a many-hued canopy.

Now will children's laughter ever from coffins flow; now will a strong wind ever come victoriously to all mortal weariness: of this you are yourself the pledge and the prophet!

They themselves did you dream, your enemies: that was your sorest dream.

But as you awoke from them and came to yourself, so shall they awaken from themselves – and come to you!'

Thus spoke the disciple; and all the others then thronged around Zarathustra, grasped him by the hands, and tried to persuade him to leave his bed and his sadness, and return to them. Zarathustra, however, sat upright on his couch, with an absent look. Like one returning from long foreign sojourn did he look on his disciples, and examined their features; but still he knew them not. When, however, they raised him,

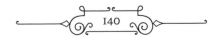

and set him upon his feet, behold, all on a sudden his eye changed; he understood everything that had happened, stroked his beard, and said with a strong voice:

'Well! This has just its time; but see to it, my disciples, that we have a good repast; and without delay! Thus do I mean to make amends for bad dreams!

The soothsayer, however, shall eat and drink at my side: and verily, I will yet show him a sea in which he can drown himself!'

Thus spoke Zarathustra. Then did he gaze long into the face of the disciple who had been the dream-interpreter, and shook his head.

42. Redemption

WHEN Zarathustra went one day over the great bridge, then did the cripples and beggars surround him, and a hunchback spoke thus to him:

'Behold, Zarathustra! Even the people learn from you, and acquire faith in your teaching: but for them to believe fully in you, one thing is still needful – you must first of all convince us cripples! Here have you now a fine selection, and verily, an opportunity with more than one forelock! The blind can you heal, and make the lame run; and from him who has too much behind, could you well, also, take away a little; – that, I think, would be the right method to make the cripples believe in Zarathustra!'

Zarathustra, however, answered thus to him who so spoke: "When one takes his hump from the hunchback, then does one take from him his spirit – so do the people teach. And when one gives the blind man eyes, then does he see too many bad things on the earth: so that he curses him who healed him. He, however, who makes the lame man run, inflicts upon him the greatest injury; for hardly can he run, when his vices run away with him – so do the people teach concerning

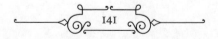

cripples. And why should not Zarathustra also learn from the people, when the people learn from Zarathustra?

It is, however, the small thing to me since I have been amongst men, to see one person lacking an eye, another an ear, and a third a leg, and that others have lost the tongue, or the nose, or the head.

I see and have seen worse things, and divers things so hideous, that I should neither like to speak of all matters, nor even keep silent about some of them: namely, men who lack everything, except that they have too much of one thing – men who are nothing more than a big eye, or a big mouth, or a big belly, or something else big, reversed cripples, I call such men.

And when I came out of my solitude, and for the first time passed over this bridge, then I could not trust my eyes, but looked again and again, and said at last: "That is an ear! An ear as big as a man!" I looked still more attentively – and actually there did move under the ear something that was pitiably small and poor and slim. And in truth this immense ear was perched on a small thin stalk – the stalk, however, was a man! A person putting a glass to his eyes, could even recognize further a small envious countenance, and also that a bloated little soul dangled at the stalk. The people told me, however, that the big ear was not only a man, but a great man, a genius. But I never believed in the people when they spoke of great men – and I hold to my belief that it was a reversed cripple, who had too little of everything, and too much of one thing.'

When Zarathustra had spoken thus to the hunchback, and to those of whom the hunchback was the mouthpiece and advocate, then did he turn to his disciples in profound dejection, and said:

'My friends, I walk amongst men as amongst the fragments and limbs of human beings!

This is the terrible thing to my eye, that I find man broken up, and scattered about, as on a battle- and butcher-ground.

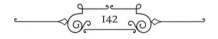

And when my eye flees from the present to the bygone, it finds ever the same: fragments and limbs and fearful chances – but no men!

The present and the bygone upon earth – ah! my friends – that is my most unbearable trouble; and I should not know how to live, if I were not a seer of what is to come.

A seer, a purposer, a creator, a future itself, and a bridge to the future – and alas! also as it were a cripple on this bridge: all that is Zarathustra.

And you also asked yourselves often: "Who is Zarathustra to us? What shall he be called by us?" And like me, did you give yourselves questions for answers.

Is he a promiser? Or a fulfiller? A conqueror? Or an inheritor? A harvest? Or a ploughshare? A physician? Or a healed one?

Is he a poet? Or a genuine one? An emancipator? Or a subjugator? A good one? Or an evil one?

I walk amongst men as the fragments of the future: that future which I contemplate.

And it is all my poetisation and aspiration to compose and collect into unity what is fragment and riddle and fearful chance.

And how could I endure to be a man, if man were not also the composer, and riddle-reader, and redeemer of chance!

To redeem what is past, and to transform every "It was" into "Thus would I have it!" – that only do I call redemption!

Will – so is the emancipator and joy-bringer called: thus have I taught you, my friends! But now learn this likewise: the Will itself is still a prisoner.

Willing emancipates: but what is that called which still puts the emancipator in chains?

"It was": thus is the Will's teeth-gnashing and most lonesome tribulation called. Impotent towards what has been done – it is a malicious spectator of all that is past.

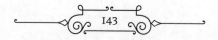

Not backward can the Will will; that it cannot break time and time's desire – that is the Will's most lonesome tribulation.

Willing emancipates: what does Willing itself create in order to get free from its tribulation and mock at its prison?

Ah, a fool becomes every prisoner! Foolishly delivers itself also the imprisoned Will.

That time does not run backward – that is its animosity: "That which was": so is the stone which it cannot roll called.

And thus does it roll stones out of animosity and ill-humour, and takes revenge on whatever does not, like it, feel rage and ill-humour.

Thus did the Will, the emancipator, become a torturer; and on all that is capable of suffering it takes revenge, because it cannot go backward.

This, yes, this alone is revenge itself: the Will's antipathy to time, and its "It was."

A great folly dwells in our Will; and it became a curse to all humanity, that this folly acquired spirit!

The spirit of revenge: my friends, that has hitherto been man's best contemplation; and where there was suffering, it was claimed there was always penalty.

"Penalty," so calls itself revenge. With a lying word it feigns a good conscience.

And because in the willer himself there is suffering, because he cannot will backwards – thus was Willing itself, and all life, claimed – to be penalty!

And then did cloud after cloud roll over the spirit, until at last madness preached: "Everything perishes, therefore everything deserves to perish!"

"And this itself is justice, the law of time – that he must devour his children:" thus did madness preach.

"Morally are things ordered according to justice and penalty. Oh,

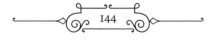

where is there deliverance from the flux of things and from the 'existence' of penalty?" Thus did madness preach.

"Can there be deliverance when there is eternal justice? Alas, unrollable is the stone, 'It was': eternal must also be all penalties!" Thus did madness preach.

"No deed can be annihilated: how could it be undone by the penalty! This, this is what is eternal in the 'existence' of penalty, that existence also must be eternally recurring deed and guilt!

Unless the Will should at last deliver itself, and Willing become non-Willing:" but you know, my brothers, this fabulous song of madness!

Away from those fabulous songs did I lead you when I taught you: "The Will is a creator."

All "It was" is a fragment, a riddle, a fearful chance – until the creating Will says thereto: "But thus would I have it."

Until the creating Will says thereto: "But thus do I will it! Thus shall I will it!"

But did it ever speak thus? And when does this take place? Has the Will been unharnessed from its own folly?

Has the Will become its own deliverer and joy-bringer? Has it unlearned the spirit of revenge and all teeth-gnashing?

And who has taught it reconciliation with time, and something higher than all reconciliation?

Something higher than all reconciliation must the Will will which is the Will to Power: but how does that take place? Who has taught it also to will backwards?'

—But at this point it chanced that Zarathustra suddenly paused, and looked like a person in the greatest alarm. With terror in his eyes did he gaze on his disciples; his glances pierced as with arrows their thoughts and arrear-thoughts. But after a brief space he again laughed, and said soothedly:

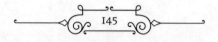

'It is difficult to live amongst men, because silence is so difficult – especially for a babbler.'

Thus spoke Zarathustra. The hunchback, however, had listened to the conversation and had covered his face during the time; but when he heard Zarathustra laugh, he looked up with curiosity, and said slowly:

'But why does Zarathustra speak otherwise to us than to his disciples?'

Zarathustra answered: 'What is there to be wondered at! With hunchbacks one May well speak in a hunchbacked way!'

'Very good,' said the hunchback; 'and with pupils one may well tell tales out of school.

But why does Zarathustra speak otherwise to his pupils – than to himself?'

43. Manly Prudence

'NOT the height, it is the declivity that is terrible!

The declivity, where the gaze shoots downwards, and the hand grasps upwards. There does the heart become giddy through its double will.

Ah, friends, do you divine also my heart's double will?

This, this is my declivity and my danger, that my gaze shoots towards the summit, and my hand would rather clutch and lean – on the depth!

To man clings my will; with chains do I bind myself to man, because I am pulled upwards to the Superman: for there does my other will tend.

And therefore do I live blindly among men, as if I knew them not: that my hand may not entirely lose belief in firmness.

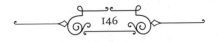

I know not you men: this gloom and consolation is often spread around me.

I sit at the gateway for every rogue, and ask: Who wishes to deceive me?

This is my first manly prudence, that I allow myself to be deceived, so as not to be on my guard against deceivers.

Ah, if I were on my guard against man, how could man be an anchor to my ball! Too easily would I be pulled upwards and away!

This providence is over my fate, that I have to be without foresight.

And he who would not languish amongst men, must learn to drink out of all glasses; and he who would keep clean amongst men, must know how to wash himself even with dirty water.

And thus spoke I often to myself for consolation: "Courage! Cheer up! old heart! An unhappiness has failed to befall you: enjoy that as thy – happiness!"

This, however, is my other manly prudence: I am more forbearing to the vain than to the proud.

Is not wounded vanity the mother of all tragedies? Where, however, pride is wounded, there there grows up something better than pride.

That life may be fair to behold, its game must be well played; for that purpose, however, it needs good actors.

Good actors have I found all the vain ones: they play, and wish people to be fond of beholding them – all their spirit is in this wish.

They represent themselves, they invent themselves; in their neighbourhood I like to look upon life – it cures of melancholy.

Therefore am I forbearing to the vain, because they are the physicians of my melancholy, and keep me attached to man as to a drama.

And further, who conceives the full depth of the modesty of the vain man! I am favourable to him, and sympathetic on account of his modesty.

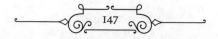

From you would he learn his belief in himself; he feeds upon your glances, he eats praise out of your hands.

Your lies does he even believe when you lie favourably about him: for in its depths sighs his heart: "What am I?"

And if that be the true virtue which is unconscious of itself – well, the vain man is unconscious of his modesty!

This is, however, my third manly prudence: I am not put out of conceit with the wicked by your timorousness.

I am happy to see the marvels the warm sun hatches: tigers and palms and rattlesnakes.

Also amongst men there is a beautiful brood of the warm sun, and much that is marvellous in the wicked.

In truth, as your wisest did not seem to me so very wise, so found I also human wickedness below the fame of it.

And oft did I ask with a shake of the head: Why still rattle, you rattlesnakes?

There is still a future even for evil! And the warmest south is still undiscovered by man.

How many things are now called the worst wickedness, which are only twelve feet broad and three months long! Some day, however, will greater dragons come into the world.

For that the Superman may not lack his dragon, the super-dragon that is worthy of him, there must still much warm sun glow on moist virgin forests!

Out of your wild cats must tigers have evolved, and out of your poison-toads, crocodiles: for the good hunter shall have a good hunt!

And verily, you good and just! In you there is much to be laughed at, and especially your fear of what has hitherto been called "the devil!"

So alien are you in your souls to what is great, that to you the Superman would be frightful in his goodness!

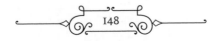

And you wise and knowing ones, you would flee from the solar-glow of the wisdom in which the Superman joyfully baths his nakedness!

You highest men who have come within my ken! This is my doubt of you, and my secret laughter: I suspect you would call my Superman – a devil!

Ah, I became tired of those highest and best ones: from their "height" did I long to be up, out, and away to the Superman!

A horror came over me when I saw those best ones naked: then there grew for me the pinions to soar away into distant futures.

Into more distant futures, into more southern souths than ever artist dreamed of: there, where gods are ashamed of all clothes!

But disguised do I want to see you, you neighbours and fellowmen, and well-attired and vain and estimable, as "the good and just;" –

And disguised will I myself sit amongst you – that I may mistake you and myself: for that is my last manly prudence.'

Thus spoke Zarathustra.

44. *The Stillest Hour*

'WHAT has happened to me, my friends? You see me troubled, driven forth, unwillingly obedient, ready to go – alas, to go away from you!

Yes, once more must Zarathustra retire to his solitude: but unjoyously this time does the bear go back to his cave!

What has happened to me? Who orders this? – Ah, my angry mistress wishes it so; she spoke to me. Have I ever named her name to you?

Yesterday towards evening there spoke to me my still hour: that is the name of my terrible mistress.

And thus did it happen – for everything must I tell you, that your heart may not harden against the suddenly departing one!

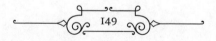

Do you know the terror of him who falls asleep?

To the very toes he is terrified, because the ground gives way under him, and the dream begins.

This do I speak to you in parable. Yesterday at the still hour did the ground give way under me: the dream began.

The hour-hand moved on, the timepiece of my life drew breath – never did I hear such stillness around me, so that my heart was terrified.

Then was there spoken to me without voice: "You know it, Zarathustra?"

And I cried in terror at this whispering, and the blood left my face: but I was silent.

Then was there once more spoken to me without voice: "You know it, Zarathustra, but you do not speak it!"

And at last I answered, like one defiant: "Yes, I know it, but I will not speak it!"

Then was there again spoken to me without voice: "You will not, Zarathustra? Is this true? Conceal yourself not behind your defiance!"

And I wept and trembled like a child, and said: 'Ah, I would indeed, but how can I do it! Exempt me only from this! It is beyond my power!'

Then was there again spoken to me without voice: "What matter about yourself, Zarathustra! Speak your word, and perish!"

And I answered: "Ah, is it my word? Who am I? I await the worthier one; I am not worthy even to perish by it."

Then was there again spoken to me without voice: "What matter about yourself? You are not yet humble enough for me. Humility has the hardest skin."

And I answered: "What has not the skin of my humility endured! At the foot of my height do I dwell: how high are my summits, no one has yet told me. But well do I know my valleys."

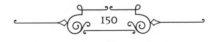

Then was there again spoken to me without voice: "O Zarathustra, he who has to remove mountains removes also valleys and plains."

And I answered: "As yet has my word not removed mountains, and what I have spoken has not reached man. I went, indeed, to men, but not yet have I attained to them."

Then was there again spoken to me without voice: "What know you thereof! The dew falls on the grass when the night is most silent."

And I answered: "They mocked me when I found and walked in my own path; and certainly did my feet then tremble.

And thus did they speak to me: you forgot the path before, now do you also forget how to walk!"

Then was there again spoken to me without voice: "What matter about their mockery! You are one who have unlearned to obey: now shall you command!

Know you not who is most needed by all? He who commands great things.

To execute great things is difficult: but the more difficult task is to command great things.

This is your most unpardonable obstinacy: you have the power, and you will not rule."

And I answered: "I lack the lion's voice for all commanding."

Then was there again spoken to me as a whispering: 'It is the still words which bring the storm. Thoughts that come with doves' footsteps guide the world.

O Zarathustra, you shall go as a shadow of that which is to come: thus will you command, and in commanding go foremost."

And I answered: "I am ashamed."

Then was there again spoken to me without voice: "You must yet become a child, and be without shame.

The pride of youth is still upon you; late have you become young: but he who would become a child must overcome even his youth."

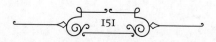

And I considered a long while, and trembled. At last, however, did I say what I had said at first. "I will not."

Then did a laughing take place all around me. Alas, how that laughing lacerated my bowels and cut into my heart!

And there was spoken to me for the last time: "O Zarathustra, your fruits are ripe, but you are not ripe for your fruits!

So must you go again into solitude: for you shall yet become mellow."

And again was there a laughing, and it fled: then did it become still around me, as with a double stillness. I lay, however, on the ground, and the sweat flowed from my limbs.

—Now have you heard all, and why I have to return into my solitude. Nothing have I kept hidden from you, my friends.

But even this have you heard from me, who is still the most reserved of men – and will be so!

Ah, my friends! I should have something more to say to you! I should have something more to give to you! Why do I not give it? Am I then a niggard?'

When, however, Zarathustra had spoken these words, the violence of his pain, and a sense of the nearness of his departure from his friends came over him, so that he wept aloud; and no one knew how to console him. In the night, however, he went away alone and left his friends.

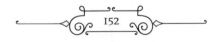

Part Three

45. The Wanderer

THEN, when it was about midnight, Zarathustra went his way over the ridge of the isle, that he might arrive early in the morning at the other coast; because there he meant to embark. For there was a good roadstead there, in which foreign ships also liked to anchor: those ships took many people with them, who wished to cross over from the Blessed isles. So when Zarathustra thus ascended the mountain, he thought on the way of his many solitary wanderings from youth onwards, and how many mountains and ridges and summits he had already climbed.

'I am a wanderer and mountain-climber', said he to his heart. 'I love not the plains, and it seems I cannot long sit still.

And whatever may still overtake me as fate and experience – a wandering will be therein, and a mountain-climbing: in the end one experiences only oneself.

The time is now past when accidents could befall me; and what *could* now fall to my lot which would not already be my own!

It returns only, it comes home to me at last – my own Self, and such of it as has been long abroad, and scattered among things and accidents.

And one thing more do I know: I stand now before my last summit, and before that which has been longest reserved for me. Ah, my hardest path must I ascend! Ah, I have begun my most lonesome wandering!

Yet he who is of my nature does not avoid such an hour: the hour

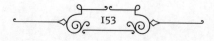

that says to him: Now only do you go the way to your greatness! Summit and abyss – these are now comprised together!

You go the way to your greatness: now has it become your last refuge, what was hitherto your last danger!

You go the way to your greatness: it must now be your best courage that there is no longer any path behind you!

You go the way to your greatness: here shall no one steal after you! Your foot itself has effaced the path behind you, and over it stands written: Impossibility.

And if all ladders henceforth fail you, then must you learn to mount upon your own head: how could you mount upward otherwise?

Upon your own head, and beyond your own heart! Now must the gentlest in you become the hardest.

He who has always much-indulged himself, sickens at last by his much-indulgence. Praises on what makes hardy! I do not praise the land where butter and honey – flow!

To learn to look away from oneself, is necessary in order to see many things – this hardiness is needed by every mountain-climber.

Yet he who is obtrusive with his eyes as a discerner, how can he ever see more of anything than its foreground!

But you, O Zarathustra, would view the ground of everything, and its background: thus must you mount even above yourself – up, upwards, until you have even your stars under you!

Yes! To look down upon myself, and even upon my stars: that only would I call my summit, that has remained for me as my last summit!'

Thus spoke Zarathustra to himself while ascending, comforting his heart with harsh maxims: for he was sore at heart as he had never been before. And when he had reached the top of the mountain-ridge, behold, there lay the other sea spread out before him; and he stood still and was long silent. The night, however, was cold at this height, and clear and starry.

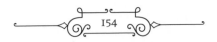

'I recognize my destiny', said he at last, sadly. 'Well! I am ready. Now has my last lonesomeness begun.

Ah, this sombre, sad sea, below me! Ah, this sombre nocturnal vexation! Ah, fate and sea! To you must I now go down!

Before my highest mountain do I stand, and before my longest wandering: therefore must I first go deeper down than I ever ascended:

—Deeper down into pain than I ever ascended, even into its darkest flood! So wills my fate. Well! I am ready.

Whence come the highest mountains? So did I once ask. Then did I learn that they come out of the sea.

That testimony is inscribed on their stones, and on the walls of their summits. Out of the deepest must the highest come to its height.'

Thus spoke Zarathustra on the ridge of the mountain where it was cold: when, however, he came into the vicinity of the sea, and at last stood alone amongst the cliffs, then had he become weary on his way, and eagerer than ever before.

'Everything as yet sleeps', said he; 'even the sea sleeps. Drowsily and strangely does its eye gaze upon me.

But it breaths warmly – I feel it. And I feel also that it dreams. It tosses about dreamily on hard pillows.

Hark! Hark! How it groans with evil recollections! Or evil expectations?

Ah, I am sad along with you, you dusky monster, and angry with myself even for your sake.

Ah, that my hand has not strength enough! Gladly, indeed, would I free you from evil dreams!'

And while Zarathustra thus spoke, he laughed at himself with melancholy and bitterness. 'What! Zarathustra', said he, 'will you even sing consolation to the sea?

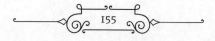

Ah, you amiable fool, Zarathustra, you too-blindly confiding one! But thus have you ever been: ever have you approached confidently all that is terrible.

Every monster would you caress. A whiff of warm breath, a little soft tuft on its paw: and immediately were you ready to love and lure it.

Love is the danger of the most lonesome one, love to anything, if it only live! Laughable, verily, is my folly and my modesty in love!'

Thus spoke Zarathustra, and laughed thereby a second time. Then, however, he thought of his abandoned friends – and as if he had done them a wrong with his thoughts, he upbraided himself because of his thoughts. And forthwith it came to pass that the laugher wept – with anger and longing wept Zarathustra bitterly.

46. *The Vision and the Riddle*

1

WHEN it got abroad among the sailors that Zarathustra was on board the ship – for a man who came from the Blessed isles had gone on board along with him, there was great curiosity and expectation. But Zarathustra kept silent for two days, and was cold and deaf with sadness; so that he neither answered looks nor questions. On the evening of the second day, however, he again opened his ears, though he still kept silent: for there were many curious and dangerous things to be heard on board the ship, which came from afar, and was to go still further. Zarathustra, however, was fond of all those who make distant voyages, and dislike to live without danger. And behold! When listening, his own tongue was at last loosened, and the ice of his heart broke. Then did he begin to speak thus:

'To you, the daring venturers and adventurers, and whoever has embarked with cunning sails upon frightful seas,

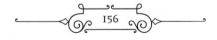

To you the enigma-intoxicated, the twilight-enjoyers, whose souls are allured by flutes to every treacherous gulf:

—For you dislike to grope at a thread with cowardly hand; and where you can divine, there do you hate to calculate.

To you only do I tell the enigma that I saw – the vision of the most lonesome one.

Gloomily walked I lately in corpse-coloured twilight – gloomily and sternly, with compressed lips. Not only one sun had set for me.

A path which ascended daringly among boulders, an evil, lonesome path, which neither herb nor shrub any longer cheered, a mountain-path, crunched under the daring of my foot.

Mutely marching over the scornful clinking of pebbles, trampling the stone that let it slip: thus did my foot force its way upwards.

Upwards: in spite of the spirit that drew it downwards, towards the abyss, the spirit of gravity, my devil and archenemy.

Upwards: although it sat upon me, half-dwarf, half-mole; para-lysed, paralysing; dripping lead in my ear, and thoughts like drops of lead into my brain.

"O Zarathustra," it whispered scornfully, syllable by syllable, 'you stone of wisdom! you threw yourself high, but every thrown stone must – fall!

O Zarathustra, you stone of wisdom, you sling-stone, you star-destroyer! Yourself threw you so high, but every thrown stone – must fall!

Condemned of yourself, and to your own stoning: O Zarathustra, far indeed threw you your stone – but upon yourself will it recoil!"

Then was the dwarf silent; and it lasted long. The silence, however, oppressed me; and to be thus in pairs, one is verily lonesomer than when alone!

I ascended, I ascended, I dreamt, I thought, but everything oppressed me. A sick one did I resemble, whom bad torture wearies, and a worse dream reawakens out of his first sleep.

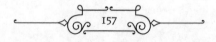

But there is something in me which I call courage: it has hitherto slain for me every dejection. This courage at last bade me stand still and say: "Dwarf! Thou! Or I!"—

For courage is the best killer, courage which attacks: for in every attack there is sound of triumph. Man, however, is the most courageous animal: thereby has he overcome every animal. With sound of triumph has he overcome every pain; human pain, however, is the sorest pain.

Courage kills also giddiness at abysses: and where does man not stand at abysses! Is not seeing itself – seeing abysses?

Courage is the best killer: courage kills also fellow-suffering. Fellow-suffering, however, is the deepest abyss: as deeply as man looks into life, so deeply also does he look into suffering.

Courage, however, is the best killer, courage which attacks: it kills even death itself; for it says: "Was that life? Well! Once more!"

In such speech, however, there is much sound of triumph. He who has ears to hear, let him hear.'

2

'"Halt, dwarf!" said I. "Either I – or you! I, however, am the stronger of the two: you knowest not my abysmal thought! It – could you not endure!"

Then happened that which made me lighter: for the dwarf sprang from my shoulder, the prying sprite! And it squatted on a stone in front of me. There was however a gateway just where we halted.

"Look at this gateway! Dwarf!" I continued, "it has two faces. Two roads come together here: these has no one yet gone to the end of.

This long lane backwards: it continues for an eternity. And that long lane forward – that is another eternity.

They are antithetical to one another, these roads; they directly abut on one another: and it is here, at this gateway that they come together. The name of the gateway is inscribed above: 'This Moment.'

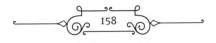

But should one follow them further – and ever further and further on, think you, dwarf, that these roads would be eternally antithetical?"

"Everything straight lies," murmured the dwarf, contemptuously. "All truth is crooked; time itself is a circle."

"You spirit of gravity!" said I wrathfully, "do not take it too lightly! Or I shall let you squat where you squat, Haltfoot, and I carried you high!"

"Observe," continued I, "This Moment! From the gateway, This Moment, there runs a long eternal lane backwards: behind us lies an eternity.

Must not whatever can run its course of all things, have already run along that lane? Must not whatever can happen of all things have already happened, resulted, and gone by?

And if everything has already existed, what think you, dwarf, of This Moment? Must not this gateway also – have already existed?

And are not all things closely bound together in such wise that This Moment draws all coming things after it? Consequently – itself also?

For whatever can run its course of all things, also in this long lane outward – must it once more run!

And this slow spider which creeps in the moonlight, and this moonlight itself, and you and I in this gateway whispering together, whispering of eternal things – must we not all have already existed?

—And must we not return and run in that other lane out before us, that long weird lane – must we not eternally return?"

Thus did I speak, and always more softly: for I was afraid of my own thoughts, and arrear-thoughts. Then, suddenly did I hear a dog howl near me.

Had I ever heard a dog howl thus? My thoughts ran back. Yes! When I was a child, in my most distant childhood:

—Then did I hear a dog howl thus. And saw it also, with hair

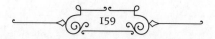

bristling, its head upwards, trembling in the still midnight, when even dogs believe in ghosts:

—So that it excited my commiseration. For just then went the full moon, silent as death, over the house; just then did it stand still, a glowing globe – at rest on the flat roof, as if on someone's property:

Thereby had the dog been terrified: for dogs believe in thieves and ghosts. And when I again heard such howling, then did it excite my commiseration once more.

Where was now the dwarf? And the gateway? And the spider? And all the whispering? Had I dreamt? Had I awakened? 'Twixt rugged rocks did I suddenly stand alone, dreary in the dreariest moonlight.

But there lay a man! And there! The dog leaping, bristling, whining – now did it see me coming – then did it howl again, then did it cry: had I ever heard a dog cry so for help?

And verily, what I saw, the like had I never seen. A young shepherd did I see, writhing, choking, quivering, with distorted countenance, and with a heavy black serpent hanging out of his mouth.

Had I ever seen so much loathing and pale horror on one countenance? He had perhaps gone to sleep? Then had the serpent crawled into his throat – there had it bitten itself fast.

My hand pulled at the serpent, and pulled: in vain! I failed to pull the serpent out of his throat. Then there cried out of me: "Bite! Bite! Its head off! Bite!" – so cried it out of me; my horror, my hatred, my loathing, my pity, all my good and my bad cried with one voice out of me.

You daring ones around me! You venturers and adventurers, and whoever of you have embarked with cunning sails on unexplored seas! You enigma-enjoyers!

Solve to me the enigma that I then beheld, interpret to me the vision of the most lonesome one!

For it was a vision and a foresight: what did I then behold in parable? And who is it that must come some day?

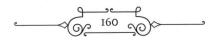

Who is the shepherd into whose throat the serpent thus crawled? Who is the man into whose throat all the heaviest and blackest will thus crawl?

—The shepherd however bit as my cry had admonished him; he bit with a strong bite! Far away did he spit the head of the serpent: and sprang up.

No longer shepherd, no longer man – a transfigured being, a light-surrounded being, that laughed! Never on earth laughed a man as he laughed!

O my brothers, I heard a laughter which was no human laughter, and now gnaws a thirst at me, a longing that is never allayed.

My longing for that laughter gnaws at me: oh, how can I still endure to live! And how could I endure to die at present!'

Thus spoke Zarathustra.

47. *Involuntary Bliss*

WITH such enigmas and bitterness in his heart did Zarathustra sail o'er the sea. When, however, he was four day-journeys from the Blessed isles and from his friends, then had he overcame all his pain: triumphantly and with firm foot did he again accept his fate. And then talked Zarathustra in this wise to his exulting conscience:

'Alone am I again, and like to be so, alone with the pure heaven, and the open sea; and again is the afternoon around me.

On an afternoon did I find my friends for the first time; on an afternoon, also, did I find them a second time: at the hour when all light becomes stiller.

For whatever happiness is still on its way 'twixt heaven and earth, now seeks for lodging a luminous soul: with happiness has all light now become stiller.

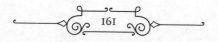

O afternoon of my life! Once did my happiness also descend to the valley that it might seek a lodging: then did it find those open hospitable souls.

O afternoon of my life! What did I not surrender that I might have one thing: this living plantation of my thoughts, and this dawn of my highest hope!

Companions did the creator once seek, and children of his hope: and lo, it turned out that he could not find them, except he himself should first create them.

Thus am I in the midst of my work, to my children going, and from them returning: for the sake of his children must Zarathustra perfect himself.

For in one's heart one loves only one's child and one's work; and where there is great love to oneself, then is it the sign of pregnancy: so have I found it.

Still are my children verdant in their first spring, standing nigh one another, and shaken in common by the winds, the trees of my garden and of my best soil.

And verily, where such trees stand beside one another, there are Blessed isles!

But one day will I take them up, and put each by itself alone: that it may learn solitude and defiance and prudence.

Gnarled and crooked and with flexible hardness shall it then stand by the sea, a living lighthouse of unconquerable life.

Yonder where the storms rush down into the sea, and the snout of the mountain drinks water, shall each on a time have his day and night watches, for his testing and recognition.

Recognized and tested shall each be, to see if he be of my type and lineage: if he be master of a long will, silent even when he speaks, and giving in such wise that he takes in giving:

—So that he may one day become my companion, a fellow-creator

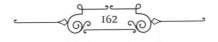

and fellow-enjoyer with Zarathustra: such a one as writes my will on my law-tablets, for the fuller perfection of all things.

And for his sake and for those like him, must I perfect myself: therefore do I now avoid my happiness, and present myself to every misfortune – for my final testing and recognition.

And verily, it were time that I went away; and the wanderer's shadow and the longest tedium and the still hour – have all said to me: "It is the highest time!"

The word blew to me through the keyhole and said "Come!" The door sprang subtly open to me, and said "Go!"

But I lay enchained to my love for my children: desire spread this snare for me – the desire for love – that I should become the prey of my children, and lose myself in them.

Desiring – that is now for me to have lost myself. I possess you, my children! In this possessing shall everything be assurance and nothing desire.

But brooding lay the sun of my love upon me, in his own juice stewed Zarathustra, then did shadows and doubts fly past me.

For frost and winter I now longed: "Oh, that frost and winter would again make me crack and crunch!" sighed I: then arose icy mist out of me.

My past burst its tomb, many pains buried alike woke up: fully slept had they merely, concealed in corpse-clothes.

So called everything to me in signs: "It is time!" But I – heard not, until at last my abyss moved, and my thought bit me.

Ah, abysmal thought, which are my thought! When shall I find strength to hear you burrowing, and no longer tremble?

To my very throat throbs my heart when I hear them burrowing! Your muteness even is like to strangle me, you abysmal mute one!

As yet have I never ventured to call you up; it has been enough

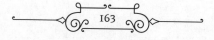

that I – have carried you about with me! As yet have I not been strong enough for my final lion-wantonness and playfulness.

Sufficiently formidable to me has your weight ever been: but one day shall I yet find the strength and the lion's voice which will call you up!

When I shall have overcome myself therein, then will I overcome myself also in that which is greater; and a victory shall be the seal of my perfection!

Meanwhile do I sail along on uncertain seas; chance flatters me, smooth-tongued chance; forward and backward do I gaze, still see I no end.

As yet has the hour of my final struggle not come to me – or does it come to me perhaps just now? With insidious beauty do sea and life gaze upon me round about:

O afternoon of my life! O happiness before eventide! O haven upon high seas! O peace in uncertainty! How I distrust all of you!

Distrustful am I of your insidious beauty! Like the lover am I, who distrusts too sleek smiling.

As he pushes the best-beloved before him – tender even in severity, the jealous one, so do I push this blissful hour before me.

Away with you, you blissful hour! With you has there come to me an involuntary bliss! Ready for my severest pain do I here stand: at the wrong time have you come!

Away with you, you blissful hour! Rather harbour there – with my children! Hasten! and bless them before eventide with my happiness!

There, already approaches eventide: the sun sinks. Away – my happiness!'

Thus spoke Zarathustra. And he waited for his misfortune the whole night; but he waited in vain. The night remained clear and calm, and happiness itself came closer and closer to him. Towards morning, however, Zarathustra laughed to his heart, and said mockingly:

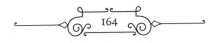

'Happiness runs after me. That is because I do not run after women. Happiness, however, is a woman.'

48. *Before Sunrise*

'O HEAVEN above me, you pure, you deep heaven! You abyss of light! Gazing on you, I tremble with divine desires.

Up to your height to toss myself – that is my depth! In your purity to hide myself – that is my innocence!

The God veils his beauty: thus hide you your stars. You speak not: thus proclaim you your wisdom to me.

Mute o'er the raging sea have you risen for me today; your love and your modesty make a revelation to my raging soul.

In that you came to me beautiful, veiled in your beauty, in that you spoke to me mutely, obvious in your wisdom:

Oh, how could I fail to divine all the modesty of your soul! Before the sun did you come to me – the most lonesome one.

We have been friends from the beginning: to us are grief, gruesomeness, and ground common; even the sun is common to us.

We do not speak to each other, because we know too much: we keep silent to each other, we smile our knowledge to each other.

Are you not the light of my fire? Have you not the sister-soul of my insight?

Together did we learn everything; together did we learn to ascend beyond ourselves to ourselves, and to smile uncloudedly:

—Uncloudedly to smile down out of luminous eyes and out of miles of distance, when under us constraint and purpose and guilt stream like rain.

And wandered I alone, for what did my soul hunger by night and in labyrinthine paths? And climbed I mountains, whom did I ever seek, if not you, upon mountains?

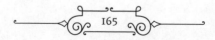

And all my wandering and mountain-climbing: a necessity was it merely, and a makeshift of the unhandy one: to fly only, wants my entire will, to fly into you!

And what have I hated more than passing clouds, and whatever taints you? And my own hatred have I even hated, because it tainted you!

The passing clouds I detest – those stealthy cats of prey: they take from you and me what is common to us – the vast unbounded Yes – and Amen – saying.

These mediators and mixers we detest – the passing clouds: those half-and-half ones, that have neither learned to bless nor to curse from the heart.

Rather will I sit in a tub under a closed heaven, rather will I sit in the abyss without heaven, than see you, you luminous heaven, tainted with passing clouds!

And oft have I longed to pin them fast with the jagged gold-wires of lightning, that I might, like the thunder, beat the drum upon their kettle-bellies:

—An angry drummer, because they rob me of your Yes and Amen! you heaven above me, you pure, you luminous heaven! You abyss of light! Because they rob you of my Yes and Amen.

For rather will I have noise and thunders and tempest-blasts, than this discreet, doubting cat-repose; and also amongst men do I hate most of all the soft-treaders, and half-and-half ones, and the doubting, hesitating, passing clouds.

And "he who cannot bless shall learn to curse!" – this clear teaching dropt to me from the clear heaven; this star stands in my heaven even in dark nights.

I, however, am a blesser and a Yes-sayer, if you be but around me, you pure, you luminous heaven! You abyss of light! Into all abysses do I then carry my beneficent Yes-saying.

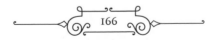

A blesser have I become and a Yes-sayer: and therefore strove I long and was a striver, that I might one day get my hands free for blessing.

This, however, is my blessing: to stand above everything as its own heaven, its round roof, its azure bell and eternal security: and blessed is he who thus blesses!

For all things are baptized at the font of eternity, and beyond good and evil; good and evil themselves, however, are but fugitive shadows and damp afflictions and passing clouds.

It is a blessing and not a blasphemy when I teach that "above all things there stands the heaven of chance, the heaven of innocence, the heaven of hazard, the heaven of wantonness."

"Of Hazard" – that is the oldest nobility in the world; that gave I back to all things; I emancipated them from bondage under purpose.

This freedom and celestial serenity did I put like an azure bell above all things, when I taught that over them and through them, no "eternal Will" – wills.

This wantonness and folly did I put in place of that Will, when I taught that "In everything there is one thing impossible – rationality!"

A little reason, to be sure, a germ of wisdom scattered from star to star – this leaven is mixed in all things: for the sake of folly, wisdom is mixed in all things!

A little wisdom is indeed possible; but this blessed security have I found in all things, that they prefer – to dance on the feet of chance.

O heaven above me! You pure, you lofty heaven! This is now your purity to me, that there is no eternal reason-spider and reason-cobweb: That you are to me a dancing-floor for divine chances, that you are to me a table of the Gods, for divine dice and dice-players!

But you blush? Have I spoken unspeakable things? Have I abused, when I meant to bless you?

Or is it the shame of being two of us that makes you blush! Do you bid me go and be silent, because now – day comes?

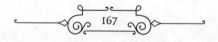

The world is deep: and deeper than e'er the day could read. Not everything may be uttered in presence of day. But day comes: so let us part!

O heaven above me, you modest one! You glowing one! O you, my happiness before sunrise! The day comes: so let us part!'

Thus spoke Zarathustra.

49. *Virtue That Diminishes*

1

WHEN Zarathustra was again on the continent, he did not go straightway to his mountains and his cave, but made many wanderings and questionings, and ascertained this and that; so that he said of himself jestingly: 'Lo, a river that flows back to its source in many windings!' For he wanted to learn what had taken place among men during the interval: whether they had become greater or smaller. And once, when he saw a row of new houses, he marvelled, and said:

'What do these houses mean? No great soul put them up as its simile!

Did perhaps a silly child take them out of its toy-box? Would that another child put them again into the box!

And these rooms and chambers – can men go out and in there? They seem to be made for silk dolls; or for dainty-eaters, who perhaps let others eat with them.'

And Zarathustra stood still and meditated. At last he said sorrowfully: 'There has everything become smaller!

Everywhere do I see lower doorways: he who is of my type can still go therethrough, but – he must stoop!

Oh, when shall I arrive again at my home, where I shall no longer have to stoop – shall no longer have to stoop before the small ones!' – And Zarathustra sighed, and gazed into the distance.

The same day, however, he spoke on the virtue that makes small.

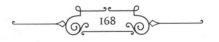

2

'I pass through this people and keep my eyes open: they do not forgive me for not envying their virtues.

They bite at me, because I say to them that for small people, small virtues are necessary – and because it is hard for me to understand that small people are necessary!

Here am I still like a cock in a strange farm-yard, at which even the hens peck: but on that account I am not unfriendly to the hens.

I am courteous towards them, as towards all small annoyances; to be prickly towards what is small, seems to me wisdom for hedgehogs.

They all speak of me when they sit around their fire in the evening – they speak of me, but no one thinks – of me!

This is the new stillness which I have experienced: their noise around me spreads a mantle over my thoughts.

They shout to one another: "What is this gloomy cloud about to do to us? Let us see that it does not bring a plague upon us!"

And recently did a woman seize upon her child that was coming to me: "Take the children away," cried she, "such eyes scorch children's souls."

They cough when I speak: they think coughing an objection to strong winds – they divine nothing of the boisterousness of my happiness!

"We have not yet time for Zarathustra" – so they object; but what matter about a time that "has no time" for Zarathustra?

And if they should altogether praise me, how could I go to sleep on their praise? A girdle of spines is their praise to me: it scratches me even when I take it off.

And this also did I learn among them: the praiser does as if he gave back; in truth, however, he wants more to be given him!

Ask my foot if their lauding and luring strains please it! To such measure and ticktack, it likes neither to dance nor to stand still.

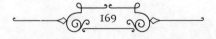

To small virtues would they rather lure and laud me; to the tick-tack of small happiness would they rather persuade my foot.

I pass through this people and keep my eyes open; they have become smaller, and ever become smaller: the reason thereof is their doctrine of happiness and virtue.

For they are moderate also in virtue, because they want comfort. With comfort, however, moderate virtue only is compatible.

To be sure, they also learn in their way to stride on and stride forward: that, I call their hobbling. – Thereby they become a hindrance to all who are in haste.

And many of them go forward, and look backwards thereby, with stiffened necks: those do I like to run up against.

Foot and eye shall not lie, nor give the lie to each other. But there is much lying among small people.

Some of them will, but most of them are willed. Some of them are genuine, but most of them are bad actors.

There are actors without knowing it amongst them, and actors without intending it, the genuine ones are always rare, especially the genuine actors.

Of man there is little here: therefore do their women masculinize themselves. For only he who is man enough, will – save the woman in woman.

And this hypocrisy found I worst amongst them, that even those who command feign the virtues of those who serve.

"I serve, you serve, we serve" – so chants here even the hypocrisy of the rulers – and alas! if the first lord be only the first servant!

Ah, even upon their hypocrisy did my eyes' curiosity alight; and well did I divine all their fly – happiness, and their buzzing around sunny window-panes.

So much kindness, so much weakness do I see. So much justice and pity, so much weakness.

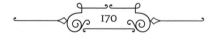

Round, fair, and considerate are they to one another, as grains of sand are round, fair, and considerate to grains of sand.

Modestly to embrace a small happiness – that do they call 'submission'! and at the same time they peer modestly after a new small happiness.

In their hearts they want simply one thing most of all: that no one hurt them. Thus do they anticipate every one's wishes and do well to every one.

That, however, is cowardice, though it be called "virtue."

And when they chance to speak harshly, those small people, then do I hear therein only their hoarseness – every draught of air makes them hoarse.

Shrewd indeed are they, their virtues have shrewd fingers. But they lack fists: their fingers do not know how to creep behind fists.

Virtue for them is what makes modest and tame: therewith have they made the wolf a dog, and man himself man's best domestic animal.

"We set our chair in the midst" – so says their smirking to me – "and as far from dying gladiators as from satisfied swine."

That, however, is – mediocrity, though it be called moderation.'

3

'I pass through this people and let fall many words: but they know neither how to take nor how to retain them.

They wonder why I came not to revile venery and vice; and verily, I came not to warn against pickpockets either!

They wonder why I am not ready to abet and whet their wisdom: as if they had not yet enough of wiseacres, whose voices grate on my ear like slate-pencils!

And when I call out: "Curse all the cowardly devils in you, that would rather whimper and fold the hands and adore" – then do they shout: "Zarathustra is godless."

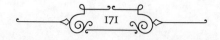

And especially do their teachers of submission shout this; – but precisely in their ears do I love to cry: "Yes! I am Zarathustra, the godless!"

Those teachers of submission! Wherever there is anything puny, or sickly, or scabby, there do they creep like lice; and only my disgust prevents me from cracking them.

Well! This is my sermon for their ears: I am Zarathustra the godless, who says: "Who is more godless than I, that I may enjoy his teaching?"

I am Zarathustra the godless: where do I find my equal? And all those are my equals who give to themselves their Will, and divest themselves of all submission.

I am Zarathustra the godless! I cook every chance in my pot. And only when it has been quite cooked do I welcome it as my food.

And verily, many a chance came imperiously to me: but still more imperiously did my Will speak to it, then did it lie imploringly upon its knees—

—Imploring that it might find home and heart with me, and saying flatteringly: 'See, O Zarathustra, how friend only comes to friend!'—

But why talk I, when no one has my ears! And so will I shout it out to all the winds:

You ever become smaller, you small people! You crumble away, you comfortable ones! You will yet perish—

—By your many small virtues, by your many small omissions, and by your many small submissions!

Too tender, too yielding: so is your soil! But for a tree to become great, it seeks to twine hard roots around hard rocks!

Also what you omit weaves at the web of all the human future; even your naught is a cobweb, and a spider that lives on the blood of the future.

And when you take, then is it like stealing, you small virtuous ones; but even among knaves honour says that "one shall only steal when one cannot rob."

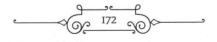

"It gives itself" – that is also a doctrine of submission. But I say to you, you comfortable ones, that it takes to itself, and will ever take more and more from you!

Ah, that you would renounce all half-willing, and would decide for idleness as you decide for action!

Ah, that you understood my word: 'Do ever what you will – but first be such as can will.

Love ever your neighbour as yourselves – but first be such as love themselves—

—Such as love with great love, such as love with great contempt!" Thus speaks Zarathustra the godless.

But why talk I, when no one has my ears! It is still an hour too early for me here.

My own forerunner am I among this people, my own cockcrow in dark lanes.

But their hour comes! And there comes also mine! Hourly do they become smaller, poorer, unfruitfuller, poor herbs! poor earth!

And soon shall they stand before me like dry grass and prairie, and verily, weary of themselves – and panting for fire, more than for water!

O blessed hour of the lightning! O mystery before noontide! Running fires will I one day make of them, and heralds with flaming tongues:

—Herald shall they one day with flaming tongues: It comes, it is nigh, the great noontide!'

Thus spoke Zarathustra.

50. The Mount of Olives

'WINTER, a bad guest, sits with me at home; blue are my hands with his friendly hand-shaking.

I honour him, that bad guest, but gladly leave him alone. Gladly do I run away from him; and when one runs well, then one escapes him!

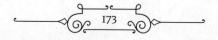

With warm feet and warm thoughts do I run where the wind is calm – to the sunny corner of my olive-mount.

There do I laugh at my stern guest, and am still fond of him; because he clears my house of flies, and quiets many little noises.

For he suffers it not if a gnat wants to buzz, or even two of them; also the lanes makes he lonesome, so that the moonlight is afraid there at night.

A hard guest is he, but I honour him, and do not worship, like the tenderlings, the pot-bellied fire-idol.

Better even a little teeth-chattering than idol-adoration! So wills my nature. And especially have I a grudge against all ardent, steaming, steamy fire-idols.

Him whom I love, I love better in winter than in summer; better do I now mock at my enemies, and more heartily, when winter sits in my house.

Heartily, verily, even when I creep into bed: there, still laughs and wantons my hidden happiness; even my deceptive dream laughs.

I, a – creeper? Never in my life did I creep before the powerful; and if ever I lied, then did I lie out of love. Therefore am I glad even in my winter-bed.

A poor bed warms me more than a rich one, for I am jealous of my poverty. And in winter she is most faithful to me.

With a wickedness do I begin every day: I mock at the winter with a cold bath: on that account grumbles my stern house-mate.

Also do I like to tickle him with a wax-taper, that he may finally let the heavens emerge from ashy-grey twilight.

For especially wicked am I in the morning: at the early hour when the pail rattles at the well, and horses neigh warmly in grey lanes:

Impatiently do I then wait, that the clear sky may finally dawn for me, the snow-bearded winter-sky, the hoary one, the white-head,

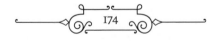

—The winter-sky, the silent winter-sky, which often stifles even its sun!

Did I perhaps learn from it the long clear silence? Or did it learn it from me? Or has each of us created it himself?

Of all good things the origin is a thousandfold, all good roguish things spring into existence for joy: how could they always do so – for once only!

A good roguish thing is also the long silence, and to look, like the winter-sky, out of a clear, round-eyed countenance:

—Like it to stifle one's sun, and one's inflexible solar will: verily, this art and this winter-roguishness have I learned well!

My best-loved wickedness and art is it, that my silence has learned not to betray itself by silence.

Clattering with diction and dice, I outwit the solemn assistants: all those stern watchers, shall my will and purpose elude.

That no one might see down into my depth and into my ultimate will – for that purpose did I create the long clear silence.

Many a shrewd one did I find: he veiled his countenance and made his water muddy, that no one might see therethrough and thereunder.

But precisely to him came the shrewder distrusters and nut-crackers: precisely from him did they fish his best-concealed fish!

But the clear, the honest, the transparent – these are for me the wisest silent ones: in them, so profound is the depth that even the clearest water does not – betray it.

You snow-bearded, silent, winter-sky, you round-eyed whitehead above me! Oh, you heavenly parable of my soul and its wantonness!

And must I not conceal myself like one who has swallowed gold – lest my soul should be ripped up?

Must I not wear stilts, that they may overlook my long legs – all those enviers and injurers around me?

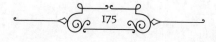

Those dingy, fire-warmed, used-up, green-tinted, ill-natured souls – how could their envy endure my happiness!

Thus do I show them only the ice and winter of my peaks – and not that my mountain winds all the solar girdles around it!

They hear only the whistling of my winter-storms: and know not that I also travel over warm seas, like longing, heavy, hot south-winds.

They commiserate also my accidents and chances: but my word says: "Suffer the chance to come to me: innocent is it as a little child!"

How could they endure my happiness, if I did not put around it accidents, and winter-privations, and bear-skin caps, and enmantling snowflakes!

—If I did not myself commiserate their pity, the pity of those enviers and injurers!

—If I did not myself sigh before them, and chatter with cold, and patiently let myself be swathed in their pity!

This is the wise waggish-will and good-will of my soul, that it conceals not its winters and glacial storms; it conceals not its chilblains either.

To one man, solitude is the flight of the sick one; to another, it is the flight from the sick ones.

Let them hear me chattering and sighing with winter-cold, all those poor squinting knaves around me! With such sighing and chattering do I flee from their heated rooms.

Let them sympathize with me and sigh with me on account of my chilblains: "At the ice of knowledge will he yet freeze to death!" – so they mourn.

Meanwhile do I run with warm feet here and there on my olive-mount: in the sunny corner of my olive-mount do I sing, and mock at all pity.'

Thus sang Zarathustra.

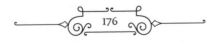

51. *Passing By*

THUS slowly wandering through many peoples and divers cities, did Zarathustra return by round-about roads to his mountains and his cave. And behold, thereby came he unawares also to the gate of the great city. Here, however, a foaming fool, with extended hands, sprang forward to him and stood in his way. It was the same fool whom the people called 'the ape of Zarathustra:' for he had learned from him something of the expression and modulation of language, and perhaps liked also to borrow from the store of his wisdom. And the fool talked thus to Zarathustra:

'O Zarathustra, here is the great city: here have you nothing to seek and everything to lose.

Why would you wade through this mire? Have pity upon your foot! Spit rather on the gate of the city, and – turn back!

Here is the hell for hermits' thoughts: here are great thoughts seethed alive and boiled small.

Here do all great sentiments decay: here may only rattle-boned sensations rattle!

Smell you not already the shambles and cookshops of the spirit? Steams not this city with the fumes of slaughtered spirit?

See you not the souls hanging like limp dirty rags? – And they make newspapers also out of these rags!

Hear you not how spirit has here become a verbal game? Loathsome verbal swill does it vomit forth! And they make newspapers also out of this verbal swill.

They hound one another, and know not where! They inflame one another, and know not why! They tinkle with their pinchbeck, they jingle with their gold.

They are cold, and seek warmth from distilled waters: they are inflamed, and seek coolness from frozen spirits; they are all sick and sore through public opinion.

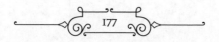

All lusts and vices are here at home; but here there are also the virtuous; there is much appointable appointed virtue:

Much appointable virtue with scribe-fingers, and hardy sitting-flesh and waiting-flesh, blessed with small breast-stars, and padded, haunchless daughters.

There is here also much piety, and much faithful spittle-licking and spittle-backing, before the God of Hosts.

"From on high," drips the star, and the gracious spittle; for the high, longs every starless bosom.

The moon has its court, and the court has its moon-calves: to all, however, that comes from the court do the mendicant people pray, and all appointable mendicant virtues.

"I serve, you serve, we serve" – so prays all appointable virtue to the prince: that the merited star may at last stick on the slender breast!

But the moon still revolves around all that is earthly: so revolves also the prince around what is earthliest of all – that, however, is the gold of the shopman.

The God of the Hosts of war is not the God of the golden bar; the prince proposes, but the shopman – disposes!

By all that is luminous and strong and good in you, O Zarathustra! Spit on this city of shopmen and return back!

Here flows all blood putridly and tepidly and frothily through all veins: spit on the great city, which is the great slum where all the scum froths together!

Spit on the city of compressed souls and slender breasts, of pointed eyes and sticky fingers –

—On the city of the obtrusive, the brazen – faced, the pen – demagogues and tongue – demagogues, the overheated ambitious:

Where everything maimed, ill-famed, lustful, untrustful, over – mellow, sickly-yellow and seditious, festers perniciously:

—Spit on the great city and turn back!'

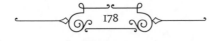

Here, however, did Zarathustra interrupt the foaming fool, and shut his mouth.

'Stop this at once!' called out Zarathustra, 'long have your speech and your species disgusted me!

Why did you live so long by the swamp, that you yourself had to become a frog and a toad?

Flows there not a tainted, frothy, swamp-blood in your own veins, when you have thus learned to croak and revile?

Why went you not into the forest? Or why did you not till the ground? Is the sea not full of green islands?

I despise your contempt; and when you warned me – why did you not warn yourself?

Out of love alone shall my contempt and my warning bird take wing; but not out of the swamp!

They call you my ape, you foaming fool: but I call you my grunting-pig, by your grunting, you spoil even my praise of folly.

What was it that first made you grunt? Because no one sufficiently flattered you: therefore did you seat yourself beside this filth, that you might have cause for much grunting,

—That you might have cause for much vengeance! For vengeance, you vain fool, is all your foaming; I have divined you well!

But your fools'-word injures me, even when you are right! And even if Zarathustra's word were a hundred times justified, you would ever – do wrong with my word!'

Thus spoke Zarathustra. Then did he look on the great city and sighed, and was long silent. At last he spoke thus:

'I loathe also this great city, and not only this fool. Here and there – there is nothing to better, nothing to worsen.

Woe to this great city! And I would that I already saw the pillar of fire in which it will be consumed!

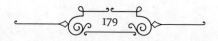

For such pillars of fire must precede the great noontide. But this has its time and its own fate.

This precept, however, give I to you, in parting, you fool: Where one can no longer love, there should one – pass by!'

Thus spoke Zarathustra, and passed by the fool and the great city.

52. *The Apostates*

1

'AH, LIES everything already withered and grey which but lately stood green and many-hued on this meadow! And how much honey of hope did I carry hence into my beehives!

Those young hearts have already all become old – and not old even! Only weary, ordinary, comfortable: they declare it: "We have again become pious."

Of late did I see them run forth at early morn with valorous steps: but the feet of their knowledge became weary, and now do they malign even their morning valour!

Many of them once lifted their legs like the dancer; to them winked the laughter of my wisdom: then did they bethink themselves. Just now have I seen them bent down – to crawl before the cross.

Around light and liberty did they once flutter like gnats and young poets. A little older, a little colder: and already are they mystifiers, and mumblers and mollycoddles.

Did perhaps their hearts despond, because solitude had swallowed me like a whale? Did their ear perhaps hearken yearningly-long for me in vain, and for my trumpet-notes and herald-calls?

—Ah! Ever are there but few of those whose hearts have persistent courage and exuberance; and in such remains also the spirit patient. The rest, however, are cowardly.

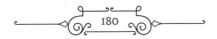

The rest: these are always the great majority, the common-place, the superfluous, the all-too-many – those all are cowardly!

Him who is of my type, will also the experiences of my type meet on the way: so that his first companions must be corpses and fools.

His second companions, however – they will call themselves his believers, will be a living host, with much love, much folly, much unbearded veneration.

To those believers shall he who is of my type among men not bind his heart; in those spring-times and many-hued meadows shall he not believe, who knows the fickly faint-hearted human species!

Could they do otherwise, then would they also will otherwise. The half-and-half spoil every whole. That leaves become withered, what is there to lament about that!

Let them go and fall away, O Zarathustra, and do not lament! Better even to blow amongst them with rustling winds,

—Blow amongst those leaves, O Zarathustra, that everything withered may run away from you the faster!'

2

'"We have again become pious" – so do those apostates confess; and some of them are still too pusillanimous thus to confess. To them I look into the eye, before them I say it to their face and to the blush on their cheeks: You are those who again pray!

It is shameful to pray! Not for all, but for you, and me, and whoever has his conscience in his head. For you it is shameful to pray!

You know it well: the faint-hearted devil in you, which would rather fold its arms, and place its hands in its bosom, and take it easier: this faint-hearted devil persuades you that "there is a God!"

Thereby, however, do you belong to the light-dreading type, to whom light never permits repose: now must you daily thrust your head deeper into obscurity and vapour!

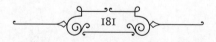

And verily, you choose the hour well: for just now do the nocturnal birds again fly abroad. The hour has come for all light-dreading people, the vesper hour and leisure hour, when they do not – "take leisure."

I hear it and smell it: it has come – their hour for hunt and procession, not indeed for a wild hunt, but for a tame, lame, snuffling, soft-treaders', soft-prayers' hunt.

—For a hunt after susceptible simpletons: all mouse-traps for the heart have again been set! And whenever I lift a curtain, a night-moth rushes out of it.

Did it perhaps squat there along with another night-moth? For everywhere do I smell small concealed communities; and wherever there are closets there are new devotees therein, and the atmosphere of devotees.

They sit for long evenings beside one another, and say: "Let us again become like little children and say, 'good God!'" – ruined in mouths and stomachs by the pious confectioners.

Or they look for long evenings at a crafty, lurking cross-spider, that preaches prudence to the spiders themselves, and teaches that "under crosses it is good for web-spinning!"

Or they sit all day at swamps with angle-rods, and on that account think themselves profound; but whoever fishes where there are no fish, I do not even call him superficial!

Or they learn in godly-gay style to play the harp with a hymn – poet, who would rather harp himself into the heart of young girls: for he has tired of old girls and their praises.

Or they learn to shudder with a learned semi-madcap, who waits in darkened rooms for spirits to come to him – and the spirit runs away entirely!

Or they listen to an old roving howl- and growl-piper, who has learned from the sad winds the sadness of sounds; now pips he as the wind, and preaches sadness in sad strains.

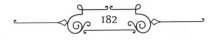

And some of them have even become night-watchmen: they know now how to blow horns, and go about at night and awaken old things which have long fallen asleep.

Five words about old things did I hear last night at the garden-wall: they came from such old, sorrowful, arid night-watchmen.

"For a father he cares not sufficiently for his children: human fathers do this better!"—

"He is too old! He now cares no more for his children," – answered the other night-watchman.

"Has he then children? No one can prove it unless he himself prove it! I have long wished that he would for once prove it thoroughly."

"Prove? As if he had ever proved anything! Proving is difficult to him; he lays great stress on one's believing him."

"Ay! Ay! Belief saves him; belief in him. That is the way with old people! So it is with us also!"—

—Thus spoke to each other the two old night-watchmen and light-scarers, and tooted then sorrowfully on their horns: so did it happen last night at the garden-wall.

To me, however, did the heart writhe with laughter, and was like to break; it knew not where to go, and sunk into the midriff.

It will be my death yet – to choke with laughter when I see asses drunken, and hear night-watchmen thus doubt about God.

Has the time not long since passed for all such doubts? Who may nowadays awaken such old slumbering, light-shunning things!

With the old Deities has it long since come to an end: and verily, a good joyful Deity-end had they!

They did not "twilight" themselves to death – that do people fabricate! On the contrary, they – laughed themselves to death once on a time!

That took place when the ungodliest utterance came from a God

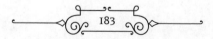

himself – the utterance: 'There is but one God! You shall have no other gods before me!'—

—An old grim-beard of a God, a jealous one, forgot himself in such wise:

And all the gods then laughed, and shook upon their thrones, and exclaimed: "Is it not just divinity that there are gods, but no God?"

He that has an ear let him hear.'

Thus talked Zarathustra in the city he loved, which is surnamed The Pied Cow. For from here he had but two days to travel to reach once more his cave and his animals; his soul, however, rejoiced unceasingly on account of the nighness of his return home.

53. The Return Home

'O SOLITUDE! My home, solitude! Too long have I lived wildly in wild remoteness, to return to you without tears!

Now threaten me with the finger as mothers threaten; now smile upon me as mothers smile; now say just: "Who was it that like a whirlwind once rushed away from me?

—Who when departing called out: 'Too long have I sat with solitude; there have I unlearned silence!' That have you learned now – surely?

O Zarathustra, everything do I know; and that you were more forsaken amongst the many, you unique one, than you ever were with me!

One thing is forsakenness, another matter is solitude: that have you now learned! And that amongst men you will ever be wild and strange:

—Wild and strange even when they love you: for above all they want to be treated indulgently!

Here, however, are you at home and house with yourself; here

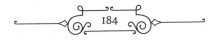

can you utter everything, and unbosom all motives; nothing is here ashamed of concealed, congealed feelings.

Here do all things come caressingly to your talk and flatter you: for they want to ride upon your back. On every simile do you here ride to every truth.

Honestly and openly may you here talk to all things: and verily, it sounds as praise in their ears, for one to talk to all things – directly!

Another matter, however, is forsakenness. For, do you remember, O Zarathustra? When your bird screamed overhead, when you stood in the forest, irresolute, ignorant where to go, beside a corpse:

—When you spoke: 'Let my animals lead me! More dangerous have I found it among men than among animals:' – That was forsakenness!

And do you remember, O Zarathustra? When you sat in your isle, a well of wine giving and granting amongst empty buckets, giving and distributing amongst the thirsty:

– Until at last you alone sat thirsty amongst the drunken ones, and wailed nightly: 'Is taking not more blessed than giving? And stealing yet more blessed than taking?' – That was forsakenness!

And do you remember, O Zarathustra? When your still hour came and drove you forth from yourself, when with wicked whispering it said: 'Speak and perish!'—

—When it disgusted you with all your waiting and silence, and discouraged your humble courage: That was forsakenness!' –

O solitude! My home, solitude! How blessedly and tenderly speaks your voice to me!

We do not question each other, we do not complain to each other; we go together openly through open doors.

For all is open with you and clear; and even the hours run here on lighter feet. For in the dark, time weighs heavier upon one than in the light.

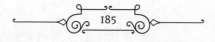

Here fly open to me all beings' words and word-cabinets: here all being wants to become words, here all becoming wants to learn of me how to talk.

Down there, however – all talking is in vain! There, forgetting and passing-by are the best wisdom: that have I learned now!

He who would understand everything in man must handle everything. But for that I have too clean hands.

I do not like even to inhale their breath; alas! That I have lived so long among their noise and bad breaths!

O blessed stillness around me! O pure odours around me! How from a deep breast this stillness fetches pure breath! How it hearkens, this blessed stillness!

But down there – there speaks everything, there is everything misheard. If one announce one's wisdom with bells, the shopmen in the marketplace will out-jingle it with pennies!

Everything among them talks; no one knows any longer how to understand. Everything falls into the water; nothing falls any longer into deep wells.

Everything among them talks, nothing succeeds any longer and accomplishes itself. Everything cackles, but who will still sit quietly on the nest and hatch eggs?

Everything among them talks, everything is out-talked. And that which yesterday was still too hard for time itself and its tooth, hangs today, outchamped and outchewed, from the mouths of the men of today.

Everything among them talks, everything is betrayed. And what was once called the secret and secrecy of profound souls, belongs today to the street-trumpeters and other butterflies.

O human hubbub, you wonderful thing! You noise in dark streets! Now are you again behind me: my greatest danger lies behind me!

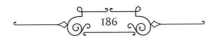

In indulging and pitying lay ever my greatest danger; and all human hubbub wishes to be indulged and tolerated.

With suppressed truths, with fool's hand and befooled heart, and rich in petty lies of pity: thus have I ever lived among men.

Disguised did I sit amongst them, ready to misjudge myself that I might endure them, and willingly saying to myself: 'You fool, you do not know men!"

One unlearns men when one lives amongst them: there is too much foreground in all men – what can far-seeing, far-longing eyes do there!

And, fool that I was, when they misjudged me, I indulged them on that account more than myself, being habitually hard on myself, and often even taking revenge on myself for the indulgence.

Stung all over by poisonous flies, and hollowed like the stone by many drops of wickedness: thus did I sit among them, and still said to myself: "Innocent is everything petty of its pettiness!"

Especially did I find those who call themselves "the good," the most poisonous flies; they sting in all innocence, they lie in all innocence; how could they – be just towards me!

He who lives amongst the good – pity teaches him to lie. Pity makes stifling air for all free souls. For the stupidity of the good is unfathomable.

To conceal myself and my riches – that did I learn down there: for every one did I still find poor in spirit. It was the lie of my pity, that I knew in every one.

—That I saw and scented in every one, what was enough of spirit for him, and what was too much!

Their stiff wise men: I call them wise, not stiff – thus did I learn to slur over words.

The grave-diggers dig for themselves diseases. Under old rubbish rest bad vapours. One should not stir up the marsh. One should live on mountains.

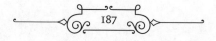

With blessed nostrils do I again breathe mountain-freedom. Freed at last is my nose from the smell of all human hubbub!

With sharp breezes tickled, as with sparkling wine, sneezes my soul – sneezes, and shouts self-congratulatingly: "Health to you!"'

Thus spoke Zarathustra.

54. The Three Evils

1

'IN MY dream, in my last morning-dream, I stood today on a promontory – beyond the world; I held a pair of scales, and weighed the world.

Alas, that the rosy dawn came too early to me: she glowed me awake, the jealous one! Jealous is she always of the glows of my morning-dream.

Measurable by him who has time, weighable by a good weigher, attainable by strong pinions, divinable by divine nutcrackers: thus did my dream find the world:

My dream, a bold sailor, half-ship, half-hurricane, silent as the butterfly, impatient as the falcon: how had it the patience and leisure today for world-weighing!

Did my wisdom perhaps speak secretly to it, my laughing, wide-awake day-wisdom, which mocks at all "infinite worlds"? For it says: "Where force is, there becomes number the master: it has more force."

How confidently did my dream contemplate this finite world, not new-fangledly, not old-fangledly, not timidly, not entreatingly:

—As if a big round apple presented itself to my hand, a ripe golden apple, with a coolly-soft, velvety skin: thus did the world present itself to me:

—As if a tree nodded to me, a broad-branched, strong-willed

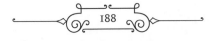

tree, curved as a recline and a foot-stool for weary travellers: thus did the world stand on my promontory:

—As if delicate hands carried a casket towards me – a casket open for the delectation of modest adoring eyes: thus did the world present itself before me today:

—Not riddle enough to scare human love from it, not solution enough to put to sleep human wisdom: a humanly good thing was the world to me today, of which such bad things are said!

How I thank my morning-dream that I thus at today's dawn, weighed the world! As a humanly good thing did it come to me, this dream and heart-comforter!

And that I may do the like by day, and imitate and copy its best, now will I put the three worst things on the scales, and weigh them humanly well.

He who taught to bless taught also to curse: what are the three best cursed things in the world? These will I put on the scales.

Voluptuousness, passion for power, and selfishness: these three things have hitherto been best cursed, and have been in worst and falsest repute – these three things will I weigh humanly well.

Well! Here is my promontory, and there is the sea – it rolls here to me, shaggily and fawningly, the old, faithful, hundred-headed dog-monster that I love!

Well! Here will I hold the scales over the weltering sea: and also a witness do I choose to look on – you, the hermit-tree, you, the strong-odoured, broad-arched tree that I love!

On what bridge goes the now to the hereafter? By what constraint do the high stoop to the low? And what enjoins even the highest still – to grow upwards?

Now stand the scales poised and at rest: three heavy questions have I thrown in; three heavy answers carries the other scale.'

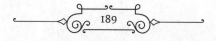

2

'Voluptuousness: to all hair-shirted despisers of the body, a sting and stake; and, cursed as "the world," by all the afterworldly: for it mocks and befools all erring, misinferring teachers.

Voluptuousness: to the rabble, the slow fire at which it is burnt; to all wormy wood, to all stinking rags, the prepared heat and stew furnace.

Voluptuousness: to free hearts, a thing innocent and free, the garden-happiness of the earth, all the future's thanks – overflow to the present.

Voluptuousness: only to the withered a sweet poison; to the lion-willed, however, the great cordial, and the reverently saved wine of wines.

Voluptuousness: the great symbolic happiness of a higher happiness and highest hope. For to many is marriage promised, and more than marriage,

—To many that are more unknown to each other than man and woman: and who has fully understood how unknown to each other are man and woman!

Voluptuousness: but I will have hedges around my thoughts, and even around my words, lest swine and libertine should break into my gardens!

Passion for power: the glowing scourge of the hardest of the heart-hard; the cruel torture reserved for the cruel themselves; the gloomy flame of living pyres.

Passion for power: the wicked gadfly which is mounted on the vainest peoples; the scorner of all uncertain virtue; which rides on every horse and on every pride.

Passion for power: the earthquake which breaks and upbreaks all that is rotten and hollow; the rolling, rumbling, punitive demolisher of whited sepulchres; the flashing interrogative-sign beside premature answers.

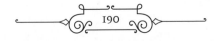

Passion for power: before whose glance man creeps and crouches and drudges, and becomes lower than the serpent and the swine: until at last great contempt cries out of him,

Passion for power: the terrible teacher of great contempt, which preaches to their face to cities and empires: "Away with you!" – until a voice cries out of themselves: "Away with me!"

Passion for power: which, however, mounts alluringly even to the pure and lonesome, and up to self-satisfied elevations, glowing like a love that paints purple felicities alluringly on earthly heavens.

Passion for power: but who would call it passion, when the height longs to stoop for power! Nothing sick or diseased is there in such longing and descending!

That the lonesome height may not forever remain lonesome and self-sufficing; that the mountains may come to the valleys and the winds of the heights to the plains:

Oh, who could find the right prenomen and honouring name for such longing! "Giving virtue" – thus did Zarathustra. Once name the unnamable.

And then it happened also, and verily, it happened for the first time! That his word blessed selfishness, the wholesome, healthy self-ishness, that springs from the powerful soul:

—From the powerful soul, to which the high body appertains, the handsome, triumphing, refreshing body, around which everything becomes a mirror:

—The pliant, persuasive body, the dancer, whose symbol and epitome is the self-enjoying soul. Of such bodies and souls the self-enjoyment calls itself "virtue."

With its words of good and bad does such self-enjoyment shelter itself as with sacred groves; with the names of its happiness does it banish from itself everything contemptible.

Away from itself does it banish everything cowardly; it says: "Bad

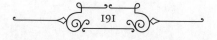

– that is cowardly!" Contemptible seem to it the ever-solicitous, the sighing, the complaining, and whoever pick up the most trifling advantage.

It despises also all bitter-sweet wisdom: for verily, there is also wisdom that blooms in the dark, a night-shade wisdom, which ever sighs: "All is vain!"

Shy distrust is regarded by it as base, and every one who wants oaths instead of looks and hands: also all over-distrustful wisdom, for such is the mode of cowardly souls.

Baser still it regards the obsequious, doggish one, who immediately lies on his back, the submissive one; and there is also wisdom that is submissive, and doggish, and pious, and obsequious.

Hateful to it altogether, and a loathing, is he who will never defend himself, he who swallows down poisonous spittle and bad looks, the all-too-patient one, the all-endurer, the all-satisfied one: for that is the mode of slaves. Whether they be servile before gods and divine spurnings, or before men and stupid human opinions: at all kinds of slaves does it spit, this blessed selfishness!

Bad: thus does it call all that is spirit-broken, and sordidly-servile – constrained, blinking eyes, depressed hearts, and the false submissive style, which kisses with broad cowardly lips.

And spurious wisdom: so does it call all the wit that slaves, and hoary-headed and weary ones affect; and especially all the cunning, spurious-witted, curious-witted foolishness of priests!

The spurious wise, however, all the priests, the world-weary, and those whose souls are of feminine and servile nature – oh, how has their game all along abused selfishness!

And precisely that was to be virtue and was to be called virtue – to abuse selfishness! And "selfless" – so did they wish themselves with good reason, all those world-weary cowards and cross-spiders!

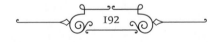

But to all those comes now the day, the change, the sword of judgment, the great noontide: then shall many things be revealed!

And he who proclaims the ego wholesome and sacred, and selfishness blessed, verily, he, the prognosticator, speaks also what he knows: "Behold, it comes, it is night, the great noontide!'"

Thus spoke Zarathustra.

55. The Spirit of Gravity

1

'MY MOUTHPIECE – is of the people: too coarsely and cordially do I talk for Angora rabbits. And still stranger sounds my word to all ink-fish and pen-foxes.

My hand – is a fool's hand: woe to all tables and walls, and whatever has room for fool's sketching, fool's scrawling!

My foot – is a horse-foot; therewith do I trample and trot over stick and stone, in the fields up and down, and am bedevilled with delight in all fast racing.

My stomach – is surely an eagle's stomach? For it prefers lamb's flesh. Certainly it is a bird's stomach.

Nourished with innocent things, and with few, ready and impatient to fly, to fly away – that is now my nature: why should there not be something of bird-nature therein!

And especially that I am hostile to the spirit of gravity, that is bird-nature: verily, deadly hostile, supremely hostile, originally hostile! Oh, where has my hostility not flown and misflown!

Thereof could I sing a song – and will sing it: though I be alone in an empty house, and must sing it to my own ears.

Other singers are there, to be sure, to whom only the full house makes the voice soft, the hand eloquent, the eye expressive, the heart wakeful: those do I not resemble.

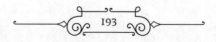

2

He who one day teaches men to fly will have shifted all landmarks; to him will all landmarks themselves fly into the air; the earth will he christen anew – as "the light body."

The ostrich runs faster than the fastest horse, but it also thrusts its head heavily into the heavy earth: thus is it with the man who cannot yet fly.

Heavy to him are earth and life, and so wills the spirit of gravity! But he who would become light, and be a bird, must love himself: thus do I teach.

Not, to be sure, with the love of the side and infected, for with them stinks even self-love!

One must learn to love oneself – thus do I teach – with a wholesome and healthy love: that one may endure to be with oneself, and not go roving about.

Such roving about christens itself "brotherly love"; with these words has there hitherto been the best lying and dissembling, and especially by those who have been burdensome to every one.

And verily, it is no commandment for today and tomorrow to learn to love oneself. Rather is it of all arts the finest, subtlest, last and patientest.

For to its possessor is all possession well concealed, and of all treasure-pits one's own is last excavated – so causes the spirit of gravity.

Almost in the cradle are we apportioned with heavy words and worths: "good" and "evil" – so calls itself this dowry. For the sake of it we are forgiven for living.

And therefore suffers one little children to come to one, to forbid them betimes to love themselves – so causes the spirit of gravity.

And we – we bear loyally what is apportioned to us, on hard shoulders, over rugged mountains! And when we sweat, then do people say to us: "Yes, life is hard to bear!"

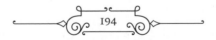

But man himself only is hard to bear! The reason thereof is that he carries too many extraneous things on his shoulders. Like the camel kneels he down, and lets himself be well laden.

Especially the strong load-bearing man in whom reverence resides. Too many extraneous heavy words and worths loads he upon himself – then seems life to him a desert!

And verily! Many a thing also that is our own is hard to bear! And many internal things in man are like the oyster – repulsive and slippery and hard to grasp;—

So that an elegant shell, with elegant adornment, must plead for them. But this art also must one learn: to have a shell, and a fine appearance, and sagacious blindness!

Again, it deceives about many things in man, that many a shell is poor and pitiable, and too much of a shell. Much concealed goodness and power is never dreamt of; the choicest dainties find no tasters!

Women know that, the choicest of them: a little fatter a little leaner – oh, how much fate is in so little!

Man is difficult to discover, and to himself most difficult of all; often lies the spirit concerning the soul. So causes the spirit of gravity.

He, however, has discovered himself who says: This is my good and evil: therewith has he silenced the mole and the dwarf, who say: "Good for all, evil for all."

Neither do I like those who call everything good, and this world the best of all. Those do I call the all – satisfied.

All-satisfiedness, which knows how to taste everything, that is not the best taste! I honour the refractory, fastidious tongues and stomachs, which have learned to say "I" and "Yes" and "No."

To chew and digest everything, however – that is the genuine swine-nature! Ever to say YEA – that has only the ass learned, and those like it!

Deep yellow and hot red – so wants my taste – it mixes blood

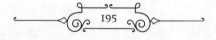

with all colours. Yet he who whitewashes his house, betrays to me a whitewashed soul.

With mummies, some fall in love; others with phantoms: both alike hostile to all flesh and blood – oh, how repugnant are both to my taste! For I love blood.

And there will I not reside and abide where every one spits and spews: that is now my taste, rather would I live amongst thieves and perjurers. Nobody carries gold in his mouth.

Still more repugnant to me, however, are all lick-spittles; and the most repugnant animal of man that I found, did I christen "parasite": it would not love, and would yet live by love.

Unhappy do I call all those who have only one choice: either to become evil beasts, or evil beast-tamers. Amongst such would I not build my tabernacle.

Unhappy do I also call those who have ever to wait, they are repugnant to my taste – all the toll-gatherers and traders, and kings, and other landkeepers and shopkeepers.

I learned waiting also, and thoroughly so, but only waiting for myself. And above all did I learn standing and walking and running and leaping and climbing and dancing.

This however is my teaching: he who wishes one day to fly, must first learn standing and walking and running and climbing and dancing: one does not fly into flying!

With rope-ladders learned I to reach many a window, with nimble legs did I climb high masts: to sit on high masts of perception seemed to me no small bliss;—

—To flicker like small flames on high masts: a small light, certainly, but a great comfort to cast-away sailors and ship-wrecked ones!

By divers ways and wendings did I arrive at my truth; not by one ladder did I mount to the height where my eye roves into my remoteness.

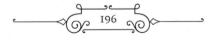

And unwillingly only did I ask my way – that was always counter to my taste! Rather did I question and test the ways themselves.

A testing and a questioning has been all my travelling: and verily, one must also learn to answer such questioning! That, however, is my taste:

—Neither a good nor a bad taste, but my taste, of which I have no longer either shame or secrecy.

"This – is now my way, where is yours?" Thus did I answer those who asked me "the way." For the way – it does not exist!'

Thus spoke Zarathustra.

56. Old and New Tablets

1

'HERE do I sit and wait, old broken law-tablets around me and also new half-written law-tablets. When comes my hour?

—The hour of my descent, of my down-going: for once more will I go to men.

For that hour do I now wait: for first must the signs come to me that it is my hour – namely, the laughing lion with the flock of doves.

Meanwhile do I talk to myself as one who has time. No one tells me anything new, so I tell myself my own story.'

2

'When I came to men, then found I them resting on an old infatuation: all of them thought they had long known what was good and bad for men.

An old wearisome business seemed to them all talk of virtue; and he who wished to sleep well spoke of "good" and "bad" before retiring to rest.

This somnolence did I disturb when I taught that no one yet knows what is good and bad: unless it be the creator!

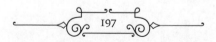

—It is he, however, who creates man's goal, and gives to the earth its meaning and its future: he only effects it that anything is good or bad.

And I bade them upset their old academic chairs, and wherever that old infatuation had sat; I bade them laugh at their great moralists, their saints, their poets, and their saviours.

At their gloomy sages did I bid them laugh, and whoever had sat admonishing as a black scarecrow on the tree of life.

On their great grave-highway did I seat myself, and even beside the carrion and vultures – and I laughed at all their bygone and its mellow decaying glory.

Like penitential preachers and fools did I cry wrath and shame on all their greatness and smallness. Oh, that their best is so very small! Oh, that their worst is so very small! Thus did I laugh.

Thus did my wise longing, born in the mountains, cry and laugh in me; a wild wisdom, verily! My great pinion-rustling longing.

And oft did it carry me off and up and away and in the midst of laughter; then flew I quivering like an arrow with sun-intoxicated rapture:

—Out into distant futures, which no dream has yet seen, into warmer souths than ever sculptor conceived, where gods in their dancing are ashamed of all clothes:

(That I may speak in parables and halt and stammer like the poets: and verily I am ashamed that I have still to be a poet!)

Where all becoming seemed to me dancing of gods, and wantoning of gods, and the world unloosed and unbridled and fleeing back to itself:

—As an eternal self-fleeing and re-seeking of one another of many gods, as the blessed self-contradicting, recommuning, and re-fraternizing with one another of many gods:

Where all time seemed to me a blessed mockery of moments, where necessity was freedom itself, which played happily with the goad of freedom:

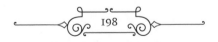

Where I also found again my old devil and arch-enemy, the spirit of gravity, and all that it created: constraint, law, necessity and consequence and purpose and will and good and evil:

For must there not be that which is danced over, danced beyond? Must there not, for the sake of the nimble, the nimblest, be moles and clumsy dwarfs?'

3

'There was it also where I picked up from the path the word "Superman," and that man is something that must be overcome.

—That man is a bridge and not a goal – rejoicing over his noontides and evenings, as advances to new rosy dawns:

—The Zarathustra word of the great noontide, and whatever else I have hung up over men like purple evening-afterglows.

Also new stars did I make them see, along with new nights; and over cloud and day and night, did I spread out laughter like a gay-coloured canopy.

I taught them all my poetization and aspiration: to compose and collect into unity what is fragment in man, and riddle and fearful chance;—

—As composer, riddle-reader, and redeemer of chance, did I teach them to create the future, and all that has been – to redeem by creating.

The past of man to redeem, and every "It was" to transform, until the Will says: "But so did I will it! So shall I will it –"

—This did I call redemption; this alone taught I them to call redemption.—

Now do I await my redemption – that I may go to them for the last time.

For once more will I go to men: amongst them will my sun set; in dying will I give them my choicest gift!

From the sun did I learn this, when it goes down, the exuberant one: gold does it then pour into the sea, out of inexhaustible riches,

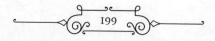

—So that the poorest fisherman rows even with golden oars! For this did I once see, and did not tire of weeping in beholding it.—

Like the sun will also Zarathustra go down: now sits he here and waits, old broken law–tablets around him, and also new law-tablets – half-written.'

4

'Behold, here is a new table; but where are my brothers who will carry it with me to the valley and into hearts of flesh?

Thus demands my great love to the remotest ones: be not considerate of your neighbour! Man is something that must be overcome.

There are many divers ways and modes of overcoming: see you thereto! But only a fool thinks: "man can also be overleapt."

Overcome yourself even in your neighbour: and a right which you can seize upon, shall you not allow to be given you!

What you do can no one do to you again. Lo, there is no requital.

He who cannot command himself shall obey. And many a one can command himself, but still sorely lacks self-obedience!'

5

'Thus wishes the type of noble souls: they desire to have nothing gratuitously, least of all, life.

He who is of the rabble wishes to live gratuitously; we others, however, to whom life has given itself – we are ever considering what we can best give in return!

And verily, it is a noble dictum which says: "What life promises us, that promise will we keep – to life!"

One should not wish to enjoy where one does not contribute to the enjoyment. And one should not wish to enjoy!

For enjoyment and innocence are the most bashful things. Neither

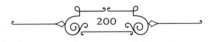

like to be sought for. One should have them, but one should rather seek for guilt and pain!'

6

'O my brothers, he who is a firstling is ever sacrificed. Now, however, are we firstlings!

We all bleed on secret sacrificial altars, we all burn and broil in honour of ancient idols.

Our best is still young: this excites old palates. Our flesh is tender, our skin is only lambs' skin: how could we not excite old idol-priests!

In ourselves dwells he still, the old idol-priest, who broils our best for his banquet. Ah, my brothers, how could firstlings fail to be sacrifices!

But so wishes our type; and I love those who do not wish to preserve themselves, the down-going ones do I love with my entire love: for they go beyond.'

7

'To be true – that can few be! And he who can, will not! Least of all, however, can the good be true.

Oh, those good ones! Good men never speak the truth. For the spirit, thus to be good, is a malady.

They yield, those good ones, they submit themselves; their heart repeats, their soul obeys: yet he who obeys, does not listen to himself!

All that is called evil by the good, must come together in order that one truth may be born. O my brothers, are you also evil enough for this truth?

The daring venture, the prolonged distrust, the cruel No, the tedium, the cutting-into-the-quick – how seldom do these come together! Out of such seed, however – is truth produced!

Beside the bad conscience has hitherto grown all knowledge! Break up, break up, you discerning ones, the old law-tablets!'

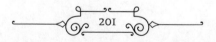

8

'When the water has planks, when gangways and railings o'erspan the stream, verily, he is not believed who then says: 'All is in flux.'

But even the simpletons contradict him. "What?" say the simpletons, "all in flux? Planks and railings are still over the stream!

Over the stream all is stable, all the values of things, the bridges and bearings, all 'good' and 'evil': these are all stable!"—

Comes, however, the hard winter, the stream-tamer, then learn even the wittiest distrust, and verily, not only the simpletons then say: 'Should not everything – stand still?'

"Fundamentally stands everything still" – that is an appropriate winter doctrine, good cheer for an unproductive period, a great comfort for winter-sleepers and fireside-loungers.

"Fundamentally stands everything still": but contrary thereto, preaches the thawing wind!

The thawing wind, a bullock, which is no ploughing bullock – a furious bullock, a destroyer, which with angry horns breaks the ice! The ice however – breaks gangways!

O my brothers, is not everything at present in flux? Have not all railings and gangways fallen into the water? Who would still hold on to "good" and "evil"?

"Woe to us! Hail to us! The thawing wind blows!" – Thus preach, my brothers, through all the streets!'

9

'There is an old illusion – it is called good and evil. Around soothsayers and astrologers has hitherto revolved the orbit of this illusion.

Once did one believe in soothsayers and astrologers; and therefore did one believe, "Everything is fate: you shall, for you must!"

Then again did one distrust all soothsayers and astrologers; and

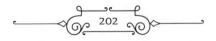

therefore did one believe, 'Everything is freedom: you can, for you will!'

O my brothers, concerning the stars and the future there has hitherto been only illusion, and not knowledge; and therefore concerning good and evil there has hitherto been only illusion and not knowledge!'

10

'"You shall not rob! You shall not kill!" – such precepts were once called sacred; before them did one bow the knee and the head, and take off one's shoes.

But I ask you: Where have there ever been better robbers and killers in the world than such sacred precepts?

Is there not even in all life – robbing and killing? And for such precepts to be called sacred, was not truth itself thereby – slain?

—Or was it a sermon of death that called sacred what contradicted and dissuaded from life? – O my brothers, break up, break up for me the old law-tablets!'

11

'It is my sympathy with all the past that I see it is abandoned,

—Abandoned to the favour, the spirit and the madness of every generation that comes, and reinterprets all that has been as its bridge!

A great potentate might arise, an artful prodigy, who with approval and disapproval could strain and constrain all the past, until it became for him a bridge, a harbinger, a herald, and a cock-crowing.

This however is the other danger, and my other sympathy: he who is of the rabble, his thoughts go back to his grandfather, with his grandfather, however, does time cease.

Thus is all the past abandoned: for it might some day happen for the rabble to become master, and drown all time in shallow waters.

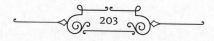

Therefore, O my brothers, a new nobility is needed, which shall be the adversary of all rabble and potentate rule, and shall inscribe anew the word "noble" on new law-tablets.

For many noble ones are needed, and many kinds of noble ones, for a new nobility! Or, as I once said in parable: "That is just divinity, that there are gods, but no God!"

12

'O my brothers, I consecrate you and point you to a new nobility: you shall become procreators and cultivators and sowers of the future;—

—Verily, not to a nobility which you could purchase like traders with traders' gold; for little worth is all that has its price.

Let it not be your honour henceforth whence you come, but where you go! Your Will and your feet which seek to overcome you – let these be your new honour!

Not that you have served a prince – of what account are princes now! nor that you have become a bulwark to that which stands, that it may stand more firmly.

Not that your family have become courtly at courts, and that you have learned – gay-coloured, like the flamingo – to stand long hours in shallow pools:

(For ability-to-stand is a merit in courtiers; and all courtiers believe that to blessedness after death pertains – permission-to-sit!)

Nor even that a Spirit called Holy, led your forefathers into promised lands, which I do not praise: for where the worst of all trees grew – the cross, in that land there is nothing to praise!

– And verily, wherever this "Holy Spirit" led its knights, always in such campaigns did – goats and geese, and wry-heads and guy-heads run foremost!

O my brothers, not backward shall your nobility gaze, but outward! Exiles shall you be from all fatherlands and forefather-lands!

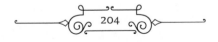

Your children's land shall you love: let this love be your new nobility, the undiscovered in the remotest seas! For it do I bid your sails search and search!

To your children shall you make amends for being the children of your fathers: all the past shall you thus redeem! This new table do I place over you!'

13

'"Why should one live? All is vain! To live – that is to thresh straw; to live – that is to burn oneself and yet not get warm."

Such ancient babbling still passes for 'wisdom'; because it is old, however, and smells mustily, therefore is it the more honoured. Even mould ennobles.

Children might thus speak: they shun the fire because it has burnt them! There is much childishness in the old books of wisdom.

And he who ever 'threshes straw,' why should he be allowed to rail at threshing! Such a fool one would have to muzzle!

Such persons sit down to the table and bring nothing with them, not even good hunger: and then do they rail: 'All is vain!'

But to eat and drink well, my brothers, is verily no vain art! Break up, break up for me the law-tablets of the never-joyous ones!'

14

'"To the clean are all things clean" – thus say the people. I, however, say to you: To the swine all things become swinish!

Therefore preach the visionaries and bowed-heads (whose hearts are also bowed down): "The world itself is a filthy monster."

For these are all unclean spirits; especially those, however, who have no peace or rest, unless they see the world from the backside – the afterworldly!

To those do I say it to the face, although it sound unpleasantly:

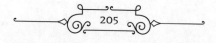

the world resembles man, in that it has a backside, so much is true!

There is in the world much filth: so much is true! But the world itself is not therefore a filthy monster!

There is wisdom in the fact that much in the world smells badly: loathing itself creates wings, and fountain-divining powers!

In the best there is still something to loathe; and the best is still something that must be overcome!

O my brothers, there is much wisdom in the fact that much filth is in the world!'

15

'Such sayings did I hear pious afterworldly speak to their consciences, and verily without wickedness or guile, although there is nothing more guileful in the world, or more wicked.

"Let the world be as it is! Raise not a finger against it!"

"Let whoever will choke and stab and skin and scrape the people: raise not a finger against it! Thereby will they learn to renounce the world."

"And your own reason – this shall you yourself stifle and choke; for it is a reason of this world, thereby will you learn yourself to renounce the world."—

—Shatter, shatter, O my brothers, those old law-tablets of the pious! Tatter the maxims of the world-maligners!'

16

'"He who learns much unlearns all violent cravings" – that do people now whisper to one another in all the dark lanes.

"Wisdom wearies, nothing is worth while; you shall not crave!" – this new table found I hanging even in the public markets.

Break up for me, O my brothers, break up also that new table!

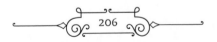

The weary-o'-the-world put it up, and the preachers of death and the jailer: for lo, it is also a sermon for slavery:

Because they learned badly and not the best, and everything too early and everything too fast; because they ate badly: from thence has resulted their ruined stomach; –

—For a ruined stomach, is their spirit: it persuades to death! For verily, my brothers, the spirit is a stomach!

Life is a well of delight, but to him in whom the ruined stomach speaks, the father of affliction, all fountains are poisoned.

To discern: that is delight to the lion-willed! But he who has become weary, is himself merely "willed"; with him play all the waves.

And such is always the nature of weak men: they lose themselves on their way. And at last asks their weariness: "Why did we ever go on the way? All is indifferent!"

To them sounds it pleasant to have preached in their ears: "Nothing is worth while! You shall not will!" That, however, is a sermon for slavery.

O my brothers, a fresh blustering wind comes Zarathustra to all way-weary ones; many noses will he yet make sneeze!

Even through walls blows my free breath, and into prisons and imprisoned spirits!

Willing emancipates: for willing is creating: so do I teach. And only for creating shall you learn!

And also the learning shall you learn only from me, the learning well! He who has ears let him hear!'

17

There stands the boat – there goes it over, perhaps into vast nothing-ness – but who wills to enter into this "Perhaps"?

None of you want to enter into the death-boat! How should you then be world-weary ones!

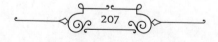

World-weary ones! And have not even withdrawn from the earth! Eager did I ever find you for the earth, amorous still of your own earth-weariness!

Not in vain does your lip hang down: a small worldly wish still sits on it! And in your eye – floats there not a little cloud of unforgotten earthly bliss?

There are on the earth many good inventions, some useful, some pleasant: for their sake is the earth to be loved.

And many such good inventions are there, that they are like woman's breasts: useful at the same time, and pleasant.

You world-weary ones, however! You earth-idlers! You, shall one beat with stripes! With stripes shall one again make you sprightly limbs.

For if you be not invalids, or decrepit creatures, of whom the earth is weary, then are you sly sloths, or dainty, sneaking pleasure-cats. And if you will not again run gaily, then shall you – pass away!

To the incurable shall one not seek to be a physician: thus teaches Zarathustra: so shall you pass away!

But more courage is needed to make an end than to make a new verse: that do all physicians and poets know well.'

18

'O my brothers, there are law-tablets which weariness framed, and law-tablets which slothfulness framed, corrupt slothfulness: although they speak similarly, they want to be heard differently.

See this languishing one! Only a span-breadth is he from his goal; but from weariness has he lain down obstinately in the dust, this brave one!

From weariness yawns he at the path, at the earth, at the goal, and at himself: not a step further will he go, this brave one!

Now glows the sun upon him, and the dogs lick at his sweat: but he lies there in his obstinacy and preferrs to languish:

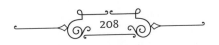

—A span-breadth from his goal, to languish! You will have to drag him into his heaven by the hair of his head – this hero!

Better still that you let him lie where he has lain down, that sleep may come to him, the comforter, with cooling patter-rain.

Let him lie, until of his own accord he awakens, until of his own accord he repudiates all weariness, and what weariness has taught through him!

Only, my brothers, see that you scare the dogs away from him, the idle skulkers, and all the swarming vermin:

—All the swarming vermin of the "cultured," that – feast on the sweat of every hero!'

19.

'I form circles around me and sacred boundaries; ever fewer ascend with me ever higher mountains: I build a mountain-range out of ever holier mountains.

But wherever you would ascend with me, O my brothers, take care lest a parasite ascend with you!

A parasite: that is a reptile, a creeping, cringing reptile, that tries to fatten on your infirm and sore places.

And this is its art: it divines where ascending souls are weary, in your trouble and dejection, in your sensitive modesty, does it build its loathsome nest.

Where the strong are weak, where the noble are all-too-gentle – there builds it its loathsome nest; the parasite lives where the great have small sore-places.

What is the highest of all species of being, and what is the lowest? The parasite is the lowest species; yet he who is of the highest species feeds most parasites.

For the soul which has the longest ladder, and can go deepest down: how could there fail to be most parasites upon it?

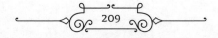

—The most comprehensive soul, which can run and stray and rove furthest in itself; the most necessary soul, which out of joy flings itself into chance:

—The soul in Being, which plunges into Becoming; the possessing soul, which seeks to attain desire and longing:

—The soul fleeing from itself, which overtakes itself in the widest circuit; the wisest soul, to which folly speaks most sweetly:

—The soul most self – loving, in which all things have their current and counter – current, their ebb and their flow: oh, how could the loftiest soul fail to have the worst parasites?'

20

'O my brothers, am I then cruel? But I say: What falls, that shall one also push!

Everything of today – it falls, it decays; who would preserve it! But I – I wish also to push it!

Know you the delight which rolls stones into precipitous depths? – Those men of today, see just how they roll into my depths!

A prelude am I to better players, O my brothers! An example! Do according to my example!

And him whom you do not teach to fly, teach I pray you – to fall faster!'

21

'I love the brave: but it is not enough to be a swordsman, one must also know whereon to use swordsmanship!

And often is it greater bravery to keep quiet and pass by, that thereby one may reserve oneself for a worthier foe!

You shall only have foes to be hated; but not foes to be despised: you must be proud of your foes. Thus have I already taught.

For the worthier foe, O my brothers, shall you reserve yourselves: therefore must you pass by many a one,

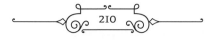

—Especially many of the rabble, who din your ears with noise about people and peoples.

Keep your eye clear of their For and Against! There is there much right, much wrong: he who looks on becomes wroth.

Therein viewing, therein hewing – they are the same thing: therefore depart into the forests and lay your sword to sleep!

Go your ways! and let the people and peoples go theirs! Gloomy ways, verily, on which not a single hope glints any more!

Let there the trader rule, where all that still glitters is – traders' gold. It is the time of kings no longer: that which now calls itself the people is unworthy of kings.

See how these peoples themselves now do just like the traders: they pick up the small advantage out of all kinds of rubbish!

They lay lures for one another, they lure things out of one another, that they call "good neighbourliness." O blessed remote period when a people said to itself: "I will be – master over peoples!"

For, my brothers, the best shall rule, the best also wills to rule! And where the teaching is different, there – the best is lacking.'

22

'If they had – bread for nothing, alas! For what would they cry! Their maintainment – that is their true entertainment; and they shall have it hard!

Beasts of prey, are they: in their "working" – there is even plundering, in their "earning" – there is even over-reaching! Therefore shall they have it hard!

Better beasts of prey shall they thus become, subtler, cleverer, more man-like: for man is the best beast of prey.

All the animals has man already robbed of their virtues: that is why of all animals it has been hardest for man.

Only the birds are still beyond him. And if man should yet learn to fly, alas! To what height – would his rapacity fly!'

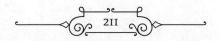

23

'Thus would I have man and woman: fit for war, the one; fit for maternity, the other; both, however, fit for dancing with head and legs.

And lost be the day to us in which a measure has not been danced. And false be every truth which has not had laughter along with it!'

24

'Your marriage-arranging: see that it be not a bad arranging! You have arranged too hastily: so there follows therefrom – marriage-breaking!

And better marriage-breaking than marriage-bending, marriage-lying! Thus spoke a woman to me: "Indeed, I broke the marriage, but first did the marriage break – me!"

The badly paired found I ever the most revengeful: they make every one suffer for it that they no longer run singly.

On that account want I the honest ones to say to one another: "We love each other: let us see to it that we maintain our love! Or shall our pledging be blundering?"

—"Give us a set term and a small marriage, that we may see if we are fit for the great marriage! It is a great matter always to be twain."

Thus do I counsel all honest ones; and what would be my love to the Superman, and to all that is to come, if I should counsel and speak otherwise!

Not only to propagate yourselves onwards but upwards – thereto, O my brothers, may the garden of marriage help you!'

25

'He who has grown wise concerning old origins, lo, he will at last seek after the fountains of the future and new origins.

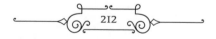

O my brothers, not long will it be until new peoples shall arise and new fountains shall rush down into new depths.

For the earthquake – it chokes up many wells, it causes much languishing: but it brings also to light inner powers and secrets.

The earthquake discloses new fountains. In the earthquake of old peoples new fountains burst forth.

And whoever calls out: "Lo, here is a well for many thirsty ones, one heart for many longing ones, one will for many instruments": around him collects a people, that is to say, many attempting ones.

Who can command, who must obey – that is there attempted! Ah, with what long seeking and solving and failing and learning and re-attempting!

Human society: it is an attempt – so I teach – a long seeking: it seeks however the ruler!

—An attempt, my brothers! And no "contract"! Destroy, I pray you, destroy that word of the soft-hearted and half-and-half!'

26

'O my brothers! With whom lies the greatest danger to the whole human future? Is it not with the good and just?

—As those who say and feel in their hearts: "We already know what is good and just, we possess it also; woe to those who still seek thereafter!"

And whatever harm the wicked may do, the harm of the good is the harmfulest harm!

And whatever harm the world-maligners may do, the harm of the good is the harmfulest harm!

O my brothers, into the hearts of the good and just looked some one once on a time, who said: "They are the Pharisees." But people did not understand him.

The good and just themselves were not free to understand him;

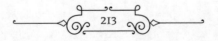

their spirit was imprisoned in their good conscience. The stupidity of the good is unfathomably wise.

It is the truth, however, that the good must be Pharisees – they have no choice!

The good must crucify him who creates his own virtue! That is the truth!

The second one, however, who discovered their country – the country, heart and soil of the good and just, it was he who asked: "Whom do they hate most?"

The creator, hate they most, him who breaks the law-tablets and old values, the breaker, him they call the law-breaker.

For the good – they cannot create; they are always the beginning of the end:

—They crucify him who writes new values on new law-tablets, they sacrifice to themselves the future – they crucify the whole human future!

The good – they have always been the beginning of the end.'

27

'O my brothers, have you also understood this word? And what I once said of the "last man"?—

With whom lies the greatest danger to the whole human future? Is it not with the good and just?

Break up, break up, I pray you, the good and just! O my brothers, have you understood also this word?'

28

'You flee from me? You are frightened? You tremble at this word?

O my brothers, when I enjoined you to break up the good, and the law-tablets of the good, then only did I embark man on his high seas.

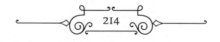

And now only comes to him the great terror, the great outlook, the great sickness, the great nausea, the great seasickness.

False shores and false securities did the good teach you; in the lies of the good were you born and bred. Everything has been radically contorted and distorted by the good.

But he who discovered the country of "man," discovered also the country of "man's future." Now shall you be sailors for me, brave, patient!

Keep yourselves up betimes, my brothers, learn to keep yourselves up! The sea storms: many seek to raise themselves again by you.

The sea storms: all is in the sea. Well! Cheer up! You old seaman-hearts!

What of fatherland! There strives our helm where our children's land is! Therewards, stormier than the sea, storms our great longing!'

29

'"Why so hard!" – said to the diamond one day the charcoal; "are we then not near relatives?"—

Why so soft? O my brothers; thus do I ask you: are you then not – my brothers?

Why so soft, so submissive and yielding? Why is there so much negation and abnegation in your hearts? Why is there so little fate in your looks?

And if you will not be fates and inexorable ones, how can you one day – conquer with me?

And if your hardness will not glance and cut and chip to pieces, how can you one day – create with me?

For the creators are hard. And blessed must it seem to you to press your hand upon millenniums as upon wax,

—Blessed to write upon the will of millenniums as upon brass, harder than brass, nobler than brass. Entirely hard is only the noblest.

This new table, O my brothers, put I up over you: Become hard!'

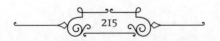

30

'O you, my Will! You change of every need, my needfulness! Preserve me from all small victories!

You fatedness of my soul, which I call fate! you In-me! Over-me! Preserve and spare me for one great fate!

And your last greatness, my Will, spare it for your last – that you may be inexorable in your victory! Ah, who has not perished to his victory!

Ah, whose eye has not bedimmed in this intoxicated twilight! Ah, whose foot has not faltered and forgotten in victory – how to stand!

—That I may one day be ready and ripe in the great noon-tide: ready and ripe like the glowing ore, the lightning-bearing cloud, and the swelling milk-udder:

—Ready for myself and for my most hidden Will: a bow eager for its arrow, an arrow eager for its star:

—A star, ready and ripe in its noontide, glowing, pierced, blessed, by annihilating sun-arrows:

—A sun itself, and an inexorable sun-will, ready for annihilation in victory!

O Will, you change of every need, my needfulness! Spare me for one great victory!'

Thus spoke Zarathustra.

57. The Convalescent

1

ONE morning, not long after his return to his cave, Zarathustra sprang up from his couch like a madman, crying with a frightful voice, and acting as if someone still lay on the couch who did not wish to rise. Zarathustra's voice also resounded in such a manner that his animals

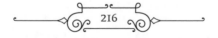

came to him frightened, and out of all the neighbouring caves and lurking-places all the creatures slipped away – flying, fluttering, creeping or leaping, according to their variety of foot or wing. Zarathustra, however, spoke these words:

'Up, abysmal thought out of my depth! I am your cock and morning dawn, you overslept reptile: Up! Up! My voice shall soon crow you awake!

Unbind the fetters of your ears: listen! For I wish to hear you! Up! Up! There is thunder enough to make the very graves listen!

And rub the sleep and all the dimness and blindness out of your eyes! Hear me also with your eyes: my voice is a medicine even for those born blind.

And once you are awake, then shall you ever remain awake. It is not my custom to awake great-grandmothers out of their sleep that I may bid them – sleep on!

You stir, stretch yourself, wheeze? Up! Up! Not wheeze, shall you, but speak to me! Zarathustra calls you, Zarathustra the godless!

I, Zarathustra, the advocate of living, the advocate of suffering, the advocate of the circuit – you do I call, my most abysmal thought!

Joy to me! you come, I hear you! My abyss speaks, my lowest depth have I turned over into the light!

Joy to me! Come here! Give me your hand – ha! let be! aha! – Disgust, disgust, disgust – alas to me!'

2

Hardly, however, had Zarathustra spoken these words, when he fell down as one dead, and remained long as one dead. When however he again came to himself, then was he pale and trembling, and remained lying; and for long he would neither eat nor drink. This condition continued for seven days; his animals, however, did not leave him day

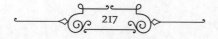

nor night, except that the eagle flew forth to fetch food. And what it fetched and foraged, it laid on Zarathustra's couch: so that Zarathustra at last lay among yellow and red berries, grapes, rosy apples, sweet-smelling herbage, and pine-cones. At his feet, however, two lambs were stretched, which the eagle had with difficulty carried off from their shepherds.

At last, after seven days, Zarathustra raised himself upon his couch, took a rosy apple in his hand, smelt it and found its smell pleasant. Then did his animals think the time had come to speak to him.

'O Zarathustra,' said they, 'now have you lain thus for seven days with heavy eyes: will you not set yourself again upon your feet?

Step out of your cave: the world waits for you as a garden. The wind plays with heavy fragrance which seeks for you; and all brooks would like to run after you.

All things long for you, since you have remained alone for seven days – step forth out of your cave! All things want to be your physicians!

Did perhaps a new knowledge come to you, a bitter, grievous knowledge? Like leavened dough lay you, your soul arose and swelled beyond all its bounds.'

—O my animals, answered Zarathustra, talk on thus and let me listen! It refreshes me so to hear your talk: where there is talk, there is the world as a garden to me.

How charming it is that there are words and tones; are not words and tones rainbows and seeming bridges 'twixt the eternally separated?

To each soul belongs another world; to each soul is every other soul a back-world.

Among the most alike does semblance deceive most delightfully: for the small gap is most difficult to bridge over.

For me – how could there be an outside-of-me? There is no

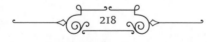

outside! But this we forget on hearing tones; how delightful it is that we forget!

Have not names and tones been given to things that man may refresh himself with them? It is a beautiful folly, speaking; therewith dances man over everything.

How lovely is all speech and all falsehoods of tones! With tones dances our love on variegated rainbows.'

'O Zarathustra,' said then his animals, 'to those who think like us, things all dance themselves: they come and hold out the hand and laugh and flee – and return.

Everything goes, everything returns; eternally rolls the wheel of existence. Everything dies, everything blossoms forth again; eternally runs on the year of existence.

Everything breaks, everything is integrated anew; eternally builds itself the same house of existence. All things separate, all things again greet one another; eternally true to itself remains the ring of existence.

Every moment begins existence, around every "Here" rolls the ball "There." The middle is everywhere. Crooked is the path of eternity.'—

—'O you wags and barrel-organs!' answered Zarathustra, and smiled once more, how well do you know what had to be fulfilled in seven days:

—And how that monster crept into my throat and choked me! But I bit off its head and spat it away from me.

And you – you have made a lyre-lay out of it? Now, however, do I lie here, still exhausted with that biting and spitting-away, still sick with my own salvation.

And you looked on at it all? O my animals, are you also cruel? Did you like to look at my great pain as men do? For man is the cruel animal.

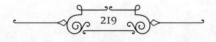

At tragedies, bull-fights, and crucifixions has he hitherto been happiest on earth; and when he invented his hell, behold, that was his heaven on earth.

When the great man cries: immediately runs the little man there, and his tongue hangs out of his mouth for very lusting. Yet he calls it his "pity."

The little man, especially the poet – how passionately does he accuse life in words! Hearken to him, but do not fail to hear the delight which is in all accusation!

Such accusers of life – them life overcomes with a glance of the eye. "You love me?" says the insolent one; "wait a little, as yet have I no time for you."

Towards himself man is the cruel animal; and in all who call themselves "sinners" and "bearers of the cross" and "penitents," do not overlook the voluptuousness in their plaints and accusations!

And I myself – do, I thereby want to be man's accuser? Ah, my animals, this only have I learned hitherto, that for man his evil is necessary for his best,

—That all that is evil is the best power, and the hardest stone for the highest creator; and that man must become better and more evil:

Not to this torture-stake was I tied, that I know man is bad, but I cried, as no one has yet cried:

"Ah, that his evil is so very small! Ah, that his best is so very small!"

The great disgust at man – it strangled me and had crept into my throat: and what the soothsayer had presaged: "All is alike, nothing is worth while, knowledge strangles."

A long twilight limped on before me, a fatally weary, fatally intoxicated sadness, which spoke with yawning mouth.

"Eternally he returns, the man of whom you are weary, the small man" – so yawned my sadness, and dragged its foot and could not go to sleep.

A cavern, became the human earth to me; its breast caved in;

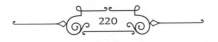

everything living became to me human dust and bones and mouldering past.

My sighing sat on all human graves, and could no longer arise: my sighing and questioning croaked and choked, and gnawed and nagged day and night:

—"Ah, man returns eternally! The small man returns eternally!"

Naked had I once seen both of them, the greatest man and the small man: all too like one another – all too human, even the greatest man!

All too small, even the greatest man! That was my disgust at man! And the eternal return also of the small man! That was my disgust at all existence!

Ah, Disgust! Disgust! Disgust!' – Thus spoke Zarathustra, and sighed and shuddered; for he remembered his sickness. Then did his animals prevent him from speaking further.

'Do not speak further, you convalescent!' – so answered his animals, 'but go out where the world waits for you like a garden.

Go out to the roses, the bees, and the flocks of doves! Especially, however, to the singing-birds, to learn singing from them!

For singing is for the convalescent; the sound ones may talk. And when the sound also want songs, then want they other songs than the convalescent.'

—'O you wags and barrel – organs, do be silent!' answered Zarathustra, and smiled at his animals. 'How well you know what consolation I created for myself in seven days!

That I have to sing once more – that consolation did I create for myself, and this convalescence: would you also make another lyre-lay thereof?'

—'Do not talk further,' answered his animals once more; 'rather, you convalescent, prepare for yourself first a lyre, a new lyre! For behold, O Zarathustra! For your new lays there are needed new lyres.

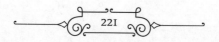

Sing and bubble over, O Zarathustra, heal your soul with new lays: that you may bear your great fate, which has not yet been any one's fate!

For your animals know it well, O Zarathustra, who you are and must become: behold, you are the teacher of the eternal return, that is now your fate!

That you must be the first to teach this teaching – how could this great fate not be your greatest danger and infirmity!

Behold, we know what you teach: that all things eternally return, and ourselves with them, and that we have already existed times without number, and all things with us.

You teach that there is a great year of Becoming, a prodigy of a great year; it must, like a sand-glass, ever turn up anew, that it may anew run down and run out:

—So that all those years are like one another in the greatest and also in the small, so that we ourselves, in every great year, are like ourselves in the greatest and also in the small.

And if you would now die, O Zarathustra, behold, we know also how you would then speak to yourself: but your animals beseech you not to die yet!

You would speak, and without trembling, buoyant rather with bliss, for a great weight and worry would be taken from you, you patientest one!

"Now do I die and disappear," would you say, "and in a moment I am nothing. Souls are as mortal as bodies.

But the plexus of causes returns in which I am intertwined, it will again create me! I myself pertain to the causes of the eternal return.

I come again with this sun, with this earth, with this eagle, with this serpent – not to a new life, or a better life, or a similar life:

—I come again eternally to this identical and selfsame life, in

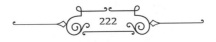

its greatest and its small, to teach again the eternal return of all things,

—To speak again the word of the great noontide of earth and man, to announce again to man the Superman.

I have spoken my word. I break down by my word: so wills my eternal fate – as announcer do I perish!

The hour has now come for the down-goer to bless himself. Thus – ends Zarathustra's down-going".'—

When the animals had spoken these words they were silent and waited, so that Zarathustra might say something to them; but Zarathustra did not hear that they were silent. On the contrary, he lay quietly with closed eyes like a person sleeping, although he did not sleep; for he communed just then with his soul. The serpent, however, and the eagle, when they found him silent in such wise, respected the great stillness around him, and prudently retired.

58. The Great Longing

'O MY soul, I have taught you to say "today" as "once on a time" and "formerly," and to dance your measure over every Here and There and Yonder.

O my soul, I delivered you from all by-places, I brushed down from you dust and spiders and twilight.

O my soul, I washed the petty shame and the by-place virtue from you, and persuaded you to stand naked before the eyes of the sun.

With the storm that is called "spirit" did I blow over your surging sea; all clouds did I blow away from it; I strangled even the strangler called "sin."

O my soul, I gave you the right to say No like the storm, and

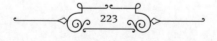

to say Yes as the open heaven says Yes: calm as the light remain you, and now walk through denying storms.

O my soul, I restored to you liberty over the created and the uncreated; and who knows, as you know, the voluptuousness of the future?

O my soul, I taught you the contempt which does not come like worm-eating, the great, the loving contempt, which loves most where it contemns most.

O my soul, I taught you so to persuade that you persuade even the grounds themselves to you: like the sun, which persuades even the sea to its height.

O my soul, I have taken from you all obeying and knee-bending and homage-paying; I have myself given you the names, "Change of need" and "Fate."

O my soul, I have given you new names and gay-coloured play-things, I have called you "Fate" and "the Circuit of circuits" and "the Navel-string of time" and "the Azure bell."

O my soul, to your domain gave I all wisdom to drink all new wines, and also all immemorially old strong wines of wisdom.

O my soul, every sun shed I upon you, and every night and every silence and every longing: then grew you up for me as a vine.

O my soul, exuberant and heavy do you now stand forth, a vine with swelling udders and full clusters of brown golden grapes:

—Filled and weighted by your happiness, waiting from super-abundance, and yet ashamed of your waiting.

O my soul, there is nowhere a soul which could be more loving and more comprehensive and more extensive! Where could future and past be closer together than with you?

O my soul, I have given you everything, and all my hands have become empty by you: and now! Now say you to me, smiling and full of melancholy: "Which of us owes thanks?

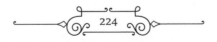

—Does the giver not owe thanks because the receiver received? Is giving not a necessity? Is receiving not – pitying?"

O my soul, I understand the smiling of your melancholy: your over-abundance itself now stretches out longing hands!

Your fullness looks forth over raging seas, and seeks and waits: the longing of over-fullness looks forth from the smiling heaven of your eyes!

And verily, O my soul! Who could see your smiling and not melt into tears? The angels themselves melt into tears through the over-graciousness of your smiling.

Your graciousness and over-graciousness, is it which will not complain and weep: and yet, O my soul, longs your smiling for tears, and your trembling mouth for sobs.

"Is not all weeping complaining? And all complaining, accusing?" Thus speak you to yourself; and therefore, O my soul, will you rather smile than pour forth your grief –

—Than in gushing tears pour forth all your grief concerning your fulness, and concerning the craving of the vine for the vintager and vintage-knife!

But will you not weep, will you not weep forth your purple melancholy, then will you have to sing, O my soul! Behold, I smile myself, who foretell you this:

—You will have to sing with passionate song, until all seas turn calm to hearken to your longing,

—Until over calm longing seas the bark glides, the golden marvel, around the gold of which all good, bad, and marvellous things frisk:

—Also many large and small animals, and everything that has light marvellous feet, so that it can run on violet-blue paths,

—Towards the golden marvel, the spontaneous bark, and its master: he, however, is the vintager who waits with the diamond vintage-knife,

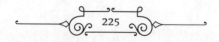

—Your great deliverer, O my soul, the nameless one – for whom future songs only will find names! And verily, already has your breath the fragrance of future songs,

—Already glow you and dream, already drink you thirstily at all deep echoing wells of consolation, already reposes your melancholy in the bliss of future songs!—

O my soul, now have I given you all, and even my last possession, and all my hands have become empty by you: that I bade you sing, behold, that was my last thing to give!

That I bade you sing, say now, say: which of us now – owes thanks? – Better still, however: sing to me, sing, O my soul! And let me thank you!'

Thus spoke Zarathustra.

59. *The Second Dance Song*

1

'INTO thy eyes gazed I lately, O Life: gold saw I gleam in your night-eyes, my heart stood still with delight:

—A golden bark saw I gleam on darkened waters, a sinking, drinking, reblinking, golden swing-bark!

At my dance-frantic foot, do you cast a glance, a laughing, questioning, melting, thrown glance:

Twice only moved you your rattle with your little hands – then did my feet swing with dance-fury.

My heels reared aloft, my toes they hearkened, you they would know: has not the dancer his ear – in his toe!

To you did I spring: then fled you back from my bound; and towards me waved your fleeing, flying tresses round!

Away from you did I spring, and from your snaky tresses: then stood you there half-turned, and in your eye caresses.

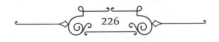

With crooked glances – do you teach me crooked courses; on crooked courses learn my feet – crafty fancies!

I fear you near, I love you far; your flight allures me, your seeking secures me: I suffer, but for you, what would I not gladly bear!

For you, whose coldness inflames, whose hatred misleads, whose flight enchains, whose mockery – pleads:

—Who would not hate you, you great bindress, inwindress, temptress, seekress, findress! Who would not love you, you innocent, impatient, wind-swift, child-eyed sinner!

Where pull you me now, you paragon and tomboy? And now fool you me fleeing; you sweet romp does annoy!

I dance after you, I follow even faint traces lonely. Where are you? Give me your hand! Or your finger only!

Here are caves and thickets: we shall go astray! Halt! Stand still! See you not owls and bats in fluttering fray?

You bat! You owl! You would play me foul? Where are we? From the dogs have you learned thus to bark and howl.

You gnash on me sweetly with little white teeth; your evil eyes shoot out upon me, your curly little mane from underneath!

This is a dance over stock and stone: I am the hunter, will you be my hound, or my chamois anon?

Now beside me! And quickly, wickedly springing! Now up! And over! Alas! I have fallen myself overswinging!

Oh, see me lying, you arrogant one, and imploring grace! Gladly would I walk with you – in some lovelier place!

—In the paths of love, through bushes variegated, quiet, trim! Or there along the lake, where gold-fishes dance and swim!

You are now a-weary? There above are sheep and sun-set stripes: is it not sweet to sleep – the shepherd pipes?

You are so very weary? I carry you there; let just your arm sink!

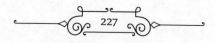

And are you thirsty – I should have something; but your mouth would not like it to drink!

—Oh, that cursed, nimble, supple serpent and lurking-witch! Where are you gone? But in my face do I feel through your hand, two spots and red blotches itch!

I am verily weary of it, ever your sheepish shepherd to be. You witch, if I have hitherto sung to you, now shall you – cry to me!

To the rhythm of my whip shall you dance and cry! I forget not my whip? – Not I!'—

2

'Then did Life answer me thus, and kept thereby her fine ears closed:

"O Zarathustra! Crack not so terribly with your whip! You know surely that noise kills thought, and just now there came to me such delicate thoughts.

We are both of us genuine ne'er-do-wells and ne'er-do-ills. Beyond good and evil found we our island and our green meadow – we two alone! Therefore must we be friendly to each other!

And even should we not love each other from the bottom of our hearts, must we then have a grudge against each other if we do not love each other perfectly?

And that I am friendly to you, and often too friendly, that know you: and the reason is that I am envious of your Wisdom. Ah, this mad old fool, Wisdom!

If your Wisdom should one day run away from you, ah! Then would also my love run away from you quickly."—

Then did Life look thoughtfully behind and around, and said softly: "O Zarathustra, you are not faithful enough to me!

You love me not nearly so much as you say; I know you think of soon leaving me.

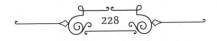

There is an old heavy, heavy, booming-clock: it booms by night up to your cave:

—When you hear this clock strike the hours at midnight, then think you between one and twelve thereon—

—You think thereon, O Zarathustra, I know it – of soon leaving me!"—

"Yes," answered I, hesitatingly, "but you know it also" – And I said something into her ear, in amongst her confused, yellow, foolish tresses.

"You know that, O Zarathustra? That knows no one—"

And we gazed at each other, and looked at the green meadow o'er which the cool evening was just passing, and we wept together. – Then, however, was Life dearer to me than all my Wisdom had ever been.'

Thus spoke Zarathustra.

3

One!

'O man! Take heed!'

Two!

'What says deep midnight's voice indeed?'

Three!

'I slept my sleep—

Four!

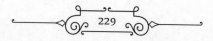

'From deepest dream I've woke and plead:'

Five!

'The world is deep,'

Six!

'And deeper than the day could read.'

Seven!

'Deep is its woe—'

Eight!

'Joy – deeper still than grief can be:'

Nine!

'Woe says: Hence! Go!'

Ten!

'But joys all want eternity—'

Eleven!

'Want deep profound eternity!'

Twelve!

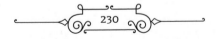

60. The Seven Seals
(or, The Yes and Amen Song)

1

'IF I be a diviner and full of the divining spirit which wanders on high mountain-ridges, 'twixt two seas,

Wanders 'twixt the past and the future as a heavy cloud – hostile to sultry plains, and to all that is weary and can neither die nor live:

Ready for lightning in its dark bosom, and for the redeeming flash of light, charged with lightnings which say Yes! which laugh Yes! ready for divining flashes of lightning:

—Blessed, however, is he who is thus charged! And verily, long must he hang like a heavy tempest on the mountain, who shall one day kindle the light of the future!

Oh, how could I not be ardent for Eternity and for the marriage-ring of rings – the ring of the return?

Never yet have I found the woman by whom I should like to have children, unless it be this woman whom I love: for I love you, O Eternity!

For I love you, O Eternity!'

2

'If ever my wrath has burst graves, shifted landmarks, or rolled old shattered law-tablets into precipitous depths:

If ever my scorn has scattered mouldered words to the winds, and if I have come like a besom to cross-spiders, and as a cleansing wind to old charnel-houses:

If ever I have sat rejoicing where old gods lie buried, world-blessing, world-loving, beside the monuments of old world-maligners:

—For even churches and gods' – graves do I love, if only heaven

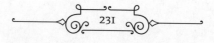

looks through their ruined roofs with pure eyes; gladly do I sit like grass and red poppies on ruined churches –

Oh, how could I not be ardent for Eternity, and for the marriage – ring of rings – the ring of the return?

Never yet have I found the woman by whom I should like to have children, unless it be this woman whom I love: for I love you, O Eternity!

For I love you, O Eternity!'

3

'If ever a breath has come to me of the creative breath, and of the heavenly necessity which compels even chances to dance star-dances:

If ever I have laughed with the laughter of the creative lightning, to which the long thunder of the deed follows, grumbling, but obedient:

If ever I have played dice with the gods at the divine table of the earth, so that the earth quaked and ruptured, and snorted forth fire-streams:

—For a divine table is the earth, and trembling with new active dictums and dice-casts of the gods:

Oh, how could I not be ardent for Eternity, and for the marriage-ring of rings – the ring of the return?

Never yet have I found the woman by whom I should like to have children, unless it be this woman whom I love: for I love you, O Eternity!

For I love you, O Eternity!'

4

'If ever I have drunk a full draught of the foaming spice – and confection-bowl in which all things are well mixed:

If ever my hand has mingled the furthest with the nearest, fire with spirit, joy with sorrow, and the harshest with the kindest:

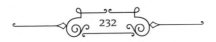

If I myself am a grain of the saving salt which makes everything in the confection-bowl mix well:

—For there is a salt which unites good with evil; and even the evilest is worthy, as spicing and as final over-foaming:

Oh, how could I not be ardent for Eternity, and for the marriage-ring of rings – the ring of the return?

Never yet have I found the woman by whom I should like to have children, unless it be this woman whom I love: for I love you, O Eternity!

For I love you, O Eternity!'

5

'If I be fond of the sea, and all that is of the sea, and fondest of it when it angrily contradicts me:

If the exploring delight be in me, which impels sails to the undiscovered, if the seafarer's delight be in my delight:

If ever my rejoicing has called out: "The shore has vanished, now has fallen from me the last chain—

The boundless roars around me, far away sparkle for me space and time, well! Cheer up! Old heart!"—

Oh, how could I not be ardent for Eternity, and for the marriage-ring of rings – the ring of the return?

Never yet have I found the woman by whom I should like to have children, unless it be this woman whom I love: for I love you, O Eternity!

For I love you, O Eternity!'

6

'If my virtue be a dancer's virtue, and if I have often sprung with both feet into golden-emerald rapture:

If my wickedness be a laughing wickedness, at home among rose-banks and hedges of lilies:

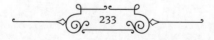

—or in laughter is all evil present, but it is sanctified and absolved by its own bliss:

And if it be my Alpha and Omega that everything heavy shall become light, everybody a dancer, and every spirit a bird: and verily, that is my Alpha and Omega!

Oh, how could I not be ardent for Eternity, and for the marriage-ring of rings – the ring of the return?

Never yet have I found the woman by whom I should like to have children, unless it be this woman whom I love: for I love you, O Eternity!

For I love you, O Eternity!'

7

'If ever I have spread out a tranquil heaven above me, and have flown into my own heaven with my own pinions:

If I have swum playfully in profound luminous distances, and if my freedom's avian wisdom has come to me:

—Thus however speaks avian wisdom: 'Lo, there is no above and no below! Throw yourself about, outward, backward, you light one! Sing! Speak no more!

—Are not all words made for the heavy? Do not all words lie to the light ones? Sing! speak no more!'—

Oh, how could I not be ardent for Eternity, and for the marriage-ring of rings – the ring of the return?

Never yet have I found the woman by whom I should like to have children, unless it be this woman whom I love: for I love you, O Eternity!

For I love you, O Eternity!'

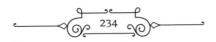

Part Four

61. The Honey Sacrifice

—AND again passed moons and years over Zarathustra's soul, and he heeded it not; his hair, however, became white. One day when he sat on a stone in front of his cave, and gazed calmly into the distance – one there gazes out on the sea, and away beyond sinuous abysses, then went his animals thoughtfully round about him, and at last set themselves in front of him.

'O Zarathustra,' said they, 'gaze you out perhaps for your happiness?' – 'Of what account is my happiness!' answered he, 'I have long ceased to strive any more for happiness, I strive for my work.' – 'O Zarathustra,' said the animals once more, 'that say you as one who has overmuch of good things. Lie you not in a sky-blue lake of happiness?' – 'You wags,' answered Zarathustra, and smiled, 'how well did you choose the simile! But you know also that my happiness is heavy, and not like a fluid wave of water: it presses me and will not leave me, and is like molten pitch.'—

Then went his animals again thoughtfully around him, and placed themselves once more in front of him. 'O Zarathustra,' said they, 'it is consequently *for that reason* that you yourself always becomes yellower and darker, although your hair looks white and flaxen? Lo, you sit in your pitch!' – 'What do you say, my animals?' said Zarathustra, laughing; 'verily I reviled when I spoke of pitch. As it happens with me, so is it with all fruits that turn ripe. It is the *honey* in my veins that makes my blood thicker, and also my soul stiller.' – 'So will it

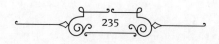

be, O Zarathustra,' answered his animals, and pressed up to him; 'but will you not today ascend a high mountain? The air is pure, and today one sees more of the world than ever.' – 'Yes, my animals,' answered he, 'you counsel admirably and according to my heart: I will today ascend a high mountain! But see that honey is there ready to hand, yellow, white, good, ice-cool, golden-comb-honey. For know that when aloft I will make the honey-sacrifice.'—

When Zarathustra, however, was aloft on the summit, he sent his animals home that had accompanied him, and found that he was now alone: then he laughed from the bottom of his heart, looked around him, and spoke thus:

'That I spoke of sacrifices and honey-sacrifices, it was merely a ruse in talking and verily, a useful folly! Here aloft can I now speak freer than in front of mountain-caves and hermits' domestic animals.

What to sacrifice! I squander what is given me, a squanderer with a thousand hands: how could I call that – sacrificing?

And when I desired honey I only desired bait, and sweet mucus and mucilage, for which even the mouths of growling bears, and strange, sulky, evil birds, water:

—The best bait, as huntsmen and fishermen require it. For if the world be as a gloomy forest of animals, and a pleasure-ground for all wild huntsmen, it seems to me rather – and preferably – a fathomless, rich sea;

—A sea full of many – hued fishes and crabs, for which even the gods might long, and might be tempted to become fishers in it, and casters of nets, so rich is the world in wonderful things, great and small!

Especially the human world, the human sea: towards it do I now throw out my golden angle-rod and say: Open up, you human abyss!

Open up, and throw to me your fish and shining crabs! With my best bait shall I allure to myself today the strangest human fish!

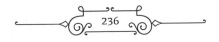

—My happiness itself do I throw out into all places far and wide 'twixt orient, noontide, and occident, to see if many human fish will not learn to hug and tug at my happiness;—

Until, biting at my sharp hidden hooks, they have to come up to my height, the motleyest abyss-groundlings, to the wickedest of all fishers of men.

For this am I from the heart and from the beginning – drawing, here-drawing, upward-drawing, upbringing; a drawer, a trainer, a training-master, who not in vain counselled himself once on a time: "Become what you are!"

Thus may men now come up to me; for as yet do I await the signs that it is time for my down-going; as yet do I not myself go down, as I must do, amongst men.

Therefore do I here wait, crafty and scornful upon high mountains, no impatient one, no patient one; rather one who has even unlearnt patience, because he no longer "suffers."

For my fate gives me time: it has forgotten me perhaps? Or does it sit behind a big stone and catch flies?

And verily, I am well-disposed to my eternal fate, because it does not hound and hurry me, but leaves me time for merriment and mischief; so that I have today ascended this high mountain to catch fish.

Did ever any one catch fish upon high mountains? And though it be a folly what I here seek and do, it is better so than that down below I should become solemn with waiting, and green and yellow—

—A posturing wrath – snorter with waiting, a holy howl – storm from the mountains, an impatient one that shouts down into the valleys: "Hearken, else I will scourge you with the scourge of God!"

Not that I would have a grudge against such wrathful ones on that account: they are well enough for laughter to me! Impatient must they now be, those big alarm-drums, which find a voice now or never!

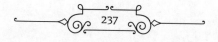

Myself, however, and my fate – we do not talk to the Present, neither do we talk to the Never: for talking we have patience and time and more than time. For one day must it yet come, and may not pass by.

What must one day come and may not pass by? Our great Hazar, that is to say, our great, remote human-kingdom, the Zarathustra-kingdom of a thousand years—

How remote may such "remoteness" be? What does it concern me? But on that account it is none the less sure to me – , with both feet stand I secure on this ground;

—On an eternal ground, on hard primary rock, on this highest, hardest, primary mountain-ridge, to which all winds come, as to the storm-parting, asking Where? and Whence? and Where?

Here laugh, laugh, my hearty, healthy wickedness! From high mountains cast down your glittering scorn-laughter! Allure for me with your glittering the finest human fish!

And whatever belongs to me in all seas, my in-and-for-me in all things – fish that out for me, bring that up to me: for that do I wait, the wickedest of all fish-catchers. Out! out! my fishing-hook! In and down, you bait of my happiness! Drip your sweetest dew, you honey of my heart! Bite, my fishing-hook, into the belly of all black affliction!

Look out, look out, my eye! Oh, how many seas round about me, what dawning human futures! And above me – what rosy red stillness! What unclouded silence!'

62. The Cry of Distress

THE next day sat Zarathustra again on the stone in front of his cave, whilst his animals roved about in the world outside to bring home new food, also new honey: for Zarathustra had spent and wasted the old honey to the very last particle. When he thus sat, however, with a stick in his hand, tracing the shadow of his figure on the earth, and

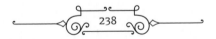

reflecting – verily! Not upon himself and his shadow, all at once he startled and shrank back: for he saw another shadow beside his own. And when he hastily looked around and stood up, behold, there stood the soothsayer beside him, the same whom he had once given to eat and drink at his table, the proclaimer of the great weariness, who taught: 'All is alike, nothing is worth while, the world is without meaning, knowledge strangles.' But his face had changed since then; and when Zarathustra looked into his eyes, his heart was startled once more: so much evil announcement and ashy-grey lightnings passed over that countenance.

The soothsayer, who had perceived what went on in Zarathustra's soul, wiped his face with his hand, as if he would wipe out the impression; the same did also Zarathustra. And when both of them had thus silently composed and strengthened themselves, they gave each other the hand, as a token that they wanted once more to recognize each other.

'Welcome here,' said Zarathustra, 'you soothsayer of the great weariness, not in vain shall you once have been my messmate and guest. Eat and drink also with me today, and forgive it that a cheerful old man sits with you at table!' – 'A cheerful old man?' answered the soothsayer, shaking his head, 'but whoever you are, or would be, O Zarathustra, you have been here aloft the longest time, in a little while your bark shall no longer rest on dry land!' – 'Do I then rest on dry land?' – asked Zarathustra, laughing. – 'The waves around your mountain,' answered the soothsayer, 'rise and rise, the waves of great distress and affliction: they will soon raise your bark also and carry you away.' – Then was Zarathustra silent and wondered. – 'Do you still hear nothing?' continued the soothsayer: 'does it not rush and roar out of the depth?' – Zarathustra was silent once more and listened: then heard he a long, long cry, which the abysses threw to one another and passed on; for none of them wished to retain it: so evil did it sound.

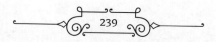

'You ill announcer,' said Zarathustra at last, 'that is a cry of distress, and the cry of a man; it may come perhaps out of a black sea. But what does human distress matter to me! My last sin which has been reserved for me, know you what it is called?'

—'Pity!' answered the soothsayer from an overflowing heart, and raised both his hands aloft – 'O Zarathustra, I have come that I may seduce you to your last sin!'—

And hardly had those words been uttered when there sounded the cry once more, and longer and more alarming than before – also much nearer. 'Hear you? Hear you, O Zarathustra?' called out the soothsayer, 'the cry concerns you, it calls you: Come, come, come; it is time, it is the highest time!'—

Zarathustra was silent then, confused and staggered; at last he asked, like one who hesitates in himself: 'And who is it that there calls me?'

'But you know it, certainly,' answered the soothsayer warmly, 'why do you conceal yourself? It is the higher man that cries for you!'

'The higher man?' cried Zarathustra, horror-stricken: 'What wants he? What wants he? The higher man! What wants he here?' – and his skin covered with perspiration.

The soothsayer, however, did not heed Zarathustra's alarm, but listened and listened in the downward direction. When, however, it had been still there for a long while, he looked behind, and saw Zarathustra standing trembling.

'O Zarathustra,' he began, with sorrowful voice, 'you do not stand there like one whose happiness makes him giddy: you will have to dance lest you tumble down!

But although you should dance before me, and leap all your side-leaps, no one may say to me: "Behold, here dances the last joyous man!"

In vain would any one come to this height who sought him here:

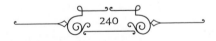

caves would he find, indeed, and back-caves, hiding-places for hidden ones; but not lucky mines, nor treasure-chambers, nor new gold-veins of happiness.

Happiness – how indeed could one find happiness among such buried-alive and solitary ones! Must I yet seek the last happiness on the Blessed isles, and far away among forgotten seas?

But all is alike, nothing is worth while, no seeking is of service, there are no longer any Blessed isles!'—

Thus sighed the soothsayer; with his last sigh, however, Zarathustra again became serene and assured, like one who has come out of a deep chasm into the light. 'No! No! Three times No!' exclaimed he with a strong voice, and stroked his beard – 'that do I know better! There are still Blessed isles! Silence then, you sighing sorrow-sack!

Cease to splash, you rain – cloud of the forenoon! Do I not already stand here wet with your misery, and drenched like a dog?

Now do I shake myself and run away from you, that I may again become dry: thereat may you not wonder! Do I seem to you discourteous? Here however is my court.

But as regards the higher man: well! I shall seek him at once in those forests: from thence came his cry. Perhaps he is there hard beset by an evil beast.

He is in my domain: therein shall he receive no scath! And verily, there are many evil beasts about me.'—

With those words Zarathustra turned around to depart. Then said the soothsayer: 'O Zarathustra, you are a rogue!

I know it well: you would rather be rid of me! Rather would you run into the forest and lay snares for evil beasts!

But what good will it do you? In the evening will you have me again: in your own cave will I sit, patient and heavy like a block – and wait for you!'

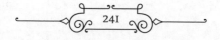

'So be it!' shouted back Zarathustra, as he went away: 'and what is mine in my cave belongs also to you, my guest!

Should you however find honey therein, well! Just lick it up, you growling bear, and sweeten your soul! For in the evening we want both to be in good spirits; – In good spirits and joyful, because this day has come to an end! And you yourself shall dance to my lays, as my dancing-bear.

Thou dost not believe this? Thou shakest thy head? Well! Cheer up, old bear! But I also – am a soothsayer.'

Thus spoke Zarathustra.

63. Talk with the Kings

1

ERE Zarathustra had been an hour on his way in the mountains and forests, he saw all at once a strange procession. Right on the path which he was about to descend came two kings walking, bedecked with crowns and purple girdles, and variegated like flamingoes: they drove before them a laden ass. 'What do these kings want in my domain?' said Zarathustra in astonishment to his heart, and hid himself hastily behind a thicket. When however the kings approached to him, he said half-aloud, like one speaking only to himself: 'Strange! Strange! How does this harmonize? Two kings do I see – and only one ass!'

Then the two kings made a halt; they smiled and looked towards the spot whence the voice proceeded, and afterwards looked into each other's faces. 'Such things do we also think among ourselves,' said the king on the right, 'but we do not utter them.'

The king on the left, however, shrugged his shoulders and answered: 'That may perhaps be a goat-herd. Or an hermit who has lived too long among rocks and trees. For no society at all spoils also good manners.'

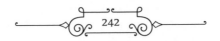

'Good manners?' replied angrily and bitterly the other king: 'what then do we run out of the way of? Is it not "good manners"? Our "good society"?

Better, verily, to live among hermits and goat-herds, than with our gilded, false, over-rouged rabble – though it call itself 'good society.'

—Though it call itself "nobility." But there all is false and foul, above all the blood – thanks to old evil diseases and worse curers.

The best and dearest to me at present is still a sound peasant, coarse, artful, obstinate and enduring: that is at present the noblest type.

The peasant is at present the best; and the peasant type should be master! But it is the kingdom of the rabble – I no longer allow anything to be imposed upon me. The rabble, however – that means, hodgepodge.

Rabble-hodgepodge: therein is everything mixed with everything, saint and swindler, gentleman and Jew, and every beast out of Noah's ark.

Good manners! Everything is false and foul with us. No one knows any longer how to reverence: it is that precisely that we run away from. They are fulsome obtrusive dogs; they gild palm-leaves.

This loathing chokes me, that we kings ourselves have become false, draped and disguised with the old faded pomp of our ancestors, show-pieces for the stupidest, the craftiest, and whosoever at present trafficks for power.

We are not the first men – and have nevertheless to stand for them: of this imposture have we at last become weary and disgusted.

From the rabble have we gone out of the way, from all those bawlers and scribe – blowflies, from the trader-stench, the ambition-fidgeting, the bad breath: fie, to live among the rabble;

—Fie, to stand for the first men among the rabble! Ah, loathing! Loathing! Loathing! What does it now matter about us kings!'—

'Thine old sickness seizes you,' said here the king on the left,

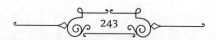

'thy loathing seizes you, my poor brother. You know, however, that some one hears us.'

Immediately then, Zarathustra, who had opened ears and eyes to this talk, rose from his hiding-place, advanced towards the kings, and thus began:

'He who hearkens to you, he who gladly hearkens to you, is called Zarathustra.

I am Zarathustra who once said: "What does it now matter about kings!" Forgive me; I rejoiced when you said to each other: "What does it matter about us kings!"

Here, however, is my domain and jurisdiction: what may you be seeking in my domain? Perhaps, however, you have found on your way what I seek: namely, the higher man.'

When the kings heard this, they beat upon their breasts and said with one voice: 'We are recognized!

With the sword of your utterance severest you the thickest darkness of our hearts. You have discovered our distress; for behold, we are on our way to find the higher man—

—The man that is higher than we, although we are kings. To him do we convey this ass. For the highest man shall also be the highest lord on earth.

There is no sorer misfortune in all human destiny, than when the mighty of the earth are not also the first men. Then everything becomes false and distorted and monstrous.

And when they are even the last men, and more beast than man, then riseth and riseth the populace in honour, and at last says even the populace-virtue: "Lo, I alone am virtue!"—

'What have I just heard?' answered Zarathustra. 'What wisdom in kings! I am enchanted, and verily, I have already promptings to make a rhyme thereon:

—Even if it should happen to be a rhyme not suited for every

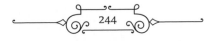

one's ears. I unlearned long ago to have consideration for long ears. Well then! Well now!

(Here, however, it happened that the ass also found utterance: it said distinctly and with malevolence, YE-A.)

'Twas once – methinks year one of our blessed Lord, –
Drunk without wine, the Sybil thus deplored:
'How ill things go!
Decline! Decline! Ne'er sank the world so low!
Rome now has turned harlot and harlot-stew,
Rome's Caesar a beast, and God – has turned Jew!'

2

With those rhymes of Zarathustra the kings were delighted; the king on the right, however, said: 'O Zarathustra, how well it was that we set out to see you!

For thine enemies showed us thy likeness in their mirror: there lookedst thou with the grimace of a devil, and sneeringly: so that we were afraid of thee.

But what good did it do! Always didst thou prick us anew in heart and ear with thy sayings. Then did we say at last: What does it matter how he look!

We must hear him; him who teaches: "You shall love peace as a means to new wars, and the short peace more than the long!"

No one ever spoke such warlike words: "What is good? To be brave is good. It is the good war that hallows every cause."

O Zarathustra, our fathers' blood stirred in our veins at such words: it was like the voice of spring to old wine-casks.

When the swords ran among one another like red-spotted serpents, then did our fathers become fond of life; the sun of every peace seemed to them languid and lukewarm, the long peace, however, made them ashamed.

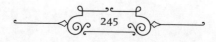

How they sighed, our fathers, when they saw on the wall brightly furbished, dried-up swords! Like those they thirsted for war. For a sword thirsts to drink blood, and sparkles with desire.'—

—When the kings thus discoursed and talked eagerly of the happiness of their fathers, there came upon Zarathustra no little desire to mock at their eagerness: for evidently they were very peaceable kings whom he saw before him, kings with old and refined features. But he restrained himself. 'Well!' said he, 'there leads the way, there lies the cave of Zarathustra; and this day is to have a long evening! At present, however, a cry of distress calls me hastily away from you.

It will honour my cave if kings want to sit and wait in it: but, to be sure, you will have to wait long!

Well! What of that! Where does one at present learn better to wait than at courts? And the whole virtue of kings that has remained to them – is it not called today: Ability to wait?'

Thus spoke Zarathustra.

64. The Leech

AND Zarathustra went thoughtfully on, further and lower down, through forests and past moory bottoms; as it happens, however, to every one who meditates upon hard matters, he trod thereby unawares upon a man. And lo, there spurted into his face all at once a cry of pain, and two curses and twenty bad invectives, so that in his fright he raised his stick and also struck the trodden one. Immediately afterwards, however, he regained his composure, and his heart laughed at the folly he had just committed.

'Pardon me,' said he to the trodden one, who had got up enraged, and had seated himself, 'pardon me, and hear first of all a parable.

As a wanderer who dreams of remote things on a lonesome

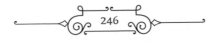

highway, runs unawares against a sleeping dog, a dog which lies in the sun:

—As both of them then start up and snap at each other, like deadly enemies, those two beings mortally frightened – so did it happen to us.

And yet! And yet – how little was lacking for them to caress each other, that dog and that lonesome one! Are they not both – lonesome ones!'

—'Whoever thou art,' said the trodden one, still enraged, 'thou treadest also too nigh me with thy parable, and not only with thy foot!

Lo! am I then a dog?' – And then the sitting one got up, and pulled his naked arm out of the swamp. For at first he had lain outstretched on the ground, hidden and indiscernible, like those who lie in wait for swamp-game.

'But whatever are you about' called out Zarathustra in alarm, for he saw a deal of blood streaming over the naked arm, 'what has hurt you? Has an evil beast bit you, you unfortunate one?'

The bleeding one laughed, still angry, 'What matter is it to you!' said he, and was about to go on. 'Here am I at home and in my province. Let him question me whoever will: to a dolt, however, I shall hardly answer.'

'You are mistaken,' said Zarathustra sympathetically, and held him fast; 'you are mistaken. Here you are not at home, but in my domain, and therein shall no one receive any hurt.

Call me however what you wilt – I am who I must be. I call myself Zarathustra.

Well! Up there is the way to Zarathustra's cave: it is not far, will you not attend to your wounds at my home?

It has gone badly with you, you unfortunate one, in this life: first a beast bit you, and then – a man trod upon you!' –

When however the trodden one had heard the name of Zarathustra he was transformed. 'What happens to me!' he exclaimed,

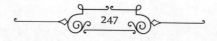

'who preoccupies me so much in this life as this one man, namely Zarathustra, and that one animal that lives on blood, the leech?

For the sake of the leech did I lie here by this swamp, like a fisher, and already had my outstretched arm been bitten ten times, when there bites a still finer leech at my blood, Zarathustra himself!

O happiness! O miracle! Praised be this day which enticed me into the swamp! Praised be the best, the livest cupping-glass, that at present lives; praised be the great conscience-leech Zarathustra!'—

Thus spoke the trodden one, and Zarathustra rejoiced at his words and their refined reverential style. 'Who are you?' asked he, and gave him his hand, 'there is much to clear up and elucidate between us, but already methinks pure clear day is dawning.'

'I am the spiritually conscientious one,' answered he who was asked, 'and in matters of the spirit it is difficult for any one to take it more rigorously, more restrictedly, and more severely than I, except him from whom I learnt it, Zarathustra himself.

Better know nothing than half-know many things! Better be a fool on one's own account, than a sage on other people's approbation! I – go to the basis:

—What matter if it be great or small? If it be called swamp or sky? A handbreadth of basis is enough for me, if it be actually basis and ground!

—A handbreadth of basis: there can one stand. In the true knowing-knowledge there is nothing great and nothing small.'

'Then you are perhaps an expert on the leech?' asked Zarathustra; 'and you investigate the leech to its ultimate basis, you conscientious one?'

'O Zarathustra,' answered the trodden one, 'that would be something immense; how could I presume to do so!

That, however, of which I am master and knower, is the brain of the leech: that is my world!

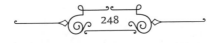

And it is also a world! Forgive it, however, that my pride here finds expression, for here I have not my equal. Therefore said I: "here am I at home."

How long have I investigated this one thing, the brain of the leech, so that here the slippery truth might no longer slip from me! Here is my domain!

—For the sake of this did I cast everything else aside, for the sake of this did everything else become indifferent to me; and close beside my knowledge lies my black ignorance.

My spiritual conscience requires from me that it should be so – that I should know one thing, and not know all else: they are a loathing to me, all the semi-spiritual, all the hazy, hovering, and visionary.

Where my honesty ceases, there am I blind, and want also to be blind. Where I want to know, however, there want I also to be honest – namely, severe, rigorous, restricted, cruel and inexorable.

Because you once said, O Zarathustra: "Spirit is life which itself cuts into life"; – that led and allured me to your doctrine. And verily, with my own blood have I increased my own knowledge!'

—'As the evidence indicates,' broke in Zarathustra; for still was the blood flowing down on the naked arm of the conscientious one. For there had ten leeches bitten into it.

'O you strange fellow, how much does this very evidence teach me – namely, you yourself! And not all, perhaps, might I pour into your rigorous ear!

Well then! We part here! But I would rather find you again. Up there is the way to my cave: tonight shall you there by my welcome guest!

Fain would I also make amends to your body for Zarathustra treading upon you with his feet: I think about that. Just now, however, a cry of distress calls me hastily away from you.'

Thus spoke Zarathustra.

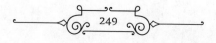

65. *The Magician*

1

WHEN however Zarathustra had gone round a rock, then saw he on the same path, not far below him, a man who threw his limbs about like a maniac, and at last tumbled to the ground on his belly. 'Halt!' said then Zarathustra to his heart, 'he there must surely be the higher man, from him came that dreadful cry of distress, I will see if I can help him.' When, however, he ran to the spot where the man lay on the ground, he found a trembling old man with fixed eyes; and in spite of all Zarathustra's efforts to lift him and set him again on his feet, it was all in vain. The unfortunate one, also, did not seem to notice that some one was beside him; on the contrary, he continually looked around with moving gestures, like one forsaken and isolated from all the world. At last, however, after much trembling, and convulsion, and curling-himself-up, he began to lament thus:

'Who warm'th me, who lov'th me still?
Give ardent fingers!
Give heartening charcoal-warmers!
Prone, outstretched, trembling,
Like him, half dead and cold, whose feet one warm'th—
And shaken, ah! By unfamiliar fevers,
Shivering with sharpened, icy-cold frost-arrows,
By you pursued, my fancy!
Ineffable! Recondite! Sore-frightening!
You huntsman 'hind the cloud-banks! Now lightning-struck by you,
You mocking eye that me in darkness watches:
—Thus do I lie,

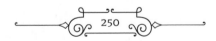

Bend myself, twist myself, convulsed
With all eternal torture,
And smitten
By you, cruel huntsman,
You unfamiliar – God…

Smite deeper!
Smite yet once more!
Pierce through and rend my heart!
What mean'th this torture
With dull, indented arrows?
Why look'st you hither,
Of human pain not weary,
With mischief-loving, godly flash-glances?
Not murder will you,
But torture, torture?
For why – me torture,
You mischief-loving, unfamiliar God?

Ha! Ha!
You stealest nigh
In midnight's gloomy hour?…
What will you?
Speak!
You crowd me, pressest –
Ha! Now far too closely!
You hearst me breathing,
You o'erhearst my heart,
You ever jealous one! – Of what, pray, ever jealous?
Off! Off!
For why the ladder?

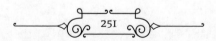

Would you get in?
To heart in-clamber?
To mine own secretest
Conceptions in-clamber?
Shameless one! You unknown one! Thief!
What seekst you by your stealing?
What seekst you by your hearkening?
What seekst you by your torturing?
You torturer!
You – hangman-God!
Or shall I, as the mastiffs do,
Roll me before you?
And cringing, enraptured, frantical,
My tail friendly – waggle!

In vain!
Goad further!
Cruel goader!
No dog – your game just am I,
Cruel huntsman!
Your proudest of captives,
You robber 'hind the cloud-banks...
Speak finally!
You lightning-veiled one! You unknown one! Speak!
What will you, highway-ambusher, from – me?
What will you, unfamiliar – God?
What?
Ransom-gold?
How much of ransom-gold? Solicit much – that bid'th my pride!
And be concise – that bid'th mine other pride!

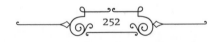

Ha! Ha!
Me – wantst you? me?
—Entire?...

Ha! Ha!
And torturest me, fool that you are,
Dead-torturest quite my pride?
Give love to me – who warm'th me still?
Who lov'th me still?
Give ardent fingers
Give heartening charcoal-warmers,
Give me, the most lonesome,
The ice (ah! seven-fold frozen ice
For very enemies,
For foes, do make one thirst).
Give, yield to me,
Cruel foe,
—Yourself!—

Away!
There fled he surely,
My final, only comrade,
My greatest foe,
Mine unfamiliar—
My hangman – God!...

—No!
Come you back!
With all of your great tortures! To me the last of lonesome ones,
Oh, come you back!
All my hot tears in streamlets trickle

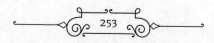

Their course to you!
And all my final hearty fervour—
Up-glow'th to you!
Oh, come you back,
Mine unfamiliar God! my pain!
My final bliss!'

2

—Here, however, Zarathustra could no longer restrain himself; he took his staff and struck the wailer with all his might. 'Stop this,' cried he to him with wrathful laughter, 'stop this, you stage-player! You false coiner! you liar from the very heart! I know you well!

I will soon make warm legs to you, you evil magician: I know well how – to make it hot for such as you!'

—'Leave off,' said the old man, and sprang up from the ground, 'strike me no more, O Zarathustra! I did it only for amusement!

That kind of thing belongs to my art. You yourself, I wanted to put to the proof when I gave this performance. And verily, you have well detected me!

But you yourself – have given me no small proof of yourself: you are hard, you wise Zarathustra! Hard strike you with your "truths," your cudgel forces from me – this truth!'

—'Flatter not,' answered Zarathustra, still excited and frowning, 'you stage-player from the heart! you are false: why speak you – of truth!

You peacock of peacocks, you sea of vanity; what did you represent before me, you evil magician; whom was I meant to believe in when you wailed in such wise?'

'The penitent in spirit,' said the old man, 'it was him – I represented; you yourself once created this expression—

—The poet and magician who at last turns his spirit against

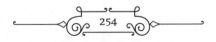

himself, the transformed one who freezes to death by his bad science and conscience.

And just acknowledge it: it was long, O Zarathustra, before you discovered my trick and lie! You believed in my distress when you held my head with both your hands,

—I heard you lament "we have loved him too little, loved him too little!" Because I so far deceived you, my wickedness rejoiced in me.'

'You may have deceived subtler ones than I,' said Zarathustra sternly. 'I am not on my guard against deceivers; I have to be without precaution: so wills my lot.

You, however, must deceive: so far do I know you! You must ever be equivocal, trivocal, quadrivocal, and quinquivocal! Even what you have now confessed, is not nearly true enough nor false enough for me!

You bad false coiner, how could you do otherwise! Your very malady would you whitewash if you showed yourself naked to your physician.

Thus did you whitewash your lie before me when you said: "I did so only for amusement!" There was also seriousness therein, you are something of a penitent-in-spirit!

I divine you well: you have become the enchanter of all the world; but for yourself you have no lie or artifice left, you are disenchanted to yourself!

You have reaped disgust as your one truth. No word in you is any longer genuine, but your mouth is so: that is to say, the disgust that cleaves to your mouth.'—

—'Who are you at all!' cried here the old magician with defiant voice, 'who dares to speak thus to me, the greatest man now living?' – and a green flash shot from his eye at Zarathustra. But immediately after he changed, and said sadly:

'O Zarathustra, I am weary of it, I am disgusted with my arts, I

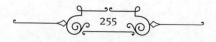

am not great, why do I dissemble! But you know it well – I sought for greatness!

A great man I wanted to appear, and persuaded many; but the lie has been beyond my power. On it do I collapse.

O Zarathustra, everything is a lie in me; but that I collapse – this my collapsing is genuine!'—

'It honours you,' said Zarathustra gloomily, looking down with sidelong glance, 'it honours you that you sought for greatness, but it betrays you also. You are not great.

You bad old magician, that is the best and the honestest thing I honour in you, that you have become weary of yourself, and have expressed it: "I am not great."

Therein do I honour you as a penitent-in-spirit, and although only for the twinkling of an eye, in that one moment wast you – genuine.

But tell me, what seek you here in my forests and rocks? And if you have put yourself in my way, what proof of me would you have?

—Wherein did you put me to the test?'

Thus spoke Zarathustra, and his eyes sparkled. But the old magician kept silence for a while; then said he: 'Did I put you to the test? I – seek only.

O Zarathustra, I seek a genuine one, a right one, a simple one, an unequivocal one, a man of perfect honesty, a vessel of wisdom, a saint of knowledge, a great man!

Know you it not, O Zarathustra? I seek Zarathustra.'

—And here there arose a long silence between them: Zarathustra, however, became profoundly absorbed in thought, so that he shut his eyes. But afterwards coming back to the situation, he grasped the hand of the magician, and said, full of politeness and policy:

'Well! Up there leads the way, there is the cave of Zarathustra. In it may you seek him whom you would rather find.

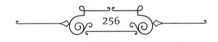

And ask counsel of my animals, my eagle and my serpent: they shall help you to seek. My cave however is large.

I myself, to be sure – I have as yet seen no great man. That which is great, the acutest eye is at present insensible to it. It is the kingdom of the rabble.

Many a one have I found who stretched and inflated himself, and the people cried: "Behold; a great man!" But what good do all bellows do! The wind comes out at last.

At last bursts the frog which has inflated itself too long: then comes out the wind. To prick a swollen one in the belly, I call good pastime. Hear that, you boys!

Our today is of the popular: who still knows what is great and what is small! Who could there seek successfully for greatness! A fool only: it succeeds with fools.

You seek for great men, you strange fool? Who taught that to you? Is today the time for it? Oh, you bad seeker, why do you – tempt me?'—

Thus spoke Zarathustra, comforted in his heart, and went laughing on his way.

66. Out of Service

NOT long, however, after Zarathustra had freed himself from the magician, he again saw a person sitting beside the path which he followed, namely a tall, black man, with a haggard, pale countenance: this man grieved him exceedingly. 'Alas,' said he to his heart, 'there sits disguised affliction; methinks he is of the type of the priests: what do they want in my domain?

What! Hardly have I escaped from that magician, and must another necromancer again run across my path,

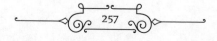

—Some sorcerer with laying-on-of-hands, some sombre wonder-worker by the grace of God, some anointed world-maligner, whom, may the devil take!

But the devil is never at the place which would be his right place: he always comes too late, that cursed dwarf and club-foot!'—

Thus cursed Zarathustra impatiently in his heart, and considered how with averted look he might slip past the black man. But behold, it came about otherwise. For at the same moment had the sitting one already perceived him; and not unlike one whom an unexpected happiness overtakes, he sprang to his feet, and went straight towards Zarathustra.

'Whoever you are, you traveller,' said he, 'help a strayed one, a seeker, an old man, who may here easily come to grief!

The world here is strange to me, and remote; wild beasts also did I hear howling; and he who could have given me protection – he is himself no more.

I was seeking the pious man, a saint and an hermit, who, alone in his forest, had not yet heard of what all the world knows at present.'

'What does all the world know at present?' asked Zarathustra. 'Perhaps that the old God no longer lives, in whom all the world once believed?'

'You say it,' answered the old man sorrowfully. 'And I served that old God until his last hour.

Now, however, am I out of service, without master, and yet not free; likewise am I no longer merry even for an hour, except it be in recollections.

Therefore did I ascend into these mountains, that I might finally have a festival for myself once more, as becomes an old pope and church-father: for know it, that I am the last pope! A festival of pious recollections and divine services.

Now, however, is he himself dead, the most pious of men, the

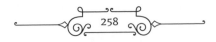

saint in the forest, who praised his God constantly with singing and mumbling.

He himself found I no longer when I found his cot – but two wolves found I therein, which howled on account of his death, for all animals loved him. Then did I haste away.

Had I thus come in vain into these forests and mountains? Then did my heart determine that I should seek another, the most pious of all those who believe not in God, my heart determined that I should seek Zarathustra!'

Thus spoke the hoary man, and gazed with keen eyes at him who stood before him. Zarathustra however seized the hand of the old pope and regarded it a long while with admiration.

'Lo! You venerable one,' said he then, 'what a fine and long hand! That is the hand of one who has ever dispensed blessings. Now, however, does it hold fast him whom you seek, me, Zarathustra.

It is I, the ungodly Zarathustra, who says: "Who is ungodlier than I, that I may enjoy his teaching?"'—

Thus spoke Zarathustra, and penetrated with his glances the thoughts and arrear-thoughts of the old pope. At last the latter began:

'He who most loved and possessed him has now also lost him most:

—Lo, I myself am surely the most godless of us at present? But who could rejoice at that!'—

—'You served him to the last?' asked Zarathustra thoughtfully, after a deep silence, 'you know how he died? Is it true what they say, that sympathy choked him;

—That he saw how man hung on the cross, and could not endure it; – that his love to man became his hell, and at last his death?'—

The old pope however did not answer, but looked aside timidly, with a painful and gloomy expression.

'Let him go,' said Zarathustra, after prolonged meditation, still looking the old man straight in the eye.

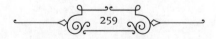

'Let him go, he is gone. And though it honours you that you speak only in praise of this dead one, yet you know as well as I who he was, and that he went curious ways.'

'To speak before three eyes,' said the old pope cheerfully (he was blind of one eye), 'in divine matters I am more enlightened than Zarathustra himself – and may well be so.

My love served him long years, my will followed all his will. A good servant, however, knows everything, and many a thing even which a master hides from himself.

He was a hidden God, full of secrecy. He did not come by his son otherwise than by secret ways. At the door of his faith stands adultery.

Whoever extolls him as a God of love, does not think highly enough of love itself. Did not that God want also to be judge? But the loving one loves irrespective of reward and requital.

When he was young, that God out of the Orient, then was he harsh and revengeful, and built himself a hell for the delight of his favourites.

At last, however, he became old and soft and mellow and pitiful, more like a grandfather than a father, but most like a tottering old grandmother.

There did he sit shrivelled in his chimney-corner, fretting on account of his weak legs, world-weary, will-weary, and one day he suffocated of his all-too-great pity.' –

'You old pope,' said here Zarathustra interposing, 'have you seen that with your eyes? It could well have happened in that way: in that way, and also otherwise. When gods die they always die many kinds of death.

Well! At all events, one way or other – he is gone! He was counter to the taste of my ears and eyes; worse than that I should not like to say against him.

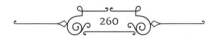

I love everything that looks bright and speaks honestly. But he – you know it, you old priest, there was something of your type in him, the priest-type – he was equivocal.

He was also indistinct. How he raged at us, this wrath-snorter, because we understood him badly! But why did he not speak more clearly?

And if the fault lay in our ears, why did he give us ears that heard him badly? If there was dirt in our ears, well! Who put it in them?

Too much miscarried with him, this potter who had not learned thoroughly! That he took revenge on his pots and creations, however, because they turned out badly – that was a sin against good taste.

There is also good taste in piety: this at last said: "Away with such a God! Better to have no God, better to set up destiny on one's own account, better to be a fool, better to be God oneself!"'

—'What do I hear!' said then the old pope, with intent ears; 'O Zarathustra, you are more pious than you believe, with such an unbelief! Some god in you has converted you to your ungodliness.

Is it not your piety itself which no longer lets you believe in a God? And your over-great honesty will yet lead you even beyond good and evil!

Behold, what has been reserved for you? You have eyes and hands and mouth, which have been predestined for blessing from eternity. One does not bless with the hand alone.

Near to you, though you profess to be the ungodliest one, I feel a hale and holy odour of long benedictions: I feel glad and grieved thereby.

Let me be your guest, O Zarathustra, for a single night! Nowhere on earth shall I now feel better than with you!'—

'Amen! So shall it be!' said Zarathustra, with great astonishment; 'up there leads the way, there lies the cave of Zarathustra.

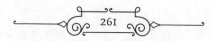

Gladly would I conduct you there myself, you venerable one; for I love all pious men. But now a cry of distress calls me hastily away from you.

In my domain shall no one come to grief; my cave is a good haven. And best of all would I like to put every sorrowful one again on firm land and firm legs.

Who, however, could take your melancholy off your shoulders? For that I am too weak. Long, verily, should we have to wait until some one re-awoke your God for you.

For that old God lives no more: he is indeed dead.'—

Thus spoke Zarathustra.

67. *The Ugliest Man*

—AND again did Zarathustra's feet run through mountains and forests, and his eyes sought and sought, but nowhere was he to be seen whom they wanted to see – the sorely distressed sufferer and crier. On the whole way, however, he rejoiced in his heart and was full of gratitude. 'What good things,' said he, 'has this day given me, as amends for its bad beginning! What strange interlocutors have I found!

At their words will I now chew a long while as at good corn; small shall my teeth grind and crush them, until they flow like milk into my soul!'—

When, however, the path again curved round a rock, all at once the landscape changed, and Zarathustra entered into a realm of death. Here bristled aloft black and red cliffs, without any grass, tree, or bird's voice. For it was a valley which all animals avoided, even the beasts of prey, except that a species of ugly, thick, green serpent came here to die when they became old. Therefore the shepherds called this valley: 'Serpent-death.'

Zarathustra, however, became absorbed in dark recollections, for

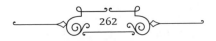

it seemed to him as if he had once before stood in this valley. And much heaviness settled on his mind, so that he walked slowly and always more slowly, and at last stood still. Then, however, when he opened his eyes, he saw something sitting by the wayside shaped like a man, and hardly like a man, something nondescript. And all at once there came over Zarathustra a great shame, because he had gazed on such a thing. Blushing up to the very roots of his white hair, he turned aside his glance, and raised his foot that he might leave this ill-starred place. Then, however, became the dead wilderness vocal: for from the ground a noise welled up, gurgling and rattling, as water gurgles and rattles at night through stopped-up water-pipes; and at last it turned into human voice and human speech: it sounded thus:

'Zarathustra! Zarathustra! Read my riddle! Say, say! What is the revenge on the witness?

I entice you back; here is smooth ice! See to it, see to it, that your pride does not here break its legs!

You think yourself wise, you proud Zarathustra! Read then the riddle, you hard nut-cracker, the riddle that I am! Say then: who am I!'

—When however Zarathustra had heard these words, what think you then took place in his soul? Pity overcame him; and he sank down all at once, like an oak that has long withstood many tree-fellers, heavily, suddenly, to the terror even of those who meant to fell it. But immediately he got up again from the ground, and his countenance became stern.

'I know you well,' said he, with a brazen voice, 'you are the murderer of God! Let me go.

You could not endure him who beheld you, who ever beheld you through and through, you ugliest man. You took revenge on this witness!'

Thus spoke Zarathustra and was about to go; but the nondescript grasped at a corner of his garment and began anew to gurgle and seek for words. 'Stay,' said he at last—

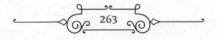

—'Stay! Do not pass by! I have divined what axe it was that struck you to the ground: hail to you, O Zarathustra, that you are again upon your feet!

You have divined, I know it well, how the man feels who killed him, the murderer of God. Stay! Sit down here beside me; it is not to no purpose.

To whom would I go but to you? Stay, sit down! Do not however look at me! Honour thus – my ugliness!

They persecute me: now are you my last refuge. Not with their hatred, not with their bailiffs; – Oh, such persecution would I mock at, and be proud and cheerful!

Has not all success hitherto been with the well-persecuted ones? And he who persecutes well learns readily to be obsequent – when once he is – put behind! But it is their pity—

—Their pity is it from which I flee away and flee to you. O Zarathustra, protect me, you, my last refuge, you sole one who divined me:

—You have divined how the man feels who killed him. Stay! And if you will go, you impatient one, go not the way that I came. That way is bad.

Are you angry with me because I have already racked language too long? Because I have already counselled you? But know that it is I, the ugliest man,

—Who have also the largest, heaviest feet. Where I have gone, the way is bad. I tread all paths to death and destruction.

But that you passed me by in silence, that you blushed – I saw it well: thereby did I know you as Zarathustra.

Every one else would have thrown to me his alms, his pity, in look and speech. But for that – I am not beggar enough: that did you divine.

For that I am too rich, rich in what is great, frightful, ugliest, most unutterable! Your shame, O Zarathustra, honoured me!

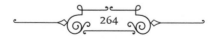

With difficulty did I get out of the crowd of the pitiful, that I might find the only one who at present teaches that "pity is obtrusive" – yourself, O Zarathustra!

—Whether it be the pity of a God, or whether it be human pity, it is offensive to modesty. And unwillingness to help may be nobler than the virtue that rushes to do so.

That however – namely, pity – is called virtue itself at present by all petty people: they have no reverence for great misfortune, great ugliness, great failure.

Beyond all these do I look, as a dog looks over the backs of thronging flocks of sheep. They are petty, good-wooled, good-willed, grey people.

As the heron looks contemptuously at shallow pools, with backward-bent head, so do I look at the throng of grey little waves and wills and souls.

Too long have we acknowledged them to be right, those petty people: so we have at last given them power as well; – and now do they teach that "good is only what petty people call good."

And "truth" is at present what the preacher spoke who himself sprang from them, that singular saint and advocate of the petty people, who testified of himself: "I – am the truth."

That shameless one has long made the petty people greatly puffed up, he who taught no small error when he taught: "I – am the truth."

Has a shameless one ever been answered more courteously? – You, however, O Zarathustra, passed him by, and said: "No! No! Three times No!"

You warned against his error; you warned – the first to do so – against pity: not every one, not none, but yourself and your type.

You are ashamed of the shame of the great sufferer; and verily when you say: "From pity there comes a heavy cloud; take heed, you men!"

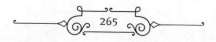

—When you teach: "All creators are hard, all great love is beyond their pity:" O Zarathustra, how well versed do you seem to me in weather-signs!

You yourself, however, warn yourself also against your pity! For many are on their way to you, many suffering, doubting, despairing, drowning, freezing ones—

I warn you also against myself. You have read my best, my worst riddle, myself, and what I have done. I know the axe that fells you.

But he – had to die: he looked with eyes which beheld everything, he beheld men's depths and dregs, all his hidden ignominy and ugliness.

His pity knew no modesty: he crept into my dirtiest corners. This most prying, over-intrusive, over-pitiful one had to die.

He ever beheld me: on such a witness I would have revenge – or not live myself.

The God who beheld everything, and also man: that God had to die! Man cannot endure it that such a witness should live.'

Thus spoke the ugliest man. Zarathustra however got up, and prepared to go on: for he felt frozen to the very bowels.

'You nondescript,' said he, 'you warned me against your path. As thanks for it I praise mine to you. Behold, up there is the cave of Zarathustra.

My cave is large and deep and has many corners; there finds he that is most hidden his hiding-place. And close beside it, there are a hundred lurking-places and by-places for creeping, fluttering, and hopping creatures.

You outcast, who have cast yourself out, you will not live amongst men and men's pity? Well then, do like me! Thus will you learn also from me; only the doer learns.

And talk first and foremost to my animals! The proudest animal

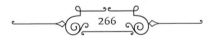

and the wisest animal – they might well be the right counsellors for us both!'—

Thus spoke Zarathustra and went his way, more thoughtfully and slowly even than before: for he asked himself many things, and hardly knew what to answer.

'How poor indeed is man,' thought he in his heart, 'how ugly, how wheezy, how full of hidden shame!

They tell me that man loves himself. Ah, how great must that self-love be! How much contempt is opposed to it!

Even this man has loved himself, as he has despised himself, a great lover methinks he is, and a great despiser.

No one have I yet found who more thoroughly despised himself: even that is elevation. Alas, was this perhaps the higher man whose cry I heard?

I love the great despisers. Man is something that has to be overcome.'—

68. *The Voluntary Beggar*

WHEN Zarathustra had left the ugliest man, he was chilled and felt lonesome: for much coldness and lonesomeness came over his spirit, so that even his limbs became colder thereby. When, however, he wandered on and on, uphill and down, at times past green meadows, though also sometimes over wild stony couches where once perhaps an impatient brook had made its bed, then he turned all at once warmer and heartier again.

'What has happened to me?' he asked himself, 'something warm and living quickens me; it must be in the neighbourhood.

Already am I less alone; unconscious companions and brothers rove around me; their warm breath touches my soul.'

When, however, he spied about and sought for the comforters

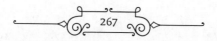

of his lonesomeness, behold, there were cows there standing together on an eminence, whose proximity and smell had warmed his heart. The cows, however, seemed to listen eagerly to a speaker, and took no heed of him who approached. When, however, Zarathustra was quite near to them, then did he hear plainly that a human voice spoke in the midst of the cows, and apparently all of them had turned their heads towards the speaker.

Then ran Zarathustra up speedily and drove the animals aside; for he feared that someone had here met with harm, which the pity of the kine would hardly be able to relieve. But in this he was deceived; for behold, there sat a man on the ground who seemed to be persuading the animals to have no fear of him, a peaceable man and Preacher-on-the-Mount, out of whose eyes kindness itself preached. 'What do you seek here?' called out Zarathustra in astonishment.

'What do I here seek?' answered he: 'the same that you seek, you mischief-maker; that is to say, happiness upon earth.

To that end, however, I would rather learn of these cows. For I tell you that I have already talked half a morning to them, and just now were they about to give me their answer. Why do you disturb them?

Except we be converted and become as cattle, we shall in no wise enter into the kingdom of heaven. For we ought to learn from them one thing: ruminating.

And verily, although a man should gain the whole world, and yet not learn one thing, ruminating, what would it profit him! He would not be rid of his affliction,

—His great affliction: that, however, is at present called disgust. Who has not at present his heart, his mouth and his eyes full of disgust? You also! You also! But behold these cows!' –

Thus spoke the Preacher-on-the-Mount, and turned then his own look towards Zarathustra – for hitherto it had rested lovingly on the

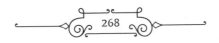

cows: then, however, he put on a different expression. 'Who is this with whom I talk?' he exclaimed, frightened, and sprang up from the ground.

'This is the man without disgust, this is Zarathustra himself, the overcomer of the great disgust, this is the eye, this is the mouth, this is the heart of Zarathustra himself.'

And whilst he thus spoke he kissed with o'erflowing eyes the hands of him with whom he spoke, and behaved altogether like one to whom a precious gift and jewel has fallen unawares from heaven. The cattle, however, gazed at it all and wondered.

'Speak not of me, you strange one; you amiable one!' said Zarathustra, and restrained his affection, 'speak to me firstly of yourself! Are you not the voluntary beggar who once cast away great riches,

—Who was ashamed of his riches and of the rich, and fled to the poorest to give upon them his abundance and his heart? But they received him not.'

'But they received me not,' said the voluntary beggar, 'you know it, forsooth. So I went at last to the animals and to those cows.'

'Then learned you,' interrupted Zarathustra, 'how much harder it is to give properly than to take properly, and that giving well is an art – the last, subtlest master-art of kindness.

'Especially nowadays,' answered the voluntary beggar: 'at present, that is to say, when everything low has become rebellious and exclusive and haughty in its manner – in the manner of the rabble.

For the hour has come, you know it, for the great, evil, long, slow mob-and-slave-insurrection: it extends and extends!

Now does it provoke the lower classes, all benevolence and petty giving; and the overrich may be on their guard!

Whoever at present drip, like bulgy bottles out of all-too-small necks: of such bottles at present one willingly breaks the necks.

Wanton avidity, bilious envy, careworn revenge, rabble-pride: all

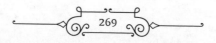

these struck my eye. It is no longer true that the poor are blessed. The kingdom of heaven, however, is with the cows.'

'And why is it not with the rich?' asked Zarathustra temptingly, while he kept back the cattle which sniffed familiarly at the peaceful one.

'Why do you tempt me?' answered the other. 'You know it yourself better even than I. What was it drove me to the poorest, O Zarathustra? Was it not my disgust at the richest?

—At the culprits of riches, with cold eyes and rank thoughts, who pick up profit out of all kinds of rubbish – at this rabble that stinks to heaven,

—At this gilded, falsified rabble, whose fathers were pickpockets, or carrion-crows, or rag-pickers, with wives compliant, lewd and forgetful: for they are all of them not far different from harlots—

Rabble above, rabble below! What are "poor" and "rich" at present! That distinction did I unlearn, then did I flee away further and ever further, until I came to those cows.'

Thus spoke the peaceful one, and puffed himself and perspired with his words: so that the cattle wondered anew. Zarathustra, however, kept looking into his face with a smile, all the time the man talked so severely – and shook silently his head.

'You do violence to yourself, you Preacher-on-the-Mount, when you use such severe words. For such severity neither your mouth nor your eye have been given you.

Nor, methinks, has your stomach either: to it all such rage and hatred and foaming-over is repugnant. Your stomach wants softer things: you are not a butcher.

Rather seem you to me a plant-eater and a root-man. Perhaps you grind corn. Certainly, however, you are averse to fleshly joys, and you love honey.'

'You have divined me well,' answered the voluntary beggar, with

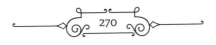

lightened heart. 'I love honey, I also grind corn; for I have sought out what tastes sweetly and makes pure breath:

—Also what requires a long time, a day's-work and a mouth's-work for gentle idlers and sluggards.

Furthest, to be sure, have those cows carried it: they have created ruminating and lying in the sun. They also abstain from all heavy thoughts which inflate the heart.'

—'Well!' said Zarathustra, 'you should also see my animals, my eagle and my serpent, their like do not at present exist on earth.

Behold, there leads the way to my cave: be tonight its guest. And talk to my animals of the happiness of animals,

—Until I myself come home. For now a cry of distress calls me hastily away from you. Also, should you find new honey with me, ice-cold, golden-comb-honey, eat it!

Now, however, take leave at once of your cattle, you strange one! You amiable one! Though it be hard for you. For they are your warmest friends and preceptors!'—

—'One excepted, whom I hold still dearer,' answered the voluntary beggar. 'You yourself are good, O Zarathustra, and better even than a cow!'

'Away, away with you! you evil flatterer!' cried Zarathustra mischievously, 'why do you spoil me with such praise and flattery – honey?'

'Away, away from me!' cried he once more, and heaved his stick at the fond beggar, who, however, ran nimbly away.

69. The Shadow

SCARCELY however was the voluntary beggar gone in haste, and Zarathustra again alone, when he heard behind him a new voice which called out: 'Stay! Zarathustra! Do wait! It is myself, O Zarathustra,

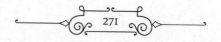

myself, your shadow!' But Zarathustra did not wait; for a sudden irritation came over him on account of the crowd and the crowding in his mountains. 'Where has my lonesomeness gone?' spoke he.

'It is verily becoming too much for me; these mountains swarm; my kingdom is no longer of this world; I require new mountains.

My shadow calls me? What matter about my shadow! Let it run after me! I – run away from it.'

Thus spoke Zarathustra to his heart and ran away. But the one behind followed after him, so that immediately there were three runners, one after the other – namely, foremost the voluntary beggar, then Zarathustra, and thirdly, and hindmost, his shadow. But not long had they run thus when Zarathustra became conscious of his folly, and shook off with one jerk all his irritation and detestation.

'What!' said he, 'have not the most ludicrous things always happened to us old hermits and saints?

My folly has grown big in the mountains! Now do I hear six old fools' legs rattling behind one another!

But does Zarathustra need to be frightened by his shadow? Also, methinks that after all it has longer legs thin mine.'

Thus spoke Zarathustra, and, laughing with eyes and entrails, he stood still and turned round quickly – and behold, he almost thereby threw his shadow and follower to the ground, so closely had the latter followed at his heels, and so weak was he. For when Zarathustra scrutinized him with his glance he was frightened as by a sudden apparition, so slender, swarthy, hollow and worn out did this follower appear.

'Who are you?' asked Zarathustra vehemently, 'what do you here? And why call you yourself my shadow? You are not pleasing to me.'

'Forgive me,' answered the shadow, 'that it is I; and if I please you not – well, O Zarathustra! Therein do I admire you and your good taste.

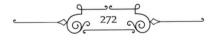

A wanderer am I, who have walked long at your heels; always on the way, but without a goal, also without a home: so that verily, I lack little of being the eternally Wandering Jew, except that I am not eternal and not a Jew.

What? Must I ever be on the way? Whirled by every wind, un-settled, driven about? O earth, you have become too round for me!

On every surface have I already sat, like tired dust have I fallen asleep on mirrors and window-panes: everything takes from me, nothing gives; I become thin – I am almost equal to a shadow.

After you, however, O Zarathustra, did I fly and hie longest; and though I hid myself from you, I was nevertheless your best shadow: wherever you have sat, there sat I also.

With you have I wandered about in the remotest, coldest worlds, like a phantom that voluntarily haunts winter roofs and snows.

With you have I pushed into all the forbidden, all the worst and the furthest: and if there be anything of virtue in me, it is that I have had no fear of any prohibition.

With you have I broken up whatever my heart revered; all boundary-stones and statues have I o'erthrown; the most dangerous wishes did I pursue, verily, beyond every crime did I once go.

With you did I unlearn the belief in words and worths and in great names. When the devil casts his skin, does not his name also fall away? It is also skin. The devil himself is perhaps – skin.

"Nothing is true, all is permitted": so said I to myself. Into the coldest water did I plunge with head and heart. Ah, how oft did I stand there naked on that account, like a red crab!

Ah, where have gone all my goodness and all my shame and all my belief in the good! Ah, where is the lying innocence which I once possessed, the innocence of the good and of their noble lies!

Too oft, verily, did I follow close to the heels of truth: then did

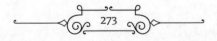

it kick me on the face. Sometimes I meant to lie, and behold! Then only did I hit – the truth.

Too much has become clear to me: now it does not concern me any more. Nothing lives any longer that I love, how should I still love myself?

"To live as I incline, or not to live at all": so do I wish; so wishes also the holiest. But alas! how have I still – inclination?

Have I – still a goal? A haven towards which my sail is set?

A good wind? Ah, he only who knows where he sails, knows what wind is good, and a fair wind for him.

What still remains to me? A heart weary and flippant; an unstable will; fluttering wings; a broken backbone.

This seeking for my home: O Zarathustra, do you know that this seeking has been my home-sickening; it eats me up.

"Where is – my home?" For it do I ask and seek, and have sought, but have not found it. O eternal everywhere, O eternal nowhere, O eternal – in-vain!'

Thus spoke the shadow, and Zarathustra's countenance lengthened at his words. 'You are my shadow!' said he at last sadly.

'Your danger is not small, you free spirit and wanderer! you have had a bad day: see that a still worse evening does not overtake you!

To such unsettled ones as you, seems at last even a prisoner blessed. Did you ever see how captured criminals sleep? They sleep quietly, they enjoy their new security.

Beware lest in the end a narrow faith capture you, a hard, rigorous delusion! For now everything that is narrow and fixed seduces and tempts you.

You have lost your goal. Alas, how will you forego and forget that loss? Thereby – have you also lost your way!

You poor rover and rambler, you tired butterfly! Will you have a rest and a home this evening? Then go up to my cave!

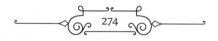

There leads the way to my cave. And now will I run quickly away from you again. Already lies as it were a shadow upon me.

I will run alone, so that it may again become bright around me. Therefore must I still be a long time merrily upon my legs. In the evening, however, there will be – dancing with me!'—

Thus spoke Zarathustra.

70. *At Noontide*

—AND Zarathustra ran and ran, but he found no one else, and was alone and ever found himself again; he enjoyed and quaffed his solitude, and thought of good things – for hours. About the hour of noontide, however, when the sun stood exactly over Zarathustra's head, he passed an old, bent and gnarled tree, which was encircled round by the ardent love of a vine, and hidden from itself; from this there hung yellow grapes in abundance, confronting the wanderer. Then he felt inclined to quench a little thirst, and to break off for himself a cluster of grapes. When, however, he had already his arm out-stretched for that purpose, he felt still more inclined for something else – namely, to lie down beside the tree at the hour of perfect noontide and sleep.

This Zarathustra did; and no sooner had he laid himself on the ground in the stillness and secrecy of the variegated grass, than he had forgotten his little thirst, and fell asleep. For as the aphorism of Zarathustra says: 'One thing is more necessary than the other.' Only that his eyes remained open: for they never grew weary of viewing and admiring the tree and the love of the vine. In falling asleep, however, Zarathustra spoke thus to his heart:

'Hush! Hush! Has not the world now become perfect? What has happened to me?

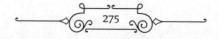

As a delicate wind dances invisibly upon parqueted seas, light, feather-light, so – dances sleep upon me.

No eye does it close to me, it leaves my soul awake. Light is it, verily, feather-light.

It persuades me, I know not how, it touches me inwardly with a caressing hand, it constrains me. Yes, it constrains me, so that my soul stretches itself out:

—How long and weary it becomes, my strange soul! Has a seventh-day evening come to it precisely at noontide? Has it already wandered too long, blissfully, among good and ripe things?

It stretches itself out, long – longer! It lies still, my strange soul. Too many good things has it already tasted; this golden sadness oppresses it, it distorts its mouth.

—As a ship that puts into the calmest cove: it now draws up to the land, weary of long voyages and uncertain seas. Is not the land more faithful?

As such a ship hugs the shore, tugs the shore: then it suffices for a spider to spin its thread from the ship to the land. No stronger ropes are required there.

As such a weary ship in the calmest cove, so do I also now repose, nigh to the earth, faithful, trusting, waiting, bound to it with the lightest threads.

O happiness! O happiness! Will you perhaps sing, O my soul? You lie in the grass. But this is the secret, solemn hour, when no shepherd plays his pipe.

Take care! Hot noontide sleeps on the fields. Do not sing! Hush! The world is perfect.

Do not sing, you prairie-bird, my soul! Do not even whisper! Lo – hush! The old noontide sleeps, it moves its mouth: does it not just now drink a drop of happiness—

—An old brown drop of golden happiness, golden wine?

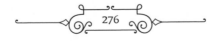

Something whisks over it, its happiness laughs. Thus – laughs a God. Hush!

—"For happiness, how little suffices for happiness!" Thus spoke I once and thought myself wise. But it was a blasphemy: that have I now learned. Wise fools speak better.

The least thing precisely, the gentlest thing, the lightest thing, a lizard's rustling, a breath, a whisk, an eye-glance – little makes up the best happiness. Hush!

—What has befallen me: Hark! has time flown away? Do I not fall? Have I not fallen – hark! into the well of eternity?

—What happens to me? Hush! It stings me – alas – to the heart? To the heart! Oh, break up, break up, my heart, after such happiness, after such a sting!

—What? has not the world just now become perfect? Round and ripe? Oh, for the golden round ring – where does it fly? Let me run after it! Quick!

Hush—' (and here Zarathustra stretched himself, and felt that he was asleep.)

'Up!' said he to himself, 'you sleeper! you noontide sleeper! Well then, up, you old legs! It is time and more than time; many a good stretch of road is still awaiting you—

Now have you slept your fill; for how long a time? A half-eternity! Well then, up now, my old heart! For how long after such a sleep may you – remain awake?'

(But then did he fall asleep anew, and his soul spoke against him and defended itself, and lay down again) – 'Leave me alone! Hush! Has not the world just now become perfect? Oh, for the golden round ball!'

'Get up,' said Zarathustra, 'you little thief, you sluggard! What! Still stretching yourself, yawning, sighing, failing into deep wells?

Who are you then, O my soul!' (and here he became frightened, for a sunbeam shot down from heaven upon his face.)

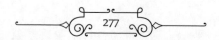

'O heaven above me,' said he sighing, and sat upright, 'you gaze at me? You hearken to my strange soul?

When will you drink this drop of dew that fell down upon all earthly things, when will you drink this strange soul –

—When, you well of eternity! You joyous, awful, noontide abyss! When will you drink my soul back into you?'

Thus spoke Zarathustra, and rose from his couch beside the tree, as if awakening from a strange drunkenness: and behold! There stood the sun still exactly above his head. One might, however, rightly infer therefrom that Zarathustra had not then slept long.

71. *The Greeting*

IT WAS late in the afternoon only when Zarathustra, after long useless searching and strolling about, again came home to his cave. When, however, he stood over against it, not more than twenty paces therefrom, the thing happened which he now least of all expected: he heard anew the great cry of distress. And extraordinary! This time the cry came out of his own cave. It was a long, manifold, peculiar cry, and Zarathustra plainly distinguished that it was composed of many voices: although heard at a distance it might sound like the cry out of a single mouth.

Then Zarathustra rushed forward to his cave, and behold! What a spectacle awaited him after that concert! For there did they all sit together whom he had passed during the day: the king on the right and the king on the left, the old magician, the pope, the voluntary beggar, the shadow, the intellectually conscientious one, the sorrowful soothsayer, and the ass; the ugliest man, however, had set a crown on his head, and had put round him two purple girdles, for he liked, like all ugly ones, to disguise himself and play the handsome person. In the midst, however, of that sorrowful company stood Zarathustra's

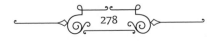

eagle, ruffled and disquieted, for it had been called upon to answer too much for which its pride had not any answer; the wise serpent however hung round its neck.

All this did Zarathustra behold with great astonishment; then however he scrutinized each individual guest with courteous curiosity, read their souls and wondered anew. In the meantime the assembled ones had risen from their seats, and waited with reverence for Zarathustra to speak. Zarathustra however spoke thus:

'You despairing ones! You strange ones! So it was your cry of distress that I heard? And now do I know also where he is to be sought, whom I have sought for in vain today: the higher man:

—In my own cave sits he, the higher man! But why do I wonder! Have not I myself allured him to me by honey-offerings and artful lure-calls of my happiness?

But it seems to me that you are badly adapted for company: you make one another's hearts fretful, you that cry for help, when you sit here together? There is one that must first come,

—One who will make you laugh once more, a good jovial fool, a dancer, a wind, a wild romp, some old fool: what think ye?

Forgive me, however, you despairing ones, for speaking such trivial words before you, unworthy, verily, of such guests! But you do not divine what makes my heart wanton:

—You yourselves do it, and your aspect, forgive it me! For every one becomes courageous who beholds a despairing one. To encourage a despairing one – every one thinks himself strong enough to do so.

To myself have you given this power, a good gift, my honourable guests! An excellent guest's-present! Well, do not then upbraid when I also offer you something of mine.

This is my empire and my dominion: that which is mine, however, shall this evening and tonight be yours. My animals shall serve you: let my cave be your resting-place!

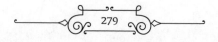

At house and home with me shall no one despair: in my purlieus do I protect every one from his wild beasts. And that is the first thing which I offer you: security!

The second thing, however, is my little finger. And when you have that, then take the whole hand also, yes and the heart with it! Welcome here, welcome to you, my guests!'

Thus spoke Zarathustra, and laughed with love and mischief. After this greeting his guests bowed once more and were reverentially silent; the king on the right, however, answered him in their name.

'O Zarathustra, by the way in which you have given us your hand and your greeting, we recognize you as Zarathustra. You have humbled yourself before us; almost have you hurt our reverence:

—Who however could have humbled himself as you have done, with such pride? That uplifts us ourselves; a refreshment is it, to our eyes and hearts.

To behold this, merely, gladly would we ascend higher mountains than this. For as eager beholders have we come; we wanted to see what brightens dim eyes.

And lo! Now is it all over with our cries of distress. Now are our minds and hearts open and enraptured. Little is lacking for our spirits to become wanton.

There is nothing, O Zarathustra, that grows more pleasingly on earth than a lofty, strong will: it is the finest growth. An entire landscape refreshes itself at one such tree.

To the pine do I compare him, O Zarathustra, which grows up like you – tall, silent, hardy, solitary, of the best, supplest wood, stately,

—In the end, however, grasping out for its dominion with strong, green branches, asking weighty questions of the wind, the storm, and whatever is at home on high places;

—Answering more weightily, a commander, a victor! Oh! Who should not ascend high mountains to behold such growths?

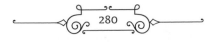

At your tree, O Zarathustra, the gloomy and ill-constituted also refresh themselves; at your look even the wavering become steady and heal their hearts.

And verily, towards your mountain and your tree do many eyes turn today; a great longing has arisen, and many have learned to ask: "Who is Zarathustra?"

And those into whose ears you have at any time dripped your song and your honey: all the hidden ones, the lone-dwellers and the twain-dwellers, have simultaneously said to their hearts:

"Does Zarathustra still live? It is no longer worth while to live, everything is indifferent, everything is useless: or else – we must live with Zarathustra!

Why does he not come who has so long announced himself?" Thus do many people ask; "has solitude swallowed him up? Or should we perhaps go to him?"

Now does it come to pass that solitude itself becomes fragile and breaks open, like a grave that breaks open and can no longer hold its dead. Everywhere one sees resurrected ones.

Now do the waves rise and rise around your mountain, O Zarathustra. And however high be your height, many of them must rise up to you: your boat shall not rest much longer on dry ground.

And that we despairing ones have now come into your cave, and already no longer despair: it is but a prognostic and a presage that better ones are on the way to you,

—For they themselves are on the way to you, the last remnant of God among men – that is to say, all the men of great longing, of great loathing, of great satiety,

—All who do not want to live unless they learn again to hope – unless they learn from you, O Zarathustra, the great hope!'

Thus spoke the king on the right, and seized the hand of Zarathustra in order to kiss it; but Zarathustra checked his veneration,

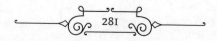

and stepped back frightened, fleeing as it were, silently and suddenly into the far distance. After a little while, however, he was again at home with his guests, looked at them with clear scrutinizing eyes, and said:

'My guests, you higher men, I will speak plain language and plainly with you. It is not for you that I have waited here in these mountains.'

('"Plain language and plainly?' Good God!" said here the king on the left to himself; "one sees he does not know the good Occidentals, this sage out of the Orient!

But he means 'blunt language and bluntly' – well! That is not the worst taste in these days!")

'You may, verily, all of you be higher men,' continued Zarathustra; 'but for me – you are neither high enough, nor strong enough.

For me, that is to say, for the inexorable which is now silent in me, but will not always be silent. And if you appertain to me, still it is not as my right arm.

For he who himself stands, like you, on sickly and tender legs, wishes above all to be treated indulgently, whether he be conscious of it or hide it from himself.

My arms and my legs, however, I do not treat indulgently, I do not treat my warriors indulgently: how then could you be fit for my warfare?

With you I should spoil all my victories. And many of you would tumble over if you but heard the loud beating of my drums.

Moreover, you are not sufficiently beautiful and well-born for me. I require pure, smooth mirrors for my doctrines; on your surface even my own likeness is distorted.

On your shoulders presses many a burden, many a recollection; many a mischievous dwarf squats in your corners. There is concealed rabble also in you.

And though you be high and of a higher type, much in you is

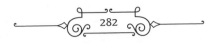

crooked and misshapen. There is no smith in the world that could hammer you right and straight for me.

You are only bridges: may higher ones pass over upon you! You signify steps: so do not upbraid him who ascends beyond you into his height!

Out of your seed there may one day arise for me a genuine son and perfect heir: but that time is distant. You yourselves are not those to whom my heritage and name belong.

Not for you do I wait here in these mountains; not with you may I descend for the last time. You have come to me only as a presage that higher ones are on the way to me,

—Not the men of great longing, of great loathing, of great satiety, and that which you call the remnant of God;

—No! No! Three times No! For others do I wait here in these mountains, and will not lift my foot from thence without them;

—For higher ones, stronger ones, triumphanter ones, merrier ones, for such as are built squarely in body and soul: laughing lions must come!

O my guests, you strange ones – have you yet heard nothing of my children? And that they are on the way to me?

Do speak to me of my gardens, of my Blessed isles, of my new beautiful race – why do you not speak to me thereof?

This guests'-present do I solicit of your love, that you speak to me of my children. For them am I rich, for them I became poor: what have I not surrendered.

What would I not surrender that I might have one thing these children, this living plantation, these life-trees of my will and of my highest hope!'

Thus spoke Zarathustra, and stopped suddenly: for his longing came over him, and he closed his eyes and his mouth, because of the agitation of his heart. And all his guests also were silent, and stood

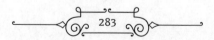

still and confounded: except only that the old soothsayer made signs with his hands and his gestures.

72. *The Last Supper*

FOR at this point the soothsayer interrupted the greeting of Zarathustra and his guests: he pressed forward as one who had no time to lose, seized Zarathustra's hand and exclaimed: 'But Zarathustra!

One thing is more necessary than the other, so say you yourself: well, one thing is now more necessary to me than all others.

A word at the right time: did you not invite me to table? And here are many who have made long journeys. You do not mean to feed us merely with speeches?

Besides, all of you have thought too much about freezing, drowning, suffocating, and other bodily dangers: none of you, however, have thought of my danger, namely, perishing of hunger—'

(Thus spoke the soothsayer. When Zarathustra's animals, however, heard these words, they ran away in terror. For they saw that all they had brought home during the day would not be enough to fill the one soothsayer.)

'Likewise perishing of thirst,' continued the soothsayer. 'And although I hear water splashing here like words of wisdom – that is to say, plenteously and unweariedly, I – want wine!

Not every one is a born water-drinker like Zarathustra. Neither does water suit weary and withered ones: we deserve wine – it alone gives immediate vigour and improvised health!'

On this occasion, when the soothsayer was longing for wine, it happened that the king on the left, the silent one, also found expression for once. 'We took care,' said he, 'about wine, I, along with my brother the king on the right: we have enough of wine, a whole ass-load of it. So there is nothing lacking but bread.'

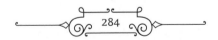

'Bread,' replied Zarathustra, laughing when he spoke, 'it is precisely bread that hermits have not. But man does not live by bread alone, but also by the flesh of good lambs, of which I have two:

—These shall we slaughter quickly, and cook spicily with sage: it is so that I like them. And there is also no lack of roots and fruits, good enough even for the fastidious and dainty, nor of nuts and other riddles for cracking.

Thus will we have a good repast in a little while. But whoever wishes to eat with us must also give a hand to the work, even the kings. For with Zarathustra even a king may be a cook.'

This proposal appealed to the hearts of all of them, save that the voluntary beggar objected to the flesh and wine and spices.

'Just hear this glutton Zarathustra!' said he jokingly: 'does one go into caves and high mountains to make such repasts?

Now indeed do I understand what he once taught us: "Blessed be moderate poverty!" And why he wishes to do away with beggars.'

'Be of good cheer,' replied Zarathustra, 'as I am. Abide by your customs, you excellent one: grind your corn, drink your water, praise your cooking, if only it make you glad!

I am a law only for my own; I am not a law for all. Yet he who belongs to me must be strong of bone and light of foot,

—Joyous in fight and feast, no sulker, no John o' Dreams, ready for the hardest task as for the feast, healthy and hale.

The best belongs to mine and me; and if it be not given us, then do we take it: the best food, the purest sky, the strongest thoughts, the fairest women!'—

Thus spoke Zarathustra; the king on the right however answered and said: 'Strange! Did one ever hear such sensible things out of the mouth of a wise man?

And verily, it is the strangest thing in a wise man, if over and above, he be still sensible, and not an ass.'

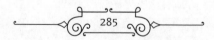

Thus spoke the king on the right and wondered; the ass however, with ill-will, said YE-A to his remark. This however was the beginning of that long repast which is called 'The Supper' in the history-books. At this there was nothing else spoken of but *the higher man*.

73. The Higher Man

1

'WHEN I came to men for the first time, then did I commit the hermit folly, the great folly: I appeared on the marketplace.

And when I spoke to all, I spoke to none. In the evening, however, rope-dancers were my companions, and corpses; and I myself almost a corpse.

With the new morning, however, there came to me a new truth: then did I learn to say: "Of what account to me are marketplace and rabble and rabble-noise and long rabble-ears!"

You higher men, learn this from me: On the marketplace no one believes in higher men. But if you will speak there, very well! The rabble, however, blinks: "We are all equal."

"You higher men," – so blinks the rabble – "there are no higher men, we are all equal; man is man, before God – we are all equal!"

Before God! Now, however, this God has died. Before the rabble, however, we will not be equal. You higher men, away from the marketplace!

2

'Before God! Now however this God has died! You higher men, this God was your greatest danger.

Only since he lay in the grave have you again arisen. Now only comes the great noontide, now only does the higher man become – master!

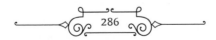

Have you understood this word, O my brothers? You are frightened: do your hearts turn giddy? does the abyss here yawn for you? does the hellhound here yelp at you?

Well! Take heart! you higher men! Now only travails the mountain of the human future. God has died: now do we desire – the Superman to live.'

3

'The most careful ask today: "How is man to be maintained?" Zarathustra however asks, as the first and only one: "How is man to be overcome?"

The Superman, I have at heart; that is the first and only thing to me – and not man: not the neighbour, not the poorest, not the sorriest, not the best.

O my brothers, what I can love in man is that he is an over-going and a down-going. And also in you there is much that makes me love and hope.

In that you have despised, you higher men, that makes me hope. For the great despisers are the great reverers.

In that you have despaired, there is much to honour. For you have not learned to submit yourselves, you have not learned petty policy.

For today have the petty people become master: they all preach submission and humility and policy and diligence and consideration and the long et cetera of petty virtues.

Whatever is of the effeminate type, whatever originates from the servile type, and especially the rabble-mishmash: that wishes now to be master of all human destiny – O disgust! Disgust! Disgust!

That asks and asks and never tires: "How is man to maintain himself best, longest, most pleasantly?" Thereby – are they the masters of today.

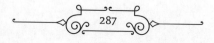

These masters of today – overcome them, O my brothers – these petty people: they are the Superman's greatest danger!

Overcome, you higher men, the petty virtues, the petty policy, the sand-grain considerateness, the ant-hill trumpery, the pitiable comfortableness, the "happiness of the greatest number"—!

And rather despair than submit yourselves. And verily, I love you, because you know not today how to live, you higher men! For thus do you live – best!'

4

'Have you courage, O my brothers? Are you stout-hearted? Not the courage before witnesses, but hermit and eagle courage, which not even a God any longer beholds?

Cold souls, mules, the blind and the drunken, I do not call stout-hearted. He has heart who knows fear, but vanquishes it; who sees the abyss, but with pride.

He who sees the abyss, but with eagle's eyes, he who with eagle's talons grasps the abyss: he has courage.'—

5

'"Man is evil" – so said to me for consolation, all the wisest ones. Ah, if only it be still true today! For the evil is man's best force.

"Man must become better and eviler" – so do I teach. The evilest is necessary for the Superman's best.

It may have been well for the preacher of the petty people to suffer and be burdened by men's sin. I, however, rejoice in great sin as my great consolation.

Such things, however, are not said for long ears. Every word, also, is not suited for every mouth. These are fine far-away things: at them sheep's claws shall not grasp!'

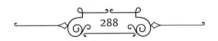

6

'You higher men, think you that I am here to put right what you have put wrong?

Or that I wished henceforth to make snugger couches for you sufferers? Or show you restless, miswandering, misclimbing ones, new and easier footpaths?

No! No! Three times No! Always more, always better ones of your type shall perish, for you shall always have it worse and harder. Thus only—

—Thus only grows man aloft to the height where the lightning strikes and shatters him: high enough for the lightning!

Towards the few, the long, the remote go forth my soul and my seeking: of what account to me are your many little, short miseries!

You do not yet suffer enough for me! For you suffer from yourselves, you have not yet suffered from man. You would lie if you spoke otherwise! None of you suffers from what I have suffered.'—

7

'It is not enough for me that the lightning no longer does harm. I do not wish to conduct it away: it shall learn – to work for me.

My wisdom has accumulated long like a cloud, it becomes stiller and darker. So does all wisdom which shall one day bear lightnings.

To these men of today will I not be light, nor be called light. Them – will I blind: lightning of my wisdom! Put out their eyes!'

8

'Do not will anything beyond your power: there is a bad falseness in those who will beyond their power.

Especially when they will great things! For they awaken distrust in great things, these subtle false-coiners and stage-players:

– Until at last they are false towards themselves, squint-eyed,

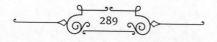

whited cankers, glossed over with strong words, parade virtues and brilliant false deeds.

Take good care there, you higher men! For nothing is more precious to me, and rarer, than honesty.

Is this today not that of the rabble? The rabble however knows not what is great and what is small, what is straight and what is honest: it is innocently crooked, it ever lies.'

9

'Have a good distrust today you, higher men, you enheartened ones! You open-hearted ones! And keep your reasons secret! For this today is that of the rabble.

What the rabble once learned to believe without reasons, who could – refute it to them by means of reasons?

And on the marketplace one convinces with gestures. But reasons make the rabble distrustful.

And when truth has once triumphed there, then ask yourselves with good distrust: "What strong error has fought for it?"

Be on your guard also against the learned! They hate you, because they are unproductive! They have cold, withered eyes before which every bird is unplumed.

Such persons vaunt about not lying: but inability to lie is still far from being love to truth. Be on your guard!

Freedom from fever is still far from being knowledge! Refrigerated spirits I do not believe in. He who cannot lie, does not know what truth is.'

10

'If you would go up high, then use your own legs! Do not get yourselves carried aloft; do not seat yourselves on other people's backs and heads!

You have mounted, however, on horseback? You now ride briskly

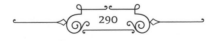

up to your goal? Well, my friend! But your lame foot is also with you on horseback!

When you reach your goal, when you alight from your horse: precisely on your height, you higher man, then will you stumble!'

11

'You creators, you higher men! One is only pregnant with one's own child.

Do not let yourselves be imposed upon or put upon! Who then is your neighbour? Even if you act "for your neighbour" – you still do not create for him!

Unlearn, I pray you, this "for," you creators: your very virtue wishes you to have naught to do with "for" and "on account of" and "because." Against these false little words shall you stop your ears.

"For one's neighbour," is the virtue only of the petty people: there it is said "like and like," and "hand washes hand": they have neither the right nor the power for your self-seeking!

In your self-seeking, you creators, there is the foresight and foreseeing of the pregnant! What no one's eye has yet seen, namely, the fruit – this, shelters and saves and nourishes your entire love.

Where your entire love is, namely, with your child, there is also your entire virtue! Your work, your will is your "neighbour": let no false values impose upon you!'

12

'You creators, you higher men! Whoever has to give birth is sick; whoever has given birth, however, is unclean.

Ask women: one gives birth, not because it gives pleasure. The pain makes hens and poets cackle.

You creators, in you there is much uncleanliness. That is because you have had to be mothers.

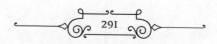

A new child: oh, how much new filth has also come into the world! Go apart! He who has given birth shall wash his soul!'

13

'Be not virtuous beyond your powers! And seek nothing from yourselves opposed to probability!

Walk in the footsteps in which your fathers' virtue has already walked! How would you rise high, if your fathers' will should not rise with you?

Yet he who would be a firstling, let him take care lest he also become a lastling! And where the vices of your fathers are, there should you not set up as saints!

He whose fathers were inclined for women, and for strong wine and flesh of wildboar swine; what would it be if he demanded chastity of himself?

A folly would it be! Much, verily, does it seem to me for such a one, if he should be the husband of one or of two or of three women.

And if he founded monasteries, and inscribed over their portals: "The way to holiness," – I should still say: What good is it! it is a new folly!

He has founded for himself a penance-house and refuge-house: much good may it do! But I do not believe in it.

In solitude there grows what any one brings into it – also the brute in one's nature. Thus is solitude inadvisable to many.

Has there ever been anything filthier on earth than the saints of the wilderness? Around them was not only the devil loose – but also the swine.'

14

'Shy, ashamed, awkward, like the tiger whose spring has failed – thus, you higher men, have I often seen you slink aside. A cast which you made had failed.

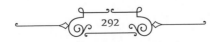

But what does it matter, you dice-players! You had not learned to play and mock, as one must play and mock! Do we not ever sit at a great table of mocking and playing?

And if great things have been a failure with you, have you yourselves therefore – been a failure? And if you yourselves have been a failure, has man therefore – been a failure? If man, however, has been a failure: well then! never mind!'

15

'The higher its type, always the seldomer does a thing succeed. You higher men here, have you not all – been failures?

Be of good cheer; what does it matter? How much is still possible! Learn to laugh at yourselves, as you ought to laugh!

What wonder even that you have failed and only half – succeeded, you half-shattered ones! Do not – man's future strive and struggle in you?

Man's furthest, profoundest, star-highest issues, his prodigious powers – do not all these foam through one another in your vessel?

What wonder that many a vessel shatters! Learn to laugh at yourselves, as you ought to laugh! You higher men, Oh, how much is still possible!

And verily, how much has already succeeded! How rich is this earth in small, good, perfect things, in well-constituted things!

Set around you small, good, perfect things, you higher men. Their golden maturity heals the heart. The perfect teaches one to hope.'

16

'What has hitherto been the greatest sin here on earth? Was it not the word of him who said: "Woe to them that laugh now!"

Did he himself find no cause for laughter on the earth? Then he sought badly. A child even finds cause for it.

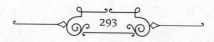

He – did not love sufficiently: otherwise would he also have loved us, the laughing ones! But he hated and hooted us; wailing and teeth-gnashing did he promise us.

Must one then curse immediately, when one does not love? That – seems to me bad taste. Thus did he, however, this absolute one. He sprang from the rabble.

And he himself just did not love sufficiently; otherwise would he have raged less because people did not love him. All great love does not seek love: it seeks more.

Go out of the way of all such absolute ones! They are a poor sickly type, a rabble-type: they look at this life with ill-will, they have an evil eye for this earth.

Go out of the way of all such absolute ones! They have heavy feet and sultry hearts: they do not know how to dance. How could the earth be light to such ones!'

17

'Tortuously do all good things come nigh to their goal. Like cats they curve their backs, they purr inwardly with their approaching happiness, all good things laugh.

His step betrays whether a person already walks on his own path: just see me walk! Yet he who comes nigh to his goal, dances.

And verily, a statue have I not become, not yet do I stand there stiff, stupid and stony, like a pillar; I love fast racing.

And though there be on earth fens and dense afflictions, he who has light feet runs even across the mud, and dances, as upon well-swept ice.

Lift up your hearts, my brothers, high, higher! And do not forget your legs! Lift up also your legs, you good dancers, and better still, if you stand upon your heads!'

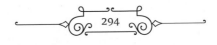

18

'This crown of the laughter, this rose-garland crown: I myself have put on this crown, I myself have consecrated my laughter. No one else have I found today potent enough for this.

Zarathustra the dancer, Zarathustra the light one, who beckons with his pinions, one ready for flight, beckoning to all birds, ready and prepared, a blissfully light-spirited one:

Zarathustra the soothsayer, Zarathustra the sooth-laugher, no impatient one, no absolute one, one who loves leaps and side-leaps; I myself have put on this crown!'

19

'Lift up your hearts, my brothers, high, higher! And do not forget your legs! Lift up also your legs, you good dancers, and better still if you stand upon your heads!

There are also heavy animals in a state of happiness, there are club-footed ones from the beginning. Curiously do they exert themselves, like an elephant which endeavours to stand upon its head.

Better, however, to be foolish with happiness than foolish with misfortune, better to dance awkwardly than walk lamely. So learn, I pray you, my wisdom, you higher men: even the worst thing has two good reverse sides,

—Even the worst thing has good dancing-legs: so learn, I pray you, you higher men, to put yourselves on your proper legs!

So unlearn, I pray you, the sorrow-sighing, and all the rabble – sadness! Oh, how sad the fools of the rabble seem to me today! This today, however, is that of the rabble.'

20

'Do like to the wind when it rushes forth from its mountain-caves: to its own piping will it dance; the seas tremble and leap under its footsteps.

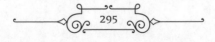

That which gives wings to asses, that which milks the lionesses: praised be that good, unruly spirit, which comes like a hurricane to all the present and to all the rabble,

—Which is hostile to thistle-heads and puzzle-heads, and to all withered leaves and weeds: praised be this wild, good, free spirit of the storm, which dances upon fens and afflictions, as upon meadows!

Which hates the consumptive rabble-dogs, and all the ill-constituted, sullen brood: praised be this spirit of all free spirits, the laughing storm, which blows dust into the eyes of all the melanopic and melancholic!

You higher men, the worst thing in you is that you have none of you learned to dance as you ought to dance – to dance beyond yourselves! What does it matter that you have failed!

How many things are still possible! So learn to laugh beyond yourselves! Lift up your hearts, you good dancers, high! Higher! And do not forget the good laughter!

This crown of the laughter, this rose-garland crown: to you, my brothers, do I cast this crown! Laughing have I consecrated; you higher men, learn, I pray you – to laugh!'

74. *The Song of Melancholy*

1

WHEN Zarathustra spoke these sayings, he stood nigh to the entrance of his cave; with the last words, however, he slipped away from his guests, and fled for a little while into the open air.

'O pure odours around me,' cried he, 'O blessed stillness around me! But where are my animals? Here, here, my eagle and my serpent!

Tell me, my animals: these higher men, all of them – do they

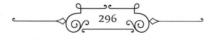

perhaps not smell well? O pure odours around me! Now only do I know and feel how I love you, my animals.'

—And Zarathustra said once more: 'I love you, my animals!' The eagle, however, and the serpent pressed close to him when he spoke these words, and looked up to him. In this attitude were they all three silent together, and sniffed and sipped the good air with one another. For the air here outside was better than with the higher men.

2

Hardly, however, had Zarathustra left the cave when the old magician got up, looked cunningly about him, and said: 'He is gone!

And already, you higher men – let me tickle you with this complimentary and flattering name, as he himself does – already does my evil spirit of deceit and magic attack me, my melancholy devil,

—Which is an adversary to this Zarathustra from the very heart: forgive it for this! Now does it wish to beseech before you, it has just its hour; in vain do I struggle with this evil spirit.

To all of you, whatever honours you like to assume in your names, whether you call yourselves "the free spirits" or "the conscientious," or "the penitents of the spirit," or "the unfettered," or "the great longers,"

—To all of you, who like me suffer from the great loathing, to whom the old God has died, and as yet no new God lies in cradles and swaddling clothes – to all of you is my evil spirit and magic – devil favourable.

I know you, you higher men, I know him, I know also this fiend whom I love in spite of me, this Zarathustra: he himself often seems to me like the beautiful mask of a saint,

—Like a new strange mummery in which my evil spirit, the melancholy devil, delights: I love Zarathustra, so does it often seem to me, for the sake of my evil spirit.

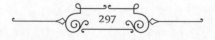

But already does it attack me and constrain me, this spirit of melancholy, this evening-twilight devil: and verily, you higher men, it has a longing—

—Open your eyes! It has a longing to come naked, whether male or female, I do not yet know: but it comes, it constrains me, alas! Open your wits!

The day dies out, to all things comes now the evening, also to the best things; hear now, and see, you higher men, what devil – man or woman – this spirit of evening-melancholy is!'

Thus spoke the old magician, looked cunningly about him, and then seized his harp.

3

'In evening's limpid air,
What time the dew's soothings
To the earth downpour,
Invisibly and unheard—
For tender shoe-gear wear
The soothing dews, like all that's kind-gentle:
Bethinkst you then, bethinkst you, burning heart,
How once you thirstedest
For heaven's kindly teardrops and dew's down-droppings,
All singed and weary thirstedest,
What time on yellow grass-pathways
Wicked, occidental sunny glances
Through sombre trees about you sported,
Blindingly sunny glow-glances, gladly-hurting?

"Of truth the wooer? You?" – so taunted they—
No! Merely poet!
A brute insidious, plundering, grovelling,

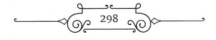

That aye must lie,
That wittingly, wilfully, aye must lie:
For booty lusting,
Motley masked,
Self-hidden, shrouded,
Himself his booty—
He – of truth the wooer?
No! Mere fool! Mere poet!
Just motley speaking,
From mask of fool confusedly shouting,
Circumambling on fabricated word-bridges,
On motley rainbow-arches,
'Twixt the spurious heavenly,
And spurious earthly,
Round us roving, round us soaring,
Mere fool! Mere poet!

He – of truth the wooer?
Not still, stiff, smooth and cold,
Become an image,
A godlike statue,
Set up in front of temples,
As a God's own door-guard:
No! Hostile to all such truthfulness-statues,
In every desert homelier than at temples,
With cattish wantonness,
Through every window leaping
Quickly into chances,
Every wild forest a-sniffing,
Greedily-longingly, sniffing,
That you, in wild forests,

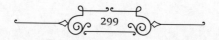

'Mong the motley-speckled fierce creatures,
Shouldest rove, sinful-sound and fine-coloured,
With longing lips smacking,
Blessedly mocking, blessedly hellish, blessedly blood-thirsty,
Robbing, skulking, lying – roving:

Or to eagles like which fixedly,
Long adown the precipice look,
Adown their precipice:
Oh, how they whirl down now,
Thereunder, therein,
To ever deeper profoundness whirling!
Then,
Sudden,
With aim aright,
With quivering flight,
On lambkins pouncing,
Headlong down, sore-hungry,
For lambkins longing,
Fierce 'gainst all lamb – spirits,
Furious-fierce all that look
Sheeplike, or lambeyed, or crisp-woolly,
—Grey, with lambsheep kindliness!

Even thus,
Eaglelike, pantherlike,
Are the poet's desires,
Are your own desires 'neath a thousand guises.
You fool! You poet!
You who all mankind viewed—
So God, as sheep:

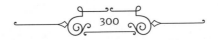

The God to rend within mankind,
As the sheep in mankind,
And in rending laughing—

That, that is your own blessedness!
Of a panther and eagle – blessedness!
Of a poet and fool – the blessedness!—

In evening's limpid air,
What time the moon's sickle,
Green, 'twixt the purple-glowings,
And jealous, steal'th forth:
—Of day the foe,
With every step in secret,
The rosy garland-hammocks
Downsickling, till they've sunken
Down nightwards, faded, downsunken:

Thus had I sunken one day
From mine own truth-insanity,
From mine own fervid day-longings,
Of day aweary, sick of sunshine,
—Sunk downwards, evenwards, shadowwards:
By one sole trueness
All scorched and thirsty:
—Bethinkst you still, bethinkst you, burning heart,
How then you thirstedest?
That I should banned be
From all the trueness!
Mere fool! Mere poet!'

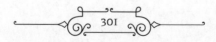

75. Science

THUS sang the magician; and all who were present went like birds unawares into the net of his artful and melancholy voluptuousness. Only the spiritually conscientious one had not been caught: he at once snatched the harp from the magician and called out: 'Air! Let in good air! Let in Zarathustra! you make this cave sultry and poisonous, you bad old magician!

You seduce, you false one, you subtle one, to unknown desires and deserts. And alas, that such as you should talk and make ado about the truth!

Alas, to all free spirits who are not on their guard against such magicians! It is all over with their freedom: you teach and tempt back into prisons,

—You old melancholy devil, out of your lament sounds a lurement: you resemble those who with their praise of chastity secretly invite to voluptuousness!'

Thus spoke the conscientious one; the old magician, however, looked about him, enjoying his triumph, and on that account put up with the annoyance which the conscientious one caused him. 'Be still!' said he with modest voice, 'good songs want to re-echo well; after good songs one should be long silent.

Thus do all those present, the higher men. You, however, have perhaps understood but little of my song? In you there is little of the magic spirit.'

'You praise me,' replied the conscientious one, 'in that you separate me from yourself; very well! But, you others, what do I see? You still sit there, all of you, with lusting eyes:

You free spirits, where has your freedom gone! You almost seem to me to resemble those who have long looked at bad girls dancing naked: your souls themselves dance!

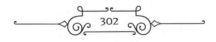

In you, you higher men, there must be more of that which the magician calls his evil spirit of magic and deceit: we must indeed be different.

And verily, we spoke and thought long enough together before. Zarathustra came home to his cave, for me not to be unaware that we are different.

We seek different things even here aloft, you and I. For I seek more security; on that account have I come to Zarathustra. For he is still the most steadfast tower and will—

—Today, when everything totters, when all the earth quakes. You, however, when I see what eyes you make, it almost seems to me that you seek more insecurity,

—More horror, more danger, more earthquake. You long (it almost seems so to me – forgive my presumption, you higher men)—

—You long for the worst and dangerousest life, which frightens me most, for the life of wild beasts, for forests, caves, steep mountains and labyrinthine gorges.

And it is not those who lead out of danger that please you best, but those who lead you away from all paths, the misleaders. But if such longing in you be actual, it seems to me nevertheless to be impossible.

For fear – that is man's original and fundamental feeling; through fear everything is explained, original sin and original virtue. Through fear there grew also my virtue, that is to say: Science.

For fear of wild animals – that has been longest fostered in man, inclusive of the animal which he conceals and feares in himself: Zarathustra calls it "the beast inside."

Such prolonged ancient fear, at last become subtle, spiritual and intellectual – at present, me thinks, it is called Science.'—

Thus spoke the conscientious one; but Zarathustra, who had just come back into his cave and had heard and divined the last conversation, threw a handful of roses to the conscientious one, and laughed

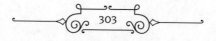

on account of his 'truths.' 'Why!' he exclaimed, 'what did I hear just now? it seems to me, you are a fool, or else I myself am one: and quietly and quickly will I Put your "truth" upside down.

For fear – is an exception with us. Courage, however, and adventure, and delight in the uncertain, in the unattempted – courage seems to me the entire primitive history of man.

The wildest and most courageous animals has he envied and robbed of all their virtues: thus only did he become – man.

This courage, at last become subtle, spiritual and intellectual, this human courage, with eagle's pinions and serpent's wisdom: this, it seems to me, is called at present – '

'Zarathustra!' cried all of them there assembled, as if with one voice, and burst out at the same time into a great laughter; there arose, however, from them as it were a heavy cloud. Even the magician laughed, and said wisely: 'Well! It is gone, my evil spirit!

And did I not myself warn you against it when I said that it was a deceiver, a lying and deceiving spirit?

Especially when it shows itself naked. But what can I do with regard to its tricks! Have I created it and the world?

Well! Let us be good again, and of good cheer! And although Zarathustra looks with evil eye – just see him! he dislikes me:

—Ere night comes will he again learn to love and laud me; he cannot live long without committing such follies.

He – loves his enemies: this art knows he better than any one I have seen. But he takes revenge for it – on his friends!'

Thus spoke the old magician, and the higher men applauded him; so that Zarathustra went round, and mischievously and lovingly shook hands with his friends, like one who has to make amends and apologize to every one for something. When however he had thereby come to the door of his cave, lo, then had he again a longing for the good air outside, and for his animals, and wished to steal out.

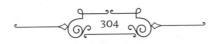

76. *Among Daughters of the Desert*

1

'GO NOT away!' said then the wanderer who called himself Zarathustra's shadow, 'abide with us – otherwise the old gloomy affliction might again fall upon us.

Now has that old magician given us of his worst for our good, and lo! The good, pious pope there has tears in his eyes, and has quite embarked again upon the sea of melancholy.

Those kings may well put on a good air before us still: for that have they learned best of us all at present! Had they however no one to see them, I wager that with them also the bad game would again commence,

—The bad game of drifting clouds, of damp melancholy, of curtained heavens, of stolen suns, of howling autumn-winds,

—The bad game of our howling and crying for help! Abide with us, O Zarathustra! Here there is much concealed misery that wishes to speak, much evening, much cloud, much damp air!

You have nourished us with strong food for men, and powerful aphorisms: do not let the weakly, womanly spirits attack us anew at dessert!

You alone make the air around you strong and clear. Did I ever find anywhere on earth such good air as with you in your cave?

Many lands have I seen, my nose has learned to test and estimate many kinds of air: but with you do my nostrils taste their greatest delight!

Unless it be, unless it be —, do forgive an old recollection! Forgive me an old after-dinner song, which I once composed amongst daughters of the desert:

For with them was there equally good, clear, Oriental air; there was I furthest from cloudy, damp, melancholy Old-Europe!

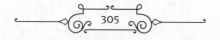

Then did I love such Oriental maidens and other blue kingdoms of heaven, over which hang no clouds and no thoughts.

You would not believe how charmingly they sat there, when they did not dance, profound, but without thoughts, like little secrets, like beribboned riddles, like dessert-nuts—

Many-hued and foreign, forsooth! But without clouds: riddles which can be guessed: to please such maidens I then composed an after-dinner psalm.'

Thus spoke the wanderer who called himself Zarathustra's shadow; and before any one answered him, he had seized the harp of the old magician, crossed his legs, and looked calmly and sagely around him: with his nostrils, however, he inhaled the air slowly and questioningly, like one who in new countries tastes new foreign air. Afterward he began to sing with a kind of roaring.

2.

'The deserts grow: woe him who does them hide!

—Ha!
Solemnly!
In effect solemnly!
A worthy beginning!
Afric manner, solemnly!
Of a lion worthy,
Or perhaps of a virtuous howl-monkey—
—But it's naught to you,
You friendly damsels dearly loved,
At whose own feet to me,
The first occasion,
To a European under palm-trees,
At seat is now granted. Selah.

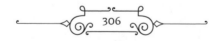

Wonderful, truly!
Here do I sit now,
The desert nigh, and yet I am
So far still from the desert,
Even in naught yet deserted:
That is, I'm swallowed down
By this the small oasis:
—It opened up just yawning,
Its loveliest mouth agape,
Most sweet-odoured of all mouthlets:
Then fell I right in,
Right down, right through – in 'mong you,
You friendly damsels dearly loved! Selah.
Hail! Hail! To that whale, fishlike,
If it thus for its guest's convenience
Made things nice! (you well know,
Surely, my learned allusion?)
Hail to its belly,
If it had e'er
A such loveliest oasis-belly
As this is: though however I doubt about it,
—With this come I out of Old-Europe,
That doubt'th more eagerly than do any
Elderly married woman.
May the Lord improve it!
Amen!

Here do I sit now,
In this the small oasis,
Like a date indeed,
Brown, quite sweet, gold-suppurating,

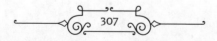

For rounded mouth of maiden longing,
But yet still more for youthful, maidlike,
Ice-cold and snow-white and incisory
Front teeth: and for such assuredly,
Pine the hearts all of ardent date-fruits. Selah.

To the there-named south-fruits now,
Similar, all-too-similar,
Do I lie here; by little
Flying insects
Round-sniffled and round-played,
And also by yet littler,
Foolisher, and peccabler
Wishes and phantasies,
Environed by you,
You silent, presentientest
Maiden-kittens,
Dudu and Suleika,
—Round sphinxed, that into one word
I may crowd much feeling:
(Forgive me, O God,
All such speech-sinning!)
—Sit I here the best of air sniffling,
Paradisal air, truly,
Bright and buoyant air, golden-mottled,
As goodly air as ever
From lunar orb downfell—
Be it by hazard,
Or supervened it by arrogancy?
As the ancient poets relate it.
But doubter, I'm now calling it

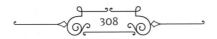

In question: with this do I come indeed
Out of Europe,
That doubt'th more eagerly than do any
Elderly married woman.
May the Lord improve it!
Amen.

This the finest air drinking,
With nostrils out-swelled like goblets,
Lacking future, lacking remembrances,
Thus do I sit here, ye
Friendly damsels dearly loved,
And look at the palm-tree there,
How it, to a dance-girl, like,
Do bow and bend and on its haunches bob,
—One does it too, when one view'th it long!
To a dance-girl like, who as it seem'th to me,
Too long, and dangerously persistent,
Always, always, just on single leg has stood?
—Then forgot she thereby, as it seem'th to me,
The other leg?
For vainly I, at least,
Did search for the amissing
Fellow-jewel
—Namely, the other leg—
In the sanctified precincts,
Nigh her very dearest, very tenderest,
Flapping and fluttering and flickering skirting.
Yes, if you should, you beauteous friendly ones,
Quite take my word:
She hath, alas! Lost it!

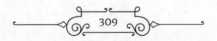

Hu! Hu! Hu! Hu! Hu!
It is away!
For ever away!
The other leg!
Oh, pity for that loveliest other leg!
Where may it now tarry, all-forsaken weeping?
The most lonesome leg?
In fear perhaps before a
Furious, yellow, blond and curled
Leonine monster? Or perhaps even
Gnawed away, nibbled badly—
Most wretched, woeful! Woeful! Nibbled badly! Selah.

Oh, weep you not,
Gentle spirits!
Weep you not, ye
Date-fruit spirits! Milk-bosoms!
You sweetwood-heart
Purselets!
Weep you no more,
Pallid Dudu!
Be a man, Suleika! Bold! Bold!
—Or else should there perhaps
Something strengthening, heart-strengthening,
Here most proper be?
Some inspiring text?
Some solemn exhortation?
Ha! Up now! Honour!
Moral honour! European honour!
Blow again, continue,

Bellows-box of virtue!
Ha!
Once more your roaring,
Your moral roaring!
As a virtuous lion
Nigh the daughters of deserts roaring!
—For virtue's out-howl,
You very dearest maidens,
Is more than every
European fervour, European hot-hunger!
And now do I stand here,
As European,
I can't be different, God's help to me!
Amen!

The deserts grow: woe him who do them hide!'

77. *The Awakening*

1

AFTER the song of the wanderer and shadow, the cave became all at once full of noise and laughter: and since the assembled guests all spoke simultaneously, and even the ass, encouraged thereby, no longer remained silent, a little aversion and scorn for his visitors came over Zarathustra, although he rejoiced at their gladness. For it seemed to him a sign of convalescence. So he slipped out into the open air and spoke to his animals.

'Where has their distress now gone?' said he, and already did he himself feel relieved of his petty disgust – 'with me, it seems that they have unlearned their cries of distress!

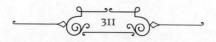

—Though, alas! Not yet their crying.' And Zarathustra stopped his ears, for just then did the YE-A of the ass mix strangely with the noisy jubilation of those higher men.

'They are merry,' he began again, 'and who knows? perhaps at their host's expense; and if they have learned of me to laugh, still it is not my laughter they have learned.

But what matter about that! They are old people: they recover in their own way, they laugh in their own way; my ears have already endured worse and have not become peevish.

This day is a victory: he already yields, he flees, the spirit of gravity, my old arch-enemy! How well this day is about to end, which began so badly and gloomily!

And it is about to end. Already comes the evening: over the sea rides it here, the good rider! How it bobs, the blessed one, the home-returning one, in its purple saddles!

The sky gazes brightly there, the world lies deep. Oh, all you strange ones who have come to me, it is already worth while to have lived with me!'

Thus spoke Zarathustra. And again came the cries and laughter of the higher men out of the cave: then began he anew:

'They bite at it, my bait takes, there departs also from them their enemy, the spirit of gravity. Now do they learn to laugh at themselves: do I hear rightly?

My virile food takes effect, my strong and savoury sayings: and verily, I did not nourish them with flatulent vegetables! But with warrior-food, with conqueror-food: new desires did I awaken.

New hopes are in their arms and legs, their hearts expand. They find new words, soon will their spirits breathe wantonness.

Such food may sure enough not be proper for children, nor even

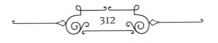

for longing girls old and young. One persuades their bowels otherwise; I am not their physician and teacher.

The disgust departs from these higher men; well! That is my victory. In my domain they become assured; all stupid shame flees away; they empty themselves.

They empty their hearts, good times return to them, they keep holiday and ruminate, they become thankful.

That do I take as the best sign: they become thankful. Not long will it be before they create festivals, and put up memorials to their old joys.

They are convalescents!' Thus spoke Zarathustra joyfully to his heart and gazed outward; his animals, however, pressed up to him, and honoured his happiness and his silence.

2

All on a sudden however, Zarathustra's ear was frightened: for the cave which had hitherto been full of noise and laughter, became all at once still as death; – his nose, however, smelt a sweet-scented vapor and incense-odour, as if from burning pinecones.

'What happens? What are they about?' he asked himself, and stole up to the entrance, that he might be able unobserved to see his guests. But wonder upon wonder! What was he then obliged to behold with his own eyes!

'They have all of them become pious again, they pray, they are mad!' – said he, and was astonished beyond measure. And forsooth! All these higher men, the two kings, the pope out of service, the evil magician, the voluntary beggar, the wanderer and shadow, the old soothsayer, the spiritually conscientious one, and the ugliest man – they all lay on their knees like children and credulous old women, and worshipped the ass. And just then began the ugliest man to gurgle and snort, as if

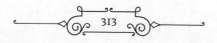

something unutterable in him tried to find expression; when, however, he had actually found words, behold! it was a pious, strange litany in praise of the adored and censed ass. And the litany sounded thus:

'Amen! And glory and honour and wisdom and thanks and praise and strength be to our God, from everlasting to everlasting!

—The ass, however, here brayed YE-A.

He carried our burdens, he has taken upon him the form of a servant, he is patient of heart and never says No; and he who loves his God chastises him.

—The ass, however, here brayed YE-A.

He speaks not: except that he ever says Yes to the world which he created: thus does he extol his world. It is his artfulness that speaks not: thus is he rarely found wrong.

—The ass, however, here brayed YE-A.

Uncomely goes he through the world. Grey is the favourite colour in which he wraps his virtue. Has he spirit, then does he conceal it; every one, however, believes in his long ears.

—The ass, however, here brayed YE-A.

What hidden wisdom it is to wear long ears, and only to say Yes and never No! Has he not created the world in his own image, namely, as stupid as possible?

—The ass, however, here brayed YE-A.

You go straight and crooked ways; it concerns you little what seems straight or crooked to us men. Beyond good and evil is your domain. It is your innocence not to know what innocence is.

—The ass, however, here brayed YE-A.

Lo! How you spurn none from you, neither beggars nor kings. You suffer little children to come to you, and when the bad boys decoy you, then say you simply, YE-A.

—The ass, however, here brayed YE-A.

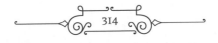

You love she-asses and fresh figs, you are no food-despiser. A thistle tickles your heart when you chance to be hungry. There is the wisdom of a God therein.

—The ass, however, here brayed YE-A.

78. *The Ass Festival*

1

AT THIS place in the litany, however, Zarathustra could no longer control himself; he himself cried out YE-A, louder even than the ass, and sprang into the midst of his maddened guests. 'Whatever are you about, you grown-up children?' he exclaimed, pulling up the praying ones from the ground. 'Alas, if any one else, except Zarathustra, had seen you:

Every one would think you the worst blasphemers, or the very most foolish old women, with your new belief!

And you yourself, you old pope, how is it in accordance with you, to adore an ass in such a manner as God?'—

'O Zarathustra,' answered the pope, 'forgive me, but in divine matters I am more enlightened even than you. And it is right that it should be so.

Better to adore God so, in this form, than in no form at all! Think over this saying, my exalted friend: you will readily divine that in such a saying there is wisdom.

He who said "God is a Spirit" – made the greatest stride and slide hitherto made on earth towards unbelief: such a dictum is not easily amended again on earth!

My old heart leaps and bounds because there is still something to adore on earth. Forgive it, O Zarathustra, to an old, pious pontiff-heart!'

—'And you,' said Zarathustra to the wanderer and shadow, 'you

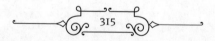

call and think yourself a free spirit? And you here practise such idolatry and hierolatry?

Worse verily, do you here than with your bad brown girls, you bad, new believer!'

'It is sad enough,' answered the wanderer and shadow, 'you are right: but how can I help it! The old God lives again, O Zarathustra, you mayst say what you wilt.

The ugliest man is to blame for it all: he has reawakened him. And if he say that he once killed him, with Gods death is always just a prejudice.'

—'And you,' said Zarathustra, 'you bad old magician, what did you do! Who ought to believe any longer in you in this free age, when you believe in such divine donkeyism?

It was a stupid thing that you didst; how could you, a shrewd man, do such a stupid thing!'

'O Zarathustra,' answered the shrewd magician, 'you are right, it was a stupid thing, it was also repugnant to me.'

—'And you even,' said Zarathustra to the spiritually conscientious one, 'consider, and put your finger to your nose! Does nothing go against your conscience here? Is your spirit not too cleanly for this praying and the fumes of those devotees?'

'There is something therein,' said the spiritually conscientious one, and put his finger to his nose, 'there is something in this spectacle which even does good to my conscience.

Perhaps I dare not believe in God: certain it is however, that God seems to me most worthy of belief in this form.

God is said to be eternal, according to the testimony of the most pious: he who has so much time takes his time. As slow and as stupid as possible: thereby can such a one nevertheless go very far.

And he who has too much spirit might well become infatuated with stupidity and folly. Think of yourself, O Zarathustra!

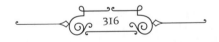

You yourself – verily! Even you could well become an ass through superabundance of wisdom.

Does not the true sage willingly walk on the crookedest paths? The evidence teaches it, O Zarathustra, your own evidence!'

—'And you yourself, finally,' said Zarathustra, and turned towards the ugliest man, who still lay on the ground stretching up his arm to the ass (for he gave it wine to drink). 'Say, you nondescript, what have you been about!

You seem to me transformed, your eyes glow, the mantle of the sublime covers your ugliness: what did you do?

Is it then true what they say, that you have again awakened him? And why? Was he not for good reasons killed and made away with?

You yourself seem to me awakened: what did you do? Why did you turn round? Why did you get converted? Speak, you nondescript!'

'O Zarathustra,' answered the ugliest man, 'you are a rogue!

Whether he yet lives, or again lives, or is thoroughly dead – which of us both knows that best? I ask you.

One thing however do I know, from yourself did I learn it once, O Zarathustra: he who wants to kill most thoroughly, laughs.

"Not by wrath but by laughter does one kill" – thus spoke you once, O Zarathustra, you hidden one, you destroyer without wrath, you dangerous saint, you are a rogue!'

2

Then, however, did it come to pass that Zarathustra, astonished at such merely roguish answers, jumped back to the door of his cave, and turning towards all his guests, cried out with a strong voice:

'O you wags, all of you, you fools! Why do you dissemble and disguise yourselves before me!

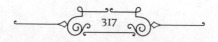

How the hearts of all of you convulsed with delight and wickedness, because you had at last become again like little children – namely, pious,

—Because you at last did again as children do – namely, prayed, folded your hands and said "good God"!

But now leave, I pray you, this nursery, my own cave, where today all childishness is carried on. Cool down, here outside, your hot child-wantonness and heart-tumult!

To be sure: except you become as little children you shall not enter into that kingdom of heaven.' (And Zarathustra pointed aloft with his hands.)

'But we do not at all want to enter into the kingdom of heaven: we have become men, so we want the kingdom of earth.'

3

And once more began Zarathustra to speak. 'O my new friends,' said he, 'you strange ones, you higher men, how well do you now please me,

—Since you have again become joyful! You have, verily, all blossomed forth: it seems to me that for such flowers as you, new festivals are required.

—A little valiant nonsense, some divine service and ass-festival, some old joyful Zarathustra fool, some blusterer to blow your souls bright. Forget not this night and this ass-festival, you higher men! That did you create when with me, that do I take as a good omen, such things only the convalescents create!

And should you celebrate it again, this ass-festival, do it from love to yourselves, do it also from love to me! And in remembrance of me!'

Thus spoke Zarathustra.

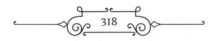

79. *The Drunken Song*

1

MEANWHILE one after another had gone out into the open air, and into the cool, thoughtful night; Zarathustra himself, however, led the ugliest man by the hand, that he might show him his night-world, and the great round moon, and the silvery waterfalls near his cave. There they at last stood still beside one another; all of them old people, but with comforted, brave hearts, and astonished in themselves that it was so well with them on earth; the mystery of the night, however, came closer and closer to their hearts. And anew Zarathustra thought to himself: 'Oh, how well do they now please me, these higher men!' – but he did not say it aloud, for he respected their happiness and their silence.

Then, however, there happened that which in this astonishing long day was most astonishing: the ugliest man began once more and for the last time to gurgle and snort, and when he had at length found expression, behold! there sprang a question plump and plain out of his mouth, a good, deep, clear question, which moved the hearts of all who listened to him.

'My friends, all of you,' said the ugliest man, 'what think ye? For the sake of this day – I am for the first time content to have lived my entire life.

And that I testify so much is still not enough for me. It is worth while living on the earth: one day, one festival with Zarathustra, has taught me to love the earth.

"Was that – life?" will I say to death. "Well! Once more!"

My friends, what think ye? Will you not, like me, say to death: "Was that – life? For the sake of Zarathustra, well! Once more!"'—

Thus spoke the ugliest man; it was not, however, far from midnight. And what took place then, think ye? As soon as the higher men heard his question, they became all at once conscious of their transformation

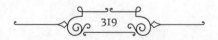

and convalescence, and of him who was the cause thereof: then did they rush up to Zarathustra, thanking, honouring, caressing him, and kissing his hands, each in his own peculiar way; so that some laughed and some wept. The old soothsayer, however, danced with delight; and though he was then, as some narrators suppose, full of sweet wine, he was certainly still fuller of sweet life, and had renounced all weariness. There are even those who narrate that the ass then danced: for not in vain had the ugliest man previously given it wine to drink. That may be the case, or it may be otherwise; and if in truth the ass did not dance that evening, there nevertheless happened then greater and rarer wonders than the dancing of an ass would have been. In short, as the aphorism of Zarathustra says: 'What does it matter!'

2

When, however, this took place with the ugliest man, Zarathustra stood there like one drunken: his glance dulled, his tongue faltered and his feet staggered. And who could divine what thoughts then passed through Zarathustra's soul? Apparently, however, his spirit retreated and fled in advance and was in remote distances, and as it were 'wandering on high mountain-ridges,' as it stands written, ''twixt two seas,

—Wandering 'twixt the past and the future as a heavy cloud.' Gradually, however, while the higher men held him in their arms, he came back to himself a little, and resisted with his hands the crowd of the honouring and caring ones; but he did not speak. All at once, however, he turned his head quickly, for he seemed to hear something: then laid he his finger on his mouth and said: 'Come!'

And immediately it became still and mysterious round about; from the depth however there came up slowly the sound of a clock-bell. Zarathustra listened thereto, like the higher men; then, however, laid he his finger on his mouth the second time, and said again: 'Come! Come! It is getting on to midnight!' – and his voice had changed. But

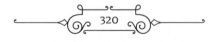

still he had not moved from the spot. Then it became yet stiller and more mysterious, and everything hearkened, even the ass, and Zarathustra's noble animals, the eagle and the serpent, likewise the cave of Zarathustra and the big cool moon, and the night itself. Zarathustra, however, laid his hand upon his mouth for the third time, and said:

'Come! Come! Come! Let us now wander! It is the hour: let us wander into the night!'

3

'You higher men, it is getting on to midnight: then will I say something into your ears, as that old clock-bell says it into my ear,

—As mysteriously, as frightfully, and as cordially as that midnight clock-bell speaks it to me, which has experienced more than one man:

—Which has already counted the smarting throbbings of your fathers' hearts – ah! ah! How it sighs! how it laughs in its dream! The old, deep, deep midnight!

Hush! Hush! Then is there many a thing heard which may not be heard by day; now however, in the cool air, when even all the tumult of your hearts has become still,

—Now does it speak, now is it heard, now does it steal into overwakeful, nocturnal souls: ah! ah! How the midnight sighs! How it laughs in its dream!

—Hear you not how it mysteriously, frightfully, and cordially speaks to you, the old deep, deep midnight?

O man, take heed!'

4

'Woe to me! Where has time gone? Have I not sunk into deep wells? The world sleeps—

Ah! Ah! The dog howls, the moon shins. Rather will I die, rather will I die, than say to you what my midnight-heart now thinks.

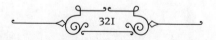

Already have I died. It is all over. Spider, why spin you around me? Will you have blood? Ah! Ah! The dew falls, the hour comes – The hour in which I frost and freeze, which asks and asks and asks: "Who has sufficient courage for it?

—Who is to be master of the world? Who is going to say: Thus shall you flow, you great and small streams!"

—The hour approaches: O man, you higher man, take heed! This talk is for fine ears, for your ears – what says deep midnight's voice indeed?'

5

'It carries me away, my soul dances. Day's-work! Day's-work! Who is to be master of the world?

The moon is cool, the wind is still. Ah! Ah! Have you already flown high enough? You have danced: a leg, nevertheless, is not a wing.

You good dancers, now is all delight over: wine has become lees, every cup has become brittle, the sepulchres mutter.

You have not flown high enough: now do the sepulchres mutter: "Free the dead! Why is it so long night? Does not the moon make us drunken?"

You higher men, free the sepulchres, awaken the corpses! Ah, why does the worm still burrow? There approaches, there approaches, the hour,

—There booms the clock-bell, there thrills still the heart, there burrows still the wood-worm, the heart-worm. Ah! Ah! The world is deep!'

6

'Sweet lyre! Sweet lyre! I love your tone, your drunken, ranunculine tone! How long, how far has come to me your tone, from the distance, from the ponds of love!

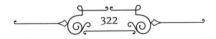

You old clock-bell, you sweet lyre! Every pain has torn your heart, father-pain, fathers'-pain, forefathers'-pain; your speech has become ripe,

—Ripe like the golden autumn and the afternoon, like my hermit heart – now say you: The world itself has become ripe, the grape turns brown,

—Now does it wish to die, to die of happiness. You higher men, do you not feel it? There wells up mysteriously an odour,

—A perfume and odour of eternity, a rosy-blessed, brown, gold-wine-odour of old happiness.

—Of drunken midnight-death happiness, which sings: the world is deep, and deeper than the day could read!'

7

'Leave me alone! Leave me alone! I am too pure for you. Touch me not! has not my world just now become perfect?

My skin is too pure for your hands. Leave me alone, you dull, doltish, stupid day! Is not the midnight brighter?

The purest are to be masters of the world, the least known, the strongest, the midnight-souls, who are brighter and deeper than any day.

O day, you grope for me? you feel for my happiness? For you am I rich, lonesome, a treasure-pit, a gold chamber?

O world, you want me? Am I worldly for you? Am I spiritual for you? Am I divine for you? But day and world, you are too coarse,

—Have cleverer hands, grasp after deeper happiness, after deeper unhappiness, grasp after some God; grasp not after me:

—My unhappiness, my happiness is deep, you strange day, but yet am I no God, no God's-hell: deep is its woe.'

8

'God's woe is deeper, you strange world! Grasp at God's woe, not at me! What am I! A drunken sweet lyre,

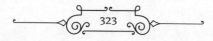

—A midnight-lyre, a bell-frog, which no one understands, but which must speak before deaf ones, you higher men! For you do not understand me!

Gone! Gone! O youth! O noontide! O afternoon! Now have come evening and night and midnight, the dog howls, the wind:

—Is the wind not a dog? It whines, it barks, it howls. Ah! Ah! How she sighs! How she laughs, how she wheezes and pants, the midnight!

How she just now speaks soberly, this drunken poetess! Has she perhaps overdrunk her drunkenness? Has she become overawake? does she ruminate?

—Her woe does she ruminate over, in a dream, the old, deep midnight – and still more her joy. For joy, although woe be deep, joy is deeper still than grief can be.'

9

'You grape-vine! Why do you praise me? Have I not cut you! I am cruel, you bleedest: what means your praise of my drunken cruelty?

"Whatever has become perfect, everything mature – wants to die!" So say you. Blessed, blessed be the vintner's knife! But everything immature wants to live: alas!

Woe says: "Hence! Go! Away, you woe!" But everything that suffers wants to live, that it may become mature and lively and longing,

—Longing for the further, the higher, the brighter. "I want heirs," so says everything that suffers, "I want children, I do not want myself,"

Joy, however, does not want heirs, it does not want children, joy wants itself, it wants eternity, it wants recurrence, it wants everything eternally-like-itself.

Woe says: "Break, bleed, you heart! Wander, you leg! You wing, fly! Onward! Upward! you pain!" Well! Cheer up! O my old heart: Woe says: "Hence! Go!"'

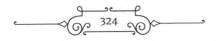

10

'You higher men, what think ye? Am I a soothsayer? Or a dreamer? Or a drunkard? Or a dream-reader? Or a midnight-bell?

Or a drop of dew? Or a fume and fragrance of eternity? Hear you it not? Smell you it not? Just now has my world become perfect, midnight is also midday,

Pain is also a joy, curse is also a blessing, night is also a sun, go away! Or you will learn that a sage is also a fool.

Said you ever Yes to one joy? O my friends, then said you Yes also to all woe. All things are enlinked, enlaced and enamoured,

—Wanted you ever once to come twice; said you ever: "You please me, happiness! Instant! Moment!" then wanted you all to come back again!

—All anew, all eternal, all enlinked, enlaced and enamoured, Oh, then did you love the world,

—You eternal ones, you love it eternally and for all time: and also to woe do you say: Hence! Go! but come back! For joys all want – eternity!'

11

'All joy wants the eternity of all things, it wants honey, it wants lees, it wants drunken midnight, it wants graves, it wants grave-tears' consolation, it wants gilded evening-red—

—What does not joy want! It is thirstier, heartier, hungrier, more frightful, more mysterious, than all woe: it wants itself, it bites into itself, the ring's will wriths in it,

—It wants love, it wants hate, it is over-rich, it gives, it throws away, it begs for some one to take from it, it thanks the taker, it would rather be hated,

—So rich is joy that it thirsts for woe, for hell, for hate, for shame, for the lame, for the world, for this world, Oh, you know it indeed!

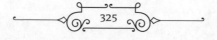

You higher men, for you does it long, this joy, this irrepressible, blessed joy – for your woe, you failures! For failures, longs all eternal joy.

For joys all want themselves, therefore do they also want grief! O happiness, O pain! Oh break, you heart! You higher men, do learn it, that joys want eternity.

—Joys want the eternity of all things, they want deep, profound eternity!'

12

'Have you now learned my song? Have you divined what it would say? Well! Cheer up! You higher men, sing now my roundelay!

Sing now yourselves the song, the name of which is "Once more," the signification of which is "To all eternity!" – sing, you higher men, Zarathustra's roundelay!

O man! Take heed!
What says deep midnight's voice indeed?
"I slept my sleep,
From deepest dream I've woke, and plead:
The world is deep,
And deeper than the day could read.
Deep is its woe,
Joy – deeper still than grief can be:
Woe says: Hence! Go!
But joys all want eternity,
Want deep, profound eternity!"'

80. The Sign

IN THE morning, however, after this night, Zarathustra jumped up from his couch, and, having girded his loins, he came out of his cave glowing and strong, like a morning sun coming out of gloomy mountains.

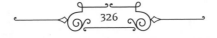

'You great star,' spoke he, as he had spoken once before, 'you deep eye of happiness, what would be all your happiness if you had not those for whom you shine!

And if they remained in their chambers whilst you are already awake, and come and give and distribute, how would your proud modesty upbraid for it!

Well! They still sleep, these higher men, whilst I am awake: they are not my proper companions! Not for them do I wait here in my mountains.

At my work I want to be, at my day: but they understand not what are the signs of my morning, my step – is not for them the awakening-call.

They still sleep in my cave; their dream still drinks at my drunken songs. The audient ear for me – the obedient ear, is yet lacking in their limbs.'

– This had Zarathustra spoken to his heart when the sun arose: then looked he inquiringly aloft, for he heard above him the sharp call of his eagle. 'Well!' called he upwards, 'thus is it pleasing and proper to me. My animals are awake, for I am awake.

My eagle is awake, and like me honours the sun. With eagle-talons does it grasp at the new light. You are my proper animals; I love you.

But still do I lack my proper men!'—

Thus spoke Zarathustra; then, however, it happened that all on a sudden he became aware that he was flocked around and fluttered around, as if by innumerable birds, the whizzing of so many wings, however, and the crowding around his head was so great that he shut his eyes. And verily, there came down upon him as it were a cloud, like a cloud of arrows which pours upon a new enemy. But behold, here it was a cloud of love, and showered upon a new friend.

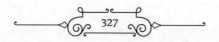

'What happens to me?' thought Zarathustra in his astonished heart, and slowly seated himself on the big stone which lay close to the exit from his cave. But while he grasped about with his hands, around him, above him and below him, and repelled the tender birds, behold, there then happened to him something still stranger: for he grasped thereby unawares into a mass of thick, warm, shaggy hair; at the same time, however, there sounded before him a roar, a long, soft lion-roar.

'The sign comes,' said Zarathustra, and a change came over his heart. And in truth, when it turned clear before him, there lay a yellow, powerful animal at his feet, resting its head on his knee, unwilling to leave him out of love, and doing like a dog which again finds its old master. The doves, however, were no less eager with their love than the lion; and whenever a dove whisked over its nose, the lion shook its head and wondered and laughed.

When all this went on Zarathustra spoke only a word: 'My children are nigh, my children', then he became quite mute. His heart, however, was loosed, and from his eyes there dropped down tears and fell upon his hands. And he took no further notice of anything, but sat there motionless, without repelling the animals further. Then flew the doves to and fro, and perched on his shoulder, and caressed his white hair, and did not tire of their tenderness and joyousness. The strong lion, however, licked always the tears that fell on Zarathustra's hands, and roared and growled shyly. Thus did these animals do.

All this went on for a long time, or a short time: for properly speaking, there is no time on earth for such things. Meanwhile, however, the higher men had awakened in Zarathustra's cave, and marshalled themselves for a procession to go to meet Zarathustra, and give him their morning greeting: for they had found when they awakened that he no longer tarried with them. When, however, they reached the door of the cave and the noise of their steps had preceded them, the lion started violently; it turned away all at once from Zarathustra, and roaring wildly, sprang towards the cave.

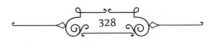

The higher men, however, when they heard the lion roaring, cried all aloud as with one voice, fled back and vanished in an instant.

Zarathustra himself, however, stunned and strange, rose from his seat, looked around him, stood there astonished, inquired of his heart, bethought himself, and remained alone. 'What did I hear?' said he at last, slowly, 'What happened to me just now?'

But soon there came to him his recollection, and he took in at a glance all that had taken place between yesterday and today. 'Here is indeed the stone,' said he, and stroked his beard, 'on it sat I yester-morn; and here came the soothsayer to me, and here heard I first the cry which I heard just now, the great cry of distress.

O you higher men, your distress was it that the old soothsayer foretold to me yester-morn,

—To your distress did he want to seduce and tempt me: "O Zarathustra," said he to me, "I come to seduce you to your last sin."

To my last sin?' cried Zarathustra, and laughed angrily at his own words: 'What has been reserved for me as my last sin?'

—And once more Zarathustra became absorbed in himself, and sat down again on the big stone and meditated. Suddenly he sprang up,

'Fellow-suffering! Fellow-suffering with the higher men!' he cried out, and his countenance changed into brass. 'Well! That – has had its time!

My suffering and my fellow-suffering – what matter about them! Do I then strive after happiness? I strive after my work!

Well! The lion has come, my children are nigh, Zarathustra has grown ripe, my hour has come:

This is my morning, my day begins: arise now, arise, you great noontide!'

Thus spoke Zarathustra and left his cave, glowing and strong, like a morning sun coming out of gloomy mountains.

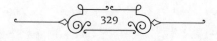

Ecce Homo

Translated by
Gerta Valentine

CONTENTS

PREFACE

1.

SINCE, sooner or later, I shall have to approach mankind with one of the most difficult tasks that has ever been asked of it, it seems inevitable that I must tell you *who I am*. It should really be known already: after all, I did present plenty of 'evidence'. However, the disproportion between the greatness of my task and the *triviality* of my peers has manifested itself in that I have not been heard, nor even been seen. I live on my own credit; is it perhaps just a preconception that I actually live?... I only need to speak to one of those 'learned men' that come visiting the Upper Engadine during the summer to become convinced that I do not live... Under such circumstances there is a duty against which my way of life, and quintessentially even more so my instincts revolt, that is to say: *Listen to me! for I am who I am. Above all, do not take me for someone else!*

2.

FOR instance, I am by no means a bogey man, nor am I a moral monster – far from it, I am actually the opposite to the type of man that hitherto has been admired as virtuous. Between you and me, I am really quite proud of it. I am a follower of the philosopher Dionysus; I should prefer to be a satyr rather than a saint. Just read this book to see what I mean. Perhaps I was able to throw some light on this polarity in a happy and

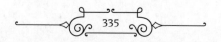

philanthropic way, perhaps this was the only point of this book. The last thing *I* should promise is to try and 'improve' mankind. You will not find me erecting new idols! The old may come to realize what it means to have feet of clay! To *topple* Idols (my word for 'ideals') comes somewhat closer to my craft. They deprived reality of its worth, its meaning, its truthfulness to the same extent to which they have *fabricated* an ideal world... The 'true world' and the 'apparent world', or to say it more plainly: the *fabricated* world and reality... The *lie* of the ideal has until now been the curse on reality; mankind itself has on account of it become dishonest and false down to its basest instincts – to the point of worshipping the *opposite* values from those which alone would guarantee success, a future, the lofty *right* to a future.

3.

THOSE who can breathe the air of my writing know that it is the air at the top of the mountains, a *strong* air. You have to be made for it, otherwise there is no small danger of catching cold from it. Ice is all around you, the loneliness is immense – but how quietly all things lie in the light! How freely you breathe! How much you feel lies *beneath* you! – Philosophy, as I have so far understood and lived it, is the voluntary life among ice and high mountains – seeking all that is foreign and dubious in existence, all that which so far has been outlawed by morality. From long experience, acquired on such a journey through *the forbidden*, I learned to look at the causes, which until now prompted moralizing and idealizing, in a very different light than may have been desired: the *hidden* history of the philosophers, the psychology of their great names became clear to me.

How much truth can the mind *bear*, how much truth does it *dare* to take in? This became more and more my real yardstick. Error (– faith in the ideal –) is not blindness, error is *cowardice*... Every accomplishment, every step forward in knowledge is a *consequence* of

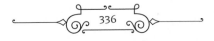

courage, from being hard on yourself, from your own cleanliness... I do not refute ideals, I merely put on gloves when I deal with them... We strive for the *forbidden*: under this sign, my philosophy shall triumph one day for they have basically always forbidden the truth alone.

<h1 style="text-align:center">4.</h1>

MY *Zarathustra* is unique among my books. With it, I gave mankind the most precious gift that it has been given up to now. This book, its voice spanning thousands of years, is not only the loftiest book in existence, a true mountain air book – the whole fact of what man is lies incredibly far *beneath* him – it is actually also the *deepest*, born out of the innermost wealth of truth, an inexhaustible well, where no pail will descend without coming up again brimming with gold and goodness. Here speaks no 'prophet', none of those dreadful hybrids of sickness and will to power commonly known as religious founders. Above all, you have to *hear* the tone coming from that mouth, this peaceful tone, as it should be *heard*, so you do not misjudge the sense of its wisdom in some wretched way.

'It is the stillest words which bring about the storm; thoughts that creep up on you with the footsteps of doves steer the world.

The figs are falling from the trees, they are good and sweet; and as they fall, their red skin bursts.

I am a north wind to ripe figs.

Thus, like figs, these teachings fall into your laps, my friends; now you drink their juice and their sweet meat.

Autumn is around us and pure sky and afternoon.'

It is no fanatic that speaks here, this is not 'preaching', there is no *faith* required here: drop by drop, word upon word falls from an immeasurable abundance of light and depth of happiness – their timing is a tender slow movement. Such things will only reach the chosen few; it is a privilege without equal to be a listener here; nobody should

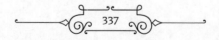

expect as a matter of course to have an ear for Zarathustra... In view of all that, is Zarathustra not a *seducer* after all?... But what does he himself say as he returns for the first time to his solitude? Precisely the opposite of everything that any old 'sage', 'saint', 'world-redeemer' or other Decadent would say in such a case... Not only does he talk differently, he actually *is* different...

'I shall now go away to be alone, my disciples. You too will go now and be alone. That is how I wish it.

Depart from me and defend yourself against Zarathustra. And better still: be ashamed of him! Perhaps he has deceived you. Man of knowledge must not just love his enemies, he must also be able to hate his friends.

You reward your teacher poorly if you always remain a pupil. And why do you not wish to pluck at my laurels?

You venerate me: but what if your veneration should one day *collapse*? Beware lest a statue crushes you!

You say, you believe in Zarathustra? But why does Zarathustra matter!

You are my believers, but why do believers matter!

You had not even looked for each other: yet you found me.

That is the way with all believers; that is why all beliefs matter so little.

Now I bid you to lose me and to find yourselves and only *when you have all denied me* shall I come back to you.'

Friedrich Nietzsche

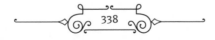

ON THIS perfect day, when all is ripening and not only the grape turns brown, a sunbeam lit my life: I looked back, looked outwards and never saw so many and such good things all at once. Not in vain did I bury today my forty-fourth year – I *had the right* to bury it – all that was life in it has been saved, and is immortal. The *Re-evaluation of Values*, the *Songs of Zarathustra* and, for a break, *The Twilight of the Idols* – all gifts of this year, indeed of its last quarter. *How could I not be grateful to my whole life?* And so I am about to tell myself the story of my life.

Chapter I
WHY I AM SO WISE

1.

THE happiness of my existence, its uniqueness perhaps, lies in its inevitable end: I am, to put it in the form of a riddle, as my own father, already dead; as my own mother, I am still alive and grow old. This duality, taken as it were from the highest and lowest rungs of the ladder of life, at once decadent and a *beginning* – this, if anything, explains that neutrality, that freedom from involvement in the general problems of life, which are perhaps so typical for me. I have always had a keener nose for early indications of the rise and downfall than any other person; in this I am the perfect teacher – I know both, I am both.

My father died at thirty-six: he was delicate, lovable, and morbid, as any being that is only meant to live for a brief spell – a gentle reminder of life rather than life itself. During the same year in which his life declined, mine too declined: in my thirty-sixth year I reached the lowest point of my vitality – I was still alive but could not see three steps ahead of me. At that time – it was in 1879 – I resigned my professorship in Basel, lived throughout the summer like a shadow in St Moritz and the following winter, the most sun-starved of my life, *as* a shadow in Naumburg. This was the lowest point of my existence; *The Wanderer and his Shadow* was the product of this period. No doubt, I was an expert in shadows then...

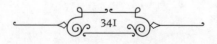

The following winter, my first winter in Genoa, brought forth that sweetness and spirituality which almost always goes hand in hand with an extreme physical weakness: my book *Dawn*. The perfect brightness and cheerfulness, even exuberance of the spirit that this work reflects, is not, in my case, just consistent with the most profound physiological weakness, but also with an excess of suffering. In the midst of the agony caused by three days of headaches accompanied by violent attacks of nausea with hopeless retching of bile – I was possessed of extraordinary dialectical clarity and in utter cold blood I thought things through, which in a healthier frame of mind I would not have been smart enough, not *cold* enough a mountaineer to do. My readers may know how far I regard dialectic as a symptom of decadence, for instance in the most notorious case of all: the case of Socrates.

All the morbid disturbances of the intellect, even that semi-stupor which follows a fever, have remained alien to me to this very day, and I had to inform myself first on their nature and frequency, looking it up in books. My blood runs slowly through my veins. No-one has ever seen me run a temperature. A doctor who treated me over a longer period as a neurotic patient finally decided: 'No, there is nothing the matter with your nerves; quite simply, I am the one who is nervous.' There is absolutely no sign of any local degeneration; no stomach upset caused by organ failure, despite the profound weakness of the gastric systems which comes from my general exhaustion. Even my eye trouble, sometimes coming dangerously close to blindness, is just an effect, not a cause, so that as my physical strength increased, my visual power also increased.

A long, much too long, number of years means recovery for me, unfortunately though, it also means relapse, decline, a spell of decadence. After all this, need I say that I am *experienced* in matters of decadence? I know it backwards! Even that finely spun craft of apprehension and comprehension in general, that feeling for nuances, that

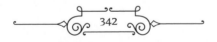

psychology of 'seeing what is around the corner' and whatever else I may be able to do, was first learned at that point, and it is the very gift of that period during which everything in me became refined, observation itself as well as the organs of observation. To look upon *healthier* concepts and values from the standpoint of the sick man and, conversely, to look down from the abundance and self-confidence of a *rich* life down into the secret workings of the instinct of decadence – that has been my main task, the one I worked longest at, in which if anything at all, I became expert. I have it at my fingertips now, I have the ability to *change perspectives*, the main reason perhaps, why I alone could achieve a *Re-evaluation of Values*.

2.

IF YOU accept that I am decadent, I am also the opposite. My argument for this amongst other things is that I always instinctively choose the *proper* means to fight bad conditions: whilst the Decadent, as such, invariably chooses those means that are to his disadvantage. Overall, then, I was of sound health, but looked at more closely, I was decadent. That energy for absolute isolation and extraction from a life of habit, the way I forced myself no longer to be indulged, to be waited on hand and foot, to be *pampered* – all that proves the absolute certainty of my instincts *that was*, above all, essential for me at that time. I took myself in hand, I healed myself: this can only be done on the condition – as every physician will admit – that we are *basically healthy*. A typically morbid being cannot become healthy at all, much less heal himself: whereas for a typically healthy being illness can even be a strong *stimulus* to life, for an even richer life. This, indeed, is how I *now* regard my long period of illness: I discovered life afresh, as it were, myself included; I tasted all good and even trifling things in such a way that others cannot easily do – I created my philosophy from my will for health, for *life*...

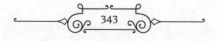

For I must ask you to take note of this; it was during those years when my life-force was at its lowest ebb that I *ceased* being a pessimist: the instinct of self-recovery forbade me to adopt a philosophy of poverty and discouragement... Now, how can we basically recognize *brilliance*? We recognize that a brilliant or first-rate human being is agreeable to our senses: that he is made of a matter at once hard yet sweet and fragrant. He enjoys only what is conducive to him; his pleasure, his desire ceases as soon as the level of what is good for him has been overstepped. He divines remedies against injuries, he uses serious accidents to his own advantage; that which does not kill him makes him stronger. He instinctively gathers his *sum-total* from all that he sees, hears and experiences. He is a selective principle, he discards much. He is always in *his own* company, whether he deals with books, people or landscapes: he honours his *choices* by *acknowledging* them, by *trusting* them. He reacts slowly to all types of stimuli, with the very slowness bred in him by long years of caution and deliberate pride – he tests the stimulus that meets him head-on; no compromise is required. He believes in neither 'misfortune' nor 'guilt'; he copes with himself and others; he knows *when to let go* – he is strong enough to turn everything to his greatest advantage.

Well then, I am the opposite of a Decadent: for I just described none other than *myself*.

3.

I REGARD it as a great privilege to have had such a father; the peasants he preached to (for, after having lived for some years at the Altenburg Court, he spent his last years of life as a preacher) said of him that this is how the angels must have looked – and with this I will touch on the question of race.

I am a Polish nobleman without a drop of bad blood, least of all German blood. If I search for the most shocking contrast to myself,

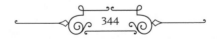

the unfathomable pettiness of the instincts, I always find my mother and sister – to believe myself kindred to such bitches would be blaspheming my divinity. The treatment that I have received from my mother and sister fills me with unutterable horror to this very day; there is a totally hellish machine at work here, operating with infallible certainty at the precise moment when I am most vulnerable – at my loftiest moments. For then I lack any strength to defend myself against such vipers! The physiological closeness makes such age-old disharmony possible – but I confess that the deepest objection against any 'reincarnation' and my real thoughts when staring into the abyss, are always of my mother and sister.

However, even as a Pole I am an incredible throwback. You would have to go back centuries to find this noblest race that ever lived on earth as sensitive as I have described them. Everything that is called noble these days gives me a feeling of superiority and distinction – I would not allow the young German Emperor the honour of being my coachman. There is one single case where I acknowledge my equal and I admit it with profound gratitude: Madame Cosima Wagner is by far the noblest nature; and, I may as well admit it, I hold true that Richard Wagner was the man by far closest akin to me; the rest – silence!

All prevailing concepts about degrees of relationship are an utter physiological nonsense. Even today the Pope insists on this absurdity for his own purposes. We are least akin to our parents; indeed it would be the utmost mark of vulgarity to be too akin to our parents. Loftier natures can trace their true origins infinitely farther back; from them a great deal had to be gathered, hoarded and heaped over long periods of time. The great individuals are the oldest; I do not understand why, but Julius Caesar could have been my father – or Alexander, that Dionysus incarnate... At the very moment of writing this, someone has sent me the head of Dionysus through the mail...

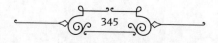

4.

I NEVER understood the art of being antagonistic – this, too, I owe to my marvellous father – even though at times it could have been very useful to me. However unchristian this may seem, I do not even feel antagonism against myself. You can look at my life from any angle and rarely will you find traces of any ill will towards me (apart from that one single case perhaps), though too many traces of *good will*...

Even my experiences with those that everyone else fares badly with are without exception positive; I tame every beast, I can even make buffoons behave demurely. During the seven years in which I taught classical Greek to a top form at the Grammar school in Basel, I never needed to administer a punishment. Even the laziest worked hard for me in my class. If chance comes my way, I will take it, but I have to be spontaneous to take control of myself. Whatever the instrument, however badly tuned, even if as much out of tune as only the instrument 'man' can be – I would have to be ill if I could not squeeze something worth listening to out of it. And as often as not, I have been told by the 'instruments' themselves that they had thought themselves incapable of such a tune...

Most beautifully perhaps by that Heinrich von Stein who died unforgivably young, and who, after dutifully obtaining permission, turned up and stayed for three days in Sils-Maria, explaining to everyone that he had *not* just come to look at the Engadine. This fine human being, who waded deep into Wagnerian mires (and also into those of Dürer!) with all the impetuous simplicity of a Prussian nobleman, became a different man during these three days, changed by a tempest of freedom like one who has been suddenly lifted to *his* full height and given wings to fly with. I told him over and again that it was the good mountain air up here that did it, that everyone felt like that, that after all, you were not some 6,000 ft above Bayreuth for nothing – but he would not believe me...

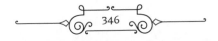

If, in spite of that, some small and not so small misdemeanours have been committed against me, it was not an act of 'will', least of all of *ill* will: rather, as I have already indicated, I could complain of good will that has done no little mischief in my life. My experiences give me a right to feel generally suspicious of the so-called 'selfless' instincts, the whole concept of 'neighbourly love', that is always ready to offer advice or to break into action. I deem it a weakness in itself, an individual case of inability to resist temptations – only the Decadent call *compassion* a virtue. I accuse the compassionate of easily losing modesty, respect, the sensitivity to keep their distance; compassion smells very quickly of the mob and is indistinguishable from bad manners – compassionate hands can at times be interfering in a downright destructive way with a great destiny, the growing isolation amongst the wounded and the *privilege* of a great wrong. I count conquering compassion among the *noble* virtues: with the 'Temptation of Zarathustra' I wrote a poem where a great cry of distress reaches his ear, where compassion assaults him and tries to entice him away from *himself* like a final sin. To keep control of himself at this point, to remain adamant that the *magnitude* of his task must not be belittled by lower and more short-sighted impulses which affect the so-called selfless deeds, that is the test, perhaps the ultimate test, which Zarathustra must pass – the real *proof* of power.

5.

AND in yet another respect I am once more my father over again and thus the continuation of his life following his so untimely death. Like every man who has never lived amongst equals and to whom therefore the notion of 'retaliation' is just as foreign as the notion of 'equal rights', I do not allow myself to safeguard or protect myself when small or even gross acts of foolishness have been committed against me – naturally, neither do I defend or justify myself. My kind of retaliation is quickly to send prudence to run after stupidity, perhaps

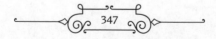

it will catch up with it. To put it as a parable: I eat a pot of jam in order to get rid of a *sour* taste... Just let anyone speak ill of me, I shall 'retaliate', don't doubt it: it won't take me long to find an opportunity to offer my thanks to the 'perpetrator' (occasionally even for the misdeed itself) – or to *ask* him for something, which can be more gracious even than *offering* something...

Moreover, it seems to me that the rudest word, the rudest letter, is still kinder, still more virtuous than silence. Those who are silent are almost always lacking in delicacy and refinement of the heart; silence is an objection, swallowing grievances makes for a bad character – it even upsets the stomach. All those who are silent suffer from dyspepsia.

As you see, I do not wish to underestimate rudeness, it is by far the most *human* form of contradiction and amidst the modern fashion for pampering, one of our most important virtues.

If you are rich enough for it, it may even be your good fortune to be in the wrong. A god descending to this earth could *do* nothing but wrong; not to bring punishment on himself but to take on the *guilt* – only that would make him divine.

6.

TO BE free of resentment, to be aware of resentment – who knows how much I ultimately have to thank my long illness for, even for that. The problem is not an easy one: you have to have experienced it from strength as well as from weakness. If anything has to be upheld against illness, against weakness, it is that man's actual sense of salvation, that is to say his *instinct for war and taking up arms* has been worn out. We know how to break free from nothingness, we know how to cope with nothingness, we know how to push nothingness away from us – it all hurts. Man and things crowd in, all experiences strike too deep, memory is a festering wound. Illness itself is a form of resentment.

In the face of that, the sick man has only one great remedy – I

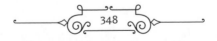

call it *Russian fatalism*, that fatalism without revolt with which a Russian soldier lies down in the snow at the end of a campaign that was all too hard; to accept nothing further, to take nothing on, nothing in – to cease reacting altogether...

The great sense in such fatalism (that is not always merely the courage to die, for it can be life-saving under deadly circumstances) lies in reducing the metabolism, slowing it down as a form of will to hibernate. If we take this reasoning a few steps further, we arrive at the fakir who sleeps for weeks in a tomb. Because we would wear ourselves out much too quickly *if* we reacted in any way, we don't react at all: that is the principle. And nothing burns us up faster than the emotion of resentment. Anger, morbid sensitivity, the inability to force revenge, the yearning, the thirst for revenge, the concoction of all types of poison – this, surely, is for the exhausted the most detrimental way to react: it involves a rapid consumption of nervous energy, a pathological increase of harmful secretions, for instance that of bile into the stomach. Resentment is *all that is* forbidden to the sick man – it is his *worst evil*: unfortunately, it is also what he most desires.

That was recognized by that profound physician Buddha. His 'religion' which should rather be called a *hygiene system* to avoid any confusion with such a wretched thing as Christianity, works because it depends on the conquest of resentment: to free the soul of it – this is the first step towards recovery. 'Animosity is not ended by animosity, animosity is ended by friendship'; thus begins Buddha's doctrine – this is *not* the voice of morality but of physiology. Resentment born of weakness is harmful to no-one more than to the weak man himself – conversely, with a fundamentally rich nature it is a *superfluous* emotion, which, if kept under control, is almost a proof of riches. Those readers who know how seriously my philosophy has taken up the fight against the feelings of revenge and rancour, even taking on the doctrine of 'free will' (the fight against Christianity is merely a small part of it),

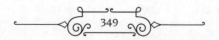

will understand why I emphasise my own personal attitude, my *instinctive confidence* in practicality at precisely this point. During my decadent period I *denied* myself these feelings as being harmful; as soon as life offered once again wealth and pride, I denied them myself as being beneath me. That 'Russian fatalism' of which I spoke manifested itself in such a way that for years I clung tenaciously to almost unbearable conditions, locations, dwellings, societies, once fate had sent them my way; it was better than changing them, better than *feeling* they could be changed – better than rebelling against them...

Anyone who interfered with my fatalism, who tried forcefully to awaken me, would have been my mortal enemy in those days; in truth, it would have been fatally dangerous every time. Thinking of yourself as a destiny, not wanting to be 'other' than you are – that is under such circumstances the *highest wisdom*.

7.

NOW, war is a different matter altogether. I am essentially a warrior. To wage war is one of my instincts. Talent for animosity, to actually *be* an enemy – this, perhaps, presupposes a strong nature; in any case it is a precondition of every strong nature. It needs resistances, therefore it *seeks* out resistance: *aggressive* pathos is just as necessary for strength as resentment and rancour for weakness. Women, for instance, are vengeful: that is due to their weakness, as much as to their sensitivity to others' distress.

The strength of the aggressor, in a way, has its *measure* in the opposition he requires; any increase in strength makes itself known when seeking out a mightier opponent or, indeed, problem – for a philosopher who is a warrior will also do battle with problems. The task is *not* to overcome opponents at all costs, but only those against whom you must pit all your strength, subtlety and fighting skill – opponents who are *your equals*... Equality before the enemy – that is

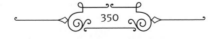

the main condition to fight a *fair* duel. Where you have contempt, you *cannot* wage war; where you are in command, where you can see someone *beneath* you, you *should not* wage war. My war tactics can be summed up in four theorems. Firstly: I only ever engage with causes that are winnable – if necessary, I wait until they win. Secondly: I only ever engage with causes where I would find no allies, where I stand alone – where I compromise only myself... I have never publicly taken a single step which did not compromise me: that is my criterion for doing right. Thirdly: I never attack people – I use a person merely as a powerful magnifying glass that allows me to make visible a general but insidious and elusive calamity.

In this way I attacked David Strauss, or to put it more plainly, the *success* of a senile book amongst the 'cultured classes' of Germany – thereby catching this culture red-handed...

In this way I attacked Wagner, or to put it more plainly, the hypocrisy, the semi-refined instinct of our 'culture' which confuses the artful with richness, the late with the great. Fourthly: I only ever attack things from which all personal differences are excluded, where any background of bad experience is lacking. On the contrary, to attack is to me a proof of good-will, in some circumstances even of gratitude. It is an honour, a reward, if I associate my name with a matter or a person, notwithstanding whether I am for it or against it. If I wage war on Christianity I have a right to do so, because it's not going to kill me and they're not going to stop me – the most serious Christians were always favourably disposed towards me. I myself, the strictest opponent of Christianity, am far from minded to bear grudges against individuals for what has been the undoing of centuries.

8.

MAY I point out to you one more trait of my character, which causes me no little difficulty in my dealings with men? I have a perfectly

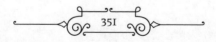

uncanny sense of purity so that I can register, even *smell* the approach
or – may I say? – the innermost region, the 'entrails' of every soul in
a physical way... This sensitivity of mine has psychological antennae
with which I probe and handle every secret: the *hidden* filth at the
bottom of many a character. Perhaps caused by bad genes but glossed
over by breeding, it is nevertheless obvious to me almost at a glance.
If I am right, those who offend my sense of purity also sense my
disgust themselves; that does not make them smell any better... To
be treated with extreme fairness is a precondition for my existence; I
should perish in impure conditions (I got used to swimming and
bathing and splashing, as it were, incessantly in water, in some perfectly
transparent and glistening element). That is why dealing with men is
no small test of my patience; my humanity *does not* consist of empa-
thizing with men's nature but to *endure* that I empathize – my humanity
is a constant test of my willpower...

However, I do need *seclusion*, that is to say, healing, being myself
again, breathing free, light, playful air... All of my *Zarathustra* is a
song in praise of seclusion, or, if you get my meaning, of *purity* –
fortunately not about *pure folly*. Those with an eye for colour would
call him adamantine; the *loathing* for mankind, for the 'rabble' was
always my greatest danger... Do you wish to hear what Zarathustra
has to say when he talks of being *set free* of *loathing*?

'What could have happened to me? How have I freed myself
from loathing? Who renewed my sight? How did I soar to such heights,
above the rabble sitting by the well?

Was it my loathing that gave me wings and water-divining powers?

Truly, I had to fly to the loftiest heights to find once again that
fount of desire!

Ah, but I found it, my brothers! Here in the loftiest height the
fount of my desire wells up for me, and there is a life in which the
rabble cannot have a share.

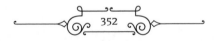

You flow almost too fast for me, my fount of desire! And often you empty the cup again by wanting to refill it.

And yet I must learn to approach you with greater modesty – my heart overflows all too wildly at the sight of you – my heart, on which my summer's heat is burning; the short, hot, sad, overly blissful one – how my summer heart longs for your chill.

Gone is the lingering sadness of my spring! Gone are the snow-flakes of my wickedness in June! I have become all summer and a summer's noon.

A summer in loftiest heights with ice-cold springs and blissful silence: come, my friends, come that this silence may be still more blissful.

For this is *our* height and our home – we all live here, where it is too high and steep for any of the impure and their thirst. Look with your pure eyes into the fount of my desire, friends! Why should that cloud it? Why, it will smile at you in its *own* purity.

On the tree of future we shall build our nest; eagles will carry food to us recluses in their beaks.

Truly, this is no food that the impure are allowed to share! Like fire it would burn their mouths.

Truly, we do not prepare homes for the impure! Our happiness would be like icy caves to their bodies and spirits.

And like strong winds we shall live above them, neighbours to the eagles, neighbours of the snow, neighbours of the sun: this is the way strong winds live.

And like a wind I shall yet blow amongst them one day and take their spirits' breath away with mine: that is the dictate of my future.

Truly, Zarathustra is a strong wind on all and every plain, and his advice to all his friends and all that spit and spout is this: beware of spitting *against* the wind!…'

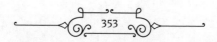

Chapter 2
WHY I AM SO CLEVER

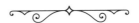

1.

WHY do I know *more* than other people? Why, in general, am I so clever? I have never wasted my time pondering questions that are not really questions. For instance, I have no personal experiences of real *religious* difficulties. It completely escapes me why I should be a 'sinner'. Similarly, I don't have a reliable criterion by which to work out what a bad conscience consists of: from where I stand, a bad conscience does not appear of great value to me… I would rather not leave anything that I have done *afterwards* in the lurch; I would prefer to omit a bad ending, or its *consequences*, from any form of evaluation. A bad ending makes you lose the vision you had in sight, a bad conscience is in my view some form of *evil eye*. To respect something that didn't work all the more because it didn't work – that is rather closer to my set of morals.

'God', 'immortality of the soul', 'redemption', 'heaven', these are all terms for which I never had any time and to which I never paid any attention, even as a child – was I perhaps not enough of a child for that?

For me, atheism is not at all a result, even less an event: to me it is instinctive. I am much too inquisitive, too sceptical, and too high-spirited to put up with an obvious if coarse answer. God is such a coarse and obvious answer, a lack of delicacy towards us thinkers – at heart He is just a coarse command not to think: thou shalt not think!

Now, the question of nutrition is a very different matter to me;

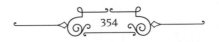

on that the 'salvation of mankind' is truly dependent, much more so than on some theological musing. For practical purposes we could put it like this: 'How precisely must you feed yourself to attain your maximum power, a truly enlightened virtue, a virtue free of moral input?'

Here, my personal experiences are the worst possible; I am surprised that I did not become aware of this question earlier, that I have learned to 'reason' from these experiences only at such a late stage. The utter worthlessness of our German culture alone – its 'idealism' – can explain to some extent why of all people I was so backward here, almost revelling in this backwater. This 'culture', which teaches you from the start to lose sight of *reality*, so that you may aim for quite difficult, so-called 'ideal' goals; for instance 'classical education' (as if it was not already doomed to unite the two concepts: 'Classical' and 'German'). Actually, this is quite funny: imagine a man from Leipzig with a classical education!

As it is, in moral terms I have eaten *a very poor diet* until very recently: that is 'impersonally', 'selflessly', 'altruistically' – for the good of the cooks and other fellow Christians. For instance, because of the cuisine of Leipzig as well as my first involvement with the works of Schopenhauer (1865), I seriously shunned my 'will to live'. Think – to upset my stomach on account of a poor diet – such a problem seemed to be amazingly well solved by this type of cuisine (it is said that the year 1866 had brought about a change in this department).

But as to German cuisine in general – what can it not be accused of! Serving soup *before* the main meal (still called *alla tedesca* in 16th-century Venetian cookery books); meat boiled to death, vegetables full of grease and made stodgy with flour; the degeneration of pastries into solid bulk! Add to this the almost bestial, postprandial habits of the ancient, although not just the *ancient* Germans, you will understand the origin of the *German* mind – it is founded in disordered innards. The German mind is a sore stomach; it cannot take any more.

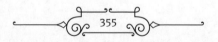

But even the *English* diet that, compared with the German or the French one, seems to me a 'return to nature' (that is, to cannibalism), is deeply repugnant to my innermost self; I think it makes the mind heavy-footed, gives it the feet of English women... My favourite cuisine is that of *Piedmont*.

Alcohol does not agree with me; a glass of wine or beer a day is enough to turn my life into a valley of tears – my adversaries live in Munich. I confess that I came to understand all this a little late, even though I have *experienced* it since childhood. As a boy I believed that drinking wine, like smoking tobacco, was simply youthful vanity, which would then turn into a bad habit. Perhaps the wine of Naumburg vineyards was partly responsible for my harsh judgment. To believe that wine is *cheering* I would have to be a Christian, in other words I would have to believe in what to me is utterly absurd.

Oddly enough, whereas *small* doses of alcohol depress me deeply, *large* quantities turn me almost into a sailor on leave. Even as a boy I could hold my own in this respect. To compose and even transcribe a long Latin essay in a single night, keen to emulate my role model Sallust in austerity and terseness and then to pour some strong drink all over it, this was not incompatible with my physiology even as a pupil of the venerable grammar school Schulpforta, perhaps not even to that of Sallust – however much it was frowned upon by that venerable school... But later in life I decided against any form of 'spirit' as a drink; like Richard Wagner who converted me, I, an opponent of vegetarianism from experience, cannot urge all those with a *fine* mind strongly enough to entirely abstain from alcohol. Water is good enough... I prefer locations where I have an opportunity to drink water fresh from a fountain, for instance in Nice, Turin and Sils; I keep a small glass by me wherever I go.

In wine lies the truth – here too I seem to be at odds with the rest of the world about the concept of 'truth' – for me, the spirit floats above *water*. Let me give you a few more pieces of advice from my

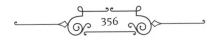

set of moral codes. A big meal is easier to digest than a small one. A main condition for a good digestive system is the fact that the stomach has to work in its entirety. You ought *to know* the size of your stomach. For the same reasons I advise against those lengthy meals, which I call interrupted sacrificial feasts and which are served at the *table d'hôte*.

No snacking in between, no coffee, coffee is depressing. Tea is only good in the morning, in small quantities but strong. If too weak, even by a grain or two, tea can be very harmful and leave you indisposed for the whole day. Everyone has their own limits, sometimes within the narrowest and most delicate margins. In a very irritating climate I advise against drinking tea first thing in the morning. If at all possible, drink a cup of strong cocoa, any cocoa butter extracted, an hour beforehand. *Sit* on your bottom as little as possible; trust no thought that is not born in the open and in free motion, when all your muscles are engaged. All prejudices come from the bowels. The bottom – I said it before – is the true *sin* against the Holy Spirit.

2.

THE question of nutrition is closely related to that of *location* and *climate*. None of us can live everywhere at the same time, and those of us who have to perform great tasks which require all our strength have an even more limited choice. The influence of climate upon the *metabolism*, slowing it down or speeding it up, is so great that a wrong choice of location and climate not only alienates you from your task but can even prevent you from taking it up altogether: you would never even know it. Thus, animal strength has never been developed enough to feel that exuberant freedom which enables you to recognize: Only I can do *that*.

Even the least sluggishness of the bowels, once a habit, is more than enough to turn the genius into something mediocre, something 'German'. The climate of Germany alone is sufficient to discourage the strongest and most heroic bowels. The timing of the metabolism

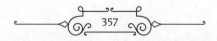

is in precise relation to the agility or slowness of the mind's *feet*: after all, the 'mind' itself is only a form of this metabolism. Put together locations where ingenious people live and always have lived, where wit, cleverness, and irony were part of happiness, where genius is almost compelled to dwell: all of these places have an exquisitely dry atmosphere. Paris, Provence, Florence, Jerusalem, Athens (these names prove something: Genius is *dependent* on dry air, on clear skies), in other words, on a rapid metabolism, on being able to continuously supply itself with great, even enormous quantities of power. I have a case in mind where a great and open mind became narrow, repressed, pedantic and cranky, simply because it lacked a fine instinct for climate. I myself might have become such a case, if illness had not forced me to reason and to reflect upon reason realistically. Now long practice has taught me to read the effects of climatic and meteorological origin on myself as on a very precise and reliable instrument, so that after a journey even as short as that from Turin to Milan I can calculate the change in the degree of atmospheric humidity by observing my body, and I remember with horror the *sinister* fact that apart from the last ten years, the most dangerous years, my life was always spent at the wrong locations, places that should have been forbidden to me: Naumburg, Schulpforta, Thuringia in general, Leipzig, Basel – so many disastrous places for my constitution. If I have not a single pleasant memory of my childhood and youth it would be foolish to blame it at this point on so-called 'moral' causes, as for instance the incontestable lack of *compatible* company; for this lack exists today just as it did then and it does not stop me from being cheerful and brave. But it was the ignorance of the functioning of the body, that confounded 'idealism', that was the real curse of my life, superfluous and stupid, from which no good would come, for which there can be no compensation, no agreement. The consequences of this 'idealism' explain all my blunders, the great aberrations of instinct and the 'modesties' that diverted me from

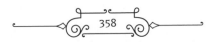

my task, the fact that I became a professor of linguistics – why not at least a medical doctor or anything else that could have opened my eyes? During my stay in Basel, my whole intellectual routine, including my daily schedule, was a completely pointless abuse of extraordinary powers, without any sort of compensation for the strength I had spent, without even giving a thought about its exhaustion and how to replace it. I completely lacked any subtle egotism; I did not take care of my imperious instinct; I was everyone's equal – it was a 'selflessness' that did not observe distance – something I will never forgive myself for. When I had almost reached the end (*because* I very nearly did reach it), I began to reflect on this basic absurdity of my life, which was 'idealism'. It was my *illness* that brought me to reason.

3.

CHOICE of nutrition, choice of climate and location: the third choice, where you must not at any price go wrong, is *your* choice of *recreation*. Here again, depending on the uniqueness of your mind, the limits of what is permitted (that is to say *useful*) are ever more restricted. In my case, general *reading* is part of my recreation, therefore it is part of that which allows me to escape from myself, that lets me stroll through alien sciences and souls – something I no longer take seriously. Indeed, reading allows me to recover from my seriousness. When I work very intensely, you do not find books near me: I wouldn't dream of letting anyone talk to me or even think in my presence. After all, that is just what reading means…

Has anyone ever noticed that, that during that profound tension to which the state of pregnancy condemns the mind and basically the entire organism, chance and every kind of external stimulus strike much too vehemently and 'penetrate' too deeply? You must try to avoid accidents and external stimuli as far as possible: to brick yourself in is one of the first instinctive precautions of spiritual pregnancy.

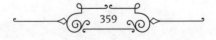

Would I permit an *alien* thought to secretly climb over my brick wall? – After all, that is just what reading means...

Periods of work and productivity are followed by a period of recreation: come on, you pleasant, you witty, you clever books! – Will they be German books?

I must go back six months to catch myself with a book in my hand. What was it this time? An excellent work by Victor Brochard, *Les Sceptiques Grecs*. The sceptics, the only *venerable* types amongst the two-faced, indeed quintuple-faced race of philosophers!

Otherwise, I almost always take refuge in the same books, not very many really, such books that seem to have been written for me. Perhaps it is not in my nature to read many or a wide variety of books: a library makes me ill. Neither is it in my nature to love many or, indeed, a wide variety of things. Suspicion, even hostility towards new books, is more likely to be one of my instincts than 'tolerance', 'generosity' and other types of 'brotherly love'. Ultimately, it is to a few old French authors that I return again and again; I only believe in French culture and regard everything in Europe that calls itself 'culture' as a misunderstanding, not to mention German culture.

The few instances of highly educated people I have encountered in Germany were of French origin, in particular Cosima Wagner, who as far as I am concerned was by far the leading voice in matters of taste.

The fact that I do not read Pascal but that I *love* him, as the most instructive victim of Christianity – slowly murdered, first in body, then in mind, as the sum of the logic of the most horrific form of inhuman cruelty; that I have something of Montaigne's mischievousness in my spirit and, who knows?, perhaps in my body too; that my artist's taste cannot but defend men like Molière, Corneille and Racine and this not entirely without wrath against a wild genius like Shakespeare – all this does not finally prevent me from regarding even the modern French writers as charming company. I cannot imagine any other century in

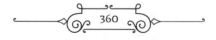

history in which such a group of inquisitive yet subtle psychologists could have been gathered than in present-day Paris. Randomly, since their number is by no means small. I name Paul Bourget, Pierre Loti, Gyp, Meilhac, Anatole France, Jules Lemaître, or, singling out one of strong race, a genuine Latin of whom I am particularly fond, Guy de Maupassant. Between ourselves, I prefer *this* generation even to their great masters since they have all been corrupted by German philosophy (Taine for instance by Hegel, whom he has to thank for misunder-standing great men and times). Wherever Germany reaches out to, she *corrupts* culture. It was the war that 'redeemed' the spirit of France.

Stendhal (one of the happiest accidents of my life, for everything in it of lasting value came to me by chance, never because of recommendation) is invaluable with his anticipatory psychologist's eye, his grasp of facts, reminiscent of the greatest of all masters (Napoleon); and last but not least as an honest atheist, a rare figure in France, almost impossible to find – with all due respect to Prosper Mérimée… Perhaps I am myself jealous of Stendhal? He has taken the best atheist joke I could possibly have made away from me: 'God's only excuse is that he does not exist'… I myself have said somewhere: What was hitherto the greatest objection to life? *God…*'

4.

IT WAS Heinrich Heine who defined the meaning of a lyrical poet for me. In vain do I search all areas throughout the past millennia for a similarly sweet and passionate music. He possessed that divine wick-edness without which I cannot image perfection; I assess men and races according to how closely they associate god with Satyr – and how they handle the German language! One day it will be said that Heine and I were by far the top jugglers of the German language, infinitely outstripping everything ordinary Germans could do with it.

I must be closely related to *Byron's* Manfred: I found all these

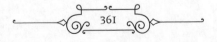

abysses in my own soul – at the mere age of thirteen I was ready to read this work. I have nothing to say, just a contemptuous glance for those who dare to speak of Faust in the same breath as Manfred. The Germans are *incapable* of any notion of greatness: look at Schumann. Angry with this sickly Saxon, I actually composed a counter-overture to Manfred, of which Hans von Bülow declared he had never seen the like before: raping the muse of music, that's what it is, he said.

Searching for the best formula to do Shakespeare justice, I only ever come up with: 'He conceived the character of Caesar.' You cannot conjecture a thing like that – you either are him or you are not. The great poet *only* draws from his own experience – up to the point where he cannot bear to look at his own work later on. Whenever I reread my *Zarathustra* I must pace to and fro in my room for half an hour, unable to control my sobs.

I know of no more heartbreaking literature than that of Shakespeare: how he must have suffered to need to play the clown so badly; do you understand *Hamlet*? It is not doubt, but *certainty* that drives you mad... But to feel like that you must be deep, must be abysmal, must be a philosopher... We are all *afraid* of the truth... And let me tell you this: I know instinctively for certain that Lord Bacon is the originator, the self-torturer, of this most sinister type of literature: why should *I* bother about the pitiful chattering of American blockheads and half-wits? But the power for the greatest visionary realism is not only compatible with the greatest strength for action, with the monstrous, the crime – *it actually anticipates it*... We don't by far know enough about Lord Bacon, the first realist in the very sense of the word, to know *everything* he did, *everything* he aimed for, how he himself felt about *everything*... You critics can all go to hell! If I had called my Zarathustra something else, Richard Wagner for example, the acumen of two millennia would not have been enough to divine that the author of *Human, All Too Human* is the inventor of Zarathustra...

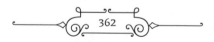

5.

WHILE speaking of the recreational pursuits of my life I need to express my gratitude for him who afforded me by far the deepest and dearest forms of escape. This has been without doubt my intimate relationship with Richard Wagner. All other human relationships were fair enough; but I would not miss the days in Tribschen from my life – days of trust, of happiness, of marvellous opportunities and above all – of *deep* moments... I do not know what others made of Wagner, but nothing ever cast a cloud over *our* friendship.

This brings me back to France – I cannot give any reasons, I can only contemptuously pucker my mouth when I look to Wagnerians and their ilk, who think they honour Wagner by believing him to be like *themselves*... Since I am what I am, instinctively alienated from all things German (to the point that the mere presence of a German will make me constipated), the first meeting with Wagner was also my first sigh of relief ever. I felt him, I revered him as a *foreigner*, as the antithesis of, and a living protest against, all 'German virtues'.

We, who were children in the stagnant air of the 1850s, are necessarily pessimists with regard to the notion of 'German'; we cannot be anything else but revolutionaries – we will not accept any condition in which a *creep* will be at the top. I am totally oblivious to his attire – whether he is robed in scarlet or puts on a uniform. Well then! Wagner was a revolutionary – he ran away from the Germans...

The *artist* has no home in Europe except in Paris; the predilection for all the five senses which is a condition of Wagner's art, that sensitivity to nuance, the psychological morbidity, these can only be found in Paris. Nowhere else is there this passion for form, this seriousness about stage-setting, which is Parisian seriousness par excellence. The Germans have no idea of the extraordinary ambition that lives in the soul of a Parisian artist... Germans are good-natured – Wagner was certainly not... But I have already written enough on the subject of

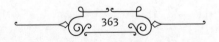

Wagner, where he stands, where he comes from (see *Beyond Good and Evil*, 'Aphorism 2'): it is the late French Romanticists, that high-flying and heaven-aspiring bunch of artists like Delacroix and Berlioz, who are essentially sick, terminally so, pure fanatics of *expression*, virtuosos to the last... Who was the first *intelligent* follower of Wagner, pray? Charles Baudelaire, the very man who first understood Delacroix, that archetypal Decadent in whom a whole generation of artists has recognized itself – perhaps he was also the last...

What was it that I could not forgive Wagner for? That he *condescended* to the Germans – that he became a German Imperialist... Whoever Germany reaches out to – she will *corrupt* their culture.

6.

ALL things considered, I would never have survived my youth without Wagner's music. For I was *condemned* to live amongst Germans. If you wish to escape from unbearable oppression, you need Hashish. Well then, I needed Wagner. Wagner is the antidote to everything essentially German, but it is a poison nevertheless, I do not deny it. As soon as there was a piano arrangement of *Tristan* available (thank you, Mr von Bülow), I was a Wagnerite. The older works of Wagner, I felt, were beneath me, they were too common, too 'German'... But to this day I am looking for works of a similar dangerous fascination to *Tristan*, that horrifying yet sweet quality of infinity. I am searching among all the arts, but in vain. All the mysteries of Leonardo da Vinci are forgotten at the first note of *Tristan*. It is absolutely the very highest point in Wagner's work, he recovered from it with the *Mastersingers* and the *Ring* cycle. To recuperate – that is a retrograde step in a nature like that of Wagner...

I thank my lucky stars that I lived at the right time and in particular amongst Germans, to have been able to appreciate this work – that is how strongly the curiosity of a psychologist has a hold on me. The world must be a poor place for those that have never been sick enough

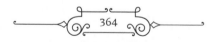

for the 'salaciousness of hell'; it is permissible, almost imperative to use a mystic formula here.

I believe that I know better than anyone else the prodigious feats of which Wagner is capable, the fifty worlds of unknown ecstasies to which only he could soar. Strong as I am now and able to use even the most dubious and dangerous things to my advantage to become even more powerful, I see Wagner as the great benefactor of my life. We are related in that we suffered more than any other men of this century, even made each other suffer, and that will bring together our names once again for all eternity. For, just as Wagner as a German is simply a misconception, so surely am I and always will be. Two hundred years of psychological and artistic discipline are required, my dear Germans... But it is all too late...

7.

ONE more word for my most select readers: what do I actually ask of music? It should be bright yet profound, like an October's afternoon; it should be individual, carefree, tender, like a dainty, sweet woman full of mischief and grace... I will never accept that Germans *can* know the meaning of music. The musicians generally accepted as Germans are all *foreigners*: Slavs, Croats, Italians, Dutchmen or Jews; or else they are Germans of a strong race now *extinct*, like Heinrich Schütz, Bach and Handel. I myself am still enough of a Pole to give up all the music in the world for that of Chopin. I would make three exceptions here: with Wagner's *Siegfried Idyll* and perhaps with some works of Liszt too, who with his noble orchestration has the advantage over all other musicians; and finally also with all those that grew up beyond the Alps – *my side*... I would not miss Rossini for the world, even less my Southern counterpart in music, my Venetian maestro, Pietro Gasti. And when I say beyond the Alps, I really only mean Venice. Whenever I want to find another word for music, I inevitably come to say Venice.

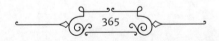

I do not know the difference between tears and music; I cannot think of joy or the *South* without the tremble of real fear.

> On the bridge I stood
> in recent muggy night,
> from afar a song
> came: like golden drops
> across the trembling rim.
> Gondolas, lights, music
> drunkenly they swam far into the dusk
>
> My soul, strings finely tuned,
> sang a boating song
> invisibly moved,
> secretly along,
> trembling in bright bliss
> – was someone listening in?

8.

IN ALL this – in the choice of food, location, climate and recreation – the instinct for self-preservation dominates, expressing itself most obviously as an instinct for *self-defence*. Not to see, not to hear most things, but to keep them at arm's length – this is the foremost prudence, the first evidence that you are not here by chance but out of necessity. The common word for this instinct of self-defence is *taste*. It is imperative not just to say 'no' where a 'yes' would be an act of 'unselfishness', but also to say *'no' as little as possible*. Depart, detach yourself from situations where again and again it would be necessary to say 'no'. That is because the discharge of defensive energy, however slight, regular and habitual it has become, causes an extraordinary and absolutely superfluous loss. Our *greatest* energy discharge consists of the most

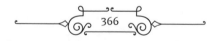

frequent small ones. The defence, the keeping-at-arm's-length is a discharge – and make no mistake here – of strength *wasted* for negative ends. Simply by being constantly on your guard, you can become weak enough not to be able to defend yourself any longer.

Suppose I were to step out of my house and, instead of the quiet and noble city of Turin, were to encounter a provincial German town: why, my instinct would have to shut down, to repress everything that would force itself upon it from this downtrodden and cowardly world. Or if I were to find a German metropolis, this structure of vice in which nothing grows but where everything, good or bad, has been forcibly imported. What choice would I have then but to become a *hedgehog*? – But to have quills is a sheer waste, a twofold luxury even if I choose not to have quills but *open* hands instead...

Another form of prudence and self-defence is to react as *seldom as possible* and to avoid situations and conditions where you are condemned, as it were, to suspend your 'liberty' and initiative and become a mere bundle of reactions. For example, when we are dealing with books. The scholar who actually does little else but pore over books (he reads on average 200 books a day), in the end loses all his ability to think for himself. If he does not pore, he does not think! Whenever he thinks, he *answers* to a stimulus (a thought he has read) – and finally all he does is react. The scholar devotes all his energy to affirming or denying or reviewing all that has already been thought – he no longer thinks for himself... His instinct for self-defence has become brittle, otherwise he would defend himself against books. The scholar is a Decadent. I have seen it with my own eyes: gifted, generous and free-spirited natures, no more than thirty and already 'wrecks' from too much reading; nothing but matchsticks that you have to strike so that they emit a spark or 'thought'.

To read a *book* first thing in the morning at daybreak, at the dawn of your strength – that I call a vice!

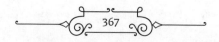

9.

AT THIS point a direct answer to the question *how we become what we are* can no longer be evaded. And with that I touch upon the master stroke of the art of self-preservation – *Selfishness*… Let us assume that our task, the purpose, the *destiny* of the task exceeds by far an average norm, then there could be no greater danger but to come face-to-face *with* this task. To become what you are presupposes that you do not have the remotest idea *what* you are. From this point of view, even the *blunders* in your life have a unique meaning and value, the occasional deviation or straying from the path, the hesitations, the 'modesties', the seriousness, wasted upon tasks that are beyond *the* main task. This outlines a great prudence, possibly even the highest prudence; whereas 'Know Yourself' would be a sure way to lead to downfall, to forget yourself, to *misunderstand* yourself, to belittle yourself, to limit and moderate yourself becomes reason itself. In moral terms: neighbourly love and living for others and other things *may* be the means of protection to maintain the most rigorous egoism. This is the exception where I, against all my self-imposed rules and conviction, take the part of the 'selfless' instincts: here they are engaged in the service of *egoism* and *self-discipline*.

The whole surface of consciousness (for consciousness is a surface) has to be kept free of any of the great imperatives. Beware even of every striking word or gesture! They all endanger the instinct to 'know itself' too soon. Meanwhile the organizing 'idea', destined to rule, continues to grow below; it becomes commanding; it leads you slowly *back* from deviations and aberrations; it prepares *individual* qualities and capacities that may one day be indispensable as the means to the whole – gradually, it develops all *serviceable* faculties before it indicates any trace of the dominant task of 'goal', 'purpose' and 'meaning'.

Viewed from this angle, my life is simply amazing. The task to *re-evaluate all values* required perhaps more abilities than could ever be found combined in one individual, and above all, also contrasting

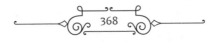

abilities that would at the same time not be mutually inimical, if not destructive. The ranking of abilities, distancing, the art of separating without creating hostility, to confuse nothing, to 'reconcile' nothing, to be enormously diverse yet the opposite of chaos – all this was the main condition and the long secret workings and artistic nature of my instinct. Its superior *guardianship* was so strong that at no time could I have any notion of what was growing within me – suddenly all my abilities *burst forth*: ripe and absolutely perfect. I fail to remember ever having exerted myself; there is truly no trace of a *struggle* in my life; I am the opposite of a heroic character. To 'want' something, to 'strive' for something, to focus on a 'purpose' or a 'wish', all these things I do not know from experience. Even at this moment I look out upon my future – a *wide* future – as upon a calm sea; there is no foam of desire upon it. I have not the slightest wish that anything should change from the way it is; I myself do not wish to change. But I have always been like that. I never wished for anything. I am someone who can say at the age of forty-four that he was never interested in *honours*, *women* or *money*. Not that these things were lacking… For instance, one fine day I found myself to be a university professor! I never even thought about it; after all, I was only twenty-four years old. In the same way, only two years earlier I suddenly was a philologist, in the sense that my *first* philological work, my beginning in every sense, was required by my teacher Ritschl to be printed in his magazine *Rheinisches Museum*. (*Ritschl* – I say it full of veneration – was the only genial scholar whom I have ever met. He possessed that pleasant notoriety that distinguishes us Thuringians and that makes even a German a nice person – we prefer to use secret and hidden paths to get to the truth. These words should not be taken as a slur upon my fellow countryman, the *intelligent* Leopold von Ranke.)

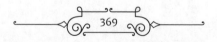

10.

AT THIS point you may ask me why I actually told you all these trivial and on the whole irrelevant details; I would seem to be harming my own cause, all the more so since I claim to represent great tasks. Let me say this to you: such small things as diet, location, climate, recreation, the whole casuistry of self-love, are by far more important than anything else that has been hitherto considered essential by us. Here in particular, we have to start to *rethink*. All those things that mankind has until now thought about with such earnestness are not even realities; they are mere fancies, indeed *lies*, arising from the bad instincts of sick and in the truest sense harmful natures: such concepts as 'god', 'soul', 'virtue', 'sin', 'the hereafter', 'truth', 'eternal life'... And yet we looked for the greatness of human nature, its 'divinity' in them... All questions of politics, of the social order, of education have been thoroughly falsified because the most harmful people were accepted by us as great men, by being taught to despise the so-called 'trivial' matters, which are really the fundamental concerns of life... Our current culture is highly ambiguous... The German emperor is in league with the Pope, as if the Pope was not the representative of the mortal enemy of life! What has been built today will not stand three years from now.

If I put my abilities to the test, never mind that what follows, a regime change or a new development as never seen before, I more than any other mortal can claim to be great. If I now compare myself with those people who were hitherto considered the 'first' among men, the difference becomes tangible. I do not even count these so-called 'first' men among human beings – for me they are the waste product of mankind, fiends deformed by disease and instincts of revenge; they are all monsters, rotten to the core and sick beyond cure, avenging themselves on life... I choose to be their very opposite. It is my prerogative to be highly sensitive to any indication of healthy instincts. There is not a single morbid trait in me; even during my long and

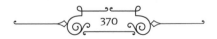

serious illness I have never become morbid. You will look in vain for a trace of fanaticism in my character. No-one is able to point out even a single instance in my life where I was presumptuous or pathetic. The pathos of gestures is *not* part of greatness; whoever needs gestures is *false*… Beware of the picturesque!

Life became easiest for me whenever it demanded the most from me. Those who saw me during the seventy days of this autumn when, without interruption, I performed so many things of the first order that no-one can match it or do better, things that will be representative for centuries to come, will not have noticed a single sign of tension in me, but rather my exuberant wellbeing and cheerfulness.

Never did I eat with greater enjoyment, never did I sleep better. I know no better means to deal with great tasks but *play*; this is an essential prerequisite and a sign of greatness. The slightest constraint, a gloomy expression, any harsh sound from the throat are all objections to a person, but how much more so to his work!… We must have no nerves… Even to *suffer* from loneliness is an objection – I personally have only ever suffered from being 'crowded out'.

At an absurdly young age, when I was only seven, I already knew that I could never be stirred by human speech. Did anyone see me sad because of it? Today, I still feel the same affability towards everyone, I give my attention even to the most lowly born, and in all this there is not an ounce of arrogance or contempt. Those whom I despise will soon *know* that I despise them, my mere existence angers those with bad blood in them. My formula for greatness in man is to *embrace your destiny*, to alter nothing, either in the future, or in the past, or in all eternity. Do not simply endure necessity and even less, hide it, but *love* it – all idealism is a falsehood in the face of necessity.

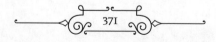

Chapter 3
WHY I WRITE SUCH EXCELLENT BOOKS

1.

I AM one thing, my books are another... Before I talk about them, I would like to touch upon the question about whether or *not* they are understood. I do it as casually as is fitting, since the time for this question has not yet come, really. For me, too, the time has not yet come, some of us are born posthumously.

One day, there will have to be institutions where men can live and teach as I myself know how to live and teach: perhaps then they will also establish professorships for the interpretation of *Zarathustra*. But I would be completely contradicting myself, if I expected ears *and hands* for my truths today. Not only does it seem understandable that no-one listens to me yet, that no-one knows what to do with me, it also seems to me quite right that it is so. I do not wish to be taken for someone else – and I too must not take myself for someone else.

Let me say it once again, there have been very few instances of 'ill will' in my life, even less of literary 'ill will'. However, there have been far too many of *pure stupidity*... To pick up a book of mine seems to me to be one of the rarest honours man can pay himself – I even assume he takes his shoes off first, or his boots... When Doctor Heinrich von Stein once seriously complained not to have understood a single word of my *Zarathustra*, I told him that that was as it should be: to have understood just six sentences or better; to have *lived* them,

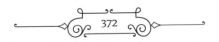

372

would lift a man on to a higher level among mortals than 'modern man' could reasonably hope for. How *could* I, with *this* feeling for distance, even wish to be read by 'modern men' as I know them! My triumph is precisely the opposite to that of Schopenhauer's 'read and be read' – I say, 'I am not read, I shall not read.'

Not that I wish to underestimate the fun that I had when I met with the *innocence* of people saying no to my books. Even this very summer, at a time when I could perhaps upset the apple cart of all literature together with my weighty, far too weighty literature, a professor from Berlin University told me good-naturedly that I should find a new form of writing: nobody would read anything like that.

In the end it was not Germany but Switzerland that came up with the two most extreme cases: an essay by a Dr V Widman in the Bernese newspaper *Bund* about *Beyond Good and Evil* as 'Nietzsche's dangerous book' and a general account about all my books by a Mr Karl Spitteler in the very same newspaper are the highlight of my life – I shall not say why… The latter spoke of my *Zarathustra* as 'an advanced *exercise in style*', for example, and suggested I should also try and add some substance. Dr Widman expressed his respect for the courage of my endeavour to abolish all decent feelings.

Thanks to a little trick of chance, every sentence here was, with admirable consistency, a truth stood on its head: at bottom there was nothing else to do but to 're-evaluate values', to hit the nail on the head as far as I was concerned in a remarkable fashion – instead of hitting my head with a nail. I shall try to explain myself all the more.

In the end, no-one can learn any more from matters, books included, than he already knows. Without access to events, you will not have an ear for them. Let us take an extreme case and suppose a book contains only events that lie entirely outside the range of general or even less general experiences and suppose it is the first language for a new series of experiences. In such a case nothing really will be

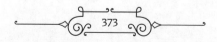

heard at all and thanks to an acoustic delusion, you will think that since you hear nothing *there is nothing there*. This, at least, is my usual experience, and proves, if you like, the *originality* of my experience. Whoever thought they had understood something in my work will have appropriated something from it in his own image – quite often the opposite of me, for instance an 'idealist'; whoever understood nothing I wrote will deny that I am worth considering at all.

The word '*Superman*' as a definition of a type of greatest perfection in contrast to 'modern' man or 'good' man, to Christians and other nihilists – a word that in the mouth of Zarathustra, the *destroyer* of morality, acquires a very profound meaning – was in all innocence understood almost everywhere in the light of those values that the figure of Zarathustra stood against – I mean as an 'idealistic' type of higher human being – half 'saint', half 'genius'... Other learned cattle have accused me of Darwinism because of this definition; it was even seen as belonging to that 'hero cult' of Carlyle's, that great unconscious and involuntary swindler, which was so maliciously rejected by me. Once I whispered in someone's ear he should look to Cesare Borgia rather than Parsifal and he could not believe his ears.

You must forgive me my lack of any curiosity as far as reviews of my books are concerned, in particular when they appear in newspapers. My friends and publishers know this and do not mention them to me. In one particular case, however, I once found out about all the sins committed against one of my books – it was *Beyond Good and Evil*. I could tell a pretty story about that. Would you believe that the *Nationalzeitung* (a Prussian newspaper – this information is for my readers from abroad; I myself read only the *Journal des Débats*) in all seriousness regarded this book as a 'sign of the times', a piece of right and proper *Junker philosophy*, which its organ the *Kreuz* newspaper simply lacked the courage to come up with?

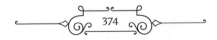

2.

THIS was mentioned for the benefit of Germans, for I have readers everywhere – all highly educated minds, characters in top positions and with great responsibilities on their shoulders; among my readers are even some true geniuses. In Vienna, in St Petersburg, in Stockholm, in Copenhagen, in Paris and in New York – everywhere I have been discovered, but *not* in Europe's plain country: in Germany... And let me be honest, I am even happier about my non-readers, those that have neither heard my name nor of the word 'philosophy', but wherever I go, here in Turin for instance, all faces light up and soften. The thing that so far has flattered me most is that old peddler women will not rest until they have picked for me the very sweetest bunch from amongst their grapes. *For this* you must be a philosopher.

Not for nothing are the Poles called the Frenchmen of the Slavs. A lovely Russian woman will not mistake my origins for a moment. I am no use at being pompous; at best I can go as far as embarrassment... To think in German, to feel in German – I can do it all, but *that* is too much for me... My former tutor Ritschl went so far as to say that I planned even my philological treatises like a Parisian novelist – that they were absurdly thrilling. In Paris itself people are surprised about *'toutes mes audaces et finesses'* – to quote Monsieur Taine; I am afraid that even in the highest forms of the dithyramb, the hymn of praise to Dionysus, you will find traces of that ingredient that can never be stupid, never be 'German' – it is called 'wit'... I can do no other, so help me God! Amen. We all know, some even know from experience, what a long-ear is. Well, I dare to assert that I have the tiniest ears. This is of no little interest to the ladies – am I right that they feel understood by me?... I am the supreme *anti-ass* and as such a world-historical beast – I am in Greek, and not only in Greek, the *Antichrist*...

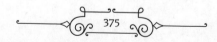

3.

I KNOW on the whole my privileges as a writer; in a few cases I was even assured how much the habitual reading of my books would 'ruin' the taste buds. It is simply unbearable to read any other books, least of all philosophical ones. It is a distinction beyond all comparison to enter this elegant and delicate world – you certainly do not need to be a German; it is in short a distinction that must be earned. Anyone, however, akin to me in *loftiness* of will, experiences the true ecstasies of learning by reading them: for I swoop from heights where no bird ever flew, I know abysses where no foot ever lost its footing. I was told it was not possible to put any book of mine down – even that I disturbed a good night's sleep... There is absolutely no prouder or at the same time more subtle kind of book: it achieves here and there the highest that can be achieved on earth, cynicism; you have to conquer it with the most delicate fingerstrokes, using them like the most valiant fists. Every weakness of the soul will bar you from it for good and ever, even a belly-ache; you do not need nerves but you have to have a cheerful abdomen. Not just poverty, the stuffy air in a soul excludes you from it, but much more so cowardice, the unclean and the secret longing for revenge deep down in the bowels: one word from me drives all bad instincts into full view. Among my acquaintances are several test animals, which I use to sample their very varied and instructive reactions to my books. Those who wish to have nothing to do with their contents, my so-called friends for example, become 'impersonal', they wish me luck to have 'done it once again' – apparently there is improvement because of a happier ring to the books... These completely reprobate 'spirits', these 'beautiful souls', liars all in the extreme, have absolutely no idea what to do with these books – therefore they feel they are *beneath* them – a consistent reaction of all 'beautiful souls'. The cattle among my acquaintances, the mere Germans, if you don't mind my saying so, let me know that they are

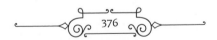

not always of my opinion but that they agree here and there, for instance... I have heard this even with regard to my *Zarathustra*.

Similarly, every 'feminist' in a person, even in a man, closes the gate as far as I am concerned: never will you enter the labyrinth of daring knowledge. You have to be completely ruthless with yourself, must be used to great *hardness*, to remain cheerful and merry among all these implacable truths. If I conjure up the picture of a perfect reader, he always becomes a monster of courage and curiosity, yet also of subtlety, cunning and prudence – a born adventurer and explorer. After all, I can not describe any better than *Zarathustra* did *who* I am actually addressing: those few he was prepared to reveal his riddle to.

'To you, you bold explorers and experimenters and who ever else embarked beneath cunning sails on dreadful seas,

– to you, you drunk, with riddles revelling in twilight, whose souls are being lured by flutes down every treacherous abyss,

– for you do not want to grope your way along a thread with a coward's hand, and where you are able to *divine*, you hate to *open up*...'

4.

AT THE same time, I wish to make a general comment about my *art of style*. The meaning of every style is to *communicate* a state of mind, an inner tension of pathos through symbols, including the timing of these symbols – that is the character of every style; and in view of the fact that the multitude of states of mind in me is enormous, I have also many styles at my disposal – in short, the most diverse art of style that ever was available to man. Any style is *good* which genuinely communicates a state of mind, which does not make a mistake when using symbols, the timing of symbols, and the *moods* – all phrasing is to do with creating moods. Here my instinct is impeccable.

Good style *in itself* is a folly, mere 'idealism' or 'beautiful *in itself*' for instance, or 'goodness *in itself*' or 'the thing *itself*'... This is assuming

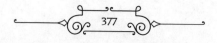

that there are ears to hear – that they are *capable* and worthy of such pathos, that there are still plenty who are *worth* communicating with… Meanwhile my Zarathustra, for example, is still searching for such people – ah, he will have to go looking for a long time yet! – You have to *deserve* to listen to him… And until then, there will be nobody who will understand the *art* that has been squandered here. No-one else has lavished newer, more extraordinary, more genuinely original forms of art on to the world. That this was possible in the German language had yet to be substantiated; I myself would have dismissed it most emphatically. Before me, nobody knew what the German language was capable of – what any language is capable of.

The art of *grand* rhythm and *grand style* of phrasing, expressing a tremendous swing in sublime and superhuman passion, was first discovered by me: with a hymn of praise entitled 'The Seven Seals' which is the last discourse of the third part of *Zarathustra*. With that I soared thousands of miles above everything which hitherto has been called poetry.

5.

THE fact that my books are written by a psychologist, unparalleled in history, is perhaps the first impression a good reader may get, a reader such as I deserve, and one who reads me as the good old philologists used to read their Horace. Those doctrines that are really accepted by all the world, not to speak of the la-di-da philosophers, moralists and other blockheads and cabbages, seem to me but naive blunders – for example that belief that 'altruistic' and 'egoistic' are opposites, while the ego itself is merely a 'supreme swindle', an 'ideal'… There are *no such things* as egoistic or altruistic deeds: both terms are a psychological nonsense. Or the proposition 'man strives for happiness'… or 'happiness is the reward of virtue'… or 'joy and misery are opposite values'… Morality, the femme fatale, has falsified all psychology and *outmoralized*

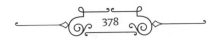

it until only that horrible humbug that love must be 'altruistic' was left... You have to have a firm grip of *yourself*, stand steadfastly on both legs, otherwise you *cannot* love at all. Women know that all too well: they don't give a damn for unselfish and merely objective men... May I dare to say that I know women? That this is part of my Dionysian heritage? Who knows, perhaps I am the first psychologist of the eternal-feminine. They all love me – which is old hat (not counting the damaged, the 'emancipated' ones, who haven't got what it takes to have children). Luckily I am not willing to let myself be torn to bits – your typical woman tears those she loves to bits... I know these amiable maenads... Oh, what a dangerous, sly, subterranean little beast she is! And at the same time so lovely!... A little woman pursuing her revenge would even destroy fate.

Woman is inexpressibly more wicked than man, but also cleverer. Goodness in a woman is already a form of *degeneration*... A so-called 'beautiful soul' in a woman is essentially a physiological disease – I shall not go any further, otherwise this would become a medical discourse. The struggle for *equal* rights is actually a symptom of disease; every doctor knows it. Women, the more feminine they are, fight with all their might against rights in general: the natural order of things, in the eternal *war* between the sexes she always has the greatest advantage.

Have you ever listened to my definition of love? It is the only one worthy of a philosopher. Love is conducted like war because it is at heart the deadly hatred of the sexes. Have you heard my reply to the question of how a woman can be *cured*, saved? Give her a child. Women need children, to her a man is merely a means to an end: thus spoke Zarathustra.

'The emancipation of woman' is the instinctive hatred of the *misshapen* – that is to say, infertile – women for her fertile sisters; the fight against 'man' is only ever a means, an excuse, a strategy. In raising themselves to the level of 'women *per se*', of 'supreme woman', of

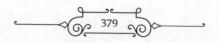

'ideal woman', they try to bring down the general level of women's rank; and there is no surer way of doing so than higher education, wearing trousers and the voting rights of cattle. To tell the truth, the emancipated are the *anarchists* in the world of the 'eternal-feminine', the failures and losers whose lowest instinct is revenge... A whole species of the ugliest type of 'idealism', incidentally, can also be found among men; for instance with Henrik Ibsen, that typical old maid, it is aimed at *poisoning* the clear conscience and the natural spirit in sexual love... And not to leave any doubt about my heartfelt and strict views on these matters I will give you another clause from my code of morality against *vice*: I use the word 'vice' to fight any form of perversion, but if you prefer a finer word, use 'idealism'. The clause reads: 'Preaching of chastity is a public incitement to perverse acts. All contempt for sexual matters, all sullying of them by applying the concept "unclean" is itself a crime against life – it is the actual crime against the holy spirit of life.'

6.

TO GIVE you an idea of my role as a psychologist, I give you a curious bit of psychological analysis from my book *Beyond Good and Evil* – but I forbid any conjectures as to whom I may or may not describe in this passage.

> 'The Genius of the heart, as that great recluse possesses it, the divine tempter and born pied piper of consciences, whose voice is able to descend right down into the underworld of every soul, who does not speak a word or cast a glance without some seductive power or trick, whose exquisite skill enables him to seem, not what he is but what is to those who follow him yet *one more* compulsion to press ever closer to him, to follow him ever more enthusiastically and whole-

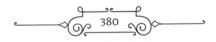

heartedly... The genius of the heart, who makes all loud and self-satisfied things fall silent and listen out, who smoothes the rough souls and lets them taste a new longing: to lie still, like a mirror, that the low sky may be reflected in them... The genius of the heart, who teaches the clumsy and over-hasty hand to hesitate and to grasp more tenderly, who senses the hidden and forgotten treasure, the drop of goodness and sweet spirituality beneath thick black ice and who is a divining rod for every grain of gold that was buried for years and years, imprisoned under heaps of mud and sand... The genius of the heart, whose very touch enriches everyone, not with gifts and surprises, not by the wealth and stealth of others, but richer in themselves, more aware of themselves than before, opened up, caressed and sounded out by a soft westerly wind, perhaps even less sure, more tender, more fragile, more broken, but full of hopes that have not yet a name, full of new will and flowing forth, full of new unwillingness and flowing back.'

THE BIRTH OF TRAGEDY.

1.

TO BE fair to *The Birth of Tragedy* (1872) we have to overlook a few things. Whatever was wrong with the book gave it its *effect* and fascination, that is to say its practical application to *Wagnerism* as if that were a symptom of an *ascent*. Because of it, this book was an event in Wagner's life; it was only from then on that the name of Wagner evoked great hopes. People still remind me of this today, occasionally even in the context of *Parsifal*, how it is really *my* fault that the movement became a *cult* and excited such high opinions.

I found on several occasions that the book was referred to as the

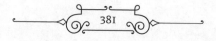

'Rebirth of Tragedy from the Spirit of Music'; people had only ears for a new formula for the art, the intention, the task of *Wagner*, and because of it they did not notice what was truly valuable in the book. 'Hellenism and Pessimism', that would have been a less ambiguous title, suggesting a first instruction of how the Greeks coped with pessimism – how they *overcame* it... Precisely their tragedies prove that the Greeks were *no* pessimists: Schopenhauer went wrong here, in precisely the same way as he went wrong in all other things.

If looked at with some degree of objectivity, *The Birth of Tragedy* seems anachronistic; you would never dream that it was *begun* amid the thunder of the Battle of Wörth. I have thought through these problems before the walls of Metz, on cold September nights while on duty as a medical orderly. The book seems to be some fifty years older than it really is. Politically it is indifferent, 'un-German' you would say today. It smells offensively of Hegel, but some of the formulas have the doleful whiff of Schopenhauer. It is a 'concept' – the antithesis of the Dionysian and the Apollonian translated into metaphysics; history itself is the development of this 'concept' whereby in tragedy this polarity has been sublimated into a unity. These things have never before faced each other and are now suddenly juxtaposed; they are used to illuminate each other and are now *comprehensible*... Opera, for example, and the revolution.

The two decisive *innovations* of the book are firstly that Greeks have understood the Dionysian phenomenon; for the first time a psychological analysis is given and it is considered to be the root of all Greek art. The other is the understanding of Socratism: Socrates is recognized for the first time as an instrument of Greek disintegration, as a typical Decadent. 'Rationality' *versus* instinct. 'Rationality' is at any price seen as a dangerous, life-undermining power.

On the matter of Christianity there is a profound and hostile silence throughout the book. It is neither Apollonian nor Dionysian;

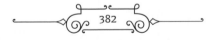

it *denies* all *aesthetic* values – the only values that *The Birth of Tragedy* recognizes; it is nihilistic in its truest sense, while the ultimate limit of affirmation is attained in the Dionysian symbol. Once the Christian priests are even alluded to as a 'spiteful kind of dwarf' dwelling 'deep, deep beneath the earth'.

2.

THIS beginning is strange beyond belief. As far as I know, I myself had *discovered* the only metaphor and counterpart in history, and thus I became the first to understand the amazing phenomenon of the Dionysian. Similarly, in recognizing Socrates as a Decadent, I could prove unequivocally how little the security of my psychological grasp would be endangered by any moral idiosyncrasy; regarding Morality itself as a symptom of decadence is an innovation and unique in the history of knowledge. How high had I jumped with these two insights above the wretched and shallow chatter about optimism versus pessimism. I was the first to see the actual polarity: the degenerating instinct that turns against life with subliminal vengefulness (Christianity, the philosophy of Schopenhauer, in a sense even the philosophy of Plato, the whole of idealism in its typical form) versus the formula of *supreme affirmation* born out of abundance, of profusion, to say 'yes' without reserve, say 'yes' to suffering itself, to guilt, to all that is dubious and strange in existence itself... This ultimate, most joyous, most wantonly extravagant 'yes' to life is not just the ultimate insight, it is also the *most profound*, the one most strongly confirmed and upheld by truth and science. Nothing needs to be taken away, nothing is superfluous – as it is, the aspects of existence rejected by the Christians and other nihilists are of an infinitely higher order in the hierarchy of values than even that which the instinct of decadence could approve of. To understand this requires *courage* and, as a condition for that, an excess of *strength*; for precisely as far as courage *may* dare to go governed by

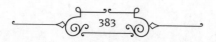

precisely that strength, you will come closer to the truth. Knowledge, saying 'yes' to reality, is just as necessary for the strong as cowardice and the *flight* from reality – the 'ideal' – is for the weak, who are inspired by weakness... It is not given to them to know that the Decadents *need* the lie, it is one of the conditions for their survival.

Whoever does not merely understand the word 'Dionysian' but sees *himself* described by the word 'Dionysian' has no need to refute Plato or Christianity or Schopenhauer – he can *smell the decay.*

3.

I FINALLY explained in my book *The Twilight of the Idols* the extent to which I have discovered the concept of the 'tragic', the ultimate knowledge of the psychology of tragedy. 'Saying "Yes" to life even with its most alien and difficult problems; the will to live rejoicing in its own boundlessness even while *sacrificing* its most superior types – *that* is what I called Dionysian, that was how I saw the bridge to the psychology of the *tragic* poet. *Not* to be rid of fear and pity, not to purge myself of a dangerous effect by its vehement discharge as Aristotle misunderstood it, but the eternal joy of becoming in itself beyond all fear and pity, that joy that included even *joy in destroying.*'

In this sense I have the right to see myself as the first *tragical philosopher* – that is to say, the extreme antithesis and polar opposite of a pessimistic philosopher. Before I came along, this translation of the Dionysian into philosophical pathos did not exist: *the tragic wisdom was lacking* – I looked in vain for signs of it even among the *great* Greeks of philosophy, those that lived two centuries before Socrates. I retained some doubt in the case of Heraclitus, in whose presence I felt altogether warmer and more comfortable then anywhere else. The affirmative answer to death *and destruction*, which is the decisive feature of a Dionysian philosophy, saying 'yes' to opposition and war, of *becoming* along with radical rejection even of the concept of *'being'* –

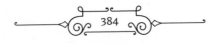

all this is definitively more closely related to me than anything else thought to date. The doctrine of the 'eternal recurrence', that is to say of the unconditional and infinite circuit of all things – this doctrine of Zarathustra *could* already have been taught by Heraclitus. Stoicism, having inherited almost all their fundamental ideas of Heraclitus, shows traces of it.

4.

THIS book offers tremendous hope. Ultimately, I have no reason to withdraw the hope for a Dionysian future from music. Let us look a century ahead and assume that my assault on two thousand years of unnaturalness and abuse of mankind is successful. That new denomination of life, which takes the greatest of all tasks, the advancement of mankind, into its hands, including the merciless destruction of all that is degenerative and parasitic, will make that *abundance of life* on earth (from which the Dionysian state must also grow again) once again possible. I promise a *tragic age*: the greatest art of saying 'Yes' to life, tragedy itself, will be reborn when mankind has weathered the recognition of the hardest but most necessary war *without suffering on its account...*

A psychologist might still add that the Wagnerian music I heard in my youth had absolutely nothing to do with Wagner, that when I described the Dionysian music I described what *I* had heard – that I instinctively had to translate and transfigure everything into the new spirit that I had within me. The evidence for that, *as convincing as any evidence can be*, is my essay 'Wagner in Bayreuth' – all psychologically decisive passages only speak of me, you can happily insert my name or the word 'Zarathustra' whenever the text mentions Wagner. The entire picture of the artist *in praise of Dionysus* is the picture of the *pre-existent* poet of Zarathustra, sketched with incredible profundity and without touching in the slightest on Wagnerian reality. Wagner himself was aware of that; he did not recognize himself in this essay.

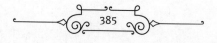

Similarly, 'the idea of Bayreuth' was transformed into something that is no mystery to those who know my Zarathustra: into that *great noon*, at which the most select will consecrate themselves for the greatest of all tasks. Who can say? The vision of a feast I shall yet live to see... The pathos of the first pages is world-historical; the *glance* spoken of on the seventh page is Zarathustra's distinctive glance; Wagner, Bayreuth, the whole provincial German wretchedness are a cloud in which an infinite mirage of the future is reflected. Even psychologically all decisive traits of my own nature are projected into that of Wagner, the side-by-side proximity of the brightest and the most calamitous forces, the will to power as no man ever possessed it before, the ruthless bravery in the spirit, the unlimited power to learn without suppressing the will to act. All in this essay is a prophetic announcement: the impending rebirth of the Greek spirit, the necessity of the new Alexanders who will *tie* the Gordian knot of Greek culture once again... Listen to the world-historical emphasis, with which the concept 'tragic attitude' is introduced at the end of section 4: this essay is full of world-historical emphasis. This is the most foreign sounding 'objectivity' possible: the absolute certainty about what I *am* projected on some chance reality – the truth about me spoken from some gruesome depth. At the beginning of section 9, the *style* of Zarathustra is described in dramatic detail and anticipated; and never will there be a more magnificent expression for the *event* of Zarathustra, an act of tremendous purification and consecration of humanity, than can be found in section 6.

The Untimely Meditations

1.

THE four *Untimely Meditations* are by all means militant. They prove that I was not some 'Jack the dreamer' or fantasist but that I actually enjoy drawing a sword – or is it just that my wrists are dangerously

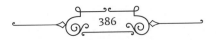

flexible. The *first* assault (1873) was aimed at German culture upon which even then I looked down with merciless contempt, since it was without meaning, without substance and without aim: a mere 'public opinion'. There is no more malignant error of judgement than to believe that the great military success of the Germans was to prove anything in favour of this culture – least of all *its* triumph over France... The *second* Meditation (1874) illuminates the dangerous element in how we make science operate, gnawing at life and poisoning it; life is made *sick* by this dehumanized grinding of gears and mechanism, the 'impersonality' of the worker, and the false economy of the 'division of labour'. The *aim* is lost; culture, ways and means, how modern methods of science are *barbarized*... This essay recognized for the first time that the 'sense of history' of which this century is so proud is a sickness, a typical symptom of decay. In the *third* and *fourth* Meditations two images of the most extreme *self-love* and *self-discipline* are offered in contrast as a pointer to a *higher* concept of culture; to restore the concept of culture – Schopenhauer and Wagner, *or*, in a word, Nietzsche. These untimely types are beyond comparison, since they are full of a sovereign contempt for all that surrounds them by the name of 'the German Empire', 'Culture', 'Christianity', 'Bismarck', 'Success'...

2.

OF THESE four attacks, the first was extraordinarily successful. The commotion it made was splendid in every sense. I had touched the sore point of a victorious nation – that their victory was *not* a cultural event but perhaps something entirely different... The response came from all sides, not just from the old friends of David Strauss whom I had ridiculed as the archetypal cultural philistine and self-satisfied ass, in short as the author of his beer-hall gospel *The Old and New Faith* (the expression 'cultural philistine' taken from my essay has since become part of the German language). These old friends, citizens of Württemberg and

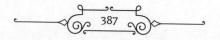

Swabia, whom I deeply hurt by making fun of their prodigy, their Strauss, replied in as plain and uncouth a manner as I could have hoped for. The replies from Prussia were more prudent – after all, they were of true Prussian Blue. The rudest reply came from a Leipzig newspaper, the notorious *Grenzboten*. It caused me some difficulties to restrain the indignant Baselers from taking action. Only a few old gentlemen were unconditionally on my side, acting from mixed and often unfathomable motives. Ewald from Göttingen was one of them and he suggested that my assault had had fatal consequences for Strauss. Also the old Hegelian Bruno Bauer, who from then on was one of my most attentive readers. During his last years he liked to refer to me, for example, when giving von Treitschke, the Prussian historiographer, a steer on whom he might ask for information about the concept of 'culture', which he seemed to have lost. The most thoughtful, also the lengthiest comments about the essay and its author, come from an old disciple of the philosopher von Baader, a Professor Hoffmann from Würzburg. On reading my essay, he predicted a great destiny for me – bringing about a kind of crisis and ultimate decision with regard to the problem of atheism, whose most instinctive and ruthless convert he assumed me to be. It was atheism that led me to Schopenhauer.

By far the most acutely heard and most keenly felt was an extraordinarily strong and brave plea on my behalf by the usually very moderate Karl Hillebrand, this last *humane* German with knowledge of how to put pen to paper. His piece was first published in the *Augsburger Zeitung*; these days you will find a somewhat amended version in his collected essays. He described the essay as an event, a turning point, a dawning of awareness, an excellent sign, as a *true* return of German earnestness and German passion for all things intellectual.

Hillebrand was full of praise for the style of the essay, for its maturity, for its perfect tact in distinguishing between the person and the issue; he honoured it by calling it the best polemical essay written

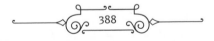

in German – since the skill of polemics is so dangerous and inadvisable, in particular for Germans. Backing me up to the hilt, even intensifying the comments I had dared to make against the galloping barbarization of the German language ('these days they act the purist and can no longer form a sentence'), with the same contempt for the 'top writers' of this nation, he concluded with an expression of his admiration for my *courage*, that 'supreme courage which is determined to put the people's favourites in the dock'…

The effects of this essay are of almost incalculable value to my life. So far, nobody has tried to quarrel with it. There is a silence; in Germany I am treated with a certain gloomy caution: for years I have made use of an unconditional freedom of speech which today nobody, least of all in the German Empire, seems to be at *liberty* to do. My paradise lies in 'the shadow of my sword'… In all truth, I only put into practice one of Stendhal's principles: he advises us to enter any society with a *duel*. And how I had picked my opponent! The foremost German freethinker!… Indeed, an altogether new type of libertine spirit was expressed for a first time in this way; to this day nothing is more foreign and less related to me than the whole European and American species of '*libre penseur*'. I am much more thoroughly at odds with these incorrigible blockheads and fools and their 'modern ideas' than with any of their opponents. They also want in their way to 'improve' mankind in their own image; they would fight an irreconcilable war against what I am and what I *want*, if only they understood it – however, all of them still believe in the 'ideal'… I am the first *immoralist*.

3.

I CANNOT say that the *Untimely Meditations* with titles like 'Schopenhauer' or 'Wagner' would contribute much to an understanding or even just raise the relevant psychological questions in either case,

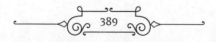

give or take the odd exception. Thus, for example, the essay describes the elementary in Wagner's character with profound instinctive certainty as an actor's talent that only draws conclusions from its means and purposes. I did not really want to dwell on psychology in these essays but to pursue a unique problem of education, a new concept of *self-discipline, self-defence* to the point of hardness; a path to greatness and to world-historical tasks that must be expressed for a first time. Broadly speaking, I caught hold of two famous and as yet undiagnosed types, the way we grab an opportunity when it presents itself in order to say something; in order to have at hand a few more formulas, symbols, means of expression. This is finally, and with a wisdom that seems uncanny to me, suggested in section 7 in the third Untimely Meditation; Plato used Socrates in this way, as a sign language for Plato.

Now that I am looking back from some distance upon the conditions which these essays bear witness to, I cannot deny that they speak really only of me. The essay 'Wagner in Bayreuth' is a vision of my future, but in 'Schopenhauer as Educator' I describe my innermost biography, my *becoming*. Above all, though, it was about my *promise*!... *What* I am today, *where* I am today (at a giddy height where I no longer speak with words but with lightning bolts) – how far away was I from this at the time!

But I *saw* the land; I did not deceive myself for a moment about the way, the sea, the danger – *and* the success! The great calm of the promise, this happy gaze into a future that should not remain just a promise! Here, every word is based on experience, is deep, is inward; the most painful is there too – it contains words that are virtually dripping with blood. But a wind of *great* freedom blows above it all; the wound itself is no objection.

I see the philosopher as a terrible explosive endangering everything. My concept of the 'philosopher' is worlds removed from any concept that would include even a Kant, not to mention the academic 'rumi-

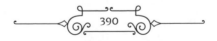

nants' and other professors of philosophy: this essay offers an invaluable lesson, even if it must be admitted that at bottom it is not 'Schopenhauer as Educator' but 'Nietzsche as Educator' who is speaking. Considering that in those days my trade was that of a scholar and perhaps that I was *good at it*, it is not entirely without significance that an austere sample of scholar-psychology suddenly reveals itself in this essay – it expresses the *feeling of distance*, the absolute certainty I felt about what was to be my life's work and what could be dismissed as just means to an end. I was clever enough to have been many things in many different places in order to make myself singular – to arrive at one thing. For a time I also *had* to become a scholar.

HUMAN, ALL TOO HUMAN.
WITH TWO SEQUELS

1.

HUMAN, All Too Human is the monument to a crisis. It calls itself a book for *free* spirits: almost every sentence marks some kind of victory – I liberated myself with it from anything in my nature that *does not belong*. Idealism does not belong to me – the title reads 'where *you* see ideal things, *I* see – the human, ah, the all too human!' I know mankind *better*... The term 'free spirit' cannot have any other meaning here but that it is *liberated*, a spirit that took control of itself once again. The tone, the sound of voice, has completely changed; you will find the book clever, detached, occasionally hard and mocking. A certain spirituality kept in *good* taste seems to maintain the upper hand over a more passionate undercurrent. In this context, the publication of the book in 1878 can actually be seen as an excuse to celebrate the hundredth anniversary of the death of Voltaire. For Voltaire, contrary to all those who wrote after him, was above all an aristocrat of the mind – just like me.

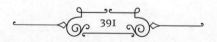

The name Voltaire on one of my essays – that really meant progress – *towards me*... If you look more closely, you will discover a merciless spirit that knows all the hideouts of the ideal, where it has its secret dungeons and also therefore where it can still lurk in safety. With a torch in both hands (for once its light is steady), you will shine through the dark into this *underworld* of the ideal. This is war, but a war without gunpowder and smoke, without bellicose attitudes, without pathos and torn limbs – all that would still be 'idealism'. One mistake after another is calmly laid on ice, the ideal is not refuted – it simply *freezes to death*. Here, for example, the 'genius' freezes to death, a little further on it is the 'saint'; under a huge icicle the 'hero'; and in the end 'belief' freezes to death, the so-called 'conviction', 'pity' too cools down considerably – almost everywhere 'the matter in itself' freezes to death...

2.

THE beginnings of this book go right back to the weeks of the first Bayreuth festivals; a profound alienation from all that surrounded me there is one of its preconditions. Those who have any notion of the visions I had already encountered then can imagine how I felt, when one day I woke up in Bayreuth. It was as if in a dream... Where was I? I recognized nothing, I hardly recognized Wagner. In vain did I leaf through my memories: Tribschen, a distant island of the blessed – not a trace of similarity. The incomparable days when the foundation stone was laid, the small *elect* group of people that celebrated it and whose sensitivity I could take for granted – not a trace of similarity. *What had happened?* – They had translated Wagner into German! The Wagnerian had become Wagner's master!

German art! the *German* Master! *German* beer!... We others, who know only too well what subtle artist and what cosmopolitanism of taste is exclusively addressed by Wagner's art, were beside ourselves

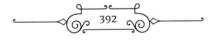

to find Wagner decorated with German 'virtues'. I understand, indeed, I know the Wagnerian; I have 'experienced' three generations from the late Brendel onwards who confused Wagner with Hegel down to the 'idealists' of *Bayreuther Blätter* who confused Wagner with themselves. I have heard every kind of confession of 'beautiful souls' about Wagner. A kingdom for one sensible word!

In truth, a hair-raising company! All philistines and cabbages – endlessly charming! No deformed monster is missing, not even the anti-Semite. Poor Wagner! Where had he ended up – he would have been better off in a herd of swine! But among Germans!... For the instruction of future generations we should really take a true Bayreuth citizen, stuff him, or, even better, preserve him in surgical spirit since spirit is needed – with the label underneath reading, 'This is the "spirit" on which the German Empire is founded...'

Enough, I left in the midst of it all for a couple of weeks, very abruptly, even though a charming Parisian tried to console me. The only apology I offered Wagner was a fatalistic telegram. In a place called Klingenbrunn, hidden away in the deep Bohemian forest, I dragged a deep depression and contempt for the Germans around like a sickness *and* from time to time I would write a sentence or two in my notebook, under the general title 'The Ploughshare', aphorisms of strong psychological content that may perhaps still be found in *Human, All Too Human*.

3.

WHAT I decided at that time was not, as you may think, a break with Wagner – I felt a total aberration of my instincts of which the odd mistake, be it now Wagner or the chair at the University of Basel, was just another symptom. I became extremely *impatient* with myself; I realized that it was high time to reflect on *myself*. All at once I saw with terrible clarity how much time I had already wasted – how useless

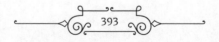

and arbitrary my whole existence as a philologist appeared in relation to my task. This false modesty embarrassed me… Ten years had passed in which the *nourishment* of my mind had truly ceased, in which I had learned nothing useful at all, in which I had forgotten absurd amounts for the sake of the rags and bones of learnedness. To crawl scrupulously with terrible eyesight through the metrics of Antiquity – that is what I had come to!

I looked at myself with overwhelming pity – how thin and emaciated I was: my learning simply lacked *realities* and my 'idealities' were not worth a damn! An almost all-consuming thirst took hold of me: from then on I really pursued nothing more than physiology, medicine and natural sciences – and I only returned to properly historical studies when the greater task compelled me to do so. It was then that I also realized for the first time the connection between an activity chosen against your better judgement, a so-called 'vocation' to which one is *barely* called, and that need for a dulling of the feeling of despondency and hunger by means of a narcotic art – for instance Wagnerian Art. As I carefully looked around me, I discovered that a large number of young men are in the same state of distress: one step against nature virtually *compels* another one. In German, in the 'German Empire' to speak unambiguously, all too many are condemned to choose vocations too early, and then to *waste away* under the heavy load, unable to shake it off. These people long for Wagner as a drug – they forget themselves, they lose themselves for a moment… what am I saying – *for five or six hours*!

4.

IT WAS then that my instinct decided inexorably against giving way, being a follower, being confused about myself. Any form of life, even the most unfavourable conditions like illness and poverty – they all seemed to me preferable to the unworthy 'selflessness' which I got

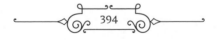

mixed up with, originally because of ignorance and *youth*, and which I stuck to later because of inertia and a so-called 'sense of duty'. Here I was helped in a way that I cannot praise enough and just in time by my father's *malignant* heritage – basically a predestination to an early death. My illness *slowly set me free* – it spared me having to break away or take any violent or offensive step. I did not lose any goodwill then, but actually gained some. My illness also gave me the right to change all my habits completely; it allowed, even *commanded* me to forget; it granted me the necessity of lying still, of leisure, of waiting and being patient... But that means thinking!... My eyes themselves put an end to all that book-reading, in plain language: to philology. I was saved from the 'book', for years I did not read a thing – the *greatest* favour I ever did myself.

My most profound self, buried and silenced, as it were, by a constant barrage of *having* to listen to other selves (and that means reading!) woke up slowly, timidly, full of doubt – but at least *it was talking again*. Never have I been as happy as during the sickest and most painful periods of my life: just look at *Dawn* or even *The Wanderer and His Shadow* to understand what this 'return to *myself*' meant: a supreme kind of *recovery*... The other kind, my cure, was merely a consequence of it.

5.

HUMAN, All Too Human, this monument to a rigorous self-discipline with which I abruptly ended all those effeminacies like 'supreme swindle', 'idealism', 'beautiful feelings' that had somehow wormed their way inside me, was for the most part written in Sorrento; I finished its final version during the winter months in Basel, under far less pleasant conditions than those in Sorrento. Actually, it is *Peter Gast*, a student at the University of Basel and very fond of me, who is responsible for this. I dictated it with my head bandaged, and in

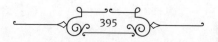

pain; he transcribed and corrected it – he was really the writer while I was merely the author. When the book was finally finished – to the amazement of the sick man – I also sent two copies to Bayreuth. By an extraordinary coincidence I received at the same time a beautiful copy of the *Parsifal* text dedicated to me by Richard Wagner with the inscription: 'To my dear friend Friedrich Nietzsche, from Richard Wagner, member of the Church Council'. To my ears, this crossing of the two books had an ominous ring. Did it not sound as if we had crossed *swords*?... Anyway, we both seemed to feel it, for we both remained silent.

Around that time the first *Bayreuth Blätter* appeared: I understood *what* I should have realized long ago – Incredible! Wagner had turned to religion...

6.

WHAT I then (1876) thought of myself, with what tremendous certainty I had my task and its world-historical aspect in my grasp, is testified by the book in general and by one passage in particular; only, once again with my inborn cunning I avoided the little word 'I' and showered with world-historical glory, this time not Schopenhauer or Wagner, but one of my friends, the excellent Dr Paul Rée – luckily far too sophisticated a creature to be deceived... *others* were less refined – I have always recognized the hopeless amongst my readers (for example, the typical German professor) by their reaction to this passage – they always had to see the whole book as a form of higher realism... In fact, the contents contradicted five or six propositions of my friend: you may wish to read the preface to my *On the Genealogy of Morals*.

The passage reads: 'But what is the main proposition at which one of the boldest and coldest thinkers has arrived, the author of the book *On the Origin of Moral Feelings* (read Nietzsche, the first

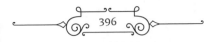

immoralist) in virtue of his radical and penetrating analyses of human activity? "Moral man is no closer to the intelligible world than the physical man – since there is no intelligible world...'" This sentence, grown hard and sharp-edged under the hammer blow of historical recognition (read *Re-evaluation of all Values*) may perhaps one day, in some future (1890), serve as the axe aimed at the roots of the 'metaphysical needs' of humanity – but whether this is a blessing or a curse, who can say? However, it stands as a proposition of tremendous consequences, fruitful and dreadful at the same time and looking into the world possessed of that *double perspective* which all great insights share...

Dawn.

THOUGHTS ON MORALITY AS A PREJUDICE

1.

WITH this book I begin my crusade against *morality*. Not that it smells in the least of gunpowder; you will notice very different, much lovelier scents, assuming that you have a reasonably sensitive nose. The guns are neither big nor small; if the effect of the book is negative, then its means are all the less so; these means that effect a conclusion, *not* a gunshot. To take leave in this book with a cautious reserve from all that was hitherto honoured and even worshipped under the name of morality in no way contradicts the fact that it contains not a single negative word, no attack, no spite – indeed, there it lies in the sunshine, well-rounded and happy, like some sea urchin basking in the sun among rocks. Ultimately, I myself was this sea urchin; almost each sentence of the book was first thought, was *hatched out* among that jumble of rocks near Genoa where I was alone and still in secret bond with the sea. Even now, whenever I touch that book by chance, almost every sentence becomes part of a net with

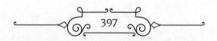

which I can pull something unique back from the depths: its entire skin trembling with tender thrills of memory. The skill which distinguishes it is not least that it detains things for a little while, things that otherwise scurry past, weightlessly and noiselessly, moments I privately call divine lizards – not with the cruelty of that young Greek god who simply speared the poor little lizard, but all the same, I work with something pointed, with a pen... 'There are so many dawns that have not yet risen' – with this *Indian* inscription this book opens its doors. Where does its originator *seek* that new morning, that delicate red as yet undiscovered that will rise another day – what do I say, a whole series, a whole world of new days!? In a *re-evaluation of all values*, in liberation from all moral values, in saying 'Yes' and trusting all that has hitherto been forbidden, despised and cursed. This book, which says so firmly '*Yes*' pours out its light, its love, its tenderness for many wicked things; it gives them a 'soul', a 'good conscience', the lofty right and *privilege* of existence. Morality is not attacked, it is merely no longer in the picture... This book closes with 'don't you think?' – it is the only book that closes with 'don't you think?'...

2.

MY LIFE'S work lies in preparing humanity for a moment of intense self-examination, a *time of reckoning* when it will look backwards and outwards, then emerge from the dominion of chance and priests and for the first time ask itself the fundamental questions about 'Why?' and 'For What?' – this task is the necessary consequence of the knowledge that humanity is *not* capable of setting itself on the right path, that it is *not* in any way subject to divine rule; on the contrary, that actually precisely among their most holy regarded values the instinct for denial, the instinct for decadence, has been seductively in charge. The question concerning the origin of moral value is therefore for me a question of *the first order*, because it is crucial for the future of humanity. The demand that we

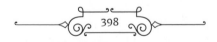

should all *believe* ourselves basically in safe hands, that a book, the Bible, offers us a definitive assurance of divine governance and wisdom in the destiny of man, is translated back into reality, the will to suppress the truth about the pitiable opposite of all this, namely that so far humanity has been in the *worst* of hands and that it has been governed by the losers, two-faced vengeful ones, the so-called 'saints', these slanderers of the world and violators of men. The ultimate proof that the priest (and this includes the *clandestine* priest, the philosopher) is not just master of a certain religious community, but has become master in general, and that the morality of decadence, the will to the end, has been accepted as morality *itself*, is the fact that absolute value is afforded to all that is non-egoistic, and hostility to all that is egoistic. Those who do not agree with me at this point are in my opinion *infected*… But all the world disagrees with me… For a physiologist such a juxtaposition of values simply leaves no doubt. When even the least important organ within an organism fails to enforce its self-preservation, its restoration of energy, its 'egoism' with perfect certainty, then the whole will degenerate. The physiologist demands the degenerated part is *cut out*; he denies any solidarity with it, he has not the slightest pity for it.

However, it is precisely the *degeneration* of the whole, of humanity, that the priest *desires*; that is why he *conserves* what degenerates – that is his price for his governance… What is the point of those concepts of lies, the *ancillary* concepts of morality: 'soul', 'spirit', 'free will', 'God', if not to ruin humanity physiologically?… If you deflect seriousness from self-preservation, the build-up of physical strength, *that is of life*, if anaemia is construed as an ideal and contempt for the body as 'the salvation of the soul', what else is this if not a *recipe* for decadence? – The loss of the centre of gravity, the resistance to the natural instincts, in a word 'selflessness' – that is what until now was called *morality*… With *Dawn* I first took up the fight against the morality that would unself man.

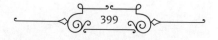

THE JOYFUL SCIENCE.

DAWN is a positive book, profound but full of light and kindness. This is also true and to the highest degree of *The Joyful Science*; in almost every sentence, thoughtfulness and sense of mischief are lovingly combined in this book. A poem expressing thanks for the most wonderful January I ever lived through – the whole book is a gift – reveals most clearly from what sheer depth 'science' drew to become *joyful...*

> You, who with your spear aflame
> crushed the ice around my soul
> that rushing to the sea it came
> of its highest hope and goal:
> ever brighter, full of grace
> in its loving bond, but free –
> will it sing you songs of praise
> my beloved January.

Who can doubt what is meant here by 'highest hope' when at the close of the fourth book the crystalline beauty of the first words of *Zarathustra* rise in their shining glory? Or on reading the granite-like sentences at the end of the third book with which for the first time destiny is given a formula *for all time*? 'The Songs of Prince Outlaw', most of it was written in Sicily, remind us explicitly of the Provençal notion of *The Joyful Science*, that group of *singer, knight and free spirit* which distinguishes that wonderful early culture of Provence from all ambiguous cultures – in particular the last poem 'To the Mistral', an exuberant song in which, with respect, morality is freely trodden on, is perfectly typical for Provence.

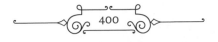

Thus spoke Zarathustra.
A book for all and no-one

1.

I SHALL now tell you the story of *Zarathustra*. The basic *idea* of the book, the notion of *eternal recurrence*, this highest formula of affirmation that could ever have been achieved, was conceived in August of 1881: it was drafted on a sheet of paper with the inscription: '6,000 feet beyond men and time'. I myself walked on that day from Lake Silvaplana through the forests; at a powerful pyramid-shaped boulder near Surlei I stopped to rest. There I had this thought: if I count back a few months from this day, I will discover, like an omen, a sudden and extremely decisive change in my taste, especially in music. You may of course altogether count *Zarathustra* as music – certainly a renaissance of the art of *listening* was a precondition for it. In a little mountain spa near Vicenza, Recoaro, where I spent the spring of 1881, I, together with my friend, the young musician Peter Gast, another 'reborn' one, discovered that the phoenix of music flew past us with a lighter and more brilliant plumage than he had ever displayed before. But if I go forward from that day to the sudden birth under the most unlikely conditions in February 1883 (the final part, from which I quoted a few sentences in my *preface*, was finished in precisely that sacred hour in which Richard Wagner died in Venice), we arrive at eighteen months for the pregnancy. This figure of exactly eighteen months might suggest, at least to Buddhists, that I am really a female elephant.

The Joyful Science, its hundred indications showing that it is near to something quite incomparable, belongs to the interval period; in the end it even starts *Zarathustra* off, and it also delivers the fundamental concept of *Zarathustra* in the penultimate passage of the fourth book. Similarly, that 'Hymn to Life' (for mixed choir and orchestra) was composed during this interval; its score was published two years

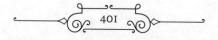

ago by EW Fritzsch in Leipzig. One symptom for my state of mind that year perhaps worth noting was the pure *positive* pathos that was particularly strong within me then; I called it the tragic pathos. The time will come when it will be sung in my memory. The text (I have to make this clear since this is currently often misunderstood) is not by me; it is the surprising inspiration of a young Russian woman who was my friend at that time, a Miss Lou von Salomé. If you can make any sense of the final words of this poem you will be able to imagine why I preferred and admired it – it has greatness. Pain is *not* held to be an objection to life: 'If you have no joy to give me, well then, *you still have your pain...*'

Perhaps my music, too, has some greatness when it comes to this passage (top note of the oboe, C sharp, not C: misprint). The following winter I stayed in that pretty quiet bay of Rapallo near Genoa, which is wedged between Chiavari and the foothills of Portofino. My health was not at its best back then: the winter was cold and excessively wet; a little hostel right next to the sea, so that the high waves made it impossible for me to sleep at night, was in just about every way the opposite of what I would have wished for. Nevertheless, and almost to prove my doctrine that anything of decision-making importance happens 'in spite of' and not 'because of', this winter and its inclement conditions saw my *Zarathustra* come into being.

In the morning I would climb upwards and southwards on the splendid road to Zoagli, right to the top, looking past pine trees to get a magnificent view of the sea. In the afternoon, whenever my health permitted it, I walked around the whole bay from Santa Margherita all the way to Portofino. This town and its landscape came even closer to my heart because of the great love which the unforgettable German Emperor Frederick III felt for them; by chance I was in this coastal region again in the autumn of 1886, when he visited this small forgotten world of happiness for a last time. It was on these

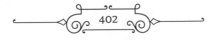

two walks that Zarathustra first came to me, in particular as a type: indeed, he *overcame* me…

2.

TO UNDERSTAND this type we must first become familiar with his physiological condition: this is what I call *great health*. I cannot explain this concept better, more *personally* than I already did, that is to say in one of the final sections of the fifth book of *The Joyful Science*: 'Being new, nameless, incomprehensible, we premature births of an as yet unproven future need for a new goal also a new means – namely a new health, stronger, more seasoned, tougher, more audacious and more joyful than any previous one. Whoever has a soul that longs to have experienced the whole range of values and desires to date, and to have sailed around all the coast of this ideal "Mediterranean"; whoever wants to know from the adventures of his own more authentic experience how an explorer and conqueror of the ideal feels, and also an artist, a saint, a legislator, a sage, a scholar, a pious man, a sooth-sayer and a recluse of the old style – needs one thing above everything else: *great health* – a condition that we not merely have but also acquire continually. This condition we must acquire because it is relinquished again and again, and must be relinquished. And now, after having long been on our way in this manner, we Argonauts of the ideal, with more daring perhaps than is prudent, and having suffered shipwreck and damage often enough, but we are, to repeat it, healthier than they would like us to be, dangerously healthy, always regaining health – it will seem to us as if, as a reward, we have now confronted an as yet undiscovered country whose boundaries nobody has surveyed yet, something beyond all the lands and nooks of the ideal so far, a world so abundantly rich in beauty, strangeness, dubiousness, dreadfulness and heavenliness that our curiosity as well as our longing to possess it has got beside itself – oh, nothing will satisfy us now! After such

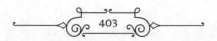

sights and with such ravenous hunger for knowledge and conscience, how could we still be satisfied with *present-day man*? That is bad enough, but it is inevitable that we find it difficult to remain serious when we look at his worthiest goals and hopes, and perhaps we do not even bother to look any more.

'Another ideal runs ahead of us, an odd, tempting, dangerous ideal to which we should not wish to persuade anybody because we do not readily grant *the right to it* to anyone: the ideal of a spirit who plays naively – that is to say not deliberately but out of overflowing power and abundance – with all that was hitherto called holy, good, untouchable, divine; for whom those supreme things which the people naturally accept as the measure of their values, signify danger, decay, humiliation, or at least recreation, blindness, and temporary self-oblivion; the ideal of a human-superhuman well-being and benevolence that will often appear *inhuman* (for example, when it confronts all previous earthly seriousness, all previous solemnity in gesture, word, tone, eye, morality, and sense of duty, as if it were their most lifelike and unintended parody) and with which in spite of all of this perhaps *great seriousness* will really begin, the real question mark will be set for the first time, the destiny of the soul will take a turn, the hand of the clock will move on, the tragedy will *take its course...*'

3.

HAS anyone at the end of the 19th century a clear idea of what poets of strong ages called *inspiration*? If not, I shall describe it. If you had the least remains of superstition in you, you could indeed hardly reject the idea you are merely the plaything and mouthpiece of, and medium for, overpowering forces. The concept of revelation in the sense that suddenly with incredible certainty and subtlety something becomes *visible*, audible, something that shakes you to the core and takes you over, merely describes the facts. You listen out, you do not seek; you

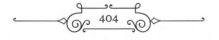

take, you do not ask who gives; like lightning a thought flashes up, urging, unfaltering – I never had a choice. It is a rapture – its tremendous tension may occasionally find relief in floods of tears, now the pace quickens unintentionally, now it slows down; a complete frenzy while being distinctly aware of countless subtle thrills that make your skin tingle right down to your toes; a depth of happiness in which the most poignant and most dismal do not seem to be at odds, but rather a condition, challenged, a *much-needed* splash of colour within such an excess of light; an instinct for rhythmic relationships reaching across wide spaces – length, the need for *all-embracing* rhythm is almost the measure of the force of inspiration, a kind of counterpoint to its pressure and tension...

Everything happens completely involuntarily but as in a gale of yearning for freedom, of absoluteness, of power, of divinity... The randomness of image and simile is strangest of all; there is no longer a notion of what is an image or a simile, everything offers itself as the nearest, the most obvious, the simplest expression. It really seems, to bring something that Zarathustra said to mind, as if the things came by themselves and offered themselves as similes ('here come all things with caresses to your discourse and flatter you: for they want to ride on your back. On every simile you ride to every truth. Here the words and receptacles of words all burst open for you; all being wishes to become word, all becoming wishes to learn from you how to speak'). This is *my* experience of inspiration; I do not doubt that you have to go back thousands of years to find anyone who could tell me, 'It is mine too'.

4.

AFTERWARDS I was ill for a few weeks in Genoa. Then there followed a melancholy spring in Rome where I put up with life – it was not easy. Basically, I was hugely irritated by this location, the most

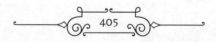

unsuitable location in the world for the poet of *Zarathustra*, where I was not by choice. I tried to get away – I wanted to go to *Aquila*, precisely the opposite of Rome, founded as an act of hostility to Rome, as I shall one day found a place in memory of an atheist and enemy of the church of the first order, one of those closest related to me, the great Emperor Frederick II of the Hohenstaufen dynasty. But somehow I could not escape the capital: I had to go back again. In the end, after I had given up trying to find an *anti-Christian* region, I resigned myself to the Piazza Barberini. I fear that in order to avoid bad smells as much as possible, I even asked in the residence of the King of Italy itself whether they did not have a quiet room for a philosopher.

On a loggia high above that Piazza, from which you have a view over all of Rome and can listen to the fountain running deep below, I composed that loneliest of lonely songs that has ever been written, 'The Night Song'; at that time a melody of inexpressible melancholy was always in my head and I used the words 'death from immortality' in the chorus...

That summer, back home at the sacred spot where the first lightning flash of *Zarathustra* had dazzled me, I found *Zarathustra II*. I only needed ten days: I never needed any more time, for the first or for the third and the final section either. In the following winter under the peaceful sky of Nice that sparkled above me for the first time in my life, I found *Zarathustra III* – and was finished; scarcely a year was all it took. Many hidden places and heights in the landscape around Nice are made very special for me by unforgettable moments; that decisive passage titled 'On Old and New Tablets' was composed during the difficult climb from the station to the marvellous Moorish aerie, Eza – I was always fittest when on top of my creative force. The *body* is inspired; let us keep the 'soul' out of it... I was often seen to dance; in those days I could walk in the mountains for seven, eight hours

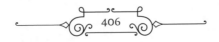

without feeling in the least bit tired. I slept well, I laughed much – I was at the height of my vigour and patience.

5.

APART from these ten-day oeuvres, the years during and in particular *after* my *Zarathustra* were a calamity beyond comparison. You pay dearly to be immortal: you have to die several times during your lifetime.

There is something that I would call the grudge of greatness: everything that is great, a work, a deed, will turn, once completed, *against* the one who accomplished it, and precisely because he accomplished it, he has become *weak* – he cannot bear his deed any longer, he can no longer face it. To have put something *behind* you that you were never permitted to choose, something into which the destiny of mankind has been knotted – and now you labour *under* it!… It almost crushes you. The grudge of Greatness! Then there is the eerie silence around you. Loneliness has seven skins – nothing can penetrate it. You meet people, greet friends: new bleakness, no-one looks you in the eye. At best this is a form of rebellion. I experienced such a rebellion; it was of a different nature but from almost everyone close to me: it seems that nothing is more insulting than to create a sudden distance – those *noble* natures who cannot live without worshipping someone are rare. Thirdly, there is the absurd sensitivity of the skin to small barbs, a kind of helplessness before everything petty. This seems to me due to an enormous squandering of all defensive energies, which are a condition for every *creative* deed, every deed that stems from our most authentic, inmost, nethermost regions. The *limited* abilities to defend yourself are thereby as good as suspended; no energy goes back into them. Moreover, I dare to suggest that our digestive system is hampered, we are less keen to move, that we are all too susceptible to chills as well as mistrust – mistrust which in many cases

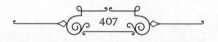

is merely an error caused by illness. In such a condition I once sensed the close presence of a herd of cows even before I set eyes on them, because milder, more philanthropic thoughts came back to me: *they* had warmth...

6.

THIS work stands very much on its own. Let us leave the poets out of it, perhaps nothing has ever been done from such an abundance of energy. My concept of the 'Dionysian' became a *supreme deed* here; all human action up to now seems poor and relative in comparison. The least we can say is that a Goethe, a Shakespeare would be unable to breathe even for a moment at this incredible height of passion, that Dante is merely a believer compared with Zarathustra and not one who first *creates* truth, a *world-governing* spirit and destiny – that the poets of the Vedic texts are priests and not even worthy of tying the shoelaces of Zarathustra and it does not give the slightest idea of the distance, of the *mountain blue* solitude in which this work dwells. Zarathustra has for ever a right to say, 'I draw circles around me and sacred boundaries; fewer and fewer climb with me on ever higher mountains – I build a mountain range out of ever more sacred mountains.' Add up the spirit and goodness of all great souls: all of them together would not be able to speak like Zarathustra. The scale on which he ascends and descends is tremendous; he has seen further, strives to go further, *could* go further than any other human being. He contradicts with his every word, this most positive of all minds; in him all opposites are blended into a new unity. The highest and the lowest energies of human nature, the sweetest, airiest and most dreadful ones surge forth from a well with immortal certainty. Until then, you do not know what height is, what depth is, you know even less what truth is. There is not a moment in this revelation of truth that has already been anticipated or conjectured by one of the greatest. Before

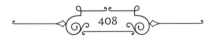

Zarathustra, there was no wisdom, no soul searching, no art of oratory; even everyday matters, the most humdrum, speak of extraordinary things. Aphorisms are trembling with passion; eloquence becomes music; lightning bolts are hurled into hitherto unfathomed futures. The most powerful capacity for simile that has existed so far is poor and a mere toy compared with this return of language to the nature of symbolism.

Look, how Zarathustra descends and says something kind to everyone! How gently his hands touch even his antagonists, the priests, and how he suffers *with* them. Here, man is overcome every moment that passes, the concept of 'Superman' has here become the greatest reality – whatever has been great in man up to now lies *beneath* him at an infinite distance. The peaceful, the light-footed, the omnipresence of wickedness and high spirits and all other things typical of the type of Zarathustra, has never been dreamed of as being essential to greatness. Precisely in this immense space with its access to the contradictory, Zarathustra feels himself to be *the supreme type of all beings*; and if you hear his definition of it, you will not bother trying to look for a simile for him.

'– the soul which has the longest ladder and can go down
　　the deepest,
the most comprehensive soul which can walk and go astray
　　and roam furthest within itself,
the one most necessary, which flings itself with joyful passion
　　into chance,
the soul as being, which *will* strive to become, the one as
　　having, which *will* strive to want and desire,
the one in flight from itself, closing in on itself in the widest
　　possible circle,
the wisest soul, enticed most sweetly by folly,
the one that loves itself the most, in which all matters have

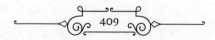

their currents and counter-currents, their low and high tides.'

But that is the concept of Dionysus himself. Another contemplation led us to precisely this point. The psychological problem with the type of Zarathustra is, how he who says 'No' and *does* 'No' to everything to which we have until now said 'Yes' to an unheard-of degree, can nevertheless be the opposite of a No-saying spirit; how the spirit bearing the most terrible fate, a doomed task, can nevertheless be the lightest and the most ethereal – Zarathustra is a dancer. How he who has the hardest, the most dreadful insight into reality, who thought the 'most abysmal thought' nevertheless does not consider it an objection to existence, not even to its eternal recurrence – but rather one reason more for *being himself* the eternal 'Yes' to all things, 'the tremendous, boundless saying of "Yes" and "Amen"'... 'Into all abysses I still carry the blessings of my "Yes"'... *But that is the concept of Dionysus once again.*

7.

WHAT language will such a spirit speak when he speaks to himself? The language of the *dithyramb*, the song of praise to Dionysus. I am the inventor of the dithyramb. Listen all to how Zarathustra talks to himself before *sunrise* (III, 18): such emerald happiness, such divine tenderness had no tongue before me. Even the profoundest sadness of such a Dionysus still becomes a song of his praise; take for instance 'The Night Song' – the immortal lament at being condemned by the abundance of light and power, by his *sun* nature, not to love.

'It is night: now all fountains speak louder. And my soul too is a fountain.

It is night: only now all songs of lovers are roused. And my soul too is the song of a lover.

Something not stilled, which cannot be stilled is within me that

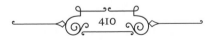

wants to raise its voice. A desire for love is within me that itself speaks the language of love.

I am light: ah, that I were night! But this is my loneliness: I am girded by light.

Ah, that I were dark and of the night! How I would suck at the breasts of light!

And I would even bless you yourselves, you little twinkling stars and glow-worms up there! – and be overjoyed because of your gifts of light.

But I live in my own light, I drink the flames that break out of me back into myself.

I do not know the happiness of those who take, and I have often dreamed that stealing must be still more blissful than taking.

This is my poverty that my hand never rests from giving; that is my envy that I see waiting eyes and the illuminated nights of longing.

Oh misery of all givers; eclipse of my sun; craving to crave; ravenous hunger while filling up!

They take from me: but do I still touch their soul? There is a chasm between taking and giving, and the smallest chasm is the last to be bridged.

Hunger grows out of my beauty: I should like to hurt those for whom I light the way, I should like to rob those to whom I gave – thus I hunger for wickedness.

Withdrawing my hand just as the other hand reaches out to it, like a waterfall that hesitates even as it plunges: this is how I hunger for wickedness.

Such revenge is plotted by my abundance, such spite wells up out of my loneliness.

My happiness in giving died while giving; my virtue became weary of itself in its abundance.

Those who always give are in danger of losing their shame; those

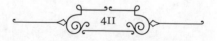

who always hand out grow callouses on heart and hand from all that handing out.

My eye no longer sheds tears because of the shame of those asking; my hand has become too hard for the trembling of filled hands.

Where have the tears in my eyes gone and the downiness of my heart? Oh the loneliness of all givers, the silence of all who shine!

Many suns circle in barren space: to all that is dark they speak with their light – to me they do not speak.

This is the hostility of the light towards those who shine: merciless, it travels in its orbit.

Unjust to those who shine in its innermost heart, cold towards suns – thus travels every sun.

The suns travel like a storm in their orbits; they follow their implacable will – that is their coldness. Oh it is only you, you dark ones, you of the night, who create warmth from that which shines! Only you drink milk and refreshment from the udders of light.

Ah, ice is around me, my hand is burned by iciness; thirst is within me, which pines for your thirst.

It is night: ah, that I must be light! And thirst for things of the night! And loneliness!

It is night: now my longing breaks out of me like a well – I long for speech.

It is night: now all fountains talk louder. And my soul too is a fountain.

It is night: now all songs of lovers are roused. And my soul too is the song of a lover.'

8.

NOTHING like this has ever been written, ever been felt or *suffered*: this is how a god, a Dionysus, suffers. The answer to such a song of

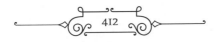

solar solitude in the light would be Ariadne... Who apart from me knows what Ariadne is!... No one so far knows the solution of such riddles, I doubt that anyone ever even saw it as riddle. Zarathustra defines once, with rigour, his task – it is mine too – so that we cannot be mistaken as to the *meaning*; he *says 'Yes'* to the point of justification, to the point of redemption of all things past too.

'I travel amongst men as amongst fragments of the future: the future which I envisage.

And that is all my poetry and striving, that I can write poetry and gather all at once what is fragment and riddle and dreadful chance.

And how could I bear to be human if man was not also a poet, and solver of riddles and redeemer of the future?

To redeem those from the past and to turn every "it was" into a "that is how I wanted it": that alone I should call redemption.'

In another passage he defines as rigorously as possible what for him alone 'man' can be – *not* an object of love or, worse, compassion – Zarathustra even mastered the *great disgust* for man: man to him is a shapeless thing, a material, an ugly stone that needs a sculptor.

'No longer to *want* and no longer to *appreciate* and no longer to *create*: oh that this great weariness might always remain far from me!

In knowledge too I only feel my will's joy in begetting and becoming and if there is innocence in my knowledge, it is because the *will to beget* is part of it.

This will has lured me away from God and the gods: what is there to create if gods – were there?

But my fervent will to create drives me again and again towards man; thus is the hammer driven to the stone.

Ah, you men, within the stone sleeps an image for me to see, the image of all images! Ah, that it must sleep in the hardest, ugliest stone.

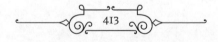

Now my hammer rages brutally against its prison. Pieces of rock rain from the stone: what is that to me!

I want to perfect it, for a shadow came to me – once, the quietest and lightest of all things came to me!

The beauty of superman came to me as a shadow: what are the gods to me now!...'

I wish to stress a final point: the line in italics demands it. Among the conditions for a Dionysian task is most certainly the hardness of the hammer, *the joy even in destroying*. The imperative 'Harden!', the certainty deep below *that all creators are hard* is the distinctive mark of a Dionysian nature.

BEYOND GOOD AND EVIL
PROLOGUE TO A PHILOSOPHY OF THE FUTURE

1.

MY TASK for the following years has been as strictly sketched out as is possible. Now that the Yes-saying part has been achieved, it is the turn of the No-saying, *No*-doing part, the re-evaluation of the previous values themselves, the great war – the evocation of a day for the big decision. This includes the slow turning round to look for my peers, to those strong enough to offer me their help *destroying*.

From then on, all my writings are fishhooks: perhaps I am as good an angler as anyone else?... If I caught nothing, it's not my fault. *There just weren't any fish...*

2.

IN ALL that matters, this book (1886) is a *critique of modernity*, including modern science, modern art, even modern politics, whilst pointing to an antagonistic type that has very little in common with modern man: a noble, Yes-saying type. In this latter sense, the book

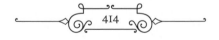

is a *school for gentlemen*, the term here being used in a more spiritual and radical sense than ever before. You have to have inbuilt courage to put up with it and never have known fear... All those things on which this era prides itself are seen as conflicting with this type, making them almost seem like bad manners: the famous 'objectivity' for instance, the 'compassion with all suffering', the 'historical sense' with its slavish devotion to all things foreign, subservience to inferior notions and 'all concepts of science'. If you keep in mind that the book was written *after Zarathustra*, you may be able to imagine where it comes from. The eye, compelled by a tremendous urge to look out into the *far* distance (and Zarathustra is even more farsighted than the Tsar) is here forced to focus sharply on what is close at hand: our own age and *environment*. You will find in every detail and in particular in outline a *deliberate* renunciation of those instincts which made a *Zarathustra* possible. Refinement of form, intention and the *art of being silent* are emphasized; psychology is handled with deliberate hardness and cruelty – the book has not a single kind word...

All that is restful: who can conceive in the end *which* type of rest makes such a waste of goodness necessary as is found in *Zarathustra*?... Theologically speaking – listen well, because I seldom speak as a theologian – it was God Himself who, at the end of His day's work, coiled Himself up as a snake beneath the tree of knowledge: that was His way of resting from His task of being God... He had made everything too beautiful. The devil is simply God's idleness on every seventh day.

The Genealogy of Morals.
A POLEMICAL PAPER

THE three treatises which make up this genealogy are, as regards expression, intention and technique of the unexpected, perhaps the

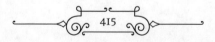

most sinister that have ever been written. Dionysus, as we know, is also the god of darkness.

This is a starting line that is *calculated* to lead you astray every time – cool, scientific, even ironical, deliberately pushy and deliberately reticent. Gradually the atmosphere becomes restless, there is the odd flash of lightning, very uncomfortable truths make themselves heard from afar with a dull rumbling sound – until finally with ferocious speed the moment comes where all is driven forward with terrible intensity. And at the last, amongst dreadful detonations, a *new* truth peeps at you through thick clouds.

The truth of the *first* treatise is the psychology of Christianity: the birth of Christianity out of the spirit of resentment, not, as may have been believed, out of 'spirit' – it is a countermovement in its nature, the grand uprising against domination by *noble* values. The *second* treatise deals with the psychology of *conscience*: this is *not*, as may well have been believed, 'the voice of God in man', but the instinct of cruelty turning in on itself after it can no longer release itself to the outside world. Cruelty is here revealed, for the first time, as one of the oldest and most indispensable elements of culture. The *third* treatise is a reply to the question as to the origin of the tremendous power of the ascetic ideal, the priest ideal, even though it is a *harmful* ideal in every sense, the will to annihilation and an ideal of decadence. This is the reply: it is powerful *not* because God's presence is behind the priest, which may well have been believed, but for lack of something better and because so far it has been the only ideal – after all, it has no competition. 'For man would rather aspire to nothingness than *not* aspire at all'… Above all, *apart from* Zarathustra there was no *counter-ideal*.

You get my meaning. Three decisive psychological overtures for a re-evaluation of all values. This book contains the first psychology of the priest.

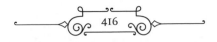

THE TWILIGHT OF THE IDOLS.
HOW TO PHILOSOPHIZE WITH A SLEDGEHAMMER

1.

THIS book of less than 150 pages, both cheerful and fatalistic in its tone (a demon laughing at you, so to speak, and the work of so few days that I cannot even be bothered to tell you how many) is altogether an exception amongst books: there is no book richer in substance, more independent, more dazzling – more wicked! If you wish to get an idea of how everything stood on its head in front of me, start by reading this work. What is called '*idol*' in the title is simply everything that hitherto has been called truth. *The Twilight of the Idols* – in plain language: the old truth is coming to an end...

2.

THERE is no reality, no 'notion of an ideal' that has not been touched upon in this book (touched! what cautious euphemism!). Not just the *eternal* idols, but also the very recent and therefore most senile ones: 'Modern ideas' for instance. A powerful wind blows between the trees and everywhere fruit – truths – drops down. It smacks of the windfall of an autumn all too fruitful: you trip over truths, you even crush some to death – there are just too many...

However, what you can grasp is no longer questionable, these are decisions. I alone hold the yardstick for 'truths' in my hands, I alone *can* decide. It is as if a *second* consciousness had grown within me, as if my 'will' had cast a light upon the *downward* slope along which it has been running for ages... The *downward* slope – they called it the road to the 'truth'... All 'dark urges' have been dealt with, indeed, the *good* human being was least aware of the righteous path.

And in all seriousness, nobody before me knew of the righteous path, the path leading upwards: I alone pointed towards hopes, tasks

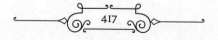

and recommended paths of culture – *I am the herald of these good tidings...* And therefore I am also destiny.

3.

IMMEDIATELY after finishing this work and without losing a single day, I took upon myself the formidable task of the *re-evaluation* with a supreme feeling of pride which nothing could equal. Aware of my immortality at every moment, I engraved sign after sign into brass tablets with the certainty of fate. The preface was written on 3rd September 1888. When, after finishing it, I stepped outside into the morning air, I found the most lovely day I have ever lived through in the Upper Engadine – clear, glowing in its colours and with all its contrasts, all hues available between the icy north and the south.

Owing to a delay caused by floods, I did not leave Sils-Maria until 20th September, so in the end I was the only visitor in this delectable spot, which in my gratitude I wish to make immortal. After an eventful journey, including one narrow escape from death in the waters of Lake Como, which was flooded when I reached it in the dead of night, I arrived in Turin, to which I was *guided*, on the afternoon of the 21st, and it was from that time on my home.

I took the same lodgings I had occupied in the spring, on Via Carlo Alberto 6, III, opposite the mighty Palazzo Carignano where Vittorio Emanuele was born; it has a view of the Piazza Carlo Alberto and to the hills beyond it. Without hesitating and without being swayed for one moment, I returned to my work: only the last quarter of the book still remained to be written. The 30th September, Victory!, was the seventh day and a God could take it easy, walking along the River Po. The same day, I wrote the preface for my *Twilight of the Idols* for which I had corrected the proofs at leisure during the month of September.

Never before have I lived through an autumn like that, nor even

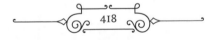

imagined that such glory could be possible – a Claude Lorrain painting extended to infinity, every day of an equally incredible perfection.

THE WAGNER CASE
A MUSICIAN'S PROBLEM.

1.

TO DO this essay justice you have to suffer from the fatal affliction of music as from an open wound. *From what* do I suffer, when I suffer from the fatal affliction of music? I suffer because music has been deprived of its transfiguring, positive character – because it has become the music of decadence and is no longer the flute of Dionysus...

Supposing, however, that you feel that the cause of music is very much your *own* cause, your *own* tale of woe, then you will find this essay considerate and extremely mild in tone. To be cheerful in such cases and self-deprecating in a good-humoured way, in other words, to speak the truth whilst laughing whereby the truth would justify the hardest language, that is humanitarianism itself. Who would seriously doubt that I, old war horse that I am, will bring out my big guns against Wagner? – I restrained myself from any decisive action in this cause – I loved Wagner!

In the end this is an attack on a more subtle 'unknown figure' who cannot be easily divined by anyone in the sense that I wish to insinuate (really! I have to expose 'unknown figures' of a very different calibre to some adventurer in music). However, it is even more so an attack on the German nation, whose mind is becoming lazier and less instinctive but ever more *honest* and continues to feed itself with an enviable appetite on polarities, gulping 'faith', as well as scholarship, 'Christian love', as well as anti-Semitism, the will to power (the 'Empire') as well as the Gospel of the Humble without any sign of indigestion... This lack of judgement in choosing between these

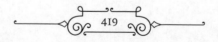

opposites! This ventral neutrality and 'selflessness'. This fairness of the German *taste bud* that will level everything – that finds everything tasty... Without any doubt, the Germans are idealists! When I last visited Germany, I found German taste occupied with trying to put Wagner and the Trumpeter of Säckingen on the same level; I myself was witness as the citizens of Leipzig founded a Liszt society in honour of one of the most genuine and German musicians (in the old sense of the term German, not an 'imperial' German), Master *Heinrich Schütz*, in order to foster and spread '*listed* church music'... Without any doubt, Germans are idealists!

2.

BUT nothing shall stop me from becoming rude and telling the Germans a few hard truths: *who else will do it?* I speak of their historical perversion. Not only have German historians lost altogether the *grand view* for the course and values of culture and have, to a man, become buffoons of politics (or the church): they have even *outlawed* this grand view. First and foremost you have to be 'German', of 'good race', then you may settle all historical values and non-values by arbitration.

'German' is an argument; 'Germany, Germany above all' is a principle; the Germans represent the 'moral world order' in history. In relation to the Roman Empire they are the bringers of freedom, in relation to the 18th century they are the restorers of morality, of the 'categorical imperative'... There is an imperial German historiography, even, I fear, an anti-Semitic one, a *court* historiography, and Mr von Treitschke does not seem to be embarrassed by it...

The other day, an idiotic judgement of *history*, a proposition by the (fortunately) deceased Swabian aesthetician Vischer went the rounds of the German newspapers as a 'truth' that every German had to *accept*: 'The Renaissance *and* the Reformation – both together they constitute a whole – the aesthetic rebirth *and* the moral rebirth'. Such

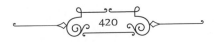

announcements make me lose my patience and I feel inclined, even duty bound, to tell the Germans once and for all *what* else they have already on their conscience. *Every great cultural crime for four centuries is what they have on their conscience*!... And always from the same cause – from their innermost *cowardice* in the face of reality, which has become cowardice in the face of truth, from their now instinctive lack of truthfulness, from 'idealism'... The Germans have cheated Europe of the harvest, of the meaning of the last *great* era – the Renaissance – at a moment when a higher order of values, noble, life- and future-affirming values had been victorious at the seat of anti-ethical values, the *values of decline – and entered deeply into the instincts of those that dwelled there*. Luther, this calamity of a monk, restored the church and, much, much worse, Christianity, at the moment *of its fall*... Christianity, this *negation of the will to live* that became a religion! Luther, an impossible monk who precisely because of his 'impossibleness' attacked the church and thus – as a consequence – restored it. The Catholics would have good reason to celebrate Luther Festivals, to compose Luther plays! Luther... and the 'moral rebirth'! To hell with all psychology! Without doubt, the Germans are idealists.

Twice before, when incredible courage and willpower just managed to attain a decent, an unambiguous, a completely scientific mode of thinking, the Germans have known how to find rat runs back to the old 'ideal', to reconciliations between truth and 'ideal', at bottom formulas for the right to reject science, for the right to *lie*: in the form of Leibniz and Kant – these two largest stumbling blocks of Europe's intellectual integrity. Finally, when on the cusp between two decadent centuries a sweeping force of genius and will made itself known, strong enough to unite Europe, a political and *economic* union for the purpose of global government, the Germans with their 'Wars of Liberation' cheated Europe of the meaning, the miracle of meaning in the person of Napoleon – they thereby have on their conscience all that followed,

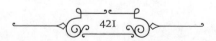

all that we see today, this sickness and lack of reason *inimical to culture* – nationalism – this national neurosis which Europe suffers from, reinforcing Europe's system of mini-states, of *petty* politics: they have made Europe lose its mind, its reason – they have led it into a blind alley. Does anyone apart from me know a way out of this blind alley?... A task, *great* enough to *unite* people once again?

3.

AND last but not least, why should I not voice my suspicion? In my case too, the Germans will try once again everything to breed a mouse from a tremendous destiny. So far, they have shown themselves up for what they are with regards to me; I doubt that they will do any better in the future. What I wouldn't give to be wrong here, to be a *bad* prophet!...

My natural readers and listeners even now are Russians, Scandinavians and the French – will this always be the case? The Germans have entered nothing but ambiguous names into the history of the quest for knowledge; they have only ever produced 'unconscious' frauds (this befits Fichte, Schelling, Schopenhauer, Hegel, Schleiermacher as well as it does Kant and Leibniz – they are all only pulling the wool over our eyes); they shall never be privileged to be counted as one with the first spirit of *integrity* in the history of the spirit, the spirit which does justice to the truth of fraudulence of four thousand years. The 'German spirit' seems stuffy to me: I breathe with difficulty near this psychological squalor that has become instinctive and is revealed by every word and in every countenance of a German. They have never lived through a 17th century of tough self-examination like the French – a La Rochefoucauld, a Descartes, are a hundred times superior to the best German in integrity – to this day they have not had a psychologist. But psychology is almost a yardstick for the *cleanliness* or *squalor* of a race... And if you are not

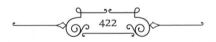

even clean, how can you have *depth*? You will never get to the bottom of it with a German, almost as with women, *there is none*, that is all there is to it. They are not even shallow. What is called 'deep' in Germany is precisely this instinctive squalor turned against themselves of which I have just spoken: they *do not want* to see themselves clearly. Might I suggest to use the word 'German' as an international coinage for this psychological depravity?

For example, at this very moment the German Emperor calls it his 'Christian duty' to free the slaves in Africa: we other Europeans would then simply be calling this 'German'… Have the Germans produced even a single book of any depth? They do not even have a notion of depth in a book. I have met scholars who thought of Kant as deep; I am afraid that at the Prussian court, Mr von Treitschke is considered deep. And on occasions when I praised Stendhal as a deep psychologist, I have met German university professors who asked me how to spell his name…

4.

AND why should I not go all the way? I like to make a clean sweep of things. I even have the ambition of appearing to be the supreme rejecter of Germans. Even at twenty-six I expressed my mistrust of the German character (Third Untimely Meditation, section 6) – I can't stand the Germans. If I had to invent a type of person who antagonizes all my instincts, he would always turn into a German.

The acid test for me is whether a man can see things as they are, whether he recognizes rank, degree or the hierarchy which is natural to people, whether he *distinguishes*: if so, he is a gentleman; otherwise he belongs hopelessly to the broad-minded, oh such good-natured category of the scoundrel. But that is what the Germans are – scoundrels – oh, they are so very good-natured… You debase yourself when associating with Germans: the Germans make everyone *look equal*.

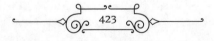

Not counting my association with a few artists, in particular with Richard Wagner, I have not spent one good hour with a German... If the most profound spirit of all time were to appear among Germans, some silly goose would believe that her not-so-beautiful soul deserved at least as much attention... I can't bear this race which is always bad company, has no feelings for nuances (oh dear! I am a nuance), has no life in its feet and cannot even walk... Ultimately, the Germans have no feet at all, just legs... They have no idea how common they are, but this is the superlative of vulgarity – they are not even *ashamed* of being merely Germans... They have to join in every conversation, they think of themselves as decision-makers, I am afraid that they have reached a decision even with regards to me...

My whole life is essentially the proof for all this. In vain do I look for some sign of tact, of sensitivity in their treatment of me. From Jews, yes, but never ever from a German. My nature demands that I am kind and gentle towards everyone – it is my *right*, not to differentiate – however, that does not stop me keeping my eyes open. I do not exclude anyone, least of all my friends – in the end I hope that this has not diminished my humanity towards them. There are five or six things which have always been a point of honour with me.

Nevertheless it remains true that almost every letter that has reached me for some years now strikes me as a piece of cynicism: there is more cynicism in goodwill for me than in any hatred... I tell every one of my friends to his face that he has never thought it worthwhile to *study* any of my books; I take it from the smallest sign that they don't even know what they are about. As for my Zarathustra, who of my friends would have seen more in him than a forbidden, fortunately perfectly meaningless presumption?...

Ten years, and nobody in Germany took it upon himself to defend my name against the absurd silence under which it was buried: it was a foreigner, a Dane, who was the first to have sufficient refinement of

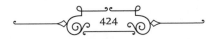

instinct and enough courage to take up arms against my so-called friends... Which German university these days would offer lectures on my philosophy as did Dr Georg Brandes in Copenhagen, who therewith once more proved himself a true psychologist?

As it is, I myself never suffered on account of all this; *necessaries* do not hurt me – love of destiny is my inmost nature. However, that does not preclude my love of irony, even world-historical irony. And thus, approximately two years before the shattering lightning bolt of *re-evaluation* which will convulse the earth, I have sent *The Wagner Case* into the world: let the Germans one more time assault me and this time *once and for all*! There is just about enough time left!

Has it been achieved? I am delighted, my dear Teutonic gentlemen, I must pay you my compliments... Just now, lest my friends be left out, one of my old girlfriends wrote to me that she now laughs at me... And this at a moment when an indescribable responsibility weighs on me – when no word can be too carefully chosen, no-one can look with sufficient awe at me. For I carry the destiny of mankind on my shoulders...

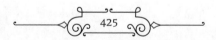

Chapter 4
WHY I AM DESTINY

1.

I KNOW my fate. One day, my name will be associated with the memory of something tremendous – a crisis without equal on earth, the most profound collision of conscience, a decision that was conjured up *against* everything that mankind has ever believed in and held sacred. I am no man, I am dynamite.

Yet for all that I am not a founder of a religion – religions are for the rabble. Whenever I come into contact with a religious person, I have to wash my hands afterwards. I don't *want* 'believers'; I think I am too wicked to believe in myself; I never address crowds... I am terribly afraid that one day I will be *canonized*: they will work out why I published this book *beforehand*, it is to prevent being taken the wrong way... I do not want to be a saint, I would sooner be a buffoon... Perhaps I am a buffoon... And yet or perhaps not yet (for there is nothing more false than a saint), the truth speaks out of me. But my truth is *terrible*: for until now they have called *lies* the truth. *Re-evaluation of all Values*: that is my formula for an act of supreme self-examination of mankind that became my flesh and my genius. It is my fate that I have to be the first *decent* person, that I find myself opposing the falsehood of thousands of years...

I was the first to *discover* the truth by being the first to find out that a lie is a lie – I could smell it... My genius lies in my nostrils...

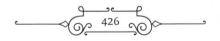

I dispute in a way that has never been done before and yet I am the opposite of a negative spirit. I am the bringer of glad tidings like no-one before me; I know tasks so enormous that hitherto no term could do justice to them, I alone will offer hope once again. For all that, I am necessarily also a man of destiny. For when truth declares war on the lies of thousands of years, we shall have upheavals, a convulsion of earthquakes, a moving of mountains and valleys the like of which has never been dreamed of. The concept of politics will have merged entirely with a war of ghosts, all power structures of the old society will have been blown to bits – all of them are founded on lies: there will be wars the like of which have never been seen on earth. I alone am responsible for *great politics* on earth.

2.

DO YOU WANT a formula for a destiny such that becomes *Son of Man*? – You will find it in my *Zarathustra*.

'*– and whoever wants to become a creator in good or evil, must first be a destroyer and dismantle values.*

Therefore the greatest evil is part of the greatest goodness: but this is being creative.'

I am by far the most awful human being that ever lived. However, that does not mean I will not also be the kindest. I know the pleasure in *destroying* to a degree that is in line with my strength to destroy – in both respects I obey my Dionysian nature which does not know how to separate doing 'No' from saying 'Yes'. I am the first *immoralist* – that makes me the perfect *destroyer*.

3.

NO-ONE asked me but they should have asked me what the name of Zarathustra means when I speak it, I, the first immoralist: for the tremendous uniqueness of that historical Persian lies precisely in his

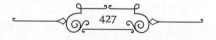

contradictions. Zarathustra first saw the true wheel of fate in the fight with good and evil – the transmission of morality into metaphysics, as a force, a cause, a purpose in itself – that is *his* work. But this question is at heart already the reply. Zarathustra *created* this most fatal mistake – morality – therefore he also had to be the first to *recognize* it. Not just because he has more experience than any other thinker in this field, after all the whole history is the experimental dispute of the doctrine of the so-called 'ethical world order'; no, it is more important to say that Zarathustra is more truthful than any other thinker. His teaching and his teaching alone recognizes truth as the highest virtue; it means, it is the opposite of the *cowardice* of the 'idealist', who runs away from reality. Zarathustra is more courageous than all other thinkers put together and he *is able to shoot with arrow and bow* – that is the Persian virtue. Do you get my meaning?... Self-conquest of morality has its roots in truth, the self-conquest of the moralist in his opposite – in *me* – that is to say, when I speak the name of Zarathustra.

4.

BASICALLY there are two negations in my definition of *immoralist*: firstly, I deny a type of man that has so far been considered the very best, the *good*, the *complaisant*, the *charitable*; and then I negate a type of morality which became prevalent and predominant as morality itself – the morality of decadence or, to put it more plainly, *Christian* morality. It would be permissible to see the second objection as the more important one, since the overrating of goodness and kindness on a large scale is to my mind already the consequence of decadence, a symptom of weakness, incompatible with the force-gathering and positive life: negating and *destroying* are conditions of saying 'Yes'.

For now, I shall stick to the psychology of the good person. To

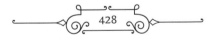

estimate how much an archetypal person is worth, you have to calculate the price that his keep will cost – you have to know the conditions he needs for his existence. The condition for the existence of the good is the *lie* – put differently, not *wanting* to look reality in the face at any cost, in particular *not* in such a way as to ever challenge complaisant instincts, and even less in such a way as to put up with the interference of short-sightedly good-natured ones. To consider any *difficulties* in general as an objection, as something that has to be abolished, is absolute nonsense, and on a large scale a true calamity in its consequences, destined to be stupid – almost as stupid as if trying to abolish bad weather – say from pity for the poor… In the overall system, the calamities of reality (in its effects, in desires, in the will to power) are to an incalculable measure more important than that form of petty happiness which people call 'goodness'. You actually have to be quite forbearing to the latter to give it some space, since it is based on instinctive falseness. I will find a major occasion to demonstrate how the historical consequences of *optimism*, this spawn of great men, have been sinister beyond belief. Zarathustra, who was the first to grasp that the optimist is just as decadent as the pessimist, and perhaps more harmful, says, *'Good men never speak the truth. Treacherous coastlines and assurances have been taught to you by the good; in the lies of the good you were hatched and huddled. Everything is riddled through and through with, and twisted by, the lies of the good.'*

Luckily, the world has not been built on such instincts that only good-natured herd animals may find their narrow happiness in it, to demand that all should become 'good men', herd animals, blue-eyed, complaisant, 'beautiful souls' – or, as Mr Herbert Spencer would have it, altruistic – that would deprive existence of its *great* character and would castrate humanity and reduce us all to a stagnant state of misery.

And they have tried to! Precisely this they called morality… In this

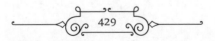

sense, Zarathustra calls the good now 'the last men', now the 'beginning of the end'; above all, he considers this type of man the most harmful, because they enforce their existence at the expense of *truth* as well as at the expense of the *future*.

' – The good – are unable to *create*; they are always the beginning of the end;

– they crucify him who writes *new* values on new tablets; they sacrifice the future to themselves; they crucify the future of all of man!

– The good – have always been the beginning of the end...

– And whatever harm those who sling mud at the world may do, *the harm done by the good is the most harmful harm.*'

5.

ZARATHUSTRA, the first psychologist of the good, is therefore a friend of the wicked. When a decadent type of man has risen to the rank of finest character, this could only happen at the expense of its counterpart, the strong and self-confident type. When the herd animal radiates purest virtue, the exceptional man must have been reduced to the level of the wicked. If falseness monopolizes the word 'truth' at any price, the really truthful man is bound to be branded with the worst names. Zarathustra leaves no doubt here: he says that it had been precisely the perception of the good, 'the very best' that made him shudder at the sight of man in general; from *this* dislike he had grown his wings, 'to soar off into distant futures' – he does not conceal the fact that *his* type of man, a relatively superhuman type, is superhuman precisely in relation to the *good* – that the good and just would call his superman *the devil*.

'You men of highest rank whom my eyes looked upon, this is my doubt in you and my secret mirth: I assume you would call my superman: the devil! You are so estranged in your soul from all that is great that superman would be terrifying to you in his goodness.' It

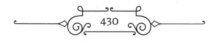

is at this point and nowhere else that you must make a start to grasp what Zarathustra wants: this type of man of his own conception, conceives reality *as it is*: it is strong enough for that – this type is not estranged or removed from reality, it is reality *itself* and exemplifies all that is terrible and questionable in it – *only in that way can man attain greatness…*

6.

BUT here is yet another sense in which I have chosen the word *immoralist* for myself as a symbol and badge of honour; I am proud of knowing this word that sets me apart from all of humanity. Nobody has as yet felt *Christian* morality to be *beneath* him: for this you need great height, a farsightedness, a hitherto unheard of psychological depth and profundity. Christian morality has until now been the femme fatale to all thinkers – they were in her service.

Who has entered before me the lairs from which the poisonous stench of this type of ideal (of world slandering) rises? Who even dared to suspect that these are lairs in the first place? Who among philosophers was actually a *psychologist* before me and not rather the opposite, a 'superior swindler' and 'idealist'? There was no psychology at all before me. To be the first here can also be a curse – it is at all events a destiny: *for you are also the first to despise…* The *distaste* for mankind is my danger…

7.

DID you get my meaning?

What defines me and sets me apart from the rest of humanity is the fact that I *exposed* Christian morality. That is why I needed a word that would be a challenge to everyone. The fact that they did not open their eyes earlier at this point is to me the greatest stain on man's conscience; it is a self-deception that has become instinct, that is a

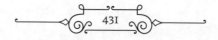

fundamental principle *to close* their eyes to everything that happens, to every causality, to every reality, as psychological fraudulence that borders on criminality. Blindness to Christianity is the *absolute crime* – the crime *against life*…

Thousands of years have passed and all people, the first and the last, the philosophers and the old women, they are all as bad as each other as far as this matter is concerned – apart from five or six moments in history (I am the seventh). The Christian has so far been *the* 'moral being', a rare curiosity and, *as* the 'moral being' more absurd, false, vain, frivolous and *acting more to his own disadvantage* than even the greatest rejecter of mankind could dream up. Christian morality, the most malignant form of the will to lie, the true femme fatale of mankind, corrupted it. It is *not* the error as such which horrifies me when I look at this fact, *not* the lack of 'good will' for two millennia, of discipline, of decency, of spiritual courage, revealed by its victory – it is the lack of naturalness and the utterly horrific fact that *perversion* itself received the highest honours as morality and was left to govern humanity as law and categorical imperative… To fail to such an extent – *not* as individuals, *not* as people, but as humanity!… That they taught us to despise the primary instincts of life, that they made up a 'soul' and a 'spirit' to abuse the body, that they taught us to find something unclean in the precondition for life – sexuality; that even in the most profound quality for any growth, strict self-interest (even the word is pejorative!), they seek the evil principle, and that, conversely, they regard the *higher* value, what am I saying, the *absolute* value, in the typical signs of decline and contradictory instincts, that is to say in 'selflessness', in loss of gravity, in 'depersonalization' and 'charity' (addictive charity!)… What? Is humanity itself decadent? Was it always?

One thing is certain, that it has been *taught* only decadent values as supreme values. The losing of the Self-morality is the absolute

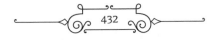

morality of decline, the fact 'I am losing myself' has been translated into the imperative 'you must all lose yourself' – and *not just* into the imperative!… The only morality that has been taught so far is to lose your Self and it reveals a will to end all – it is a basic negation of life.

This could leave open the possibility that humanity is not degenerating, but only that type of parasitic man, the *priest*, who with lies and deceptions about morality became the definer of values – who divined that Christian morality would be his means to *power*… And indeed, *this* is my discovery: the teachers, the leaders of mankind, theologians all of them, were also Decadents on the whole: *hence* the re-evaluation of all values into hostility to life, *hence* morality… *definition of morality*: morality – the idiosyncrasy of Decadents with the hidden agenda to take revenge on life – successfully. I find this definition very important.

<h2 style="text-align:center">8.</h2>

DID you get my meaning?

Everything I have just said, I said five years ago with Zarathustra as my mouthpiece. The *uncovering* of Christian morality is an event unparalleled, a true catastrophe. He who enlightens the world about it is a *force majeure*, a destiny – he breaks the history of mankind in two. You live *before* him or you live *after* him.

The lightning bolt of truth struck precisely that which was held in highest esteem: whoever understands *what* has been destroyed may look down on his hands to see whether he still has something left to hold. All that was called 'truth' up to now has been recognized as the most harmful, insidious and underhand form of lie: the sacred pretext of 'improving' humanity as an uncanny attempt to *suck* the blood of life itself – morality as *vampirism*…

Whoever uncovers morality also discovers the lack of value in all values in which we believe or have believed. He no longer sees anything

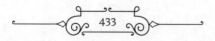

venerable in the most venerated, even *canonized* type of man. He sees the most fatal type of crippled existence in them, fatal because they fascinate…

The concept of 'God', invented as an anti-climax to life, stands for all that is harmful, poisonous, slandering and the deathly hostility against life in one dreadful unity. The concept of 'other world' or 'better world' was invented to devalue the *only* world in existence, in order not to keep a single aim, reason or task for our earthly reality. The concept of our 'soul', 'spirit' and finally even 'immortal soul' were invented to make us despise our body, to render it sick, 'holy', to meet all things that deserve to be taken seriously: the questions of nourishment, accommodation, education, nursing care, hygiene and weather, with dreadful flippancy! Instead of health the idea of 'salvation of the soul' (a folly wedged between pathological use of penitence and redemption-hysteria of manic depressive intensity) was invented together with the associated instrument of torture, the concept of 'free will', to confuse the instincts that make mistrust of our instincts second nature. The concept of the 'selfless' and 'self-denial' are the defining signs of decadence; the *attraction* of the harmful, the *inability* to evaluate your own usefulness and self-destruction were turned into proof of value itself, into 'duty', into 'holiness', into what is 'divine' in man! Finally, and this is the most terrible, the concept of the *good* man takes the side of all that is weak, sick, misshapen and suffering, of all those that ought to perish – the law of selection is crossed and an ideal born out of opposition to those proud and well-made, those who say 'Yes', those who are sure of the future, who safeguard the future – this is now called *evil*… And all this was believed and called *morality*! *Ecrasez l'infâme!*

9.

DID you get my meaning? – *Dionysus versus the man on the Cross.*

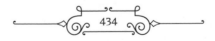

Beyond Good and Evil

Translated by
Helen Zimmern

CONTENTS

PREFACE

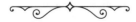

SUPPOSING that Truth is a woman – what then? Is there not ground for suspecting that all philosophers, in so far as they have been dogmatists, have failed to understand women – that the terrible seriousness and clumsy importunity with which they have usually paid their addresses to Truth, have been unskilled and unseemly methods for winning a woman? Certainly she has never allowed herself to be won; and at present every kind of dogma stands with sad and discouraged mien – *if*, indeed, it stands at all! For there are scoffers who maintain that it has fallen, that all dogma lies on the ground – nay more, that it is at its last gasp. But to speak seriously, there are good grounds for hoping that all dogmatizing in philosophy, whatever solemn, whatever conclusive and decided airs it has assumed, may have been only a noble puerilism and tyronism; and probably the time is at hand when it will be once and again understood *what* has actually sufficed for the basis of such imposing and absolute philosophical edifices as the dogmatists have hitherto reared: perhaps some popular superstition of immemorial time (such as the soul-superstition, which, in the form of subject- and ego-superstition, has not yet ceased doing mischief): perhaps some play upon words, a deception on the part of grammar, or an audacious generalization of very restricted, very personal, very human – all-too-human facts. The philosophy of the dogmatists, it is to be hoped, was only a promise for thousands of years afterwards, as

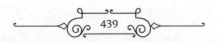

was astrology in still earlier times, in the service of which probably more labour, gold, acuteness and patience have been spent than on any actual science hitherto: we owe to it, and to its 'super-terrestrial' pretensions in Asia and Egypt, the grand style of architecture. It seems that in order to inscribe themselves upon the heart of humanity with everlasting claims, all great things have first to wander about the earth as enormous and awe-inspiring caricatures: dogmatic philosophy has been a caricature of this kind – for instance, the Vedanta doctrine in Asia, and Platonism in Europe. Let us not be ungrateful to it, although it must certainly be confessed that the worst, the most tiresome and the most dangerous of errors hitherto has been a dogmatist error – namely, Plato's invention of Pure Spirit and the Good in Itself. But now when it has been surmounted, when Europe, rid of this nightmare, can again draw breath freely and at least enjoy a healthier – sleep, we, *whose duty is wakefulness itself*, are the heirs of all the strength which the struggle against this error has fostered. It amounted to the very inversion of truth, and the denial of the *perspective* – the fundamental condition – of life, to speak of Spirit and the Good as Plato spoke of them; indeed one might ask, as a physician: 'How did such a malady attack that finest product of antiquity, Plato? Had the wicked Socrates really corrupted him? Was Socrates after all a corrupter of youths, and deserved his hemlock?' But the struggle against Plato, or – to speak plainer, and for the 'people' – the struggle against the ecclesiastical oppression of millenniums of Christianity *(for Christianity is Platonism for the 'people')*, produced in Europe a magnificent tension of soul, such as had not existed anywhere previously; with such a tensely strained bow one can now aim at the furthest goals. As a matter of fact, the European feels this tension as a state of distress, and twice attempts have been made in grand style to unbend the bow: once by means of Jesuitism, and the second time by means of democratic enlightenment – which, with the aid of liberty of the press and

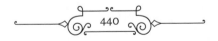

newspaper reading, might, in fact, bring it about that the spirit would not so easily find itself in 'distress'! (The Germans invented gunpowder – all credit to them! but they again made things square – they invented printing.) But we, who are neither Jesuits, nor democrats nor even sufficiently Germans, we *good Europeans*, and free, *very* free spirits – we have it still, all the distress of spirit and all the tension of its bow! And perhaps also the arrow, the duty, and, who knows? *The goal to aim at...*

Friedrich Nietzsche, Sils Maria Upper Engadine, June, 1885.

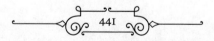

CHAPTER I
PREJUDICES OF PHILOSOPHERS

1

THE Will to Truth, which is to tempt us to many a hazardous enterprise, the famous Truthfulness of which all philosophers have hitherto spoken with respect, what questions has this Will to Truth not laid before us! What strange, perplexing, questionable questions! It is already a long story; yet it seems as if it were hardly commenced. Is it any wonder if we at last grow distrustful, lose patience and turn impatiently away? That this Sphinx teaches us at last to ask questions ourselves? *Who* is it really that puts questions to us here? *What* really is this 'Will to Truth' in us? In fact we made a long halt at the question as to the origin of this Will – until at last we came to an absolute standstill before a yet more fundamental question. We inquired about the *value* of this Will. Granted that we want the truth: *why not rather* untruth? And uncertainty? Even ignorance? The problem of the value of truth presented itself before us – or was it we who presented ourselves before the problem? Which of us is the Oedipus here? Which the Sphinx? It would seem to be a rendezvous of questions and notes of interrogation. And could it be believed that it at last seems to us as if the problem had never been propounded before, as if we were the first to discern it, get a sight of it, and *risk raising* it? For there is risk in raising it, perhaps there is no greater risk.

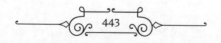

2

'*HOW could* anything originate out of its opposite? For example, truth out of error? or the Will to Truth out of the will to deception? or the generous deed out of selfishness? or the pure sun-bright vision of the wise man out of covetousness? Such genesis is impossible; whoever dreams of it is a fool, nay, worse than a fool; things of the highest value must have a different origin, an origin of *their* own – in this transitory, seductive, illusory, paltry world, in this turmoil of delusion and cupidity, they cannot have their source. But rather in the lap of Being, in the intransitory, in the concealed God, in the 'Thing-in-itself – *there* must be their source, and nowhere else!' – This mode of reasoning discloses the typical prejudice by which metaphysicians of all times can be recognized, this mode of valuation is at the back of all their logical procedure; through this 'belief' of theirs, they exert themselves for their 'knowledge', for something that is in the end solemnly christened 'the Truth'. The fundamental belief of metaphysicians is *the belief in antitheses of values*. It never occurred even to the wariest of them to doubt here on the very threshold (where doubt, however, was most necessary); though they had made a solemn vow, '*de omnibus dubitandum*'. For it may be doubted, firstly, whether antitheses exist at all; and secondly, whether the popular valuations and antitheses of value upon which metaphysicians have set their seal, are not perhaps merely superficial estimates, merely provisional perspectives, besides being probably made from some corner, perhaps from below – 'frog perspectives', as it were, to borrow an expression current among painters. In spite of all the value which may belong to the true, the positive and the unselfish, it might be possible that a higher and more fundamental value for life generally should be assigned to pretence, to the will to delusion, to selfishness and cupidity. It might even be possible that *what* constitutes the value of those good and respected things, consists precisely in their being insidiously related, knotted and crocheted to these evil and apparently opposed things – perhaps even in being essentially identical with them. Perhaps! But who wishes to

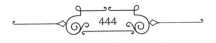

concern himself with such dangerous 'Perhapses'! For that investigation one must await the advent of a new order of philosophers, such as will have other tastes and inclinations, the reverse of those hitherto prevalent – philosophers of the dangerous 'Perhaps' in every sense of the term. And to speak in all seriousness, I see such new philosophers beginning to appear.

3

HAVING kept a sharp eye on philosophers, and having read between their lines long enough, I now say to myself that the greater part of conscious thinking must be counted among the instinctive functions, and it is so even in the case of philosophical thinking; one has here to learn anew, as one learned anew about heredity and 'innateness'. As little as the act of birth comes into consideration in the whole process and procedure of heredity, just as little is 'being-conscious' *opposed* to the instinctive in any decisive sense; the greater part of the conscious thinking of a philosopher is secretly influenced by his instincts, and forced into definite channels. And behind all logic and its seeming sovereignty of movement, there are valuations, or to speak more plainly, physiological demands, for the maintenance of a definite mode of life. For example, that the certain is worth more than the uncertain, that illusion is less valuable than 'truth': such valuations, in spite of their regulative importance for *us*, might notwithstanding be only superficial valuations, special kinds of *niaiserie*, such as may be necessary for the maintenance of beings such as ourselves. Supposing, in effect, that man is not just the 'measure of things'.

4

THE falseness of an opinion is not for us any objection to it: it is here, perhaps, that our new language sounds most strangely. The question is, how far an opinion is life-furthering, life-preserving, species-preserving, perhaps species-rearing; and we are fundamentally inclined to maintain that the falsest opinions (to which the synthetic judgments a priori belong),

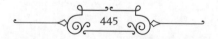

are the most indispensable to us, that without a recognition of logical fictions, without a comparison of reality with the purely *imagined* world of the absolute and immutable, without a constant counterfeiting of the world by means of numbers, man could not live – that the renunciation of false opinions would be a renunciation of life, a negation of life. *To recognize untruth as a condition of life*; that is certainly to impugn the traditional ideas of value in a dangerous manner, and a philosophy which ventures to do so, has thereby alone placed itself beyond good and evil.

5

THAT which causes philosophers to be regarded half-distrustfully and half-mockingly, is not the oft-repeated discovery how innocent they are – how often and easily they make mistakes and lose their way, in short, how childish and childlike they are, – but that there is not enough honest dealing with them, whereas they all raise a loud and virtuous outcry when the problem of truthfulness is even hinted at in the remotest manner. They all pose as though their real opinions had been discovered and attained through the self-evolving of a cold, pure, divinely indifferent dialectic (in contrast to all sorts of mystics, who, fairer and foolisher, talk of 'inspiration'); whereas, in fact, a prejudiced proposition, idea, or 'suggestion', which is generally their heart's desire abstracted and refined, is defended by them with arguments sought out after the event. They are all advocates who do not wish to be regarded as such, generally astute defenders, also, of their prejudices, which they dub 'truths', – and *very* far from having the conscience which bravely admits this to itself, very far from having the good taste of the courage which goes so far as to let this be understood, perhaps to warn friend or foe, or in cheerful confidence and self-ridicule. The spectacle of the Tartuffery of old Kant, equally stiff and decent, with which he entices us into the dialectic by-ways that lead (more correctly mislead) to his 'categorical imperative' – makes us fastidious ones smile, we who find no small amusement in spying out the subtle

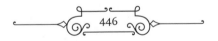

tricks of old moralists and ethical preachers. Or, still more so, the hocus-pocus in mathematical form, by means of which Spinoza has, as it were, clad his philosophy in mail and mask – in fact, the 'love of *his* wisdom', to translate the term fairly and squarely – in order thereby to strike terror at once into the heart of the assailant who should dare to cast a glance on that invincible maiden, that Pallas Athene: – how much of personal timidity and vulnerability does this masquerade of a sickly recluse betray!

<h1 style="text-align:center">6</h1>

IT HAS gradually become clear to me what every great philosophy up till now has consisted of – namely, the confession of its originator, and a species of involuntary and unconscious auto-biography; and moreover that the moral (or immoral) purpose in every philosophy has constituted the true vital germ out of which the entire plant has always grown. Indeed, to understand how the abstrusest metaphysical assertions of a philosopher have been arrived at, it is always well (and wise) to first ask oneself: 'What morality do they (or does he) aim at?' Accordingly, I do not believe that an 'impulse to knowledge' is the father of philosophy; but that another impulse, here as elsewhere, has only made use of knowledge (and mistaken knowledge!) as an instrument. But whoever considers the fundamental impulses of man with a view to determining how far they may have here acted as *inspiring genii* (or as demons and cobolds), will find that they have all practiced philosophy at one time or another, and that each one of them would have been only too glad to look upon itself as the ultimate end of existence and the legitimate *lord* over all the other impulses. For every impulse is imperious, and as *such*, attempts to philosophize. To be sure, in the case of scholars, in the case of really scientific men, it may be otherwise – 'better', if you will; there there may really be such a thing as an 'impulse to knowledge', some kind of small, independent clockwork, which, when well wound up, works away industriously to that end, *without* the rest of the scholarly impulses taking any material part therein. The

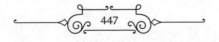

actual 'interests' of the scholar, therefore, are generally in quite another direction – in the family, perhaps, or in money-making or in politics; it is, in fact, almost indifferent at what point of research his little machine is placed, and whether the hopeful young worker becomes a good philologist, a mushroom specialist or a chemist; he is not *characterized* by becoming this or that. In the philosopher, on the contrary, there is absolutely nothing impersonal; and above all, his morality furnishes a decided and decisive testimony as to *who he is*, – that is to say, in what order the deepest impulses of his nature stand to each other.

7

HOW malicious philosophers can be! I know of nothing more stinging than the joke Epicurus took the liberty of making on Plato and the Platonists; he called them *Dionysiokolakes*. In its original sense, and on the face of it, the word signifies 'Flatterers of Dionysius' – consequently, tyrants' accessories and lick-spittles; besides this, however, it is as much as to say, 'They are all *actors*, there is nothing genuine about them' (for *Dionysiokolax* was a popular name for an actor). And the latter is really the malignant reproach that Epicurus cast upon Plato: he was annoyed by the grandiose manner, the *mise en scène* style of which Plato and his scholars were masters – of which Epicurus was not a master! He, the old schoolteacher of Samos, who sat concealed in his little garden at Athens, and wrote three hundred books, perhaps out of rage and ambitious envy of Plato, who knows! Greece took a hundred years to find out who the garden-god Epicurus really was. Did she ever find out?

8

THERE is a point in every philosophy at which the 'conviction' of the philosopher appears on the scene; or, to put it in the words of an ancient mystery:

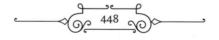

Adventavit asinus,
Pulcher et fortissimus.

9

YOU desire to *live* 'according to Nature'? Oh, you noble Stoics, what fraud of words! Imagine to yourselves a being like Nature, boundlessly extravagant, boundlessly indifferent, without purpose or consideration, without pity or justice, at once fruitful and barren and uncertain: imagine to yourselves *indifference* as a power – how *could* you live in accordance with such indifference? To live – is not that just endeavouring to be otherwise than this Nature? Is not living valuing, preferring, being unjust, being limited, endeavouring to be different? And granted that your imperative, 'living according to Nature', means actually the same as 'living according to life' – how could you do *differently*? Why should you make a principle out of what you yourselves are, and must be? In reality, however, it is quite otherwise with you: while you pretend to read with rapture the canon of your law in Nature, you want something quite the contrary, you extraordinary stage-players and self-deluders! In your pride you wish to dictate your morals and ideals to Nature, to Nature herself, and to incorporate them therein; you insist that it shall be Nature 'according to the Stoa', and would like everything to be made after your own image, as a vast, eternal glorification and generalism of Stoicism! With all your love for truth, you have forced yourselves so long, so persistently, and with such hypnotic rigidity to see Nature *falsely*, that is to say, Stoically, that you are no longer able to see it otherwise – and to crown all, some unfathomable superciliousness gives you the Bedlamite hope that *because* you are able to tyrannize over yourselves – Stoicism is self-tyranny – Nature will also allow herself to be tyrannized over: is not the Stoic a *part* of Nature?... But this is an old and everlasting story: what happened in old times with the Stoics still happens today, as soon as ever a philosophy begins to believe in itself. It always creates the world in its own image; it cannot do other-

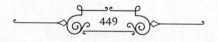

wise; philosophy is this tyrannical impulse itself, the most spiritual Will to Power, the will to 'creation of the world', the will to the *causa prima*.

10

THE eagerness and subtlety, I should even say craftiness, with which the problem of 'the real and the apparent world' is dealt with at present throughout Europe, furnishes food for thought and attention; and he who hears only a 'Will to Truth' in the background, and nothing else, cannot certainly boast of the sharpest ears. In rare and isolated cases, it may really have happened that such a Will to Truth – a certain extravagant and adventurous pluck, a metaphysician's ambition of the forlorn hope – has participated therein: that which in the end always prefers a handful of 'certainty' to a whole cartload of beautiful possibilities; there may even be puritanical fanatics of conscience, who prefer to put their last trust in a sure nothing, rather than in an uncertain something. But that is Nihilism, and the sign of a despairing, mortally wearied soul, notwithstanding the courageous bearing such a virtue may display. It seems, however, to be otherwise with stronger and livelier thinkers who are still eager for life. In that they side *against* appearance, and speak superciliously of 'perspective', in that they rank the credibility of their own bodies about as low as the credibility of the ocular evidence that 'the earth stands still', and thus, apparently, allowing with complacency their securest possession to escape (for what does one at present believe in more firmly than in one's body?), – who knows if they are not really trying to win back something which was formerly an even securer possession, something of the old domain of the faith of former times, perhaps the 'immortal soul', perhaps 'the old God', in short, ideas by which they could live better, that is to say, more vigorously and more joyously, than by 'modern ideas'? There is *distrust* of these modern ideas in this mode of looking at things, a disbelief in all that has been constructed yesterday and today; there is perhaps some slight admixture of satiety and scorn, which can no longer endure the *bric-a-brac*

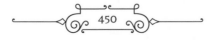

of ideas of the most varied origin, such as so-called Positivism at present throws on the market; a disgust of the more refined taste at the village-fair motleyness and patchiness of all these reality-philosophasters, in whom there is nothing either new or true, except this motleyness. Therein it seems to me that we should agree with those sceptical anti-realists and knowledge-microscopists of the present day; their instinct, which repels them from *modern* reality, is unrefuted... what do their retrograde by-paths concern us! The main thing about them is *not* that they wish to go 'back', but that they wish to get *away* therefrom. A little *more* strength, swing, courage and artistic power, and they would be *off* – and not back!

11

IT SEEMS to me that there is everywhere an attempt at present to divert attention from the actual influence which Kant exercised on German philosophy, and especially to ignore prudently the value which he set upon himself. Kant was first and foremost proud of his Table of Categories; with it in his hand he said: 'This is the most difficult thing that could ever be undertaken on behalf of metaphysics'. Let us only understand this 'could be'! He was proud of having *discovered* a new faculty in man, the faculty of synthetic judgment a priori. Granting that he deceived himself in this matter; the development and rapid flourishing of German philosophy depended nevertheless on his pride, and on the eager rivalry of the younger generation to discover if possible something – at all events 'new faculties' – of which to be still prouder! – But let us reflect for a moment – it is high time to do so. 'How are synthetic judgments a priori *possible*?' Kant asks himself – and what is really his answer? '*By means of a means* (faculty)' – but unfortunately not in five words, but so circumstantially, imposingly and with such display of German profundity and verbal flourishes, that one altogether loses sight of the comical *niaiserie allemande* involved in such an answer. People were beside themselves with delight over this new faculty, and the jubilation reached its climax when

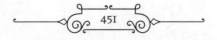

Kant further discovered a moral faculty in man – for at that time Germans were still moral, not yet dabbling in the 'Politics of hard fact'. Then came the honeymoon of German philosophy. All the young theologians of the Tübingen institution went immediately into the groves – all seeking for 'faculties'. And what did they not find – in that innocent, rich and still youthful period of the German spirit, to which Romanticism, the malicious fairy, piped and sang, when one could not yet distinguish between 'finding' and 'inventing'! Above all a faculty for the 'transcendental'; Schelling christened it, intellectual intuition, and thereby gratified the most earnest longings of the naturally pious-inclined Germans. One can do no greater wrong to the whole of this exuberant and eccentric movement (which was really youthfulness, notwithstanding that it disguised itself so boldly, in hoary and senile conceptions), than to take it seriously, or even treat it with moral indignation. Enough, however – the world grew older, and the dream vanished. A time came when people rubbed their foreheads, and they still rub them today. People had been dreaming, and first and foremost – old Kant. 'By means of a means (faculty)' – he had said, or at least meant to say. But, is that – an answer? An explanation? Or is it not rather merely a repetition of the question? How does opium induce sleep? 'By means of a means (faculty)', namely the *virtus dormitiva*, replies the doctor in Molière,

> *Quia est in eo virtus dormitiva,*
> *Cujus est natura sensus assoupire.*

But such replies belong to the realm of comedy, and it is high time to replace the Kantian question, 'How are synthetic judgments *a priori* possible?' by another question, 'Why is belief in such judgments necessary?' – in effect, it is high time that we should understand that such judgments must be *believed* to be true, for the sake of the preservation of creatures like ourselves; though they still might naturally be *false* judg-

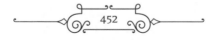

ments! Or, more plainly spoken, and roughly and readily – synthetic judgments a priori should not 'be possible' at all; we have no right to them; in our mouths they are nothing but false judgments. Only, of course, the belief in their truth is necessary, as plausible belief and ocular evidence belonging to the perspective view of life. And finally, to call to mind the enormous influence which 'German philosophy' – I hope you understand its right to inverted commas (goosefeet)? – has exercised throughout the whole of Europe, there is no doubt that a certain *virtus dormitiva* had a share in it; thanks to German philosophy, it was a delight to the noble idlers, the virtuous, the mystics, the artists, the three-fourths Christians and the political obscurantists of all nations, to find an antidote to the still overwhelming sensualism which overflowed from the last century into this, in short – *'sensus assoupire'*...

12

AS REGARDS materialistic atomism, it is one of the best-refuted theories that have been advanced, and in Europe there is now perhaps no one in the learned world so unscholarly as to attach serious signification to it, except for convenient everyday use (as an abbreviation of the means of expression) – thanks chiefly to the Pole Boscovich: he and the Pole Copernicus have hitherto been the greatest and most successful opponents of ocular evidence. For while Copernicus has persuaded us to believe, contrary to all the senses, that the earth does *not* stand fast, Boscovich has taught us to abjure the belief in the last thing that 'stood fast' of the earth – the belief in 'substance', in 'matter', in the earth-residuum and parti-cle-atom: it is the greatest triumph over the senses that has hitherto been gained on earth. One must, however, go still further, and also declare war, relentless war to the knife, against the 'atomistic requirements' which still lead a dangerous after-life in places where no one suspects them, like the more celebrated 'metaphysical requirements': one must also above all give the finishing stroke to that other and more portentous atomism which

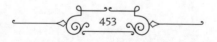

Christianity has taught best and longest, the *soul-atomism*. Let it be permitted to designate by this expression the belief which regards the soul as something indestructible, eternal, indivisible, as a monad, as an *atomon*: *this* belief ought to be expelled from science! Between ourselves, it is not at all necessary to get rid of 'the soul' thereby, and thus renounce one of the oldest and most venerated hypotheses – as happens frequently to the clumsiness of naturalists, who can hardly touch on the soul without immediately losing it. But the way is open for new acceptations and refinements of the soul-hypothesis; and such conceptions as 'mortal soul', and 'soul of subjective multiplicity', and 'soul as social structure of the instincts and passions', want henceforth to have legitimate rights in science. In that the *new* psychologist is about to put an end to the superstitions which have hitherto flourished with almost tropical luxuriance around the idea of the soul, he is really, as it were, thrusting himself into a new desert and a new distrust – it is possible that the older psychologists had a merrier and more comfortable time of it; eventually, however, he finds that precisely thereby he is also condemned to *invent* – and, who knows? perhaps to *discover* the new.

13

PSYCHOLOGISTS should bethink themselves before putting down the instinct of self-preservation as the cardinal instinct of an organic being. A living thing seeks above all to *discharge* its strength – life itself is *Will to Power*; self-preservation is only one of the indirect and most frequent *results* thereof. In short, here, as everywhere else, let us beware of *superfluous* teleological principles! – one of which is the instinct of self-preservation (we owe it to Spinoza's inconsistency). It is thus, in effect, that method ordains, which must be essentially economy of principles.

14

IT IS perhaps just dawning on five or six minds that natural philosophy is only a world-exposition and world-arrangement (according to us, if I

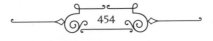

may say so!) and *not* a world-explanation; but in so far as it is based on belief in the senses, it is regarded as more, and for a long time to come must be regarded as more – namely, as an explanation. It has eyes and fingers of its own, it has ocular evidence and palpableness of its own: this operates fascinatingly, persuasively and *convincingly* upon an age with fundamentally plebeian tastes – in fact, it follows instinctively the canon of truth of eternal popular sensualism. What is clear, what is 'explained'? Only that which can be seen and felt – one must pursue every problem thus far. Obversely, however, the charm of the Platonic mode of thought, which was an *aristocratic* mode, consisted precisely in *resistance* to obvious sense-evidence – perhaps among men who enjoyed even stronger and more fastidious senses than our contemporaries, but who knew how to find a higher triumph in remaining masters of them: and this by means of pale, cold, grey conceptional networks which they threw over the motley whirl of the senses – the mob of the senses, as Plato said. In this overcoming of the world, and interpreting of the world in the manner of Plato, there was an *enjoyment* different from that which the physicists of today offer us – and likewise the Darwinists and anti-teleologists among the physiological workers, with their principle of the 'smallest possible effort', and the greatest possible blunder. 'Where there is nothing more to see or to grasp, there is also nothing more for men to do' – that is certainly an imperative different from the Platonic one, but it may notwithstanding be the right imperative for a hardy, laborious race of machinists and bridge-builders of the future, who have nothing but *rough* work to perform.

15

TO STUDY physiology with a clear conscience, one must insist on the fact that the sense-organs are not phenomena in the sense of the idealistic philosophy; as such they certainly could not be causes! Sensualism, therefore, at least as regulative hypothesis, if not as heuristic principle. What? And others say even that the external world is the work of our

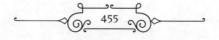

organs? But then our body, as a part of this external world, would be the work of our organs! But then our organs themselves would be the work of our organs! It seems to me that this is a complete *reductio ad absurdum*, if the conception *causa sui* is something fundamentally absurd. Consequently, the external world is *not* the work of our organs – ?

16

THERE are still harmless self-observers who believe that there are 'immediate certainties'; for instance, 'I think', or as the superstition of Schopenhauer puts it, 'I will'; as though cognition here got hold of its object purely and simply as 'the thing in itself', without any falsification taking place either on the part of the subject or the object. I would repeat it, however, a hundred times, that 'immediate certainty', as well as 'absolute knowledge' and the 'thing in itself', involve a *contradictio in adjecto*; we really ought to free ourselves from the misleading significance of words! The people on their part may think that cognition is knowing all about things, but the philosopher must say to himself: 'When I analyze the process that is expressed in the sentence, "I think", I find a whole series of daring assertions, the argumentative proof of which would be difficult, perhaps impossible: for instance, that it is *I* who think, that there must necessarily be something that thinks, that thinking is an activity and operation on the part of a being who is thought of as a cause, that there is an "ego", and finally, that it is already determined what is to be designated by thinking – that *I know* what thinking is. For if I had not already decided within myself what it is, by what standard could I determine whether that which is just happening is not perhaps "willing" or "feeling"? In short, the assertion "I think", assumes that I *compare* my state at the present moment with other states of myself which I know, in order to determine what it is; on account of this retrospective connection with further "knowledge", it has, at any rate, no immediate certainty for me.' – In place of the 'immediate certainty' in which the people may believe

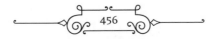

in the special case, the philosopher thus finds a series of metaphysical questions presented to him, veritable conscience questions of the intellect, to wit: 'From whence did I get the notion of "thinking"? Why do I believe in cause and effect? What gives me the right to speak of an "ego", and even of an "ego" as cause, and finally of an "ego" as cause of thought?' He who ventures to answer these metaphysical questions at once by an appeal to a sort of *intuitive* perception, like the person who says, 'I think, and know that this, at least, is true, actual and certain' – will encounter a smile and two notes of interrogation in a philosopher nowadays. 'Sir,' the philosopher will perhaps give him to understand, 'it is improbable that you are not mistaken, but why should it be the truth?'

17

WITH regard to the superstitions of logicians, I shall never tire of emphasizing a small, terse fact, which is unwillingly recognized by these credulous minds – namely, that a thought comes when 'it' wishes, and not when 'I' wish; so that it is a *perversion* of the facts of the case to say that the subject 'I' is the condition of the predicate 'think'. *One* thinks; but that this 'one' is precisely the famous old 'ego', is, to put it mildly, only a supposition, an assertion, and assuredly not an 'immediate certainty'. After all, one has even gone too far with this 'one thinks' – even the 'one' contains an *interpretation* of the process, and does not belong to the process itself. One infers here according to the usual grammatical formula – 'To think is an activity; every activity requires an agency that is active; consequently'... It was pretty much on the same lines that the older atomism sought, besides the operating 'power', the material particle wherein it resides and out of which it operates – the atom. More rigorous minds, however, learnt at last to get along without this 'earth-residuum', and perhaps some day we shall accustom ourselves, even from the logician's point of view, to get along without the little 'one' (to which the worthy old 'ego' has refined itself).

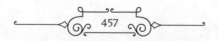

18

IT IS certainly not the least charm of a theory that it is refutable; it is precisely thereby that it attracts the more subtle minds. It seems that the hundred-times-refuted theory of the 'free will' owes its persistence to this charm alone; some one is always appearing who feels himself strong enough to refute it.

19

PHILOSOPHERS are accustomed to speak of the will as though it were the best-known thing in the world; indeed, Schopenhauer has given us to understand that the will alone is really known to us, absolutely and completely known, without deduction or addition. But it again and again seems to me that in this case Schopenhauer also only did what philosophers are in the habit of doing – he seems to have adopted a *popular prejudice* and exaggerated it. Willing – seems to me to be above all something *complicated*, something that is a unity only in name – and it is precisely in a name that popular prejudice lurks, which has got the mastery over the inadequate precautions of philosophers in all ages. So let us for once be more cautious, let us be 'unphilosophical': let us say that in all willing there is firstly a plurality of sensations, namely, the sensation of the condition *'away from which* we go', the sensation of the condition *'towards which* we go', the sensation of this *'from'* and *'towards'* itself, and then besides, an accompanying muscular sensation, which, even without our putting in motion 'arms and legs', commences its action by force of habit, directly we 'will' anything. Therefore, just as sensations (and indeed many kinds of sensations) are to be recognized as ingredients of the will, so, in the second place, thinking is also to be recognized; in every act of the will there is a ruling thought; – and let us not imagine it possible to sever this thought from the 'willing', as if the will would then remain over! In the third place, the will is not only a complex of sensation and thinking, but it is above all an *emotion*, and in fact the emotion of the command. That

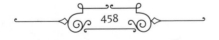

which is termed 'freedom of the will' is essentially the emotion of supremacy in respect to him who must obey: 'I am free, 'he' must obey' – this consciousness is inherent in every will; and equally so the straining of the attention, the straight look which fixes itself exclusively on one thing, the unconditional judgment that 'this and nothing else is necessary now', the inward certainty that obedience will be rendered – and whatever else pertains to the position of the commander. A man who *wills* commands something within himself which renders obedience, or which he believes renders obedience. But now let us notice what is the strangest thing about the will, – this affair so extremely complex, for which the people have only one name. Inasmuch as in the given circumstances we are at the same time the commanding *and* the obeying parties, and as the obeying party we know the sensations of constraint, impulsion, pressure, resistance and motion, which usually commence immediately after the act of will; inasmuch as, on the other hand, we are accustomed to disregard this duality, and to deceive ourselves about it by means of the synthetic term 'I': a whole series of erroneous conclusions, and consequently of false judgments about the will itself, has become attached to the act of willing – to such a degree that he who wills believes firmly that willing *suffices* for action. Since in the majority of cases there has only been exercise of will when the effect of the command – consequently obedience, and therefore action – was to be *expected*, the *appearance* has translated itself into the sentiment, as if there were a *necessity of effect*; in a word, he who wills believes with a fair amount of certainty that will and action are somehow one; he ascribes the success, the carrying out of the willing, to the will itself, and thereby enjoys an increase of the sensation of power which accompanies all success. 'Freedom of Will' – that is the expression for the complex state of delight of the person exercising volition, who commands and at the same time identifies himself with the executor of the order – who, as such, enjoys also the triumph over obstacles, but thinks within himself that it was really his own will that overcame them. In this way the person exercising volition

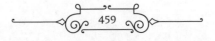

adds the feelings of delight of his successful executive instruments, the useful 'underwills' or under-souls – indeed, our body is but a social structure composed of many souls – to his feelings of delight as commander. *L'effet c'est moi*. what happens here is what happens in every well-constructed and happy commonwealth, namely, that the governing class identifies itself with the successes of the commonwealth. In all willing it is absolutely a question of commanding and obeying, on the basis, as already said, of a social structure composed of many 'souls', on which account a philosopher should claim the right to include willing-as-such within the sphere of morals – regarded as the doctrine of the relations of supremacy under which the phenomenon of 'life' manifests itself.

20

THAT the separate philosophical ideas are not anything optional or autonomously evolving, but grow up in connection and relationship with each other; that, however suddenly and arbitrarily they seem to appear in the history of thought, they nevertheless belong just as much to a system as the collective members of the fauna of a Continent – is betrayed in the end by the circumstance: how unfailingly the most diverse philosophers always fill in again a definite fundamental scheme of *possible* philosophies. Under an invisible spell, they always revolve once more in the same orbit, however independent of each other they may feel themselves with their critical or systematic wills, something within them leads them, something impels them in definite order the one after the other – to wit, the innate methodology and relationship of their ideas. Their thinking is, in fact, far less a discovery than a re-recognizing, a remembering, a return and a home-coming to a far-off, ancient common-household of the soul, out of which those ideas formerly grew: philosophizing is so far a kind of atavism of the highest order. The wonderful family resemblance of all Indian, Greek and German philosophizing is easily enough explained. In fact, where there is affinity of language, owing to the common philosophy of

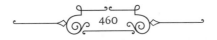

grammar – I mean owing to the unconscious domination and guidance of similar grammatical functions – it cannot but be that everything is prepared at the outset for a similar development and succession of philosophical systems, just as the way seems barred against certain other possibilities of world-interpretation. It is highly probable that philosophers within the domain of the Ural-Altaic languages (where the conception of the subject is least developed) look otherwise 'into the world', and will be found on paths of thought different from those of the Indo-Germans and Mussulmans, the spell of certain grammatical functions is ultimately also the spell of *physiological* valuations and racial conditions. – So much by way of rejecting Locke's superficiality with regard to the origin of ideas.

21

THE *causa sui* is the best self-contradiction that has yet been conceived, it is a sort of logical violation and unnaturalness; but the extravagant pride of man has managed to entangle itself profoundly and frightfully with this very folly. The desire for 'freedom of will' in the superlative, metaphysical sense, such as still holds sway, unfortunately, in the minds of the half-educated, the desire to bear the entire and ultimate responsibility for one's actions oneself, and to absolve God, the world, ancestors, chance and society therefrom, involves nothing less than to be precisely this *causa sui*, and, with more than Munchausen daring, to pull oneself up into existence by the hair, out of the slough of nothingness. If any one should find out in this manner the crass stupidity of the celebrated conception of 'free will' and put it out of his head altogether, I beg of him to carry his 'enlightenment' a step further, and also put out of his head the contrary of this monstrous conception of 'free will': I mean 'non-free will', which is tantamount to a misuse of cause and effect. One should not wrongly *materialize* 'cause' and 'effect', as the natural philosophers do (and whoever like them naturalize in thinking at present), according to the prevailing mechanical doltishness which makes the cause press and push until it

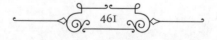

'effects' its end; one should use 'cause' and 'effect' only as pure *conceptions*, that is to say, as conventional fictions for the purpose of designation and mutual understanding, – *not* for explanation. In 'being-in-itself' there is nothing of 'casual-connection', of 'necessity', or of 'psychological non-freedom'; there the effect does *not* follow the cause, there 'law' does not obtain. It is *we* alone who have devised cause, sequence, reciprocity, relativity, constraint, number, law, freedom, motive and purpose; and when we interpret and intermix this symbol-world, as 'being-in-itself', with things, we act once more as we have always acted – *mythologically*. The 'non-free will' is mythology; in real life it is only a question of *strong* and *weak* wills. – It is almost always a symptom of what is lacking in himself, when a thinker, in every 'causal-connection' and 'psychological necessity', manifests something of compulsion, indigence, obsequiousness, oppression and non-freedom; it is suspicious to have such feelings – the person betrays himself. And in general, if I have observed correctly, the 'non-freedom of the will' is regarded as a problem from two entirely opposite standpoints, but always in a profoundly *personal* manner: some will not give up their 'responsibility', their belief in *themselves*, the personal right to *their* merits, at any price (the vain races belong to this class); others on the contrary, do not wish to be answerable for anything, or blamed for anything, and owing to an inward self-contempt, seek to *get out of the business*, no matter how. The latter, when they write books, are in the habit at present of taking the side of criminals; a sort of socialistic sympathy is their favourite disguise. And as a matter of fact, the fatalism of the weak-willed embellishes itself surprisingly when it can pose as '*la religion de la souffrance humaine*'; that is *its* 'good taste'.

22

LET me be pardoned, as an old philologist who cannot desist from the mischief of putting his finger on bad modes of interpretation, but 'Nature's conformity to law', of which you physicists talk so proudly, as though –

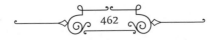

why, it exists only owing to your interpretation and bad 'philology'. It is no matter of fact, no 'text', but rather just a naively humanitarian adjustment and perversion of meaning, with which you make abundant concessions to the democratic instincts of the modern soul! 'Everywhere equality before the law – Nature is not different in that respect, nor better than we': a fine instance of secret motive, in which the vulgar antagonism to everything privileged and autocratic – likewise a second and more refined atheism – is once more disguised. *'Ni dieu, ni maître'* – that, also, is what you want; and therefore 'Cheers for natural law!' – is it not so? But, as has been said, that is interpretation, not text; and somebody might come along, who, with opposite intentions and modes of interpretation, could read out of the same 'Nature', and with regard to the same phenomena, just the tyrannically inconsiderate and relentless enforcement of the claims of power – an interpreter who should so place the unexceptionalness and unconditionalness of all 'Will to Power' before your eyes, that almost every word, and the word 'tyranny' itself, would eventually seem unsuitable, or like a weakening and softening metaphor – as being too human; and who should, nevertheless, end by asserting the same about this world as you do, namely, that it has a 'necessary' and 'calculable' course, *not*, however, because laws obtain in it, but because they are absolutely *lacking*, and every power effects its ultimate consequences every moment. Granted that this also is only interpretation – and you will be eager enough to make this objection? – well, so much the better.

23

ALL psychology hitherto has run aground on moral prejudices and timidities, it has not dared to launch out into the depths. In so far as it is allowable to recognize in that which has hitherto been written, evidence of that which has hitherto been kept silent, it seems as if nobody had yet harboured the notion of psychology as the Morphology and *Development – doctrine of the Will to Power*, as I conceive of it. The power of moral

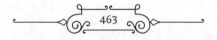

prejudices has penetrated deeply into the most intellectual world, the world apparently most indifferent and unprejudiced, and has obviously operated in an injurious, obstructive, blinding and distorting manner. A proper physio-psychology has to contend with unconscious antagonism in the heart of the investigator, it has 'the heart' against it; even a doctrine of the reciprocal conditionalness of the 'good' and the 'bad' impulses, causes (as refined immorality) distress and aversion in a still strong and manly conscience – still more so, a doctrine of the derivation of all good impulses from bad ones. If, however, a person should regard even the emotions of hatred, envy, covetousness and imperiousness as life-conditioning emotions, as factors which must be present, fundamentally and essentially, in the general economy of life (which must, therefore, be further developed if life is to be further developed), he will suffer from such a view of things as from sea-sickness. And yet this hypothesis is far from being the strangest and most painful in this immense and almost new domain of dangerous knowledge; and there are in fact a hundred good reasons why every one should keep away from it who *can* do so! On the other hand, if one has once drifted hither with one's bark, well! very good! now let us set our teeth firmly! let us open our eyes and keep our hand fast on the helm! We sail away right *over* morality, we crush out, we destroy perhaps the remains of our own morality by daring to make our voyage thither – but what do *we* matter. Never yet did a *profounder* world of insight reveal itself to daring travellers and adventurers, and the psychologist who thus 'makes a sacrifice' – it is *not* the *sacrifizio dell' intelletto*, on the contrary! – will at least be entitled to demand in return that psychology shall once more be recognized as the queen of the sciences, for whose service and equipment the other sciences exist. For psychology is once more the path to the fundamental problems.

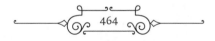

CHAPTER II
THE FREE SPIRIT

24

O SANCTA simplicitas! In what strange simplification and falsification man lives! One can never cease wondering when once one has got eyes for beholding this marvel! How we have made everything around us clear and free and easy and simple! how we have been able to give our senses a passport to everything superficial, our thoughts a godlike desire for wanton pranks and wrong inferences! – how from the beginning, we have contrived to retain our ignorance in order to enjoy an almost inconceivable freedom, thoughtlessness, imprudence, heartiness and gaiety – in order to enjoy life! And only on this solidified, granite-like foundation of ignorance could knowledge rear itself hitherto, the will to knowledge on the foundation of a far more powerful will, the will to ignorance, to the uncertain, to the untrue! Not as its opposite, but – as its refinement! It is to be hoped, indeed, that *language*, here as elsewhere, will not get over its awkwardness, and that it will continue to talk of opposites where there are only degrees and many refinements of gradation; it is equally to be hoped that the incarnated Tartuffery of morals, which now belongs to our unconquerable 'flesh and blood', will turn the words round in the mouths of us discerning ones. Here and there we understand it, and laugh at the way in which precisely the best knowledge seeks most to retain us in this *simplified*, thoroughly artificial, suitably imagined and suitably falsified world: at

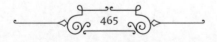

the way in which, whether it will or not, it loves error, because, as living itself, it loves life!

25

AFTER such a cheerful commencement, a serious word would fain be heard; it appeals to the most serious minds. Take care, ye philosophers and friends of knowledge, and beware of martyrdom! Of suffering 'for the truth's sake'! even in your own defence! It spoils all the innocence and fine neutrality of your conscience; it makes you headstrong against objections and red rags; it stupefies, animalizes and brutalizes, when in the struggle with danger, slander, suspicion, expulsion and even worse consequences of enmity, ye have at last to play your last card as protectors of truth upon earth – as though 'the Truth' were such an innocent and incompetent creature as to require protectors! and you of all people, ye knights of the sorrowful countenance, Messrs Loafers and Cobweb-spinners of the spirit! Finally, ye know sufficiently well that it cannot be of any consequence if *ye* just carry your point; ye know that hitherto no philosopher has carried his point, and that there might be a more laudable truthfulness in every little interrogative mark which you place after your special words and favourite doctrines (and occasionally after yourselves) than in all the solemn pantomime and trumping games before accusers and law-courts! Rather go out of the way! Flee into concealment! And have your masks and your ruses, that ye may be mistaken for what you are, or somewhat feared! And pray, don't forget the garden, the garden with golden trellis-work! And have people around you who are as a garden – or as music on the waters at eventide, when already the day becomes a memory. Choose the *good* solitude, the free, wanton, lightsome solitude, which also gives you the right still to remain good in any sense whatsoever! How poisonous, how crafty, how bad, does every long war make one, which cannot be waged openly by means of force! How

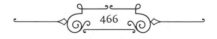

personal does a long fear make one, a long watching of enemies, of possible enemies! These pariahs of society, these long-pursued, badly persecuted ones – also the compulsory recluses, the Spinozas or Giordano Brunos – always become in the end, even under the most intellectual masquerade, and perhaps without being themselves aware of it, refined vengeance-seekers and poison-brewers (just lay bare the foundation of Spinoza's ethics and theology!), not to speak of the stupidity of moral indignation, which is the unfailing sign in a philosopher that the sense of philosophical humour has left him. The martyrdom of the philosopher, his 'sacrifice for the sake of truth', forces into the light whatever of the agitator and actor lurks in him; and if one has hitherto contemplated him only with artistic curiosity, with regard to many a philosopher it is easy to understand the dangerous desire to see him also in his deterioration (deteriorated into a 'martyr', into a stage-and-tribune-bawler). Only, that it is necessary with such a desire to be clear *what* spectacle one will see in any case – merely a satyric play, merely an epilogue farce, merely the continued proof that the long, real tragedy *is at an end*, supposing that every philosophy has been a long tragedy in its origin.

26

EVERY select man strives instinctively for a citadel and a privacy, where he is *free* from the crowd, the many, the majority – where he may forget 'men who are the rule', as their exception; – exclusive only of the case in which he is pushed straight to such men by a still stronger instinct, as a discerner in the great and exceptional sense. Whoever, in intercourse with men, does not occasionally glisten in all the green and grey colours of distress, owing to disgust, satiety, sympathy, gloominess and solitariness, is assuredly not a man of elevated tastes; supposing, however, that he does not voluntarily take all this burden and disgust upon himself, that he persistently avoids it, and remains, as I said, quietly and proudly

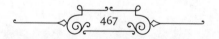

hidden in his citadel, one thing is then certain: he was not made, he was not predestined for knowledge. For as such, he would one day have to say to himself: 'The devil take my good taste! but "the rule" is more interesting than the exception – than myself, the exception!' And he would go *down*, and above all, he would go 'inside'. The long and serious study of the *average* man – and consequently much disguise, self-overcoming, familiarity and bad intercourse (all intercourse is bad intercourse except with one's equals): – that constitutes a necessary part of the life-history of every philosopher; perhaps the most disagreeable, odious and disappointing part. If he is fortunate, however, as a favourite child of knowledge should be, he will meet with suitable auxiliaries who will shorten and lighten his task; I mean so-called cynics, those who simply recognize the animal, the commonplace and 'the rule' in themselves, and at the same time have so much spirituality and ticklishness as to make them talk of themselves and their like *before witnesses* – sometimes they wallow, even in books, as on their own dung-hill. Cynicism is the only form in which base souls approach what is called honesty; and the higher man must open his ears to all the coarser or finer cynicism, and congratulate himself when the clown becomes shameless right before him, or the scientific satyr speaks out. There are even cases where enchantment mixes with the disgust – namely, whereby a freak of nature, genius is bound to some such indiscreet billy-goat and ape, as in the case of the Abbé Galiani, the profoundest, acutest and perhaps also filthiest man of his century – he was far profounder than Voltaire, and consequently also, a good deal more silent. It happens more frequently, as has been hinted, that a scientific head is placed on an ape's body, a fine exceptional understanding in a base soul, an occurrence by no means rare, especially among doctors and moral physiologists. And whenever anyone speaks without bitterness, or rather quite innocently, of man as a belly with two requirements, and a head with one; whenever anyone sees, seeks and *wants* to see only hunger, sexual instinct and vanity as the real and only motives

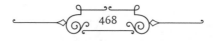

of human actions; in short, when anyone speaks 'badly' – and not even 'ill' – of man, then ought the lover of knowledge to hearken attentively and diligently; he ought, in general, to have an open ear wherever there is talk without indignation. For the indignant man, and he who perpetually tears and lacerates himself with his own teeth (or, in place of himself, the world, God or society), may indeed, morally speaking, stand higher than the laughing and self-satisfied satyr, but in every other sense he is the more ordinary, more indifferent and less instructive case. And no one is such a *liar* as the indignant man.

27

IT IS difficult to be understood, especially when one thinks and lives *gangasrotogati** among those only who think and live otherwise – namely, *kurmagati*†, or at best 'frog-like', *mandeikagati*‡ (I do everything to be 'difficultly understood' myself!) – and one should be heartily grateful for the good will to some refinement of interpretation. As regards 'the good friends', however, who are always too easy-going, and think that as friends they have a right to ease, one does well at the very first to grant them a playground and romping-place for misunderstanding – one can thus laugh still; or get rid of them altogether, these good friends – and laugh then also!

28

WHAT is most difficult to render from one language into another is the *tempo* of its style, which has its basis in the character of the race, or to speak more physiologically, in the average *tempo* of the assimilation of its nutriment. There are honestly meant translations, which, as involuntary vulgarizations, are almost falsifications of the original,

---

* Like the River Ganges: *presto.*

† Like the tortoise: *lento.*

‡ Like the frog: *staccato.*

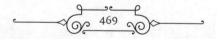

merely because its lively and merry *tempo* (which overleaps and obviates all dangers in word and expression) could not also be rendered. A German is almost incapacitated for *presto* in his language; consequently also, as may be reasonably inferred, for many of the most delightful and daring *nuances* of free, free-spirited thought. And just as the buffoon and satyr are foreign to him in body and conscience, so Aristophanes and Petronius are untranslatable for him. Everything ponderous, viscous and pompously clumsy, all long-winded and wearying species of style, are developed in profuse variety among Germans – pardon me for stating the fact that even Goethe's prose, in its mixture of stiffness and elegance, is no exception, as a reflection of the 'good old time' to which it belongs, and as an expression of German taste at a time when there was still a 'German taste', which was a rococo-taste *in moribus et artibus*. Lessing is an exception, owing to his histrionic nature, which understood much, and was versed in many things; he who was not the translator of Bayle to no purpose, who took refuge willingly in the shadow of Diderot and Voltaire, and still more willingly among the Roman comedy-writers – Lessing loved also free-spiritism in the *tempo*, and flight out of Germany. But how could the German language, even in the prose of Lessing, imitate the *tempo* of Machiavelli, who in his '*Il Principe*' makes us breathe the dry, fine air of Florence, and cannot help presenting the most serious events in a boisterous *allegrissimo*, perhaps not without a malicious artistic sense of the contrast he ventures to present – long, heavy, difficult, dangerous thoughts and a *tempo* of the gallop, and of the best, wantonest humour? Finally, who would venture on a German translation of Petronius, who, more than any great musician hitherto, was a master of *presto* in invention, ideas and words? What matter in the end about the swamps of the sick, evil world or of the 'ancient world', when like him, one has the feet of a wind, the rush, the breath, the emancipating scorn of a wind, which makes everything healthy, by making everything

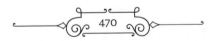

run! And with regard to Aristophanes – that transfiguring, complementary genius, for whose sake one *pardons* all Hellenism for having
existed, provided one has understood in its full profundity *all* that
there requires pardon and transfiguration; there is nothing that has
caused me to meditate more on *Plato's* secrecy and sphinx-like nature,
than the happily preserved *petit fait* that under the pillow of his
death-bed there was found no 'Bible', nor anything Egyptian,
Pythagorean or Platonic – but a book of Aristophanes. How could
even Plato have endured life – a Greek life which he repudiated –
without an Aristophanes!

29

IT IS the business of the very few to be independent; it is a privilege
of the strong. And whoever attempts it, even with the best right, but
without being *obliged* to do so, proves that he is probably not only
strong, but also daring beyond measure. He enters into a labyrinth,
he multiplies a thousandfold the dangers which life in itself already
brings with it; not the least of which is that no one can see how and
where he loses his way, becomes isolated, and is torn piecemeal by
some minotaur of conscience. Supposing such a one comes to grief,
it is so far from the comprehension of men that they neither feel it,
nor sympathize with it. And he cannot any longer go back! He cannot
even go back again to the sympathy of men!

30

OUR deepest insights must – and should – appear as follies, and under
certain circumstances as crimes, when they come unauthorizedly to
the ears of those who are not disposed and predestined for them. The
exoteric and the esoteric, as they were formerly distinguished by
philosophers – among the Indians, as among the Greeks, Persians and
Mussulmans, in short, wherever people believed in gradations of rank

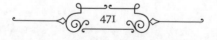

and *not* in equality and equal rights – are not so much in contradis-
tinction to one another in respect to the exoteric class, standing
without, and viewing, estimating, measuring and judging from the
outside, and not from the inside; the more essential distinction is that
the class in question views things from below upwards – while the
esoteric class views things *from above downwards*. There are heights of
the soul from which tragedy itself no longer appears to operate trag-
ically; and if all the woe in the world were taken together, who would
dare to decide whether the sight of it would *necessarily* seduce and
constrain to sympathy, and thus to a doubling of the woe?... That
which serves the higher class of men for nourishment or refreshment,
must be almost poison to an entirely different and lower order of
human beings. The virtues of the common man would perhaps mean
vice and weakness in a philosopher; it might be possible for a highly
developed man, supposing him to degenerate and go to ruin, to acquire
qualities thereby alone, for the sake of which he would have to be
honoured as a saint in the lower world into which he had sunk. There
are books which have an inverse value for the soul and the health
according as the inferior soul and the lower vitality, or the higher and
more powerful, make use of them. In the former case they are
dangerous, disturbing, unsettling books, in the latter case they are
herald-calls which summon the bravest to *their* bravery. Books for the
general reader are always ill-smelling books, the odour of paltry people
clings to them. Where the populace eat and drink, and even where
they reverence, it is accustomed to stink. One should not go into
churches if one wishes to breathe *pure* air.

31

IN OUR youthful years we still venerate and despise without the art
of *nuance*, which is the best gain of life, and we have rightly to do hard
penance for having fallen upon men and things with Yea and Nay.

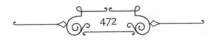

Everything is so arranged that the worst of all tastes, *the taste for the unconditional*, is cruelly befooled and abused, until a man learns to introduce a little art into his sentiments, and prefers to try conclusions with the artificial, as do the real artists of life. The angry and reverent spirit peculiar to youth appears to allow itself no peace, until it has suitably falsified men and things, to be able to vent its passion upon them: youth in itself even, is something falsifying and deceptive. Later on, when the young soul, tortured by continual disillusions, finally turns suspiciously against itself – still ardent and savage even in its suspicion and remorse of conscience: how it upbraids itself, how impatiently it tears itself, how it revenges itself for its long self-blinding, as though it had been a voluntary blindness! In this transition one punishes oneself by distrust of one's sentiments; one tortures one's enthusiasm with doubt, one feels even the good conscience to be a danger, as if it were the self-concealment and lassitude of a more refined uprightness; and above all, one espouses upon principle the cause *against* 'youth'. – A decade later, and one comprehends that all this was also still – youth!

32

THROUGHOUT the longest period of human history – one calls it the prehistoric period – the value or non-value of an action was inferred from its *consequences*; the action in itself was not taken into consideration, any more than its origin; but pretty much as in China at present, where the distinction or disgrace of a child redounds to its parents, the retro-operating power of success or failure was what induced men to think well or ill of an action. Let us call this period the *pre-moral* period of mankind; the imperative, 'know thyself!' was then still unknown. – In the last ten thousand years, on the other hand, on certain large portions of the earth, one has gradually got so far, that one no longer lets the consequences of an action, but its origin, decide with regard to its worth: a great achievement as a whole, an important refinement of vision and of crite-

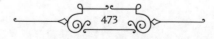

rion, the unconscious effect of the supremacy of aristocratic values and of the belief in 'origin', the mark of a period which may be designated in the narrower sense as the *moral* one: the first attempt at self-knowledge is thereby made. Instead of the consequences, the origin – what an inversion of perspective! And assuredly an inversion effected only after long struggle and wavering! To be sure, an ominous new superstition, a peculiar narrowness of interpretation, attained supremacy precisely thereby: the origin of an action was interpreted in the most definite sense possible, as origin out of an *intention*; people were agreed in the belief that the value of an action lay in the value of its intention. The intention as the sole origin and antecedent history of an action: under the influence of this prejudice moral praise and blame have been bestowed, and men have judged and even philosophized almost up to the present day. – Is it not possible, however, that the necessity may now have arisen of again making up our minds with regard to the reversing and fundamental shifting of values, owing to a new self-consciousness and acuteness in man – is it not possible that we may be standing on the threshold of a period which to begin with, would be distinguished negatively as *ultra-moral*: nowadays when, at least among us immoralists, the suspicion arises that the decisive value of an action lies precisely in that which is *not intentional*, and that all its intentionalness, all that is seen, sensible or 'sensed' in it, belongs to its surface or skin – which, like every skin, betrays something, but *conceals* still more? In short, we believe that the intention is only a sign or symptom, which first requires an explanation – a sign, moreover, which has too many interpretations, and consequently hardly any meaning in itself alone: that morality, in the sense in which it has been understood hitherto, as intention-morality, has been a prejudice, perhaps a prematureness or preliminariness, probably something of the same rank as astrology and alchemy, but in any case something which must be surmounted. The surmounting of morality, in a certain sense even the self-mounting of morality – let that be the

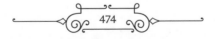

name for the long-secret labour which has been reserved for the most refined, the most upright and also the most wicked consciences of today, as the living touchstones of the soul.

33

IT CANNOT be helped: the sentiment of surrender, of sacrifice for one's neighbour, and all self-renunciation-morality, must be mercilessly called to account, and brought to judgment; just as the aesthetics of 'disinterested contemplation', under which the emasculation of art nowadays seeks insidiously enough to create itself a good conscience. There is far too much witchery and sugar in the sentiments 'for others' and '*not* for myself', for one not needing to be doubly distrustful here, and for one asking promptly: 'Are they not perhaps – *deceptions*?' – That they *please* – him who has them, and him who enjoys their fruit, and also the mere spectator – that is still no argument in their *favour*, but just calls for caution. Let us therefore be cautious!

34

AT WHATEVER standpoint of philosophy one may place oneself nowadays, seen from every position, the *erroneousness* of the world in which we think we live is the surest and most certain thing our eyes can light upon: we find proof after proof thereof, which would fain allure us into surmises concerning a deceptive principle in the 'nature of things'. He, however, who makes thinking itself, and consequently 'the spirit', responsible for the falseness of the world – an honourable exit, which every conscious or unconscious *advocatus dei* avails himself of – he who regards this world, including space, time, form and move- ment, as falsely *deduced*, would have at least good reason in the end to become distrustful also of all thinking; has it not hitherto been playing upon us the worst of scurvy tricks? and what guarantee would it give that it would not continue to do what it has always been doing? In all

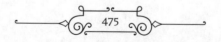

seriousness, the innocence of thinkers has something touching and respect-inspiring in it, which even nowadays permits them to wait upon consciousness with the request that it will give them *honest* answers: for example, whether it be 'real' or not, and why it keeps the outer world so resolutely at a distance, and other questions of the same description. The belief in 'immediate certainties' is a *moral naïveté* which does honour to us philosophers; but – we have now to cease being *'merely* moral' men! Apart from morality, such belief is a folly which does little honour to us! If in middle-class life an ever-ready distrust is regarded as the sign of a 'bad character', and consequently as an imprudence, here among us, beyond the middle-class world and its Yeas and Nays, what should prevent our being imprudent and saying: the philosopher has at length a *right* to 'bad character', as the being who has hitherto been most befooled on earth – he is now under *obligation* to distrustfulness, to the wickedest squinting out of every abyss of suspicion. – Forgive me the joke of this gloomy grimace and turn of expression; for I myself have long ago learned to think and estimate differently with regard to deceiving and being deceived, and I keep at least a couple of pokes in the ribs ready for the blind rage with which philosophers struggle against being deceived. Why *not?* It is nothing more than a moral prejudice that truth is worth more than semblance; it is, in fact, the worst proved supposition in the world. So much must be conceded: there could have been no life at all except upon the basis of perspective estimates and semblances; and if, with the virtuous enthusiasm and stupidity of many philosophers, one wished to do away altogether with the 'seeming world' – well, granted that *you* could do that, – at least nothing of your 'truth' would thereby remain! Indeed, what is it that forces us in general to the supposition that there is an essential opposition of 'true' and 'false'? Is it not enough to suppose degrees of seemingness, and as it were lighter and darker shades and tones of semblance – different *valeurs*, as the painters say? Why might not the world *which concerns us* – be a

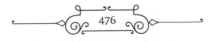

fiction? And to any one who suggested: 'But to a fiction belongs an originator?' – might it not be bluntly replied: *Why*? May not this 'belong' also belong to the fiction? Is it not at length permitted to be a little ironical towards the subject, just as towards the predicate and object? Might not the philosopher elevate himself above faith in grammar? All respect to governesses, but is it not time that philosophy should renounce governess-faith?

35

O VOLTAIRE! O humanity! O idiocy! There is something ticklish in 'the truth', and in the *search* for the truth; and if man goes about it too humanely – '*il ne cherche le vrai que pour faire le bien*' – I wager he finds nothing!

36

SUPPOSING that nothing else is 'given' as real but our world of desires and passions, that we cannot sink or rise to any other 'reality' but just that of our impulses – for thinking is only a relation of these impulses to one another: – are we not permitted to make the attempt and to ask the question whether this which is 'given' does not *suffice*, by means of our counterparts, for the understanding even of the so-called mechanical (or 'material') world? I do not mean as an illusion, a 'semblance', a 'representation' (in the Berkeleyan and Schopenhauerian sense), but as possessing the same degree of reality as our emotions themselves – as a more primitive form of the world of emotions, in which everything still lies locked in a mighty unity, which afterwards branches off and develops itself in organic processes (naturally also, refines and debilitates) – as a kind of instinctive life in which all organic functions, including self-regulation, assimilation, nutrition, secretion and change of matter, are still synthetically united with one another – as a *primary form* of life? – In the end, it is not

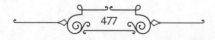

only permitted to make this attempt, it is commanded by the conscience of *logical method*. Not to assume several kinds of causality, so long as the attempt to get along with a single one has not been pushed to its furthest extent (to absurdity, if I may be allowed to say so): that is a morality of method which one may not repudiate nowadays – it follows 'from its definition', as mathematicians say. The question is ultimately whether we really recognize the will as *operating*, whether we believe in the causality of the will; if we do so – and fundamentally our belief *in this* is just our belief in causality itself – we *must* make the attempt to posit hypothetically the causality of the will as the only causality. 'Will' can naturally only operate on 'will' – and not on 'matter' (not on 'nerves', for instance): in short, the hypothesis must be hazarded, whether will does not operate on will wherever 'effects' are recognized – and whether all mechanical action, inasmuch as a power operates therein, is not just the power of will, the effect of will. Granted, finally, that we succeeded in explaining our entire instinctive life as the development and ramification of one fundamental form of will – namely, the Will to Power, as *my* thesis puts it; granted that all organic functions could be traced back to this Will to Power, and that the solution of the problem of generation and nutrition – it is one problem – could also be found therein: one would thus have acquired the right to define *all* active force unequivocally as *Will to Power*. The world seen from within, the world defined and designated according to its 'intelligible character' – it would simply be 'Will to Power', and nothing else.

37

'WHAT? Does not that mean in popular language: God is disproved, but not the devil?' – On the contrary! On the contrary, my friends! And who the devil also compels you to speak popularly!

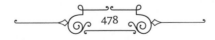

38

AS HAPPENED finally in all the enlightenment of modern times with the French Revolution (that terrible farce, quite superfluous when judged close at hand, into which, however, the noble and visionary spectators of all Europe have interpreted from a distance their own indignation and enthusiasm so long and passionately, *until the text has disappeared under the interpretation*), so a noble posterity might once more misunderstand the whole of the past, and perhaps only thereby make *its* aspect endurable. – Or rather, has not this already happened? Have not we ourselves been – that 'noble posterity'? And, in so far as we now comprehend this, is it not – thereby already past?

39

NOBODY will very readily regard a doctrine as true merely because it makes people happy or virtuous – excepting, perhaps, the amiable 'Idealists', who are enthusiastic about the good, true and beautiful, and let all kinds of motley, coarse and good-natured desirabilities swim about promiscuously in their pond. Happiness and virtue are no arguments. It is willingly forgotten, however, even on the part of thoughtful minds, that to make unhappy and to make bad are just as little counter-arguments. A thing could be *true*, although it were in the highest degree injurious and dangerous; indeed, the fundamental constitution of existence might be such that one succumbed by a full knowledge of it – so that the strength of a mind might be measured by the amount of 'truth' it could endure – or to speak more plainly, by the extent to which it *required* truth attenuated, veiled, sweetened, damped and falsified. But there is no doubt that for the discovery of certain *portions* of truth the wicked and unfortunate are more favourably situated and have a greater likelihood of success; not to speak of the wicked who are happy – a species about whom moralists are silent. Perhaps severity and craft are more favourable conditions for the development of strong,

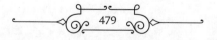

independent spirits and philosophers than the gentle, refined, yielding good-nature and habit of taking things easily, which are prized, and rightly prized in a learned man. Presupposing always, to begin with, that the term 'philosopher' be not confined to the philosopher who writes books, or even introduces *his* philosophy into books! – Stendhal furnishes a last feature of the portrait of the free-spirited philosopher, which for the sake of German taste I will not omit to underline – for it is *opposed* to German taste. '*Pour être bon philosophe,*' says this last great psychologist, '*il faut être sec, clair, sans illusion. Un banquier, qui a fait fortune, a une partie du caractère requis pour faire des découvertes en philosophie, c'est-à-dire pour voir clair dans ce qui est.*'

40

EVERYTHING that is profound loves the mask: the profoundest things have a hatred even of figure and likeness. Should not the *contrary* only be the right disguise for the shame of a God to go about in? A question worth asking! – it would be strange if some mystic has not already ventured on the same kind of thing. There are proceedings of such a delicate nature that it is well to overwhelm them with coarseness and make them unrecognizable; there are actions of love and of an extravagant magnanimity after which nothing can be wiser than to take a stick and thrash the witness soundly: one thereby obscures his recollection. Many a one is able to obscure and abuse his own memory, in order at least to have vengeance on this sole party in the secret: shame is inventive. They are not the worst things of which one is most ashamed: there is not only deceit behind a mask – there is so much goodness in craft. I could imagine that a man with something costly and fragile to conceal, would roll through life clumsily and rotundly like an old, green, heavily hooped wine cask: the refinement of his shame requiring it to be so. A man who has depths in his shame meets his destiny and his delicate decisions upon paths which few ever reach, and with regard to the

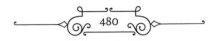

existence of which his nearest and most intimate friends may be ignorant; his mortal danger conceals itself from their eyes, and equally so
his regained security. Such a hidden nature, which instinctively employs
speech for silence and concealment, and is inexhaustible in evasion of
communication, *desires* and insists that a mask of himself shall occupy
his place in the hearts and heads of his friends; and supposing he does
not desire it, his eyes will some day be opened to the fact that there is
nevertheless a mask of him there – and that it is well to be so. Every
profound spirit needs a mask; nay, more, around every profound spirit
there continually grows a mask, owing to the constantly false, that is
to say, *superficial* interpretation of every word he utters, every step he
takes, every sign of life he manifests.

41

ONE must subject oneself to one's own tests that one is destined for
independence and command, and do so at the right time. One must
not avoid one's tests, although they constitute perhaps the most
dangerous game one can play, and are in the end tests made only
before ourselves and before no other judge. Not to cleave to any
person, be it even the dearest – every person is a prison and also a
recess. Not to cleave to a fatherland, be it even the most suffering
and necessitous – it is even less difficult to detach one's heart from a
victorious fatherland. Not to cleave to a sympathy, be it even for higher
men, into whose peculiar torture and helplessness chance has given
us an insight. Not to cleave to a science, though it tempt one with
the most valuable discoveries, apparently specially reserved for us. Not
to cleave to one's own liberation, to the voluptuous distance and
remoteness of the bird, which always flies further aloft in order always
to see more under it – the danger of the flier. Not to cleave to our
own virtues, nor become as a whole a victim to any of our specialties,
to our 'hospitality' for instance, which is the danger of dangers for

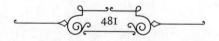

highly developed and wealthy souls, who deal prodigally, almost indifferently with themselves, and push the virtue of liberality so far that it becomes a vice. One must know how *to conserve oneself* – the best test of independence.

42

A NEW order of philosophers is appearing; I shall venture to baptize them by a name not without danger. As far as I understand them, as far as they allow themselves to be understood – for it is their nature to *wish* to remain something of a puzzle – these philosophers of the future might rightly, perhaps also wrongly, claim to be designated as 'tempters'. This name itself is after all only an attempt, or, if it be preferred, a temptation.

43

WILL they be new friends of 'truth', these coming philosophers? Very probably, for all philosophers hitherto have loved their truths. But assuredly they will not be dogmatists. It must be contrary to their pride, and also contrary to their taste, that their truth should still be truth for every one – that which has hitherto been the secret wish and ultimate purpose of all dogmatic efforts. 'My opinion is *my* opinion: another person has not easily a right to it' – such a philosopher of the future will say, perhaps. One must renounce the bad taste of wishing to agree with many people. 'Good' is no longer good when one's neighbour takes it into his mouth. And how could there be a 'common good'! The expression contradicts itself; that which can be common is always of small value. In the end things must be as they are and have always been – the great things remain for the great, the abysses for the profound, the delicacies and thrills for the refined, and, to sum up shortly, everything rare for the rare.

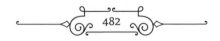

44

NEED I say expressly after all this that they will be free, *very* free spirits, these philosophers of the future – as certainly also they will not be merely free spirits, but something more, higher, greater and fundamentally different, which does not wish to be misunderstood and mistaken? But while I say this, I feel under *obligation* almost as much to them as to ourselves (we free spirits who are their heralds and forerunners), to sweep away from ourselves altogether a stupid old prejudice and misunderstanding, which, like a fog, has too long made the conception of 'free spirit' obscure. In every country of Europe, and the same in America, there is at present something which makes an abuse of this name: a very narrow, prepossessed, enchained class of spirits, who desire almost the opposite of what our intentions and instincts prompt – not to mention that in respect to the *new* philosophers who are appearing, they must still more be closed windows and bolted doors. Briefly and regrettably, they belong to the *levellers*, these wrongly named 'free spirits' – as glib-tongued and scribe-fingered slaves of the democratic taste and its 'modern ideas': all of them men without solitude, without personal solitude, blunt honest fellows to whom neither courage nor honourable conduct ought to be denied; only, they are not free, and are ludicrously superficial, especially in their innate partiality for seeing the cause of almost *all* human misery and failure in the old forms in which society has hitherto existed – a notion which happily inverts the truth entirely! What they would fain attain with all their strength, is the universal, green-meadow happiness of the herd, together with security, safety, comfort and alleviation of life for everyone, their two most frequently chanted songs and doctrines are called 'Equality of Rights' and 'Sympathy with all Sufferers' – and suffering itself is looked upon by them as something which must be *done away with*. We opposite ones, however, who have opened our eye and conscience to the question how and where the plant 'man' has

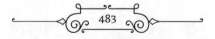

hitherto grown most vigorously, believe that this has always taken place under the opposite conditions, that for this end the dangerousness of his situation had to be increased enormously, his inventive faculty and dissembling power (his 'spirit') had to develop into subtlety and daring under long oppression and compulsion, and his Will to Life had to be increased to the unconditioned Will to Power – we believe that severity, violence, slavery, danger in the street and in the heart, secrecy, stoicism, tempter's art and devilry of every kind, – that everything wicked, terrible, tyrannical, predatory and serpentine in man, serves as well for the elevation of the human species as its opposite: – we do not even say enough when we only say *this much*; and in any case we find ourselves here, both with our speech and our silence, at the *other* extreme of all modern ideology and gregarious desirability, as their antipodes perhaps? What wonder that we 'free spirits' are not exactly the most communicative spirits? that we do not wish to betray in every respect *what* a spirit can free itself from, and *where* perhaps it will then be driven? And as to the import of the dangerous formula, 'Beyond Good and Evil', with which we at least avoid confusion, we *are* something else than '*libres-penseurs*', '*liberi pensatori*', 'free-thinkers', and whatever these honest advocates of 'modern ideas' like to call themselves. Having been at home, or at least guests, in many realms of the spirit, having escaped again and again from the gloomy, agreeable nooks in which preferences and prejudices, youth, origin, the accident of men and books, or even the weariness of travel seemed to confine us; full of malice against the seductions of dependency which lie concealed in honours, money, positions or exaltation of the senses; grateful even for distress and the vicissitudes of illness, because they always free us from some rule, and its 'prejudice', grateful to the God, devil, sheep and worm in us; inquisitive to a fault, investigators to the point of cruelty, with unhesitating fingers for the intangible, with teeth and stomachs for the most

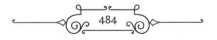

indigestible, ready for any business that requires sagacity and acute senses, ready for every adventure, owing to an excess of 'free will'; with anterior and posterior souls, into the ultimate intentions of which it is difficult to pry, with foregrounds and backgrounds to the end of which no foot may run; hidden ones under the mantles of light, appropriators, although we resemble heirs and spendthrifts, arrangers and collectors from morning till night, misers of our wealth and our full-crammed drawers, economical in learning and forgetting, inventive in scheming; sometimes proud of tables of categories, sometimes pedants, sometimes night owls of work even in full day; yea, if necessary, even scarecrows – and it is necessary nowadays, that is to say, inasmuch as we are the born, sworn, jealous friends of *solitude*, of our own profoundest midnight and midday solitude: – such kind of men are we, we free spirits! And perhaps *ye* are also something of the same kind, ye coming ones? ye *new* philosophers?

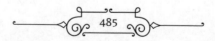

CHAPTER III
THE RELIGIOUS MOOD

45

THE human soul and its limits, the range of man's inner experiences hitherto attained, the heights, depths and distances of these experiences, the entire history of the soul *up to the present time*, and its still unexhausted possibilities: this is the preordained hunting-domain for a born psychologist and lover of a 'big hunt'. But how often must he say despairingly to himself: 'A single individual! alas, only a single individual! and this great forest, this virgin forest!' So he would like to have some hundreds of hunting assistants and fine trained hounds, that he could send into the history of the human soul, to drive *his* game together. In vain: again and again he experiences, profoundly and bitterly, how difficult it is to find assistants and dogs for all the things that directly excite his curiosity. The evil of sending scholars into new and dangerous hunting-domains, where courage, sagacity and subtlety in every sense are required, is that they are no longer serviceable just when the '*big hunt*', and also the great danger commences, – it is precisely then that they lose their keen eye and nose. In order, for instance, to divine and determine what sort of history the problem of *knowledge and conscience* has hitherto had in the souls of *homines religiosi*, a person would perhaps himself have to possess as profound, as bruised, as immense an experience as the intellectual conscience of Pascal; and then he would still require that wide-spread heaven of clear, wicked spirituality, which, from

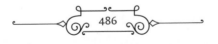

above, would be able to oversee, arrange and effectively formulize this mass of dangerous and painful experiences. – But who could do me this service! And who would have time to wait for such servants! – they evidently appear too rarely, they are so improbable at all times! Eventually one must do everything *oneself* in order to know something; which means that one has *much* to do! – But a curiosity like mine is once for all the most agreeable of vices – pardon me! I mean to say that the love of truth has its reward in heaven, and already upon earth.

46

FAITH, such as early Christianity desired, and not infrequently achieved in the midst of a sceptical and southernly free-spirited world, which had centuries of struggle between philosophical schools behind it and in it, counting besides the education in tolerance which the *Imperium Romanum* gave – this faith is *not* that sincere, austere slave-faith by which perhaps a Luther or a Cromwell, or some other northern barbarian of the spirit remained attached to his God and Christianity; it is much rather the faith of Pascal, which resembles in a terrible manner a continuous suicide of reason – a tough, long-lived, worm-like reason, which is not to be slain at once and with a single blow. The Christian faith from the beginning, is sacrifice: the sacrifice of all freedom, all pride, all self-confidence of spirit; it is at the same time subjection, self-derision and self-mutilation. There is cruelty and religious Phoenicianism in this faith, which is adapted to a tender, many-sided and very fastidious conscience, it takes for granted that the subjection of the spirit is indescribably *painful,* that all the past and all the habits of such a spirit resist the *absurdissimum,* in the form of which 'faith' comes to it. Modern men, with their obtuseness as regards all Christian nomenclature, have no longer the sense for the terribly superlative conception which was implied to an antique taste by the paradox of the formula, 'God on the Cross'. Hitherto there had never and nowhere

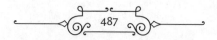

been such boldness in inversion, nor anything at once so dreadful, questioning and questionable as this formula: it promised a transvaluation of all ancient values. – It was the Orient, the *profound* Orient, it was the Oriental slave who thus took revenge on Rome and its noble, light-minded toleration, on the Roman 'Catholicism' of non-faith; and it was always not the faith, but the freedom from the faith, the half-stoical and smiling indifference to the seriousness of the faith, which made the slaves indignant at their masters and revolt against them. 'Enlightenment' causes revolt: for the slave desires the unconditioned, he understands nothing but the tyrannous, even in morals; he loves as he hates, without *nuance*, to the very depths, to the point of pain, to the point of sickness – his many *hidden* sufferings make him revolt against the noble taste which seems to *deny* suffering. The scepticism with regard to suffering, fundamentally only an attitude of aristocratic morality, was not the least of the causes, also, of the last great slave-insurrection which began with the French Revolution.

47

WHEREVER the religious neurosis has appeared on the earth so far, we find it connected with three dangerous prescriptions as to regimen: solitude, fasting and sexual abstinence – but without its being possible to determine with certainty which is cause and which is effect, or *if* any relation at all of cause and effect exists there. This latter doubt is justified by the fact that one of the most regular symptoms among savage as well as among civilized peoples is the most sudden and excessive sensuality; which then with equal suddenness transforms into penitential paroxysms, world-renunciation and will-renunciation: both symptoms perhaps explainable as disguised epilepsy? But nowhere is it *more* obligatory to put aside explanations: around no other type has there grown such a mass of absurdity and superstition, no other type seems to have been more interesting to men and even to philosophers – perhaps it is time to become

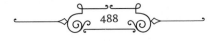

just a little indifferent here, to learn caution, or, better still, to look away, *to go away* – Yet in the background of the most recent philosophy, that of Schopenhauer, we find almost as the problem in itself, this terrible note of interrogation of the religious crisis and awakening. How is the negation of will *possible*? how is the saint possible? – that seems to have been the very question with which Schopenhauer made a start and became a philosopher. And thus it was a genuine Schopenhauerian consequence, that his most convinced adherent (perhaps also his last, as far as Germany is concerned), namely, Richard Wagner, should bring his own life-work to an end just here, and should finally put that terrible and eternal type upon the stage as Kundry, *type vécu*, and as it loved and lived, at the very time that the mad-doctors in almost all European countries had an opportunity to study the type close at hand, wherever the religious neurosis – or as I call it, 'the religious mood' – made its latest epidemical outbreak and display as the 'Salvation Army'. – If it be a question, however, as to what has been so extremely interesting to men of all sorts in all ages, and even to philosophers, in the whole phenomenon of the saint, it is undoubt-edly the appearance of the miraculous therein – namely, the immediate *succession of opposites*, of states of the soul regarded as morally antithetical: it was believed here to be self-evident that a 'bad man' was all at once turned into a 'saint', a good man. The hitherto existing psychology was wrecked at this point; is it not possible it may have happened principally because psychology had placed itself under the dominion of morals, because it *believed* in oppositions of moral values, and saw, read and *inter-preted* these oppositions into the text and facts of the case? What? 'Miracle' only an error of interpretation? A lack of philology?

48

IT SEEMS that the Latin races are far more deeply attached to their Catholicism than we Northerners are to Christianity generally, and that consequently unbelief in Catholic countries means something quite

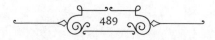

different from what it does among Protestants – namely, a sort of revolt against the spirit of the race, while with us it is rather a return to the spirit (or non-spirit) of the race. We Northerners undoubtedly derive our origin from barbarous races, even as regards our talents for religion – we have *poor* talents for it. One may make an exception in the case of the Celts, who have theretofore furnished also the best soil for Christian infection in the North: the Christian ideal blossomed forth in France as much as ever the pale sun of the North would allow it. How strangely pious for our taste are still these later French sceptics, whenever there is any Celtic blood in their origin! How Catholic, how un-German does Auguste Comte's Sociology seem to us, with the Roman logic of its instincts! How Jesuitical, that amiable and shrewd cicerone of Port Royal, Sainte-Beuve, in spite of all his hostility to Jesuits! And even Ernest Renan: how inaccessible to us Northerners does the language of such a Renan appear, in whom every instant the merest touch of religious thrill throws his refined voluptuous and comfortably couching soul off its balance! Let us repeat after him these fine sentences – and what wickedness and haughtiness is immediately aroused by way of answer in our probably less beautiful but harder souls, that is to say, in our more German souls! – '*Disons donc hardiment que la religion est un produit de l'homme normal, que l'homme est le plus dans le vrai quand il est le plus religieux et le plus assuré d'une destinée infinie.... C'est quand il est bon qu'il veut que la virtu corresponde à un order éternal, c'est quand il contemple les choses d'une manière désintéressee qu'il trouve la mort révoltante et absurde. Comment ne pas supposer que c'est dans ces moments-là, que l'homme voit le mieux?'*... These sentences are so extremely *antipodal* to my ears and habits of thought, that in my first impulse of rage on finding them, I wrote on the margin, '*la niaiserie religieuse par excellence!*' – until in my later rage I even took a fancy to them, these sentences with their truth absolutely inverted! It is so nice and such a distinction to have one's own antipodes!

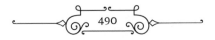

49

THAT which is so astonishing in the religious life of the ancient Greeks is the irrestrainable stream of *gratitude* which it pours forth – it is a very superior kind of man who takes *such* an attitude towards nature and life. – Later on, when the populace got the upper hand in Greece, *fear* became rampant also in religion; and Christianity was preparing itself.

50

THE passion for God: there are churlish, honest-hearted and importunate kinds of it, like that of Luther – the whole of Protestantism lacks the Southern *delicatezza*. There is an Oriental exaltation of the mind in it, like that of an undeservedly favoured or elevated slave, as in the case of St Augustine, for instance, who lacks in an offensive manner, all nobility in bearing and desires. There is a feminine tenderness and sensuality in it, which modestly and unconsciously longs for a *unio mystica et physica*, as in the case of Madame de Guyon. In many cases it appears, curiously enough, as the disguise of a girl's or youth's puberty; here and there even as the hysteria of an old maid, also as her last ambition. The Church has frequently canonized the woman in such a case.

51

THE mightiest men have hitherto always bowed reverently before the saint, as the enigma of self-subjugation and utter voluntary privation – why did they thus bow? They divined in him – and as it were behind the questionableness of his frail and wretched appearance – the superior force which wished to test itself by such a subjugation; the strength of will, in which they recognized their own strength and love of power, and knew how to honour it: they honoured something in themselves when they honoured the saint. In addition to this, the contemplation of the saint suggested to them a suspicion: such an enormity of self-negation and anti-naturalness will not have been coveted for nothing – they have said,

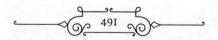

inquiringly. There is perhaps a reason for it, some very great danger, about which the ascetic might wish to be more accurately informed through his secret interlocutors and visitors? In a word, the mighty ones of the world learned to have a new fear before him, they divined a new power, a strange, still unconquered enemy: – it was the 'Will to Power' which obliged them to halt before the saint. They had to question him.

52

IN THE Jewish 'Old Testament', the book of divine justice, there are men, things and sayings on such an immense scale, that Greek and Indian literature has nothing to compare with it. One stands with fear and reverence before those stupendous remains of what man was formerly, and one has sad thoughts about old Asia and its little out-pushed peninsula Europe, which would like, by all means, to figure before Asia as the 'Progress of Mankind'. To be sure, he who is himself only a slender, tame house-animal, and knows only the wants of a house-animal (like our cultured people of today, including the Christians of 'cultured' Christianity), need neither be amazed nor even sad amid those ruins – the taste for the Old Testament is a touchstone with respect to 'great' and 'small': perhaps he will find that the New Testament, the book of grace, still appeals more to his heart (there is much of the odour of the genuine, tender, stupid beadsman and petty soul in it). To have bound up this New Testament (a kind of *rococo* of taste in every respect) along with the Old Testament into one book, as the 'Bible', as 'The Book in Itself', is perhaps the greatest audacity and 'sin against the Spirit' which literary Europe has upon its conscience.

53

WHY Atheism nowadays? 'The father' in God is thoroughly refuted; equally so 'the judge', 'the rewarder'. Also his 'free will': he does not hear – and even if he did, he would not know how to help. The worst

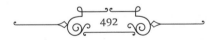

is that he seems incapable of communicating himself clearly; is he uncertain? – This is what I have made out (by questioning and listening at a variety of conversations) to be the cause of the decline of European theism; it appears to me that though the religious instinct is in vigorous growth, – it rejects the theistic satisfaction with profound distrust.

54

WHAT does all modern philosophy mainly do? Since Descartes – and indeed more in defiance of him than on the basis of his procedure – an *attentat* has been made on the part of all philosophers on the old conception of the soul, under the guise of a criticism of the subject and predicate conception – that is to say, an *attentat* on the fundamental presupposition of Christian doctrine. Modern philosophy, as epistemological scepticism, is secretly or openly *anti-Christian*, although (for keener ears, be it said) by no means anti-religious. Formerly, in effect, one believed in 'the soul' as one believed in grammar and the grammatical subject: one said, 'I' is the condition, 'think' is the predicate and is conditioned – to think is an activity for which one *must* suppose a subject as cause. The attempt was then made, with marvellous tenacity and subtlety, to see if one could not get out of this net, – to see if the opposite was not perhaps true: 'think' the condition, and 'I' the conditioned; 'I', therefore, only a synthesis which has been *made* by thinking itself. *Kant* really wished to prove that, starting from the subject, the subject could not be proved – nor the object either: the possibility of an *apparent existence* of the subject, and therefore of 'the soul', may not always have been strange to him, – the thought which once had an immense power on earth as the Vedanta philosophy.

55

THERE is a great ladder of religious cruelty, with many rounds; but three of these are the most important. Once on a time men sacrificed

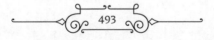

human beings to their God, and perhaps just those they loved the best
– to this category belong the firstling sacrifices of all primitive religions,
and also the sacrifice of the Emperor Tiberius in the Mithra-Grotto on
the Island of Capri, that most terrible of all Roman anachronisms. Then,
during the moral epoch of mankind, they sacrificed to their God the
strongest instincts they possessed, their 'nature'; *this* festal joy shines in
the cruel glances of ascetics and 'anti-natural' fanatics. Finally, what still
remained to be sacrificed? Was it not necessary in the end for men to
sacrifice everything comforting, holy, healing, all hope, all faith in hidden
harmonies, in future blessedness and justice? Was it not necessary to
sacrifice God himself, and out of cruelty to themselves to worship stone,
stupidity, gravity, fate, nothingness? To sacrifice God for nothingness
– this paradoxical mystery of the ultimate cruelty has been reserved for
the rising generation; we all know something thereof already.

56

WHOEVER, like myself, prompted by some enigmatical desire, has
long endeavoured to go to the bottom of the question of pessimism
and free it from the half-Christian, half-German narrowness and
stupidity in which it has finally presented itself to this century, namely,
in the form of Schopenhauer's philosophy; whoever, with an Asiatic
and super-Asiatic eye, has actually looked inside, and into the most
world-renouncing of all possible modes of thought – beyond good
and evil, and no longer like Buddha and Schopenhauer, under the
dominion and delusion of morality, – whoever has done this, has
perhaps just thereby, without really desiring it, opened his eyes to
behold the opposite ideal: the ideal of the most world-approving,
exuberant and vivacious man, who has not only learnt to compromise
and arrange with that which was and is, but wishes to have it again
as it was and is, for all eternity, insatiably calling out *da capo*, not only
to himself, but to the whole piece and play; and not only the play, but

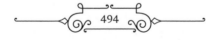

actually to him who requires the play – and makes it necessary; because he always requires himself anew – and makes himself necessary. – What? And this would not be – *circulus vitiosus deus?*

57

THE distance, and as it were the space around man, grows with the strength of his intellectual vision and insight: his world becomes profounder; new stars, new enigmas and notions are ever coming into view. Perhaps everything on which the intellectual eye has exercised its acuteness and profundity has just been an occasion for its exercise, something of a game, something for children and childish minds. Perhaps the most solemn conceptions that have caused the most fighting and suffering, the conceptions 'God' and 'sin', will one day seem to us of no more importance than a child's plaything or a child's pain seems to an old man; – and perhaps another plaything and another pain will then be necessary once more for 'the old man' – always childish enough, an eternal child!

58

HAS it been observed to what extent outward idleness, or semi-idleness, is necessary to a real religious life (alike for its favourite microscopic labour of self-examination, and for its soft placidity called 'prayer', the state of perpetual readiness for the 'coming of God'), I mean the idle-ness with a good conscience, the idleness of olden times and of blood, to which the aristocratic sentiment that work is *dishonouring* – that it vulgarizes body and soul – is not quite unfamiliar? And that consequently the modern, noisy, time-engrossing, conceited, foolishly proud labori-ousness educates and prepares for 'unbelief' more than anything else? Among these, for instance, who are at present living apart from religion in Germany, I find 'free-thinkers' of diversified species and origin, but above all a majority of those in whom laboriousness from generation

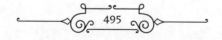

to generation has dissolved the religious instincts; so that they no longer know what purpose religions serve, and only note their existence in the world with a kind of dull astonishment. They feel themselves already fully occupied, these good people, be it by their business or by their pleasures, not to mention the 'Fatherland', and the newspapers, and their 'family duties'; it seems that they have no time whatever left for religion; and above all, it is not obvious to them whether it is a question of a new business or a new pleasure – for it is impossible, they say to themselves, that people should go to church merely to spoil their tempers. They are by no means enemies of religious customs; should certain circumstances, State affairs perhaps, require their participation in such customs, they do what is required, as so many things are done – with a patient and unassuming seriousness, and without much curiosity or discomfort; – they live too much apart and outside to feel even the necessity for a *for* or *against* in such matters. Among those indifferent persons may be reckoned nowadays the majority of German Protestants of the middle classes, especially in the great laborious centres of trade and commerce; also the majority of laborious scholars, and the entire University personnel (with the exception of the theologians, whose existence and possibility there always gives psychologists new and more subtle puzzles to solve). On the part of pious, or merely church-going people, there is seldom any idea of *how much* good-will, one might say arbitrary will, is now necessary for a German scholar to take the problem of religion seriously; his whole profession (and as I have said, his whole workmanlike laboriousness, to which he is compelled by his modern conscience) inclines him to a lofty and almost charitable serenity as regards religion, with which is occasionally mingled a slight disdain for the 'uncleanliness' of spirit which he takes for granted wherever anyone still professes to belong to the Church. It is only with the help of history (*not* through his own personal experience, therefore) that the scholar succeeds in bringing himself to a respectful seriousness, and to a certain

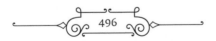

timid deference in presence of religions; but even when his sentiments have reached the stage of gratitude towards them, he has not personally advanced one step nearer to that which still maintains itself as Church or as piety; perhaps even the contrary. The practical indifference to religious matters in the midst of which he has been born and brought up, usually sublimates itself in his case into circumspection and cleanliness, which shuns contact with religious men and things; and it may be just the depth of his tolerance and humanity which prompts him to avoid the delicate trouble which tolerance itself brings with it. – Every age has its own divine type of naïveté, for the discovery of which other ages may envy it: and how much naïveté – adorable, childlike and boundlessly foolish naïveté is involved in this belief of the scholar in his superiority, in the good conscience of his tolerance, in the unsuspecting, simple certainty with which his instinct treats the religious man as a lower and less valuable type, beyond, before and *above* which he himself has developed – he, the little arrogant dwarf and mob-man, the sedulously alert, head-and-hand drudge of 'ideas', of 'modern ideas'!

59

WHOEVER has seen deeply into the world has doubtless divined what wisdom there is in the fact that men are superficial. It is their preservative instinct which teaches them to be flighty, lightsome and false. Here and there one finds a passionate and exaggerated adoration of 'pure forms' in philosophers as well as in artists: it is not to be doubted that whoever has *need* of the cult of the superficial to that extent, has at one time or another made an unlucky dive *beneath* it. Perhaps there is even an order of rank with respect to those burnt children, the born artists who find the enjoyment of life only in trying to *falsify* its image (as if taking wearisome revenge on it); one might guess to what degree life has disgusted them, by the extent to which they wish to see its image falsified, attenuated, ultrified and deified;

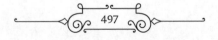

– one might reckon the *homines religiosi* among the artists, as their *highest* rank. It is the profound, suspicious fear of an incurable pessimism which compels whole centuries to fasten their teeth into a religious interpretation of existence: the fear of the instinct which divines that truth might be attained *too soon*, before man has become strong enough, hard enough, artist enough… Piety, the 'Life in God', regarded in this light, would appear as the most elaborate and ultimate product of the *fear* of truth, as artist-adoration and artist-intoxication in presence of the most logical of all falsifications, as the will to the inversion of truth, to untruth at any price. Perhaps there has hitherto been no more effective means of beautifying man than piety; by means of it man can become so artful, so superficial, so iridescent and so good, that his appearance no longer offends.

60

TO LOVE mankind *for God's sake* – this has so far been the noblest and remotest sentiment to which mankind has attained. That love to mankind, without any redeeming intention in the background, is only an *additional* folly and brutishness, that the inclination to this love has first to get its proportion, its delicacy, its grain of salt and sprinkling of ambergris from a higher inclination: – whoever first perceived and 'experienced' this, however his tongue may have stammered as it attempted to express such a delicate matter, let him for all time be holy and respected, as the man who has so far flown highest and gone astray in the finest fashion!

61

THE philosopher, as *we* free spirits understand him – as the man of the greatest responsibility, who has the conscience for the general development of mankind, – will use religion for his disciplining and educating work, just as he will use the contemporary political and

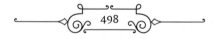

economic conditions. The selecting and disciplining influence – destructive, as well as creative and fashioning – which can be exercised by means of religion is manifold and varied, according to the sort of people placed under its spell and protection. For those who are strong and independent, destined and trained to command, in whom the judgment and skill of a ruling race is incorporated, religion is an additional means for overcoming resistance in the exercise of authority – as a bond which binds rulers and subjects in common, betraying and surrendering to the former the conscience of the latter, their inmost heart, which would fain escape obedience. And in the case of the unique natures of noble origin, if by virtue of superior spirituality they should incline to a more retired and contemplative life, reserving to themselves only the more refined forms of government (over chosen disciples or members of an order), religion itself may be used as a means for obtaining peace from the noise and trouble of managing *grosser* affairs, and for securing immunity from the *unavoidable* filth of all political agitation. The Brahmins, for instance, understood this fact. With the help of a religious organization, they secured to themselves the power of nominating kings for the people, while their sentiments prompted them to keep apart and outside, as men with a higher and super-regal mission. At the same time, religion gives inducement and opportunity to some of the subjects to qualify themselves for future ruling and commanding the slowly ascending ranks and classes, in which, through fortunate marriage customs, volitional power and delight in self-control are on the increase. To them religion offers sufficient incentives and temptations to aspire to higher intellectuality, and to experience the sentiments of authoritative self-control, of silence and of solitude. Asceticism and Puritanism are almost indispensable means of educating and ennobling a race which seeks to rise above its hereditary baseness and work itself upwards to future supremacy. And finally, to ordinary men, to the majority of the people, who exist for service and general utility, and are only so far

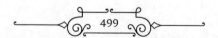

entitled to exist, religion gives invaluable contentedness with their lot and condition, peace of heart, ennoblement of obedience, additional social happiness and sympathy, with something of transfiguration and embellishment, something of justification of all the commonplaceness, all the meanness, all the semi-animal poverty of their souls. Religion, together with the religious significance of life, sheds sunshine over such perpetually harassed men, and makes even their own aspect endurable to them, it operates upon them as the Epicurean philosophy usually operates upon sufferers of a higher order, in a refreshing and refining manner, almost *turning* suffering *to account*, and in the end even hallowing and vindicating it. There is perhaps nothing so admirable in Christianity and Buddhism as their art of teaching even the lowest to elevate themselves by piety to a seemingly higher order of things, and thereby to retain their satisfaction with the actual world in which they find it difficult enough to live – this very difficulty being necessary.

62

TO BE sure – to make also the bad counter-reckoning against such religions, and to bring to light their secret dangers – the cost is always excessive and terrible when religions do *not* operate as an educational and disciplinary medium in the hands of the philosopher, but rule voluntarily and *paramountly*, when they wish to be the final end, and not a means along with other means. Among men, as among all other animals, there is a surplus of defective, diseased, degenerating, infirm and necessarily suffering individuals; the successful cases, among men also, are always the exception; and in view of the fact that man is *the animal not yet properly adapted to his environment*, the rare exception. But worse still. The higher the type a man represents, the greater is the improbability that he will *succeed*; the accidental, the law of irrationality in the general constitution of mankind, manifests itself most terribly in its destructive effect on the higher orders of men, the

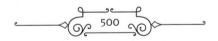

conditions of whose lives are delicate, diverse and difficult to determine. What, then, is the attitude of the two greatest religions above-mentioned to the *surplus* of failures in life? They endeavour to preserve and keep alive whatever can be preserved; in fact, as the religions *for sufferers*, they take the part of these upon principle; they are always in favour of those who suffer from life as from a disease, and they would fain treat every other experience of life as false and impossible. However highly we may esteem this indulgent and preservative care (inasmuch as in applying to others, it has applied, and applies also to the highest and usually the most suffering type of man), the hitherto *paramount* religions – to give a general appreciation of them – are among the principal causes which have kept the type of 'man' upon a lower level – they have preserved too much *that which should have perished*. One has to thank them for invaluable services; and who is sufficiently rich in gratitude not to feel poor at the contemplation of all that the 'spiritual men' of Christianity have done for Europe hitherto! But when they had given comfort to the sufferers, courage to the oppressed and despairing, a staff and support to the helpless, and when they had allured from society into convents and spiritual penitentiaries the broken-hearted and distracted: what else had they to do in order to work systematically in that fashion, and with a good conscience, for the preservation of all the sick and suffering, which means, in deed and in truth, to work for the *deterioration of the European race?* To *reverse* all estimates of value – *that* is what they had to do! And to shatter the strong, to spoil great hopes, to cast suspicion on the delight in beauty, to break down everything autonomous, manly, conquering and imperious – all instincts which are natural to the highest and most successful type of 'man' – into uncertainty, distress of conscience and self-destruction; forsooth, to invert all love of the earthly and of supremacy over the earth, into hatred of the earth and earthly things – *that* is the task the Church imposed on itself, and was

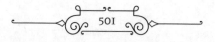

obliged to impose, until, according to its standard of value, 'unworld-liness', 'unsensuousness', and 'higher man' fused into one sentiment. If one could observe the strangely painful, equally coarse and refined comedy of European Christianity with the derisive and impartial eye of an Epicurean god, I should think one would never cease marvelling and laughing; does it not actually seem that some single will has ruled over Europe for eighteen centuries in order to make a *sublime abortion* of man? He, however, who, with opposite requirements (no longer Epicurean) and with some divine hammer in his hand, could approach this almost voluntary degeneration and stunting of mankind, as exemplified in the European Christian (Pascal, for instance), would he not have to cry aloud with rage, pity and horror: 'Oh, you bunglers, presumptuous pitiful bunglers, what have you done! Was that a work for your hands? How you have hacked and botched my finest stone! What have you presumed to do!' – I should say that Christianity has hitherto been the most portentous of presumptions. Men, not great enough, nor hard enough, to be entitled as artists to take part in fashioning *man*; men, not sufficiently strong and far-sighted to *allow*, with sublime self-constraint, the obvious law of the thousandfold failures and perishings to prevail; men, not sufficiently noble to see the radically different grades of rank and intervals of rank that separate man from man: – *such* men, with their 'equality before God', have hitherto swayed the destiny of Europe; until at last a dwarfed, almost ludicrous species has been produced, a gregarious animal, something obliging, sickly, mediocre, the European of the present day.

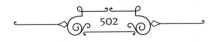

CHAPTER IV
APOPHTHEGMS AND INTERLUDES

63

HE WHO is a thorough teacher takes things seriously – and even himself – only in relation to his pupils.

64

'KNOWLEDGE for its own sake' – that is the last snare laid by morality: we are thereby completely entangled in morals once more.

65

THE charm of knowledge would be small, were it not so much shame has to be overcome on the way to it.

65A

WE ARE most dishonourable towards our God: he is not *permitted* to sin.

66

THE tendency of a person to allow himself to be degraded, robbed, deceived and exploited might be the diffidence of a God among men.

67

LOVE to one only is a barbarity, for it is exercised at the expense of all others. Love to God also!

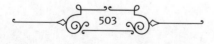

68

'I DID that,' says my memory. 'I could not have done that,' says my pride, and remains inexorable. Eventually – the memory yields.

69

ONE has regarded life carelessly, if one has failed to see the hand that – kills with leniency.

70

IF A man has character, he has also his typical experience, which always recurs.

71

THE Sage as Astronomer. – So long as thou feelest the stars as an 'above thee', thou lackest the eye of the discerning one.

72

IT IS not the strength, but the duration of great sentiments that makes great men.

73

HE WHO attains his ideal, precisely thereby surpasses it.

73A

MANY a peacock hides his tail from every eye – and calls it his pride.

74

A MAN of genius is unbearable, unless he possess at least two things besides: gratitude and purity.

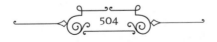

75

THE degree and nature of a man's sensuality extends to the highest altitudes of his spirit.

76

UNDER peaceful conditions the militant man attacks himself.

77

WITH his principles a man seeks either to dominate, or justify, or honour, or reproach, or conceal his habits: two men with the same principles probably seek fundamentally different ends therewith.

78

HE WHO despises himself, nevertheless esteems himself thereby, as a despiser.

79

A SOUL which knows that it is loved, but does not itself love, betrays its sediment: its dregs come up.

80

A THING that is explained ceases to concern us. – What did the God mean who gave the advice, 'Know thyself!' Did it perhaps imply: 'Cease to be concerned about thyself! become objective!' – And Socrates? – And the 'scientific man'?

81

IT IS terrible to die of thirst at sea. Is it necessary that you should so salt your truth that it will no longer – quench thirst?

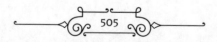

82

'SYMPATHY for all' – would be harshness and tyranny for *thee*, my good neighbour.

83

INSTINCT. – When the house is on fire one forgets even the dinner. – Yes, but one recovers it from among the ashes.

84

WOMAN learns how to hate in proportion as she – forgets how to charm.

85

THE same emotions are in man and woman, but in different *tempo*; on that account man and woman never cease to misunderstand each other.

86

IN THE background of all their personal vanity, women themselves have still their impersonal scorn – for 'woman'.

87

FETTERED Heart, Free Spirit – When one firmly fetters one's heart and keeps it prisoner, one can allow one's spirit many liberties: I said this once before. But people do not believe it when I say so, unless they know it already.

88

ONE begins to distrust very clever persons when they become embarrassed.

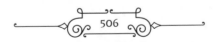

89

DREADFUL experiences raise the question whether he who experiences them is not something dreadful also.

90

HEAVY, melancholy men turn lighter, and come temporarily to their surface, precisely by that which makes others heavy – by hatred and love.

91

SO COLD, so icy, that one burns one's finger at the touch of him! Every hand that lays hold of him shrinks back! – And for that very reason many think him red-hot.

92

WHO has not, at one time or another – sacrificed himself for the sake of his good name?

93

IN affability there is no hatred of men, but precisely on that account a great deal too much contempt of men.

94

THE maturity of man – that means, to have reacquired the seriousness that one had as a child at play.

95

TO BE ashamed of one's immorality is a step on the ladder at the end of which one is ashamed also of one's morality.

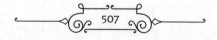

96

ONE should part from life as Ulysses parted from Nausicaa – blessing it rather than in love with it.

97

WHAT? A great man? I always see merely the play-actor of his own ideal.

98

WHEN one trains one's conscience, it kisses one while it bites.

99

THE Disappointed One Speaks. – 'I listened for the echo and I heard only praise.'

100

WE ALL feign to ourselves that we are simpler than we are, we thus relax ourselves away from our fellows.

101

A DISCERNING one might easily regard himself at present as the animalization of God.

102

DISCOVERING reciprocal love should really disenchant the lover with regard to the beloved. 'What! *She* is modest enough to love even you? Or stupid enough? Or – or – '

103

THE Danger in Happiness. – 'Everything now turns out best for me, I now love every fate: – who would like to be my fate?'

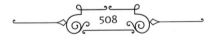

104

NOT their love of humanity, but the impotence of their love, prevents the Christians of today – burning us.

105

THE *pia fraus* is still more repugnant to the taste (*the 'piety'*) of the free spirit (the 'pious man of knowledge') than the *impia fraus*. Hence the profound lack of judgment, in comparison with the Church, characteristic of the type 'free spirit' – as *its* non-freedom.

106

BY MEANS of music the very passions enjoy themselves.

107

A SIGN of strong character, when once the resolution has been taken, to shut the ear even to the best counter-arguments. Occasionally, therefore, a will to stupidity.

108

THERE is no such thing as moral phenomena, but only a moral interpretation of phenomena.

109

THE criminal is often enough not equal to his deed: he extenuates and maligns it.

110

THE advocates of a criminal are seldom artists enough to turn the beautiful terribleness of the deed to the advantage of the doer.

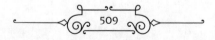

111

OUR vanity is most difficult to wound just when our pride has been wounded.

112

TO HIM who feels himself preordained to contemplation and not to belief, all believers are too noisy and obtrusive; he guards against them.

113

'YOU want to prepossess him in your favour? Then you must be embarrassed before him.'

114

THE immense expectation with regard to sexual love, and the coyness in this expectation, spoils all the perspectives of women at the outset.

115

WHERE there is neither love nor hatred in the game, woman's play is mediocre.

116

THE great epochs of our life are at the points when we gain courage to rebaptize our badness as the best in us.

117

THE will to overcome an emotion, is ultimately only the will of another, or of several other, emotions.

118

THERE is an innocence of admiration: it is possessed by him to whom it has not yet occurred that he himself may be admired some day.

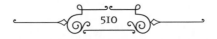

119

OUR loathing of dirt may be so great as to prevent our cleaning ourselves – 'justifying' ourselves.

120

SENSUALITY often forces the growth of love too much, so that its root remains weak, and is easily torn up.

121

IT IS a curious thing that God learned Greek when he wished to turn author – and that he did not learn it better.

122

TO REJOICE on account of praise is in many cases merely politeness of heart – and the very opposite of vanity of spirit.

123

EVEN concubinage has been corrupted – by marriage.

124

HE WHO exults at the stake, does not triumph over pain, but because of the fact that he does not feel pain where he expected it. A parable.

125

WHEN we have to change an opinion about any one, we charge heavily to his account the inconvenience he thereby causes us.

126

A NATION is a detour of nature to arrive at six or seven great men. – Yes, and then to get round them.

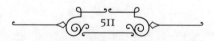

127

IN THE eyes of all true women science is hostile to the sense of shame. They feel as if one wished to peep under their skin with it – or worse still! under their dress and finery.

128

THE more abstract the truth you wish to teach, the more must you allure the senses to it.

129

THE devil has the most extensive perspectives for God; on that account he keeps so far away from him: – the devil, in effect, as the oldest friend of knowledge.

130

WHAT a person *is* begins to betray itself when his talent decreases, – when he ceases to show what he *can* do. Talent is also an adornment; an adornment is also a concealment.

131

THE sexes deceive themselves about each other: the reason is that in reality they honour and love only themselves (or their own ideal, to express it more agreeably). Thus man wishes woman to be peaceable: but in fact woman is *essentially* unpeaceable, like the cat, however well she may have assumed the peaceable demeanour.

132

ONE is punished best for one's virtues.

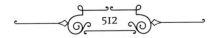

133

HE WHO cannot find the way to *his* ideal, lives more frivolously and shamelessly than the man without an ideal.

134

FROM the senses originate all trustworthiness, all good conscience, all evidence of truth.

135

PHARISAISM is not a deterioration of the good man; a considerable part of it is rather an essential condition of being good.

136

THE one seeks an *accoucheur* for his thoughts, the other seeks someone whom he can assist: a good conversation thus originates.

137

IN INTERCOURSE with scholars and artists one readily makes mistakes of opposite kinds: in a remarkable scholar one not infrequently finds a mediocre man; and often, even in a mediocre artist, one finds a very remarkable man.

138

WE DO the same when awake as when dreaming: we only invent and imagine him with whom we have intercourse – and forget it immediately.

139

IN REVENGE and in love woman is more barbarous than man.

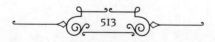

140

ADVICE as a riddle. – 'If the band is not to break, bite it first – secure to make!'

141

THE belly is the reason why man does not so readily take himself for a God.

142

THE chastest utterance I ever heard: *'Dans le véritable amour c'est l'âmi qui enveloppe le corps.'*

143

OUR vanity would like what we do best to pass precisely for what is most difficult to us. – Concerning the origin of many systems of morals.

144

WHEN a woman has scholarly inclinations there is generally something wrong with her sexual nature. Barrenness itself conduces to a certain virility of taste; man, indeed, if I may say so, is 'the barren animal'.

145

COMPARING man and woman generally, one may say that woman would not have the genius for adornment, if she had not the instinct for the *secondary* role.

146

HE WHO fights with monsters should be careful lest he thereby become a monster. And if thou gaze long into an abyss, the abyss will also gaze into thee.

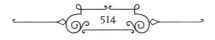

147

FROM old Florentine novels – moreover, from life: *Buona femmina e mala femmina vuol bastone.* – Sacchetti, Nov. 86.

148

TO SEDUCE their neighbour to a favourable opinion, and afterwards to believe implicitly in this opinion of their neighbour – who can do this conjuring trick so well as women?

149

THAT which an age considers evil is usually an unseasonable echo of what was formerly considered good – the atavism of an old ideal.

150

AROUND the hero everything becomes a tragedy; around the demigod everything becomes a satyr-play; and around God everything becomes – what? perhaps a 'world'?

151

IT IS not enough to possess a talent: one must also have your permission to possess it; – eh, my friends?

152

'WHERE there is the tree of knowledge, there is always Paradise': so say the most ancient and the most modern serpents.

153

WHAT is done out of love always takes place beyond good and evil.

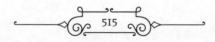

154

OBJECTION, evasion, joyous distrust and love of irony are signs of health; everything absolute belongs to pathology.

155

THE sense of the tragic increases and declines with sensuousness.

156

INSANITY in individuals is something rare – but in groups, parties, nations and epochs it is the rule.

157

THE thought of suicide is a great consolation: by means of it one gets successfully through many a bad night.

158

NOT only our reason, but also our conscience, truckles to our strongest impulse – the tyrant in us.

159

ONE *must* repay good and ill; but why just to the person who did us good or ill?

160

ONE no longer loves one's knowledge sufficiently after one has communicated it.

161

POETS act shamelessly towards their experiences: they exploit them.

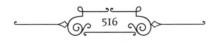

162

'OUR fellow-creature is not our neighbour, but our neighbour's neighbour': – so thinks every nation.

163

LOVE brings to light the noble and hidden qualities of a lover – his rare and exceptional traits: it is thus liable to be deceptive as to his normal character.

164

JESUS said to his Jews: 'The law was for servants; – love God as I love him, as his Son! What have we Sons of God to do with morals!'

165

IN SIGHT of Every Party. – A shepherd has always need of a bell-wether – or he has himself to be a wether occasionally.

166

ONE may indeed lie with the mouth; but with the accompanying grimace one nevertheless tells the truth.

167

TO VIGOROUS men intimacy is a matter of shame – and something precious.

168

CHRISTIANITY gave Eros poison to drink; he did not die of it, certainly, but degenerated to Vice.

169

TO TALK much about oneself may also be a means of concealing oneself.

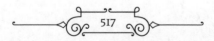

170

IN PRAISE there is more obtrusiveness than in blame.

171

PITY has an almost ludicrous effect on a man of knowledge, like tender hands on a Cyclops.

172

ONE occasionally embraces someone or other, out of love to mankind (because one cannot embrace all); but this is what one must never confess to the individual.

173

ONE does not hate as long as one disesteems, but only when one esteems equal or superior.

174

YE UTILITARIANS – ye, too, love the *utile* only as a *vehicle* for your inclinations, – ye, too, really find the noise of its wheels insupportable!

175

ONE loves ultimately one's desires, not the thing desired.

176

THE vanity of others is only counter to our taste when it is counter to our vanity.

177

WITH regard to what 'truthfulness' is, perhaps nobody has ever been sufficiently truthful.

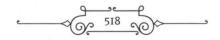

178

ONE does not believe in the follies of clever men: what a forfeiture of the rights of man!

179

THE consequences of our actions seize us by the forelock, very indifferent to the fact that we have meanwhile 'reformed'.

180

THERE is an innocence in lying, which is the sign of good faith in a cause.

181

IT IS inhuman to bless when one is being cursed.

182

THE familiarity of superiors embitters one, because it may not be returned.

183

'I AM affected, not because you have deceived me, but because I can no longer believe in you.'

184

THERE is a haughtiness of kindness, which has the appearance of wickedness.

185

'I DISLIKE him.' – Why? – 'I am not a match for him.' – Did anyone ever answer so?

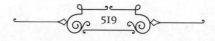

CHAPTER V
THE NATURAL HISTORY
OF MORALS

186

THE moral sentiment in Europe at present is perhaps as subtle, belated, diverse, sensitive and refined, as the 'Science of Morals' belonging thereto is recent, initial, awkward and coarse-fingered: – an interesting contrast, which sometimes becomes incarnate and obvious in the very person of a moralist. Indeed, the expression, 'Science of Morals' is, in respect to what is designated thereby, far too presumptuous and counter to *good* taste, – which is always a foretaste of more modest expressions. One ought to avow with the utmost fairness *what* is still necessary here for a long time, *what* is alone proper for the present: namely, the collection of material, the comprehensive survey and classification of an immense domain of delicate sentiments of worth and distinctions of worth, which live, grow, propagate and perish – and perhaps attempts to give a clear idea of the recurring and more common forms of these living crystallizations – as preparation for a *theory of types* of morality. To be sure, people have not hitherto been so modest. All the philosophers, with a pedantic and ridiculous seriousness, demanded of themselves something very much higher, more pretentious and ceremonious, when they concerned themselves with morality as a science: they wanted to *give a basis* to morality – and every philosopher hitherto has believed that he has given it a basis; morality itself, however, has been regarded as something 'given'. How far from their awkward pride was the seem-

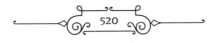

ingly insignificant problem – left in dust and decay – of a description of forms of morality, notwithstanding that the finest hands and senses could hardly be fine enough for it! It was precisely owing to moral philosophers' knowing the moral facts imperfectly, in an arbitrary epitome, or an accidental abridgement – perhaps as the morality of their environment, their position, their church, their *Zeitgeist*, their climate and zone – it was precisely because they were badly instructed with regard to nations, eras and past ages, and were by no means eager to know about these matters, that they did not even come in sight of the real problems of morals – problems which only disclose themselves by a comparison of *many* kinds of morality. In every 'Science of Morals' hitherto, strange as it may sound, the problem of morality itself has been *omitted*: there has been no suspicion that there was anything problematic there! That which philosophers called 'giving a basis to morality', and endeavoured to realize, has, when seen in a right light, proved merely a learned form of good *faith* in prevailing morality, a new means of its *expression*, consequently just a matter-of-fact within the sphere of a definite morality, yea, in its ultimate motive, a sort of denial that it is *lawful* for this morality to be called in question – and in any case the reverse of the testing, analyzing, doubting and vivisecting of this very faith. Hear, for instance, with what innocence – almost worthy of honour – Schopenhauer represents his own task, and draw your conclusions concerning the scientificness of a 'Science' whose latest master still talks in the strain of children and old wives: 'The principle,' he says (page 136 of the *Grundprobleme der Ethik**), 'the axiom about the purport of which all moralists are *practically* agreed: *neminem laede, immo omnes quantum potes juva* – is *really* the proposition which all moral teachers strive to establish,… the *real* basis of ethics which has been sought, like the philosopher's stone, for centuries.' – The difficulty of establishing

* Pages 54–55 of Schopenhauer's *Basis of Morality*, translated by Arthur B. Bullock, M.A. (1903).

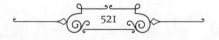

the proposition referred to may indeed be great – it is well known that Schopenhauer also was unsuccessful in his efforts; and whoever has thoroughly realized how absurdly false and sentimental this proposition is, in a world whose essence is Will to Power, may be reminded that Schopenhauer, although a pessimist, *actually* – played the flute… daily after dinner: one may read about the matter in his biography. A question by the way: a pessimist, a repudiator of God and of the world, who *makes a halt* at morality – who assents to morality, and plays the flute to *laede-neminem* morals, what? Is that really – a pessimist?

187

APART from the value of such assertions as 'there is a categorical imperative in us', one can always ask: What does such an assertion indicate about him who makes it? There are systems of morals which are meant to justify their author in the eyes of other people; other systems of morals are meant to tranquilize him, and make him self-satisfied; with other systems he wants to crucify and humble himself, with others he wishes to take revenge, with others to conceal himself, with others to glorify himself and gave superiority and distinction, – this system of morals helps its author to forget, that system makes him, or something of him, forgotten, many a moralist would like to exercise power and creative arbitrariness over mankind, many another, perhaps, Kant especially, gives us to understand by his morals that 'what is estimable in me, is that I know how to obey – and with you it *shall* not be otherwise than with me!' In short, systems of morals are only a *sign-language of the emotions*.

188

IN CONTRAST to *laisser-aller*, every system of morals is a sort of tyranny against 'nature' and also against 'reason'; that is, however, no objection, unless one should again decree by some system of morals,

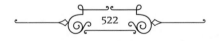

that all kinds of tyranny and unreasonableness are unlawful What is essential and invaluable in every system of morals, is that it is a long constraint. In order to understand Stoicism, or Port-Royal or Puritanism, one should remember the constraint under which every language has attained to strength and freedom – the metrical constraint, the tyranny of rhyme and rhythm. How much trouble have the poets and orators of every nation given themselves! – not excepting some of the prose writers of today, in whose ear dwells an inexorable conscientiousness – 'for the sake of a folly', as utilitarian bunglers say, and thereby deem themselves wise – 'from submission to arbitrary laws', as the anarchists say, and thereby fancy themselves 'free', even free-spirited. The singular fact remains, however, that everything of the nature of freedom, elegance, boldness, dance and masterly certainty, which exists or has existed, whether it be in thought itself, or in administration, or in speaking and persuading, in art just as in conduct, has only developed by means of the tyranny of such arbitrary law; and in all seriousness, it is not at all improbable that precisely this is 'nature' and 'natural' – and not *laisser-aller*! Every artist knows how different from the state of letting himself go, is his 'most natural' condition, the free arranging, locating, disposing and constructing in the moments of 'inspiration' – and how strictly and delicately he then obeys a thousand laws, which, by their very rigidness and precision, defy all formulation by means of ideas (even the most stable idea has, in comparison therewith, something floating, manifold and ambiguous in it). The essential thing 'in heaven and in earth' is, apparently (to repeat it once more), that there should be long *obedience* in the same direction, there thereby results, and has always resulted in the long run, something which has made life worth living; for instance, virtue, art, music, dancing, reason, spirituality – anything whatever that is transfiguring, refined, foolish or divine. The long bondage of the spirit, the distrustful constraint in the communicability of ideas, the discipline

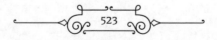

which the thinker imposed on himself to think in accordance with the rules of a church or a court, or conformable to Aristotelian premises, the persistent spiritual will to interpret everything that happened according to a Christian scheme, and in every occurrence to rediscover and justify the Christian God: – all this violence, arbitrariness, severity, dreadfulness and unreasonableness, has proved itself the disciplinary means whereby the European spirit has attained its strength, its remorseless curiosity and subtle mobility; granted also that much irrecoverable strength and spirit had to be stifled, suffocated and spoilt in the process (for here, as everywhere, 'nature' shows herself as she is, in all her extravagant and *indifferent* magnificence, which is shocking, but nevertheless noble). That for centuries European thinkers only thought in order to prove something – nowadays, on the contrary, we are suspicious of every thinker who 'wishes to prove something' – that it was always settled beforehand what *was to be* the result of their strictest thinking, as it was perhaps in the Asiatic astrology of former times, or as it is still at the present day in the innocent, Christian-moral explanation of immediate personal events 'for the glory of God', or 'for the good of the soul': – this tyranny, this arbitrariness, this severe and magnificent stupidity, has *educated* the spirit; slavery, both in the coarser and the finer sense, is apparently an indispensable means even of spiritual education and discipline. One may look at every system of morals in this light: it is 'nature' therein which teaches to hate the *laisser-aller*, the too great freedom, and implants the need for limited horizons, for immediate duties – it teaches the *narrowing of perspectives*, and thus, in a certain sense, that stupidity is a condition of life and development. 'Thou must obey some one, and for a long time; *otherwise* thou wilt come to grief, and lose all respect for thyself' – this seems to me to be the moral imperative of nature, which is certainly neither 'categorical', as old Kant wished (consequently the 'otherwise'), nor does it address itself to the individual (what does

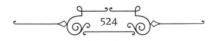

nature care for the individual!), but to nations, races, ages and ranks; above all, however, to the animal 'man' generally, to *mankind*.

189

INDUSTRIOUS races find it a great hardship to be idle: it was a master stroke of *English* instinct to hallow and begloom Sunday to such an extent that the Englishman unconsciously hankers for his week- and work-day again: – as a kind of cleverly devised, cleverly intercalated *fast*, such as is also frequently found in the ancient world (although, as is appropriate in southern nations, not precisely with respect to work). Many kinds of fasts are necessary; and wherever powerful influences and habits prevail, legislators have to see that intercalary days are appointed, on which such impulses are fettered, and learn to hunger anew. Viewed from a higher standpoint, whole generations and epochs, when they show themselves infected with any moral fanaticism, seem like those intercalated periods of restraint and fasting, during which an impulse learns to humble and submit itself – at the same time also to *purify* and *sharpen* itself; certain philosophical sects likewise admit of a similar interpretation (for instance, the Stoa, in the midst of Hellenic culture, with the atmosphere rank and overcharged with Aphrodisiacal odours). – Here also is a hint for the explanation of the paradox, why it was precisely in the most Christian period of European history, and in general only under the pressure of Christian sentiments, that the sexual impulse sublimated into love (*amour-passion*).

190

THERE is something in the morality of Plato which does not really belong to Plato, but which only appears in his philosophy, one might say, in spite of him: namely, Socratism, for which he himself was too noble. 'No one desires to injure himself, hence all evil is done unwittingly. The evil man inflicts injury on himself; he would not do so,

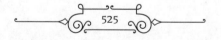

however, if he knew that evil is evil. The evil man, therefore, is only evil through error; if one free him from error one will necessarily make him – good.' – This mode of reasoning savours of the *populace*, who perceive only the unpleasant consequences of evil-doing, and practically judge that 'it is *stupid* to do wrong'; while they accept 'good' as identical with 'useful and pleasant', without further thought. As regards every system of utilitarianism, one may at once assume that it has the same origin, and follow the scent: one will seldom err. – Plato did all he could to interpret something refined and noble into the tenets of his teacher, and above all to interpret himself into them – he, the most daring of all interpreters, who lifted the entire Socrates out of the street, as a popular theme and song, to exhibit him in endless and impossible modifications – namely, in all his own disguises and multi-plicities. In jest, and in Homeric language as well, what is the Platonic Socrates, if not – πρόοὺε Πλάτων ἄπσέυ τε Πλάτων μέσσῃ Χίμαιρα.

191

THE old theological problem of 'Faith' and 'Knowledge', or more plainly, of instinct and reason – the question whether, in respect to the valuation of things, instinct deserves more authority than ration-ality, which wants to appreciate and act according to motives, according to a 'Why', that is to say, in conformity to purpose and utility – it is always the old moral problem that first appeared in the person of Socrates, and had divided men's minds long before Christianity. Socrates himself, following, of course, the taste of his talent – that of a surpassing dialectician – took first the side of reason; and, in fact, what did he do all his life but laugh at the awkward incapacity of the noble Athenians, who were men of instinct, like all noble men, and could never give satisfactory answers concerning the motives of their actions? In the end, however, though silently and secretly, he laughed also at himself: with his finer conscience and introspection, he found

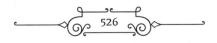

in himself the same difficulty and incapacity. 'But why' – he said to himself – 'should one on that account separate oneself from the instincts! One must set them right, and the reason *also* – one must follow the instincts, but at the same time persuade the reason to support them with good arguments.' This was the real *falseness* of that great and mysterious ironist; he brought his conscience up to the point that he was satisfied with a kind of self-outwitting: in fact, he perceived the irrationality in the moral judgment. – Plato, more innocent in such matters, and without the craftiness of the plebeian, wished to prove to himself, at the expenditure of all his strength – the greatest strength a philosopher had ever expended – that reason and instinct lead spontaneously to one goal, to the good, to 'God'; and since Plato, all theologians and philosophers have followed the same path – which means that in matters of morality, instinct (or as Christians call it, 'Faith', or as I call it, 'the herd') has hitherto triumphed. Unless one should make an exception in the case of Descartes, the father of rationalism (and consequently the grandfather of the Revolution), who recognized only the authority of reason: but reason is only a tool, and Descartes was superficial.

192

WHOEVER has followed the history of a single science, finds in its development a clue to the understanding of the oldest and commonest processes of all 'knowledge and cognizance': there, as here, the premature hypotheses, the fictions, the good stupid will to 'belief' and the lack of distrust and patience are first developed – our senses learn late, and never learn completely, to be subtle, reliable and cautious organs of knowledge. Our eyes find it easier on a given occasion to produce a picture already often produced, than to seize upon the divergence and novelty of an impression: the latter requires more force, more 'morality'. It is difficult and painful for the ear to listen to anything

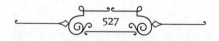

new; we hear strange music badly. When we hear another language spoken, we involuntarily attempt to form the sounds into words with which we are more familiar and conversant – it was thus, for example, that the Germans modified the spoken word *arcubalista* into *armbrust* (cross-bow). Our senses are also hostile and averse to the new; and generally, even in the 'simplest' processes of sensation, the emotions *dominate* – such as fear, love, hatred and the passive emotion of indolence. – As little as a reader nowadays reads all the single words (not to speak of syllables) of a page – he rather takes about five out of every twenty words at random, and 'guesses' the probably appropriate sense to them – just as little do we see a tree correctly and completely in respect to its leaves, branches, colour and shape; we find it so much easier to fancy the chance of a tree. Even in the midst of the most remarkable experiences, we still do just the same; we fabricate the greater part of the experience, and can hardly be made to contemplate any event, *except* as 'inventors' thereof. All this goes to prove that from our fundamental nature and from remote ages we have been – *accustomed to lying*. Or, to express it more politely and hypocritically, in short, more pleasantly – one is much more of an artist than one is aware of. – In an animated conversation, I often see the face of the person with whom I am speaking so clearly and sharply defined before me, according to the thought he expresses, or which I believe to be evoked in his mind, that the degree of distinctness far exceeds the *strength* of my visual faculty – the delicacy of the play of the muscles and of the expression of the eyes *must* therefore be imagined by me. Probably the person put on quite a different expression, or none at all.

193

QUIDQUID luce fuit, tenebris agit: but also contrariwise. What we experience in dreams, provided we experience it often, pertains at last just as much to the general belongings of our soul as anything 'actually'

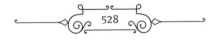

experienced; by virtue thereof we are richer or poorer, we have a requirement more or less, and finally, in broad daylight, and even in the brightest moments of our waking life, we are ruled to some extent by the nature of our dreams. Supposing that someone has often flown in his dreams, and that at last, as soon as he dreams, he is conscious of the power and art of flying as his privilege and his peculiarly enviable happiness; such a person, who believes that on the slightest impulse, he can actualize all sorts of curves and angles, who knows the sensation of a certain divine levity, an 'upwards' without effort or constraint, a 'downwards' without descending or lowering – without *trouble*! – how could the man with such dream-experiences and dream-habits fail to find 'happiness' differently coloured and defined, even in his waking hours! How could he fail – to long *differently* for happiness? 'Flight', such as is described by poets, must, when compared with his own 'flying', be far too earthly, muscular, violent, far too 'troublesome' for him.

194

THE difference among men does not manifest itself only in the difference of their lists of desirable things – in their regarding different good things as worth striving for, and being disagreed as to the greater or less value, the order of rank, of the commonly recognized desirable things: – it manifests itself much more in what they regard as actually *having* and *possessing* a desirable thing. As regards a woman, for instance, the control over her body and her sexual gratification serves as an amply sufficient sign of ownership and possession to the more modest man; another with a more suspicious and ambitious thirst for possession, sees the 'questionableness', the mere apparentness of such ownership, and wishes to have finer tests in order to know especially whether the woman not only gives herself to him, but also gives up for his sake what she has or would like to have – only *then* does he look upon her as 'possessed.' A third, however, has not even here got to the limit of his distrust and his desire for possession: he asks himself whether the woman, when she gives up everything for him, does not perhaps do so for a phantom of him; he wishes first to be thoroughly, indeed, profoundly well known; in order to be loved at all he ventures to let himself be found out. Only then does he feel the beloved one fully in his possession, when she no longer deceives herself about him, when she loves him just as much for the sake of his devilry and concealed insatiability, as for his goodness, patience and spirituality. One man would like to possess a nation, and he finds all the higher arts of Cagliostro and Catalina suitable for his purpose. Another, with a more refined thirst for possession, says to himself: 'One may not deceive where one desires to possess' – he is irritated and impatient at the idea that a mask of him should rule in the hearts of the people: 'I must, therefore, *make* myself known, and first of all learn to know myself!' Among helpful and charitable people, one almost always finds the awkward craftiness which first gets up suitably him who has to be helped, as though, for instance, he should 'merit' help, seek just *their* help and would show himself deeply grateful, attached and subservient to them for all help. With these conceits, they take control of the needy as a property, just as in general they are charitable and helpful out of a desire for property. One finds them jealous when they are crossed or forestalled in their charity. Parents involuntarily make something like themselves out of their children – they call that 'education'; no mother doubts at the bottom of her heart that the child she has borne is thereby her property, no father hesitates about his right to *his own* ideas and notions of worth. Indeed, in former times fathers deemed it right to use their discretion concerning the life or death of the newly born (as among the ancient Germans). And like the father, so also do the teacher, the class, the priest and the prince still see in every new individual an unobjectionable opportunity for a new possession. The consequence is…

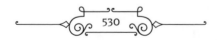

195

THE Jews – a people 'born for slavery', as Tacitus and the whole ancient world say of them; 'the chosen people among the nations', as they themselves say and believe – the Jews performed the miracle of the inversion of valuations, by means of which life on earth obtained a new and dangerous charm for a couple of millenniums. Their prophets fused into one the expressions 'rich', 'godless', 'wicked', 'violent', 'sensual', and for the first time coined the word 'world' as a term of reproach. In this inversion of valuations (in which is also included the use of the word 'poor' as synonymous with 'saint' and 'friend') the significance of the Jewish people is to be found; it is with *them* that the *slave-insurrection in morals* commences.

196

IT IS to be *inferred* that there are countless dark bodies near the sun – such as we shall never see. Among ourselves, this is an allegory; and the psychologist of morals reads the whole star-writing merely as an allegorical and symbolic language in which much may be unexpressed.

197

THE beast of prey and the man of prey (for instance, Caesar Borgia) are fundamentally misunderstood, 'nature' is misunderstood, so long as one seeks a 'morbidness' in the constitution of these healthiest of all tropical monsters and growths, or even an innate 'hell' in them – as almost all moralists have done hitherto. Does it not seem that there is a hatred of the virgin forest and of the tropics among moralists? And that the 'tropical man' must be discredited at all costs, whether as disease and deterioration of mankind, or as his own hell and self-torture? And why? In favour of the 'temperate zones'? In favour of the temperate men? The 'moral'? The mediocre? – This for the chapter: 'Morals as Timidity'.

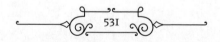

198

ALL the systems of morals which address themselves with a view to their 'happiness', as it is called – what else are they but suggestions for behaviour adapted to the degree of *danger* from themselves in which the individuals live; recipes for their passions, their good and bad propensities, in so far as such have the Will to Power and would like to play the master; small and great expediencies and elaborations, permeated with the musty odour of old family medicines and old-wife wisdom; all of them grotesque and absurd in their form – because they address themselves to 'all', because they generalize where generalization is not authorized; all of them speaking unconditionally, and taking themselves unconditionally; all of them flavoured not merely with one grain of salt, but rather endurable only, and sometimes even seductive, when they are over-spiced and begin to smell dangerously, especially of 'the other world'. That is all of little value when estimated intellectually, and is far from being 'science', much less 'wisdom'; but, repeated once more, and three times repeated, it is expediency, expediency, expediency, mixed with stupidity, stupidity, stupidity – whether it be the indifference and statuesque coldness towards the heated folly of the emotions, which the Stoics advised and fostered; or the no-more-laughing and no-more-weeping of Spinoza, the destruction of the emotions by their analysis and vivisection, which he recommended so naively; or the lowering of the emotions to an innocent mean at which they may be satisfied, the Aristotelianism of morals; or even morality as the enjoyment of the emotions in a voluntary attenuation and spiritualization by the symbolism of art, perhaps as music or as love of God, and of mankind for God's sake – for in religion the passions are once more enfranchised, provided that...; or, finally, even the complaisant and wanton surrender to the emotions, as has been taught by Hafis and Goethe, the bold letting-go of the reins, the spiritual and corporeal *licentia morum* in the exceptional cases of wise old codgers and drunkards, with whom it 'no longer has much danger'. – This also for the chapter: 'Morals as Timidity'.

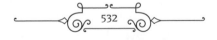

199

INASMUCH as in all ages, as long as mankind has existed, there have also been human herds (family alliances, communities, tribes, peoples, states, churches), and always a great number who obey in proportion to the small number who command – in view, therefore, of the fact that obedience has been most practiced and fostered among mankind hitherto, one may reasonably suppose that, generally speaking, the need thereof is now innate in every one, as a kind of *formal conscience* which gives the command: 'Thou shalt unconditionally do something, unconditionally refrain from something'; in short, 'Thou shalt'. This need tries to satisfy itself and to fill its form with a content, according to its strength, impatience and eagerness, it at once seizes as an omnivorous appetite with little selection, and accepts whatever is shouted into its ear by all sorts of commanders – parents, teachers, laws, class prejudices or public opinion. The extraordinary limitation of human development, the hesitation, protractedness, frequent retrogression and turning thereof, is attributable to the fact that the herd-instinct of obedience is transmitted best, and at the cost of the art of command. If one imagine this instinct increasing to its greatest extent, commanders and independent individuals will finally be lacking altogether, or they will suffer inwardly from a bad conscience, and will have to impose a deception on themselves in the first place in order to be able to command just as if they also were only obeying. This condition of things actually exists in Europe at present – I call it the moral hypocrisy of the commanding class. They know no other way of protecting themselves from their bad conscience than by playing the role of executors of older and higher orders (of predecessors, of the constitution, of justice, of the law or of God himself), or they even justify themselves by maxims from the current opinions of the herd, as 'first servants of their people', or 'instruments of the public weal'. On the other hand, the gregarious European man nowadays assumes an air

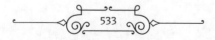

as if he were the only kind of man that is allowable; he glorifies his qualities, such as public spirit, kindness, deference, industry, temperance, modesty, indulgence, sympathy, by virtue of which he is gentle, endurable and useful to the herd, as the peculiarly human virtues. In cases, however, where it is believed that the leader and bell-wether cannot be dispensed with, attempt after attempt is made nowadays to replace commanders by the summing together of clever gregarious men all representative constitutions, for example, are of this origin. In spite of all, what a blessing, what a deliverance from a weight becoming unendurable, is the appearance of an absolute ruler for these gregarious Europeans – of this fact the effect of the appearance of Napoleon was the last great proof: the history of the influence of Napoleon is almost the history of the higher happiness to which the entire century has attained in its worthiest individuals and periods.

200

THE man of an age of dissolution which mixes the races with one another, who has the inheritance of a diversified descent in his body – that is to say, contrary, and often not only contrary, instincts and standards of value, which struggle with one another and are seldom at peace – such a man of late culture and broken lights, will, on an average, be a weak man. His fundamental desire is that the war which is *in him* should come to an end; happiness appears to him in the character of a soothing medicine and mode of thought (for instance, Epicurean or Christian); it is above all things the happiness of repose, of undisturbedness, of repletion, of final unity – it is the 'Sabbath of Sabbaths', to use the expression of the holy rhetorician, St Augustine, who was himself such a man. – Should, however, the contrariety and conflict in such natures operate as an *additional* incentive and stimulus to life – and if, on the other hand, in addition to their powerful and irreconcilable instincts, they have also inherited and indoctrinated into

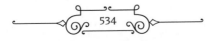

them a proper mastery and subtlety for carrying on the conflict with themselves (that is to say, the faculty of self-control and self-deception), there then arise those marvellously incomprehensible and inexplicable beings, those enigmatical men, predestined for conquering and circumventing others, the finest examples of which are Alcibiades and Caesar (with whom I should like to associate the *first* of Europeans according to my taste, the Hohenstaufen, Frederick the Second), and among artists, perhaps Leonardo da Vinci. They appear precisely in the same periods when that weaker type, with its longing for repose, comes to the front; the two types are complementary to each other, and spring from the same causes.

201

AS LONG as the utility which determines moral estimates is only gregarious utility, as long as the preservation of the community is only kept in view, and the immoral is sought precisely and exclusively in what seems dangerous to the maintenance of the community, there can be no 'morality of love to one's neighbour'. Granted even that there is already a little constant exercise of consideration, sympathy, fairness, gentleness and mutual assistance, granted that even in this condition of society all those instincts are already active which are latterly distinguished by honourable names as 'virtues', and eventually almost coincide with the conception 'morality': in that period they do not as yet belong to the domain of moral valuations – they are still *ultra-moral*. A sympathetic action, for instance, is neither called good nor bad, moral nor immoral, in the best period of the Romans; and should it be praised, a sort of resentful disdain is compatible with this praise, even at the best, directly the sympathetic action is compared with one which contributes to the welfare of the whole, to the *res publica*. After all, 'love to our neighbour' is always a secondary matter, partly conventional and arbitrarily manifested in relation to our *fear of our neighbour*. After the fabric of society

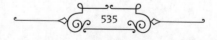

seems on the whole established and secured against external dangers, it is this fear of our neighbour which again creates new perspectives of moral valuation. Certain strong and dangerous instincts, such as the love of enterprise, foolhardiness, revengefulness, astuteness, rapacity and love of power, which up till then had not only to be honoured from the point of view of general utility – under other names, of course, than those here given – but had to be fostered and cultivated (because they were perpetually required in the common danger against the common enemies), are now felt in their dangerousness to be doubly strong – when the outlets for them are lacking – and are gradually branded as immoral and given over to calumny. The contrary instincts and inclinations now attain to moral honour, the gregarious instinct gradually draws its conclusions. How much or how little dangerousness to the community or to equality is contained in an opinion, a condition, an emotion, a disposition or an endowment – that is now the moral perspective, here again fear is the mother of morals. It is by the loftiest and strongest instincts, when they break out passionately and carry the individual far above and beyond the average, and the low level of the gregarious conscience, that the self-reliance of the community is destroyed; its belief in itself, its backbone, as it were, breaks; consequently these very instincts will be most branded and defamed. The lofty independent spirituality, the will to stand alone, and even the cogent reason, are felt to be dangers, everything that elevates the individual above the herd, and is a source of fear to the neighbour, is henceforth called *evil*; the tolerant, unassuming, self-adapting, self-equalizing disposition, the *mediocrity* of desires, attains to moral distinction and honour. Finally, under very peaceful circumstances, there is always less opportunity and necessity for training the feelings to severity and rigour; and now every form of severity, even in justice, begins to disturb the conscience; a lofty and rigorous nobleness and self-responsibility almost offends, and awakens distrust, 'the lamb', and still more 'the sheep', wins respect. There is a point of diseased mellow-

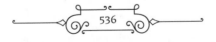

ness and effeminacy in the history of society, at which society itself takes the part of him who injures it, the part of the *criminal*, and does so, in fact, seriously and honestly. To punish, appears to it to be somehow unfair – it is certain that the idea of 'punishment' and 'the obligation to punish' are then painful and alarming to people. 'Is it not sufficient if the criminal be rendered *harmless*? Why should we still punish? Punishment itself is terrible!' – with these questions gregarious morality, the morality of fear, draws its ultimate conclusion. If one could at all do away with danger, the cause of fear, one would have done away with this morality at the same time, it would no longer be necessary, it *would not consider itself* any longer necessary! – Whoever examines the conscience of the present-day European, will always elicit the same imperative from its thousand moral folds and hidden recesses, the imperative of the timidity of the herd 'we wish that some time or other there may be *nothing more to fear*!' Some time or other – the will and the way *thereto* is nowadays called 'progress' all over Europe.

202

LET us at once say again what we have already said a hundred times, for people's ears nowadays are unwilling to hear such truths – *our* truths. We know well enough how offensive it sounds when any one plainly, and without metaphor, counts man among the animals, but it will be accounted to us almost a *crime*, that it is precisely in respect to men of 'modern ideas' that we have constantly applied the terms 'herd', 'herd-instincts', and such like expressions. What avail is it? We cannot do otherwise, for it is precisely here that our new insight is. We have found that in all the principal moral judgments, Europe has become unanimous, including likewise the countries where European influence prevails in Europe people evidently *know* what Socrates thought he did not know, and what the famous serpent of old once promised to teach – they 'know' today what is good and evil. It must

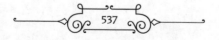

then sound hard and be distasteful to the ear, when we always insist that that which here thinks it knows, that which here glorifies itself with praise and blame, and calls itself good, is the instinct of the herding human animal: the instinct which has come and is ever coming more and more to the front, to preponderance and supremacy over other instincts, according to the increasing physiological approximation and resemblance of which it is the symptom. *Morality in Europe at present is herding-animal morality;* and therefore, as we understand the matter, only one kind of human morality, beside which, before which and after which many other moralities, and above all *higher* moralities, are or should be possible. Against such a 'possibility', against such a 'should be', however, this morality defends itself with all its strength, it says obstinately and inexorably: 'I am morality itself and nothing else is morality!' Indeed, with the help of a religion which has humoured and flattered the sublimest desires of the herding-animal, things have reached such a point that we always find a more visible expression of this morality even in political and social arrangements: the *democratic* movement is the inheritance of the Christian movement. That its *tempo*, however, is much too slow and sleepy for the more impatient ones, for those who are sick and distracted by the herding-instinct, is indicated by the increasingly furious howling, and always less disguised teeth-gnashing of the anarchist dogs, who are now roving through the highways of European culture. Apparently in opposition to the peacefully industrious democrats and Revolution-ideologues, and still more so to the awkward philosophasters and fraternity-visionaries who call themselves Socialists and want a 'free society', those are really at one with them all in their thorough and instinctive hostility to every form of society other than that of the *autonomous* herd (to the extent even of repudiating the notions 'master' and 'servant' – *ni dieu ni maître,* says a socialist formula); at one in their tenacious opposition to every special claim, every special right and privilege (this means ultimately

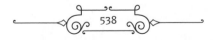

opposition to *every* right, for when all are equal, no one needs 'rights' any longer); at one in their distrust of punitive justice (as though it were a violation of the weak, unfair to the *necessary* consequences of all former society); but equally at one in their religion of sympathy, in their compassion for all that feels, lives and suffers (down to the very animals, up even to 'God' – the extravagance of 'sympathy for God' belongs to a democratic age); altogether at one in the cry and impatience of their sympathy, in their deadly hatred of suffering generally, in their almost feminine incapacity for witnessing it or *allowing* it; at one in their involuntary beglooming and heart-softening, under the spell of which Europe seems to be threatened with a new Buddhism; at one in their belief in the morality of *mutual* sympathy, as though it were morality in itself, the climax, the *attained* climax of mankind, the sole hope of the future, the consolation of the present, the great discharge from all the obligations of the past; altogether at one in their belief in the community as the *deliverer*, in the herd, and therefore in 'themselves'.

203

WE, WHO hold a different belief – we, who regard the democratic movement, not only as a degenerating form of political organization, but as equivalent to a degenerating, a waning type of man, as involving his mediocrising and depreciation: where have *we* to fix our hopes? In *new philosophers* – there is no other alternative: in minds strong and original enough to initiate opposite estimates of value, to transvalue and invert 'eternal valuations'; in forerunners, in men of the future, who in the present shall fix the constraints and fasten the knots which will compel millenniums to take *new* paths. To teach man the future of humanity as his *will*, as depending on human will, and to make preparation for vast hazardous enterprises and collective attempts in rearing and educating, in order thereby to put an end to the frightful

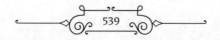

rule of folly and chance which has hitherto gone by the name of 'history' (the folly of the 'greatest number' is only its last form) – for that purpose a new type of philosopher and commander will sometime or other be needed, at the very idea of which everything that has existed in the way of occult, terrible and benevolent beings might look pale and dwarfed. The image of such leaders hovers before *our* eyes: – is it lawful for me to say it aloud, ye free spirits? The conditions which one would partly have to create and partly utilize for their genesis; the presumptive methods and tests by virtue of which a soul should grow up to such an elevation and power as to feel a *constraint* to these tasks; a transvaluation of values, under the new pressure and hammer of which a conscience should be steeled and a heart transformed into brass, so as to bear the weight of such responsibility; and on the other hand the necessity for such leaders, the dreadful danger that they might be lacking, or miscarry and degenerate: – these are *our* real anxieties and glooms, ye know it well, ye free spirits! these are the heavy distant thoughts and storms which sweep across the heaven of *our* life. There are few pains so grievous as to have seen, divined or experienced how an exceptional man has missed his way and deteriorated; but he who has the rare eye for the universal danger of 'man' himself *deteriorating*, he who like us has recognized the extraordinary fortuitousness which has hitherto played its game in respect to the future of mankind – a game in which neither the hand, nor even a 'finger of God' has participated! – he who divines the fate that is hidden under the idiotic unwariness and blind confidence of 'modern ideas', and still more under the whole of Christo-European morality – suffers from an anguish with which no other is to be compared. He sees at a glance all that could still *be made out of man* through a favourable accumulation and augmentation of human powers and arrangements; he knows with all the knowledge of his conviction how unexhausted man still is for the greatest possibilities, and how

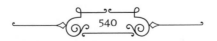

often in the past the type man has stood in presence of mysterious decisions and new paths: – he knows still better from his painfulest recollections on what wretched obstacles promising developments of the highest rank have hitherto usually gone to pieces, broken down, sunk and become contemptible. The *universal degeneracy of mankind* to the level of the 'man of the future' – as idealized by the socialistic fools and shallow-pates – this degeneracy and dwarfing of man to an absolutely gregarious animal (or as they call it, to a man of 'free society'), this brutalizing of man into a pigmy with equal rights and claims, is undoubtedly *possible*! He who has thought out this possibility to its ultimate conclusion knows *another* loathing unknown to the rest of mankind – and perhaps also a new *mission*!

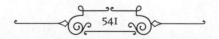

CHAPTER VI
WE SCHOLARS

204

AT THE risk that moralizing may also reveal itself here as that which it has always been – namely, resolutely *montrer ses plaies*, according to Balzac – I would venture to protest against an improper and injurious alteration of rank, which quite unnoticed, and as if with the best conscience, threatens nowadays to establish itself in the relations of science and philosophy. I mean to say that one must have the right out of one's own *experience* – experience, as it seems to me, always implies unfortunate experience? – to treat of such an important question of rank, so as not to speak of colour like the blind, or *against* science like women and artists ('Ah! this dreadful science!' sigh their instinct and their shame, 'it always *finds things out!*'). The declaration of independence of the scientific man, his emancipation from philosophy, is one of the subtler after-effects of democratic organization and disorganization: the self-glorification and self-conceitedness of the learned man is now everywhere in full bloom, and in its best springtime – which does not mean to imply that in this case self-praise smells sweetly. Here also the instinct of the populace cries, 'Freedom from all masters!' and after science has, with the happiest results, resisted theology, whose 'handmaid' it had been too long, it now proposes in its wantonness and indiscretion to lay down laws for philosophy, and in its turn to play the 'master' – what am I saying! to play the *philos-*

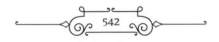

opher on its own account. My memory – the memory of a scientific man, if you please! – teems with the naïvetés of insolence which I have heard about philosophy and philosophers from young naturalists and old physicians (not to mention the most cultured and most conceited of all learned men, the philologists and schoolmasters, who are both the one and the other by profession). On one occasion it was the specialist and the Jack Horner who instinctively stood on the defensive against all synthetic tasks and capabilities; at another time it was the industrious worker who had got a scent of *otium* and refined luxuriousness in the internal economy of the philosopher, and felt himself aggrieved and belittled thereby. On another occasion it was the colour-blindness of the utilitarian, who sees nothing in philosophy but a series of *refuted* systems, and an extravagant expenditure which 'does nobody any good'. At another time the fear of disguised mysticism and of the boundary-adjustment of knowledge became conspicuous, at another time the disregard of individual philosophers, which had involuntarily extended to disregard of philosophy generally. In fine, I found most frequently, behind the proud disdain of philosophy in young scholars, the evil after-effect of some particular philosopher, to whom on the whole obedience had been foresworn, without, however, the spell of his scornful estimates of other philosophers having been got rid of – the result being a general ill-will to all philosophy. (Such seems to me, for instance, the after-effect of Schopenhauer on the most modern Germany: by his unintelligent rage against Hegel, he has succeeded in severing the whole of the last generation of Germans from its connection with German culture, which culture, all things considered, has been an elevation and a divining refinement of the *historical sense*; but precisely at this point Schopenhauer himself was poor, irreceptive and un-German to the extent of ingeniousness.) On the whole, speaking generally, it may just have been the humanness, all-too-humanness of the modern philos-

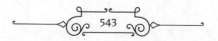

ophers themselves, in short, their contemptibleness, which has injured most radically the reverence for philosophy and opened the doors to the instinct of the populace. Let it but be acknowledged to what an extent our modern world diverges from the whole style of the world of Heraclitus, Plato, Empedocles, and whatever else all the royal and magnificent anchorites of the spirit were called, and with what justice an honest man of science *may* feel himself of a better family and origin, in view of such representatives of philosophy, who, owing to the fashion of the present day, are just as much aloft as they are down below – in Germany, for instance, the two lions of Berlin, the anarchist Eugen Dühring and the amalgamist Eduard von Hartmann. It is especially the sight of those hotchpotch philosophers, who call themselves 'realists', or 'positivists', which is calculated to implant a dangerous distrust in the soul of a young and ambitious scholar those philosophers, at the best, are themselves but scholars and specialists, that is very evident! All of them are persons who have been vanquished and *brought back again* under the dominion of science, who at one time or another claimed more from themselves, without having a right to the 'more' and its responsibility – and who now, creditably, rancorously, and vindictively, represent in word and deed, *disbelief* in the master-task and supremacy of philosophy After all, how could it be otherwise? Science flourishes nowadays and has the good conscience clearly visible on its countenance, while that to which the entire modern philosophy has gradually sunk, the remnant of philosophy of the present day, excites distrust and displeasure, if not scorn and pity. Philosophy reduced to a 'theory of knowledge', no more in fact than a diffident science of epochs and doctrine of forbearance: a philosophy that never even gets beyond the threshold, and rigorously *denies* itself the right to enter – that is philosophy in its last throes, an end, an agony, something that awakens pity. How could such a philosophy – *rule*!

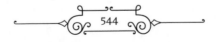

205

THE dangers that beset the evolution of the philosopher are, in fact, so manifold nowadays, that one might doubt whether this fruit could still come to maturity. The extent and towering structure of the sciences have increased enormously, and therewith also the probability that the philosopher will grow tired even as a learner, or will attach himself somewhere and 'specialize' so that he will no longer attain to his elevation, that is to say, to his superspection, his circumspection and his *despection*. Or he gets aloft too late, when the best of his maturity and strength is past, or when he is impaired, coarsened and deteriorated, so that his view, his general estimate of things, is no longer of much importance. It is perhaps just the refinement of his intellectual conscience that makes him hesitate and linger on the way, he dreads the temptation to become a dilettante, a millepede, a milleantenna; he knows too well that as a discerner, one who has lost his self-respect no longer commands, no longer *leads*; unless he should aspire to become a great play-actor, a philosophical Cagliostro and spiritual rat-catcher – in short, a misleader. This is in the last instance a question of taste, if it has not really been a question of conscience. To double once more the philosopher's difficulties, there is also the fact that he demands from himself a verdict, a Yea or Nay, not concerning science, but concerning life and the worth of life – he learns unwillingly to believe that it is his right and even his duty to obtain this verdict, and he has to seek his way to the right and the belief only through the most extensive (perhaps disturbing and destroying) experiences, often hesitating, doubting and dumbfounded. In fact, the philosopher has long been mistaken and confused by the multitude, either with the scientific man and ideal scholar, or with the religiously elevated, desensualized, desecularized visionary and God-intoxicated man; and even yet when one hears anybody praised, because he lives 'wisely', or 'as a philosopher', it hardly means anything more than

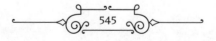

'prudently and apart'. Wisdom: that seems to the populace to be a kind of flight, a means and artifice for withdrawing successfully from a bad game; but the *genuine* philosopher – does it not seem so to *us*, my friends? – lives 'unphilosophically' and 'unwisely', above all, *imprudently*, and feels the obligation and burden of a hundred attempts and temptations of life – he risks *himself* constantly, he plays *this* bad game.

206

IN RELATION to the genius, that is to say, a being who either *engenders* or *produces* – both words understood in their fullest sense – the man of learning, the scientific average man, has always something of the old maid about him; for, like her, he is not conversant with the two principal functions of man. To both, of course, to the scholar and to the old maid, one concedes respectability, as if by way of indemnification – in these cases one emphasizes the respectability – and yet, in the compulsion of this concession, one has the same admixture of vexation. Let us examine more closely: what is the scientific man? First, a commonplace type of man, with commonplace virtues: that is to say, a non-ruling, non-authoritative and non-self-sufficient type of man; he possesses industry, patient adaptableness to rank and file, equability and moderation in capacity and requirement; he has the instinct for people like himself, and for that which they require – for instance: the portion of independence and green meadow without which there is no rest from labour, the claim to honour and consideration (which first and foremost presupposes recognition and recognizability), the sunshine of a good name, the perpetual ratification of his value and usefulness, with which the inward *distrust* which lies at the bottom of the heart of all dependent men and gregarious animals, has again and again to be overcome. The learned man, as is appropriate, has also maladies and faults of an ignoble kind: he is full of petty envy, and has a lynx-eye for the weak points in those natures to

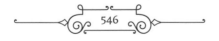

whose elevations he cannot attain. He is confiding, yet only as one who lets himself go, but does not *flow*; and precisely before the man of the great current he stands all the colder and more reserved – his eye is then like a smooth and irresponsive lake, which is no longer moved by rapture or sympathy. The worst and most dangerous thing of which a scholar is capable results from the instinct of mediocrity of his type, from the Jesuitism of mediocrity, which labours instinctively for the destruction of the exceptional man, and endeavours to break – or still better, to relax – every bent bow. To relax, of course, with consideration, and naturally with an indulgent hand – to *relax* with confiding sympathy: that is the real art of Jesuitism, which has always understood how to introduce itself as the religion of sympathy.

207

HOWEVER gratefully one may welcome the *objective* spirit – and who has not been sick to death of all subjectivity and its confounded *ipissimosity*! – in the end, however, one must learn caution even with regard to one's gratitude, and put a stop to the exaggeration with which the unselfing and depersonalizing of the spirit has recently been celebrated, as if it were the goal in itself, as if it were salvation and glorification – as is especially accustomed to happen in the pessimist school, which has also in its turn good reasons for paying the highest honours to 'disinterested knowledge'. The objective man, who no longer curses and scolds like the pessimist, the *ideal* man of learning in whom the scientific instinct blossoms forth fully after a thousand complete and partial failures, is assuredly one of the most costly instruments that exist, but his place is in the hand of one who is more powerful. He is only an instrument, we may say, he is a *mirror* – he is no 'purpose in himself'. The objective man is in truth a mirror: accustomed to prostration before everything that wants to be known, with such desires only as knowing or 'reflecting' imly – he waits until

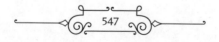

something comes, and then expands himself sensitively, so that even the light footsteps and gliding past of spiritual beings may not be lost on his surface and film. Whatever 'personality' he still possesses seems to him accidental, arbitrary or still oftener, disturbing, so much has he come to regard himself as the passage and reflection of outside forms and events. He calls up the recollection of 'himself' with an effort, and not infrequently wrongly, he readily confounds himself with other persons, he makes mistakes with regard to his own needs, and here only is he unrefined and negligent. Perhaps he is troubled about the health, or the pettiness and confined atmosphere of wife and friend, or the lack of companions and society – indeed, he sets himself to reflect on his suffering, but in vain! His thoughts already rove away to the *more general* case, and tomorrow he knows as little as he knew yesterday how to help himself. He does not now take himself seriously and devote time to himself: he is serene, *not* from lack of trouble, but from lack of capacity for grasping and dealing with *his* trouble. The habitual complaisance with respect to all objects and experiences, the radiant and impartial hospitality with which he receives everything that comes his way, his habit of inconsiderate good-nature, of dangerous indifference as to Yea and Nay: alas! there are enough of cases in which he has to atone for these virtues of his! – and as man generally, he becomes far too easily the *caput mortuum* of such virtues. Should one wish love or hatred from him – I mean love and hatred as God, woman and animal understand them – he will do what he can, and furnish what he can. But one must not be surprised if it should not be much – if he should show himself just at this point to be false, fragile, questionable and deteriorated. His love is constrained, his hatred is artificial, and rather *un tour de force*, a slight ostentation and exaggeration. He is only genuine so far as he can be objective; only in his serene totality is he still 'nature' and 'natural'. His mirroring and eternally self-polishing soul no longer

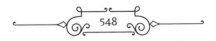

knows how to affirm, no longer how to deny; he does not command; neither does he destroy. *'Je ne méprise presque rien'* – he says, with Leibniz: let us not overlook nor undervalue the *presque*! Neither is he a model man; he does not go in advance of anyone, nor after, either; he places himself generally too far off to have any reason for espousing the cause of either good or evil. If he has been so long confounded with the *philosopher*, with the Caesarian trainer and dictator of civilization, he has had far too much honour, and what is more essential in him has been overlooked – he is an instrument, something of a slave, though certainly the sublimest sort of slave, but nothing in himself – *presque rien*! The objective man is an instrument, a costly, easily injured, easily tarnished measuring instrument and mirroring apparatus, which is to be taken care of and respected; but he is no goal, not outgoing nor upgoing, no complementary man in whom the *rest* of existence justifies itself, no termination – and still less a commencement, an engendering or primary cause, nothing hardy, powerful, self-centred, that wants to be master; but rather only a soft, inflated, delicate, movable potter's-form, that must wait for some kind of content and frame to 'shape' itself thereto – for the most part a man without frame and content, a 'selfless' man. Consequently, also, nothing for women, *in parenthesi*.

208

WHEN a philosopher nowadays makes known that he is not a sceptic – I hope that has been gathered from the foregoing description of the objective spirit? – people all hear it impatiently; they regard him on that account with some apprehension, they would like to ask so many, many questions… indeed among timid hearers, of whom there are now so many, he is henceforth said to be dangerous. With his repudiation of scepticism, it seems to them as if they heard some evil-threatening sound in the distance, as if a new kind of explosive were being tried

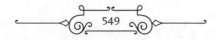

somewhere, a dynamite of the spirit, perhaps a newly discovered Russian *nihiline*, a pessimism *bonae voluntatis*, that not only denies, means denial, but – dreadful thought! *practises* denial. Against this kind of 'good-will' – a will to the veritable, actual negation of life – there is, as is generally acknowledged nowadays, no better soporific and sedative than scepticism, the mild, pleasing, lulling poppy of scepticism; and Hamlet himself is now prescribed by the doctors of the day as an antidote to the 'spirit', and its underground noises. 'Are not our ears already full of bad sounds?' say the sceptics, as lovers of repose, and almost as a kind of safety police, 'this subterranean Nay is terrible! Be still, ye pessimistic moles!' The sceptic, in effect, that delicate creature, is far too easily frightened; his conscience is schooled so as to start at every Nay, and even at that sharp, decided Yea, and feels something like a bite thereby. Yea! and Nay! – they seem to him opposed to morality; he loves, on the contrary, to make a festival to his virtue by a noble aloofness, while perhaps he says with Montaigne: 'What do I know?' Or with Socrates: 'I know that I know nothing.' Or: 'Here I do not trust myself, no door is open to me.' Or: 'Even if the door were open, why should I enter immediately?' Or: 'What is the use of any hasty hypotheses? It might quite well be in good taste to make no hypotheses at all. Are you absolutely obliged to straighten at once what is crooked? to stuff every hole with some kind of oakum? Is there not time enough for that? Has not the time leisure? Oh, ye demons, can ye not at all *wait*? The uncertain also has its charms, the Sphinx, too, is a Circe, and Circe, too, was a philosopher.' – Thus does a sceptic console himself; and in truth he needs some consolation. For scepticism is the most spiritual expression of a certain many-sided physiological temperament, which in ordinary language is called nervous debility and sickliness; it arises whenever races or classes which have been long separated, decisively and suddenly blend with one another. In the new generation, which has inherited as it were different standards and valuations in its blood, everything is disquiet, derangement, doubt

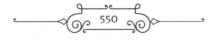

and tentativeness; the best powers operate restrictively, the very virtues prevent each other growing and becoming strong, equilibrium, ballast, and perpendicular stability are lacking in body and soul. That, however, which is most diseased and degenerated in such nondescripts is the *will*; they are no longer familiar with independence of decision, or the courageous feeling of pleasure in willing – they are doubtful of the 'freedom of the will' even in their dreams Our present-day Europe, the scene of a senseless, precipitate attempt at a radical blending of classes, and *consequently* of races, is therefore sceptical in all its heights and depths, sometimes exhibiting the mobile scepticism which springs impatiently and wantonly from branch to branch, sometimes with gloomy aspect, like a cloud overcharged with interrogative signs – and often sick unto death of its will! Paralysis of will, where do we not find this cripple sitting nowadays! And yet how bedecked oftentimes! How seductively ornamented! There are the finest gala dresses and disguises for this disease, and that, for instance, most of what places itself nowadays in the show-cases as 'objectiveness', 'the scientific spirit', '*l'art pour l'art*', and 'pure voluntary knowledge', is only decked-out scepticism and paralysis of will – I am ready to answer for this diagnosis of the European disease. – The disease of the will is diffused unequally over Europe; it is worst and most varied where civilization has longest prevailed; it decreases according as 'the barbarian' still – or again – asserts his claims under the loose drapery of Western culture. It is therefore in the France of today, as can be readily disclosed and comprehended, that the will is most infirm, and France, which has always had a masterly aptitude for converting even the portentous crises of its spirit into something charming and seductive, now manifests emphatically its intellectual ascendancy over Europe, by being the school and exhibition of all the charms of scepticism. The power to will and to persist, moreover, in a resolution, is already somewhat stronger in Germany, and again in the North of Germany it is stronger than in Central Germany; it is consid-

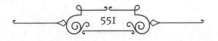

erably stronger in England, Spain and Corsica, associated with phlegm in the former and with hard skulls in the latter – not to mention Italy, which is too young yet to know what it wants, and must first show whether it can exercise will but it is strongest and most surprising of all in that immense middle empire where Europe as it were flows back to Asia – namely, in Russia. There the power to will has been long stored up and accumulated, there the will – uncertain whether to be negative or affirmative – waits threateningly to be discharged (to borrow their pet phrase from our physicists). Perhaps not only Indian wars and complications in Asia would be necessary to free Europe from its greatest danger, but also internal subversion, the shattering of the empire into small states, and above all the introduction of parliamentary imbecility, together with the obligation of everyone to read his newspaper at breakfast. I do not say this as one who desires it; in my heart I should rather prefer the contrary – I mean such an increase in the threatening attitude of Russia, that Europe would have to make up its mind to become equally threatening – namely, *to acquire one will*, by means of a new caste to rule over the Continent, a persistent, dreadful will of its own, that can set its aims thousands of years ahead; so that the long spun-out comedy of its petty-statism, and its dynastic as well as its democratic many-willed-ness, might finally be brought to a close. The time for petty politics is past; the next century will bring the struggle for the dominion of the world – the *compulsion* to great politics.

209

AS TO how far the new warlike age on which we Europeans have evidently entered may perhaps favour the growth of another and stronger kind of scepticism, I should like to express myself preliminarily merely by a parable, which the lovers of German history will already understand. That unscrupulous enthusiast for big, handsome grenadiers (who, as King of Prussia, brought into being a military and sceptical genius – and

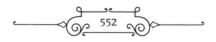

therewith, in reality, the new and now triumphantly emerged type of German), the problematic, crazy father of Frederick the Great, had on one point the very knack and lucky grasp of the genius: he knew what was then lacking in Germany, the want of which was a hundred times more alarming and serious than any lack of culture and social form – his ill-will to the young Frederick resulted from the anxiety of a profound instinct. *Men were lacking*; and he suspected, to his bitterest regret, that his own son was not man enough. There, however, he deceived himself; but who would not have deceived himself in his place? He saw his son lapsed to atheism, to the *esprit*, to the pleasant frivolity of clever Frenchmen – he saw in the background the great bloodsucker, the spider scepticism; he suspected the incurable wretchedness of a heart no longer hard enough either for evil or good, and of a broken will that no longer commands, is no longer *able* to command. Meanwhile, however, there grew up in his son that new kind of harder and more dangerous scepticism – who knows *to what extent* it was encouraged just by his father's hatred and the icy melancholy of a will condemned to solitude? – the scepticism of daring manliness, which is closely related to the genius for war and conquest, and made its first entrance into Germany in the person of the great Frederick. This scepticism despises and nevertheless grasps; it undermines and takes possession; it does not believe, but it does not thereby lose itself; it gives the spirit a dangerous liberty, but it keeps strict guard over the heart. It is the *German* form of scepticism, which, as a continued Fredericianism, risen to the highest spirituality, has kept Europe for a considerable time under the dominion of the German spirit and its critical and historical distrust. Owing to the insuperably strong and tough masculine character of the great German philologists and historical critics (who, rightly estimated, were also all of them artists of destruction and dissolution), a *new* conception of the German spirit gradually established itself – in spite of all Romanticism in music and philosophy – in which the leaning towards masculine

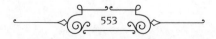

scepticism was decidedly prominent: whether, for instance, as fearlessness of gaze, as courage and sternness of the dissecting hand or as resolute will to dangerous voyages of discovery, to spiritualized North Pole expeditions under barren and dangerous skies. There may be good grounds for it when warm-blooded and superficial humanitarians cross themselves before this spirit, *cet esprit fataliste, ironique, méphistophélique*, as Michelet calls it, not without a shudder. But if one would realize how characteristic is this fear of the 'man' in the German spirit which awakened Europe out of its 'dogmatic slumber', let us call to mind the former conception which had to be overcome by this new one – and that it is not so very long ago that a masculinized woman could dare, with unbridled presumption, to recommend the Germans to the interest of Europe as gentle, good-hearted, weak-willed and poetical fools. Finally, let us only understand profoundly enough Napoleon's astonishment when he saw Goethe: it reveals what had been regarded for centuries as the 'German spirit'. '*Voilà un homme!*' – that was as much as to say: 'But this is a *man*! And I only expected to see a German!'

210

SUPPOSING, then, that in the picture of the philosophers of the future, some trait suggests the question whether they must not perhaps be sceptics in the last-mentioned sense, something in them would only be designated thereby – and *not* they themselves. With equal right they might call themselves critics, and assuredly they will be men of experiments. By the name with which I ventured to baptize them, I have already expressly emphasized their attempting and their love of attempting: is this because, as critics in body and soul, they will love to make use of experiments in a new, and perhaps wider and more dangerous sense? In their passion for knowledge, will they have to go further in daring and painful attempts than the sensitive and pampered taste of a democratic century can approve of? – There is no doubt

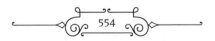

these coming ones will be least able to dispense with the serious and not unscrupulous qualities which distinguish the critic from the sceptic: I mean the certainty as to standards of worth, the conscious employment of a unity of method, the wary courage, the standing-alone and the capacity for self-responsibility; indeed, they will avow among themselves a *delight* in denial and dissection, and a certain considerate cruelty, which knows how to handle the knife surely and deftly, even when the heart bleeds. They will be *sterner* (and perhaps not always towards themselves only) than humane people may desire, they will not deal with the 'truth' in order that it may 'please' them, or 'elevate' and 'inspire' them – they will rather have little faith in '*truth*' bringing with it such revels for the feelings. They will smile, those rigorous spirits, when anyone says in their presence: 'that thought elevates me, why should it not be true?' or 'that work enchants me, why should it not be beautiful?' or 'that artist enlarges me, why should he not be great?' Perhaps they will not only have a smile, but a genuine disgust for all that is thus rapturous, idealistic, feminine and hermaphroditic, and if any one could look into their inmost hearts, he would not easily find therein the intention to reconcile 'Christian sentiments' with 'antique taste', or even with 'modern parliamentarism' (the kind of reconciliation necessarily found even among philosophers in our very uncertain and consequently very conciliatory century). Critical discipline, and every habit that conduces to purity and rigour in intellectual matters, will not only be demanded from themselves by these philosophers of the future, they may even make a display thereof as their special adornment – nevertheless they will not want to be called critics on that account. It will seem to them no small indignity to philosophy to have it decreed, as is so welcome nowadays, that 'philosophy itself is criticism and critical science – and nothing else whatever!' Though this estimate of philosophy may enjoy the approval of all the Positivists of France and Germany (and possibly it even

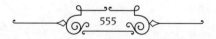

flattered the heart and taste of *Kant*: let us call to mind the titles of his principal works), our new philosophers will say, notwithstanding, that critics are instruments of the philosopher, and just on that account, as instruments, they are far from being philosophers themselves! Even the great Chinaman of Königsberg was only a great critic.

211

I INSIST upon it that people finally cease confounding philosophical workers, and in general scientific men, with philosophers – that precisely here one should strictly give 'each his own', and not give those far too much, these far too little. It may be necessary for the education of the real philosopher that he himself should have once stood upon all those steps upon which his servants, the scientific workers of philosophy, remain standing, and *must* remain standing: he himself must perhaps have been critic, and dogmatist, and historian, and besides, poet, and collector, and traveller, and riddle-reader, and moralist, and seer, and 'free spirit', and almost everything, in order to traverse the whole range of human values and estimations, and that he may *be able* with a variety of eyes and consciences to look from a height to any distance, from a depth up to any height, from a nook into any expanse. But all these are only preliminary conditions for his task; this task itself demands something else – it requires him *to create values*. The philosophical workers, after the excellent pattern of Kant and Hegel, have to fix and formalize some great existing body of valuations – that is to say, former *determinations of value*, creations of value, which have become prevalent, and are for a time called 'truths' – whether in the domain of the *logical*, the *political* (moral) or the *artistic*. It is for these investigators to make whatever has happened and been esteemed hitherto, conspicuous, conceivable, intelligible and manageable, to shorten everything long, even 'time' itself, and to *subjugate* the entire past: an immense and wonderful task, in the carrying out of which all refined pride, all tenacious will, can

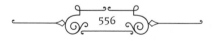

surely find satisfaction. *The real philosophers, however, are commanders and law-givers*; they say: 'Thus *shall* it be!' They determine first the Whither and the Why of mankind, and thereby set aside the previous labour of all philosophical workers, and all subjugators of the past – they grasp at the future with a creative hand, and whatever is and was, becomes for them thereby a means, an instrument and a hammer. Their 'knowing' is *creating*, their creating is a law-giving, their will to truth is – *Will to Power*. – Are there at present such philosophers? Have there ever been such philosophers? *Must* there not be such philosophers some day?...

212

IT IS always more obvious to me that the philosopher, as a man *indispensable* for the morrow and the day after the morrow, has ever found himself, and *has been obliged* to find himself, in contradiction to the day in which he lives; his enemy has always been the ideal of his day. Hitherto all those extraordinary furtherers of humanity whom one calls philosophers – who rarely regarded themselves as lovers of wisdom, but rather as disagreeable fools and dangerous interrogators – have found their mission, their hard, involuntary, imperative mission (in the end, however, the greatness of their mission), in being the bad conscience of their age. In putting the vivisector's knife to the breast of the very *virtues of their age*, they have betrayed their own secret; it has been for the sake of a *new* greatness of man, a new untrodden path to his aggrandizement. They have always disclosed how much hypocrisy, indolence, self-indulgence, and self-neglect, how much false-hood was concealed under the most venerated types of contemporary morality, how much virtue was *outlived*; they have always said: 'We must remove hence to where *you* are least at home'. In the face of a world of 'modern ideas', which would like to confine everyone in a corner, in a 'specialty', a philosopher, if there could be philosophers nowadays, would be compelled to place the greatness of man, the

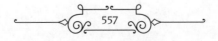

conception of 'greatness', precisely in his comprehensiveness and multifariousness, in his all-roundness; he would even determine worth and rank according to the amount and variety of that which a man could bear and take upon himself, according to the *extent* to which a man could stretch his responsibility Nowadays the taste and virtue of the age weaken and attenuate the will, nothing is so adapted to the spirit of the age as weakness of will: consequently, in the ideal of the philosopher, strength of will, sternness and capacity for prolonged resolution, must specially be included in the conception of 'greatness'; with as good a right as the opposite doctrine, with its ideal of a silly, renouncing, humble, selfless humanity, was suited to an opposite age – such as the sixteenth century, which suffered from its accumulated energy of will, and from the wildest torrents and floods of selfishness. In the time of Socrates, among men only of worn-out instincts, old conservative Athenians who let themselves go – 'for the sake of happiness', as they said, for the sake of pleasure, as their conduct indicated – and who had continually on their lips the old pompous words to which they had long forfeited the right by the life they led, *irony* was perhaps necessary for greatness of soul, the wicked Socratic assurance of the old physician and plebeian, who cut ruthlessly into his own flesh, as into the flesh and heart of the 'noble', with a look that said plainly enough. 'Do not dissemble before me! here – we are equal!' At present, on the contrary, when throughout Europe the herding-animal alone attains to honours, and dispenses honours, when 'equality of right' can too readily be transformed into equality in wrong: – I mean to say into general war against everything rare, strange and privileged, against the higher man, the higher soul, the higher duty, the higher responsibility, the creative plenipotence and lordliness – at present it belongs to the conception of 'greatness' to be noble, to wish to be apart, to be capable of being different, to stand alone, to have to live by personal initiative and the philosopher will betray something

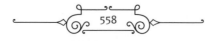

of his own ideal when he asserts: 'He shall be the greatest who can be the most solitary, the most concealed, the most divergent, the man beyond good and evil, the master of his virtues and of superabundance of will; precisely this shall be called *greatness*: as diversified as can be entire, as ample as can be full.' And to ask once more the question: Is greatness *possible* – nowadays?

213

IT IS difficult to learn what a philosopher is, because it cannot be taught: one must 'know' it by experience – or one should have the pride *not* to know it. The fact that at present people all talk of things of which they *cannot* have any experience, is true more especially and unfortunately as concerns the philosopher and philosophical matters: – the very few know them, are permitted to know them and all popular ideas about them are false. Thus, for instance, the truly philosophical combination of a bold, exuberant spirituality which runs at *presto* pace, and a dialectic rigour and necessity which makes no false step, is unknown to most thinkers and scholars from their own experience, and therefore, should anyone speak of it in their presence, it is incredible to them. They conceive of every necessity as troublesome, as a painful compulsory obedience and state of constraint; thinking itself is regarded by them as something slow and hesitating, almost as a trouble, and often enough as 'worthy of the *sweat* of the noble' – but not at all as something easy and divine, closely related to dancing and exuberance! 'To think' and to take a matter 'seriously', 'arduously' – that is one and the same thing to them; such only has been their 'experience'. – Artists have here perhaps a finer intuition; they who know only too well that precisely when they no longer do anything 'arbitrarily', and everything of necessity, their feeling of freedom, of subtlety, of power, of creatively fixing, disposing and shaping, reaches its climax – in short, that necessity and 'freedom of will' are then the

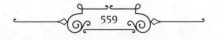

same thing with them. There is, in fine, a gradation of rank in psychical states, to which the gradation of rank in the problems corresponds; and the highest problems repel ruthlessly everyone who ventures too near them, without being predestined for their solution by the loftiness and power of his spirituality. Of what use is it for nimble, everyday intellects, or clumsy, honest mechanics and empiricists to press, in their plebeian ambition, close to such problems, and as it were into this 'holy of holies' – as so often happens nowadays! But coarse feet must never tread upon such carpets: this is provided for in the primary law of things; the doors remain closed to those intruders, though they may dash and break their heads thereon. People have always to be born to a high station, or, more definitely, they have to be *bred* for it: a person has only a right to philosophy – taking the word in its higher significance – in virtue of his descent; the ancestors, the 'blood', decide here also. Many generations must have prepared the way for the coming of the philosopher; each of his virtues must have been separately acquired, nurtured, transmitted and embodied; not only the bold, easy, delicate course and current of his thoughts, but above all the readiness for great responsibilities, the majesty of ruling glance and contemning look, the feeling of separation from the multitude with their duties and virtues, the kindly patronage and defence of whatever is misunderstood and calumniated, be it God or devil, the delight and practice of supreme justice, the art of commanding, the amplitude of will, the lingering eye which rarely admires, rarely looks up, rarely loves....

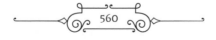

CHAPTER VII
OUR VIRTUES

214

OUR Virtues? – It is probable that we, too, have still our virtues, although naturally they are not those sincere and massive virtues on account of which we hold our grandfathers in esteem and also at a little distance from us. We Europeans of the day after tomorrow, we firstlings of the twentieth century – with all our dangerous curiosity, our multifariousness and art of disguising, our mellow and seemingly sweetened cruelty in sense and spirit – we shall presumably, *if* we must have virtues, have those only which have come to agreement with our most secret and heartfelt inclinations, with our most ardent requirements: well, then, let us look for them in our labyrinths! – where, as we know, so many things lose themselves, so many things get quite lost! And is there anything finer than to *search* for one's own virtues? Is it not almost to *believe* in one's own virtues? But this 'believing in one's own virtues' – is it not practically the same as what was formerly called one's 'good conscience', that long, respectable pigtail of an idea, which our grandfathers used to hang behind their heads, and often enough also behind their understandings? It seems, therefore, that however little we may imagine ourselves to be old-fashioned and grandfatherly respectable in other respects, in one thing we are nevertheless the worthy grandchildren of our grandfathers, we last Europeans with good consciences: we also still wear their pigtail. – Ah! if you only knew how soon, so very soon – it will be different!

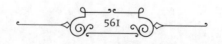

215

AS IN the stellar firmament there are sometimes two suns which determine the path of one planet, and in certain cases suns of different colours shine around a single planet, now with red light, now with green, and then simultaneously illumine and flood it with motley colours: so we modern men, owing to the complicated mechanism of our 'firmament', are determined by *different* moralities; our actions shine alternately in different colours, and are seldom unequivocal – and there are often cases, also, in which our actions are *motley-coloured*.

216

TO LOVE one's enemies? I think that has been well learnt: it takes place thousands of times at present on a large and small scale; indeed, at times the higher and sublimer thing takes place: – we learn to *despise* when we love, and precisely when we love best; all of it, however, unconsciously, without noise, without ostentation, with the shame and secrecy of goodness, which forbids the utterance of the pompous word and the formula of virtue. Morality as attitude – is opposed to our taste nowadays. This is *also* an advance, as it was an advance in our fathers that religion as an attitude finally became opposed to their taste, including the enmity and Voltairean bitterness against religion (and all that formerly belonged to freethinker-pantomime). It is the music in our conscience, the dance in our spirit, to which Puritan litanies, moral sermons and goody-goodness won't chime.

217

LET us be careful in dealing with those who attach great importance to being credited with moral tact and subtlety in moral discernment! They never forgive us if they have once made a mistake *before* us (or even with *regard* to us) – they inevitably become our instinctive calumniators and detractors, even when they still remain our 'friends.'

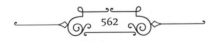

– Blessed are the forgetful: for they 'get the better' even of their blunders.

218

THE psychologists of France – and where else are there still psychologists nowadays? – have never yet exhausted their bitter and manifold enjoyment of the *betise bourgeoise*, just as though… in short, they betray something thereby. Flaubert, for instance, the honest citizen of Rouen, neither saw, heard, nor tasted anything else in the end; it was his mode of self-torment and refined cruelty. As this is growing wearisome, I would now recommend for a change something else for a pleasure – namely, the unconscious astuteness with which good, fat, honest mediocrity always behaves towards loftier spirits and the tasks they have to perform, the subtle, barbed, Jesuitical astuteness, which is a thousand times subtler than the taste and understanding of the middle-class in its best moments – subtler even than the understanding of its victims: – a repeated proof that 'instinct' is the most intelligent of all kinds of intelligence which have hitherto been discovered. In short, you psychologists, study the philosophy of the 'rule' in its struggle with the 'exception': there you have a spectacle fit for Gods and godlike malignity! Or, in plainer words, practise vivisection on 'good people', on the '*homo bonae voluntatis*', *on yourselves!*

219

THE practice of judging and condemning morally, is the favourite revenge of the intellectually shallow on those who are less so, it is also a kind of indemnity for their being badly endowed by nature, and finally, it is an opportunity for acquiring spirit and *becoming* subtle – malice spiritualizes. They are glad in their inmost heart that there is a standard according to which those who are over-endowed with intellectual goods and privileges, are equal to them, they contend for

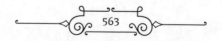

the 'equality of all before God', and almost *need* the belief in God for this purpose. It is among them that the most powerful antagonists of atheism are found. If any one were to say to them 'A lofty spirituality is beyond all comparison with the honesty and respectability of a merely moral man' – it would make them furious, I shall take care not to say so. I would rather flatter them with my theory that lofty spirituality itself exists only as the ultimate product of moral qualities, that it is a synthesis of all qualities attributed to the 'merely moral' man, after they have been acquired singly through long training and practice, perhaps during a whole series of generations, that lofty spirituality is precisely the spiritualizing of justice, and the beneficent severity which knows that it is authorized to maintain *gradations of rank* in the world, even among things – and not only among men.

220

NOW that the praise of the 'disinterested person' is so popular one must – probably not without some danger – get an idea of *what* people actually take an interest in, and what are the things generally which fundamentally and profoundly concern ordinary men – including the cultured, even the learned, and perhaps philosophers also, if appearances do not deceive. The fact thereby becomes obvious that the greater part of what interests and charms higher natures, and more refined and fastidious tastes, seems absolutely 'uninteresting' to the average man: – if, notwithstanding, he perceive devotion to these interests, he calls it désintéressé, and wonders how it is possible to act 'disinterestedly.' There have been philosophers who could give this popular astonishment a seductive and mystical, other-worldly expression (perhaps because they did not know the higher nature by experience?), instead of stating the naked and candidly reasonable truth that 'disinterested' action is very interesting and 'interested' action, provided that... 'And love?' – What! Even an action for love's sake shall be 'unegoistic'? But you fools – !

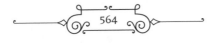

'And the praise of the self-sacrificer?' – But whoever has really offered sacrifice knows that he wanted and obtained something for it – perhaps something from himself for something from himself; that he relinquished here in order to have more there, perhaps in general to be more, or even feel himself 'more'. But this is a realm of questions and answers in which a more fastidious spirit does not like to stay: for here truth has to stifle her yawns so much when she is obliged to answer. And after all, truth is a woman; one must not use force with her.

221

'IT SOMETIMES happens,' said a moralistic pedant and trifle-retailer, 'that I honour and respect an unselfish man: not, however, because he is unselfish, but because I think he has a right to be useful to another man at his own expense.' In short, the question is always who *he* is, and who *the other* is. For instance, in a person created and destined for command, self-denial and modest retirement, instead of being virtues, would be the waste of virtues: so it seems to me. Every system of unegoistic morality which takes itself unconditionally and appeals to every one, not only sins against good taste, but is also an incentive to sins of omission, an *additional* seduction under the mask of philanthropy – and precisely a seduction and injury to the higher, rarer and more privileged types of men. Moral systems must be compelled first of all to bow before the *gradations of rank*; their presumption must be driven home to their conscience – until they thoroughly understand at last that it is *immoral* to say that 'what is right for one is proper for another'. – So said my moralistic pedant and bonhomme. Did he perhaps deserve to be laughed at when he thus exhorted systems of morals to practise morality? But one should not be too much in the right if one wishes to have the laughers on *one's own* side; a grain of wrong pertains even to good taste.

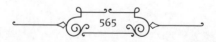

222

WHEREVER sympathy (fellow-suffering) is preached nowadays – and, if I gather rightly, no other religion is any longer preached – let the psychologist have his ears open through all the vanity, through all the noise which is natural to these preachers (as to all preachers), he will hear a hoarse, groaning, genuine note of *self-contempt*. It belongs to the overshadowing and uglifying of Europe, which has been on the increase for a century (the first symptoms of which are already specified documentarily in a thoughtful letter of Galiani to Madame d'Epinay) – *if it is not really the cause thereof!* The man of 'modern ideas', the conceited ape, is excessively dissatisfied with himself – this is perfectly certain. He suffers, and his vanity wants him only 'to suffer with his fellows'.

223

THE hybrid European – a tolerably ugly plebeian, taken all in all – absolutely requires a costume: he needs history as a storeroom of costumes. To be sure, he notices that none of the costumes fit him properly – he changes and changes. Let us look at the nineteenth century with respect to these hasty preferences and changes in its masquerades of style, and also with respect to its moments of desperation on account of 'nothing suiting' us. It is in vain to get ourselves up as romantic, or classical, or Christian, or Florentine, or *barocco* or 'national', *in moribus et artibus*: it does not 'clothe us'! But the 'spirit', especially the 'historical spirit', profits even by this desperation: once and again a new sample of the past or of the foreign is tested, put on, taken off, packed up and above all *studied* – we are the first studious age *in puncto* of 'costumes', I mean as concerns morals, articles of belief, artistic tastes and religions; we are prepared as no other age has ever been for a carnival in the grand style, for the most spiritual festival-laughter and arrogance, for the transcendental height of supreme folly and Aristophanic ridicule of the world. Perhaps we are

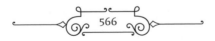

still discovering the domain of our *invention* just here, the domain where even we can still be original, probably as parodists of the world's history and as God's Merry-Andrews, – perhaps, though nothing else of the present have a future, our *laughter* itself may have a future!

224

THE *historical sense* (or the capacity for divining quickly the order of rank of the valuations according to which a people, a community or an individual has lived, the 'divining instinct' for the relationships of these valuations, for the relation of the authority of the valuations to the authority of the operating forces), – this historical sense, which we Europeans claim as our specialty, has come to us in the train of the enchanting and mad *semi-barbarity* into which Europe has been plunged by the democratic mingling of classes and races – it is only the nineteenth century that has recognized this faculty as its sixth sense. Owing to this mingling, the past of every form and mode of life, and of cultures which were formerly closely contiguous and superimposed on one another, flows forth into us 'modern souls'; our instincts now run back in all directions, we ourselves are a kind of chaos: in the end, as we have said, the spirit perceives its advantage therein. By means of our semi-barbarity in body and in desire, we have secret access everywhere, such as a noble age never had; we have access above all to the labyrinth of imperfect civilizations, and to every form of semi-barbarity that has at any time existed on earth; and in so far as the most considerable part of human civilization hitherto has just been semi-barbarity, the 'historical sense' implies almost the sense and instinct for everything, the taste and tongue for everything: whereby it immediately proves itself to be an *ignoble* sense. For instance, we enjoy Homer once more: it is perhaps our happiest acquisition that we know how to appreciate Homer, whom men of distinguished culture (as the French of the seventeenth century, like Saint-Evremond, who reproached him for his *esprit vaste*, and even

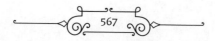

Voltaire, the last echo of the century) cannot and could not so easily appropriate – whom they scarcely permitted themselves to enjoy. The very decided Yea and Nay of their palate, their promptly ready disgust, their hesitating reluctance with regard to everything strange, their horror of the bad taste even of lively curiosity, and in general the averseness of every distinguished and self-sufficing culture to avow a new desire, a dissatisfaction with its own condition, or an admiration of what is strange: all this determines and disposes them unfavourably even towards the best things of the world which are not their property or *could not* become their prey – and no faculty is more unintelligible to such men than just this historical sense, with its truckling, plebeian curiosity. The case is not different with Shakespeare, that marvellous Spanish-Moorish-Saxon synthesis of taste, over whom an ancient Athenian of the circle of Aeschylus would have half-killed himself with laughter or irritation: but we – accept precisely this wild motleyness, this medley of the most delicate, the most coarse and the most artificial, with a secret confidence and cordiality; we enjoy it as a refinement of art reserved expressly for us, and allow ourselves to be as little disturbed by the repulsive fumes and the proximity of the English populace in which Shakespeare's art and taste lives, as perhaps on the Chiaja of Naples, where, with all our senses awake, we go our way, enchanted and voluntarily, in spite of the drain-odour of the lower quarters of the town. That as men of the 'historical sense' we have our virtues, is not to be disputed: – we are unpretentious, unselfish, modest, brave, habituated to self-control and self-renunciation, very grateful, very patient, very complaisant – but with all this we are perhaps not very 'tasteful'. Let us finally confess it, that what is most difficult for us men of the 'historical sense' to grasp, feel, taste and love, what finds us fundamentally prejudiced and almost hostile, is precisely the perfection and ultimate maturity in every culture and art, the essentially noble in works and men, their moment of smooth sea and halcyon self-sufficiency, the goldenness and coldness which all

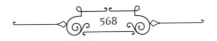

things show that have perfected themselves. Perhaps our great virtue of the historical sense is in necessary contrast to *good* taste, at least to the very bad taste; and we can only evoke in ourselves imperfectly, hesitatingly and with compulsion the small, short and happy godsends and glorifications of human life as they shine here and there: those moments and marvellous experiences when a great power has voluntarily come to a halt before the boundless and infinite, – when a super-abundance of refined delight has been enjoyed by a sudden checking and petrifying, by standing firmly and planting oneself fixedly on still trembling ground. *Proportionateness* is strange to us, let us confess it to ourselves; our itching is really the itching for the infinite, the immeasurable. Like the rider on his forward panting horse, we let the reins fall before the infinite, we modern men, we semi-barbarians – and are only in *our* highest bliss when we – *are in most danger*.

225

WHETHER it be hedonism, pessimism, utilitarianism or eudaemonism, all those modes of thinking which measure the worth of things according to *pleasure* and *pain*, that is, according to accompanying circumstances and secondary considerations, are plausible modes of thought and naïvetés, which everyone conscious of *creative* powers and an artist's conscience will look down upon with scorn, though not without sympathy. Sympathy for *you*! – to be sure, that is not sympathy as you understand it: it is not sympathy for social 'distress', for 'society' with its sick and misfortuned, for the hereditarily vicious and defective who lie on the ground around us; still less is it sympathy for the grumbling, vexed, revolutionary slave-classes who strive after power – they call it 'freedom'. *Our* sympathy is a loftier and further-sighted sympathy: – we see how *man* dwarfs himself, how *you* dwarf him! and there are moments when we view *your* sympathy with an indescribable anguish, when we resist it, – when we regard your seriousness as more dangerous than

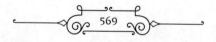

any kind of levity. You want, if possible – and there is not a more foolish 'if possible' – *to do away with suffering*; and we? – it really seems that *we* would rather have it increased and made worse than it has ever been! Well-being, as you understand it – is certainly not a goal; it seems to us an *end*; a condition which at once renders man ludicrous and contemptible – and makes his destruction *desirable*! The discipline of suffering, of *great* suffering – know ye not that it is only *this* discipline that has produced all the elevations of humanity hitherto? The tension of soul in misfortune which communicates to it its energy, its shuddering in view of rack and ruin, its inventiveness and bravery in undergoing, enduring, interpreting and exploiting misfortune, and whatever depth, mystery, disguise, spirit, artifice or greatness has been bestowed upon the soul – has it not been bestowed through suffering, through the discipline of great suffering? In man *creature* and *creator* are united: in man there is not only matter, shred, excess, clay, mire, folly, chaos; but there is also the creator, the sculptor, the hardness of the hammer, the divinity of the spectator and the seventh day – do ye understand this contrast? And that *your* sympathy for the 'creature in man' applies to that which has to be fashioned, bruised, forged, stretched, roasted, annealed, refined – to that which must necessarily *suffer*, and *is meant* to suffer? And *our* sympathy – do ye not understand what our *reverse* sympathy applies to, when it resists your sympathy as the worst of all pampering and enervation? – So it is sympathy *against* sympathy! – But to repeat it once more, there are higher problems than the problems of pleasure and pain and sympathy; and all systems of philosophy which deal only with these are naïvetés.

226

WE IMMORALISTS. – This world with which *we* are concerned, in which we have to fear and love, this almost invisible, inaudible world of delicate command and delicate obedience, a world of 'almost' in

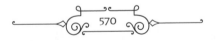

every respect, captious, insidious, sharp and tender – yes, it is well protected from clumsy spectators and familiar curiosity! We are woven into a strong net and garment of duties, and *cannot* disengage ourselves – precisely here, we are 'men of duty', even we! Occasionally, it is true, we dance in our 'chains' and betwixt our 'swords'; it is none the less true that more often we gnash our teeth under the circumstances, and are impatient at the secret hardship of our lot. But do what we will, fools and appearances say of us: 'These are men *without* duty', – we have always fools and appearances against us!

227

HONESTY, granting that it is the virtue of which we cannot rid ourselves, we free spirits – well, we will labour at it with all our perversity and love, and not tire of 'perfecting' ourselves in *our* virtue, which alone remains: may its glance some day overspread like a gilded, blue, mocking twilight this aging civilization with its dull gloomy seriousness! And if, nevertheless, our honesty should one day grow weary, and sigh, and stretch its limbs, and find us too hard, and would fain have it pleasanter, easier and gentler, like an agreeable vice, let us remain *hard*, we latest Stoics, and let us send to its help whatever devilry we have in us: – our disgust at the clumsy and undefined, our '*nitimur in vetitum*', our love of adventure, our sharpened and fastidious curiosity, our most subtle, disguised, intellectual Will to Power and universal conquest, which rambles and roves avidiously around all the realms of the future – let us go with all our 'devils' to the help of our 'God'! It is probable that people will misunderstand and mistake us on that account: what does it matter! They will say: 'Their "honesty" – that is their devilry, and nothing else!' What does it matter! And even if they were right – have not all Gods hitherto been such sanctified, re-baptized devils? And after all, what do we know of ourselves? And what the spirit that leads us wants *to be called*? (It is a question of names.) And how many spirits we harbour? Our honesty, we

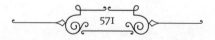

free spirits – let us be careful lest it become our vanity, our ornament and ostentation, our limitation, our stupidity! Every virtue inclines to stupidity, every stupidity to virtue; 'stupid to the point of sanctity', they say in Russia, – let us be careful lest out of pure honesty we eventually become saints and bores! Is not life a hundred times too short for us – to bore ourselves? One would have to believe in eternal life in order to...

228

I HOPE to be forgiven for discovering that all moral philosophy hitherto has been tedious and has belonged to the soporific appliances – and that 'virtue', in my opinion, has been *more* injured by the *tediousness* of its advocates than by anything else; at the same time, however, I would not wish to overlook their general usefulness. It is desirable that as few people as possible should reflect upon morals, and consequently it is very desirable that morals should not some day become interesting! But let us not be afraid! Things still remain today as they have always been: I see no one in Europe who has (or *discloses*) an idea of the fact that philosophizing concerning morals might be conducted in a dangerous, captious and ensnaring manner – that *calamity* might be involved therein. Observe, for example, the inde-fatigable, inevitable English utilitarians: how ponderously and respectably they stalk on, stalk along (a Homeric metaphor expresses it better) in the footsteps of Bentham, just as he had already stalked in the footsteps of the respectable Helvétius! (no, he was not a dangerous man, Helvétius, *ce sénateur Pococurante*, to use an expression of Galiani). No new thought, nothing of the nature of a finer turning or better expression of an old thought, not even a proper history of what has been previously thought on the subject: an *impossible* litera-ture, taking it all in all, unless one knows how to leaven it with some mischief. In effect, the old English vice called *cant*, which is *moral Tartuffism*, has insinuated itself also into these moralists (whom one

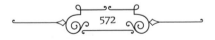

must certainly read with an eye to their motives if one *must* read them), concealed this time under the new form of the scientific spirit; moreover, there is not absent from them a secret struggle with the pangs of conscience, from which a race of former Puritans must naturally suffer, in all their scientific tinkering with morals. (Is not a moralist the opposite of a Puritan? That is to say, as a thinker who regards morality as questionable, as worthy of interrogation, in short, as a problem? Is moralizing not-immoral?) In the end, they all want *English* morality to be recognized as authoritative, inasmuch as mankind, or the 'general utility', or 'the happiness of the greatest number', – no! the happiness of *England*, will be best served thereby. They would like, by all means, to convince themselves that the striving after *English* happiness, I mean after *comfort* and *fashion* (and in the highest instance, a seat in Parliament), is at the same time the true path of virtue; in fact, that in so far as there has been virtue in the world hitherto, it has just consisted in such striving. Not one of those ponderous, conscience-stricken herding-animals (who undertake to advocate the cause of egoism as conducive to the general welfare) wants to have any knowledge or inkling of the facts that the 'general welfare' is no ideal, no goal, no notion that can be at all grasped, but is only a nostrum, – that what is fair to one *may not* at all be fair to another, that the requirement of one morality for all is really a detriment to higher men, in short, that there is a *distinction of rank* between man and man, and consequently between morality and morality. They are an unassuming and fundamentally mediocre species of men, these utilitarian Englishmen, and, as already remarked, in so far as they are tedious, one cannot think highly enough of their utility. One ought even to *encourage* them, as has been partially attempted in the following rhymes: –

> *Hail, ye worthies, barrow-wheeling,*
> *'Longer – better', aye revealing,*

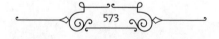

Stiffer aye in head and knee;
Unenraptured, never jesting,
Mediocre everlasting,
Sans genie et sans esprit!

229

IN THESE later ages, which may be proud of their humanity, there still remains so much fear, so much *superstition* of the fear, of the 'cruel wild beast', the mastering of which constitutes the very pride of these humaner ages – that even obvious truths, as if by the agreement of centuries, have long remained unuttered, because they have the appearance of helping the finally slain wild beast back to life again. I perhaps risk something when I allow such a truth to escape; let others capture it again and give it so much 'milk of pious sentiment'* to drink, that it will lie down quiet and forgotten, in its old corner. – One ought to learn anew about cruelty, and open one's eyes; one ought at last to learn impatience, in order that such immodest gross errors – as, for instance, have been fostered by ancient and modern philosophers with regard to tragedy – may no longer wander about virtuously and boldly. Almost everything that we call 'higher culture' is based upon the spiritualizing and intensifying of *cruelty* – this is my thesis; the 'wild beast' has not been slain at all, it lives, it flourishes, it has only been – transfigured. That which constitutes the painful delight of tragedy is cruelty; that which operates agreeably in so-called tragic sympathy, and at the basis even of everything sublime, up to the highest and most delicate thrills of metaphysics, obtains its sweetness solely from the intermingled ingredient of cruelty. What the Roman enjoys in the arena, the Christian in the ecstasies of the cross, the Spaniard at the sight of the faggot and stake, or of the bull-fight, the present-day Japanese who presses his way to the tragedy, the workman of the Parisian suburbs who has a homesickness

* An expression from Schiller's *William Tell*, Act IV, Scene 3.

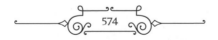

for bloody revolutions, the Wagnerienne who, with unhinged will, 'under-goes' the performance of *Tristan and Isolde* – what all these enjoy, and strive with mysterious ardour to drink in, is the philtre of the great Circe 'cruelty.' Here, to be sure, we must put aside entirely the blundering psychology of former times, which could only teach with regard to cruelty that it originated at the sight of the suffering of *others*: there is an abun-dant, superabundant enjoyment even in one's own suffering, in causing one's own suffering – and wherever man has allowed himself to be persuaded to self-denial in the *religious* sense, or to self-mutilation, as among the Phoenicians and ascetics, or in general, to desensualization, decarnalization and contrition, to Puritanical repentance-spasms, to vivisection of conscience and to Pascal-like *sacrifizia dell' intelleto*, he is secretly allured and impelled forwards by his cruelty, by the dangerous thrill of cruelty *towards himself*. – Finally, let us consider that even the seeker of knowledge operates as an artist and glorifier of cruelty, in that he compels his spirit to perceive *against* its own inclination, and often enough against the wishes of his heart: – he forces it to say Nay, where he would like to affirm, love and adore; indeed, every instance of taking a thing profoundly and fundamentally, is a violation, an intentional injuring of the fundamental will of the spirit, which instinctively aims at appearance and superficiality, – even in every desire for knowledge there is a drop of cruelty.

230

PERHAPS what I have said here about a 'fundamental will of the spirit' may not be understood without further details; I may be allowed a word of explanation. – That imperious something which is popularly called 'the spirit', wishes to be master internally and externally, and to feel itself master; it has the will of a multiplicity for a simplicity, a binding, taming, imperious and essentially ruling will. Its requirements and capacities here, are the same as those assigned by physiologists to

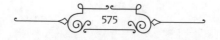

everything that lives, grows and multiplies. The power of the spirit to appropriate foreign elements reveals itself in a strong tendency to assimilate the new to the old, to simplify the manifold, to overlook or repudiate the absolutely contradictory; just as it arbitrarily re-underlines, makes prominent and falsifies for itself certain traits and lines in the foreign elements, in every portion of the 'outside world'. Its object thereby is the incorporation of new 'experiences', the assortment of new things in the old arrangements – in short, growth; or more properly, the *feeling* of growth, the feeling of increased power – is its object. This same will has at its service an apparently opposed impulse of the spirit, a suddenly adopted preference of ignorance, of arbitrary shutting out, a closing of windows, an inner denial of this or that, a prohibition to approach, a sort of defensive attitude against much that is knowable, a contentment with obscurity, with the shutting-in horizon, an acceptance and approval of ignorance: as that which is all necessary according to the degree of its appropriating power, its 'digestive power', to speak figuratively (and in fact 'the spirit' resembles a stomach more than anything else). Here also belong an occasional propensity of the spirit to let itself be deceived (perhaps with a waggish suspicion that it is *not* so and so, but is only allowed to pass as such), a delight in uncertainty and ambiguity, an exulting enjoyment of arbitrary, out-of-the-way narrowness and mystery, of the too-near, of the foreground, of the magnified, the diminished, the misshapen, the beautified – an enjoyment of the arbitrariness of all these manifestations of power. Finally, in this connection, there is the not unscrupulous readiness of the spirit to deceive other spirits and dissemble before them – the constant pressing and straining of a creating, shaping, changeable power: the spirit enjoys therein its craftiness and its variety of disguises, it enjoys also its feeling of security therein – it is precisely by its Protean arts that it is best protected and concealed! – *Counter to* this propensity for appearance, for simplification, for a disguise, for a cloak, in short, for an outside –

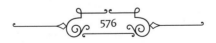

for every outside is a cloak – there operates the sublime tendency of the man of knowledge, which takes, and *insists* on taking things profoundly, variously and thoroughly; as a kind of cruelty of the intellectual conscience and taste, which every courageous thinker will acknowledge in himself, provided, as it ought to be, that he has sharpened and hardened his eye sufficiently long for introspection, and is accustomed to severe discipline and even severe words. He will say: 'There is something cruel in the tendency of my spirit': let the virtuous and amiable try to convince him that it is not so! In fact, it would sound nicer, if, instead of our cruelty, perhaps our 'extravagant honesty' were talked about, whispered about and glorified – we free, *very* free spirits – and some day perhaps *such* will actually be our – posthumous glory! Meanwhile – for there is plenty of time until then – we should be least inclined to deck ourselves out in such florid and fringed moral verbiage; our whole former work has just made us sick of this taste and its sprightly exuberance. They are beautiful, glistening, jingling, festive words: honesty, love of truth, love of wisdom, sacrifice for knowledge, heroism of the truthful – there is something in them that makes one's heart swell with pride. But we anchorites and marmots have long ago persuaded ourselves in all the secrecy of an anchorite's conscience, that this worthy parade of verbiage also belongs to the old false adornment, frippery and gold-dust of unconscious human vanity, and that even under such flattering colour and repainting, the terrible original text *homo natura* must again be recognized. In effect, to translate man back again into nature; to master the many vain and visionary interpretations and subordinate meanings which have hitherto been scratched and daubed over the eternal original text, *homo natura*; to bring it about that man shall henceforth stand before man as he now, hardened by the discipline of science, stands before the *other* forms of nature, with fearless Oedipus-eyes, and stopped Ulysses-ears, deaf to the enticements of old metaphysical bird-catchers, who have piped to him far too long: 'Thou

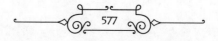

art more! thou art higher! thou hast a different origin!' – this may be a strange and foolish task, but that it is a *task*, who can deny! Why did we choose it, this foolish task? Or, to put the question differently: 'Why knowledge at all?' Everyone will ask us about this. And thus pressed, we, who have asked ourselves the question a hundred times, have not found and cannot find any better answer...

231

LEARNING alters us, it does what all nourishment does that does not merely 'conserve' – as the physiologist knows. But at the bottom of our souls, quite 'down below', there is certainly something unteachable, a granite of spiritual fate, of predetermined decision and answer to predetermined, chosen questions. In each cardinal problem there speaks an unchangeable 'I am this'; a thinker cannot learn anew about man and woman, for instance, but can only learn fully – he can only follow to the end what is 'fixed' about them in himself. Occasionally we find certain solutions of problems which make strong beliefs for *us*; perhaps they are henceforth called 'convictions.' Later on – one sees in them only footsteps to self-knowledge, guide-posts to the problem which we ourselves *are* – or more correctly to the great stupidity which we embody, our spiritual fate, the *unteachable* in us, quite 'down below'. – In view of this liberal compliment which I have just paid myself, permission will perhaps be more readily allowed me to utter some truths about 'woman as she is', provided that it is known at the outset how literally they are merely – *my* truths.

232

WOMAN wishes to be independent, and therefore she begins to enlighten men about 'woman as she is' – *this* is one of the worst developments of the general *uglifying* of Europe. For what must these clumsy attempts of feminine scientificality and self-exposure bring to light!

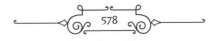

Woman has so much cause for shame; in woman there is so much pedantry, superficiality, schoolmasterliness, petty presumption, unbridledness and indiscretion concealed – study only woman's behaviour towards children! – which has really been best restrained and dominated hitherto by the *fear* of man. Alas, if ever the 'eternally tedious in woman' – she has plenty of it! – is allowed to venture forth! if she begins radically and on principle to unlearn her wisdom and art – of charming, of playing, of frightening away sorrow, of alleviating and taking easily; if she forgets her delicate aptitude for agreeable desires! Female voices are already raised, which, by Saint Aristophanes! make one afraid: – with medical explicitness it is stated in a threatening manner what woman first and last *requires* from man. Is it not in the very worst taste that woman thus sets herself up to be scientific? Enlightenment hitherto has fortunately been men's affair, men's gift – we remained therewith 'among ourselves'; and in the end, in view of all that women write about 'woman', we may well have considerable doubt as to whether woman really *desires* enlightenment about herself – and *can* desire it. If woman does not thereby seek a new *ornament* for herself – I believe ornamentation belongs to the eternally feminine? – why, then, she wishes to make herself feared: perhaps she thereby wishes to get the mastery. But she does not want truth – what does woman care for truth? From the very first, nothing is more foreign, more repugnant or more hostile to woman than truth – her great art is falsehood, her chief concern is appearance and beauty. Let us confess it, we men: we honour and love this very art and this very instinct in woman: we who have the hard task, and for our recreation gladly seek the company of beings under whose hands, glances and delicate follies, our seriousness, our gravity and profundity appear almost like follies to us. Finally, I ask the question: Did a woman herself ever acknowledge profundity in a woman's mind, or justice in a woman's heart? And is it not true that on the whole 'woman' has hitherto been most despised by woman herself, and not at all by us? – We men desire

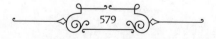

that woman should not continue to compromise herself by enlightening us; just as it was man's care and the consideration for woman, when the church decreed: *mulier taceat in ecclesia*. It was to the benefit of woman when Napoleon gave the too eloquent Madame de Staël to understand: *mulier taceat in politicis*! – and in my opinion, he is a true friend of woman who calls out to women today: *mulier taceat de muliere*!

233

IT BETRAYS corruption of the instincts – apart from the fact that it betrays bad taste – when a woman refers to Madame Roland, or Madame de Staël or Monsieur George Sand, as though something were proved thereby in favour of 'woman as she is'. Among men, these are the three comical women as they are – nothing more! – and just the best involuntary counter-arguments against feminine emancipation and autonomy.

234

STUPIDITY in the kitchen; woman as cook; the terrible thoughtlessness with which the feeding of the family and the master of the house is managed! Woman does not understand what food *means*, and she insists on being cook! If woman had been a thinking creature, she should certainly, as cook for thousands of years, have discovered the most important physiological facts, and should likewise have got possession of the healing art! Through bad female cooks – through the entire lack of reason in the kitchen – the development of mankind has been longest retarded and most interfered with: even today matters are very little better. A word to High School girls.

235

THERE are turns and casts of fancy, there are sentences, little handfuls of words, in which a whole culture, a whole society suddenly crystallizes itself. Among these is the incidental remark of Madame

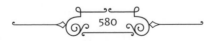

de Lambert to her son: '*Mon ami, ne vous permettez jamais que des folies, qui vous feront grand plaisir*' – the motherliest and wisest remark, by the way, that was ever addressed to a son.

236

I HAVE no doubt that every noble woman will oppose what Dante and Goethe believed about woman – the former when he sang, '*ella guardava suso, ed io in lei*', and the latter when he interpreted it, 'the eternally feminine draws us *aloft*'; for *this* is just what she believes of the eternally masculine.

237

SEVEN Apophthegms for Women:

How the longest ennui flees,
When a man comes to our knees!

Age, alas! and science staid,
Furnish even weak virtue aid.

Sombre garb and silence meet:
Dress for every dame – discreet.

Whom I thank when in my bliss?
God! – and my good tailoress!

Young, a flower-decked cavern home;
Old, a dragon thence doth roam.

Noble title, leg that's fine,
Man as well: Oh, were *he* mine!

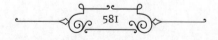

Speech in brief and sense in mass –
Slippery for the jenny-ass!

237A

WOMAN has hitherto been treated by men like birds, which, losing their way, have come down among them from an elevation: as something delicate, fragile, wild, strange, sweet and animating – but as something also which must be cooped up to prevent it flying away.

238

TO BE mistaken in the fundamental problem of 'man and woman', to deny here the profoundest antagonism and the necessity for an eternally hostile tension, to dream here perhaps of equal rights, equal training, equal claims and obligations: that is a *typical* sign of shallow-mindedness; and a thinker who has proved himself shallow at this dangerous spot – shallow in instinct! – may generally be regarded as suspicious, nay more, as betrayed, as discovered; he will probably prove too 'short' for all fundamental questions of life, future as well as present, and will be unable to descend into *any* of the depths. On the other hand, a man who has depth of spirit as well as of desires, and has also the depth of benevolence which is capable of severity and harshness, and easily confounded with them, can only think of woman as *Orientals* do: he must conceive of her as a possession, as confinable property, as a being predestined for service and accomplishing her mission therein – he must take his stand in this matter upon the immense rationality of Asia, upon the superiority of the instinct of Asia, as the Greeks did formerly; those best heirs and scholars of Asia – who, as is well known, with their *increasing* culture and amplitude of power, from Homer to the time of Pericles, became gradually *stricter* towards woman, in short, more Oriental. *How* necessary, *how* logical, even *how* humanely desirable this was, let us consider for ourselves!

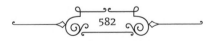

239

THE weaker sex has in no previous age been treated with so much respect by men as at present – this belongs to the tendency and fundamental taste of democracy, in the same way as disrespectfulness to old age – what wonder is it that abuse should be immediately made of this respect? They want more, they learn to make claims, the tribute of respect is at last felt to be well-nigh galling; rivalry for rights, indeed actual strife itself, would be preferred: in a word, woman is losing modesty. And let us immediately add that she is also losing taste. She is unlearning to *fear* man: but the woman who 'unlearns to fear' sacrifices her most womanly instincts. That woman should venture forward when the fear-inspiring quality in man – or more definitely, the *man* in man – is no longer either desired or fully developed, is reasonable enough and also intelligible enough; what is more difficult to understand is that precisely thereby – woman deteriorates. This is what is happening nowadays: let us not deceive ourselves about it! Wherever the industrial spirit has triumphed over the military and aristocratic spirit, woman strives for the economic and legal independence of a clerk: 'woman as clerkess' is inscribed on the portal of the modern society which is in course of formation. While she thus appropriates new rights, aspires to be 'master' and inscribes 'progress' of woman on her flags and banners, the very opposite realizes itself with terrible obviousness: *woman retrogrades*. Since the French Revolution the influence of woman in Europe has *declined* in proportion as she has increased her rights and claims; and the 'emancipation of woman', in so far as it is desired and demanded by women themselves (and not only by masculine shallow-pates), thus proves to be a remarkable symptom of the increased weakening and deadening of the most womanly instincts. There is *stupidity* in this movement, an almost masculine stupidity, of which a well-reared woman – who is always a sensible woman – might be heartily ashamed. To lose the intuition as to the ground upon which

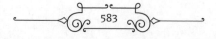

she can most surely achieve victory; to neglect exercise in the use of her proper weapons; to let-herself-go before man, perhaps even 'to the book', where formerly she kept herself in control and in refined, artful humility; to neutralize with her virtuous audacity man's faith in a *veiled*, fundamentally different ideal in woman, something eternally, necessarily feminine; to emphatically and loquaciously dissuade man from the idea that woman must be preserved, cared for, protected and indulged, like some delicate, strangely wild and often pleasant domestic animal; the clumsy and indignant collection of everything of the nature of servitude and bondage which the position of woman in the hitherto existing order of society has entailed and still entails (as though slavery were a counter-argument, and not rather a condition of every higher culture, of every elevation of culture): – what does all this betoken, if not a disintegration of womanly instincts, a defeminizing? Certainly, there are enough of idiotic friends and corrupters of woman among the learned asses of the masculine sex, who advise woman to defeminize herself in this manner, and to imitate all the stupidities from which 'man' in Europe, European 'manliness', suffers, – who would like to lower woman to 'general culture', indeed even to newspaper reading and meddling with politics. Here and there they wish even to make women into free spirits and literary workers: as though a woman without piety would not be something perfectly obnoxious or ludicrous to a profound and godless man; – almost everywhere her nerves are being ruined by the most morbid and dangerous kind of music (our latest German music), and she is daily being made more hysterical and more incapable of fulfilling her first and last function, that of bearing robust children. They wish to 'cultivate' her in general still more, and intend, as they say, to make the 'weaker sex' *strong* by culture: as if history did not teach in the most emphatic manner that the 'cultivating' of mankind and his weakening – that is to say, the weakening, dissipating and languishing of his *force of will* – have always kept pace with one another,

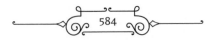

and that the most powerful and influential women in the world (and lastly, the mother of Napoleon) had just to thank their force of will – and not their schoolmasters – for their power and ascendancy over men. That which inspires respect in woman, and often enough fear also, is her *nature*, which is more 'natural' than that of man, her genuine, carnivora-like, cunning flexibility, her tiger-claws beneath the glove, her *naïveté* in egoism, her untrainableness and innate wildness, the incomprehensibleness, extent and deviation of her desires and virtues…. That which, in spite of fear, excites one's sympathy for the dangerous and beautiful cat, 'woman', is that she seems more afflicted, more vulnerable, more necessitous of love and more condemned to disillusionment than any other creature. Fear and sympathy it is with these feelings that man has hitherto stood in the presence of woman, always with one foot already in tragedy, which rends while it delights – What? And all that is now to be at an end? And the *disenchantment* of woman is in progress? The tediousness of woman is slowly evolving? Oh Europe! Europe! We know the horned animal which was always most attractive to thee, from which danger is ever again threatening thee! Thy old fable might once more become 'history' – an immense stupidity might once again overmaster thee and carry thee away! And no God concealed beneath it – no! only an 'idea', a 'modern idea'!

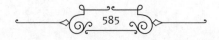

CHAPTER VIII
PEOPLES AND COUNTRIES

240

I *HEARD*, once again for the first time, Richard Wagner's overture to the *Mastersinger*: it is a piece of magnificent, gorgeous, heavy, latter-day art, which has the pride to presuppose two centuries of music as still living, in order that it may be understood: – it is an honour to Germans that such a pride did not miscalculate! What flavours and forces, what seasons and climes do we not find mingled in it! It impresses us at one time as ancient, at another time as foreign, bitter and too modern, it is as arbitrary as it is pompously traditional, it is not infrequently roguish, still oftener rough and coarse – it has fire and courage, and at the same time the loose, dun-coloured skin of fruits which ripen too late. It flows broad and full: and suddenly there is a moment of inexplicable hesitation, like a gap that opens between cause and effect, an oppression that makes us dream, almost a nightmare; but already it broadens and widens anew, the old stream of delight – the most manifold delight, – of old and new happiness; including *especially* the joy of the artist in himself, which he refuses to conceal, his astonished, happy cognizance of his mastery of the expedients here employed, the new, newly acquired, imperfectly tested expedients of art which he apparently betrays to us. All in all, however, no beauty, no South, nothing of the delicate southern clearness of the sky, nothing of grace, no dance, hardly a will to logic; a certain clum-

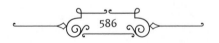

siness even, which is also emphasized, as though the artist wished to say to us: 'It is part of my intention'; a cumbersome drapery, something arbitrarily barbaric and ceremonious, a flirring of learned and venerable conceits and witticisms; something German in the best and worst sense of the word, something in the German style, manifold, formless and inexhaustible; a certain German potency and super-plenitude of soul, which is not afraid to hide itself under the *raffinements* of decadence – which, perhaps, feels itself most at ease there; a real, genuine token of the German soul, which is at the same time young and aged, too ripe and yet still too rich in futurity. This kind of music expresses best what I think of the Germans: they belong to the day before yesterday and the day after tomorrow – *they have as yet no today.*

241

WE 'GOOD Europeans', we also have hours when we allow ourselves a warm-hearted patriotism, a plunge and relapse into old loves and narrow views – I have just given an example of it – hours of national excitement, of patriotic anguish, and all other sorts of old-fashioned floods of sentiment. Duller spirits may perhaps only get done with what confines its operations in us to hours and plays itself out in hours – in a considerable time: some in half a year, others in half a lifetime, according to the speed and strength with which they digest and 'change their material'. Indeed, I could think of sluggish, hesitating races, which even in our rapidly moving Europe, would require half a century ere they could surmount such atavistic attacks of patriotism and soil-attachment, and return once more to reason, that is to say, to 'good Europeanism'. And while digressing on this possibility, I happen to become an ear-witness of a conversation between two old patriots – they were evidently both hard of hearing and consequently spoke all the louder. '*He* has as much, and knows as much, philosophy as a peasant or a corps-student,' said the one – 'he is still innocent. But what does that matter nowadays! It is the age of the masses:

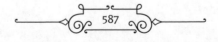

they lie on their belly before everything that is massive. And so also in *politicis*. A statesman who rears up for them a new Tower of Babel, some monstrosity of empire and power, they call "great" – what does it matter that we more prudent and conservative ones do not meanwhile give up the old belief that it is only the great thought that gives greatness to an action or affair. Supposing a statesman were to bring his people into the position of being obliged henceforth to practise "high politics", for which they were by nature badly endowed and prepared, so that they would have to sacrifice their old and reliable virtues, out of love to a new and doubtful mediocrity; – supposing a statesman were to condemn his people generally to "practise politics", when they have hitherto had something better to do and think about, and when in the depths of their souls they have been unable to free themselves from a prudent loathing of the restlessness, emptiness and noisy wranglings of the essentially politics-practising nations; – supposing such a statesman were to stimulate the slumbering passions and avidities of his people, were to make a stigma out of their former diffidence and delight in aloofness, an offence out of their exoticism and hidden permanency, were to depreciate their most radical proclivities, subvert their consciences, make their minds narrow and their tastes "national" – what! a statesman who should do all this, which his people would have to do penance for throughout their whole future, if they had a future, such a statesman would be *great*, would he?' – 'Undoubtedly!' replied the other old patriot vehemently, 'otherwise he *could not* have done it! It was mad perhaps to wish such a thing! But perhaps everything great has been just as mad at its commencement!' – 'Misuse of words!' cried his interlocutor, contradictorily – 'strong! strong! Strong and mad! *not* great!' – The old men had obviously become heated as they thus shouted their 'truths' in each other's faces, but I, in my happiness and apartness, considered how soon a stronger one may become master of the strong, and also that there is a compensation for the intellectual superficializing of a nation – namely, in the deepening of another.

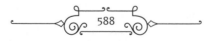

242

WHETHER we call it 'civilization', or 'humanising', or 'progress' which now distinguishes the European, whether we call it simply, without praise or blame, by the political formula: the *democratic* movement in Europe – behind all the moral and political foregrounds pointed to by such formulas, an immense *physiological process* goes on, which is ever extending: the process of the assimilation of Europeans; their increasing detachment from the conditions under which, climatically and hereditarily, united races originate, their increasing independence of every definite *milieu*, that for centuries would fain inscribe itself with equal demands on soul and body; – that is to say, the slow emergence of an essentially *super-national* and nomadic species of man, who possesses, physiologically speaking, a maximum of the art and power of adaptation as his typical distinction. This process of the *evolving European*, which can be retarded in its *tempo* by great relapses, but will perhaps just gain and grow thereby in vehemence and depth – the still-raging storm and stress of 'national sentiment' pertains to it, and also the anarchism which is appearing at present – this process will probably arrive at results on which its naïve propagators and panegyrists, the apostles of 'modern ideas', would least care to reckon. The same new conditions under which on an average a levelling and mediocrising of man will take place – a useful, industrious, variously serviceable and clever gregarious man – are in the highest degree suitable to give rise to exceptional men of the most dangerous and attractive qualities. For, while the capacity for adaptation, which is every day trying changing conditions, and begins a new work with every generation, almost with every decade, makes the *powerfulness* of the type impossible; while the collective impression of such future Europeans will probably be that of numerous, talkative, weak-willed and very handy workmen who *require* a master, a commander, as they require their daily bread; while, therefore, the democratizing of Europe will tend to the production of a type prepared for *slavery* in the

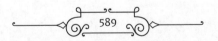

most subtle sense of the term: the *strong* man will necessarily in individual and exceptional cases, become stronger and richer than he has perhaps ever been before – owing to the unprejudicedness of his schooling, owing to the immense variety of practice, art and disguise. I meant to say that the democratizing of Europe is at the same time an involuntary arrangement for the rearing of *tyrants* – taking the word in all its meanings, even in its most spiritual sense.

243

I HEAR with pleasure that our sun is moving rapidly towards the constellation *Hercules*: and I hope that the men on this earth will do like the sun. And we foremost, we good Europeans!

244

THERE was a time when it was customary to call Germans 'deep' by way of distinction; but now that the most successful type of new Germanism is covetous of quite other honours, and perhaps misses 'smartness' in all that has depth, it is almost opportune and patriotic to doubt whether we did not formerly deceive ourselves with that commendation: in short, whether German depth is not at bottom something different and worse – and something from which, thank God, we are on the point of successfully ridding ourselves. Let us try, then, to relearn with regard to German depth; the only thing necessary for the purpose is a little vivisection of the German soul. – The German soul is above all manifold, varied in its source, aggregated and super-imposed, rather than actually built: this is owing to its origin. A German who would embolden himself to assert: 'Two souls, alas, dwell in my breast', would make a bad guess at the truth, or, more correctly, he would come far short of the truth about the number of souls. As a people made up of the most extraordinary mixing and mingling of races, perhaps even with a preponderance of the pre-Aryan element as the 'people of the centre' in every sense of the

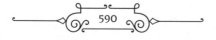

term, the Germans are more intangible, more ample, more contradictory, more unknown, more incalculable, more surprising and even more terri- fying than other peoples are to themselves: – they escape *definition*, and are thereby alone the despair of the French. It *is* characteristic of the Germans that the question: 'What is German?' never dies out among them. Kotzebue certainly knew his Germans well enough: 'We are known,' they cried jubilantly to him – but Sand also thought he knew them. Jean Paul knew what he was doing when he declared himself incensed at Fichte's lying but patriotic flatteries and exaggerations, – but it is probable that Goethe thought differently about Germans from Jean Paul, even though he acknowledged him to be right with regard to Fichte. It is a question what Goethe really thought about the Germans? – But about many things around him he never spoke explicitly, and all his life he knew how to keep an astute silence – probably he had good reason for it. It is certain that it was not the 'Wars of Independence' that made him look up more joyfully, any more than it was the French Revolution, – the event on account of which he *reconstructed* his *Faust*, and indeed the whole problem of 'man', was the appearance of Napoleon. There are words of Goethe in which he condemns with impatient severity, as from a foreign land, that which Germans take a pride in, he once defined the famous German turn of mind as 'Indulgence towards its own and others' weak- nesses'. Was he wrong? it is characteristic of Germans that one is seldom entirely wrong about them. The German soul has passages and galleries in it, there are caves, hiding-places and dungeons therein, its disorder has much of the charm of the mysterious, the German is well acquainted with the bypaths to chaos. And as everything loves its symbol, so the German loves the clouds and all that is obscure, evolving, crepuscular, damp and shrouded: it seems to him that everything uncertain, undevel- oped, self-displacing and growing is 'deep'. The German himself does not *exist*: he is *becoming*, he is 'developing himself'. 'Development' is therefore the essentially German discovery and hit in the great domain

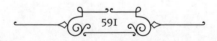

of philosophical formulas, – a ruling idea, which, together with German beer and German music, is labouring to Germanize all Europe. Foreigners are astonished and attracted by the riddles which the conflicting nature at the basis of the German soul propounds to them (riddles which Hegel systematized and Richard Wagner has in the end set to music). 'Good-natured and spiteful' – such a juxtaposition, preposterous in the case of every other people, is unfortunately only too often justified in Germany: one has only to live for a while among Swabians to know this! The clumsiness of the German scholar and his social distastefulness agree alarmingly well with his physical rope-dancing and nimble boldness, of which all the Gods have learnt to be afraid. If anyone wishes to see the 'German soul' demonstrated *ad oculos*, let him only look at German taste, at German arts and manners: what boorish indifference to 'taste'! How the noblest and the commonest stand there in juxtaposition! How disorderly and how rich is the whole constitution of this soul! The German *drags* at his soul, he drags at everything he experiences. He digests his events badly; he never gets 'done' with them; and German depth is often only a difficult, hesitating 'digestion'. And just as all chronic invalids, all dyspeptics, like what is convenient, so the German loves 'frankness' and 'honesty'; it is so *convenient* to be frank and honest! – This confidingness, this complaisance, this showing-the-cards of German *honesty*, is probably the most dangerous and most successful disguise which the German is up to nowadays: it is his proper Mephistophelean art; with this he can 'still achieve much'! The German lets himself go, and thereby gazes with faithful, blue, empty German eyes – and other countries immediately confound him with his dressing-gown! – I meant to say that, let 'German depth' be what it will – among ourselves alone we perhaps take the liberty to laugh at it – we shall do well to continue henceforth to honour its appearance and good name, and not barter away too cheaply our old reputation as a people of depth for Prussian 'smartness', and Berlin wit and sand. It is wise for a people to pose, and *let* itself be regarded, as

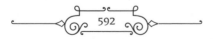

profound, clumsy, good-natured, honest and foolish: it might even be – profound to do so! Finally, we should do honour to our name – we are not called the '*tiusche Volk*' (deceptive people) for nothing...

245

THE 'good old' time is past, it sang itself out in Mozart – how happy are *we* that his *rococo* still speaks to us, that his 'good company', his tender enthusiasm, his childish delight in the Chinese and its flourishes, his courtesy of heart, his longing for the elegant, the amorous, the tripping, the tearful and his belief in the South, can still appeal to *something left* in us! Ah, sometime or other it will be over with it! – but who can doubt that it will be over still sooner with the intelligence and taste for Beethoven! For he was only the last echo of a break and transition in style, and *not*, like Mozart, the last echo of a great European taste which had existed for centuries. Beethoven is the intermediate event between an old mellow soul that is constantly breaking down, and a future over-young soul that is always *coming*; there is spread over his music the twilight of eternal loss and eternal extravagant hope, – the same light in which Europe was bathed when it dreamed with Rousseau, when it danced round the Tree of Liberty of the Revolution, and finally almost fell down in adoration before Napoleon. But how rapidly does *this* very sentiment now pale, how difficult nowadays is even the *apprehension* of this sentiment, how strangely does the language of Rousseau, Schiller, Shelley and Byron sound to our ear, in whom *collectively* the same fate of Europe was able to *speak*, which knew how to *sing* in Beethoven! – Whatever German music came afterwards, belongs to Romanticism, that is to say, to a movement which, historically considered, was still shorter, more fleeting and more superficial than that great interlude, the transition of Europe from Rousseau to Napoleon, and to the rise of democracy. Weber – but what do *we* care nowadays for *Der Freischutz* and *Oberon*! Or Marschner's *Hans Heiling* and *Vampyre*! Or even Wagner's *Tannhauser*!

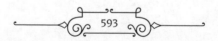

That is extinct, although not yet forgotten music. This whole music of Romanticism, besides, was not noble enough, was not musical enough, to maintain its position anywhere but in the theatre and before the masses; from the beginning it was second-rate music, which was little thought of by genuine musicians. It was different with Felix Mendelssohn, that halcyon master, who, on account of his lighter, purer, happier soul, quickly acquired admiration, and was equally quickly forgotten: as the beautiful *episode* of German music. But with regard to Robert Schumann, who took things seriously, and has been taken seriously from the first – he was the last that founded a school, – do we not now regard it as a satisfaction, a relief, a deliverance, that this very Romanticism of Schumann's has been surmounted? Schumann, fleeing into the 'Saxon Switzerland' of his soul, with a half Werther-like, half Jean-Paul-like nature (assuredly not like Beethoven! assuredly not like Byron!) – his *Manfred* music is a mistake and a misunderstanding to the extent of injustice; Schumann, with his taste, which was fundamentally a *petty* taste (that is to say, a dangerous propensity – doubly dangerous among Germans – for quiet lyricism and intoxication of the feelings), going constantly apart, timidly withdrawing and retiring, a noble weakling who revelled in nothing but anonymous joy and sorrow, from the beginning a sort of girl and *noli me tangere* – this Schumann was already merely a *German* event in music, and no longer a European event, as Beethoven had been, as in a still greater degree Mozart had been; with Schumann German music was threatened with its greatest danger, that of *losing the voice for the soul of Europe* and sinking into a merely national affair.

246

WHAT a torture are books written in German to a reader who has a *third* ear! How indignantly he stands beside the slowly turning swamp of sounds without tune and rhythms without dance, which Germans call a 'book'! And even the German who *reads* books! How lazily, how reluc-

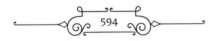

tantly, how badly he reads! How many Germans know, and consider it obligatory to know, that there is *art* in every good sentence – art which must be divined, if the sentence is to be understood! If there is a misunderstanding about its *tempo*, for instance, the sentence itself is misunderstood! That one must not be doubtful about the rhythm-determining syllables, that one should feel the breaking of the too-rigid symmetry as intentional and as a charm, that one should lend a fine and patient ear to every *staccato* and every *rubato*, that one should divine the sense in the sequence of the vowels and diphthongs, and how delicately and richly they can be tinted and retinted in the order of their arrangement – who among book-reading Germans is complaisant enough to recognize such duties and requirements, and to listen to so much art and intention in language? After all, one just 'has no ear for it'; and so the most marked contrasts of style are not heard, and the most delicate artistry is as it were *squandered* on the deaf. – These were my thoughts when I noticed how clumsily and unintuitively two masters in the art of prose-writing have been confounded: one, whose words drop down hesitatingly and coldly, as from the roof of a damp cave – he counts on their dull sound and echo; and another who manipulates his language like a flexible sword, and from his arm down into his toes feels the dangerous bliss of the quivering, over-sharp blade, which wishes to bite, hiss and cut.

247

HOW little the German style has to do with harmony and with the ear, is shown by the fact that precisely our good musicians themselves write badly. The German does not read aloud, he does not read for the ear, but only with his eyes; he has put his ears away in the drawer for the time. In antiquity when a man read – which was seldom enough – he read something to himself, and in a loud voice; they were surprised when anyone read silently, and sought secretly the reason of it. In a loud voice: that is to say, with all the swellings, inflections and variations of key and

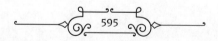

changes of *tempo*, in which the ancient *public* world took delight. The laws of the written style were then the same as those of the spoken style; and these laws depended partly on the surprising development and refined requirements of the ear and larynx; partly on the strength, endurance and power of the ancient lungs. In the ancient sense, a period is above all a physiological whole, inasmuch as it is comprised in one breath. Such periods as occur in Demosthenes and Cicero, swelling twice and sinking twice, and all in one breath, were pleasures to the men of *antiquity*, who knew by their own schooling how to appreciate the virtue therein, the rareness and the difficulty in the deliverance of such a period; – *we* have really no right to the *big* period, we modern men, who are short of breath in every sense! Those ancients, indeed, were all of them dilettanti in speaking, consequently connoisseurs, consequently critics – they thus brought their orators to the highest pitch; in the same manner as in the last century, when all Italian ladies and gentlemen knew how to sing, the virtuosoship of song (and with it also the art of melody) reached its elevation. In Germany, however (until quite recently when a kind of platform eloquence began shyly and awkwardly enough to flutter its young wings), there was properly speaking only one kind of public and *approximately* artistical discourse – that delivered from the pulpit. The preacher was the only one in Germany who knew the weight of a syllable or a word, in what manner a sentence strikes, springs, rushes, flows and comes to a close; he alone had a conscience in his ears, often enough a bad conscience: for reasons are not lacking why proficiency in oratory should be especially seldom attained by a German, or almost always too late. The masterpiece of German prose is therefore with good reason the masterpiece of its greatest preacher: the *Bible* has hitherto been the best German book. Compared with Luther's *Bible*, almost everything else is merely 'literature' – something which has not grown in Germany, and therefore has not taken and does not take root in German hearts, as the *Bible* has done.

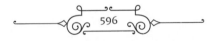

248

THERE are two kinds of geniuses: one which above all engenders and seeks to engender, and another which willingly lets itself be fructified and brings forth. And similarly, among the gifted nations, there are those on whom the woman's problem of pregnancy has devolved, and the secret task of forming, maturing and perfecting – the Greeks, for instance, were a nation of this kind, and so are the French; and others which have to fructify and become the cause of new modes of life – like the Jews, the Romans and, in all modesty be it asked: like the Germans? – nations tortured and enraptured by unknown fevers and irresistibly forced out of themselves, amorous and longing for foreign races (for such as 'let themselves be fructified'), and withal imperious, like everything conscious of being full of generative force, and consequently empowered 'by the grace of God'. These two kinds of geniuses seek each other like man and woman; but they also misunderstand each other – like man and woman.

249

EVERY nation has its own 'Tartuffery', and calls that its virtue. – One does not know – cannot know, the best that is in one.

250

WHAT Europe owes to the Jews? – Many things, good and bad, and above all one thing of the nature both of the best and the worst: the grand style in morality, the fearfulness and majesty of infinite demands, of infinite significations, the whole Romanticism and sublimity of moral questionableness – and consequently just the most attractive, ensnaring and exquisite element in those iridescences and allurements to life, in the aftersheen of which the sky of our European culture, its evening sky, now glows – perhaps glows out. For this, we artists among the spectators and philosophers, are – grateful to the Jews.

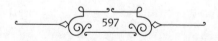

251

IT MUST be taken into the bargain, if various clouds and disturbances – in short, slight attacks of stupidity – pass over the spirit of a people that suffers and *wants* to suffer from national nervous fever and political ambition: for instance, among present-day Germans there is alternately the anti-French folly, the anti-Semitic folly, the anti-Polish folly, the Christian-romantic folly, the Wagnerian folly, the Teutonic folly, the Prussian folly (just look at those poor historians, the Sybels and Treitschkes, and their closely bandaged heads), and whatever else these little obscurations of the German spirit and conscience may be called. May it be forgiven me that I, too, when on a short daring sojourn on very infected ground, did not remain wholly exempt from the disease, but like everyone else, began to entertain thoughts about matters which did not concern me – the first symptom of political infection. About the Jews, for instance, listen to the following: – I have never yet met a German who was favourably inclined to the Jews; and however decided the repudiation of actual anti-Semitism may be on the part of all prudent and political men, this prudence and policy is not perhaps directed against the nature of the sentiment itself, but only against its dangerous excess, and especially against the distasteful and infamous expression of this excess of sentiment; – on this point we must not deceive ourselves. That Germany has amply *sufficient* Jews, that the German stomach, the German blood, has difficulty (and will long have difficulty) in disposing only of this quantity of 'Jew' – as the Italian, the Frenchman and the Englishman have done by means of a stronger digestion: – that is the unmistakable declaration and language of a general instinct, to which one must listen and according to which one must act. 'Let no more Jews come in! And shut the doors, especially towards the East (also towards Austria)!' – thus commands the instinct of a people whose nature is still feeble and uncertain, so that it could be easily wiped out, easily extinguished, by a stronger race. The Jews, however, are beyond all doubt the strongest, toughest and purest race at present

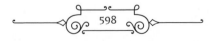

living in Europe, they know how to succeed even under the worst conditions (in fact better than under favourable ones), by means of virtues of some sort, which one would like nowadays to label as vices – owing above all to a resolute faith which does not need to be ashamed before 'modern ideas'; they alter only, *when* they do alter, in the same way that the Russian Empire makes its conquest – as an empire that has plenty of time and is not of yesterday – namely, according to the principle, 'as slowly as possible'! A thinker who has the future of Europe at heart, will, in all his perspectives concerning the future, calculate upon the Jews, as he will calculate upon the Russians, as above all the surest and likeliest factors in the great play and battle of forces. That which is at present called a 'nation' in Europe, and is really rather a *res facta* than *nata* (indeed, sometimes confusingly similar to a *res ficta et picta*), is in every case something evolving, young, easily displaced and not yet a race, much less such a race *aere perennius*, as the Jews are: such 'nations' should most carefully avoid all hot-headed rivalry and hostility! It is certain that the Jews, if they desired – or if they were driven to it, as the anti-Semites seem to wish – *could* now have the ascendancy, nay, literally the supremacy, over Europe, that they are *not* working and planning for that end is equally certain. Meanwhile, they rather wish and desire, even somewhat importunely, to be insorbed and absorbed by Europe, they long to be finally settled, authorized and respected somewhere, and wish to put an end to the nomadic life, to the 'wandering Jew'; – and one should certainly take account of this impulse and tendency, and *make advances* to it (it possibly betokens a mitigation of the Jewish instincts): for which purpose it would perhaps be useful and fair to banish the anti-Semitic bawlers out of the country. One should make advances with all prudence, and with selection; pretty much as the English nobility do. It stands to reason that the more powerful and strongly marked types of new Germanism could enter into relation with the Jews with the least hesitation, for instance, the nobleman officer from the Prussian border: it would be interesting in many ways

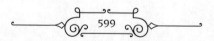

to see whether the genius for money and patience (and especially some intellect and intellectuality – sadly lacking in the place referred to) could not in addition be annexed and trained to the hereditary art of commanding and obeying – for both of which the country in question has now a classic reputation. But here it is expedient to break off my festal discourse and my sprightly Teutonomania: for I have already reached my *serious topic*, the 'European problem', as I understand it, the rearing of a new ruling caste for Europe.

252

THEY are not a philosophical race – the English: Bacon represents an *attack* on the philosophical spirit generally, Hobbes, Hume and Locke, an abasement, and a depreciation of the idea of a 'philosopher' for more than a century. It was *against* Hume that Kant uprose and raised himself; it was Locke of whom Schelling *rightly* said, '*je méprise Locke*'; in the struggle against the English mechanical stultification of the world, Hegel and Schopenhauer (along with Goethe) were of one accord; the two hostile brother-geniuses in philosophy, who pushed in different directions towards the opposite poles of German thought, and thereby wronged each other as only brothers will do. – What is lacking in England, and has always been lacking, that half-actor and rhetorician knew well enough, the absurd muddle-head, Carlyle, who sought to conceal under passionate grimaces what he knew about himself: namely, what was *lacking* in Carlyle – real *power* of intellect, real *depth* of intellectual perception, in short, philosophy. It is characteristic of such an unphilosophical race to hold on firmly to Christianity – they *need* its discipline for 'moralizing' and humanizing. The Englishman, more gloomy, sensual, headstrong and brutal than the German – is for that very reason, as the baser of the two, also the most pious: he has all the *more need* of Christianity. To finer nostrils, this English Christianity itself has still a characteristic English taint of spleen and alcoholic excess, for which, owing to good reasons, it is used

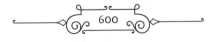

as an antidote – the finer poison to neutralize the coarser: a finer form of poisoning is in fact a step in advance with coarse-mannered people, a step towards spiritualization. The English coarseness and rustic demureness is still most satisfactorily disguised by Christian pantomime, and by praying and psalm-singing (or, more correctly, it is thereby explained and differently expressed); and for the herd of drunkards and rakes who formerly learned moral grunting under the influence of Methodism (and more recently as the 'Salvation Army'), a penitential fit may really be the relatively highest manifestation of 'humanity' to which they can be elevated: so much may reasonably be admitted. That, however, which offends even in the humanest Englishman is his lack of music, to speak figuratively (and also literally): he has neither rhythm nor dance in the movements of his soul and body; indeed, not even the desire for rhythm and dance, for 'music.' Listen to him speaking; look at the most beautiful Englishwoman *walking* – in no country on earth are there more beautiful doves and swans; finally, listen to them singing! But I ask too much...

253

THERE are truths which are best recognized by mediocre minds, because they are best adapted for them, there are truths which only possess charms and seductive power for mediocre spirits: – one is pushed to this probably unpleasant conclusion, now that the influence of respectable but mediocre Englishmen – I may mention Darwin, John Stuart Mill and Herbert Spencer – begins to gain the ascendancy in the middle-class region of European taste. Indeed, who could doubt that it is a useful thing for *such* minds to have the ascendancy for a time? It would be an error to consider the highly developed and independently soaring minds as specially qualified for determining and collecting many little common facts, and deducing conclusions from them; as exceptions, they are rather from the first in no very favourable position towards those who are 'the rules.' After all, they have more to do than merely to perceive: – in effect, they

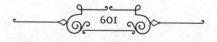

have to *be* something new, they have to *signify* something new, they have to *represent* new values! The gulf between knowledge and capacity is perhaps greater, and also more mysterious, than one thinks: the capable man in the grand style, the creator, will possibly have to be an ignorant person; – while on the other hand, for scientific discoveries like those of Darwin, a certain narrowness, aridity and industrious carefulness (in short, something English) may not be unfavourable for arriving at them. – Finally, let it not be forgotten that the English, with their profound mediocrity, brought about once before a general depression of European intelligence. What is called 'modern ideas', or 'the ideas of the eighteenth century' or 'French ideas' – that, consequently, against which the *German* mind rose up with profound disgust – is of English origin, there is no doubt about it. The French were only the apes and actors of these ideas, their best soldiers, and likewise, alas! their first and profoundest *victims*; for owing to the diabolical Anglomania of 'modern ideas', the *âme Français* has in the end become so thin and emaciated, that at present one recalls its sixteenth and seventeenth centuries, its profound, passionate strength, its inventive excellency, almost with disbelief. One must, however, maintain this verdict of historical justice in a determined manner, and defend it against present prejudices and appearances: the European *noblesse* – of sentiment, taste and manners, taking the word in every high sense – is the work and invention of *France*; the European ignobleness, the plebeianism of modern ideas – is *England's* work and invention.

254

EVEN at present France is still the seat of the most intellectual and refined culture of Europe, it is still the high school of taste; but one must know how to find this 'France of taste'. He who belongs to it keeps himself well concealed: – they may be a small number in whom it lives and is embodied, besides perhaps being men who do not stand upon the strongest legs, in part fatalists, hypochondriacs, invalids, in part persons

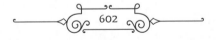

over-indulged, over-refined, such as have the *ambition* to conceal themselves. They have all something in common: they keep their ears closed in presence of the delirious folly and noisy spouting of the democratic *bourgeois*. In fact, a besotted and brutalized France at present sprawls in the foreground – it recently celebrated a veritable orgy of bad taste, and at the same time of self-admiration, at the funeral of Victor Hugo. There is also something else common to them: a predilection to resist intellectual Germanizing – and a still greater inability to do so! In this France of intellect, which is also a France of pessimism, Schopenhauer has perhaps become more at home, and more indigenous than he has ever been in Germany; not to speak of Heinrich Heine, who has long ago been reincarnated in the more refined and fastidious lyrists of Paris; or of Hegel, who at present, in the form of Taine – the *first* of living historians – exercises an almost tyrannical influence. As regards Richard Wagner, however, the more French music learns to adapt itself to the actual needs of the *âme moderne*, the more will it 'Wagnerize'; one can safely predict that beforehand, – it is already taking place sufficiently! There are, however, three things which the French can still boast of with pride as their heritage and possession, and as indelible tokens of their ancient intellectual superiority in Europe, in spite of all voluntary or involuntary Germanizing and vulgarizing of taste. *Firstly*, the capacity for artistic emotion, for devotion to 'form', for which the expression, *l'art pour l'art*, along with numerous others, has been invented: – such capacity has not been lacking in France for three centuries; and owing to its reverence for the 'small number', it has again and again made a sort of chamber music of literature possible, which is sought for in vain elsewhere in Europe. – The *second* thing whereby the French can lay claim to a superiority over Europe is their ancient, many-sided, *moralistic* culture, owing to which one finds on an average, even in the petty *romanciers* of the newspapers and chance *boulevardiers de Paris*, a psychological sensitiveness and curiosity, of which, for example, one has no conception (to say nothing of the thing itself!)

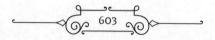

in Germany. The Germans lack a couple of centuries of the moralistic work requisite thereto, which, as we have said, France has not grudged: those who call the Germans 'naïve' on that account give them commendation for a defect. (As the opposite of the German inexperience and innocence *in voluptate psychologica*, which is not too remotely associated with the tediousness of German intercourse, – and as the most successful expression of genuine French curiosity and inventive talent in this domain of delicate thrills, Henri Beyle may be noted; that remarkable anticipatory and forerunning man, who, with a Napoleonic *tempo*, traversed *his* Europe, in fact, several centuries of the European soul, as a surveyor and discoverer thereof: – it has required two generations to *overtake* him one way or other, to divine long afterwards some of the riddles that perplexed and enraptured him – this strange Epicurean and man of interrogation, the last great psychologist of France). – There is yet a *third* claim to superiority: in the French character there is a successful half-way synthesis of the North and South, which makes them comprehend many things, and enjoins upon them other things, which an Englishman can never comprehend. Their temperament, turned alternately to and from the South, in which from time to time the Provençal and Ligurian blood froths over, preserves them from the dreadful, northern grey-in-grey, from sunless conceptual-spectrism and from poverty of blood – our *German* infirmity of taste, for the excessive prevalence of which at the present moment, blood and iron, that is to say 'high politics', has with great resolution been prescribed (according to a dangerous healing art, which bids me wait and wait, but not yet hope). – There is also still in France a preunderstanding and ready welcome for those rarer and rarely gratified men, who are too comprehensive to find satisfaction in any kind of fatherlandism, and know how to love the South when in the North and the North when in the South – the born Midlanders, the 'good Europeans'. For them *Bizet* has made music, this latest genius, who has seen a new beauty and seduction, – who has discovered a piece of the *South in music*.

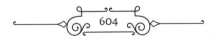

255

I HOLD that many precautions should be taken against German music. Suppose a person loves the South as I love it – as a great school of recovery for the most spiritual and the most sensuous ills, as a boundless solar profusion and effulgence which o'erspreads a sovereign existence believing in itself – well, such a person will learn to be somewhat on his guard against German music, because, in injuring his taste anew, it will also injure his health anew. Such a Southerner, a Southerner not by origin but by *belief*, if he should dream of the future of music, must also dream of it being freed from the influence of the North; and must have in his ears the prelude to a deeper, mightier and perhaps more perverse and mysterious music, a super-German music, which does not fade, pale and die away, as all German music does, at the sight of the blue, wanton sea and the Mediterranean clearness of sky – a super-European music, which holds its own even in presence of the brown sunsets of the desert, whose soul is akin to the palm tree, and can be at home and can roam with big, beautiful, lonely beasts of prey... I could imagine a music of which the rarest charm would be that it knew nothing more of good and evil; only that here and there perhaps some sailor's homesickness, some golden shadows and tender weaknesses might sweep lightly over it; an art which, from the far distance, would see the colours of a sinking and almost incomprehensible *moral* world fleeing towards it, and would be hospitable enough and profound enough to receive such belated fugitives.

256

OWING to the morbid estrangement which the nationality-craze has induced and still induces among the nations of Europe, owing also to the short-sighted and hasty-handed politicians, who with the help of this craze, are at present in power, and do not suspect to what extent the disintegrating policy they pursue must necessarily be only an

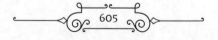

interlude policy – owing to all this and much else that is altogether unmentionable at present, the most unmistakable signs that *Europe wishes to be one*, are now overlooked, or arbitrarily and falsely misinterpreted. With all the more profound and large-minded men of this century, the real general tendency of the mysterious labour of their souls was to prepare the way for that new *synthesis*, and tentatively to anticipate the European of the future; only in their simulations, or in their weaker moments, in old age perhaps, did they belong to the 'fatherlands' – they only rested from themselves when they became 'patriots'. I think of such men as Napoleon, Goethe, Beethoven, Stendhal, Heinrich Heine, Schopenhauer: it must not be taken amiss if I also count Richard Wagner among them, about whom one must not let oneself be deceived by his own misunderstandings (geniuses like him have seldom the right to understand themselves), still less, of course, by the unseemly noise with which he is now resisted and opposed in France: the fact remains, nevertheless, that Richard Wagner and the *later French Romanticism* of the forties, are most closely and intimately related to one another. They are akin, fundamentally akin, in all the heights and depths of their requirements; it is Europe, the *one* Europe, whose soul presses urgently and longingly, outwards and upwards, in their multifarious and boisterous art – whither? into a new light? towards a new sun? But who would attempt to express accurately what all these masters of new modes of speech could not express distinctly? It is certain that the same storm and stress tormented them, that they *sought* in the same manner, these last great seekers! All of them steeped in literature to their eyes and ears – the first artists of universal literary culture – for the most part even themselves writers, poets, intermediaries and blenders of the arts and the senses (Wagner, as musician is reckoned among painters, as poet among musicians, as artist generally among actors); all of them fanatics for *expression* 'at any cost' – I specially mention Delacroix, the nearest related to Wagner;

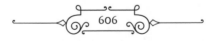

all of them great discoverers in the realm of the sublime, also of the loathsome and dreadful, still greater discoverers in effect, in display, in the art of the show-shop; all of them talented far beyond their genius, out and out *virtuosi*, with mysterious accesses to all that seduces, allures, constrains and upsets; born enemies of logic and of the straight line, hankering after the strange, the exotic, the monstrous, the crooked and the self-contradictory; as men, Tantaluses of the will, plebeian parvenus, who knew themselves to be incapable of a noble *tempo* or of a *lento* in life and action – think of Balzac, for instance, – unre-strained workers, almost destroying themselves by work; antinomians and rebels in manners, ambitious and insatiable, without equilibrium and enjoyment; all of them finally shattering and sinking down at the Christian cross (and with right and reason, for who of them would have been sufficiently profound and sufficiently original for an *anti-Christian* philosophy?); – on the whole, a boldly daring, splendidly overbearing, high-flying and aloft-up-dragging class of higher men, who had first to teach their century – and it is the century of the *masses* – the conception 'higher man'.... Let the German friends of Richard Wagner advise together as to whether there is anything purely German in the Wagnerian art, or whether its distinction does not consist precisely in coming from *super-German* sources and impulses: in which connection it may not be underrated how indispensable Paris was to the development of his type, which the strength of his instincts made him long to visit at the most decisive time – and how the whole style of his proceedings, of his self-apostolate, could only perfect itself in sight of the French socialistic original. On a more subtle compari-son it will perhaps be found, to the honour of Richard Wagner's German nature, that he has acted in everything with more strength, daring, severity and elevation than a nineteenth-century Frenchman could have done – owing to the circumstance that we Germans are as yet nearer to barbarism than the French; – perhaps even the most

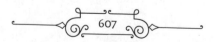

remarkable creation of Richard Wagner is not only at present, but for ever inaccessible, incomprehensible and inimitable to the whole latter-day Latin race: the figure of Siegfried, that *very free* man, who is probably far too free, too hard, too cheerful, too healthy, too *anti-Catholic* for the taste of old and mellow civilized nations. He may even have been a sin against Romanticism, this anti-Latin Siegfried: well, Wagner atoned amply for this sin in his old sad days, when – anticipating a taste which has meanwhile passed into politics – he began, with the religious vehemence peculiar to him, to preach, at least, *the way to Rome*, if not to walk therein. – That these last words may not be misunderstood, I will call to my aid a few powerful rhymes, which will even betray to less delicate ears what I mean – what I mean *counter to* the 'last Wagner' and his *Parsifal* music: –

– Is this our mode? –
From German heart came this vexed ululating?
From German body, this self-lacerating?
Is ours this priestly hand-dilation,
This incense-fuming exaltation?
Is ours this faltering, falling, shambling,
This quite uncertain ding-dong-dangling?
This sly nun-ogling, Ave-hour-bell ringing, This wholly false enraptured heaven-o'erspringing?
– Is this our mode? –
Think well! – ye still wait for admission –
For what ye hear is *Rome – Rome's faith by intuition!*

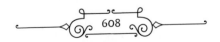

CHAPTER IX
WHAT IS NOBLE?

257

EVERY elevation of the type 'man', has hitherto been the work of an aristocratic society and so it will always be – a society believing in a long scale of gradations of rank and differences of worth among human beings, and requiring slavery in some form or other. Without the *pathos of distance,* such as grows out of the incarnated difference of classes, out of the constant out-looking and down-looking of the ruling caste on subordinates and instruments, and out of their equally constant practice of obeying and commanding, of keeping down and keeping at a distance – that other more mysterious pathos could never have arisen, the longing for an ever new widening of distance within the soul itself, the formation of ever higher, rarer, further, more extended, more comprehensive states, in short, just the elevation of the type 'man', the continued 'self-surmounting of man', to use a moral formula in a supermoral sense. To be sure, one must not resign oneself to any humanitarian illusions about the history of the origin of an aristocratic society (that is to say, of the preliminary condition for the elevation of the type 'man'): the truth is hard. Let us acknowledge unprejudicedly how every higher civilization hitherto has *originated*! Men with a still natural nature, barbarians in every terrible sense of the word, men of prey, still in possession of unbroken strength of will and desire for power, threw themselves upon weaker, more moral, more peaceful races

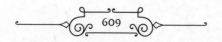

(perhaps trading or cattle-rearing communities), or upon old mellow civilizations in which the final vital force was flickering out in brilliant fireworks of wit and depravity. At the commencement, the noble caste was always the barbarian caste: their superiority did not consist first of all in their physical, but in their psychical power – they were more *complete* men (which at every point also implies the same as 'more complete beasts').

258

CORRUPTION – as the indication that anarchy threatens to break out among the instincts, and that the foundation of the emotions, called 'life', is convulsed – is something radically different according to the organization in which it manifests itself. When, for instance, an aristocracy like that of France at the beginning of the Revolution, flung away its privileges with sublime disgust and sacrificed itself to an excess of its moral sentiments, it was corruption: – it was really only the closing act of the corruption which had existed for centuries, by virtue of which that aristocracy had abdicated step by step its lordly prerogatives and lowered itself to a *function* of royalty (in the end even to its decoration and parade-dress). The essential thing, however, in a good and healthy aristocracy is that it should not regard itself as a function either of the kingship or the commonwealth, but as the *significance* and highest justification thereof – that it should therefore accept with a good conscience the sacrifice of a legion of individuals, who, *for its sake*, must be suppressed and reduced to imperfect men, to slaves and instruments. Its fundamental belief must be precisely that society is *not* allowed to exist for its own sake, but only as a foundation and scaffolding, by means of which a select class of beings may be able to elevate themselves to their higher duties, and in general to a higher *existence*: like those sun-seeking climbing plants in Java – they are called *Sipo Matador*, – which encircle an oak so long and so often with their

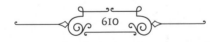

arms, until at last, high above it, but supported by it, they can unfold their tops in the open light, and exhibit their happiness.

259

TO REFRAIN mutually from injury, from violence, from exploitation, and put one's will on a par with that of others: this may result in a certain rough sense in good conduct among individuals when the necessary conditions are given (namely, the actual similarity of the individuals in amount of force and degree of worth, and their co-relation within one organization). As soon, however, as one wished to take this principle more generally, and if possible even as the *fundamental principle of society*, it would immediately disclose what it really is – namely, a Will to the *denial* of life, a principle of dissolution and decay. Here one must think profoundly to the very basis and resist all sentimental weakness: life itself is *essentially* appropriation, injury, conquest of the strange and weak, suppression, severity, obtrusion of peculiar forms, incorporation and at the least, putting it mildest, exploitation; – but why should one for ever use precisely these words on which for ages a disparaging purpose has been stamped? Even the organization within which, as was previously supposed, the individuals treat each other as equal – it takes place in every healthy aristocracy – must itself, if it be a living and not a dying organization, do all that towards other bodies, which the individuals within it refrain from doing to each other it will have to be the incarnated Will to Power, it will endeavour to grow, to gain ground, attract to itself and acquire ascendancy – not owing to any morality or immorality, but because it *lives*, and because life *is* precisely Will to Power. On no point, however, is the ordinary consciousness of Europeans more unwilling to be corrected than on this matter; people now rave everywhere, even under the guise of science, about coming conditions of society in which 'the exploiting character' is to be absent: – that sounds to my ears as if they promised to invent a mode of life which should

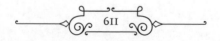

refrain from all organic functions. 'Exploitation' does not belong to a depraved, or imperfect and primitive society: it belongs to the *nature* of the living being as a primary organic function; it is a consequence of the intrinsic Will to Power, which is precisely the Will to Life. – Granting that as a theory this is a novelty – as a reality it is the *fundamental fact* of all history: let us be so far honest towards ourselves!

260

IN A tour through the many finer and coarser moralities which have hitherto prevailed or still prevail on the earth, I found certain traits recurring regularly together, and connected with one another, until finally two primary types revealed themselves to me, and a radical distinction was brought to light. There is *master-morality* and *slave-morality*, – I would at once add, however, that in all higher and mixed civilizations, there are also attempts at the reconciliation of the two moralities, but one finds still oftener the confusion and mutual misunderstanding of them, indeed sometimes their close juxtaposition – even in the same man, within one soul. The distinctions of moral values have either originated in a ruling caste, pleasantly conscious of being different from the ruled – or among the ruled class, the slaves and dependents of all sorts. In the first case, when it is the rulers who determine the conception 'good', it is the exalted, proud disposition which is regarded as the distinguishing feature, and that which determines the order of rank. The noble type of man separates from himself the beings in whom the opposite of this exalted, proud disposition displays itself: he despises them. Let it at once be noted that in this first kind of morality the antithesis 'good' and 'bad' means practically the same as 'noble' and 'despicable'; – the antithesis 'good' and 'evil' is of a different origin. The cowardly, the timid, the insignificant and those thinking merely of narrow utility are despised; moreover, also, the distrustful, with their constrained glances, the self-abasing, the dog-like kind of men who let themselves be abused, the mendicant flatterers and

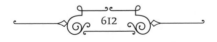

above all the liars: – it is a fundamental belief of all aristocrats that the common people are untruthful. 'We truthful ones' – the nobility in ancient Greece called themselves. It is obvious that everywhere the designations of moral value were at first applied to *men*, and were only derivatively and at a later period applied to *actions*; it is a gross mistake, therefore, when historians of morals start with questions like, 'Why have sympathetic actions been praised?' The noble type of man regards *himself* as a determiner of values; he does not require to be approved of; he passes the judgment: 'What is injurious to me is injurious in itself'; he knows that it is he himself only who confers honour on things; he is a *creator of values*. He honours whatever he recognizes in himself: such morality equals self-glorification. In the foreground there is the feeling of plenitude, of power, which seeks to overflow, the happiness of high tension, the consciousness of a wealth which would fain give and bestow: – the noble man also helps the unfortunate, but not – or scarcely – out of pity, but rather from an impulse generated by the super-abundance of power. The noble man honours in himself the powerful one, him also who has power over himself, who knows how to speak and how to keep silence, who takes pleasure in subjecting himself to severity and hardness, and has reverence for all that is severe and hard. 'Wotan placed a hard heart in my breast,' says an old Scandinavian Saga: it is thus rightly expressed from the soul of a proud Viking. Such a type of man is even proud of not being made for sympathy; the hero of the Saga therefore adds warningly: 'He who has not a hard heart when young, will never have one.' The noble and brave who think thus are the furthest removed from the morality which sees precisely in sympathy, or in acting for the good of others, or in *désintéressement*, the characteristic of the moral; faith in oneself, pride in oneself, a radical enmity and irony towards 'selflessness', belong as definitely to noble morality, as do a careless scorn and precaution in presence of sympathy and the 'warm heart'. – It is the powerful who *know* how to honour, it is their art, their domain for invention. The profound reverence for age

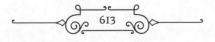

and for tradition – all law rests on this double reverence, – the belief and prejudice in favour of ancestors and unfavourable to newcomers, is typical in the morality of the powerful; and if, reversely, men of 'modern ideas' believe almost instinctively in 'progress' and the 'future', and are more and more lacking in respect for old age, the ignoble origin of these 'ideas' has complacently betrayed itself thereby. A morality of the ruling class, however, is more especially foreign and irritating to present-day taste in the sternness of its principle that one has duties only to one's equals; that one may act towards beings of a lower rank, towards all that is foreign, just as seems good to one, or 'as the heart desires', and in any case 'beyond good and evil': it is here that sympathy and similar sentiments can have a place. The ability and obligation to exercise prolonged gratitude and prolonged revenge – both only within the circle of equals, – artfulness in retaliation, *raffinement* of the idea in friendship, a certain necessity to have enemies (as outlets for the emotions of envy, quarrelsomeness, arrogance – in fact, in order to be a good *friend*): all these are typical characteristics of the noble morality, which, as has been pointed out, is not the morality of 'modern ideas', and is therefore at present difficult to realize, and also to unearth and disclose. – It is otherwise with the second type of morality, *slave-morality*. Supposing that the abused, the oppressed, the suffering, the unemancipated, the weary and those uncertain of themselves should moralize, what will be the common element in their moral estimates? Probably a pessimistic suspicion with regard to the entire situation of man will find expression, perhaps a condemnation of man, together with his situation. The slave has an unfavourable eye for the virtues of the powerful; he has a scepticism and distrust, a *refinement* of distrust of everything 'good' that is there honoured – he would fain persuade himself that the very happiness there is not genuine. On the other hand, *those* qualities which serve to alleviate the existence of sufferers are brought into prominence and flooded with light; it is here that sympathy, the kind, helping hand, the warm heart, patience, diligence,

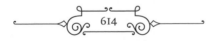

humility and friendliness attain to honour; for here these are the most useful qualities, and almost the only means of supporting the burden of existence. Slave-morality is essentially the morality of utility. Here is the seat of the origin of the famous antithesis 'good' and 'evil': – power and dangerousness are assumed to reside in the evil, a certain dreadfulness, subtlety and strength, which do not admit of being despised. According to slave-morality, therefore, the 'evil' man arouses fear; according to master-morality, it is precisely the 'good' man who arouses fear and seeks to arouse it, while the bad man is regarded as the despicable being. The contrast attains its maximum when, in accordance with the logical conse- quences of slave-morality, a shade of depreciation – it may be slight and well-intentioned – at last attaches itself to the 'good' man of this morality; because, according to the servile mode of thought, the good man must in any case be the *safe* man: he is good-natured, easily deceived, perhaps a little stupid, *un bonhomme*. Everywhere that slave-morality gains the ascendancy, language shows a tendency to approximate the significations of the words 'good' and 'stupid'. – A last fundamental difference: the desire for *freedom*, the instinct for happiness and the refinements of the feeling of liberty belong as necessarily to slave-morals and morality, as artifice and enthusiasm in reverence and devotion are the regular symp- toms of an aristocratic mode of thinking and estimating. – Hence we can understand without further detail why love *as a passion* – it is our European specialty – must absolutely be of noble origin; as is well known, its inven- tion is due to the Provençal poet-cavaliers, those brilliant, ingenious men of the '*gai saber*', to whom Europe owes so much, and almost owes itself.

261

VANITY is one of the things which are perhaps most difficult for a noble man to understand: he will be tempted to deny it, where another kind of man thinks he sees it self-evidently. The problem for him is to represent to his mind beings who seek to arouse a good opinion

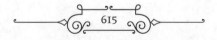

of themselves which they themselves do not possess – and consequently also do not 'deserve', – and who yet *believe* in this good opinion afterwards. This seems to him on the one hand such bad taste and so self-disrespectful, and on the other hand so grotesquely unreasonable, that he would like to consider vanity an exception, and is doubtful about it in most cases when it is spoken of. He will say, for instance: 'I may be mistaken about my value, and on the other hand may nevertheless demand that my value should be acknowledged by others precisely as I rate it: – that, however, is not vanity (but self-conceit, or, in most cases, that which is called "humility", and also "modesty").' Or he will even say: 'For many reasons I can delight in the good opinion of others, perhaps because I love and honour them, and rejoice in all their joys, perhaps also because their good opinion endorses and strengthens my belief in my own good opinion, perhaps because the good opinion of others, even in cases where I do not share it, is useful to me, or gives promise of usefulness: – all this, however, is not vanity.' The man of noble character must first bring it home forcibly to his mind, especially with the aid of history, that, from time immemorial, in all social strata in any way dependent, the ordinary man *was* only that which he *passed for*: – not being at all accustomed to fix values, he did not assign even to himself any other value than that which his master assigned to him (it is the peculiar *right of masters* to create values). It may be looked upon as the result of an extraordinary atavism, that the ordinary man, even at present, is still always *waiting* for an opinion about himself, and then instinctively submitting himself to it; yet by no means only to a 'good' opinion, but also to a bad and unjust one (think, for instance, of the greater part of the self-appreciations and self-depreciations which believing women learn from their confessors, and which in general the believing Christian learns from his Church). In fact, conformably to the slow rise of the democratic social order (and its cause, the blending of the blood of masters and slaves),

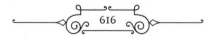

the originally noble and rare impulse of the masters to assign a value to themselves and to 'think well' of themselves, will now be more and more encouraged and extended; but it has at all times an older, ampler and more radically ingrained propensity opposed to it – and in the phenomenon of 'vanity' this older propensity overmasters the younger. The vain person rejoices over *every* good opinion which he hears about himself (quite apart from the point of view of its usefulness, and equally regardless of its truth or falsehood), just as he suffers from every bad opinion: for he subjects himself to both, he *feels* himself subjected to both, by that oldest instinct of subjection which breaks forth in him. – It is 'the slave' in the vain man's blood, the remains of the slave's craftiness – and how much of the 'slave' is still left in woman, for instance! – which seeks to *seduce* to good opinions of itself; it is the slave, too, who immediately afterwards falls prostrate himself before these opinions, as though he had not called them forth. – And to repeat it again: vanity is an atavism.

262

A *SPECIES* originates, and a type becomes established and strong in the long struggle with essentially constant *unfavourable* conditions. On the other hand, it is known by the experience of breeders that species which receive superabundant nourishment, and in general a surplus of protection and care, immediately tend in the most marked way to develop variations, and are fertile in prodigies and monstrosities (also in monstrous vices). Now look at an aristocratic commonwealth, say an ancient Greek *polis*, or Venice, as a voluntary or involuntary contrivance for the purpose of *rearing* human beings; there are there men beside one another, thrown upon their own resources, who want to make their species prevail, chiefly because they *must* prevail, or else run the terrible danger of being exterminated. The favour, the superabundance, the protection are there lacking under which variations are fostered; the species needs itself as species, as something which, precisely by virtue of its hardness, its uniformity and simplicity of structure, can in general prevail and make itself permanent in constant struggle with its neighbours, or with rebellious or rebellion-threatening vassals. The most varied experience teaches it what are the qualities to which it principally owes the fact that it still exists, in spite of all Gods and men, and has hitherto been victorious: these qualities it calls virtues, and these virtues alone it develops to maturity. It does so with severity, indeed it desires severity; every aristocratic morality is intolerant in the education of youth, in the control of women, in the marriage customs, in the relations of old and young, in the penal laws (which have an eye only for the degenerating): it counts intolerance itself among the virtues, under the name of 'justice'. A type with few, but very marked features, a species of severe, warlike, wisely silent, reserved and reticent men (and as such, with the most delicate sensibility for the charm and *nuances* of society) is thus established, unaffected by the vicissitudes of generations; the constant struggle with uniform *unfavourable* conditions is, as already remarked, the cause of a type becoming stable and hard. Finally, however, a happy state of things results, the enormous tension is relaxed; there are perhaps no more enemies among the neighbouring peoples, and the means of life, even of the enjoyment of life, are present in superabundance. With one stroke the bond and constraint of the old discipline severs: it is no longer regarded as necessary, as a condition of existence – if it would continue, it can only do so as a form of *luxury*, as an archaizing *taste*. Variations, whether they be deviations (into the higher, finer and rarer), or deteriorations and monstrosities, appear suddenly on the scene in the greatest exuberance and splendour; the individual dares to be individual and detach himself. At this turning-point of history there manifest themselves, side by side, and often mixed and entangled together, a magnificent, manifold, virgin-forest-like up-growth and

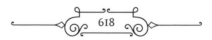

up-striving, a kind of *tropical tempo* in the rivalry of growth, and an extraordinary decay and self-destruction, owing to the savagely opposing and seemingly exploding egoisms, which strive with one another 'for sun and light', and can no longer assign any limit, restraint or forbearance for themselves by means of the hitherto existing morality. It was this morality itself which piled up the strength so enormously, which bent the bow in so threatening a manner: – it is now 'out of date', it is getting 'out of date'. The dangerous and disquieting point has been reached when the greater, more manifold, more comprehensive life *is lived beyond* the old morality; the 'individual' stands out, and is obliged to have recourse to his own law-giving, his own arts and artifices for self-preservation, self-elevation and self-deliverance. Nothing but new 'Whys', nothing but new 'Hows', no common formulas any longer, misunderstanding and disregard in league with each other, decay, deterioration and the loftiest desires frightfully entangled, the genius of the race overflowing from all the cornucopias of good and bad, a portentous simultaneousness of Spring and Autumn, full of new charms and mysteries peculiar to the fresh, still inexhausted, still unwearied corruption. Danger is again present, the mother of morality, great danger; this time shifted into the individual, into the neighbour and friend, into the street, into their own child, into their own heart, into all the most personal and secret recesses of their desires and volitions. What will the moral philosophers who appear at this time have to preach? They discover, these sharp onlookers and loafers, that the end is quickly approaching, that everything around them decays and produces decay, that nothing will endure until the day after tomorrow, except one species of man, the incurably *mediocre*. The mediocre alone have a prospect of continuing and propagating themselves – they will be the men of the future, the sole survivors; 'be like them! become mediocre!' is now the only morality which has still a significance, which still obtains a hearing.

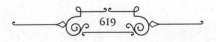

– But it is difficult to preach this morality of mediocrity! it can never avow what it is and what it desires! it has to talk of moderation and dignity and duty and brotherly love – it will have difficulty *in concealing its irony*!

263

THERE is an *instinct for rank*, which more than anything else is already the sign of a *high* rank; there is a *delight* in the *nuances* of reverence which leads one to infer noble origin and habits. The refinement, goodness and loftiness of a soul are put to a perilous test when something passes by that is of the highest rank, but is not yet protected by the awe of authority from obtrusive touches and incivilities: something that goes its way like a living touchstone, undistinguished, undiscovered and tentative, perhaps voluntarily veiled and disguised. He whose task and practice it is to investigate souls, will avail himself of many varieties of this very art to determine the ultimate value of a soul, the unalterable, innate order of rank to which it belongs: he will test it by its *instinct for reverence. Différence engendre haine*: the vulgarity of many a nature spurts up suddenly like dirty water, when any holy vessel, any jewel from closed shrines, any book bearing the marks of great destiny, is brought before it; while on the other hand, there is an involuntary silence, a hesitation of the eye, a cessation of all gestures, by which it is indicated that a soul *feels* the nearness of what is worthiest of respect. The way in which, on the whole, the reverence for the *Bible* has hitherto been maintained in Europe, is perhaps the best example of discipline and refinement of manners which Europe owes to Christianity: books of such profoundness and supreme significance require for their protection an external tyranny of authority, in order to acquire the *period* of thousands of years which is necessary to exhaust and unriddle them. Much has been achieved when the sentiment has been at last instilled into the masses (the shallow-pates and the boobies

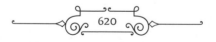

of every kind) that they are not allowed to touch everything, that there are holy experiences before which they must take off their shoes and keep away the unclean hand – it is almost their highest advance towards humanity. On the contrary, in the so-called cultured classes, the believers in 'modern ideas', nothing is perhaps so repulsive as their lack of shame, the easy insolence of eye and hand with which they touch, taste and finger everything; and it is possible that even yet there is more *relative* nobility of taste, and more tact for reverence among the people, among the lower classes of the people, especially among peasants, than among the newspaper-reading *demimonde* of intellect, the cultured class.

264

IT CANNOT be effaced from a man's soul what his ancestors have preferably and most constantly done: whether they were perhaps diligent economizers attached to a desk and a cash-box, modest and citizen-like in their desires, modest also in their virtues; or whether they were accustomed to commanding from morning till night, fond of rude pleasures and probably of still ruder duties and responsibilities; or whether, finally, at one time or another, they have sacrificed old privileges of birth and possession, in order to live wholly for their faith – for their 'God', – as men of an inexorable and sensitive conscience, which blushes at every compromise. It is quite impossible for a man *not* to have the qualities and predilections of his parents and ancestors in his constitution, whatever appearances may suggest to the contrary. This is the problem of race. Granted that one knows something of the parents, it is admissible to draw a conclusion about the child: any kind of offensive incontinence, any kind of sordid envy, or of clumsy self-vaunting – the three things which together have constituted the genuine plebeian type in all times – such must pass over to the child, as surely as bad blood; and with the help of the best education and culture one will only

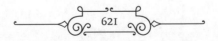

succeed in *deceiving* with regard to such heredity. – And what else does education and culture try to do nowadays! In our very democratic, or rather, very plebeian age, 'education' and 'culture' *must* be essentially the art of deceiving – deceiving with regard to origin, with regard to the inherited plebeianism in body and soul. An educator who nowadays preached truthfulness above everything else, and called out constantly to his pupils: 'Be true! Be natural! Show yourselves as you are!' – even such a virtuous and sincere ass would learn in a short time to have recourse to the *furca* of Horace, *naturam expellere*: with what results? 'Plebeianism' *usque recurret.*[*]

265

AT THE risk of displeasing innocent ears, I submit that egoism belongs to the essence of a noble soul, I mean the unalterable belief that to a being such as 'we', other beings must naturally be in subjection, and have to sacrifice themselves. The noble soul accepts the fact of his egoism without question, and also without consciousness of harshness, constraint or arbitrariness therein, but rather as something that may have its basis in the primary law of things: – if he sought a designation for it he would say: 'It is justice itself'. He acknowledges under certain circumstances, which made him hesitate at first, that there are other equally privileged ones; as soon as he has settled this question of rank, he moves among those equals and equally privileged ones with the same assurance, as regards modesty and delicate respect, which he enjoys in intercourse with himself – in accordance with an innate heavenly mechanism which all the stars understand. It is an *additional* instance of his egoism, this artfulness and self-limitation in intercourse with his equals – every star is a similar egoist; he honours *himself* in them, and in the rights which he concedes to them, he has no doubt that the exchange of honours and rights, as the *essence* of all intercourse,

* Horace's *Epistles*, I. x. 24.

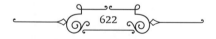

belongs also to the natural condition of things. The noble soul gives as he takes, prompted by the passionate and sensitive instinct of requital, which is at the root of his nature. The notion of 'favour' has, *inter pares*, neither significance nor good repute; there may be a sublime way of letting gifts as it were light upon one from above, and of drinking them thirstily like dew-drops; but for those arts and displays the noble soul has no aptitude. His egoism hinders him here: in general, he looks 'aloft' unwillingly – he looks either *forward*, horizontally and deliberately, or downwards – *he knows that he is on a height.*

266

'ONE can only truly esteem him who does not *look out for* himself.' – Goethe to Rath Schlosser.

267

THE Chinese have a proverb which mothers even teach their children: 'S*iao-sin*' ('*make thy heart small*'). This is the essentially fundamental tendency in latter-day civilizations. I have no doubt that an ancient Greek, also, would first of all remark the self-dwarfing in us Europeans of today – in this respect alone we should immediately be 'distasteful' to him.

268

WHAT, after all, is ignobleness? – Words are vocal symbols for ideas; ideas, however, are more or less definite mental symbols for frequently returning and concurring sensations, for groups of sensations. It is not sufficient to use the same words in order to understand one another: we must also employ the same words for the same kind of internal experiences, we must in the end have experiences *in common*. On this account the people of one nation understand one another better than those belonging to different nations, even when they use the same

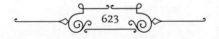

language; or rather, when people have lived long together under similar conditions (of climate, soil, danger, requirement, toil) there *originates* therefrom an entity that 'understands itself' – namely, a nation. In all souls a like number of frequently recurring experiences have gained the upper hand over those occurring more rarely: about these matters people understand one another rapidly and always more rapidly – the history of language is the history of a process of abbreviation; on the basis of this quick comprehension people always unite closer and closer. The greater the danger, the greater is the need of agreeing quickly and readily about what is necessary; not to misunderstand one another in danger – that is what cannot at all be dispensed with in intercourse. Also in all loves and friendships one has the experience that nothing of the kind continues when the discovery has been made that in using the same words, one of the two parties has feelings, thoughts, intuitions, wishes or fears different from those of the other. (The fear of the 'eternal misunderstanding': that is the good genius which so often keeps persons of different sexes from too hasty attachments, to which sense and heart prompt them – and *not* some Schopenhauerian 'genius of the species'!) Whichever groups of sensations within a soul awaken most readily, begin to speak, and give the word of command – these decide as to the general order of rank of its values, and determine ultimately its list of desirable things. A man's estimates of value betray something of the *structure* of his soul, and wherein it sees its conditions of life, its intrinsic needs. Supposing now that necessity has from all time drawn together only such men as could express similar requirements and similar experiences by similar symbols, it results on the whole that the easy *communicability* of need, which implies ultimately the undergoing only of average and *common* experiences, must have been the most potent of all the forces which have hitherto operated upon mankind. The more similar, the more ordinary people, have always had and are still having the advantage; the more select, more refined, more unique and difficultly

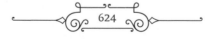

comprehensible, are liable to stand alone; they succumb to accidents in their isolation, and seldom propagate themselves. One must appeal to immense opposing forces, in order to thwart this natural, all-too-natural *progressus in simile*, the evolution of man to the similar, the ordinary, the average, the gregarious – to the *ignoble* – !

269

THE more a psychologist – a born, an unavoidable psychologist and soul-diviner – turns his attention to the more select cases and individuals, the greater is his danger of being suffocated by sympathy: he *needs* sternness and cheerfulness more than any other man. For the corruption, the ruination of higher men, of the more unusually constituted souls, is in fact, the rule: it is dreadful to have such a rule always before one's eyes. The manifold torment of the psychologist who has discovered this ruination, who discovers once, and then discovers *almost* repeatedly throughout all history, this universal inner 'desperateness' of higher men, this eternal 'too late!' in every sense – may perhaps one day be the cause of his turning with bitterness against his own lot, and of his making an attempt at self-destruction – of his 'going to ruin' himself. One may perceive in almost every psychologist a tell-tale inclination for delightful intercourse with commonplace and well-ordered men: the fact is thereby disclosed that he always requires healing, that he needs a sort of flight and forgetfulness, away from what his insight and incisiveness – from what his 'business' – has laid upon his conscience. The fear of his memory is peculiar to him. He is easily silenced by the judgment of others; he hears with unmoved countenance how people honour, admire, love and glorify, where he has *perceived* – or he even conceals his silence by expressly assenting to some plausible opinion. Perhaps the paradox of his situation becomes so dreadful that, precisely where he has learnt *great sympathy*, together with *great contempt*, the multitude, the educated and the visionaries, have on their part learnt great reverence – reverence for 'great men'

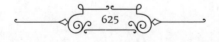

and marvellous animals, for the sake of whom one blesses and honours the fatherland, the earth, the dignity of mankind and one's own self, to whom one points the young, and in view of whom one educates them. And who knows but in all great instances hitherto just the same happened: that the multitude worshipped a God, and that the 'God' was only a poor sacrificial animal! *Success* has always been the greatest liar – and the 'work' itself is a success; the great statesman, the conqueror, the discoverer, are disguised in their creations until they are unrecognizable; the 'work' of the artist, of the philosopher, only invents him who has created it, is *reputed* to have created it; the 'great men', as they are reverenced, are poor little fictions composed afterwards; in the world of historical values spurious coinage *prevails*. Those great poets, for example, such as Byron, Musset, Poe, Leopardi, Kleist, Gogol (I do not venture to mention much greater names, but I have them in my mind), as they now appear, and were perhaps obliged to be: men of the moment, enthusiastic, sensuous and childish, light-minded and impulsive in their trust and distrust; with souls in which usually some flaw has to be concealed; often taking revenge with their works for an internal defilement, often seeking forgetfulness in their soaring from a too true memory, often lost in the mud and almost in love with it, until they become like the will-o'-the-wisps around the swamps, and *pretend to be* stars – the people then call them idealists, – often struggling with protracted disgust, with an ever-reappearing phantom of disbelief, which makes them cold, and obliges them to languish for *gloria* and devour 'faith as it is' out of the hands of intoxicated adula-tors: – what a *torment* these great artists are and the so-called higher men in general, to him who has once found them out! It is thus conceivable that it is just from woman – who is clairvoyant in the world of suffering, and also unfortunately eager to help and save to an extent far beyond her powers – that *they* have learnt so readily those outbreaks of boundless devoted *sympathy*, which the multitude, above all the reverent multitude, do not understand, and overwhelm with prying and self-gratifying inter-

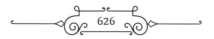

pretations. This sympathizing invariably deceives itself as to its power; woman would like to believe that love can do *everything* – it is the *superstition* peculiar to her. Alas, he who knows the heart finds out how poor, helpless, pretentious and blundering even the best and deepest love is – he finds that it rather *destroys* than saves! – It is possible that under the holy fable and travesty of the life of Jesus there is hidden one of the most painful cases of the martyrdom of *knowledge about love*: the martyrdom of the most innocent and most craving heart, that never had enough of any human love, that *demanded* love, that demanded inexorably and frantically to be loved and nothing else, with terrible outbursts against those who refused him their love; the story of a poor soul insatiated and insatiable in love, that had to invent hell to send thither those who *would not* love him – and that at last, enlightened about human love, had to invent a God who is entire love, entire *capacity* for love – who takes pity on human love, because it is so paltry, so ignorant! He who has such sentiments, he who has such *knowledge* about love – *seeks* for death! – But why should one deal with such painful matters? Provided, of course, that one is not obliged to do so.

270

THE intellectual haughtiness and loathing of every man who has suffered deeply – it almost determines the order of rank *how* deeply men can suffer – the chilling certainty, with which he is thoroughly imbued and coloured, that by virtue of his suffering he *knows more* than the shrewdest and wisest can ever know, that he has been familiar with, and 'at home' in, many distant, dreadful worlds of which '*you* know nothing'! – this silent intellectual haughtiness of the sufferer, this pride of the elect of knowledge, of the 'initiated', of the almost sacrificed, finds all forms of disguise necessary to protect itself from contact with officious and sympathizing hands, and in general from all that is not its equal in suffering. Profound suffering makes noble: it separates. – One of the

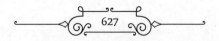

most refined forms of disguise is Epicurism, along with a certain osten-
tatious boldness of taste, which takes suffering lightly, and puts itself
on the defensive against all that is sorrowful and profound. They are
'gay men' who make use of gaiety, because they are misunderstood on
account of it – they *wish* to be misunderstood. There are 'scientific
minds' who make use of science, because it gives a gay appearance, and
because scientificness leads to the conclusion that a person is superficial
– they *wish* to mislead to a false conclusion. There are free insolent
minds which would fain conceal and deny that they are broken, proud,
incurable hearts (the cynicism of Hamlet – the case of Galiani); and
occasionally folly itself is the mask of an unfortunate *over-assured* knowledge. – From which it follows that it is the part of a more refined
humanity to have reverence 'for the mask', and not to make use of
psychology and curiosity in the wrong place.

271

THAT which separates two men most profoundly is a different sense
and grade of purity. What does it matter about all their honesty and
reciprocal usefulness, what does it matter about all their mutual good-
will: the fact still remains – they 'cannot smell each other!' The highest
instinct for purity places him who is affected with it in the most extraordinary and dangerous isolation, as a saint: for it is just holiness – the
highest spiritualization of the instinct in question. Any kind of cognizance
of an indescribable excess in the joy of the bath, any kind of ardour or
thirst which perpetually impels the soul out of night into the morning,
and out of gloom, out of 'affliction' into clearness, brightness, depth
and refinement: – just as much as such a tendency *distinguishes* – it is a
noble tendency – it also *separates*. – The pity of the saint is pity for the
filth of the human, all-too-human. And there are grades and heights
where pity itself is regarded by him as impurity, as filth.

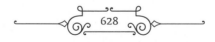

272

SIGNS of nobility: never to think of lowering our duties to the rank of duties for everybody; to be unwilling to renounce or to share our responsibilities; to count our prerogatives, and the exercise of them, among our *duties*.

273

A MAN who strives after great things, looks upon everyone whom he encounters on his way either as a means of advance, or a delay and hindrance – or as a temporary resting-place. His peculiar lofty *bounty* to his fellow-men is only possible when he attains his elevation and dominates. Impatience, and the consciousness of being always condemned to comedy up to that time – for even strife is a comedy, and conceals the end, as every means does – spoil all intercourse for him; this kind of man is acquainted with solitude, and what is most poisonous in it.

274

THE Problem of those who Wait. – Happy chances are necessary, and many incalculable elements, in order that a higher man in whom the solution of a problem is dormant, may yet take action, or 'break forth', as one might say – at the right moment. On an average it *does not* happen; and in all corners of the earth there are waiting ones sitting who hardly know to what extent they are waiting, and still less that they wait in vain. Occasionally, too, the waking call comes too late – the chance which gives 'permission' to take action – when their best youth, and strength for action have been used up in sitting still; and how many a one, just as he 'sprang up', has found with horror that his limbs are benumbed and his spirits are now too heavy! 'It is too late', he has said to himself – and has become self-distrustful and henceforth forever useless. – In the domain of genius, may not the 'Raphael without hands'

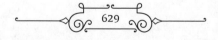

(taking the expression in its widest sense) perhaps not be the exception, but the rule? – Perhaps genius is by no means so rare: but rather the five hundred *hands* which it requires in order to tyrannize over the καιρὸς 'the right time' – in order to take chance by the forelock!

275

HE WHO does not *wish* to see the height of a man, looks all the more sharply at what is low in him, and in the foreground – and thereby betrays himself.

276

IN ALL kinds of injury and loss the lower and coarser soul is better off than the nobler soul: the dangers of the latter must be greater, the probability that it will come to grief and perish is in fact immense, considering the multiplicity of the conditions of its existence. – In a lizard a finger grows again which has been lost; not so in man. –

277

IT IS too bad! Always the old story! When a man has finished building his house, he finds that he has learnt unawares something which he *ought* absolutely to have known before he – began to build. The eternal, fatal 'Too late!' The melancholia of everything *completed* – !

278

– WANDERER, who art thou? I see thee follow thy path without scorn, without love, with unfathomable eyes, wet and sad as a plummet which has returned to the light insatiated out of every depth – what did it seek down there? – with a bosom that never sighs, with lips that conceal their loathing, with a hand which only slowly grasps: who art thou? what hast thou done? Rest thee here: this place has hospitality for everyone – refresh thyself! And whoever thou art, what is it that

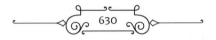

now pleases thee? What will serve to refresh thee? Only name it, whatever I have I offer thee! 'To refresh me? To refresh me? Oh, thou prying one, what sayest thou! But give me, I pray thee –' What? what? Speak out! 'Another mask! A second mask!'

279

MEN of profound sadness betray themselves when they are happy: they have a mode of seizing upon happiness as though they would choke and strangle it, out of jealousy – ah, they know only too well that it will flee from them!

280

'BAD! Bad! What? Does he not – go back?' Yes! But you misunderstand him when you complain about it. He goes back like everyone who is about to make a great spring.

281

– 'WILL people believe it of me? But I insist that they believe it of me: I have always thought very unsatisfactorily of myself and about myself, only in very rare cases, only compulsorily, always without delight in "the subject", ready to digress from "myself", and always without faith in the result, owing to an unconquerable distrust of the *possibility* of self-knowledge, which has led me so far as to feel a *contradictio in adjecto* even in the idea of "direct knowledge" which theorists allow themselves: – this matter of fact is almost the most certain thing I know about myself. There must be a sort of repugnance in me to *believe* anything definite about myself. – Is there perhaps some enigma therein? Probably; but fortunately nothing for my own teeth. – Perhaps it betrays the species to which I belong? – but not to myself, as is sufficiently agreeable to me.'

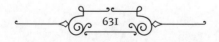

282

– 'BUT what has happened to you?' – 'I do not know,' he said, hesitatingly; 'perhaps the Harpies have flown over my table.' – It sometimes happens nowadays that a gentle, sober, retiring man becomes suddenly mad, breaks the plates, upsets the table, shrieks, raves and shocks everybody – and finally withdraws, ashamed, and raging at himself – whither? for what purpose? To famish apart? To suffocate with his memories? – To him who has the desires of a lofty and dainty soul, and only seldom finds his table laid and his food prepared, the danger will always be great – nowadays, however, it is extraordinarily so. Thrown into the midst of a noisy and plebeian age, with which he does not like to eat out of the same dish, he may readily perish of hunger and thirst – or, should he nevertheless finally 'fall to', of sudden nausea. – We have probably all sat at tables to which we did not belong; and precisely the most spiritual of us, who are most difficult to nourish, know the dangerous *dyspepsia* which originates from a sudden insight and disillusionment about our food and our messmates – the *after-dinner nausea*.

283

IF ONE wishes to praise at all, it is a delicate and at the same time a noble self-control, to praise only where one *does not* agree – otherwise in fact one would praise oneself, which is contrary to good taste: – a self-control, to be sure, which offers excellent opportunity and provocation to constant *misunderstanding*. To be able to allow oneself this veritable luxury of taste and morality, one must not live among intellectual imbeciles, but rather among men whose misunderstandings and mistakes amuse by their refinement – or one will have to pay dearly for it! – 'He praises me, *therefore* he acknowledges me to be right' – this asinine method of inference spoils half of the life of us recluses, for it brings the asses into our neighbourhood and friendship.

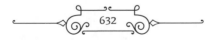

284

TO LIVE in a vast and proud tranquility; always beyond… To have, or not to have, one's emotions, one's For and Against, according to choice; to lower oneself to them for hours; to *seat* oneself on them as upon horses, and often as upon asses: – for one must know how to make use of their stupidity as well as of their fire. To conserve one's three hundred foregrounds; also one's black spectacles: for there are circumstances when nobody must look into our eyes, still less into our 'motives'. And to choose for company that roguish and cheerful vice, politeness. And to remain master of one's four virtues, courage, insight, sympathy and solitude. For solitude is a virtue with us, as a sublime bent and bias to purity, which divines that in the contact of man and man – 'in society' – it must be unavoidably impure. All society makes one somehow, somewhere, or sometime – 'commonplace'.

285

THE greatest events and thoughts – the greatest thoughts, however, are the greatest events – are longest in being comprehended: the generations which are contemporary with them do not *experience* such events – they live past them. Something happens there as in the realm of stars. The light of the furthest stars is longest in reaching man; and before it has arrived man *denies* – that there are stars there. 'How many centuries does a mind require to be understood?'– that is also a standard, one also makes a gradation of rank and an etiquette there-with, such as is necessary for mind and for star.

286

'HERE is the prospect free, the mind exalted.'* – But there is a reverse kind of man, who is also upon a height, and has also a free prospect – but looks *downwards*.

* Goethe's *Faust*, Part II, Act V. The words of Dr Marianus.

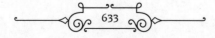

287

– WHAT is noble? What does the word 'noble' still mean for us nowadays? How does the noble man betray himself, how is he recognized under this heavy overcast sky of the commencing plebeianism, by which everything is rendered opaque and leaden? – It is not his actions which establish his claim – actions are always ambiguous, always inscrutable; neither is it his 'works.' One finds nowadays among artists and scholars plenty of those who betray by their works that a profound longing for nobleness impels them; but this very *need of* nobleness is radically different from the needs of the noble soul itself, and is in fact the eloquent and dangerous sign of the lack thereof. It is not the works, but the *belief* which is here decisive and determines the order of rank – to employ once more an old religious formula with a new and deeper meaning – it is some fundamental certainty which a noble soul has about itself, something which is not to be sought, is not to be found and perhaps, also, is not to be lost. – *The noble soul has reverence for itself.* –

288

THERE are men who are unavoidably intellectual, let them turn and twist themselves as they will, and hold their hands before their treacherous eyes – as though the hand were not a betrayer; it always comes out at last that they have something which they hide – namely, intellect. One of the subtlest means of deceiving, at least as long as possible, and of successfully representing oneself to be stupider than one really is – which in everyday life is often as desirable as an umbrella, – is called *enthusiasm*, including what belongs to it, for instance, virtue. For as Galiani said, who was obliged to know it: *vertu est enthousiasme.*

289

IN THE writings of a recluse one always hears something of the echo of the wilderness, something of the murmuring tones and timid

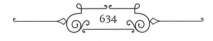

vigilance of solitude; in his strongest words, even in his cry itself, there sounds a new and more dangerous kind of silence, of concealment. He who has sat day and night, from year's end to year's end, alone with his soul in familiar discord and discourse, he who has become a cave-bear, or a treasure seeker, or a treasure guardian and dragon in his cave – it may be a labyrinth, but can also be a goldmine – his ideas themselves eventually acquire a twilight colour of their own, and an odour, as much of the depth as of the mould, something uncommunicative and repulsive, which blows chilly upon every passer-by. The recluse does not believe that a philosopher – supposing that a philosopher has always in the first place been a recluse – ever expressed his actual and ultimate opinions in books: are not books written precisely to hide what is in us? – indeed, he will doubt whether a philosopher *can* have 'ultimate and actual' opinions at all; whether behind every cave in him there is not, and must necessarily be, a still deeper cave: an ampler, stranger, richer world beyond the surface, an abyss behind every bottom, beneath every 'foundation'. Every philosophy is a foreground philosophy – this is a recluse's verdict: 'There is something arbitrary in the fact that the *philosopher* came to a stand here, took a retrospect and looked around; that he *here* laid his spade aside and did not dig any deeper – there is also something suspicious in it.' Every philosophy also *conceals* a philosophy; every opinion is also a *lurking-place*, every word is also a *mask*.

290

EVERY deep thinker is more afraid of being understood than of being misunderstood. The latter perhaps wounds his vanity; but the former wounds his heart, his sympathy, which always says: 'Ah, why would you also have as hard a time of it as I have?'

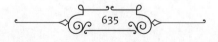

291

MAN, a *complex*, mendacious, artful and inscrutable animal, uncanny to the other animals by his artifice and sagacity, rather than by his strength, has invented the good conscience in order finally to enjoy his soul as something *simple*; and the whole of morality is a long, audacious falsification, by virtue of which generally enjoyment at the sight of the soul becomes possible. From this point of view there is perhaps much more in the conception of 'art' than is generally believed.

292

A PHILOSOPHER: that is a man who constantly experiences, sees, hears, suspects, hopes and dreams extraordinary things; who is struck by his own thoughts as if they came from the outside, from above and below, as a species of events and lightning flashes *peculiar to him*; who is perhaps himself a storm pregnant with new lightnings; a portentous man, around whom there is always rumbling and mumbling and gaping and something uncanny going on. A philosopher: alas, a being who often runs away from himself, is often afraid of himself – but whose curiosity always makes him 'come to himself' again.

293

A MAN who says: 'I like that, I take it for my own, and mean to guard and protect it from everyone'; a man who can conduct a case, carry out a resolution, remain true to an opinion, keep hold of a woman, punish and overthrow insolence; a man who has his indignation and his sword, and to whom the weak, the suffering, the oppressed and even the animals willingly submit and naturally belong; in short, a man who is a *master* by nature – when such a man has sympathy, well! *That* sympathy has value! But of what account is the sympathy of those who suffer! Or of those even who preach sympathy! There is nowadays, throughout almost the whole of Europe, a sickly irritability and sensi-

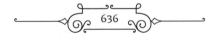

tiveness towards pain, and also a repulsive irrestrainableness in complaining, an effeminizing, which, with the aid of religion and philosophical nonsense, seeks to deck itself out as something superior – there is a regular cult of suffering. The *unmanliness* of that which is called 'sympathy' by such groups of visionaries, is always, I believe, the first thing that strikes the eye. – One must resolutely and radically taboo this latest form of bad taste; and finally I wish people to put the good amulet, '*gai saber*' ('gay science', in ordinary language), on heart and neck, as a protection against it.

294

THE Olympian Vice. – Despite the philosopher who, as a genuine Englishman, tried to bring laughter into bad repute in all thinking minds – 'Laughing is a bad infirmity of human nature, which every thinking mind will strive to overcome' (Hobbes), – I would even allow myself to rank philosophers according to the quality of their laughing – up to those who are capable of *golden* laughter. And supposing that Gods also philosophize, which I am strongly inclined to believe, owing to many reasons – I have no doubt that they also know how to laugh thereby in an overman-like and new fashion – and at the expense of all serious things! Gods are fond of ridicule: it seems that they cannot refrain from laughter even in holy matters.

295

THE genius of the heart, as that great mysterious one possesses it, the tempter-god and born rat-catcher of consciences, whose voice can descend into the netherworld of every soul, who neither speaks a word nor casts a glance in which there may not be some motive or touch of allurement, to whose perfection it pertains that he knows how to appear, – not as he is, but in a guise which acts as an *additional* constraint on his followers to press ever closer to him, to follow him more

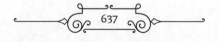

cordially and thoroughly; – the genius of the heart, which imposes silence and attention on everything loud and self-conceited, which smoothes rough souls and makes them taste a new longing – to lie placid as a mirror, that the deep heavens may be reflected in them; – the genius of the heart, which teaches the clumsy and too hasty hand to hesitate, and to grasp more delicately; which scents the hidden and forgotten treasure, the drop of goodness and sweet spirituality under thick dark ice, and is a divining-rod for every grain of gold, long buried and imprisoned in mud and sand; the genius of the heart, from contact with which everyone goes away richer; not favoured or surprised, not as though gratified and oppressed by the good things of others; but richer in himself, newer than before, broken up, blown upon and sounded by a thawing wind; more uncertain, perhaps, more delicate, more fragile, more bruised, but full of hopes which as yet lack names, full of a new will and current, full of a new ill-will and counter-current... but what am I doing, my friends? Of whom am I talking to you? Have I forgotten myself so far that I have not even told you his name? Unless it be that you have already divined of your own accord who this questionable God and spirit is, that wishes to be *praised* in such a manner? For, as it happens to everyone who from childhood onward has always been on his legs, and in foreign lands, I have also encountered on my path many strange and dangerous spirits; above all, however, and again and again, the one of whom I have just spoken: in fact, no less a personage than the god *Dionysus*, the great equivocator and tempter, to whom, as you know, I once offered in all secrecy and reverence my first-fruits – the last, as it seems to me, who has offered a *sacrifice* to him, for I have found no one who could understand what I was then doing. In the meantime, however, I have learned much, far too much, about the philosophy of this god, and, as I said, from mouth to mouth – I, the last disciple and initiate of the god Dionysus: and perhaps I might at last begin to

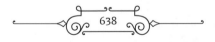

give you, my friends, as far as I am allowed, a little taste of this philosophy? In a hushed voice, as is but seemly: for it has to do with much that is secret, new, strange, wonderful and uncanny. The very fact that Dionysus is a philosopher, and that therefore gods also philosophize, seems to me a novelty which is not unensnaring, and might perhaps arouse suspicion precisely among philosophers; – among you, my friends, there is less to be said against it, except that it comes too late and not at the right time; for, as it has been disclosed to me, you are loth nowadays to believe in God and gods. It may happen, too, that in the frankness of my story I must go further than is agreeable to the strict usages of your ears? Certainly the god in question went further, very much further, in such dialogues, and was always many paces ahead of me… Indeed, if it were allowed, I should have to give him, according to human usage, fine ceremonious titles of lustre and merit, I should have to extol his courage as investigator and discoverer, his fearless honesty, truthfulness and love of wisdom. But such a god does not know what to do with all that respectable trumpery and pomp. 'Keep that', he would say, 'for thyself and those like thee, and whoever else require it! I – have no reason to cover my nakedness!' One suspects that this kind of divinity and philosopher perhaps lacks shame? – He once said: 'Under certain circumstances I love mankind' – and referred thereby to Ariadne, who was present; 'in my opinion man is an agreeable, brave, inventive animal, that has not his equal upon earth, he makes his way even through all labyrinths. I like man, and often think how I can still further advance him, and make him stronger, more evil and more profound.' – 'Stronger, more evil and more profound?' I asked in horror. 'Yes', he said again, 'stronger, more evil and more profound; also more beautiful' – and thereby the tempter-god smiled with his halcyon smile, as though he had just paid some charming compliment. One here sees at once that it is not only shame that this divinity lacks; – and in general there are good grounds for

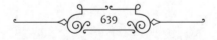

supposing that in some things the gods could all of them come to us men for instruction. We men are – more human. –

296

ALAS! what are you, after all, my written and painted thoughts! Not long ago you were so variegated, young and malicious, so full of thorns and secret spices, that you made me sneeze and laugh – and now? You have already doffed your novelty, and some of you, I fear, are ready to become truths, so immortal do they look, so pathetically honest, so tedious! And was it ever otherwise? What then do we write and paint, we mandarins with Chinese brush, we immortalizers of things which *lend* themselves to writing, what are we alone capable of painting? Alas, only that which is just about to fade and begins to lose its odour! Alas, only exhausted and departing storms and belated yellow senti-ments! Alas, only birds strayed and fatigued by flight, which now let themselves be captured with the hand – with *our* hand! We immortalize what cannot live and fly much longer, things only which are exhausted and mellow! And it is only for your *afternoon*, you, my written and painted thoughts, for which alone I have colours, many colours, perhaps, many variegated softenings, and fifty yellows and browns and greens and reds; – but nobody will divine thereby how ye looked in your morning, you sudden sparks and marvels of my solitude, you, my old, beloved – *evil* thoughts!

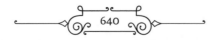